Balthasar Hubmaier

Dr. Balthasar Hubmaier

From one of a series of engravings of Anabaptist leaders drawn ca. 1606 by Christoffel van Sichem, presumably without historical basis.

Balthasar Hubmaier

Theologian of Anabaptism

Translated and edited by

H. Wayne Pipkin
and
John H. Yoder

herald press scottdale, pa
waterloo, ont

Library of Congress Cataloging-in-Publication Data
Hubmaier, Balthasar, d. 1528.
    Balthasar Hubmaier, theologian of Anabaptism / edited by H. Wayne
Pipkin and John H. Yoder.
        p. cm. — (Classics of the radical Reformation ; 5)
    Bibliography: p.
    Includes index.
    ISBN 0-8361-3103-7
    1. Anabaptists—Doctrines—Early works to 1800. I. Pipkin,
H. Wayne. II. Yoder, John Howard. III. Title. IV. Series.
    BX4930.H79 1989
    230'.97—dc19   88-28425

The paper used in this publication is recycled and meets the minimum
requirements of American National Standard for Information
Sciences—Permanence of Paper for Printed Library Materials, ANSI
Z39.48-1984.

Scripture quotations marked RSV are from the Revised Standard
Version of the Bible, copyright 1946, 1952, ° 1971, 1973 by the Division
of Christian Education of the National Council of the Churches of
Christ in the USA, and are used by permission. Other Scripture texts
are translated from Hubmaier's German.

BALTHASAR HUBMAIER
Copyright ° 1989 by Herald Press, Scottdale, PA 15683
    Published simultaneously in Canada by Herald Press,
    Waterloo, Ont. N2L 6H7. All rights reserved
Library of Congress Catalog Card Number: 88-28425
International Standard Book Number: 0-8361-3103-7
Printed in the United States of America

07 06 05 04 03 02   10 9 8 7 6 5 4

To order or request information, please call
1-800-759-4447 (individuals); 1-800-245-7894 (trade).
Website: www.mph.org

CLASSICS OF THE RADICAL REFORMATION

Cornelius J. Dyck, Editor
Institute of Mennonite Studies

In cooperation with Walter Klaassen, Conrad Grebel College, Waterloo, Ontario; John S. Oyer, Goshen College, Goshen Indiana; John H. Yoder, Notre Dame University, South Bend, Indiana; and Jarold K. Zeman, Acadia Divinity College, Wolfville, Nova Scotia.

Classics of the Radical Reformation is an English-language series of Anabaptist and free-church documents translated and annotated under the direction of the Institute of Mennonite Studies (the research agency of Associated Mennonite Biblical Seminary, 3003 Benham Ave., Elkhart, Ind.), and published by Herald Press.

1. *The Legacy of Michael Sattler.* Trans., ed. John H. Yoder, 1973.

2. *The Writings of Pilgram Marpeck.* Trans., ed. William Klassen and Walter Klaassen, 1978.

3. *Anabaptism in Outline: Selected Primary Sources.* Ed. Walter Klaassen, 1981.

4. *The Sources of Swiss Anabaptism: The Grebel Letters and Related Documents.* Ed. Leland Harder, 1985.

5. *Balthasar Hubmaier: Theologian of Anabaptism.* Trans., ed. H. Wayne Pipkin and John H. Yoder, 1989.

6. *The Writings of Dirk Philips, 1504-1568.* Trans., ed. Cornelius J. Dyck, William E. Keeney, and Alvin J. Beachy, 1992.

7. *The Anabaptist Writings of David Joris, 1535-1543.* Trans., ed. Gary K. Waite, 1993.

8. *The Essential Carlstadt.* Trans., ed. E. J. Furcha, 1995.

9. *Peter Riedemann's Hutterite Confession of Faith.* Trans., ed. John J. Friesen, 1999.

To our children

Nancy Gail Pipkin
Heather Michelle Pipkin

Rebecca Marie Yoder Neufeld
Martha Lise Yoder Maust
Daniel Christian Yoder
Elisabeth Anne Yoder
Esther Yoder Strahan
John-David Samuel Yoder

Contents

List of Illustrations

General Editor's Preface

For many years a committee of German and North American historians known as the *Täuferaktenkommission* (TAK) has published source materials of the sixteenth-century Anabaptist movement under the title *Quellen zur Geschichte der Täufer* (QGT). More recently a similar organization has begun work in the Netherlands with Dutch source materials. It is known as the *Commissie tot de Uitgave van Documenta Anabaptistica Neerlandica* (CUDAN). These developments have, obviously, been deeply rewarding to scholars and others, as the multitude of articles and books using these documents amply verifies.

There are, however, still relatively few sixteenth-century Anabaptist materials available in the English language, though their number is increasing. It is to meet this need that the Classics of the Radical Reformation (CRR) series was begun some years ago with the aim of making available in the English language a scholarly and critical edition of the primary works of major Anabaptist and free church writers of the late fifteenth, sixteenth, and early seventeenth centuries. The first volume in this series, *The Legacy of Michael Sattler* by John H. Yoder, appeared in 1973. *The Writings of Pilgram Marpeck* by William Klassen and Walter Klaassen, appeared in 1978; *Anabaptism in Outline: Selected Primary Sources* by Walter Klaassen, in 1981; and *The Sources of Swiss Anabaptism*, edited by Leland Harder, appeared in 1985.

In preparing these translations it has not been considered essential to the purposes of the series to include every known document of the writers under translation and, unless some contribution can be made to a fuller understanding of the text, it has not been considered essential to pursue at length critical textual issues. Those scholars interested in the details will, in any case, turn to the original language text. Where a choice had to be made between clarity and awkward literalism, the translators were encouraged to favor readability but without compromising the text.

It is a pleasure to express appreciation to translators-editors H. Wayne Pipkin, Director of the Institute for Baptist and Anabaptist Studies, Rüschlikon, Switzerland, and John H. Yoder of Notre Dame University for their careful and exacting work over a good number of years. It is gratifying to have Balthasar Hubmaier, one of the major theologians of sixteenth-century Anabaptism, made available to us in English in this way through the cooperation of a Baptist and a Mennonite. Appreciation is also expressed here to the Mennonite Publishing House (Herald Press), without whose commitment to the work of the church this series could not continue.

Cornelius J. Dyck, Editor, CRR
Institute of Mennonite Studies
Elkhart, Indiana

Editors' Preface

Recognition of the unique place of Balthasar Hubmaier among the writers of early Anabaptism has been evident for a century in the number of historians studying his life and works; likewise the enterprise of translation began relatively early. In 1905 Henry C. Vedder included sizable fragments of translation in his first English biography. In the 1920s W. O. Lewis visited libraries in Europe to gather photocopies which were bound and made available to scholars by William Jewell College of Liberty, Missouri, and were translated into English by Prof. G. D. Davidson of William Jewell College. Typescript and microfilm copies of Davidson's work have been used in numerous libraries.

Hubmaier was (after Hans Denck, whose writings are far fewer) the first of the early Anabaptists to have his writings appear in a full scholarly modern German edition. The translators and authors of the present collection have been privileged to work largely from that base, thereby being largely spared the burdens of textual and bibliographical research.

The choice of the title for this book—*Balthasar Hubmaier: Theologian of Anabaptism*—does not intend to suggest that Hubmaier was the only theologian, or the normative theologian, of the Anabaptist movement. Such a movement could by its nature have no normative theologian. At important points Hubmaier was not typical of majority trends in the movement, or of the views which survived. Some other authors like Pilgram Marpeck and Menno Simons were equally prolific, although they came later. Others who wrote less may have been more original, or more profound, or may be thought by some to hold more promise for later generations. Nonetheless, Hubmaier's place in the first generation of the broad movement is unique. He is the only figure of his generation with university credentials, the only one with extensive public activity before joining the Reformation, the most skilled in popular expository writing.

The editors are indebted especially to the Institute of Mennonite Studies for the moral support represented by commissioning this work in the framework of the Classics of the Radical Reformation and for the secretarial services of Evelyn Habegger and Sue DeLeon at Elkhart and Melanie Nogalski, Jeanette Hunter, Andy Chancey, Heather Pipkin, and Angela Byrskog at Rüschlikon. Generous aid in providing draft translations was received from the late Elizabeth Horsch Bender. Several participants in the Hubmaier seminars at Rüschlikon have assisted at various levels in the production and refinement of the translations as well as in the search for sources and annotations: Christoph Weichert, Jürg Rother, Walter Rappold, Margret Tepper-Di Passa, and especially Patrick Mueller and Heinz-Günther Sussdorf. Appreciation is also expressed to the Baptist Theological Seminary for financial support of the project and to the Rüschlikon faculty for support and released time to complete the translations. Finally, Dr. Leland Harder brought to bear on the task of editorial review for style consistency and precision the skills and knowledge already demonstrated in his editing the previous CRR volume, *The Sources of Swiss Anabaptism*.

Both editors have reviewed all of the material in the collection, although for each text one of us took responsibility for initial drafting of the introduction, the translation, and the notes. H. W. Pipkin was primary editor for items 7, 9, 11, 14, 17, 18, 19, 20, 22, 27, 28, and 29.

Biblical texts are translated from the German, generally without reference either to Greek or Hebrew, or to English versions. In some cases where differences were immaterial the RSV wording has been followed, with permission.

The editors would like to thank the following persons whose reviews or personal communications have made possible several corrections for the second printing: Torsten Bergsten, Dennis D. Martin, Franklin Littell, W. Glenn Jonas, Merle Schlabaugh, and Peter J. Klassen.

H. Wayne Pipkin
John H. Yoder

Introduction

Hubmaier's Career

Balthasar Hubmaier was a participant in the Anabaptist wing of the Reformation for less than three years. Baptized in Waldshut on Easter Saturday, April 15, 1525, he met his death at the stake in Vienna on March 10, 1528. In that limited time his writings and public activity gained him a well-earned reputation as the most learned and the most gifted communicator among the Anabaptists. He did not stand in the middle of the Anabaptist movement, but was without contest the most able theologian and the most visible among the leaders of those first years. He was the only Anabaptist leader who had had a public career of any significance in his earlier Catholic experience.

Hubmaier had pursued traditional theological studies to the completion of the doctorate at the University of Ingolstadt. He had also functioned as an exceptionally effective popular preacher, marked especially by devotion to the most common traits of the popular Catholicism of the time: mariolatry, the piety of the pilgrimage, and anti-Semitism. It was from this rootedness in representative Catholicism that Hubmaier was to move, along a path of which we know little, to become first Zwinglian and then Anabaptist. It was this same rootedness which made of him the fluent and effective writer of pamphlets and treatises in the field of church order whose work abundantly merits being gathered in the present volume.

His theological training prepared him for the tactics of point-by-point debate on such matters as free will and original sin, and especially on the most threatening controverted issue of infant baptism. His gifts as a popular preacher and teacher show to the best advantage in his simple polemic tracts and in his writings on church order. His life story is accessible to

English-language readers,[1] and thus we limit our introduction here to the considerations which are indispensable for situating these documents in their context.

Born probably soon after 1480 in Friedberg near Augsburg, he took from there the second surname Friedberger, sometimes latinized as *Pacimontanus*.

During his university studies at Freiburg, 1503-1506, Hubmaier learned to know as a teacher the great Catholic scholar John Eck and as a friend John Faber. Both were later to be among his most bitter Roman Catholic adversaries. Fellow students as well were Urbanus Rhegius, the later Lutheran Reformer of Augsburg, and Wolfgang Capito, later at Strasbourg.

After a brief teaching time in Schaffhausen, Hubmaier returned to Freiburg as a preacher and was ordained as a priest. Early in 1512 he followed his teacher John Eck to the University of Ingolstadt, where he was awarded a doctorate in theology in September. He was employed at Ingolstadt as theology professor, an assignment which brought with it the responsibility of priest in the largest parish church in the city. In 1515/1516 he was prorector of the University, that is, the actual administrative head, since the titular rector was regularly a prince. Before completing the year as prorector he accepted a call as cathedral preacher in Regensburg.

The five years of activity in Regensburg were marked by Hubmaier's participation in an anti-Jewish movement like those which had ravaged other German cities earlier. He became a highly popular preacher to pilgrims at the chapel built at the place where the synagogue had stood. His preaching and the reputation for miracles which the chapel's statues of Mary had acquired led to such massive attendance that the wooden chapel soon needed to be replaced by a larger building. At the end of 1520 Hubmaier left Regensburg for Waldshut.

Thus far the story contributes little to our understanding of Hubmaier's later activity as a radical Protestant theologian.

---

[1] Bergsten 1978. This work is a translation and condensation by William R. Estep, Jr., of Bergsten's definitive biography (Bergsten 1961), which rendered all earlier biographies obsolete. We shall refer directly to Bergsten's German biography only at those points which Estep has omitted.

His fame as a preacher was growing. His departure from Regensburg is unexplained, as were some of his earlier rapid movements, like his abandoning Ingolstadt at the height of his academic responsibility. Was any of this mobility a sign of what in the future was to lead him to the Reformation? Was there some no longer discernible meaning in his leaving Schaffhausen before finishing the school year, leaving Ingolstadt before finishing the academic term, and now leaving Regensburg at the height of his popularity? None of these questions can be significantly illuminated from the sources that we have.

Nor is the evidence more adequate to explain how and just when his being at Waldshut began to permit the development of sympathies with humanists and with the Zwinglian Reformation. He returned to Regensburg late in 1522, only to leave again for Waldshut in the spring of 1523. From then on he was counted as a friend and ally of Zwingli in nearby Zurich and of Oecolampad in Basel. From then on most of the narrative thread can be carried by the documents in our collection. Hubmäier's movements from late 1524 to the spring of 1526 are recounted below in the respective introduction to texts 3-13.

Upon leaving Zurich sometime after April 11, 1526, Hubmaier stopped first at Constance, where he had some friends.[2] Soon he went on to Augsburg, where in addition to Lutheran and Zwinglian Reformation styles, there was a more radically inclined circle,[3] including the recently arrived Hans Denck (from Nuremberg). It has been assumed on circumstantial grounds that it was Hubmaier who brought the practice of believers baptism to Augsburg, baptizing the Augsburg natives and Denck, thereby connecting South German Anabaptism with the earlier Swiss origins.[4] Here Hubmaier also encountered Zwingli's friend Peter Gynoraeus.[5]

---

[2] Cf. in text 12 below, p. 154.
[3] ME I, pp. 182ff.
[4] Werner Packull has objected to this assumption, on the grounds that the baptism of Denck by Hut is not clearly attested. Packull's argument supports his general concern to accentuate the diversity of the several types of Anabaptism. Packull 1973, pp. 327ff.
[5] Cf. Gynoraeus' letter to Zwingli, August 22, 1526, Z 8, pp. 688ff.

By July Hubmaier had moved on to Nikolsburg (Mikulov). The openness of the Liechtenstein family to the Reformation had already made room for the Lutheran Hans Spittelmaier[6] (early 1524) and the more Zwinglian Oswald Glaidt[7] (early 1526?). The suffragan bishop Martin Göschl was also friendly to the Reformation.[8] Hubmaier was not merely welcomed: he seems to have become the prime mover of the Reformation, which soon became Anabaptist. The next few months saw the printing of most of our texts.

The one dimension of Hubmaier's activity at Nikolsburg which does not appear overtly in his writings is his growing separation from other Anabaptists. Hans Hut, once close to Thomas Müntzer, then baptized by Denck, came to Nikolsburg a few months after Hubmaier. Their differences were immediately visible, leading to formal debate(s) and finally to the expulsion of Hut, who went on to be Anabaptism's most effective evangelist from Vienna to the Tyrol, and apparently also of Glaidt. Hut differed from Hubmaier[9] in many ways: Although Hubmaier baptized only adults, Hut considered his practice too inclusive, and the resulting congregational life insufficiently disciplined.

Hut held very clear convictions about the impending end of the age, for which believers baptism was seen as a preparation. He called for an economic order of equalization after the model of Acts (though he himself never stayed in one place to set up such a community). He seems to have held that *for the present* Christians should eschew violence, thus being recognized by the nonresistant Hutterian Brethren as their predecessor, but expected the saints to wield a righteous sword of judgment in the coming end time. To Hubmaier and his Liechtenstein patrons this was a revolutionary threat.[10]

A number of the followers of Hut and Glaidt remained in Nikolsburg. Their views of nonresistance and civil authority

---

[6] Later to become an Anabaptist: ME IV, p. 599.

[7] ME II, p. 522

[8] ME II, p. 546. See also below the foreword to item 17. The best analysis of why and how Hubmaier came to Nikolsburg is in Zeman 1969, pp. 131-176.

[9] The conflict with Hut is recounted in Bergsten 1978, pp. 361-517.

[10] See below, pp. 152 and 557, the concentration of Hubmaier's "Recantation" and "Apology" on the theme of revolution as a point of distance between him and Hut.

were not eschatologically conditioned as for Hut but were more like those of the Swiss Brethren, against which Hubmaier directed his "On the Sword." These *Stäbler* (staffbearers, contrasted to the sword-bearing *Schwertler*) were expelled from Nikolsburg in 1528, presumably at the same time that Lord Leonard had to turn Hubmaier over to the imperial authorities at Vienna. It was these refugees who for the first time pooled their goods, the event out of which the Hutterian Bruderhof evolved.

Only the Anabaptist period of Hubmaier's activity is represented here and only during this period did he have his writings printed. Letters and state records exist which throw light on the very different stories of his earlier activity in Regensburg and Waldshut,[11] but we have no writings proven to be from his pen.

Principles of Translation and Editing

For the entire corpus, fresh translations were prepared from the original texts. The translators/editors, however, took account of earlier English translations where such were known to exist. Known prior translations of individual texts are acknowledged in footnotes at the end of the respective introductions. An English version of the entire corpus, prepared in typescript by George Duiguid Davidson, then head of the language department of William Jewell College, and accessioned in the library of that college, was consulted in microfilm, as well as the editorial corrections made to it by Walter Klaassen. Earlier manuscript translations of our items 12, 15, 18, 19, 21, and 24 by Henry C. Vedder are in the library of Colgate Rochester Divinity School.[12]

All of our major texts are based, with permission, on the definitive edition of the writings of Hubmaier edited by Westin and Bergsten, cited hereafter: HS. Only a few supplementary items not in HS needed to be drawn from other sources. The translators have inserted page break numbers enclosed by slashes in the English text, e.g., /717/, to indicate the beginning of a new page in the source volumes (Z, HS).

---

[11] They are summarized in Sachsse 1914, pp. 82ff., and many are listed in Bergsten 1961, pp. 56ff.

[12] Thanks are due to Dr. Patricia Schoelles for this information.

The sequence of texts is chronological as far as the items can be dated.

The original texts were abundantly provided with notes in the margin (see specimen page facsimile, p. 128). Sometimes these functioned like subtitles, with a topic word summarizing the opposite text. Sometimes they indicated sources. Sometimes they corresponded to the function of italics by drawing attention to the most important passages on a page. Though this apparatus of marginal notes was clumsy and sometimes repetitive, nonetheless these notes have been retained in the interest of fidelity, not by reproducing in English the format of the original German page but by printing the marginalia as footnotes indicated by lowercase letters. For all details concerning printers, format, and the library location of originals, the reader will refer to HS.

The reader will note that the typography and page layout of this volume do not conform to modern standards. The editors have chosen to approximate the appearance of the original printed sources.

Hubmaier's abundant use of Scripture citations is an especially indispensable index of his attitude toward the Scripture, and of his knowledge of the biblical text. These are simply inserted into the text. Though the mode of Scripture reference in the original was only by chapter number, verse references are added by the editors where possible. A comma was inserted to separate the reference from the text; and where a Scripture reference was missing but known, we placed it in brackets.

Following the general translation principles of the CRR series, the translators have sought a middle path between strict literalism and the kind of paraphrasing which would prevent the reader from basing interpretation upon specific wordings. The varied spellings of personal and place names have been retained.

Later Protestant thought in the German language has come to make much of the distinction between *Kirche* as referring to the institutional church, visible in and administered by clergy, and *Gemeinde* as the gathered body of true believers. The translation attempts to render differences of this kind; yet the reader should remember that this distinction did not have in the sixteenth century quite the pointed clarity it has come to have since.

1

Statements at the
Second Zurich Disputation

*The "disputation" was a standard procedure to legitimate
innovation in the age of the Reformation. Borrowed from the
university promotion procedure, it provided for open debate,
impartial chairmanship and record keeping, and a right for all
to speak.[1] In a context where the established ecclesiastical
order (i.e., the bishop) and teaching authorities (the
universities) were not open to new ideas, the disputation was a
substitute frequently resorted to by Protestant governments to
legitimate change.*

*Some date Zurich's Reformation from the disputation held
January 29, 1523.[2] To prepare for that event Zwingli had presented sixty-seven theses. They were not formally debated, since
the bishop's representative Johannes Faber refused to recognize
the authority of such an assembly to deal with matters of doctrine. The meeting nonetheless had the effect of confirming the
governmental mandate to Zwingli as preacher appointed by the
Council.[3]*

*The Second Zurich Disputation, convened in October 1523,
was an effort to apply this sense of momentum and conviction
to the concrete implementation of the Reformation. The public
was already agitated about attacks on "images" (i.e., statues*

---

[1] Cf. article *Disputations* in ME I, p. 70, and Jess Yoder 1962, pp. 14-35,
118-46. Hubmaier's own "Theses Against Eck" (p. 49) begins with the
rationale and rules for a disputation. Others of his earlier writings also
called for debates to be held.

[2] E.g., Oscar Farner, who exclaims, "Zürich evangelisch!" (1954, p.356)
Jacques Courvoisier prefers November 1522 (1947, p. 91; 1963, p. 20)
when the state first claimed the right to name the clergy, making Zwingli
"the first evangelical minister." Dating a Reformation is in any case a
dubious enterprise.

[3] Zwingli himself greeted the outcome with what Bullinger called "great
joy": "Praise and thanks to God, who wants his will to reign in heaven and
on earth!" (Bullinger 1838, I 104). It was Zwingli's own later appeal to this
decision as validation and the publication of his 67 theses which gave the
January disputation its symbolic importance.

and paintings used in church and in processions) and the mass. It was at this meeting that the first discussion between Simon Stumpf and Huldrych Zwingli was recorded, in which some historians[4] have sought to identify the beginnings of Anabaptism. Hubmaier was a participant. His first two contributions were unrelated to Grebel and Stumpf.

After the disputation, someone spread the rumor that Hubmaier had claimed to be a delegate from "the four cities on the Rhine and in the Black Forest." Hubmaier wrote to the Zurich Council asking them to deny that rumor, which the Council did by a minute of early December. The Council further said that Hubmaier's presence at the disputation had been due to the moving of the Holy Spirit, and that his contribution to the disputation, as well as a sermon or two, had been irreproachable.[5] Hubmaier was clearly counted as a Zwinglian.[6]

On the Concept of Reform

Toward the end of the first day, which had been devoted to the subject of "images", chairman Sebastian Hofmeister (the Reformer of Schaffhausen) stated tentatively the conclusion to which the assembly had come, and asked whether there were any more grounds for objection to the doctrine presented by Zwingli and his colleagues.

As everyone was silent Dr. Baltassar Fridberger, pastor in Waltzhůt, rose and spoke as follows:[7]

The all powerful eternal God commanded us through Moses: If you come across the ox of your enemy or a stray donkey, lead him back to him, that is to say, to his owner; and if you see the ass of someone who hates you lying under his burden, do not go past but lift him up [Exod. 23:4f.]. Christ spoke similarly [Luke 14:5]: Which of you, if his ass or ox would fall in a pit, would not pull him out at the same hour

[4] Blanke, 1961, p. 8. John Yoder, "The Turning Point...," MQR 32, 1958, pp. 128-46.
[5] Loserth 1891, pp. 93ff. Köhler 1925, p. 318.
[6] Cf. Pipkin 1984, pp. 43ff. English translations of the texts have previously been published partially in Hošek 1891, pp. 127f.; Vedder 1905, pp. 58ff.; fully in Estep 1976, 16ff.; and Harder 1985, pp. 238ff.
[7] Z 2, pp. 716¹³-718.³

even on the sabbath day? So much more should it be taken seriously if a person is in error in matters that have to do with the salvation of his soul, or if he has fallen into a pit of error or abuse, that he should be helped.

Now it cannot be denied, but is rather public, and clearer than the sun, that for several hundred years much error and abuse has been infiltrated into Christian practices and added to them by the devil, who never rests. This has also happened on these two subjects: namely, the images of saints and the abuses of the mass. This is why the worthy, prominent, honorable, and wise /717/ Lords, Mayor, large and small Council, called "the Two Hundred," of this praiseworthy old city of Zürich, my gracious Lords, well esteemed and judged to be Christian, have undertaken to carry out a friendly brotherly conversation so that such quarreling and controversy as had arisen, in that some want to stand by the old and others by the new, might be alleviated without disturbance or disorder. All of which cannot take place more fittingly nor properly than through the proclamation of the clear Word of God as written in both Testaments. For in all divisive questions and controversies only Scripture, canonized and sanctified by God himself, should and must be the judge, no one else: or heaven and earth must fall [Matt. 24:35]. For the merciful God himself has set the judge on the judgment throne as we read in Ezekiel 44:24: "When there is a controversy men will stand in my judgment and will judge." Now the judgments of God can only be known out of the divine Word, as Scripture truly testifies to us. The Word of God judges, John 12:47-49; Deut. 17:8; Exod. 18:13-27; and 28:30.

Therefore Christ points us to the Scriptures: "Search the Scriptures. They give testimony of me, etc.," and pointed us to Moses and the prophets, whom we should hear: for he does not want to have testimony from men, John 5:39, 46.

This usage was held to by Christ himself and also by Paul and the other apostles. When they spoke against the devil or against evil men, they usually stuck Scripture under their nose as the judge of all controversial talk and thereby overcame them. For holy Scripture alone is the true light and lantern through which all human argument, darkness, and objections can be recognized. This the prophet David knew perfectly well as he said to God, "Thy Word is a lamp to my feet" [Ps.

119:105]. Christ also himself taught us the same thing: that we should take the lantern of his salutary Word in our hand, so that when the bridegroom comes we can enter into the marriage feast with him [Matt. 25:1-13]. Thus also the error and the abuses of making images and the mass shall be demonstrated only through the plumb line of the bright clear Word of God, thereby being recognized and /718/ moderated,[8] and what is built thereupon will remain finally and permanently; for the Word of God is invincible.

Here there is no one who would speak against that.[9]

After another invitation from Chairman Hofmeister, Jacob Edlibach argued that the meaning of Exodus 20 is not that images should not be made or painted but only that they should not be worshiped. He claimed that pictures move the believers to contemplation and good works. A counter question of Frantz Zingk asked how images would move people who would be blind, perhaps meaning to argue the priority of the spoken Word. The debate threatened to degenerate.

To avert this from happening Dr. Balthasar Fridberger arose[10] and read the text which stands written, Deut. 27 [15]: /719/ Moses commanded thus as ordered by God: "The Levites shall proclaim and say with a loud voice to all the people of Israel: 'Cursed is the person who makes a carved or molded image, which is an atrocity before the Lord God, and secretly places this image somewhere.' And the whole people shall say: 'Amen! So be it.' " This text or passage resolved this debate completely. All were satisfied.[11]

Implementation Through Enlightenment

Toward the end of the second day's deliberations, which had centered on the mass, a point again was reached where Zwingli's opponents no longer dared respond. In this pause Hubmaier returned to the theme of the preceding day.

---

[8] The use of the verb *gemassiget* is striking. Might Hubmaier at this time have contemplated less than a radical legal abolition of all abuses?

[9] This line is a statement by the recorder rather than Hubmaier.

[10] Z 2, pp. 718[30]-719.[8]

[11] Cf. notes 9 and 3.

Then Dr. Balthassar Fridberger arose[12] saying:

Lord Mayor and other dear brothers in Christ! Yesterday it became thoroughly clear from Scripture that there should be no images. I myself would that /761/ no image had ever come into Christendom. For the text of Exodus 20:4-6 is bright and clear. It stands firm as a wall. By means of two distinct prohibitions it expressly forbids not only worshiping the images but also making them. Still more clearly it is said in Deuteronomy 5:6-10, where God speaks by means of three distinct prohibitions: "I am the Lord your God, who brought you out of the land of Egypt, out of the house of servitude." Second: "You shall not make an image or any kind of form of all of the things that are up above in heaven or below on the earth or in the water under the earth." Third: "You shall not honor them, nor serve them, for I am the Lord your God, a jealous God." Thus we find also that God hates not only the adoration which takes place before the images but also the making of the image. Therefore he commands them to be burnt and those who make them he curses, Deut. 7:25 and 27:15. And all the people shall say: "Amen!"

Now some people in the room said: "Amen!"

Now I want to add a mosaic argument, which completely casts down the images with its two horns. That is: either it is commanded to possess images or it is not. If they are commanded, show us the Scripture and there will be no more question. If they are not commanded, then they are worthless. For everything which God has not taught us either with words or deeds is worthless and in vain. For as God alone is good [Matt. 19:17], so everything that is good must come from God alone. He who says otherwise accuses God the Father, the Son Jesus Christ, and St. Paul of lying. God the Father speaks [Deut. 12:32], "What I have commanded you, do only that, nothing more, nothing less." God the Son has said [Matt. 15:13]: "Every planting that has not been planted by my Heavenly Father will be torn out." Likewise, Paul [Rom. 14:23]: What does not arise from faith contributes to eternal damnation. Just one more thing. One of the two must be true:

---

[12] Z 2, pp. 760[31]-762.[22]

Images are useless, or useful in the church. If they are useless what do you want with them? If they are useful, then God was not telling the truth because he said in Isaiah 44:9 that images are not useful for any purpose. /762/ It is also a blasphemy to tell the people that the images call us, move us, invite us, and draw us to contemplation. For it is Christ who calls the sinner. Only he himself moves him to good deeds. He invites him to the wedding feast. God the Father is the one who draws those who come to Christ.

But now that the pictures have come into the church (which is most lamentable for me because of the manifold abuses which take place), we have to look carefully how to deal with them correctly, so that no one will be scandalized and so that brotherly Christian peace may not be troubled. For there are many persons who mightily adhere to the images. Therefore the clear holy Word of God against images and idols in Old and New Testament must be shown to the people earnestly and often with care and diligence. This will exercise its authority and power and with time will drive all the images out, for it is impossible that the Word of God should be preached and not bring works and fruits in that whereto it was sent from God [Isa. 55:10]. Thus Paul did in Athens and other places, as we find in the Acts of the Apostles. When that happens, every Christian will find in himself and recognize that the images are not any use at all. Then a whole parish congregation will gather and decide unanimously without any disorder that the images shall be moved out and laid to sleep.[13] Then the powerful Word of God will have borne its fruit, for the sake of which it went forth from God.

At the end of the second day's deliberations, when it seemed that the only remaining issue to discuss was the doctrine of purgatory, Conrad Grebel had requested that attention be given to various abuses related to the practice of the mass, inasmuch as the major issue had been the doctrine of the mass: i.e., whether it should be understood as a sacrifice. That theme became the first order of business when the session of the 28th

---

[13] It is noteworthy that Hubmaier calls for the local congregation (not necessarily "Milords" of Zurich) to make the decision in each place.

began. Conrad Grebel again opened the debate but immediately deferred to "those who can speak better."[14]

Then Dr. Baltassar Fridberger arose, speaking as follows:

Concerning numerous abuses in the mass—which I would rather call a testament of Christ or a memorial of his bitter death—without doubt this is the main point of the abuses, that we interpret the mass as a sacrifice. In order to be on record on that subject, which concerns me, and since I want to let myself be taught by all Christian believers according to God's will but only through Scripture [I conclude that] I have not been taught otherwise than that I must with my dear brothers in Christ Huldricho Zuinglen and Leone Jud confess that the mass is not a sacrifice but a proclamation of the covenant of Christ, in which there is a remembrance of his bitter suffering and his self-sacrifice, who offered himself once for all on the cross, and never more will again be offered; and that this is done by an outward visible sign and seal through which we are made completely certain of the forgiveness of our sins. And he who celebrates the mass otherwise is sealing a letter that has not yet been written.

The testimonies that move me thus to speak are found in Matthew 26:26-28; Luke 22:19ff; Mark 14:22-24; 1 Corinthians 11:23-26; Hebrews 7 and 9.

Christ speaks: *Hoc facite* ["do this"]. He does not say, *Hoc offerte* ["Sacrifice this"].

From this it follows, first of all, that the mass as a sacrifice is of no use either to the dead or the living. For as I cannot believe for someone else, so I cannot hold mass for him. Since the mass is established by Christ as a sign whereby the faith of the believing person is confirmed.

Second: Because the body and the blood of Christ are sign and seal of the Word of Christ which is spoken in the

---

[14] Z 2, pp. 768[9]-788.[9] Grebel had asked for the floor just before the session closed the previous evening. He now proposed that from the theme of the mass as such the debate should move to "many abuses which the devil has also added to this" and then yielded to "those who can speak better" (Harder 1985, p. 244). Both Conrad Grebel and Felix Mantz were quite open about their not being eloquent. That Hubmaier was ready to speak on the same theme shows how close he was to the Zwinglian movement at that time; it may indicate some prior planning.

mass, therefore /787/ the priest must not preach anything in the mass other than the pure, true, clear Word of God of which they are signs. He who celebrates mass otherwise is not properly holding mass.

Third: He who does not proclaim the Word of God is not celebrating mass. This is testified to by Christ and by Paul who learned it from him, Matthew, Luke, etc., as above: "Do this in my memory. As often as you do this you are proclaiming the death of the Lord" [1 Cor. 11:24b, 26]. The follower must be faithful or Christ is pushed aside.

Fourth: As the mass should be read in Latin to the Latins, therefore also in French to the French, in German to the Germans; for doubtless Christ did not speak Calcuttish[15] with his disciples at the Last Supper but rather aloud and understandably. Furthermore, to celebrate mass is to read a testament letter. It would be ridiculous to read a Latin letter to a German who cannot understand Latin. For to celebrate the mass quietly and not proclaim is to silence the Lord. Paul wants us to speak understandably in the church. He would rather speak five words with understanding for the benefit of the church than ten thousand which are not understood, so that the people might be instructed and might say, "Amen," 1 Cor. 14:19.

Fifth: He who properly holds the mass shall give food and drink not only to himself but also the others who are spiritually hungry and thirsty, who desire it, and that in both forms. This Christ taught us with words and deeds as he said, "Drink ye all of it!" [Matt. 26:27]. He who teaches or behaves otherwise pokes a hole in Christ's testament letter.[16] This not even an angel from heaven has a right to do, much less a human being on earth, Gal. 1:8; 3:15.

Dear pious Christians! These are my convictions, which I have been taught out of Scripture, especially having to do with images and with the mass. If they should not be right and Christian, I beg you all through Jesus Christ our only Savior, I plead and admonish you by reason of the last judgment, please correct me in a brotherly and Christian way with Scripture;

---

[15] "Calcutta" was a standard symbol for the exotic or alien. It was used as well by Zwingli.

[16] I.e., nullifies the document which "testament" signifies.

for I may err, I am a human being; but a heretic I cannot be.[17] I want—and desire from the heart—to be instructed. /788/ I want to accept that from everybody with great thanks, confess my errors and subject myself to you willingly in all obedience according to the Word of God, and also truly to follow you as followers of Christ.

I have spoken. Judge and instruct me. I pray Christ that he will grant us his grace to do so.

He also said he was never so happy all year than when he learned that there was going to be discussion here of the abuses of the mass, of which there are still many more, as Conrad Grebel had said.

---

[17] This phrase was an established proverb, cf. p. 46, n.15.

2

Eighteen Theses Concerning the Christian Life

Hubmaier prepared these Eighteen Theses *for a disputation which he proposed to conduct among the clergy of Waldshut and its environs. As noted in the introduction to item 1, the disputation was a common medieval exercise of academic theologians.[1] Perhaps taking his cue from Luther's Leipzig debate of 1519, Zwingli used the disputation as an effective technique of education and political change by which to promote the Reformation in Zurich. Its success was sealed by the disputations of January and October, 1523. Hubmaier had taken a prominent part in the second,[2] and now he was proposing a disputation for Waldshut. It differed from the Zurich disputations in several respects. Outside theologians were not invited; the civil authorities were not to act as judges; and it was not to be open to the public. Initially, only the ecclesiastical chapter of Waldshut was involved.*

The substance of the theses contains nothing specifically "Anabaptist." They largely parallel Zwingli's sixty-seven theses circulated for the disputation in January 1523.[3]

The Achtzehn Schlussreden *became Hubmaier's first published work. That some kind of dialogue actually took place is presupposed in a document of May 4, 1524. A few weeks must have elapsed between the event and that report and a few weeks before that from the publication of the* Theses *until the disputation. Thus this text may well have been completed in March.*

---

[1] Concerning the ecclesiological case for dialogue as means of renewal, cf. in addition to note 1 on p. 21 above, Yoder 1968, pp. 101ff.; Yoder 1967, pp. 300ff.; and text 4, p. 50 below. Concerning the disputation as political and forensic event, cf. Jesse Yoder 1962, and the Bergmann/Bender article "Disputations," in ME II, pp. 70ff.

[2] Cf. item 1, above, pp. 22-29.

[3] Z 1, pp. 458-65, and Z 2, pp. 1-457.

Copies now extant indicate that the work was printed on four different occasions during 1524—by three different Strasbourg printers and by one in Augsburg.[4]

Eighteen Theses concerning the whole Christian life, upon what it depends. Debated at Waldshut by Doctor Balthasser Fridberger MDXXIIII

Grace and peace in Christ Jesus, our Lord, I, Balthassar Frydberger, Doctor, etc. Pastor at Waldtshut, wish to all my chapter brethren and chaplains there:/72/

Beloved Lords and brethren: According to an ancient usage coming from the age of the apostles, when weighty matters arise concerning the faith, some of those to whom preaching God's Word has been commanded gather in a Christian attitude to confer and to weigh the Scriptures in order to continue unitedly to feed the Christian sheep according to the content of God's Word. These meetings were previously called "synods" but now are called "chapters" or "brotherhoods." Since, however, gross error and tension have arisen in these dangerous last days, touching our Christian faith not a little, and in order that we might find food and drink not only for our body but for our soul also, and might henceforth lead our sheep all the more usefully in the peace and unity of God's

---

[4] Earlier translations: Hošek 1891, pp. 129f.; Vedder 1905, pp. 69-71; Davidson 1939, pp. 1-11; and Estep 1976, pp. 23ff. Source: HS 1, pp. 71-74.

Word, and in order to set aside all slander and scandal, I therefore ask and exhort you, dear sirs and brothers, by the bond of brotherly love, by the sanctity of Christian peace, and by the name of our Lord Jesus Christ, that you look into these theses, which I have set forth after the mode of questioning and instruction, that you investigate the Scriptures and that at the next chapter assembly which we hold at Waldshūt you converse with me on these matters in a friendly, brotherly, and virtuous way. In order that we not waste much time on human teachings, on our own opinions and fancies, would you bring your Bibles or, if you have none, at least your missals, so that we may Christianly instruct one another on the grounds of the written divine Word. After which I shall provide all of you as well as I can a fraternal meal at my expense, that you not leave without food and drink. Farewell in Christ Jesus our only Savior.

1. Faith alone makes us righteous before God.
2. This faith is the knowledge of God's mercy, which he has shown us by offering his only begotten Son.[5] Here fail those who are Christian in appearance [only], who have only an historical faith in God.
3. Such faith cannot be idle, but must break forth in gratitude toward God and in all sorts of works of brotherly love toward others. This casts down all artifice such as candles, palm branches, and holy water./73/
4. Only those works are good which God has commanded, and only those are evil which he has forbidden us. Here fall away fish and flesh, cowl and tonsure.[6]
5. The mass is not a sacrifice, but a memorial of the death of Christ,[7] for which reason it cannot be offered either for the

[5] Cf. Zwingli's Thesis 2: "Summa of the gospel is that our Lord Jesus Christ, true Son of God, manifested to us the will of his heavenly Father, and that with his innocence he redeemed and reconciled us with God." Z 1, p. 458,[13-15] and Z 2, p. 27.[16ff.]
[6] Zwingli's Thesis 26 condemns cowl and tonsure, but for a different reason: because embellishment is hypocrisy. Z 2, p. 249.
[7] Cf. Zwingli's Thesis 18: "Since Christ once sacrificed himself, being eternally a pardoning valid sacrifice for the sins of all believers, it follows that the mass is not a sacrifice, but a commemoration of the sacrifice and an assurance of the redemption which Christ proved to us." Z 1, p. 460, and Z 2, pp. 111.[26ff.]

dead or for the living. Hereby requiem masses and memorial masses of the seventh day, the thirtieth day, and of the anniversary collapse.

6. As often as such commemoration is held, the death of the Lord shall be proclaimed in the tongue of every land. Here all dumb masses[8] fall on one heap.

7. Images are good for nothing. Henceforth such expenditures shall be devoted not to wood and stone, but to the living needy images of God.

8. Since every Christian believes and is baptized for himself every one should see and should judge by Scripture, whether he is being rightly fed and watered by his shepherd.

9. Since Christ alone died for our sin, in whose name alone we are baptized, so shall only he be appealed to as our sole Intercessor and Mediator. Here all pilgrimages fall away.

10. It is far better to translate a single verse of a psalm into each land's language for the people, than to sing five whole psalms in a strange language not understood by the church. Here matins, prime, terce, sext, nones, vespers, compline, and vigils disappear.

11. All teachings, which God himself did not plant, are in vain, interdicted, and shall be uprooted.[9] Hereby fall to the earth Aristotle, scholastics like Thomas, Scotus, Bonaventure, and Occam, and all teaching that does not spring forth from the Word of God.

12. The hour is coming and is now when no one will be counted a priest, /74/ except he preach the Word of God. Here fall away early masses, votive, requiem, and middle masses.[10]

13. The fellows[11] of a congregation are obligated to maintain with appropriate food and clothing and to protect those

---

[8] *Stummende messen*, celebration of the mass whereby the celebrant's words are inaudible.

[9] This implicit reference to Matt. 15:13 places Hubmaier solidly in the Zwinglian camp with regard to the theory of reformation. The Lutheran and Anglican Reformers tended to reject what is forbidden by Scripture and to retain what is not forbidden. Zwingli originally rejected all usages which were not explicitly commanded, on the basis of Matt. 15:13; Z 1, p. 549.

[10] The term *mittelmess* seems to have no English equivalent. These are forms of eucharistic celebration without a sermon.

[11] The term *fellow (kirchgenossen)* is unusual. It points to a concept of membership involving rights and obligations, different from the picture of the parish folk as a public or an audience.

who exposit to them the pure, clear, and unmixed Word of God. This destroys courtisans,[12] pensioners, members of collegia,[13] absentees, and babblers of lies and dreams.[14]

14. Whoever would look for purgatory, on which those whose God is their belly have been building for years, is seeking Moses' grave, which he shall never find.

15. To forbid marriage to priests and then tolerate their carnal immorality is to free Barabbas and to kill Christ.[15]

16. To promise chastity in human strength is nothing other than to promise to fly over the sea without wings.

17. He who denies or silences the Word of God for temporal gain trades God's blessing with Red Esau for a lentil stew, and Christ will also deny him.

18. He who does not seek his bread in the sweat of his brow is banned and unworthy of the food he eats. Hereby are cursed all loafers, whoever they be.

Truth Is Unkillable.[16]
1524

---

[12] The editors of HS (p. 74, fn. 15) suggest "benefice-chasers." The more likely meaning of the word would be, more broadly, anyone currying favor at the prince's court; but since the specific offense is being financially supported otherwise than by the congregation, the meaning in context is the same.

[13] *Incorporierter*, persons who receive financial support by virtue of being incorporated in some endowed group. Such endowments had been created by donors desirous of assuring that masses would continue to be said for them after their death.

[14] The reference is to Jeremiah 23:25-32. "Lies" (*lugender*) is a frequent pun for "legends." The sixteenth century reference may be both to the lives of saints and to accounts of visions and apparitions. The focus of polemic has shifted from people whose living is endowed to those whose message is not the gospel.

[15] Cf. Zwingli's Theses 29 Z 1, pp. 461,[22-24] 463,[26-27] and Z 2, pp. 263,[6ff.] 361.[1ff.]

[16] Cf. below, p. 42, text 3, note 12, for the various possible renderings of this epigram.

3

An Earnest Christian Appeal to Schaffhausen

Partly because of its geographical and social position, but also largely because of Hubmaier's presence and leadership, Waldshut became a center of Reformation movement parallel to that of Zwingli, Oekolampad, and Bucer in Zurich, Basel, and Strasbourg. The beginning of the Peasants' War took place in nearby Stühlingen on June 23, 1524. South German cities like Waldshut sought to take a mediating position between the peasants on the one hand and the nobles, loyal to the empire, on the other.

The sympathy of Waldshut for the Protestant movement began to cause political difficulties already in the middle of 1524. The city was under direct Austrian sovereignty, permitting far less self-determination than was enjoyed by the larger cities which were beginning to open themselves to the new ideas. In late August 1524 Hubmaier took refuge in Schaffhausen, whose reformer Sebastian Hofmeister had shared with him the status of outside participant in the Zurich disputation of October 1523. Perhaps his reason for leaving Waldshut was the hope of getting out of the way of a negotiated peace between Waldshut and the Austrians. Schaffhausen was the nearest city of the Swiss Confederacy, committed to the Protestant movement but not as prominently so as Zurich.

The Swiss city was under pressure to extradite Hubmaier to the Austrians: our text is his defense against that danger. It gives us valuable insight both into some aspects of his reforming activity and into the case for religious liberty which is the central theme of his early writings.

The Catholic cantons demanded that Hubmaier be taken prisoner and turned over to his accusers. He was therefore pleading not simply for a formal hearing, which so far as we know was never granted, but for the privilege of asylum, which was granted briefly, at least tacitly.

In these brief petitions we find much that Hubmaier later will develop further:

Artist's interpretation of Waldshut in the eighteenth century

Foto-Bauer, neben dem Ratshaus

Waldshut am Hochrhein
im 18. Jahrhundert

- *His favorite phrases, "Truth Is Unkillable" and "I may be wrong, I am human, but a heretic I cannot be, for I ask to be taught."*
- *His positive view of government as servant of God.*
- *His case for freedom of religion from control by the state.*
- *His trust in open conversation, whereby the Word of God once exposited makes its own way by convincing the congregation.*

Presumably the three "appeals" and the preface were written and submitted at different times.

By November 1524 Hubmaier was back in Waldshut, apparently having visited Zwingli in Zurich on the way back. The political climate in Waldshut had been improved by then by military support from Zurich. The presence of volunteer soldiers from Protestant Zurich accelerated the Reformation movement, aggravated the tensions with Austria, and provoked a faster pace of diplomatic negotiations in early November.

In addition to the manuscript submitted at Schaffhausen, which has survived in the archives, the text was printed in Basel sometime in 1524.[1]

To the Honorable Council of Schaffhausen, a Petition of Doctor Baldazar

Honorable, wise, gracious Lords:

I have learned by chance that your Honors[2] are going to deal with my affairs today. It is therefore my urgent request to you, my Lords, that you give earnest consideration to the three petitions that I have presented to your Honors. For I

---

[1] Earlier translations have been made by Vedder and Davidson, and selected paraphrases are found in Estep. Partial translation in Hošek 1891, pp. 133f., Vedder, 1905, pp. 82-83; Davidson 1939, pp. 11-24; Estep 1976, pp. 44-46. A first draft of the present translation was made by Elizabeth Horsch Bender. Source: HS 2, pp. 76-84.

[2] The standard complimentary term used to address a ruler, applied here as well to the Council, is E. W. for *Eure Weisheit*, literally "your Wisdom." "Your Honors" is here substituted as a rough equivalent in archaic English usage. Later in this collection the more literal "Your Wisdom" or "Your Grace" is used.

still make today the request that I made earlier; I cry and
appeal to your Honors for judgment and justice, that for God's
sake you will not deprive me of justice. Consider that the
cause is not mine but God's, whose glory and honor are at
stake, and our Christian faith. May your Honors consider this
and not my person. I cling to your reputation (concerning
which I have no doubt), which has always been highly
esteemed in the praiseworthy Confederation, namely that you
never refuse justice to anyone. Fulfill this in my case with all
fairness, so that your old and Christian reputation may not be
weakened. If on any day of my life /77/ I should have fallen
from heaven in order to appeal for justice and its implementation, I would have chosen to fall into the common Confederation. I ask nothing more of God or of your Honors
under open heaven and in public than to give and to receive
justice. But I beseech you, do not let me be discredited by the
lies invented behind my back by my detractors. My opponents
have brought an accusation to you to capture and try me, and
your Honors have taken it upon yourselves to do this to me.
Therefore I in turn appeal for justice in the good hope that
my appeal against them will likewise not be rejected. I will
vouch for and compensate for such justice more than
abundantly, with people and with money.[3] Let me face the
pastors of Apozell, Vri, Schwitz, and Baden, and the preacher
of Premgartten.[4] I want to reply to them. If I am then found
to be in the right, of which I have no doubt whatever with
God's help, then consider what deep sorrow and sin you would
be committing if you thus would unjustly sentence innocent
blood to death, which would then, with the blood of Abel, cry
aloud against you and your children forever. To say nothing of
the fact that for the whole city such a deed would result to
the third and fourth generation in mockery and injury to your
reputation. How inexpressibly great the resulting scandal
among all Christian people would be, I will let your Honors
estimate. It must also be taken into consideration that such
actions would not end with me but would spread, for my case

---

[3] Is Hubmaier offering to cover court costs?
[4] These are the most ardently Catholic towns and cantons. Hubmaier was
personally acquainted with at least some of the priests he here designates.
Bergsten 1961, p. 170.

would have made the first breach in the fence of justice. Gracious Lords, your Honors are surely aware that I did not come here with the intention of staying. But since this emergency has come upon me here, it is God's will; accordingly, may your Honors also place your wills together with mine into God's will, for verily, verily, the truth will have the victory.[5] But if I should be found to be in the wrong, your Honors have sword, fire, and water that can cut, burn, and drown here as well as elsewhere; in accord with the circumstances of the offense you should then not let me go without punishing me with prison and death, and then you could indeed answer for it to God and to everyone. Let events take their course, for the honorable city of Schaffhausen has now for several years listened with joy to the clear divine Word; but now God wants to put to a test what it has effected in us and what fruit it is bringing forth. For where Christ is, he carries his cross with him. If we cast the cross from us, then neither will Christ abide. Therefore let us all esteem God more highly than men and the eternal more than the temporal and finally trust God for this. Then he will doubtlessly care and fight for us much better than we ourselves. He will bring the truth and falsehood to light and will finally be victorious and grant us eternal bliss. I herewith commend you to God.

> Your wisdom's obedient Baldazar Fridberger,
> Doctor, Pastor at Waldshutt. /78/

---

[5] Does the "victory" of the "truth" mean only Hubmaier's being cleared? Or does he mean that God will strengthen Schaffhausen against the Austrians?

*An Earnest Christian Appeal
to the Honorable Council
of Schaffhusen, by Doctor
Baldazar Hůbmör
von Fridberg,
Pastor at Waldshůt.
Truth Is Unkillable.*[6]
1524

The First Appeal
To the Honorable Council of Schaffhusen.

Honorable, foresighted, wise, and gracious Lords:

After I had come here some time ago to your Honors' city of Schaffhusen with no other intention than to await whatever would befall me here and then to go on to some other place where I planned to settle and stay for a while, I received a warning that the authorities were about to arrest me. Although I had always looked to your Honors for grace, I then went into hiding out of inborn human fear until I could learn what it was about, although I am aware of no reason why I would be afraid. However, when one is repeatedly falsely maligned, which seemingly has happened to me in this case, I am ready and willing to answer before your Honors any demand and accusation that anyone thinks he has against me and to give and receive justice and then abide by the outcome, whether for weal or for woe. Likewise I will not in the meantime make any change in my person or my possessions[7] and will do everything required in an affair of this kind. But I hope that your Honors will show me the grace not to take me by force or to imprison me before the conclusion of the action, for I am not going to run away; on this you may depend. But if your Honors should not find this legitimate, please indicate this to

---

[6] See below, note 12.

[7] I.e., he will not dispose of his property so as to evade financial responsibility. He is evidently not yet in the hands of the authorities.

me also. In short, if I should be found innocent, I should /79/ benefit from it. Should I be found guilty, let me be punished in body and possessions in accord with the seriousness of the crime. I request the grace of a reply to this, and your, my Lords, counsel and instruction.

Your Wisdom's obedient Doctor Balthasar
Hubmor of Friedberg, Pastor
at Waldtshût.

The Second Appeal
to the Honorable Council of Schaffhausen

Honorable, foresighted, wise, and gracious Lords:
The appeal I presented to your Honors in writing you have doubtless received. I request that your Honors send it to Milords the confederates[8] so that they may see that I have happiness in God to give an account to their grace[9] with the Holy Scriptures and divine truth. I would therefore also be glad to have them bring the pastors of Lucern, Apozell, Vri, or Baden; we will then apply and expound God's Word to one another so clearly and plainly that it would itself be the judge as to which has hitherto been teaching rightly or wrongly. Every pious Christian will not only hear this but will also see, and grasp it in faith, that it is so.[10] If I am wrong, let me be punished. But if the priests are defeated, I ask now for God's sake that they may be led to recognize their error and not be punished afterwards.[11] My reason for urging so strenuously that you not imprison or force me is not that I am so deeply

---

[8] The political structure of Switzerland centered on the periodic consultations of representatives of the several cantons. "Milords the confederates" therefore refers to the next meeting of the government of the confederacy, dominated at this time by the Catholic cantons, smaller but more numerous than the ones open to the Reformation.

[9] "Their grace" may mean a trial before the confederacy.

[10] This trust in the common man's ability to see the truth once it is heard is further spelled out in text 4 below, p. 52.

[11] It was typical for Anabaptists to ask for a debate with unequal stakes. Conrad Grebel, requesting a hearing before the Zurich government, was reported as saying, "... if Master Ulrich would win out, he, Conrad, would be willing to be burned, whereas if he, Conrad would win out, he would not demand that Zwingli should be burned." Bender, Grebel, p. 151. Cf. Harder 1965, p. 422.

afraid, but that I know that it would be far more praiseworthy and comforting to the divine Word and to all Christian believers if I submit to this spiritual contest willingly and with joy than if I were forced and compelled. But this alone is my deepest regret: that your Honors have to give yourselves so much trouble in this matter on my account. But if one really considers it, it is not my cause but God's who has brought it about; to him be praise in heaven. Your Honors, do not be afraid of me, nor will I be afraid, for divine truth is unkillable. Even if it may for a time be imprisoned, scourged, crowned, crucified, and laid into a grave, it would /80/ nevertheless arise again victorious on the third day and reign and triumph forever.[12] May your Honors be herewith commended to the almighty God through our Lord Jesus Christ.

Your Wisdom's Willing Baltasar Hubmor
Doctor, etc.

The Third Appeal
to the Honorable Council of Schaffhausen

Foresighted, gracious Lords,

I am herewith sending your Honors the third appeal, beyond which I can appeal no more, with the urgent petition that you send it on to the common confederates. If you will also allow me a city messenger with a weapon I will at once send it on to the Lords now assembled at [Radolf]zell[13] and to

---

[12] This sentence represents the fullest definition in his own words of Hubmaier's personal slogan, "Truth Is Unkillable." It is the same term in the several usages on title pages and as epilogue. Other translators, on strong grounds based in contemporary usage, prefer the less literal *indestructible* or *invincible* or *immortal*. There was probably a proverbial tradition recognized by Hubmaier's readers. "Truth conquers" was a Czech Brethren slogan. "Truth prevails" was Menno's phrase. According to the preference of editor Yoder, the less elegant and more literal translation sometimes renders best the nuance of the parallel to the cross and resurrection of Christ. The point is not that truth is timeless or never dies, but that it rises again, that it cannot be kept down. There may be an allusion to Acts 2:24. Cf. below, text 7, note 10, pp. 76-77.

[13] Radolfzell on the Lake of Constance was the seat of the regional legation of the Holy Roman imperial government, to which the Helvetic Confederation rendered formal respect though no real obedience.

my gracious Lord [bishop] of Constenz. To be worthy of such
kindness in God's sight will always be my earnest endeavor.

Our God, Lord and Creator of heaven and earth, who
guards and numbers every hair of our heads, without whom
the least bird does not fall to the ground, who has also bent
his bow and flaming arrow, and forged the instrument of
eternal death, has commanded all authorities and judges
through Moses in the first chapter of Deuteronomy: "Hear
[the cases between] your brethren and judge righteously
between everyone and his brother or the sojourner. You shall
be impartial in judgment; you shall hear the small and the
great alike; you shall not respect the person of anyone, for the
judgment is God's. If a case is too hard for you, you shall
bring it to Moses that he may hear it" [Deut. 1:16b-18]. These
are the plain, clear words of God spoken through Moses,
which should be weighed well and earnestly by all who
occupy seats of authority and wear the sword at their side.
For he says first, solemnly, "Hear [the cases] between your
brethren" [Deut. 1:16a.] He said, "Hear." One must always
hear the other side too if one is to judge correctly and not
condemn without a hearing. This is God's will and is required
by nature and fraternal love; for if I would not want to be
sentenced without a hearing of my case, should I then fail to
do it toward my brother? This is what God teaches and
admonishes us when he says, "Hear /81/ your brethren, be
mindful that they are your brothers and judge justly." For
thus one judges justly when he has God and his Word before
his eyes, as if each king or judge had the book of divine law
transcribed for him (as God himself commands), "that it shall
be with him and he shall read in it the days of his life, that he
may learn to fear the Lord his God by keeping all the words
of this law and these statutes and doing them. He shall not lift
up his heart above his brethren and shall not turn aside from
the command of the divine Word, neither to the right nor to
the left," Deut. 17:19-20a. Hereby fall away all old practices,
customs, origins, ancestors, fathers, councils, and scholastics,
if they depart to the right or to the left and do not
straightway follow the divine Word.

Second, God says: "And judge righteously between every
man and his brother or the sojourner" [Deut. 1:16b]. Here
God wills that everyone be weighed on the same just scales,

disregarding whether he is a native or a foreigner. For in the word "brother" the judge, the native, and the foreigner shall come together and be as one. In these words God gives us to understand clearly that there is no validity whatever in the excuse that says: "Well, of what concern is he to us, he is not one of us, he is an outsider." No, not so; for God adds: "You shall not be respecters of persons" [Deut. 1:17a], but shall regard alike the noble, the ignoble, rich, poor, acquaintance, stranger, powerful, mighty, native-born, widows, orphans, and sojourners, and shall not look askance on one side of the case more than on the other, but you shall hear the small, the unimportant, the simple and poor like the great, the worldly-wise, splendid, and rich; that is God's will.

Third, God warns all judges and rulers that they should not be intimidated or afraid of anyone's person, for judgment is God's [Deut. 1:17b]. Here every Christian can see and understand that it is worthless to say: "Yes, I must do this, for it is the wish of my lords and rulers." No, no, that is not right! God alone is the Lord and rulers of all who sit in the seat of judgment, for judgment belongs to him and to no other. Therefore one must judge and give sentence only in accord with God's will, which can be learned only from his Word. He who now judges otherwise is not seated on the judgment seat of God but on the footstool of men, and he takes away from God that which belongs to God, namely judgment, and gives it to man. Therefore Paul also calls authority the handmaiden of God. He calls judges servants of God who are to sit and rule here on earth in God's stead. But if ever (which God forbid) anything should be commanded or forbidden which is against God's command, then God says /82/ that we should not be intimidated or fear before such a person, but cry out with Moses, "Judgment is God's" [Deut. 1:17]. Or indeed with the holy apostles, who were also forbidden by government to speak anymore in the name of Jesus: "We must obey God more than man" [Acts 5:29].

Fourth, God says through Moses: "But if a case should be too difficult for you, let it be brought before Moses" [Deut. 1:17b]. Here all Christian believers find in a parable who is to be the judge in difficult cases, such as those that concern the soul. Surely, no one but Moses in his five books. Likewise God also commands this through the prophet Ezekiel, chapter 44, where he orders that the people be taught the difference between the holy and the common and between the clean and the unclean. But if a controversy should arise, men should judge according to God's judgments, for he has for that purpose given his law and commandments. Christ has illuminated this even more clearly when he says: "They have Moses and the prophets" [Luke 16:29]. By these words he points us to the Scriptures, as he says further: "Search the Scriptures, for they will testify of me" [John 5:39]. And at another place: "If one hears my sayings and does not keep them, I do not judge him; the word that I have spoken will be his judge" [John 12:47a, 48b]. It is therefore great folly for some who falsely claim to be highly learned to want to set a judge over the divine Word, although as Paul teaches us (and Christ before him) the gathered congregation indeed may judge from the divine Word which one is a true or a false prophet, lest anyone be led astray.[14] But the living Word of God cannot suffer a judge. Nor should any Christian dare to judge it; he would then not only, like Lucifer, make himself equal to God, but also would be setting himself above God; that would indeed be unchristian presumptuousness and wickedness.

But why have I made such a lengthy introduction? For the reason that I have repeatedly, as I am well aware, been accused and denounced before the authorities as a seducer of the people, seditionary, a Lutheran, a heretic, and similar epithets. The God-fearing honorable town of Waldshût has been vilified high and wide because of my teachings, for which especially I grieve from the bottom of my heart. It is therefore my urgent plea and friendly request to all believers in Christ that henceforth no one, be he called religious or secular, should malign or injure me or the town of Waldshût, for I am willing and ready to give an account to all men for my teaching, faith, and hope as I preached there for two years. If my teaching has been right, why do they strike me /83/ and others on my account? If my teaching has been false and erroneous, I call and appeal to all Christian believers that they produce evidence of the evil and lead me again to the

---

[14] Hubmaier's Scripture sources here may have been 1 Cor. 14:29-37 and Matt. 18:18-20. Cf. text 4 below, pp. 50 ff., on how the congregation properly judges.

right path with the Word of God and show me the real Jacob's ladder that I may together with them ascend to heaven on it. For I may be wrong, I am human, but a heretic I cannot be, because I am begging for instruction.[15] If it is one's duty to lead home a straying ass or ox, much more is the same due to me, whoever might do it, in writing or orally, be it the herdsman Amos, Balaam's ass, David's mule, Tobias's dog, the wise men's star, or Saint Peter's rooster. All that matters is that I be led to an understanding of God's Word, that I may with Peter bitterly weep for my sin and error, that I will gratefully accept from anyone although (God lives) I am not aware of having preached even a single letter in these two years[16] that was without foundation in God's Word. But this I confess and of this declare myself guilty, that I have not expressed everything as perfectly as I knew; I have spared the weak in faith whom I had to bring up at that time with milk and not with stronger food.[17] With that I further appeal: Since the emergency of needing to defend myself overtook me here at Schaffhusen, so that here I appeal to everyone for justice and right, and am willing to give and to receive justice, of this I have sufficiently guaranteed assurance and will let weal and woe take their course for me. If only no violence is done meanwhile either to me or to the God-fearing town of Waldshût, I shall willingly and with joy submit to this combat of faith. I herewith beg for God's sake and by the judgment day when all must give an account of their office, all Christian emperors, kings, princes, cities, and lords, especially [I beg] the honorable, stalwart and praiseworthy Confederation, which throughout the ages has never denied anyone his legal rights,

---

[15] This is another slogan Hubmaier often repeats. Error involves no deep guilt: heresy does. The difference is not material (holding the wrong beliefs) but formal: the heretic is one who refuses to be set straight.

[16] This is the second reference in this paragraph to what Hubmaier had preached for the past "two years." We have no sources from "two years" earlier (late 1522) to identify the point in time or the key doctrinal issue with regard to which Hubmaier was conscious of moving into the Protestant camp. His statement here is the clearest basis for such an estimate. It would correspond with the end of his first stay at Waldshut. Bergsten 1961, p. 106.

[17] Hubmaier says that if anything he is guilty of wrong forbearance, *schonung*, withholding some of the truth from the weak. On *schonung* cf. Yoder 1961, p. 31; Yoder 1968, 52f., 193f.; and Harder 1985, p. 677, note 17.

and also the honorable, wise Mayor and Council of Schaffhusen and the entire Christian public, not to let me or any other Christian teacher be subject to force or compulsion in the future, but to give me a hearing, to put me face-to-face with my opponents who have charged me with being so harmful not to regard, respect, or fear any person before the law, be he lowly or great, but to judge justly, for judgment is /84/ God's [Deut. 1:17]. If I am then found to be in the wrong, let me be punished in body and life,[18] for it would be a pity to let such harmful people as I am untruthfully presented to continue to live on earth. But if my opponents are defeated, I ask once more for God's sake that they be brought to a recognition of their error, also that they cease such words of disgrace and shame, improve their teachings and life, and henceforth walk before the people with right Christian teaching in which alone souls can live, and not with human prattle, and after all this be allowed to go free of any fine or punishment. But if this, my earnest and sincere plea, should not be fulfilled (which, however, I would not expect even from the Turks), but if I should by prison, torture, sword, fire, or water be compelled [to speak] differently, or if God in other ways should withdraw his grace from me so that I would speak or confess otherwise than by God's illumination I am now minded.[19] I hereupon profess and testify before God, my heavenly Father, and before all men that I want to suffer and die as a Christian so that I may cause no one to stumble because of my behavior, whatever God may allow to befall me. Still I herewith cry to God, my heavenly Father, through Jesus Christ, my only Savior. I also beg all believers in Christ that they may help to pray with me to God that he may impart to

---

[18] Cf. note 10 above. Hubmaier does not here challenge the authority of government to punish heretics, since that discussion would get in the way of his first concern, which is to show that he is not an heretic himself. At the same time he was preparing to argue that heretics should not be killed (cf. text 5, pp. 58 ff.). The interrelation of these two positions is linked to the "unequal stakes" argument cited in note 11 above.

[19] Although the sentence is incomplete in the original, it finds its completion in the subsequent sentence. Hubmaier is aware of possible personal weakness of will in the face of persecution. He does not promise to be able to resist torture. He looks forward to the possibility that he might be driven to recant, and protests that he would wish to be ready for martyrdom.

me his grace, strength, and fortitude, and grant me a brave, undismayed, and noble spirit that I may persist in his holy Word and finally in true Christian faith commend my spirit into the hands of God, my heavenly Father, through our Lord Jesus Christ, his only begotten Son, who lives and reigns with him in the communion of God's Holy Spirit, one God. Amen.

Lord, into thy hands I commend my poor little soul.

4
Theses Against Eck

Dr. John Maier from Egg (1486-1543), usually known as Eck, was previously Hubmaier's university teacher and now the leading Catholic polemicist against the Zwinglian Reformation. On August 13, 1524, Eck addressed to the Swiss Confederacy a "Missive and Petition" against the innovations of the Reformation.[1] Zwingli's answer to Eck was dated August 31[2] and Hubmaier's parallel reaction, the present text, was in Eck's hands by September 18; Hubmaier must therefore have written it during the first days of his stay in Schaffhausen or even his last days in Waldshut.[3]

*Theses which the fly[4] Baldazar Pacimontanus
[Pastor in Waldshût]
a brother in Christ, of Huldrych Zwingli,
has offered to the elephant John Eck
at Ingolstadt, to examine them masterfully.
In a conflict of faith, where two are
in disagreement, then who should be
the proper judge?
Truth Is Unkillable. /88/*

---

[1] Z 3, No. 39, p. 304

[2] Ibid., p. 305.

[3] The text was printed in both Latin (HS 3, pp. 87-90) and German (HS 3, pp. 91-94). The Latin was the original, as befits a challenge to a debate. The German was probably not written by Hubmaier himself. The editors of HS 3 (p. 85) give various linguistic arguments against the German being Hubmaier's. Earlier translations: Hošek 1891, pp. 143ff.; Vedder 1905, p. 89; Davidson 1939, pp. 35-43.

[4] The ironic references to the fly and the elephant are only in the Latin; "Pastor in Waltzhût" is only in the German. The self-designation as "brother in Christ of Zwingli" is the first formal statement of Hubmaier's allegiance to the Reformation. The prepositional phrase "in Christ" is only in the Latin. In view of the two men's earlier personal relationship (Moore 1981), it is striking that the text does not contain more personal allusions.

Jl.

ꜰ⬥AXIOMATA⬥ꜱ

QVAE BALDAZAR PACIMONTANVS, MVSCA,
Huldrychi Zuinglij in Chriſto frater, Ioanni Eckio
Ingoldſtadienſi Elephanto, magiſtraliter
examinanda propoſuit.

In controuerſia fidei, ubi duo diſſen⸗
tiunt, quis debeat eſſe
Iudex.

cerp oimep. fer r ɛimpoɦɩp vɛriɩariſ ferrerrif

⌘ Veritas eſt immortalis. ⌘

Friderici Gibely
ꜱ 6 o 8.

Title page of the Latin printed version of the Theses.

I

Every Christian is obligated to give account for his hope and thereby of the faith which is in him to whoever desires it. (1 Pet. 3:15)[5]

II

For he who confesses Christ before men, not fearing those who kill the body, the same Christ will confess before his Father. (Matt. 10:28, 32; Mark 8:38,)

III

With the heart one believes genuinely unto righteousness; but with the mouth occurs confession unto eternal salvation. (Rom. 10:10)

IV

Unless you believe you will not understand it. I have believed; therefore I have spoken. How then will they believe Him whom they have not heard? (Isa. 6:9; Ps. 116:10; Rom. 10:14)

V

Further the decision which of two understands it more correctly is conceived in the church by the Word of God and born out of faith. When you come together, etc., the others should judge. (1 Cor. 14:26)[6]

---

[5] The verse references to each thesis are printed in the margin directly opposite the main body of the text, in very small characters. Here, to avoid footnoting all marginalia, they are reproduced in parenthesis following each thesis. Following the general practice of the time, Scripture references are given in the original only with a chapter numeral. The verse number indicated is that supplied in HS by editor Bergsten. In some cases it is not fully clear to just what section of the indicated chapter Hubmaier means to be alluding.

[6] This article V is the first which goes beyond citing specific biblical texts to state a procedural understanding regarding how to hold a meeting. It now becomes visible that Hubmaier is not simply making a statement about confession or theological affirmations. He is describing the ground rules for a theological conversation. This trust in the gathered congregation, as empowered by the Spirit to pass on the truth as exposited by prophets and teachers, is a conviction common to all the Zwinglian

VI

Still so that order may be maintained and disorderly chatter avoided, three or four men shall be properly elected out of the church, as, for instance, were Peter, Paul, Barnabas, and James. Not that they should stand in judgment over the truth of the Word, which is eternal and unchanging, but [to judge] which party comes closest to the intent of the divine Word or deviates from it. (Acts 15:2, 1 Pet. 1:23, Luke 12)[7]

VII

Thus the apostles of Christ held counsel, not for the sake of the doctrine of faith, but in order to maintain unity among the brethren. (Acts 15)[8]

VIII

Their judgment shall fall according to the plumb line of Holy Scripture. Otherwise, it would be rejected by the same authority with which it is spoken. This follows from the example of Christ, where he ruled on the heads of grain plucked by the apostles according to Scripture. (Acts 15; Matt. 15; Matt. 12:1ff.; Mark 2:23ff.; Luke 6:1ff.; 1 Sam. 21)

Reformation: Cf. Zwingli himself: "So when the prophets explain, the whole church should judge, that is: all of the others, whether he is doing it right or not. See, on what grounds the church should judge, or by what capacity, when she is just now hearing something she has never heard before? Answer: by virtue of the God who dwells in them. When God is in a man, then he understands at once what is or is not spoken to the honor of God and the welfare of the neighbor. Thus in one stroke is made clear that the pope together with all his adherents should be judged by the church, e.g., from those to whom he preaches; and he must not impose the Word upon them but they should judge him. Behold in what error the papacy is! "On the Preaching office," Z 4, pp. 395[25]-96.[3]

[7] It is not clear what is the point of the reference to Luke 12.

[8] The line between doctrine and matters of church order and practice seems to be very clear for Hubmaier. All doctrine he understands to be undebatably clear in the very words of Scripture; the realm of order and practice is that concerning which Christians need to study together. This distinction is repeated in Art. XVI.

IX

Search in Scripture, not in papal law, not councils, not fathers, not schools; for it is the discourse which Christ spoke which shall judge all things. He is the truth, the plantation, and the vine. (John 5:39; 12:48; 14:6; 15:1; Matt. 15)[9]

X

It follows therefrom that the judges should be God-learned and God-inspired. (John 6)[10]

XI

Then if they are taught by God, so as to set aside all human motivation, they are sitting with Mary at the feet of the Lord, opening the Bible with a prayerful spirit, searching the Scriptures like the noble Thessalonians to see whether things are so; /89/ like the learned scribe they are bringing forth new and old, to which they submit themselves without any speculation or disputation, receiving out of the teaching of the Lord according to the blessing of Moses. (Luke 14; Luke 10:39; James 1:5; 2 Tim. 3:15; 1 Kings 3; Acts 17:11; John 5:39; Matt. 13:52; Acts 19; 1 Cor. 11; Deut. 33)

XII

Searching the Scriptures does not take place with unspiritual chatter about innovations, nor with wordy warfare fighting until one is hoarse, but rather by illuminating the darker texts of Scripture with the clearer.[11] This is just what Christ taught us when he explained the Scripture of Moses

---

[9] The theory of reformation held by Zwingli and his friends and followers was based upon Matthew 15:13: what the Father did not plant shall be uprooted and destroyed (cf. above, p. 33, note 9). The term "planting" is thus a technical reference to those particular usages which were instituted by Christ.

[10] Within the Latin text Hubmaier uses the Greek terms *theodidactos* and *theopneustos*. In German he or his translator coins the clumsy equivalents *gotglernig* and *gotsgeystig*.

[11] That some texts which are clearer than others should be used to interpret the obscure ones is a standard principle of Reformation hermeneutics.

concerning Levirate marriage by reference to the Scripture on resurrection. (1 Tim. 6:4; Deut. 25:5ff.; Matt. 22:23ff.; Mark 12:35ff.; Luke 20:27ff.)

XIII

Blessed are they, and shall receive eternal life, who thus explicate Scripture and exercise themselves day and night in the law of the Lord. (Eccles. 14, Ps. 1:2)

XIV

The judgment on the part of the arbiters[12] shall be that one who is seated, to whom something is revealed, shall have his free right to continue; the former speaker shall then be silent. (1 Cor. 14:30)

XV

But when in fact everyone becomes silent, then the judgment of the umpires is confirmed through the silence of the church. (Acts 15:12)

XVI

The church is doubtless to be heard in such matters as concern offense or brotherly love; but in matters of faith [decision shall be made] in no other way than solely according to the rule of Scripture. (Matt. 18:15ff.; Deut. 4, 12; Rom. 14)

XVII

All persons may prophesy one by one, so that everyone may learn and all may receive encouragement. (1 Cor. 14:31)

---

[12] The Latin term *arbitros* (German, *erkennenden*) is intentionally a non-theological legal one: arbitrator, umpire, judge, witness, observer; the role is to moderate and to record the congregation's conclusion, not to lead in reaching the conclusion. Again, compare with Zwingli's *On the Preaching Office:* "Now when the prophets have spoken one after another in an orderly way, and in the meantime God has revealed the meaning of Scripture to someone sitting in the congregation, it would be proper [for him] to speak concerning the meaning of the Scripture, but with such order and discipline that if someone else begins to speak, the former one will be silent." See Z 4, p. 396.[6ff.]

XVIII

Therefore God, who is not the author of disorder but of peace, has subjected the spirit of the prophets to the prophets, as in all gatherings of the saints. (1 Cor. 14:32f.)[13]

XIX

Protect yourselves against false prophets. Watch that no one seduces you. Test the spirits, whether they are from God, and give attention to those who cause contention and offense outside of the doctrine which you have learned. Avoid the same, for they serve not Christ but their own belly. Through sweet talk and speech they seduce the heart of the innocent in order to receive twelve hundred ducats from the pope. (Matt. 7:15; 24:4; 1 John 4:1ff.; Rom. 16, 18)[14]

XX

Woe to them, for without doubt they are sons of Eli, or if you prefer, sons of Samuel. Blinded by gifts they godlessly distort the judgment of God. Phooey on Simon, Bah to Gehazi. (1 Sam. 2:12ff.; 9:3ff.; Acts 8:9ff.; 2 Kings 5:19) /90/

XXI

In this spiritual combat everyone must apply himself to prophesy and be armed with the armor of the Holy Spirit, that he might fearlessly enter the lists with Christ against Satan. (1 Cor. 14; Eph. 6; Matt. 4)

---

[13] The German *Zertrennung* suggests not only "confusion" but also "schism" or "conflict." Compare with Zwingli's *On the Preaching Office:* "For the spirits of the prophets are subject to the prophets; that is, if they are the prophets of God, they will gladly listen to those who reveal the hidden meaning of Scripture. And all of this will take place peacefully; for God is not a God of disorder and dissension but a God of peace." See Z 4p. 397.[1ff.]

[14] Editor Bergsten does not suggest whether the amount of 1,200 ducats is the size of a papal pension; some such allusion is presumably intended.

XXII

In this gathering women shall be silent and at home they should learn from their husbands, so that everything might take place properly and in order. (1 Cor. 14:34; 1 Tim. 2:2; Joel 2; 1 Cor. 11)

XXIII

But where the men are afraid and have become women, then the women should speak up and become manly, like Deborah, Hulda, Anna the prophetess, the four daughters of the evangelist Philip, and in our times Argula.[15] (Judges 4—5; 1 Chron. 34:22ff.; Luke 2:36ff.; Acts 21:9; Acts 18; Deut. 1:28ff.)

XXIV

Therefore the judges should be theologians,[16] sound in doctrine, not hooded nor capped,[17] but instructed in divine teaching by God himself, carrying the breastplate of Aaron on their breast. (Titus 1; John 6; 2 Pet. 1; Exod. 28:15ff.)

XXV

The learned ones are still to be listened to, but they are learned who like Josiah daily read the book of the law, who also have Moses and the prophets. (2 Kings 22; 2 Chron. 34; Luke 16:29)

XXVI

They who do not read the Book of the Law and the Prophets, in which the promise to us was long ago given by

---

[15] Argula of Grumbach, a Bavarian noblewoman, wrote several evangelical pamphlets, including one of 1523 directed particularly against Eck's University of Ingolstadt.

[16] The same persons as the "arbiters" above. The German here again uses *gotzglernig* (cf. note 7) but the Latin has *theologi*.

[17] I.e., neither monks nor doctors.

God the Father, should not hear[18] the process of faith nor can they be judges. (Deut. 18:15; Luke 9:35; Matt. 3; Mark 1; 1 Cor. 1)

Where is now the wise man? The scribe? The debater of this world? Eck? Let him come to us, the lordly Hercules from Ingolstatt, seized (unless I am mistaken) by Herculean disease,[19] and let him hold a disputation,[20] in the cause of faith. If he now comes, we shall praise him.

—Printed in Tiguri [Zurich] by Christophori Froschouer, November 4, 1524

---

[18] "Hear" in the judicial sense: "pass judgment on . . . ."

[19] According to legend Hercules was at times insane.

[20] Literally (in the German) "pass an examination"; the disputation was the ceremony whereby the erudition of a candidate for an academic degree was finally tested. Eck had probably presided when Hubmaier passed his doctoral disputation.

5

On Heretics and Those Who Burn Them

The probable date of the writing of this text On Heretics *would be sometime in September/October 1524 when Hubmaier had left Waldshut for temporary refuge in Schaffhausen.[1] Like the* Theses Against Eck, *it represents one of the earliest contributions to the discussion of the nature and process of the phenomenon of Reformation, the foundation and safeguards of the principle of religious liberty. At this point neither the principle nor the process of the Reformation had been defined in such a way as to distinguish between the "mainline" and the "sectarian" streams of the Reformed movement. Historians can say of this period that by then it was already too late to save the vision of a reformation carried through by the entire community of Christendom in any one place or in all of Europe, but Hubmaier is with the other Reformers in not yet having adjusted to that realism.*

One can argue that this is the first text of the Reformation directed specifically to the topic of the liberty of dissent. With the very personal Appeal to Schaffhausen *and the more procedural* Theses Against Eck, *it forms Hubmaier's trilogy on the subject.*

The text was first printed in Constance, probably very soon after the printing of Reformation literature was first authorized there in late September 1524. It was reprinted at least twice.[2]

---

[1] The occasion for Hubmaier's escape to Schaffhausen is described in Bergsten 1961, pp. 166ff. (Bergsten 1978, p. 11).

[2] Previously translated in Davidson 1939, pp. 25-35; and in Estep 1976, pp. 47ff.; with fragments in Vedder 1905, p. 84; and Klaassen 1981, p. 292. Source: HS 4, pp. 96-100.

On Heretics and Those
Who Burn Them.

A comparison
of the Scripture texts,
compiled by Dr.
Balthazer Friedberger
Pastor at Waldszhut,
for the pleasure of Brother Anthonin,[3] Vicar at
Constantz, the select
sentinel without
a trumpet.

Truth Is Unkillable.
1524

Article 1

Heretics are those who wantonly resist the Holy Scripture. The first of them was the devil, who spoke to Eve: "By no means will you die." (Gen. 3:4) Together with his followers.

Article 2

Likewise are those persons heretics who blind the Scripture, and who exposit it otherwise than the Holy Spirit demands, such as [interpreting] "a wife" as a prebend,[4]

---

[3] See note 11, below.

[4] Hubmaier here turns the accusation of heresy, as he has defined it, against the Catholic tradition. It is not clear how the tradition would have substituted the prebend [i.e., the endowed support for a priest's living] for "wife." Heinold Fast suggests an allusion to Luke 8:3, where Jesus' disciples were supported from the resources of women. Another hypothetical possibility would be an extension of Paul's appeal in 1 Cor. 9:5. In either case some link must be hypothesized permitting economic support to be ᵉquated with (or substituted for) marriage.

"pasturing" as ruling,[5] "a stone" as the rock,[6] "church" as Rome,[7] who proclaim this everywhere and force us to believe such nonsense.

Article 3

Those who are such should be overcome with holy instruction, not contentiously but gently, even though the Holy Scripture also includes wrath.

Article 4

But the wrath of Scripture is truly a spiritual flame and a loving zeal, which burns only with the Word of God.

Article 5

Should they not yield to words of authority or gospel· reasons, then avoid them and let them go on to rant and rage (Titus 3:10) so that those who are filthy may become yet more filthy. (Rev. 22:11)

Article 6

The law which condemns heretics to [execution by] fire is based upon Zion in blood and Jerusalem in wickedness.[8]

Article 7

Therefore they are taken away with sighs, so that the righteousness of God (for whose judgment they are held) will either convert them or harden them, so that the blind will

---

[5] Here the reference is certainly to John 21:15ff., used as warrant for episcopacy.

[6] The argument is standard which juxtaposed *petros* (a stone, representing Peter) and *petra* (rock, representing the church's foundation) in the appeal to Matt. 16:18 as a warrant for episcopacy.

[7] Probably also a reference to Matt. 16 as well. Thus the four denunciations of Hubmaier boil down to two errors: the claims of the Roman episcopacy and the non-Pauline form of ministerial support.

[8] Heinold Fast suggests that there may be an allusion to Micah 3:10 which reads, "Zion is built in blood and Jerusalem in iniquity."

[continue to] lead the blind [Matt. 15:14] and always both the seducers and the seduced descend further into iniquity.

Article 8

That is just what Christ intended when he said, "Let both grow up together until the harvest, lest in gathering the tares you tear up the wheat together with it." (Matt. 13:29f.) "There must be divisions so that the trustworthy among you may be manifest." (1 Cor. 11:19)

Article 9

Who, even though they resist, are not to be destroyed until Christ will say to the reapers: "Gather the tares first and bind them in bundles to be burned." (Matt. 13:30)

Article 10

The result of these words will not be negligence but a struggle as we combat without interruption, not against human beings, but against their godless teachings.

Article 11

Negligent bishops are to blame that there are divisions. "For while people were sleeping, the enemies came." (Matt. 13:25)

Article 12

Again: "Blessed [is] the man who stands watch before the bridal chamber" (Prov. 8:34), and neither sleeps "nor sits in the seat of mockers." (Psalm 1:1)

Article 13

It follows now that the inquisitors[9] are the greatest heretics of all, because counter to the teaching and example of Jesus they condemn heretics to fire; and before it is time they pull up the wheat together with the tares.

Article 14

For Christ did not come to slaughter, kill, burn, but so that those who live should live yet more abundantly. (John 10:10)

Article 15

Yea, we should pray and hope for repentance as long as a person lives in this misery.

Article 16

But a Turk or a heretic cannot be overcome by our doing, neither by sword nor by fire, but alone with patience and supplication, whereby we patiently await divine judgment.

Article 17

If we act otherwise God will consider our sword as chaff and our fire mockery. (Job 41:19)

Article 18

The entire Dominican order (to which our black and white bird[10] Anthonius[11] belongs) has fallen away from gospel

---

[9] The German term for "inquisitor" was *Ketzermeister*, i.e., heretic-masters or heretic-teachers.

[10] The reference may be to the black and white dress of the Dominican order (cf. HS, p. 98, fn. 12). It may also be to the magpie, popularly associated both with noisy cries and with stealing from the nests of other birds.

[11] Anthony was the "Vicar at Constance" to whom this writing was addressed (cf. title above). The local inquisitors were usually, although not exclusively, selected from among the members of the Dominican order.

teaching even more miserably in that it is thus far only from that order that the heretical inquisitors have come.

Article 19

If they knew of whose spirit they are, they would not so shamelessly distort the Word of God or so often shout: "Into the fire! Into the fire!" (Luke 9:54)

Article 20

Nor is it an excuse for them (as they babble) that they turn the godless[12] over to the secular authority, for whoever in this way turns someone over is even more guilty of sin. (John 19:11)

Article 21

Every Christian has a sword [to use] against the godless, namely the [sword of the] Word of God (Eph. 6:17f), but not a sword against the evildoers.

Article 22

It is fitting that secular authority puts to death the wicked (Rom. 13:4) who cause bodily harm to the defenseless. But the enemy of God[13] can harm no one, unless [that person] would not have it otherwise and would forsake the gospel.

Article 23

Christ said the same thing clearly: "Do not fear those who kill the body but are unable to kill the soul." (Matt. 10:28)

---

[12] In the next four articles Hubmaier makes the distinction between "the godless," i.e., unbelievers, dissenters, for whom prosecution and the death penalty are improper, and violent evildoers, for whom civil prosecution is fitting. Zeman 1969, p. 142, reminds us that Constance was the city where Jan Hus, the most famous Reformation martyr, had been burned at the stake. Zeman senses that Hubmaier's silence about Hus needs some explanation.

[13] HS, p. 99: gotssfind, i.e., Satan.

Article 24

The authorities judge the evildoers but not the godless, who can harm neither body nor soul but rather are useful, so that as is known God can make good out of evil.

Article 25

For faith which flows from the wellspring of the gospel lives only in the presence of testing; the rougher the test, the greater is the faith.

Article 26

But since not everyone has been taught the gospel, bishops are no less at fault than the common people: the latter in that they have not taken care to have a better shepherd, the former in that they have not fulfilled their function.

Article 27

When one blind person leads another, they both fall into the pit together according to the righteous judgment of God. (Matt. 15:14)

Article 28

Therefore to burn heretics appears to be confessing Christ (Titus 1:16), but indeed it is to deny him and is to be more abominable than Jehoiakim, the king of Judah. (Jer. 36)

Article 29

If to burn heretics is such a great evil, how much greater will be the evil, to burn to ashes the genuine proclaimers of the Word of God, without having convinced them, without having debated the truth with them.

Article 30

The greatest deception of the people is the kind of zeal for God which is invested without Scripture in the interest of the salvation of souls, the honor of the church, love for the truth, good intentions, usages or custom, episcopal decrees, and the indications of reason, all of which have been begged from the light of nature. These are lethal errors, when they are not led and directed according to Scripture.

Article 31

A person should not presume, misled by the masks of his intention, to do anything better or surer than what God said with his own mouth.

Article 32

Those who count on their own good intentions and believe that they are doing the better are like Uzzah and Peter. Jesus named the latter Satan (Matt. 16:23); the former was destroyed miserably. (2 Kings 36)[14]

Article 33

Thus Elnathan, Delaiah, and Gemariah acted wisely when they contradicted Jehoiakim, king of Judah, as he threw Jeremiah's book into the fire. (Jer. 36:25)

Article 34

The fact that after the book was burned Baruch wrote another better one on the basis of oral dictation by Jeremiah (Jer. 36:28) is God's righteous punishment for the improper burning. Thus it shall proceed so that on those who fear the frost, a cold snow will fall. (Job 6:16)

Article 35

We do not, however, hold that it is unchristian to burn books of error and irreverence, as in the deed testified to in the Acts of the Apostles (19:19). To burn innocent paper is a

---

[14]Uzzah was struck down when he reached out to steady the ark of the covenant. 2 Sam. 6; 1 Chron. 13. The reference to chapter 36 is probably a simple mistranscription.

trifle, but to demonstrate what is error and to prove the same with Scripture is an art.

Article 36

Now it appears to anyone, even to a blind person, that the law [which provides] for the burning of heretics is an invention of the devil. Truth Is Unkillable.

6

Letter to Oecolampad

The correspondence of the Reformers with each other was a powerful resource, often underestimated by their heirs, for clarifying both their theology and their strategy of Reformation. A network of courier connections linked major cities quite efficiently. Where local conditions enabled the letters to be preserved, they provide a greater concreteness and depth to our grasp of the history than do the writings they intended for print.

The letters of non-establishment theologians tended to be preserved only if they found their way into the files of an establishment person, like the letters of Conrad Grebel to Vadianus[1] or this letter from Hubmaier.

Johannes Oecolampadius (1482-1531) had studied at Heidelberg, Tübingen, and Stuttgart. He was at Basel off and on since 1515 and since 1522 could be counted as that city's Reformer, working in constant consultation with Bucer and Capito at Strasbourg and Zwingli at Zurich, as each city's government responded differently to the process of doctrinal and ecclesiastical change which they promoted. More than the others Oekolampad was a scholar, publishing editions of the church fathers. This letter testifies that Hubmaier considered himself a part of that circle, working as he was under less propitious political conditions.

Oekolampad's later career as Reformer reflected both his different personality and Basel's different politics. He differed from Zwingli and agreed with the Strasbourg Reformers in desiring an ecclesiastical discipline independent of the government. He never won a wholehearted mandate for the Reformation like that which Zurich's Council had given Zwingli already in 1523. He had his share of conversations with Anabaptists, in which he held to a generally Zwinglian-like

---

[1] The letters from Conrad Grebel to his brother-in-law Vadian form the core of the collection *The Sources of Swiss Anabaptism*, edited by Leland Harder, henceforth referred to as Harder 1985.

position despite the differences sketched above.[2] *In August 1525 he reported one such debate in a pamphlet which provoked Hubmaier's response.*[3]

To his Christian colleague, John Oekolampad, evangelist[4] of Basel, his dearly beloved brother in Christ.

Grace and peace in Christ Jesus, our Savior. You have in no way displeased me, Oekolampad, dearly beloved brother in Christ; on the contrary you have in a most generous spirit favored and benefited me with your "Demegoriae,"[5] for which we send you everlasting thanks. However, one thing I long anticipated was that you would have written more specifically on the passage about Spirit, treating the water and the blood.[6] You agreed with the writings recently put out on the Eucharist by Carlstadt[7] as being particularly striking and especially significant, even though they did not follow the usual style which you would have liked to see. In any case, they now stand as what is written. Not long ago it was from you that I willingly assumed this view; indeed I realized, or perhaps divined, that there was no difference of view between

---

[2] Cf. ME IV, p. 18, and Yoder 1962, 63ff., 120ff.

[3] Cf. below, our text 18, pp. 275ff. The first draft translation of this letter was provided graciously by Prof. William Hunt of the University of Notre Dame. Earlier translations: Hošek 1891, p. 516. Fragment in Vedder 1905, p. 108. Source: Staehelin 1927, no. 238, pp. 341-344.

[4] *Evangelist* here means neither "Scripture scholar" nor "preacher" but "protagonist of the Reformation cause."

[5] Oekolampad's text, *In Epistolam Ioannis Apostoli Catholicam primam, Ioannis Oecolampadij demegoriae, hoc est homiliae una et viginti*, printed twice in the summer of 1524, had just been printed in a third, revised edition at Basel, dated 1525.

[6] 1 John 5:8 speaks of "the Spirit, the water, and the blood" as three "witnesses" that agree. The notion of "testimony" is important in Hubmaier's theology of sacraments: cf. below, pp. 227.

[7] Andreas Bodenstein von Carlstadt had just published seven treatises on the theme of eucharistic reform. Freshly written, they had been brought to Zurich by Carlstadt's friend Gerhard Westerburg, who also brought a letter to the Zurich radicals in response to the one they had addressed to Carlstadt in September. Then Westerburg took the manuscripts to Basel and arranged for them to be printed in the first days of November. As all of them relate to the theme of the Lord's Supper, there is no reason and no way to identify just one of the seven.

Although Andreas Carlstadt figured as a "radical" in his relations to Martin Luther, with regard to the debate about sacraments, he was one of the Zwinglians. Oekolampad must have expressed himself with measured critique concerning some of Carlstadt's writings.

the two of us. At that time you always wrote to me with guarded reservation [literally: "under a certain veil"], and indeed this was then well advised; for the situation at the time demanded caution.[8]

But now the time has come to speak out openly and to everyone concerned what earlier we whispered only among ourselves. May God "the best and greatest" be blessed, for along with this new atmosphere of freedom to speak out he has also given us at the same time receptive listeners. I had quite feared that a great disturbance or lamentable rumpus about this matter might be stirred up among a people so often cruelly misled; but Christ calmed the winds. We[9] have written twenty theses on the Eucharist, also several rules on preparing the table of the Lord,[10] which writings I would willingly have sent on to you but they are no longer in my hands. Meanwhile, please write to me however you will in a few words about the initial proceedings or solemnities with which this meal should be conducted,[11] for without such direction nothing can be done.

On this day, the Doctors of Zurich[12] will assemble to compare texts of Scripture concerning the baptism of the young. This is where Zwingli with his associate Leo singing in

---

[8] This kind of "political" consideration is the type of perspective which letters convey better than do books.

[9] Hubmaier here used the editorial "we," as the letter had not hitherto. Perhaps the "we" includes the suggestion that he did this drafting together with ministerial colleagues at Waldshut.

[10] None of the later texts on the Supper (cf. items 7 and 22, above) seems to correspond to this description of "twenty theses." This is a hint of Hubmaier's way of working. He must often have prepared lists, drafts, outlines not yet meant for print.

[11] It is significant that Hubmaier's concern here is not to pursue the doctrinal debate about the meaning of the Eucharist, but to begin modifying the forms of celebrations. The doctrinal decision is already behind him when he uses the term *meal*.

[12] The Council of Zurich convened for January 17, 1525, a kind of public debate on baptism, less open and formal than those of January and October 1523, which had assured the success of the Reformation. Cf. documents 68ff. in Harder 1985 and pp. 333ff. Cf. Yoder 1962, pp. 40ff. Hubmaier's reference to "those in the white robes of the teacher" indicates that the event was primarily for theologians. It is fitting that Hubmaier should use the phrase "collate Scripture texts" to describe the debate. The city fathers had summoned the opponents of infant baptism to "prove from the pure holy Scriptures the reasons for their opinions."

harmony[13] disagrees with us. We ourselves have indeed earlier taught as well that according to the ordinance of Christ, the very young should by no means receive baptism. As a matter of fact, who instituted baptism? Of course, Christ. When? Late in Matthew's account. In what words? (Matt. 28:19): "As you go forth, teach all nations, baptizing them in the name of the Father and of the Son and of the Holy Spirit." Quite right. Why, then, do we baptize the very young? Baptism, the saying goes, is a naked sign. Why is it that we dispute so fiercely over this "sign"? The sign is assuredly also a "symbol" instituted by Christ with words significant and solemn to the highest degree: "In the name of the Father and of the Son and of the Holy Spirit." Anyone who weakens this sign or abuses it gives offense to the words with which Jesus inaugurated the sign, though of course the bonding signified by that sign and symbol (whereby for the sake of the faith and in hope of the resurrection to life eternal one binds oneself to God even unto death) should be valued more seriously than the sign itself.

But it is not possible that this significance should fit the very young; so infant baptism is a kind of vessel without wine. In baptism there is made a bond with God, to which now the Apostolic Creed attests, showing forth verily the apostolic majesty[14] and a renunciation of Satan and all his pretentiousness even unto the water, i.e., unto death. The bond made in the Lord's Supper is like it, whereby I commit myself to lay down my body and blood for his sake, as Christ did for me. And so we have the laws and the prophets. Whence I think, indeed I know, that a return to true Christianity will never be effected unless baptism and the Lord's Supper are brought back to their nature and genuine purity.

But what is an owl to the nightingale? Dearly beloved brother in Christ, clearly you hold my view; though if I am mistaken, it is your part as a brother to correct an erring dolt. For I prefer nothing under the sun than to recant, to sing as it were a palinode,[15] to do anything, indeed to refuse

---

[13] *Per diapason.* The musical allusion has several possible meanings. It might mean using the entire scale or echoing in every octave.

[14] "Apostolic majesty" must mean the authority of the apostles' proclamation, majestic by virtue of the Lord's instituting baptism.

[15] Palinode: Another song, one verse answering another, i.e., a retraction or recantation when sung by the same person.

absolutely nothing, if ever I should be instructed otherwise by you and those of like mind, who come instructed by the Word of God. May God enlighten us with his Spirit, and may it come to us ever more swiftly. Otherwise, I will persevere in this view, with the help of divine goodwill. For I am driven to this view by Christ's institution, by the Word, by faith and truth, by judgment, and by conscience. So I adjure you, my brother in Christ, to guide a straying lamb, one crying out more and more every day for one who may guide him back to the true path. Render me an account of your faith, for God's sake and for the preservation of Christ's peace. May God's Word come, may it come, and we should bow six hundred necks to it if we had so many. So come to my aid, righteous brother, with the Word of God, and witness openly to the truth. You will in no way displease me, even if of two views you declare the one against my own. I am only a man, I can fall into error which is human, longing with all my heart only to rise again to the truth.

Only one thing remains, and please do not fail in this service: Write to me whether the promise of Matthew 19:14, "Suffer the little children to come unto me, etc.," applies only to young children, or whether the Word of Christ supports me which says "for the kingdom of God is for such as them" (not for "them"), and also what the Strasbourg brothers think about this. I have written 22 theses on baptism, with 64 notes added—you will be seeing all of this very soon.

Farewell in Christ, my brother, and pardon my venial babbling, for desire to find the truth spurs me on. From our hearth at Waldshut, January 16, 1525.

Your Baldazar Pacimontanus,
     Write back to me for the love of God. I've sent a bundle of letters to Zwingli through an officer among those keeping watch for us.[16]

---

[16] Waldshut was currently being aided in its resistance to the pressures of Catholic Austria by a "volunteer" corps from Zurich; cf. Bergsten 1978, pp. 115ff. Hubmaier prevailed on them to carry papers to Zwingli, an indication that Hubmaier did not share the estrangement from Zwingli already felt by the Zurich radicals.

I like to assemble the congregation in the place of baptism,[17] bringing in the child. I exposit in the native tongue the gospel text: "Children were brought ..." (Matt. 19:13). As soon as his name has been given to him, the whole congregation on bended knee prays for the child, entrusting him to the hands of Christ, that he may be ever closer to the child and pray on his behalf. If there are parents of a sick child at a given time, who most earnestly wish the child to be baptized, I baptize it. In this matter, I take on sickness myself along with the sickly little ones, but only for a time, until better instructed. But as for interpreting the Word, I do not give ground in the least respect.

Again, farewell. And write back to me, my brother.[18]

---

[17] Hubmaier probably means that he gathers the assembly at the baptistery, so as to make the new ceremony something like the old one. But the phrase may also mean "in lieu of baptism."

[18] Oekolampad did answer, twice. A first response dated January 18 (Staehelin 1927, p. 344) defended infant baptism with several traditional arguments and sketched modestly his eucharistic practice. At about the same time he reported Hubmaier's letter to Zwingli. A second undated letter (loc. cit., 1927, no. 243, p. 357) reopened the conversations about infant baptism. He approved strongly (*placet supra modum*) of the non-baptismal dedication service which Hubmaier's letter had described.

7

Several Theses Concerning the Mass

The Theses on the Mass *were written after the January let-*
ter to Oecolampad but probably before the Public Challenge
and certainly before Easter. Characterized by Sachsse as Hub-
maier's first real theological treatise,[1] *the small essay*
represents his first published statement on the Eucharist. Hub-
maier had earlier spoken publicly on the question of the mass
at the Second Zurich Disputation as a supporter of Zwingli.[2] *In*
the January letter he mentioned to Oecolampad that he had
written twenty theses on the Eucharist as well as rules for
preparing the table of the Lord.[3] *The present text is not those*
theses but is probably a reworked treatise based on the earlier
outline. Efforts to reconstruct the original theses from this
treatise have been less than successful.[4]

The Theses *were written at the time when the reform of*
the Eucharist was under way in Waldshut as well as in Zurich,
in the latter place by the Anabaptists first and later by
Zwingli. Hubmaier himself said in the treatise that the German
mass was "not yet at the level of perfection instituted by
Christ." That was to come in Waldshut with the introduction of
the evangelical Lord's Supper at Easter. In fact, Zwingli's serv-
ice on Maundy Thursday predated Hubmaier's by only a few
days.[5]

The treatise is a positive evangelical statement, not
pointedly polemical. Hubmaier's closeness to Zwingli is
apparent in its view of the Supper as a memorial
widergedechtnüß. *Hubmaier also speaks of the Supper as a*
memorial sign, denckzaichen; *symbol,* kreyd; *and visible or*
outward emblem wortzaichen. *Windhorst has pointed to the*

---

[1] Sachsse 1914, p. 13.
[2] See text 1 above, p. 21.
[3] See text 6 above, p. 67.
[4] Bergsten evaluates Sachsse's attempts (Sachsse 1914, p. 13) as arbitrary, HS, p. 101.
[5] It is also clear that the Swiss Brethren had preceded Zwingli. For
example, see vMS, no. 50, p. 60.

influence of Carlstadt in this writing, especially in the attention given not to the presence of Christ in the Supper but to the suffering of Christ and the proclamation of his death until he comes.[6] In addition to this emphasis on the Supper as memorial and on the proclamation of the death of Christ, attention is given to the Supper as containing emblems of the love of Christ for humanity, the communal dimension of the Supper and finally, to the inner reality of Christian existence with the obligation of the Christian to be "body and blood" to one's neighbor. It is worthy of note that in this treatise Hubmaier did not yet give his attention to the issue of the meaning of the words of Christ in the institution of the Supper.[7]

Several Theses
by Dr. Paltus Fridberger
of Waldshut
To all Christians
concerning the instruction of the mass.
1525

The Supper of Christ is a commemoration of his suffering and a proclamation of his death until he comes to us again. The breaking of his bread and the drinking of the wine in the Christ meal is an outward sign or symbol instituted by Christ before his death, which signifies to us how he offered his body for us and shed his blood so that we also do the same for the sake of our neighbor. Those who do not do that perjure their oath to Christ; for where the Lord Christ went,[8] Prince and Head of his church, we do not want to follow, although we present ourselves to be members of the church in the reception of this symbol, also to do the same[9] for all those

---

[6] Windhorst 1975, p. 122.
[7] Previous translation: Davidson 1939, pp. 43-51. Source for the translation: HS 5, pp. 102-104.
[8] The term here rendered "Lord Christ" is actually "*hertzog Christus.*" Literally, it would be "Duke Christ," a relatively rare title for Christ.
[9] I.e., to offer our body for our neighbor.

who with us are members of the body of Christ, which is his church. From this it follows that the Supper is called "mass" by an invented name without any basis in Scripture. In addition one should not hold this Supper in incomprehensible tongues as it has been done until now, but in the language of each country. Although the German mass, as it is called, is not yet at the level of perfection instituted by Christ, it is still a large step nearer to that than the unintelligibly mumbled masses held until now. May God grant to us soon more grace to teach and to learn.

When Christ commands, "Take, eat, this is my body given for you," he means his mortal body, for he himself suffered for us, and not the bread on the table which he gave them to eat. Likewise his blood, and /103/ not the wine in the chalice, was poured out for us. For just such a manner of speaking did Christ use when he said to Peter, "You are Peter and on this rock," meaning himself, "will I build my church," Matt. 16:18. And the rock was Christ, 1 Cor. 10:4. Accordingly, one should always pay more attention and that more seriously to the things signified by the word symbols than to the symbols themselves. For outside of their signifying, the same mean nothing and are in vain. But the Spirit makes us alive, and the Spirit comes with the Word which then assures the human being of eternal life, as the bread and wine are word symbols of his love, by which we remember how he, Christ, was our Christ, and how we also are always to be Christ to one another. We all are one bread and one body—we all, who have fellowship in one bread and in one drink. As one little kernel does not keep its own flour, but shares it with the others, and a single grape does not keep its juice for itself, but shares it with the others, so should we Christians also act—or we eat and drink unworthily from the table of Christ. For the bread which we break means and commemorates the communion of the body of Christ with us, that he is our own, for he gave his body for us through the drink of the communion of his blood which he poured out for the forgiveness of our sin.

As we now have communion with one another in this bread and drink of the Christ meal, so also should the body and blood of all of us be shared with each other, just as the body and blood of Christ is shared with us all. This is the meaning of the word *symbol* when we eat and drink together.

Before eating from the table of the Lord, the person should test himself and recollect whether he is so minded toward his neighbor. There is a great difference between the Christ meal and another meal, although all table meals should be accepted with thanksgiving. Nevertheless, in the Christ meal one should proclaim the death of Christ, and obligate and bind oneself together with body and blood in brotherly service through this visible word symbol and not come together merely for the sake of eating and drinking. Just this Paul calls a communion or fellowship, 1 Cor.10:16. Therefore it is obvious that it is a public fraud to read masses of Our Lady, though she is worthy of all honor in God, or of other saints. Likewise it is a public abuse above all abuses to read or sing masses for the dead, likewise to keep the obsequies on the seventh day, the thirtieth day, and the anniversary of the death. For as /104/ the dead no longer eat or drink with us, so also may they not participate in the Supper. Paul says: "As often as you eat of this bread and drink from this cup" [1 Cor. 11:26.

We conclude that the bread and wine of the Christ meal are outward word symbols of an inward Christian nature here on earth, in which a Christian obligates himself to another in Christian love with regard to body and blood. Thus as the body and blood of Christ became my body and blood on the cross, so likewise shall my body and blood become the body and blood of my neighbor, and in time of need theirs become my body and blood, or we cannot boast at all to be Christians. That is the will of Christ in the Supper. Whoever now rejects the will of Christ and does not do it and hardens himself in all abuses shall rightly be punished with many plagues. Thenceforth come dearth, hail, pestilence, earthquakes, drought, dying, bloodshed, rebellion, and all kinds of miseries and adversities. That is what I believe concerning the Christ meal. Whichever Christian on earth can teach me better should show me such with Scripture for God's sake. I will wholeheartedly follow him with great thanksgiving as he follows Christ.

Truth Is Immortal.[10]

---

[10] The editors of the present volume had difficulty agreeing on a common translation of Hubmaier's epigram, "*Die Warheit ist untödtlich.*" Numerous sixteenth-century texts provide some evidence of the usage and

understanding of *untödtlich*. For example, Leo Jud's German translation of Erasmus' paraphrases of 1 Corinthians 15, published in Zurich in 1523, translated *immortalis* as *untödlich*. Elsewhere, Josua Maaler's German dictionary, *Dir Teütsch spraach* (Froschauer, 1561), defined *untödtlich* as *immortalis* or *athanatos* and *untödlichkeit* as *immortalitas*. Based on these sources and others, editor Pipkin has concluded that the proper translation of Hubmaier's epigram is, "Truth is immortal." Cf. text 3, note 12, p. 42.

8

A Public Challenge to All Believers

Following the institution of believers' baptism in Zurich,
January 21, 1525,[1] those participants in the young Anabaptist
movement who were not Zurich citizens were obliged to leave
the city. They did not simply take refuge elsewhere but scat-
tered in a planned way, visiting where they thought there
would be openness to their message. The first such place was
Schaffhausen, where the reformer Sebastian Hofmeister
sympathized with them. The city planned a debate on the sub-
ject, which, however, was canceled under pressure from
Zurich.[2] From there Wilhelm Reublin went to Waldshut, know-
ing that Hubmaier was also friendly. He probably spent
January 29-31, 1525, there.[3] Hubmaier was not baptized at that
time by Reublin, although a few citizens of Waldshut were.

Hubmaier's response was the following handbill or poster,
dated February 2, 1525, calling for a debate. It is not clear
whether it was printed separately at that time,[4] but it was
printed the following July as an appendix to Hubmaier's On the
Christian Baptism of Believers.[5]

His self-designation as "brother in Christ of Zwingli"
locates Hubmaier as an ally of the Swiss Reformation. He had
progressively become known as a friend and sympathizer of the
pattern of Reformation being promoted by Huldrych Zwingli of
Zurich, having visited with Zwingli and corresponded with his
colleagues in Basel and Strasbourg. He shared in their public
debates, most notably in the second Zurich Reformation Dis-
putation of October 26-28, 1523. At this time he stood with the
main Zwinglian Reformation party, trusting the power of the
Word of God to move local governments to implement reforma-
tion and focusing the understanding of the need for reform
upon the rejection of papal authority, the replacement of the

---

[1] Bender 1950, p. 137; Harder 1985, p. 338.
[2] Yoder 1962, p. 147. Hofmeister was sent from Schaffhausen to Basel to
be reeducated (Fast 1973, pp. 17-20).
[3] Bergsten 1961, p. 255.
[4] Hillerbrand 1962, no. 2720, follows earlier sources in locating several
copies in libraries; Westin/Bergsten HS, p. 105, say the listing is incorrect,
doubting that it was ever printed separately.
[5] Our text 11: HS, p. 118.

mass by a simple communion meal, the rejection of the use of "images" in worship, and concern for Christian morality.

However, whereas Zwingli's early doubts about the propriety of infant baptism were soon quieted by his concern for the maintenance of the visible Christian community as a civil and social order, Hubmaier further developed his negative views on the subject. He shared such convictions with the developing left wing of the Zurich Reformation, yet without participating in their meetings or in the psychological dynamics of the coming to birth of Zurich Anabaptism. He had no part in the series of private meetings and public hearings which led in January 1525 to the reaffirmation by the Zurich Council of the legal duty of infant baptism and to the birth of the Anabaptist movement through believers baptism. He first heard of the actual practice of adult baptism only a few weeks later when Wilhelm Reublin of the Zurich movement visited Waldshut, and not until Easter did Hubmaier initiate the practice of believers baptism at Waldshut. Then he did it as the official preacher of the town, in the town church, with the tacit if not formal support of the town authorities.

Hubmaier does not ask the government of Waldshut to convene a debate; he issues the challenge in his own name. Yet he does not state time and place, and it may be a pro forma challenge to which he expects no response, but which, by virtue of its having been issued, will certify his right to move on in the direction indicated.[6] *Not until Easter did he move ahead with baptisms in the name of the Waldshut congregation.*[7]

---

[6] A letter of the Waldshut government to Strasbourg (Krebs/Rott 1959, no. 375, p. 391) says that a debate convened by Hubmaier did take place. The one which did take place may have been the same as the one Hubmaier here is calling for (cf. Yoder 1959, p. 6, note 8), but it might also have been the one called for by our text 2 (p. 31 above). Bergsten (HS, p. 105, and Bergsten 1961, p. 255) says that the one which did take place had to be during Reublin's visit of January 29-31 that would date it before Hubmaier's "challenge." This would be the only possibility, *if* we knew that Reublin never returned to Waldshut between January 31 and Easter; but there is no way to know that. The dating of that "conversation" in late January is thus unlikely, for several reasons:

The very concept of a public debate, which the letter to Strasbourg says was convened by Hubmaier, demands some advance notice.

Reublin's visit of late January was Hubmaier's first contact with the news of the Anabaptist beginnings in Zurich.

A contemporary letter of Waldshut to Zurich about Reublin's visit (Bergsten 1961, p. 255, note 33) makes no reference to such conversations, in a context where one would certainly have expected a report.

[7] Earlier translation: Davidson 1939, pp. 51-55. Source: HS 6, pp. 106-107.

From Balthazar Fridberger at Waldshût,
A PUBLIC CHALLENGE
To all Believers in Christ,
Issued on February 2,
AD MDXXV.

Whoever wishes to do so, let him prove
that infants should be baptized,
and do it with German, plain, clear, and unambiguous
Scriptures
that deal only with baptism, without any addition.
Balthazar Fridberger offers
in his turn to prove
that the baptism of infants is a work without any basis
in the divine Word, and this he will do with German,
plain, clear, and unambiguous Scriptures that deal
only with baptism, without any addition.
Now let a Bible, fifty or one hundred years old,
as the right, proper, and true arbiter
be placed between these two positions.
Let it be opened
and read aloud with imploring, humble spirit,
and then let this dispute be decided and once for all
brought to a conclusion.
Thus I shall be well content for I want always to give
God the glory
and to allow his Word to be the sole judge;
to him I herewith desire to submit and subject myself
and all my teachings.

Truth Is Unkillable.[8]

---

[8] On the rendering of *Die Warheit ist untödtlich,* cf. p., text 3, note 12, and text 7, note 10, above.

9

Summa of the Entire Christian Life

The year 1525 was decisive for the personal and religious development of Hubmaier, and for the Reformation in Waldshut and the surrounding area as well as in Zurich. In January the radical challenge to Zwingli's model of reform came to an irrevocable breakthrough with the first believers' baptisms. The City Council's harsh response against the perceived threat of the Anabaptists was swift and decisive. Faced with the evidence of continued and growing impatience, Zwingli and the Council finally brought about his delayed eucharistic reforms on Maundy Thursday, April 13. Baptismal reforms were not forthcoming.

In Waldshut Hubmaier was moving on a nearly parallel course, but with a notable exception. Anabaptists who had been forced out of Zurich found a willing ear and receptive response in the reformer of Waldshut. Relations of Hubmaier not only to Zwingli, but also to the radical opposition in Zurich had been a reality for several months. Furthermore, the peasants' unrest nearby and the initial successes of the revolt, which included participants from Waldshut, may well have accelerated the adoption of Anabaptism in the city.[1] The rebellion certainly proved to be no obstacle to Hubmaier's plans.[2]

Finally on Saturday before Easter, April 15, Hubmaier was baptized by Wilhelm Reublin in his own Waldshut parish church, along with sixty other adult believers. In the course of the following week Hubmaier led Waldshut to a more thorough-going reform than had been realized anywhere in Europe.[3]

---

[1] Bergsten 1962, p. 306.

[2] For a consideration of the possible role of Hubmaier in the Peasants' Revolt, see Stayer 1985. See also Bergsten 1978, pp. 144-225. For consideration of the wider background and for an introduction into current issues of the rebellion, see Blickle 1981 and Scribner/Benecke 1979.

[3] Historians differ as to what constitutes in each major city the index of the implementation of the Reformation. If, however, we take as an index the coinciding of three basic criteria—(a) a restructuring of baptismal practice, (b) a restructuring of eucharistic practice, and (c) the validation of those changes by the civil authorities, and if permanence is not a criterion—then Waldshut's reformation was the first.

According to reports, perhaps more than 300 persons were baptized, including the majority of the City Council.[4] In addition, the evangelical Lord's Supper was celebrated during the Easter festival. This likely was influenced by the Swiss Brethren as well as by Zwingli.

Not long afterward Hubmaier turned his attention outward from Waldshut. On July 1 he published his first writing as an Anabaptist, Summa of the Christian Life. The treatise addressed the issues of infant baptism and the Lord's Supper and was dedicated to the cities of Friedberg, Regensburg, and Ingolstadt, that is, the city of his birth and two cities where he had ministered. It is possible that Hubmaier produced the tract in response to several persons in Regensburg who wished to be better instructed in the matter of the Lord's Supper and baptism. In the treatise he attacked the practices of the Roman Catholic Church, which he called the "red whore of Babylon." He excused his earlier service to her as the result of deception.

The Summa of the Christian Life appeared in two versions: first as a separate publication and second as the concluding chapter to Hubmaier's next treatise, On the Christian Baptism of Believers.[5] The second edition was revised, though not substantially. The most significant portion of the first edition to be omitted in the second was the dedication.[6]

[4] Bergsten 1978, p. 232.
[5] See below, text 11, pp. 92ff.
[6] Earlier translations: Hošek 1891, pp. 510f.; Davidson 1939, pp. 55-67. Fragments in Klaassen 1981, pp. 42, 165, 192. Source: HS 7, pp. 109-115.

Summa of the Entire Christian Life
by Baldasaren Frydberger,
now Preacher at Waldßhûtt,
Dedicated to the Three Churches at
Regenspurg, Ingoldstat, and
Fridberg,
To his dear Lords,
Brothers, and
Sisters,
in God
the Lord. /110/
Especially an Instruction concerning
Infant Baptism and the Supper.
MDXXV

Grace and peace in Christ Jesus, our only Savior. Noble, providential, and favorable Lords. Dear Lords and brothers, first of all I present to you also my humble, diligent service. I confess publicly that I have sinned against heaven and God, not only with my sinful life, which I led in all pride, fornication, and worldly luxury among you, contrary to the teaching of Christ, but also with false, ungrounded, and godless teachings, with which I instructed, fed, and tended you outside of the Word of God. And particularly, as I still well remember that I have said many useless things about infant baptism, vigils, anniversary masses, purgatory, masses, idols, bells, ringing, organs, piping, indulgences, pilgrimages, brotherhoods, sacrifices, singing, and mumbling. Nevertheless, if I may be allowed to boast with Paul in the truth, I did so unknowingly. The red whore of Babylon, with her schoolteachings, laws, and fables deceived me. But I have prayed to God who has given me everything. Therefore, dear Lords and brothers, be warned and admonished that you henceforth yourselves test and examine the prophets and preachers as to whether they go before you with God's teaching or not. Search the Scriptures;

they will give testimony of Christ and the Christian life. Do as the Thessalonians; Acts 17:11. Then you cannot fail or be led astray; and even if your pastors and preachers should offer to substitute their souls for yours, it is still not enough nor would you be helped by that. For Christ says, when a blind person leads another, both will fall into a ditch [Matt. 15:14]. It would be a small thing if the pastor alone fell, but according to the authority of the Word of Christ, the sheep would fall also.

In Summary

First: When Christ teaches the Christian life, he says, "Repent or change your lives, and believe the gospel" [Mark 1:15]. Now, it belongs to a change of life that we look into our hearts, and that we remember our deeds and our omissions. Thus, we find that we do that which God has forbidden us and we leave undone what he has commanded us to do. Yes, there is no health in us but rather poison, wounds, and all impurity, which cling to us from the beginning because we are conceived and born in sin. Thus did Job, David, Jeremiah, John, and other God-fearing people lament. Furthermore, a person finds in himself neither help, comfort, nor medicine with which he could help himself. Therefore he must despair of himself and /111/ lose heart like the man who had fallen among the killers. Such a miserable little thing is the person who ponders and recognizes himself.

Second: Then the Samaritan must come, that is, Christ Jesus. He brings along medicine, namely, wine and oil, which he pours into the wounds of the sinner. Wine: he leads the person to repentance so that he is sorry for his sins. He brings oil, by which he softens his pain and drives it away, and says, "Believe the gospel that clearly shows that I am your physician who has come into this world to make the sinner just and righteous. The gospel teaches also that I am the only giver of mercy, reconciler, intercessor, mediator, and peacemaker toward God, our father, so that whoever believes in me will not be damned but have eternal life." Through such words of comfort the sinner is enlivened again, comes to himself, becomes joyful, and henceforth surrenders himself entirely to the physician. All his sicknesses he commits, sub-

mits, and entrusts to him. As much as it is possible for a
wounded person he will also surrender to the will of the
physician. He calls upon him for healing so that what the
wounded is not able to do out of his own capacity, the
physician counsels, helps, and promotes him so that he can
follow his Word and commandment. Now before they are
believed, all these teachings, which reveal the sickness and
point to the physician, are letter and they kill. But by faith
the Spirit of God makes them alive so that they start to live,
turn green, and bear fruit. Thus in faith the water becomes
wine at the wedding. And we must first put on John's rough
coat before we may receive the tender, gentle, and sweet
little lamb Christ Jesus. Now this person surrenders himself
inwardly in the heart and intention unto a new life according
to the rule and teaching of Christ, the physician who has
made him whole, from whom he received life. Thus Paul confesses publicly that he does not live but Christ lives in him, is
life in him, and outside of Christ he confesses that he and his
works are empty, worthless, and that he is a lost sinner.

Third: After the person has now committed himself
inwardly and in faith to a new life, he then professes this also
outwardly and publicly before the Christian church, into
whose communion he lets himself be registered and counted
according to the order and institution of Christ. Therefore he
professes to the Christian church, that is, to all brothers and
sisters who live in faith in Christ, that in his heart he has
been thus inwardly instructed in the Word of Christ and so
minded that he has surrendered himself already to live henceforth according to the Word, will, and rule of Christ, to
arrange and direct his doing and leaving undone according to
him and also to fight and strive under his banner until death.
Then he lets himself be baptized with outward water in /112/
which he professes publicly his faith and his intention,
namely, that he believes he has a gracious, kind, and merciful
God and Father in heaven through Jesus Christ, with whom he
is well pleased and satisfied. He also has expressed his intention to him and committed himself already in his heart henceforth to change and amend his life. Such he testifies also
publicly with the reception of water. If he henceforth blackens or shames the faith and name of Christ with public or
offensive sins, he herewith submits and surrenders to

brotherly discipline according to the order of Christ, Matt.
18:15ff.

Fourth: Since, therefore, the person knows and confesses
that he is by nature an evil, worm-eaten, and poisoned tree,
and neither can nor wants to bring good fruit of himself, this
pledge, promise, and public testimony does not happen out of
human powers or capacities, for that would be presumptuousness or human arrogance. It rather takes place in the name of
God, the Father, and the Son, and the Holy Spirit, or in the
name of our Lord Jesus Christ, that is, in the grace and power
of God. For it is a power. From all this it follows that the outward baptism of Christ is nothing else than a public testimony
of the inner commitments with which the person confesses
and accuses himself before everybody that he is a sinner and
confesses himself to be guilty of the same. But at the same
time he fully believes that Christ through his death has forgiven him his sins and through his resurrection has made him
righteous before God, our heavenly Father. Therefore he has
already consented henceforth to confess publicly and before
everybody the faith and name of Jesus Christ. He has also
committed himself and resolved to live henceforth according
to the Word and order of Christ, but not out of human capacity, so that it may not happen to him as it did to Peter, for
"without me you can do nothing," says Christ, "except in the
power of God the Father, Son, and Holy Spirit." Now the person bursts into word and deed, proclaims and magnifies the
name and praise of Christ, so that also through us others may
be healed and saved, as we have also come to faith through
others who previously preached Christ to us in order that the
kingdom of Christ may be increased.

Here follow persecution, the cross, and all tribulation
because of the gospel in the world which hates light and life
and loves darkness. The world does not want to be an
evildoer, but righteous and just in its own works. It establishes
for itself laws, and rules by which it thinks it can be saved
and despises the unattractive, plain, /113/ and simple rule of
Christ. Here the old Adam springs forth, that is, the poisoned
nature in which we are conceived in our mother's womb and
born. The same does not give up his old trickiness, pricks up
his ears, expresses his inborn nature, and resists the Spirit
within the person, so that he does not do what he wills,

according to the Word of God. There the flesh must daily be killed since it wants only to live and reign according to its own lusts. Here the Spirit of Christ prevails and gains the victory. Then the person brings forth good fruits which give testimony of a good tree. Day and night he practices all those things which concern the praise of God and brotherly love.

This is a summary and right order of a whole Christian life which begins in the Word of God. From this follows knowledge of sin and forgiveness of the same in faith. Faith is not idle but is industrious in all good Christian works. But only those are good works which God himself has commanded us and of which he will demand a reckoning from us at the last day, Matt. 26 [25:34ff.].[7]

Fifth: After we have now recognized in faith the inestimable and inexpressible goodness of God clearly and plainly in the Word of God, then we should be thankful to God our heavenly Father, who loved the world so fervently that he did not spare his only begotten Son, but gave him for us even unto death, yes, unto death on the most shameful cross, so that we should be saved. So that we do not forget him, Christ Jesus himself, our Savior, has ordained and instituted a beautiful memorial in his Last Supper. For when he and his disciples ate together, he took bread, blessed it, and said, "Take, eat, this is my body which is given for you. Do this in remembrance of me." Likewise he took the cup and gave it to them to drink and said, "Take and drink. This is my blood which is shed for you for the forgiveness of sins. Do this in my memory." Here everybody can see that bread is bread and wine is wine, like other bread and wine. But it is instituted by Christ as a reminder and memorial. For as often as we break the bread together, distribute it and eat, we should remember his body broken for us on the cross and distributed to all those who eat and enjoy it in faith. /114/ Here it is obvious that the bread is not the body of Christ but only a reminder thereof. Likewise, the wine is not the blood of Christ but also a memorial that he shed his blood and distributed it on the cross to all believers for the washing away of our sins, as the hoop in front of the tavern is not wine, but a

---

[7] The Scripture reference is incorrect in this version. In the second version below it is correct.

remembrance thereof.[8] It is fitting that we should remember and not forget his goodness but should proclaim, shout out, and be grateful for it to all eternity. Paul admonishes us very earnestly of this when he writes to the Corinthians in 1 Corinthians 11:26: "As often as you eat the bread (notice: he takes it as bread, and it is bread) and you drink the cup, that is, the wine (notice that it is wine which is drunk) you shall proclaim the death of the Lord until he comes." Notice: he says "until he comes." From this we hear that he is not present but will come only at the hour of the last judgment, in his great majesty and glory shining visibly to everybody as the lightning from east to west.

From this it follows and is seen clearly that the Supper is nothing other than a memorial of the suffering of Christ who offered his body for our sake and shed his crimson blood on the cross to wash away our sins. But up to the present we have turned this Supper into a bear's mass[9] with mumbling and growling. We have sold the mass for huge amounts of possessions and money and, be it lamented to God, would gladly henceforth continue with it. The person who practices the Supper of Christ in that way and contemplates the suffering of Christ in a firm faith will also give thanks to God for this grace and goodness. He will surrender himself to the will of Christ, which then is that we also should do to our neighbor as he has done to us and give our body, life, property, and blood for his sake. This is the will of Christ, and since this is once more impossible for us, we should call upon God diligently for grace and strength, so that he might give them to us to make us able to fulfill his will. For if he does not give us grace, we are already lost. We are human, we have been human, and we will remain human beings until death.

O dear Lords, friends, and brothers, take to heart what I have said to you and strive for the clear, plain, and pure Word of Christ from which alone your faith comes. In it we must be

---

[8] This is a reference to the custom of hanging a hoop from a wine barrel outside the tavern to indicate the availability of new wine.

[9] Hubmaier twice uses the term "bear's mass" (*bern mess* here and *Berenmeß* at the end of text 11, *On the Christian Baptism of Believers*, see below, p. 148) to describe the mass, which is more characterized by "mumbling and growling," i.e., by unintelligible sounds, than by clearly spoken words intelligible to the laity.

saved, for the ax is already laid to the root of the tree. If there is nothing at hand, the tree will be cut down. Truly I say to you, if you fear the frost here in this time, then the snow of eternal coldness will fall upon you.[10] If you fear the coals, you will even fall into the fire. For Christ says with clear words, "He who confesses me before people, him will I confess before God, my Father. Whoever denies me before people, him I will deny before God. Do not fear those who take the body from you, which is more than earthly goods, but fear him who can take both your body and soul and cast you into eternal damnation."[11] Whoever has ears, let him hear the heavy and severe judgment of God over those who conceal and deny his Word. May the Lord God enlighten those who do not want to hear. Amen. Herewith be commended unto God.

Given at Waldshût, Saturday, after Peter and Paul, in 1525.[12]

---

[10] Allusion to Job 6:16.
[11] Hubmaier here conflates fragments of Matt. 10:28 and 10:32-33.
[12] The date was July 1.

10

Letter to the Zurich Council

A regular component of the Anabaptist witness was the request for dialogue. We have seen that the major institutional transitions of the early Reformation were marked by disputations, especially those of January and October 1523 in Zurich. As Zwingli's more radical disciples began to lose confidence in his leadership, this had first been expressed in their request to the Zurich Council that there be a public disputation to replace the now abandoned smaller meetings.[1] Zurich had called such a meeting for January 17, 1525, and at first the dissenters had hoped that Hubmaier would attend it.[2] He did not, and as a consequence was left out of the first phases of the Zurich Anabaptist movement. When he had once been drawn into Anabaptism through the work of Wilhelm Reublin at Waldshut, Hubmaier continued to consider himself to be in dialogue with Zwingli's Reformation. This letter to the Zurich Council, simultaneous with the completion of his On the Christian Baptism..., *testifies to that claim.[3]*

Grace and peace in Christ Jesus. Noble, severe, provident, honorable, and wise Lords! I recently read a booklet by Master Ulrich Zwingli concerning baptism,[4] in which he is of the opinion that he has adequately demonstrated that young children should be baptized. Just last Friday I began one of my own[5] and should if God wills be done by tomorrow, in which I thoroughly demonstrate that they should not be baptized. But now I consider the fact that such contrariety is of no use to the churches but rather brings much offense. Still

---

[1] Yoder 1962, p. 38; petition of Felix Mantz to the Zurich Council, Harder 1985, p. 311ff.

[2] vMS, no. 23, p. 33; Bergsten suggests there were no out-of-town invitations, 1961, p. 253.

[3] Source: vMS, no. 82, pp. 87-88.

[4] Cf. Z 4, no. 56, pp. 188-337.

[5] Our text 11, below.

one cannot for that reason[6] let the truth be so coarsely trampled in the mud. I and every Christian must say something according to his conscience. But in order that such[7] might occur properly (for I ascribe to Your Graces, your city, and Master Huldrich every honor), I pray Your Graces and Wisdom, for the sake of God, of the last judgment, and of the love which you have thus far had and still do for the divine Word, for which you are most famous in every land, that you assist me with a safe conduct to meet Master Ulrich. I am willing to come secretly or publicly, [with him] alone or before the entire honorable Council of Zürch, or before a few delegates chosen by Your Wisdom, in the presence of Master Leo,[8] Myconius,[9] the Commander of Küsnach,[10] and others whom you would wish to have present, [so that I might] converse and negotiate with Master Ùlrich (although I would gladly have Dr. Bastian of Schaffusen[11] with us as well), so that, whether quietly or publicly, as God wills, we might arrive at a good peace. Your Wisdom should plan a conversation, or else you will have to suffer unremitting trouble, travail, and unrest. Should it then be determined according to the Word of God that I err, then I will recant gladly and sincerely, and will henceforth assist Master Ulrich to defend and to proclaim his opinion.[12] But should it become manifest that

---

[6] I.e. for the sake of avoiding offense. Cf. above, p. 46, note 17, our reference to *schonung*.

[7] I.e. the free defense of the truth.

[8] Leo Jud, Zwingli's successor in 1519 as pilgrimage *Leutpriester* (people's priest) at Einsiedeln, since 1523 in Zurich at St. Peter's, Bible translator.

[9] Oswald Myconius, driven from Lucerne because of his sympathies with Zwingli, at Zurich since 1523, later the successor to Oekolampad as Reformer of Basel. Zwingli's first biographer.

[10] Konrad Schmid, Commander of the Johannite monastery at Küssnacht, one of the more conservative of Zwingli's colleagues. Schmid was among the patriotic preachers who died with Zwingli in the battle of Cappel in 1531. These three men formed the regular though informal inner circle of Zwingli's reforming leadership.

[11] Sebastian Hofmeister, former Franciscan, Reformer of Schaffhausen, one of the moderators of the Zurich disputation in October 1523. He was critical of infant baptism until the summer of 1525, when the Schaffhausen government ordered him to change his mind, Fast 1973, pp. 13-20

[12] There is evidence that this statement is sincere: i.e., that if convinced he had been wrong Hubmaier would become Zwingli's colleague arguing the other side. Cf. below, text 12, note 19, p. 157, and Yoder 1962, p. 159f. The authenticity of the Anabaptists' commitment to dialogue was such that the possibility of their being convinced in the course of a debate was open.

Master Ůlrich has been mistaken about infant baptism, for God's sake, he should not be ashamed to desist from it; for the truth will ultimately win out. After all, Peter stumbled after having received the Holy Spirit and did not walk according to the truth of the gospel, for which Paul admonished him, Gal. 2:11. So he should not complain if it would happen to him too. We are all errant humans; one stumbles today, another falls tomorrow. It happens for our good, that we might humble ourselves before God.

Gracious, benevolent Lords, I admonish, pray, and appeal yet again, purely for God's sake, that you bring me to Master Ůlrich. Write the [promise of safe] conduct to the honorable Council of Waldshut, so that they allow me [to come]. I hope to God that (once we are together in person) we can soon be of one mind. For I am ready in every way to yield to the bright and clear Word of God and to give God the glory, and I want to believe that the same is true of my dear brother Master Huldrich Zwingli. Farewell in God the Lord, and for God's sake may I have a favorable answer. Given at Waldshůt Monday after Huldrichi 1525.[13]

Your Graces' and Wisdom's willing Baldasar Fridberger at Waldshut.

Your Wisdom please let Master Ulrich also see my request.

---

[13] July 10, 1525.

Von dem Chꝛiſtenlichen
Lauff der glaübigen.

Durch Balthaſarn Hüeb-
möꝛ von Fribberg:
yetz zu ꝛvaldshut
aufzgangen.

Die ꝛvarheit iſt untöbtlich.

M. D. XXV.

Die lieb freüꝛvet ſich
der ꝛvarheit.

i. Coꝛin. ꝼiij. cap.

Original title page of On the Christian Baptism of Believers

11

On the Christian Baptism of Believers

In his letter of July 10, 1525, to the Zurich Council, Hubmaier mentioned that he was hard at work on a study of baptism which he hoped to finish in a day or two. On the Christian Baptism of Believers *bears the date of July 11. It was apparently written in five days. By all counts it is Hubmaier's best and most significant writing. It is a fluent, clear, and biblically based defense of believers baptism.*

It was written in specific response to Zwingli's Von der Taufe, von der Wiedertaufe, und von der Kindertaufe, which appeared in May.[1] It was dedicated to all believers in Christ. In comparison to many treatises of the day, it is moderate and thoughtful in tone. Although Zwingli is clearly the opponent, his name is never mentioned. The treatise gives all the appearance of an attempt to clarify the issues which separate Waldshut from Zurich and which finally threaten to divide the evangelical movements in South Germany and Switzerland.

Hubmaier expresses extreme reluctance in the drafting of the work. He says that he had wishes someone else had done the job and that it would have been possible for him to stay in his "burrow and cave." One thinks that it was the life of the scholar and pastor that appealed to him and not that of the polemicist.

In the treatise Hubmaier carefully searches through the New Testament for baptismal texts which then can be analyzed so as to demonstrate the dominical and apostolic bases for believers baptism. Windhorst suggests that Hubmaier was motivated to answer three specific charges of Zwingli: first, that the

---

[1] Z 4, no. 56, pp. 188-337. For partial translations see Harder 1985, pp. 362-74, and Bromiley 1953, pp. 129-75. Though Zwingli's treatise was the stimulus for Hubmaier's writing, the latter responded by setting for himself a less reactionary, more positive and programmatic task: the need for a platform statement for the young antipedobaptist movement. Later he was to refute Zwingli's argument directly (cf. below text 14, p. 172).

Anabaptists were establishing new sects; second, that they reject the legitimate role of the government; and third, that the Anabaptists assert that after baptism they do not sin.[2] In answering these charges Hubmaier appears to believe that all is not lost as far as the relationship to Zwingli is concerned. In the course of the argumentation he demonstrates his own distinctive Anabaptist point of view and to some degree distances himself from the Swiss Brethren.

According to the contemporary chronicler, Johannes Stumpf, the treatise enjoyed quick and wide distribution.[3] This may account for Zwingli's highly antagonistic response to it.[4] As will be seen below, it was not the last treatise to come forth against infant baptism in general and Zwingli in particular.

The treatise has appeared in an English translation by Estep[5] and it has often been analyzed.[6] Without doubt it represents the best of Hubmaier.

On the Christian Baptism Of Believers by Balthasar Hüebmör von Fridberg, Now of Waldshút. Truth Is Immortal. 1525 Love rejoices in the truth. 1 Cor. 13:6

To all righteous Christ-believing and pious people I, Baldazar Hüebmör von Fridberg, a servant of the Word of

---

[2] Windhorst 1976, p. 41.

[3] Gagliardi 1952, p. 284.

[4] Calvin also found it important to reply to this treatise of Hubmaier. Institutes, IV.xvi.17-23, tr. McNeill/Battles 1960, pp. 1339-46.

[5] Estep 1976, pp. 66-98. Earlier translation in Davidson 1939, pp. 67-138, and a summary in Vedder 1905, pp. 114-17. The source for our translation: HS, pp. 118-63.

[6] The most important studies of the treatise are Armour 1966, pp. 24-49; Windhorst 1976, pp. 38-90; and Sachsse 1914, pp. 16-23.

God, now at Waldshut, wish grace and peace in Christ Jesus our only Savior./119/

Beloved in God: I know and must confess with the prophet Jeremiah that the way of the human being does not lie in his own power; nor does it lie in the power of man to govern his own steps [Jer. 10:23]. The human heart undertakes also to do something for itself, but God directs and controls according to his pleasure. For I had always intended to remain alone in my barrel and cave and not at all to creep out into the light, not that I feared the light, but in order that I might remain in peace. But God ordained it differently and has pulled me out against my will to give account to anybody who requests it concerning my faith as it is in me, namely in the matter of infant baptism and the true baptism of Christ. Until now I had hoped that someone else would have done such. For I know for sure that God has preserved himself at least seven thousand men who have not bent their knee to the childish infant baptism nor have they recognized it as right, although numerous child washers do their utmost to defend the same and in addition despise the true baptism according to the institution of Christ. They further introduce a much more ungrounded, fictitious, and untrue complaint, saying: "One would thus make factions and sects, thereby abolish the government, and no longer be obedient to it."[7] Also when they asked why we let ourselves be rebaptized, though it is no rebaptism, then we answer that it has not been proven to us whether or not we have been baptized. They also spread the rumor about us that we boast we are able to sin no more after baptism.[8] They also spread many other inventions which never come into my mind or into the mind of any other orthodox and goodhearted Christian.[9] For although they decry us as factions and sects, so did it also happen with Christ, Jeremiah, Paul, and others; we are not greater than the Lord. But injustice is being done to us; we do not make factions and sects but act in this matter according to the Word of God. Neither angels, devils, nor human beings will ever be able to

---

[7] Zwingli frequently accuses the Anabaptists of forming new sects, e.g., Z 4, pp. 245,[29] 254,[15] 277,[19ff.] 328.[22ff.]

[8] Z 4, p. 208.[28ff.] Cf. Yoder 1968, p. 174.

[9] Z 4, p. 277.[23ff.]

refute that, although some rage still so much and publish against it. /120/ Thus one sees very well in their writings that they prefer to obscure and darken the clear, bright, and plain baptismal Scriptures so that one does not see their error and stumbling; rather than to bring forth and demonstrate the true understanding. One recognizes their touch[10] which does not resonate at all on the harp of Christ. May God grant us not such obscuring or glossing but the clear simple understanding of his living Word: *that* is something. In addition we confess publicly that there should be a government which carries the sword, that we want and should be obedient to the same in all things that are not contrary to God, and the more the same is Christian the more it desires from God to rule with the wisdom of Solomon so that it does not deviate either to the right nor to the left against God. Therefore we should also seriously and with great diligence pray to God for it, so that we may lead a peaceful and quiet life together in all blessedness and uprightness.

Thus we confess openly that we were not baptized in childhood. Therefore we let ourselves be baptized on the authority of the earnest command of Christ and the apostles in many places. That, however, we should boast as if we were able never more to sin after baptism and the like does violence and injustice to us, for we know that both before and after, we are poor and miserable sinners, and if we were to say that we did not sin, then we would lie and the truth would not be in us. However, if such things may have been said by some foolish people, then one should forbid the same and correct them and not make the whole of Christian baptism repulsive and annihilate it on account of their naive speaking. For although Judas Iscariot betrayed Christ, not all the disciples in the Scripture are scolded as traitors. But it is also one of the tricks which the rhetorical theologians use: We recognize them by their tricks. Therefore, dear pious Christians, let tricks be tricks. You will, your life long, not learn from these

---

[10] Ger. *griffli*. As Westin and Bergsten indicate (HS, p. 120, n. 13), it is a word used positively by Zwingli (cf. Z 4, p. 271[5]) but taken negatively by Hubmaier as "artifice, trick, ruse," as translated below. Here, however, there is a further play on words (*griff* = touch, *griffel* = finger board of a harp), suggesting a comparison with false-sounding strokes on a harp.

tricks what baptism is in the name of the Father, and the Son, and the Holy Spirit, but devote yourselves to the clear Word of God. Thus you will grasp the right basis of truth. Although I also do not reject tongues or languages for the exposition of dark passages, still for sun-clear words one needs neither tongues nor lungs.[11] Herewith I beseech and admonish you that you lay hold on the Scripture for that. It will give witness to the truth even if I had not written anything. If, however, you want to read my simplicity, then do it without /121/ any respecting of persons, of high names, of old practices, of traditions, also without any feelings which would tend to lead you away from the truth. After that, judge in your minds and consciences according to the simple Word of God. Let the Word of God alone be peacemaker and judge. Then you will not err. Be commended herewith unto God.

Waldshût on the Rhine, 11th day of July 1525.

Truth Is Immortal.

Chapter I
On Baptism

The Different Kinds of Baptism and What They Mean.
1. Baptism in water.
2. Baptism in water, for or unto change of life.
3. Baptism in the Spirit and fire.
4. To be reborn out of water and Spirit.
5. Baptism in water in the name of the Father, Son, and Holy Spirit, or in the name of our Lord Jesus Christ.[12]

1. Baptism in water according to the divine command is to pour outward water over the person who confesses his sins

---

[11] Hubmaier's play on words, *weder zungen noch lungen.*

[12] Hubmaier's beginning with the five meanings of baptism parallels Zwingli's beginning his treatise with four uses of the word *baptism* in Scripture: "First, it is used for the immersion in water whereby we are pledged individually to the Christian life. Second, it is used for the inward enlightenment and calling when we know God and cleave to him—that is the baptism of the Spirit. Third, it is used for the external teaching of salvation and external immersion in water. Finally, it is used for external baptism and internal faith, that is, for the Christian salvation and dispensation as a whole." Z 4, pp. 219^{17}-220,⁴ tr. Bromiley 1953, p. 132.

and by his own knowledge and agreement to count him among the number of sinners. Thus John baptized in Matthew 3:6 and John 1:25f.

2. Baptism in water for or unto change of life is also by divine command to pour outward water over the person who confesses his sins and by his own knowledge and agreement to count him among the number of sinners and to lead him into a new life according to the Rule of Christ, Matt. 3:11ff.

3. Baptism in the Spirit and fire is to make alive and whole again the confessing sinner with the fire of the divine Word by the Spirit of God. This takes place when the pardon of his sins has already been granted him by the life-giving Word of God. The Spirit of God makes and effects this enlivening internally in the human being. Outside of the same all teaching of the Word is a killing letter, Matt. 3:11; Luke 3:16; 2 Cor. 3:6. /122/

4. To be reborn out of water and Spirit is to help the sinner out of the fear and dread which he received when his sins were pointed out to him by the letter of the law and to give him medicine and comfort again through the Word of God which will remain for eternity, so that he will not despair, 1 Pet. 1:23. For the unbeliever this promise is a dead letter or death, but for the believer it is spirit and life, and this God alone gives to whomever he wants. He knows his own, John 3. Nobody will tear out of the hands of Christ those whom the Father has given to him. Thus Christ frightened and again comforted Prince Nicodemus, John 3:1-15.

5. Baptism in water in the name of the Father, and the Son, and the Holy Spirit, or in the name of our Lord Jesus Christ, is nothing other than a public confession and testimony of internal faith and commitment by which the person also testifies outwardly and declares before everyone that he is a sinner. He confesses himself guilty of the same, yet at the same time he wholly believes that Christ has forgiven him his sin through his death and has made him righteous through his resurrection before the face of God our heavenly Father. For that reason he already agrees to confess publicly from now on the faith and the name of Christ before everyone. He has committed himself and is determined henceforth to live according to the Word and the command of Christ, but that not according to human capacity, so that it might not happen

to him as it did to Peter. "For without me you cannot do anything," says Christ [John 15:5], but only in the power of God
the Father, the Son, and the Holy Spirit. Now, so that the
kingdom of Christ might increase, the person breaks out into
word and deed. He proclaims and magnifies the name and the
praise of Christ, so that others might also become sanctified
and be saved through him in word and faith, in the same way
as he also came to faith and the knowledge of God through
other people who preached to him about Christ. Here then
follow tribulation, temptation, persecution, the cross, and all
sorrow in the world, because of faith and because of the name
of Jesus Christ. For the world hates the light and loves the
darkness, so that a person has no comfort or support at all
except to take refuge in the Word of God. The same also happened to Christ after his baptism, according to Matthew 4:1-
11. With the same word one shields himself and protects himself from all the fiery arrows of this world, of Satan, and of
sins..

From these descriptions of the kinds of baptism anyone
can see and recognize that the word or teaching should
precede the outward baptism, along with the determination to
change one's life by the help of God. /123/ Through baptism a
person is led to the knowledge of his sins, as prior to the baptism of John, or to the knowledge of his sins, and also to the
knowledge of the pardon of them through the Lamb of God, as
prior to the baptism of Christ. This whole chapter will become
entirely obvious and clear in the following passages concerning the baptism of John and of Christ.

Chapter II
On the Office of John

There was a man sent from God whose name was John. He
came to testify, to bear witness to the light, so that all might
believe through it [John 1:6-7]. And John bore witness and
said, "I saw the Spirit descend as a dove from heaven, and it
remained on him. I did not know him; but he who sent me to
baptize with water said to me, 'He on whom you will see the
Spirit descend and remain is the one who baptizes with the
Holy Spirit.' And I saw it and bore witness that this is the Son
of God" [John 1:32-34].

This testimony consists of three points. First, he preached; second, he baptized; third, he pointed at or to Christ.

His preaching was: "Repent, change your lives, recognize your sin. The kingdom of heaven, which is the proclamation of the grace of God which he has brought about for us through his Son Christ, is at hand [Cf. Matt. 3:2]. I am a voice crying in the wilderness, 'Make straight the way of the Lord,' as the prophet Isaiah said [John 1:23]. Every valley shall be filled, and every mountain and hill shall be brought low. The uneven shall be made plain, the crooked be made straight and all flesh shall see the Savior of God [Luke 3:5-6]. The ax is already laid to the root of the trees; every tree that does not bear good fruit is cut down and thrown into the fire." And the people asked him: "What shall we do then?" He answered and said to them: "Whoever has two shirts should give to the one who has none, and he who has food, should do likewise." Tax collectors also came to be baptized, and they said to him, "Master, what then shall we do?" He said to them, "Do not cheat the people in your business." /124/ Soldiers also asked him, "What then shall we do?" And he said to them, "Do not do violence or injustice to anybody, and be content with your pay" [Luke 3:9-14].

From these words it is obvious that John preached the harsh and frightful law, the letter, sin, and death, just as the other preachers of the law and the prophets. This is shown by his words: "Recognize that you are sinners. Change your lives. You are not on the right way. Make yourselves ready and submit yourselves to the way of the Lord. Every mountain and hill shall be brought low. You have to despair in yourselves and must give up hope in your sins. Recognize yourselves that there is nothing good in you and that you also bring forth no good fruit. Now every tree that does not bear good fruit will be cut down and thrown into the fire. It is of no avail to you that you boast of being children of Abraham. God is able to raise children of Abraham from these stones. The ax is on the tree. See, what is to be your work: feed, give drink, and clothe. Do not do injustice or violence to anyone." See how all his preaching is based on the law. His rough clothing and his food also testify to just that. For he wore a garment of camel's hair, a leather belt around his loins, and his food was locusts and wild honey, Matt. 3:4. Here becomes obvious what a great wrong it is that anybody writes in appreciation of John that he preached the gospel in the same way as Christ and the other apostles did. No, that is wrong. He says, "The kingdom of God is coming near." He points to it but he did not preach it as Christ, who then announced to the believers a pardon of sins which is now present—although in this case John is more than the other prophets who have only referred to the future Christ. But John has referred to the actually present one and pointed at him with his finger that one will find the gospel with him, that is, the pardon of sins. I do not intend to ridicule anybody; ridicule is unseemly. May God enlighten us all when we have fallen, so that we may stand up again. For it is known that just as the water or pond at Jerusalem did not heal anybody unless the angel of God moved the water, John 5:2ff., in the same manner are all teachings dead which Christ does not move and make alive through his Spirit, as Paul also wrote in 2 Corinthians 3:6. Now John pointed his disciples away from himself and directed them to Christ, who takes away the sins of the world, makes alive, and pardons sins, Matt. 3:11.

Now to the second point concerning the office of John. He baptized, namely, those who went out to him where he baptized, who confessed their sins, and who also wanted to take on a new life. He pointed out to them when he listed the works in Luke 3:4ff. that they should henceforth do /125/ the works which are fitting for a life of repentance. From that one sees that John did not baptize little children but only those who confessed themselves guilty of, and recognized, their sins. Now, he baptized with water, that is, he marked all those outwardly who confessed their sins inwardly in the heart. They now were part of his fellowship and testified publicly that they were his disciples, and that there was nothing good in them. This now was a heavy blow against the Pharisaic gang. They did not want to be sinners but righteous by their own works as Scripture everywhere points out about them, Luke 7:30; 18:9ff., and in many other passages. Here the war started between John and the Pharisees.

John baptized with this water baptism as did also the other disciples of the Lord before the resurrection of Christ, for they all only pointed to Christ as the true and present physician. But after the resurrection he also gave them, as his messengers and servants, the power of forgiveness of sins and said, "Receive the Holy Spirit. To whom you remit sins, they are remitted; to whom you retain them, they are retained," John 20:22f. "Go forth and teach all people, that is, preach the gospel to all creatures and baptize them in the name of the Father, and the Son, and the Holy Spirit. For whoever believes and is baptized will be saved, but whoever does not believe will be damned," Matt. 28:19; Mark 16:16. As now before the resurrection the disciples of Christ pointed those who recognized their sins to Christ that he might forgive them and with the Word of the gospel point out to them the pardon of their sins, which he then often did. In the same way now after the resurrection they have themselves received the same office: namely, to announce the pardon of sins through Christ, who now was present no longer bodily, but henceforth in his Word and through his disciples, in which way he wants to remain among us until the end of the world. That is precisely what Christ wants to say with his words in John 20:21: "As my Father sent me, so I send you." It is as if he wanted to say, "He has given me a mandate that I should announce to all believers in me the sure pardon of their sins. Henceforth you should do the same so that all those who believe in me will not be damned but have eternal life." Here even a little child who does not yet have to pay to enter the baths understands that the baptism before the resurrection of Christ and the one after are not the same baptism in terms of witness, even though /126/ it is one water. But water is not baptism, or the whole Rhine would be baptism. That would be playing pranks with Scripture.

Here it is asked whether Christ himself also baptized. Say "No," for even though Scripture says that he baptized, John 3:22, it explains itself immediately in the fourth chapter saying, "Jesus himself did not baptize, but his disciples," John 4:2. Let it rest with this and do not unnecessarily make "teaching" out of "baptism."[13] And that without any basis in Scripture so that we are not found to be too willful or too subtle. For the same kind of thing we find in many passages of

---

[13] Zwingli had equated "teaching" with "baptizing" in Z 4, p. 221.[6ff.] Cf. also Z 4, p. 271.[19ff.]

Scripture, that one passage explains the other more clearly. In Mark 6:38 we read that the disciples said that they only had five loaves of bread; and in John 6:8f., Scripture says that Andrew had answered thus. One finds also in one passage of Scripture that all the disciples grumbled over Mary, who poured the ointment over the Lord; and yet Scripture explains itself better in John 12:4 and says that it was Judas Iscariot who did. That is a common way of speaking in the Scriptures, out of which a person seeking for glory could make much nonsense and quarrelsomeness, but in vain; it is good for nothing. Thus Christ also says in John 14:12, "He who believes in me will also do the works that I do, and greater works than these will he do." And yet it is known that we do not and cannot do anything, but he must do it through and in us, as it is written in Acts 3:12 and 14:15. And even if sometimes baptizing is taken for teaching, it would still not help anything here.

The third point concerning the office of John is that he pointed to Christ as the true physician, forgiver of sins, and healer. He cries out and says, "This is he of whom I said: 'After me will come he who was before me, for he was earlier than me.' And from his fullness we have all received grace for grace. For the law was given by Moses; grace and truth come through Jesus Christ" [John 1:15-17], that is, our grace is given to us for the sake of the grace of Christ, which is given to him, so that we might fulfill the law through him and know the Father, so that hypocrisy stops. Further he says, "Behold, the Lamb of God. I am not able to help you but the Lamb takes away the sin of the world. This is he of whom I said, 'After me comes a man who was before me, for he was earlier than me,' that is, from eternity, and I did not know him. But /127/ for this I came baptizing with water, that he might be revealed to Israel" [John 1:29-31]. Behold and grasp, all of you who have eyes and hands, that John sent his disciples away from himself. For in his preaching they do not find anything but law, sin, death, devil, and hell; and he pointed them to the Lamb of God who would proclaim to them evangelical consolation, that is, a certain forgiveness of sins. Until sinners hear this they have no peace nor rest in their consciences. It is just as if one were to tell a sick person for a long time about a good physician. He still is sick until he comes to the physician who heals him and tells him, "Go forth and be whole." So it is with Christ. He has to speak with us, or his messengers in his place; then we are made whole in our souls. Believed forgiveness of sins is the true gospel which cannot be without the Spirit of God, for the Spirit of God makes the Word alive. Faith is a work of God, John 6:29. For by faith the law of sin and of death becomes a law of the Spirit, Romans 8:2. For what was impossible to the law, God has fulfilled through Jesus Christ so that the righteousness demanded by the law might be fulfilled in us who now walk not according to the flesh but according to the Spirit.

From this it follows that the water baptism of John is nothing but a public testimony which the person receives and gives because he confesses and recognizes that he is a miserable sinner, who cannot help himself nor give himself counsel, who does nothing good but that all his righteousness is corrupt and reproachable. For that reason he despairs of himself. He must also be damned eternally, were not a foreign righteousness to come to his help. His awareness and conscience learned from the law, which is knowledge of sin, show this to him. Now John is there and points him to Christ, that in him he will find discharge of his sins, rest, peace, and security so that he not remain in despair and thus be lost eternally. In summary, God leads through John downward into hell and through Christ upward again.

Chapter III
The Passages on the Baptism of John

First, I admonish the reader to watch for the sequence of word, meaning, and understanding in all the passages which deal with the baptism of John. This now is the order put down in these passages: /128/ (1) word, (2) hearing, (3) change of life or recognition of sin, (4) baptism, (5) works.

From this order in Scripture you might see even if you were blind as a mole,[14] whether John baptized little children, or whether he baptized only those to whom he first preached, who listened to him, confessed their sins, and who decided henceforth to improve their lives. Now the passages follow:

---

[14] *Scherengschlechtig*, literally: of the species of the mole.

Matthew 3:1ff.

"At that time John the Baptist came and (a)[15] preached in the wilderness of Judea and (b) said: (c) 'Repent! The kingdom of heaven has come near and he is the one of whom the prophet Isaiah has spoken and said, "There is a voice crying in the wilderness: Prepare the way of the Lord and make his paths straight." ' Then the city of Jerusalem and the whole Judean countryside and all the territories on the Jordan went out to him, and (d) they let themselves be baptized by him in the Jordan and (e) confessed their sin. When he now saw many Pharisees and Sadducees coming to his baptism he said to them: 'You brood of vipers, who has told you that you will escape the coming wrath? See, (f) bring forth true fruits of repentance. Do not think now to say within yourselves: "We have (g) Abraham for father." I tell you: God is able to raise up children to Abraham from these stones. The axe has already been laid to the root of the trees. Therefore whichever tree does not bear good fruit will be cut down and thrown into the fire.' "

Notice here, dear Christian, how precisely the above-mentioned order is followed. Even though the confession of sins follows outwardly after baptism, it still already had preceded inwardly in the heart. For it is that which drove the people out to water baptism, as you hear from his question: "Who told you?" etc.

Luke 3:2ff.

"The (a)[b] Word of God came to John, the son of Zechariah, in the wilderness. And he came into all the areas

---

[15] The letters in the text are given by Hubmaier and correspond to marginal notations which follow the sequence or outline that Hubmaier is illustrating in this chapter.

---

[a] (a) word, (b) hearing, (c) change, (d) baptism, (e) recognition, (f) own works, (g) own faith.

[b] (a) word, (b) hearing, (c) change of life, (d) baptism, (e) own work, (f) own faith, (g) but not the young children.

around the Jordan and (b) preached the baptism of repentance for the forgiveness of sins, as it is written in the book of
the sayings of Isaiah the prophet who says: 'There is a voice
crying in the wilderness: (c) 'Prepare the way of the Lord and
make his path straight. All valleys shall be filled and all
mountains and hills shall be brought low. What is crooked
shall become straight and what is uneven shall become even.
All flesh will see the Savior of God.'

"Then he said to the people who went out /129/ to be (d)
baptized by him: 'You brood of vipers! Who has told you that
you will escape the coming wrath? See, (e) bring forth worthy
fruits of repentance, and do not propose to say to yourselves,
"We have (f) Abraham for our father." For I tell you, God is
able to raise up children to Abraham from these stones. The
axe has already been laid to the root of the trees. Whichever
tree does not bear good fruit, will be cut down and thrown
into the fire.'

"And (g) the people asked him: 'What shall we then do?'
He answered and said to them: 'Whoever has two shirts should
give to the one who has none, and whoever has food should
do the same.' Also the tax collectors came to be baptized and
said to him, 'Master, what shall we then do?' and he said to
them: 'Do violence to no one and be content with your pay.' "

Note here, the evangelist Luke has forgotten the little
children because he does not mention their asking what they
should do.

Dear, pious Christians. If there were no other passage on
earth than this one, still nobody should be so impudent and
bold to imagine (I do not want to say that he preaches and
publishes contrary to his own conscience) that John also baptized little children. It is not a question of having opinions,
thinking, and imagining; it is a question of knowing. Or I
would suppose that also Caiaphas, Annas, and Pilate went out
there and let themselves be baptized. The Scripture says:
"The people asked him." Little children cannot speak or else
John would have had to answer: "The child who has two
diapers should give one to that child who has none." Well, let
us leave this matter to God.

Luke 7:29f.

"And all the people who (a)* heard him (that is, Christ when he praised John so highly) and the tax collectors (b) acknowledged God's justice (that is, they confessed themselves to be sinners and God alone to be just) and they let themselves (c) be baptized with the baptism of John. But the Pharisees and the scribes despised the counsel of God against themselves and did not let themselves be baptized by him."

Mark 1:1ff.

"This is the beginning of the (a)ᵇ gospel of Jesus Christ, the Son of God. In Isaiah the prophet it is written: 'See, I send before you my angel who will prepare your way before you.' There is (b) a voice crying in the wilderness: (c) 'Prepare the way of the Lord and make his paths straight.' John was in the wilderness and (d) baptized and (a)ᶜ preached on the baptism of repentance for the forgiveness of sins, and the whole Judean countryside and /130/ those of Jerusalem went out to him, and they all let themselves (b) be baptized by him in the Jordan, and (c) they confessed their sins."

Here the Scripture points out two things which John practiced in the wilderness, namely preaching, and baptizing. Here the opponent cries, "Do you see that here baptism precedes preaching?" Answer: *Deo gratie*, [Thanks be to God]. Do you also see that preaching is followed by baptism? For Luke says, "And they all let themselves be baptized by him [Luke 3:21]." Away with quarreling about words! We want to take the correct sense and meaning for ourselves, so that we do not confuse anybody with strange glosses. It is the following: John was in the wilderness and baptized with water, undoubtedly nobody but those to whom he had preached beforehand and led to the recognition of their sins. Set the above-mentioned passages alongside this passage as one must do for the interpretation of the Scriptures. Then you will have

---

* (a) word, (b) recognition, (c) baptizing.
ᵇ (a) word, (b) hearing, (c) repentance, (d) baptism.
ᶜ (a) word, (b) baptism, (c) work.

to admit that I am speaking the truth and do not at all need your glosses. And after he had then baptized them he continued to preach to them and showed them the way of the baptism of repentance, that is, the recognition of sins, to the forgiveness of sins, that is, to Christ as it is clearly shown above in the third article on the office of John. Do you now see that John preached repentance before baptism and afterward; as we do not find that with him,[16] he leads us to Christ, in whom alone we can become righteous. Thus teaching precedes the baptism of Christ and follows it, Matt. 28:19. Thus, nobody is baptized by John or with the baptism of Christ unless he is instructed beforehand in the Word of God and led to the recognition of his sins, or to the recognition that they are forgiven him by Christ Jesus. Now when John had made straight a multitude by preaching and baptizing, he immediately began again with another, for that was his office.

With this the Word "and they confessed their sins" stands so strong and firm that it is sufficient in itself to prove that John baptized no children. O God, for what would one need any more proof? But these strong giants must cry out, "Yea, yea!" before they gain the victory.[17]

John 1:23ff.

"John said, 'I am (a)ᵃ a voice crying in the wilderness: "Make straight the way of the Lord," as the prophet Isaiah said.' And they who were sent were of the Pharisees. They asked him and said, 'Why then do you baptize if you are not Christ, nor Elijah, nor a prophet?'/131/ John answered them and said, 'I (b) baptize with water, but he has come among you, whom you do not know. He it is who will come after me, who was before me, the thongs of whose shoes I am not wor-

---

[16] John points forward to regeneration before baptism, he is still pointing forward to it after baptism; it follows that he (his baptism) does not impart regeneration.

[17] Hubmaier is here mocking those who celebrate the victory before it is won. *Giants* is used here as a term of derision.

ᵃ (a) word, (b) baptism, (c) instruction.

thy to untie.' This took place at Bethabara[18] on the other side of the Jordan where John baptized. The next day John sees Jesus coming to him, and says, (c) 'Behold, the Lamb of God who takes away the sin of the world.' "

Let every Christian consider here once again how John first calls himself a voice, that is, a preacher. After that he justifies his water baptism. Baptizing does not stand here for teaching as some people assume, for the Jordan itself testifies that he baptized with water. Third, after the baptism he sends his disciples away from himself to Christ and says, "Behold, the Lamb of God who takes away your sins which burden and distress you."

Acts 19:1ff.

"It happened, however, while Apollos was at Corinth, that Paul traveled through the upper countries and came to Ephesus. He found several disciples to whom he said, 'Did you receive the Holy Spirit when you became believers?' They said to him: 'We have not even heard whether there is a Holy Spirit.' And he said: 'Wherein were you baptized?' They said, 'In John's baptism.' Paul, however, said, 'John baptized with the baptism of repentance,' and told the people that they should believe in the one who would come after him, that is, in Jesus who is the Christ. When they heard this, they let themselves be baptized in the name of our Lord Jesus Christ. When Paul laid his hands on them, the Holy Spirit came on them, and they spoke with tongues and prophesied. And there were approximately twelve men."

This passage, O dear Christian, shows you such a clear, plain, and definite difference between the baptism of John and the baptism of Christ, that it is a mockery and shame that some people introduce here such obscure and confusing glosses by which they want to mix the baptism of John with his teaching, and that contrary to their previously published

---

[18] Hubmaier was using a third-century interpretation of John 1:28, attributed to Origen, that the "Bethany beyond the Jordan" was really Bethabara, to be found on the west side of the Jordan.

books.[19] But one should not play tricks like that with the treasure of the divine Word, otherwise in the end, holy theology would become Anaxagorean philosophy[20] and we would have to accept as many new beliefs as there are New Testaments being printed. For every capricious person would take without any basis in Scripture an "into" for an "in," "baptism" for "teaching," "into the name of" for "in the name of," /132/ and in the end out of a pumpkin a new Christ would have to grow.[21] Not so, dear friends. We want to present the text in the simplest way of all.

Paul had found in Ephesus several disciples of John who had come to a recognition of their sin, but they did not know yet anything about the forgiveness of sins. For even though John had directed them to Christ, they did not follow him so that they also could have heard about the forgiveness of sins by Christ. Their words prove this when they say: "We have never heard whether there is a Holy Spirit." And he asked them further wherein they had been baptized. That is the reading of the old Latin translation and the new German version, publicly printed and published.[22] They answered and said: "In the baptism of John," that is: "John baptized us and beyond that we have not gone." But Paul said: "John baptized with the baptism of repentance, that is, he pointed out sin; and those who confessed themselves to be sinners, he bap-

---

[19] Hubmaier is referring to Zwingli who in his *Commentary on True and False Religion* first developed the argument that the baptism of John and of Jesus was the same baptism in his: ". . . The baptism of John and the baptism of Christ are the same thing; for unless they were one and the same, Jesus would have rebaptized these persons through His disciples." Z 3, p. 768,[42ff.] tr. ZL, p. 191. In the same treatise Zwingli resolved the dilemma of the baptism of the disciples of John in Acts 19:1-7 by asserting that in this case, they had only been taught by John, not properly baptized. Z 3, p. 770,[15ff.] tr. ZL, p. 194ff. A useful analysis of the issue of the baptisms of John and Jesus in Hubmaier and Zwingli is Steinmetz 1979.

[20] The Greek philosopher Anaxagoras (ca. 500-428 B.C.) was a favorite name used by Reformers to refer to the Scholastics. For example, Luther called John Eck an Anaxagorean because he ". . . can prove anything he pleases from any passage of Scripture he pleases." WA 6, p.500, tr. LW 36, p. 16.

[21] Zwingli makes the distinction between being baptized "into the name" and "in the name" in Z 4, p. 271.[1ff.]

[22] Although Hubmaier occasionally uses the 1522 translation of the New Testament by Luther, he is here alluding to the Zurich translation published in 1524 by Christoph Froschauer.

tized in the water and taught them to believe in the one who would come after him, that is, in Jesus, that he is the Christ." So notice that in this passage "baptizing" may not be taken as "teaching," for it definitely says, "He baptized with the baptism of repentance."

Second, he said, he pointed out, he taught them that they should run to Christ, believe him, trust him, and call upon him. He will pardon their sins. But the twelve disciples did not pursue that. It is not enough to point somebody to Christ; he must go there, call upon him, and hear and believe in the remission of his sins. This is why Paul started at that point, and preached Christ to them, that they should believe in him. When they heard that, they believed without a doubt and let themselves be baptized in the name, that is, in the grace and power of our Lord Jesus Christ; and they testified publicly that they fully believe the remission of their sins. And then Paul laid his hands on them, and the Holy Spirit came, and they spoke in tongues and prophesied. These are works that are in general given to the new believers and the newly baptized. Now again you notice an obvious and tangible distinction between the two kinds of baptism. To sum it up: John leads his hearers into recognition of their sins. Second, he baptizes those who confess their sin and makes them his disciples. Third, he points them to Christ. Fourth, Christ forgives the sin. Fifth, all those who believe this forgiveness should be rebaptized by the apostles of Christ. That is a real rebaptism, because the baptism of John is, and /133/ is called baptism, and the baptism of Christ is also a baptism. Therefore it is correctly called rebaptism. The bath of the infants which we have hitherto taken for baptism is not a baptism, nor is it worthy of the name baptism. Therefore it is wrongly said that we let ourselves be rebaptized.

That is the correct, plain, and simple meaning of this passage. Therefore I want every Christian church and congregation to judge and discern. How blind, how blind! Why do they distress the godly, simple Christians at this point with such invented, sophistic glosses and additions. And even if in other passages baptizing was used for teaching, this passage will not bear that interpretation.

Matthew 21:25ff.

" 'Whence was the baptism of John?' Christ asked the high priests. 'Was it from God, or from men?' They thought in themselves and said: 'If we say it was from heaven,' he will say: 'Why then do you not believe him?' But if we say 'it was from men,' then we will have to fear the people. For everybody held John to be a prophet."

Here now the Scripture rippers come with their misinterpretation and say that also here the word *baptism* stands for teaching. Answer: It is to be taken for the water baptism of John, as above in John 1:26, where they also said: "If you are neither Christ, nor Elijah, nor a prophet, why then do you baptize?" He answered them and said that he was baptizing at the command of God, who had sent him to baptize by water. But they say one could have easily answered him the following: "The baptism of John was by men, because water is on the earth." O God, what childishness! Water is not baptism, or the whole Danube would be baptism, and the fishermen and sailors would be baptized daily. No, not so! He, Christ, only wants to know whether John baptized—yes, in water—by the command of God or of men. There the high scholars got stuck and were unable to answer. Therefore, let this passage stay with its simple meaning as long as neither the preceding nor the succeeding words /134/ compel or lead us differently. And even if some people have already taken baptizing here for teaching, then still this does not prove that infant baptism is right. So much for the baptism of John.

Chapter IV
On the Office of the Apostles

"Jesus said to his disciples once again: 'Peace be with you. As the Father sent me, so I send you.' And when he said this, he breathed on them and said to them: 'Receive the Holy Spirit. To whomsoever you remit their sins, to them they are remitted, and to whomsoever you retain them, to them they are retained,' " John 20:20f. "Therefore, go forth into all the world, preach the gospel to all creatures, teach all peoples, and baptize them in the name of the Father, Son, and Holy Spirit. Whoever believes and is baptized will be saved;

whoever does not believe will be damned," Mark 16:15f. and Matt. 28:19f.

From these words one understands clearly and certainly that this sending of the apostles consists of three points or commands: first, preaching; second, faith; and third, outward baptism. The preaching of the apostles was: as God promised to send the world his Word because of sin, as the prophets and Moses proclaimed this promise everywhere, God has now done that and the Word has become flesh, Jesus Christ, our Savior. He died on account of our sin and rose again for the sake of our justification, so that all who believe in him should not be lost but have eternal life, Acts 2:38; 10:34f.; John 1:14; Rom. 4:25. Thus David says: "God sent his Word and made us whole" [Ps. 107:20]. Christ also says himself: "I have come into this world not to condemn it but that it may be preserved" [John 3:17]. We have hanged Christ on the tree and have crucified him.

Dear friends, this is not only said to the actual executioners of Christ but to all of us because we are all guilty of his death, Isa. 53:4f. Truly he has suffered our sickness and borne our pains; yet we considered him as a leprous person and an outcast from God. He was wounded on account of our iniquities and crushed because of our vices. Of this Christ himself laments through the prophet Isaiah and says: "But it was you who burdened me with your sins and wearied me with your iniquities. I am the one, /135/ I am the one who blots out the sin for my own sake (for it is promised to you), and I will remember your sins never again," Isa. 43:24ff.

From these and similar discourses which the holy apostles and those sent by Christ included everywhere in their sermons, the people were moved to the recognition of their sin. And by that they also heard how Christ had suffered for them, that he paid for them and gave satisfaction for them on the cross. That again gives joy to people, enlivens the sinner, and brings him on the right path, so that he places his faith, hope, and love in God and trusts him for all good, through Jesus Christ, our Lord. Precisely for that reason, and that is the ultimate one, Christ sent out his disciples as God his father had sent him: that as he, Christ himself, said on earth to the believers, "Take heart, rise, go forth, your sins are forgiven you." Likewise his disciples should now represent him henceforth during the time of his bodily absence and guarantee to all believers a sure and certain remission of their sin through him, Jesus Christ, Rom. 5:1. Through this the believers came to rest and peace in their consciences, because they knew that through the suffering of Christ they had acquired a graceful and merciful God in heaven, to whom they were permitted to cry: "Father, Father, Rom. 8:15, our Father who is in heaven," Matt. 6:9. Whoever wants, let him read all the beautiful sermons of Peter, Paul, Stephen, and others in the Acts of the Apostles, together with the presentation of the Scriptures from the Old Testament. He will find it to be so.

The second article is faith. Therefore one preaches that people should believe and trust in God, Joel 2. Paul describes this point to the Romans in chapter 10 (10:13ff.) as follows: "Everyone who calls upon the name of the Lord will be saved. But how can they call upon him, in whom they do not believe? And how can they believe in him of whom they have heard nothing? And how can they hear without a preacher? And how can they preach if they are not sent? Thus it is written: 'How beautiful are the feet of those who proclaim peace, who proclaim good things, etc.' " So faith comes through preaching, preaching, however, through the Word of God. Therefore one preaches so that people believe, trust God, expect all good things from God our heavenly Father and believe that he is our gracious, good, gentle, benevolent, and merciful Father in heaven, who carries, protects, and shields us as a human being [shields] his child, or like a hen her chicks under her wings. This confidence and sincere trust in God through Jesus Christ, that is, through the favor, grace, and good will which God the Father has for his most-beloved Son Jesus Christ, is exactly true faith. Of this faith all the books which really describe faith thoroughly are full. It is in this faith that we should cry, pray, and call upon God that /136/ through the favor and good will which he has for his Son he might also be favorable to us. That is what it means to pray in the name of Jesus. What we ask in this way from the Father in the name of Jesus he will give us. Thereto he has guaranteed and pledged us his eternal living Word which will not fail for eternity. Before that could happen, heaven and earth would have to crumble.

If now a person who has been brought through the Word of God to recognition of his sin confesses himself to be a sinner, and is further taught by the Word of God that he should call upon God the Father for the forgiveness of his sin for the sake of Christ, and if he does that in faith and does not doubt anything, then God has cleansed his heart in this faith and trust and has remitted him all his sin. Accordingly, when he recognizes this grace and kindness, he surrenders himself to God and commits himself internally in his heart to live a new life according to the Rule of Christ. But in order to manifest to other believers in Christ his heart, mind, faith, and intention, he joins their brotherhood and churches, so that from now on he might interact with them and they again with him as with a Christian. Therefore, he accepts and gives a public testimony of his internal faith and lets himself be baptized with water. Notice, we are writing how it should be. However, whether it is always like that with those who let themselves be baptized, we want to leave to the judgment of God who knows hearts. Before him they also stand or fall who correctly or incorrectly respond to it. For where these things proceed correctly, faith must precede baptism. All Scriptures lead to this conclusion.

From that it follows that nobody can be so blind and helpless, but that he must see and grasp that no one should be baptized with water unless beforehand he confesses faith and knows how he stands with God. Saint Peter teaches that to us quite thoroughly in his first epistle in chapter 3:20ff. He says that in the time of Noah, during the building of the ark, some believing souls were also saved through water, which now also saves you in baptism, which is a sign of the former. Baptism signifies not the putting away of the flesh but the certain knowledge of a good conscience toward God through the resurrection of Jesus Christ, who ascended into heaven to the right hand of God. From this every pious Christian sees and grasps that the one who wants to be baptized with water must beforehand have the certain knowledge of a good conscience toward God through the Word of God. That is, that he is certain and sure to have a gracious and favorable God through the resurrection of Christ. From that we still have the custom of asking at baptism: "Do you believe in God the Father, etc., and in Jesus Christ, etc. Do you believe in the forgiveness of sin, the resurrection of the body, and eternal life?" And he who wants to be baptized answers: "Yes." /137/

Then water baptism follows. Not that the same cleanses the souls but rather the "yes" of a good conscience toward God which preceded inwardly in faith.

For that reason water baptism is called a baptism *in remissionem peccatorum,* Acts 2:38, that is, in forgiveness of sins. It is not that only through it or in it sin is forgiven, but by the power of the internal "Yes" in the heart, which the person proclaims publicly in the reception of water baptism, that he believes and is already sure in his heart of the remission of sins through Jesus Christ. Likewise, the baptism of John is also called a baptism of repentance, that is, the one who wants to be baptized confesses and declares himself guilty of sin. Here in particular let every Christian consider and judge how one can baptize the little babies as long as neither word, preaching, nor faith have preceded. O Christ, how far have we fallen away from your ordinances and commands. We pray to you that by grace you will help us again onto the right path.

But that one alleges to baptize infants on the grounds of a future faith is really a mocking casuistry, for under no circumstances was that the institution of Christ. He says, "Teach all nations, and then baptize them in the name of the Father, and the Son, and the Holy Spirit." One does not know whether at a later time it will be the will of the child or not. It is the same thing to baptize infants for a future faith as to hang up a barrel hoop at Easter in hope of future wine which is not to be casked until fall, and of which one does not know whether it will be ruined beforehand by hail, hoar frost, or other kinds of storms.

Now they come up with a new sophistry and call infant baptism an initial sign.ᵃ Dear one, tell me for God's sake what kind of beginning that sign stands for?[23] The beginning

---

[23]Zwingli calls infant baptism an initial sign, *anheblich zeichen,* cf. Z 4, pp. 231,[27] 237,[7] 240,[27] 241,[28] 243,[2] and 245,[21-22] tr. Bromiley 1953, pp. 141,[10] 145,[19] 148,[8] 148,[40] 149,[42] and 152.[2] For the purposes of his argument about baptism and faith, *anheblich* might more precisely be rendered "proleptic" or "anticipatory."

ᵃ Initial sign.

of the Spirit of God? Then he did not have it before. That is against you. Or the beginning of faith? You cannot say that, either. Because the Word did not precede, out of which alone faith can emerge. Or the initiation of a new life? That is not possible, either, because they do not know what is good or evil, new or old, Deut. 1:39; 1 Cor. 14:20. But now they gloss over it even more and say, It is therefore an initial sign, *ceremonii* or *teleta* (in Greek), /138/ just as if the children are being shoved into the orders. They have measured them the cowl, even though they did not know the statutes and the law, but they only learned them in their cowl.[24] Answer: whether it be Greek or cowlcuttic[25] I like the comparison very well. For as the fitting of the cowl does not make a monk and is good for nothing, but happens contrary to God, so does infant baptism not make a Christian, does not initiate a new life, but takes place counter to the institution of Christ. Away with such new tricky touches, they have nothing to do on the lute of the Word of God. One only needs to bring Scripture to Scripture. That would sound like the harp of David. Or I would almost like to ask: What if the child grows up to be a fool? What kind of initial sign would baptism then be? Now some people bring forth a foreign faith, namely that of their fathers and mothers, of their godfathers and godmothers, and say:[26] "On the same may infants be baptized." Answer: "I do not find any baptism in Scripture which is based on someone else's faith." Christ says,"The one who believes himself and is baptized." Likewise, Philip asks the treasurer: "If you believe with all your heart, you may." But one must let such people chatter; their tongue is already paid for.

Well, now they come up with another hair-splitting, subtle trickery, and assert that it has been like that in former times and that it still is like that where one is dealing with

---

[24] Zwingli wrote: It is therefore an initial sign, *ceremonii*, or *teleta* in Greek. Immediately, when the children were put into the orders they fit them the cowl: yet they did not know the laws and statutes but then only learned them in their cowls. Z 4, p. 231,[26-30] tr. Bromiley 1953, p. 141.

[25] The reference, a play on words, is at once to the language of Calcutta, i.e., gibberish to a European, and to the cowl of the monk, in this comparison an empty ceremony that is "good for nothing," as is infant baptism.

[26] In the letter to Boniface, Augustine offers a justification of the baptizing of infants on the basis of the faith of parents and godparents CIC I:1402 (canon 129), tr. Schopp 1962, v. 18, p. 130.

unbelievers.[27] There one must preach to them first; and if they believe, then baptize them. But our children have believing fathers and mothers. Therefore, /139/ one may well baptize them before they believe.[28] If these people were not too learned for me to be allowed to talk to them, then I would like to ask them two questions. First, whether our children, who have believing fathers and mothers are themselves believing or unbelieving. They cannot say that they believe because they have not heard the Word of God. Then they must be unbelieving. Then one needs to instruct them with the Word of God and lead them to faith, just as one does with other unbelievers. Second, I hear from them that there are two kinds of baptism. One for the unbelieving who first need to be instructed with the Word and then baptized and that one based in Scripture. The other one is for the children of the believers, whom one can baptize without previous instruction. Here I ask all of you together where this baptism can be found in Scripture. If you show it to me, then I will tell you the name of Melchizedek's father. But that is enough on this article. For if I wanted to answer all their empty talk, I would need days.

Third, the office of the apostles consists in the performance of the outward water baptism because Christ said, "Go forth and teach all peoples and baptize them, etc." This is said about water baptism. Nobody can deny that. What now this water baptism is, has been made sufficiently clear above in the first chapter, and in particular the water baptism which takes place in the name of the Father, and the Son, and the Holy Spirit. Also in Mark 16:15f. it is written about this office, from which it is once again clear and unmistakable that they baptize the little children without any basis in the Scriptures, for one should be taught and instructed in faith beforehand.

Do you ask now with earnest intention: "What, or how much at least, must I know if I desire to be baptized?" Answer: This, and this much, you must know from the Word of God before you let yourself be baptized: That you confess yourself a miserable sinner and guilty, that you also believe the forgiveness of your sins through Jesus Christ, and that you

---

[27] Cf. Z 4, p. 317.[27ff.]
[28] Z 4, p 318.[7-9]

give yourself into a new life with the firm resolution to improve your life and to order it according to the will of Christ, in the power of God the Father and the Son and the Holy Spirit. And if you fail in this, that you will be willing to let yourself be admonished according to the Rule of Christ, Matthew 18:15ff., so that you might grow in faith day by day like a mustard seed into the clouds of the sky. This you must know. For to know /140/ and to believe so is to believe that Jesus is the Christ, which faith is necessary before baptism, Acts 2:38; 8:37; 16:31; 19:8f. For that reason I am so dissatisfied with the water sprinklers who now pour and pour, yet no teaching has preceded.

Furthermore, I know many pious Christians who openly confess that baptism of infants has no basis in Scripture and that therefore one should not baptize them.[29] And yet neither do they see the rebaptism, which is practiced now, to be based in the Word of God. Answer: Dear pious Christians, listen. First, you err in calling the present baptism as it is practiced a rebaptism, since infant baptism is not a baptism according to your own confession nor in truth. Therefore, the present baptism is not rebaptism but a baptism. Violence and injustice are done to those of whom one says they let themselves be rebaptized. No! It is not like that. They let themselves be baptized. Let that suffice.

However, that a person who believes and has not been baptized—since infant baptism is no baptism—has the obligation to let himself be baptized, even if he might be already a hundred years old, we will prove with excellent reasons.[30]

First: Jesus Christ, our Redeemer said in Matthew 28:18f., "All power has been given to me in heaven and on earth. Go forth and teach all peoples, baptizing them in the name, etc." Here Christ commands his apostles [to do] two things in the power of the authority which God the Father has given him in heaven and on earth, namely that they should teach the people; second, that they should baptize them in the name of the Father, and the Son, and the Holy Spirit. If now these two things are commanded the apostles by Christ in such a serious

---

[29] Cf. Staehelin 1927: 355f.
[30] The section of the treatise which follows is later published by Hubmaier in *Reason and Cause*. See below, text 22.

and earnest way, with the indicated authority which God had given him, then without doubt the people are commanded to accept both of them with the same seriousness, because otherwise this command would be good for nothing and in vain. Therefore, as it is necessary to teach and to be taught, it is necessary to baptize and to be baptized. Otherwise these words, "Baptize them in the name of the Father, and the Son, and the Holy Spirit," would have to go to ruin. Before this happens heaven and earth will have to crumble.

The second reason is that water baptism has been instituted and commanded with such powerful and unfathomable words, namely in the name of the Father, and the Son, and the Holy Spirit, that nowhere else in the Old or New Testaments can we find such high words put together in such an explicit and clear way. From this we realize once again the seriousness with which Christ wills that those who have been instructed in faith should be baptized. For a serious command demands serious obedience and fulfillment. Truly, truly, I say to you, Christ did not use such precious words /141/ in vain as something which we might do or leave undone. Every pious Christian will be able to realize this for himself. But this is the way of human wisdom. What God esteems high or demands, it regards as the least.

The third reason: It is written in Mark 16:15f.: "Go forth into all the world and preach the gospel to all creatures. He who believes and is baptized will be saved but he who does not believe will be damned." Well, it is stated very clearly: (1) go, (2) preach, (3) he who believes, (4) and is baptized, (5) will be saved. Here you see a well-structured speech of which no single letter will fall. It must be kept as it is. Who then can change it? "Yes," you say, "this order is given for those to whom one needs to preach first the gospel before one baptizes them, but it is not given for infants." Answer: I like that. I am well pleased with this excuse. But now let the pedobaptizers also show me his order and command.[a] Where is it written: "Go and baptize the infants of the believers, and after six or eight years preach to them the gospel?" See, you dear pedobaptizers, you boast of an order and a baptism which has absolutely no basis in Scripture.

---

[a] Give proof.

The fourth reason: When Paul had delivered a beautiful sermon and quoted many precious passages of Scripture, his listeners went into themselves, that is, they realized that they were sinners and said to Peter and the other apostles, "You men and brethren, what shall we do?" Peter answered them, "Repent and every one let himself be baptized in the name of Jesus Christ for the forgiveness of sins. Then you will receive the gift of the Holy Spirit." Those who gladly accepted this Word, that is, those who believed (for to believe is to accept the Word) let themselves be baptized, and there were added that day about three thousand souls, Acts 2:37ff. Here all those who have eyes, see, and all those who have ears, hear that it is not enough that a person confesses his sins and amends his life, but beyond that it is necessary that he let himself be baptized in the name of Jesus Christ. Here now it is spoken about water baptism, because the story itself testifies to it with the three thousand souls who were baptized. In addition to confessing themselves guilty of their sins and accepting his word gladly, that is, believing the forgiveness of their sin, which all took place before water baptism, afterward they also had to let themselves be baptized with water, according to the institution of Christ for the forgiveness of sins. That is, they had to confess publicly that they were his disciples and that they believed the forgiveness of sins through Jesus Christ. In short, those who believe are obliged by the authority of this passage to let themselves be baptized, or otherwise Peter is lying and leading astray. That is far from him, for the words stand clear and plain: "Repent," for one thing; for the other: "and let everyone /142/ (without exception) be baptized in the name of Jesus Christ." I esteem this Scripture also as a Hercules.

The fifth reason. Paul wrote to the Hebrews in chapter 10:22f. these words: "Let us draw near (understand, to God the Father through the blood of Jesus) with a true heart, in a full faith, sprinkled in our heart from an evil conscience, and washed in our bodies with pure water; and let us hold fast to the confession of our hope without wavering." This Paul writes to the brethren of the New Testament who were not bound by the washings of the old law.

Here one can obviously see, hear, smell, taste, and grasp that all those who want to go to God through the blood of

Christ, have to go with a true heart, in a full faith, sprinkled in their hearts from an evil conscience. And this must, must, must be accompanied by the washing of the body with pure water. If you believe this, then you believe the Word of God. If you do not believe this, then tear and scratch these words out. What are they in the Book for, if they are not true? Alas, dear pedobaptist, do not tear them out. I beseech you for peace. The Words of God cannot be torn apart; they remain for eternity.

The sixth reason. Read the Acts of the Apostles and you will find in Acts 8:5ff. that the Samaritans believed Philip and thereafter they let themselves be baptized. Likewise Simon and the treasurer of Queen Candace believed and were baptized upon that faith as is written in this chapter (9ff. and 26ff.). Paul believed and was baptized thereafter, Acts 9:19. Cornelius with his household believed and received the Holy Spirit, and thereupon were they baptized with water, Acts 10:47f. and 11:15ff. Lydia, the seller of purple goods, and the jailer believed and only then they were baptized, Acts 16:14f. and 31ff. Many Corinthians believed and were baptized, Acts 18:8. The twelve men at Ephesus believed in Jesus and were baptized upon the name of the Lord Jesus, Acts 19:5ff. And in Acts 22:16 the faith and baptism of Paul are once again mentioned.

Who now wants to or can think that all those people would have let themselves be baptized if the order and serious command of Christ had not moved them to do so? Indeed they also could have said, "Yes, we do believe, yes, some of us have also already received the Holy Spirit. What need do we have of baptism? Faith saves us." No, not so. He who believes lets himself be baptized and does not continue to argue, because /143/ where water and a person to baptize him can be found, he has the order of Christ before his eyes. However, were the two not available, there faith is enough. Take an example.If the treasurer who sat beside Philip in the chariot and who had come to faith had died suddenly before they reached the water, then he would not have been saved less than after baptism. Christ wants that when he says, "He who believes and is baptized will be saved. He who does not believe will be damned." Without doubt many thousands have been saved who have not been baptized, because they had no possibility to be baptized. When now the treasurer had both the baptizer and the water available, then according to the mandate of Christ he was obliged to let himself be baptized. If he had not done so Christ would have considered him to be a despiser and transgressor of his words and he would have been punished accordingly.

The seventh argument. There has never been on earth a Christian so impertinent, godless, and proud who would say that water baptism is not a command and institution of Christ, and namely, for believers. For I can find no other baptism in Scripture. If water baptism is now an institution and creation of Christ, then he who dissolves baptism is cursed and damned by the power of the Word of Christ, for it is written: "Truly, I say to you, till heaven and earth pass away, not the smallest jot or tittle will pass from the law until all is accomplished. Whoever now breaks one of the least of these commandments and teaches people to do so, will be called the least in the kingdom of heaven," Matt. 5:18f. Here every sheep will realize that baptism is more essential than the table of the Lord, because the mandate for water baptism is phrased in the words of a law: "Go forth, teach, and baptize. He who believes is baptized. Repent, and everyone be baptized in the name of the Lord Jesus." These words one should not dissolve. But Paul says concerning the Christ meal, "As often and as much as you do this (that is left open), you shall proclaim the Lord's death (that is in the form of a law)." See here, are not those who do not want to be baptized dissolvers and mutilators of the words of Christ?

The eighth argument. Naaman came with horses and chariots and stopped before the door of Elisha's house. Elisha sent out a messenger to him and said, "Go and wash yourself seven times in the Jordan. Your flesh will be restored and you will be clean." Naaman became angry, drove away, and said: "I thought he would have come out to me and, standing there, he would have called upon the name of the Lord his God and he would have touched with his hand the place of leprosy and would have healed me. Are not the waters of Damascus better than all the waters of Israel, so that I could be washed and cleansed therein?" As he turned and drove away /144/ in a rage, his servants came to him and said, "Father, if the prophet had commanded you to do some great thing, truly, you would have done it. How much more then when he only tells you, 'Wash and be clean'?" Then he drove down and washed himself seven times according to the command of the man of God, and his flesh was again made whole like the flesh of a little child, and he became clean. Therefore he highly praised the God of Israel, 2 Kings 5:9-14. Likewise, dear pious Christians, baptism should not be despised, even though it only takes place in water. If Christ had commanded us to baptize in Malvasier wine or in balsam, then we still should do it; how much more since he says in water? For with this God makes the wisdom of this world a fool and what is exalted before people an abomination before the face of God.

The ninth argument. In being Christian, the will of God which he reveals to us in his Word is at all times to be esteemed more highly and more seriously than works themselves. For, as was just said, sometimes God demands from us the most trifling and most unattractive works in order to test us and to cast down our worldly wisdom. Was it not a simple work which he demanded from Adam and Eve that they should not eat from the fruit of precisely that tree? Was it not a foolish command that on the eighth day of their life the little boys should have the little foreskin of their penis cut off? Was it not a trifling command which God gave in Deuteronomy 23:12ff. when he said, "You shall have a place outside the camp, and when you go out for your bodily needs, carry a little shovel with you, dig a hole, sit down over it, and cover your excrement?" How do you like this "shit command," if you will pardon the expression? Foot washing was not too modest either, was it? And yet Christ said to Peter, "If I do not wash you, you will have no part in me," John 13:8. Well, dear friends, even though in the eyes of human beings these works are low, still God wants them. /145/ Samuel said to Saul in 1 Samuel 15:23, not to obey the words of the Lord is like the vice of idolatry. Therefore, watch yourselves that you walk the right way and do not say according to human wisdom, "Hey, what is it? It is still only water. What does our Lord care for water? He does not care for wine or water; heaven and earth are his." But he cares for his words and commands which he demands and wants to have fulfilled by us. Else we will have no part with him in his kingdom. See what you have to do. I have faithfully warned you.

The tenth argument. Where there is no water baptism, there is no church nor minister, neither brother nor sister, no brotherly admonition, excommunication, or reacceptance. I am speaking here of the visible church as Christ did in Matthew 18:15ff. There must also exist an outward confession or testimony through which visible brothers and sisters can know each other, since faith exists only in the heart. But when he receives the baptism of water the one who is baptized testifies publicly that he has pledged himself henceforth to live according to the Rule of Christ. By virtue of this pledge he has submitted himself to sisters, brothers, and to the church so that when he transgresses they now have the authority to admonish, punish, ban, and reaccept him. But this is not the case with those who are still outside. Listen how Paul speaks in 1 Corinthians 5:9ff. of those who are outside and of those who are inside: "I wrote to you in my letter that you must have nothing to do with immoral people. I was not thinking of the immoral people of this world, or the greedy, or robbers, or those who worship images, since then you would have to leave the world. But rather I wrote to you that you should have nothing to do with them, namely, if there is anybody who calls himself a brother but is an immoral person, a greedy person, a worshiper of images, a slanderer, a drunkard, or a robber, with those people you should also not eat. For what do I have to do with those who are outside that I should judge them? You are failing to judge those who are within. God will judge those who are outside. Put away from you those who are evil." If, however, you say, "Admonition and the power [of the keys] are practiced by the brothers and sisters in the Supper. He who wants to partake of it but is a public sinner is excluded." Answer: Now sisters and brothers, before they gather for the Supper, must be registered and have authority over each other, for one must have admonished the sinner twice beforehand. Where does this authority come from, if not from the pledge of baptism? /146/

Die schrifften von dem
Tauff Christi.

Das fünfft Capitel.

 Je bitte ich dich abermals lieber leser/das
du inn disem nachvolgenden schrifften/von
dem Tauff Christi/eben warnemest in wor
ten vnd im verstandt/diser ordnung.

i. wort. ij. Gehör. iij. Glaub.
iiij. Tauff. v. werck.

Auß diser ordnung ergründest du gewißlich/ob man
die jungen kindlin täuffen solle.
(Matthe. am. xxviij. cap.

Mir ist geben aller gwalt im hymmel vnd erden/dar
umb gand hyn/vnd ᵃleerent alle ᵇvölcker/vnd ᶜtäuf?
fent sye in dem nammen des Vatters/vnd Süns/ vnd
des heyligen Geysts/vnd leerend sye ᵈhalten alles/was
ich euch beuolhe hab.   Eben disen Wassertauff sind
ich in der gschrifft/den die Aposteln braucht haben/vnd
sunst keyn andern/nun mögen aber die kinder nit vor ge
leert werden / derhalb mag man sye/mit dem Tauff nit
täuffen/das ist vest/wie ein mur.
(Marc. am. xvj. cap.

Gand hyn in alle welt/vnd ᵃpredigend/das Euan?
gelion/allen ᵇcreaturen/ Wer da ᶜglaubt/vnd ᵈtäufft
würdt/der würdt ᶜselig/ Wer aber nit glaubt/der würt
verdampt werden.
Nun sind ich aber keyn text/der da lautet/Gand hyn

f iij

i. wort.
b
ij. Glaub
c
iij. Tauff
d
iiij werck

i. wort
b
ij. Gehör
c
iij Glaub
d
iiij. Tauff
c
v. Selig/
keit.

Page format of this portion of On the Christian Baptism of
Believers

These now are the arguments, that is, ten markstones which I have established, so that they might testify publicly that all who believe are under the obligation to let themselves be baptized according to the institution of Christ. Whoever does not do this is to be punished with many blows, as a servant knowing the will of his Lord. If now some know-it-alls object and say, "Well, even if somebody is not baptized with outward water, he can still believe, change and improve his life, and live according to the Rule of Christ. Therefore baptism is not necessary." Answer: You highly learned people should have made this objection not to me but to Christ himself, and that before he instituted baptism, so that he could have refrained from it. But at that time you were not his counselors. I realize it was a great oversight.

Chapter V
Scriptures on the Baptism of Christ

Here once again I would like to ask you, dear reader, in the following passages on the baptism of Christ to observe the following order, both in regard to the words and the meaning: (1) word, (2) hearing, (3) faith, (4) baptism, (5) work.

From this sequence you can certainly fathom whether one should baptize infants.

Matthew 28:18ff.

"All power has been given to me in heaven and on earth. Therefore, go forth and (a)* teach all (b) peoples and (c) baptize them in the name of the Father and the Son and the Holy Spirit, and teach them (d) to observe everything that I have commanded you." This and no other one is the water baptism I find in Scripture which the apostles administered. Now infants cannot be taught beforehand, therefore they should not be baptized with this baptism. That is as solid as a wall.

---

* (a) word, (b) faith, (c) baptism, (d) work.

Mark 16:15f.

"Go forth into all the world and (a)ᵃ preach the gospel
to all (b)creatures. He who (c) believes and (d) is baptized
will (e) be saved. But he who does not believe will be
damned."

I do not find, however, any passage which says: Go forth
into all the world and baptize young children and teach them
for several years. Where there is no baptizer or water available, not being baptized does /147/ not condemn.

Acts 2:36ff.

"Let all the house of Israel therefore (a)ᵇ know
assuredly that God has made this Jesus whom you have
crucified both Lord and Christ. When they (b) heard this they
were (c) pricked in the heart, and said to Peter and to the
other apostles: 'You men, dear brothers, what shall we do?'
Peter said to them: 'Repent, and let everyone of you be baptized in the name of Jesus Christ for the forgiveness of sin.
Then you will receive the gift of the Holy Spirit, etc.' Those
who gladly (d) accepted his word let themselves be (e) baptized, and there were added that day about three thousand
souls. And they remained (f) steadfast in the apostles' teaching, in the fellowship, in breaking bread, and in prayer."

Acts 8:4ff.

"Now those who were scattered went and (a)ᶜ preached
the gospel. Philip came down to a city of Samaria and
proclaimed Christ to them. But the people with one accord
gave heed to what was said by Philip: they (b) heard him, etc.

"There was previously a man named Simon in the city
who practiced magic and had bewitched the people of
Samaria, pretending to be someone great. And they all looked

ᵃ (a) word, (b) hearing, (c) faith, (d) baptism, (e) salvation.
ᵇ (a) word, (b) hearing, (c) recognition of sins, (d) faith, (e) baptism, (f)
works.
ᶜ (a) word, (b) hearing, (c) faith, (d) baptism.

up to him, from the smallest to the greatest and said: 'This is the power of God which is great.' They looked up to him because he had bewitched them with his magic for a long time. But when they (c) believed Philip's preaching on the kingdom of God and on the name of Jesus Christ, they let themselves be (d) baptized, men and women alike."

Luke mentions here men and women, but of course he forgot the young children.

Then Simon also (a)ᵃ believed, let himself be (b) baptized, and (c) followed Philip.

"Philip, however, opened his mouth and started with Scripture and (a)ᵇ preached to the treasurer the (b) gospel of Jesus. As they went along the road they came to water, and the eunuch said: 'Look, here is water. What hinders my being baptized?' Philip said: 'If you believe with all your heart, it can be.' He said, 'I (c) believe that Jesus Christ is the Son of God,' and he ordered the chariot to stop. Both Philip and the eunuch went down into the water and he (d) baptized him. When they came up out of the water, the Spirit of the Lord took Philip away and the eunuch saw him no more, but went (e) happily on his way." /148/   ᶜ

Acts 10:44ff.

"While Peter was still speaking of such things the Holy Spirit fell on all who (b)ᶜ were listening to the (a) Word of God.[31] And the believers from among the circumcised, who had come with Peter, were shocked that the gift of the Holy Spirit was poured out even on Gentiles, for they heard them speaking in tongues and magnifying God. Then Peter answered: 'Can anyone refuse water so that those who have received the Holy Spirit just as we should not be baptized?' And he ordered them to be (d) baptized in the name of the Lord. Then (e) they asked him to stay for some days."

---

[31] The reversal of sequence in the English is due to English syntax.

ᵃ (a) faith, (b) baptism, (c) works.
ᵇ (a) word, (b) hearing, (c) faith, (d) baptism, (e) works.
ᶜ (a) word, (b) hearing, (c) faith, (d) baptism, (d) works.

Acts 16:13ff.

"And on the Sabbath day we went out of the city to the water, where people were accustomed to pray, sat down, and (a)* spoke to the women who came together there. And a devout woman named Lydia, a seller of purple goods from the city of Thyatira, (b) was listening, (c) whose heart the Lord opened to give heed to what was said by Paul. And when she was (d) baptized, etc."

"The jailer, however, called for a light, rushed in, trembled, fell at the feet of Paul and Silas, brought them out, and said: 'Dear men, what must I do to be saved?' They (a)[b] said: (b) 'Believe in the Lord Jesus, then you and your household will be saved.' And they spoke the word of the Lord to him and to all that were in his house. And he took them with him the same hour of the night and washed their welts; and immediately he and his whole family let themselves (c) be baptized. Then he (d) brought them into his house, set them at the table, and rejoiced with all his household that he had come to faith in Gòd." Pay attention here to the old translations of Aldus and Erasmus.[32]

Acts 18:8ff.

"(a)[c] Crispus, however, the head of the synagogue, (b) believed in the Lord, together with his whole household, and many Corinthians who were listening believed and let themselves (c) be baptized together with his whole household." Dear one, tell me, did the young children also believe? If you say, "No," then "his whole household" must be taken to mean only the believers in the house, as it is true here and elsewhere, 1 Cor. 1:16; Acts 10:48; 16:14f. /149/

---

[32] The Aldine Bible was the first complete printed edition of the Greek Bible. It was published in 1518 by Andreas Asulanus at the press of Aldus Manutius of Venice. Erasmus published his edition of the New Testament in 1516.

---

* (a) word, (b) hearing, (c) faith, (d) baptism.
[b] (a) word, (b) faith, (c) baptism, (d) works.
[c] (a) word, (b) hearing, (c) baptism.

Acts 19:1ff.

"While Apollos was at Corinth, it happened that Paul traveled through the upper countries and came to Ephesus. He found several disciples there. He said to them: 'Did you receive the Holy Spirit when you became believers?' They said to him: 'We have not even heard that there is a Holy Spirit.' And he said: 'Wherein then were you baptized?' They said: 'In the baptism of John.' But Paul[a] (a) said: 'John baptized with the baptism of repentance and told the people that they should believe in the one who would come after him, that is, in Jesus who is the Christ.' When they (b) heard this they let themselves (c) be baptized in the name of the Lord Jesus. And when Paul laid his hands on them, the Holy Spirit came on them, and they spoke in (d) tongues and prophesied." Here if one takes "baptize" for "teach," violence and injustice are done to the text. See above, chapter 3.[33] In addition we are not proving any rebaptism from this text because we do not let ourselves be rebaptized. Therefore it would not make any difference, if "baptize" were to be taken for "teach."

Acts 22:16, again concerning the baptism of Paul:

"(a) Why do you wait? Stand up, let yourself be (b) baptized, and wash away your sin by calling on the name of the Lord."[b]

1 Corinthians 1:13ff.

"Was Paul crucified for you? Or were you baptized in the name of Paul? I thank God that I baptized none of you except Crispus and Gaius, so that no one can say I baptized in my own name. I baptized also the household of Stephanas. Beyond that I do not know if I baptized anyone."

---

[33] See above, pp. 111ff.

---

[a] (a) word, (b) hearing, (c) baptism, (d) works.
[b] (a) word, (b) baptism.

Note here that this text cannot be applied to young children, because they do not say or boast that Peter or Paul had baptized them. They are not able to speak but only cry miserably. Beyond that, it is not even certain that there were children there. Let that be proven first. Well, if it could be done with thinking, imagining, or expressing opinion, but only knowing counts.

1 Peter 3:20ff.

"In the times of Noah, during the building of the ark, in which a few, that is, eight persons, were preserved through water, which now also /150/ saves you in baptism, which signifies not the putting away of the filth of the flesh but the certain knowledge of a good conscience toward God through the resurrection of Jesus Christ, who ascended to the right hand of God in heaven and the angels, the powerful, and the mighty are subject to him."

From this passage you can obviously see that Noah's ark is a figure or shadow of baptism. But Peter nowhere mentions circumcision.

Second, the eight persons believed before they entered the ark, which the Scripture clearly shows in Genesis 6; then those who want to be baptized must believe the Word of God beforehand, or baptism will not be an ark for them.

Third, water baptism does not wash away our sin, nor does it save us, but only the certain knowledge of a good conscience toward God through the resurrection of Christ Jesus. This knowledge is nothing but the faith,[34] in which we are sure and certain that we have a gracious and favorable Father in heaven, and that before we receive the water baptism.

Fourth, from that results the question which those who desire baptism are asked: what they expect from God, what their relationship to him is, and whether they trust him to be a God who forgives their sin. In our times the question is still asked of godfathers and godmothers. But one asks the godfathers and godmothers who answer, "Yes." But the one who desires to be baptized should give this answer himself. See

---

[34] Cf. Zwingli: "For neither as water nor as external teaching does baptism save us, but faith." Z 4, p. 222,[8-9] tr. Bromiley 1953: 134.

how the devil demolished everything. May God restore them again. Amen.

See, dear pious Christian! Even if there were no Scripture on earth which states that faith should precede water baptism, its meaning and understanding would still be enough. Well, let them go. They are blind and leaders of the blind.

Hebrews 10:22f.

"(a)* Let us draw near (understand: to God through the blood of Christ) with a true heart, in a full (b) faith, (c) sprinkled in our heart from an evil conscience, and (d) washed in the body with pure water; and let us (e) hold fast to the confession of hope without wavering."

In this passage of Scripture, Christian soul, ponder the the beautiful and divine /151/ order, how Scripture tells all the different steps in such an orderly way. Therefore he would be a wicked person who would want to turn this order around and put the cart before the horse. O God, forgive us our blindness and our wickedness! Dear, friendly reader, this passage and John 5:24 move me to call outward baptism a public confession or witness. For I do not like to deal with new, sophisticated, and invented words. There is no need to invite strangers to the church feast; one finds friends enough.

From all these passages of Scripture it clearly follows that all those who baptize the previously instructed in the Word of God and believers baptize correctly and in the Christian way. But those who introduce additionally a different baptism without prior teaching are false and deceitful masters who rob us of the true baptism and show us a hoop before an inn in which there is no wine. He who has ears, let him hear. But him who is dissolute, may our Lord God cleanse. Amen.

Although there are many more passages on baptism available, nobody should worry about them. For either they deal only with the internal baptism which must precede water baptism, or they are included sufficiently in the passages dealt with above, as in John 3:23; Acts 1:5; 1 Corinthians 6:11; 10:2; 12:13; Romans 6:3-4; Galatians 3:27; Ephesians 4:5; 5:26;

---

* (a) word, (b) hearing, (c) inward baptism, (d) outward baptism, (e) works.

Colossians 2:12; Titus 3:5. He who does not believe the above-
mentioned passages will not believe the other ones either,
even if one brought him a whole shipload of them.

Chapter VI
Some Questions Are Resolved

The first question: Whether infant baptism is forbidden in
the Word of God. Answer: Yes. For baptizing believers is commanded. So by this it is already forbidden to baptize those
who do not yet believe. A comparison: Christ commanded his
apostles to preach the gospel when he said, "Preach the
gospel." By this, human teachings, laws, dreams, and legends
are already forbidden. For every institution which God the
heavenly Father /152/ has not implanted makes blind and
should be uprooted, Isa. 29; Matt. 15:13.

You say: But nowhere in Scripture is there written a clear
word that one should not baptize them.[35] Answer: It is written
clearly enough. He who has eyes, let him see it. But that it is
not written explicitly: "Do not baptize them," to this I answer: Then I may also baptize my dog and my donkey, circumcise little girls, mumble prayers and hold vigils for the dead,
call wooden idols St. Peter, or St. Peter and St. Paul, take
infants to the Lord's Supper, bless palm branches, herbs, salt,
butterfat, and water, sell the mass as a sacrifice. For it is not
prohibited anywhere in explicit words that we do these things.
Realize what a nice double popery we would set up again if it
were acceptable to juggle outside the Word of God in those
matters which concern God and the souls. You say: It is forbidden to baptize donkeys because Christ told us to baptize
people. Well, then, let us also baptize a Jew and a Turk. You
say: Yes, one should baptize people who believe. Answer:
Why, then, do you baptize infants? In addition, Christ wants
that one neither add to nor take away from his Testament,
Gal. 3:15; that no deviant teaching be introduced, 2 Pet. 2:1;
that his voice alone be heard, John 10:3. For God the Father
has given him to us so that we may hear him, Luke 9:35; Matt.
3:11; Mark 1:7-8; Deut. 18:15. For whoever is not with him is

---

[35] Z 4, p. 211.[16-17]

against him, Luke 11:23. What does not arise from faith leads to eternal condemnation, Rom. 14:23. For that reason Paul was not allowed to preach anything but that which Christ worked in him, Rom. 15:18. Our speech should be like God's speech, 1 Pet. 4:11, salted with the salt of the divine Word, Col. 4:6. For the divine power has shown us sufficiently, through the knowledge of him who called us, what we need for life and salvation, 2 Pet. 1:3f. For only Scripture, inspired for us by God, is useful for instruction as to what we should do or leave undone, 2 Tim. 3:16. God also does not want to accept any interpretation of Scripture or opinion that is invented by human will, 2 Pet. 1:20. Rather, we should teach nothing but the sound words of Christ, or we will fall into questions and word battles, out of which will arise envy, quarreling, blasphemy, /153/ evil suspicion, and the dissension of evil people, 1 Tim. 1:7; 6:3ff., and we will be led away by diverse and alien teachings, Heb. 13:9.

"Woe to the sons who leave me," says God, "who take counsel but not from me, who begin a web[36] but not through my "spirit," Isa. 30:1. We have heard the sound teachings of Christ in the above-mentioned passages, Matt. 28:18-20; Mark 16:15-18; Acts 2:22ff.; and Heb. 10:5-7. Therefore, beware and take care that no one misleads you with useless teachings and vain words. Infant baptism is such a vain word; it can be read nowhere in Scripture. Do not have fellowship with the unfruitful works of darkness but rather rebuke them, Eph. 5:11. Now infant baptism is a human trifle, as the childish pedobaptizers themselves admit. It gives nothing and takes nothing. Protect yourselves from those who, outside of the evangelical teaching, cause quarrel and offense. Depart from them, for they do not serve Christ our Lord, but their belly. Through sweet speeches and charming talks they mislead the hearts of the innocent, Rom. 16:18. The second question: Have people not always, from apostolic times until today, baptized infants, or has it not always been like that?

Answer: Even if it had always been like that, it would still not be right, because a wrong is always wrong. However, we find precisely in the books of the pope, not to mention

---

[36] *Wöpp* = cover, web, etc.

Cyprian, Augustine, and others, that it has not always been like it is today, whenever it might have started.[37] That this is true, we read in the papal decrees that more than a thousand years ago and thereafter there was again and again much discussion on account of baptism.[38] At that time it was fixed that one should baptize only twice a year, and accordingly only those who could say the creed, and that at Easter and Pentecost. There the popes bound to a specific time what Christ had left free. Beware of the papal cancer and how it has spread. You can find it in *De consecratione* ["On Consecration"], distinction 4, the following canons: "Nonratione" [Not the reason],[39] "Duo tempora" [At two times],[40] "Proprie" [Characteristically],[41] "Ante baptismum" [Before baptism][42] "Ante viginti" [Before twenty],[43] "Baptisandos" [Those to be baptized],[44] and "Non liceat" [It would not be allowed].[45] Look at what your child knows or what it answers when one asks, "Do you believe in God the Father Almighty, Creator of heaven and earth?"[46] Then it cries or wets its diapers. /154/

Moreover, if you dare exorcise the devil away from the infant and if he [the devil] rightly takes you to court and charges that you have done wrong to him, that you have accused him of being in the infant, then look, look whether you could justly take the responsibility for that.

Then it was decreed that those who wanted to be baptized had to give their names in writing, to abstain from meat

---

[37] Hubmaier later treats in considerable detail the matter of baptism in the Fathers. See below, text 17, pp. 245-274.

[38] The papal decrees to which Hubmaiaer is referring are found in the canon law of Gratian. He refers to several of the canons in the passage immediately following as well as in his treatise, *Old and New Teachers*. See below, number 17.

[39] CIC I:1364 (canon 11). Traditionally, the specific canons of canon law were cited by reference to the section or part of the collection and to the "name" of the canon, i.e., the first word or two of the selection. We will simplify the references by citing the volume, page, and canon number from the modern edition of CIC.

[40] CIC I:1365 (canon 12).

[41] CIC I:1365 (canon 13).

[42] CIC I:1382 (canon 54).

[43] CIC I:1382 (canon 55).

[44] CIC I:1383 (canon 58).

[45] CIC I:1383 (canon 59).

[46] The previously cited canon, *non liceat*, concerns the reciting of the creed before baptism.

and wine for a certain time and to present themselves on Maundy Thursday or Good Friday to the bishop or a priest, *De consecratione* [On Consecration], distinction 4, the following canons: "Baptisandi" [Those to be baptized],[47] "Baptisandos" [Those to be baptized],[48] "Non liceat 2" [It would not be allowed, sentence 2],[49] and Quaestio 1, "Legum" [of the laws].[50]

At some time it also was decreed that those who had been instructed in faith might be baptized at any time in emergencies of death, bodily sickness, siege, in wars and in droughts, *Deconsecratione* [On consecration], distinction 4, canons "Si qui" [If whoever],[51] "De catechumenis" [Concerning the catechumens],[52] "Venerabilis" [Venerable],[53] "Baptisandi" [Those to be baptized].[54] Do you see how the popes and the councils have set up one thing and thrown another down according to their whim? Now certainly at that time infants ate meat and drank wine as little as in our times. How then could they have been baptized? I also know very well what Augustine wrote to Petrus Diaconus in his chapter *Firmissime,* [Most firmly][55] eleven hundred years ago. Would to God that he had said *Impiissime,* [Most impiously] for that, then he would have spoken the truth. But that is enough said about this. In this matter we do not need the testimony of men at all. Therefore we have only answered them very briefly with their own human junk.

The third question: What happens to the unbaptized infants? Are they damned or saved? What do you read in Scripture about them? Answer: If I am to answer according to the strictness of Scripture, then Scripture says that in Adam we die, 1 Cor.15:22, and that by nature we are children of wrath, Eph. 2:3. Who would say, "My heart is pure; I am pure from sin?" Prov. 20:9. Why even the heavens are not pure nor

[47] CIC I:1383 (canon 60).
[48] CIC I:1383 (canon 58).
[49] CIC I:1383 (canon 59).
[50] CIC I:442f. (canon 9).
[51] CIC I:1370 (canon 28).
[52] CIC I:1366 (canon 15).
[53] CIC I:1367 (canon 17).
[54] CIC I:1383 (canon 60).
[55] CIC I:1362 (canon 3). In the letter to Peter the Deacon, Augustine justifies infant baptism on the basis of the doctrine of original sin.

the stars in the sight of God, Job 15:14; 25:5f. Therefore all creatures sigh and all to God for salvation, Rom. 8:19ff. Likewise, Job in chapter 3:3f. cursed the day of his birth and said, "Let the day perish when I was born and the night in which it was said, 'A child is conceived.' May that day turn to darkness, etc." Also Jeremiah 20:14f. says, "Cursed be the day when I was born, the day when my mother bore me, let it not be blessed. Cursed be the man who announced to my father, saying 'A son is born to ·you,' etc." /155/ Likewise the royal prophet David publicly confessed that he was conceived in sin and that his mother bore him in sin, Psalm 1.[56] Here you see what we are if God were to act toward us according to justice. Therefore David, who was a man after the heart of the Lord, beseeches him very earnestly not to enter into judgment with him, 1 Sam. 16:7; Acts 13:22; Psalm 143:1ff. The pious and patient Job gives the reason, saying, "I know that no human being is justified before the sight of God. If he will contend with us we will not answer him once in a thousand," Job 9:2f.

Second. Since the hand of the Lord is not short, he does what he wills and no one is permitted to ask him, "Why do you do that?" He is Lord. He has mercy upon whomever he wills; and whomever he will, he hardens and no one can resist his will. For it is not the willing nor the running, but the mercy of God. We are his lump of clay, Rom. 9:18ff. He can make out of us what he wills. Therefore I say, by the authority of these passages, that he can save the infants very well by grace since they know neither good nor evil, Deut. 1:39; 1 Cor. 14:20. And Paul writes to the Romans, "Sin is not damning in those who are in Christ Jesus, who do not walk according to sin," even though this passage probably refers only to believers, Rom. 8:1.

Third, I confess here publicly my ignorance. I am not ashamed not to know what God did not want to reveal to us with a clear and plain word. He said to me as he said to Peter, "What business is it of yours, as to what I will to do with infants? Follow me, look to my word and will," John 21:22. But yet I will humbly and earnestly beseech him that he be a merciful Father to them. I commit this into his hands. His will

---

[56] Incorrectly given in the Hubmaier original. Should be Ps. 51:7.

be done. With this I will leave it. For if he does not want it to be done, then even if one were to throw them into the water a thousand times, it would still not help because water does not save.[57] Some child washers cry that Christ said, "Let the little children come to me, of these is the kingdom of heaven," Matt. 19:14; Mark 10:14; Luke 18:16. That is wrong! They are doing violence and injustice to Scripture. It is written: For "of such" is the kingdom of heaven.[58] Christ wants to teach us humility here as he also says there to the Corinthians in 1 Corinthians 14:20 that we should be children in evil, that is, we should not be malicious or evil-minded. I want to refer you to another place where he says that we should not be unstable, like children, Eph. 4:14. But it was the custom of Christ that /156/ often he took a physical parable and led it to a spiritual meaning, as he also did with Jacob's fountain, John 4:10ff.

Furthermore, some come and say that by the faith of their fathers and mothers they are saved.[59] Dear friends, it is nothing. For it often happens that father and mother bring forth both good and bad fruit. Take, for example, Abel and Cain, Esau and Jacob. It is up to God, not to father and mother, for before they were born, God said, "Jacob I loved, but Esau I hated," Mal. 1:2f.; Rom. 9:13. It would also often grieve a child to the heart and lead him to eternal damnation if his salvation were to depend upon the faith of his father or mother, godfather or godmother.

Some now boast highly about an infused faith which God imparted to them and by which they are saved; I know nothing about that.[60] It is possible for God, just as he also purified Jeremiah and John in the wombs of their mothers.

---

[57] Cf. Zwingli's letter of June 15, 1523, to Thomas Wyttenbach: "You can wash an unbeliever a thousand times in the water of baptism, but unless he believes, it is in vain. It is faith that is required in this matter." Z 8, p. 85.[35-36]

[58] Z 4, p. 300.[5ff.]

[59] Zwingli does not make just exactly this assertion. He does say that the children of believers, since they do not know the law, are not condemned, Z 4, p. 309.[30ff.] He also says that the children of Christians are certainly, undoubtedly children of God. Z 4, p. 301.[21-22]

[60] Thomas Aquinas, in *Summa Theologica*, II-II, Question 6, art. 1, asserts that faith ". . . must needs come to him from some supernatural, principle moving him inwardly: and this is God." Pegis 1945: II:1116.

But that he is doing the same also to others—about that I have no Scripture. Therefore I let it suffice as their philosophy, but not as a theology. There is no Scripture at hand, so it does not count to suck it out of the fingers.

Finally, they continue to look for arguments and say, "There must be something to it, and without doubt it is of some use to the souls of young children that one baptizes them in the name of the Father, and the Son, and the Holy Spirit." Then I reply that it is a false, untrue statement if they say that they baptize the children in the name of the Father, etc. By that these highly learned people reveal to the whole world that they do not understand what it means to baptize in the name of the Father, and the Son, and the Holy Spirit. They think that if they pronounce the names and pour water that this is baptism. No, it is not like that, dear brethren! But baptizing in the name of the Father, and the Son, and the Holy Spirit takes place when a person first confesses that he is a sinner and guilty, when he then believes in the forgiveness of sins through Jesus Christ and therefore resolves henceforth to live according to the Rule of Christ as far as God the Father, and the Son, and the Holy Spirit will give him grace and strength, and when he now testifies all such publicly before people with the reception of the outward water: /157/ *that* is water baptism. Even if the baptizer did not pronounce these words over the baptized person, still he would be baptized. That is speaking clearly and thoroughly about baptism and not like some people do who exchange "baptism" for "teaching" and "into" for "in" and thereby obscure baptism more than explaining it in a clear way. Whether one reads "into," "on," or "in" the name, it is one thing in the true understanding. Similarly, tongues and languages are useful, but only insofar as God grants that they be used for the edification of the church, not that Scripture be obscured by them. Or henceforth we would always have to wait for the language artists,[61] as until now we had to wait for the pope and the councils. And in the end they would take away the name of Christ and his teaching and prohibit it to all those who cannot speak three or four languages. But that

---

[61] *Züngler*.

would mean to establish another "Papazare."[62] May God save us from that. Amen.

The Last Chapter
The Order of Christian Justification[63]

Until now we have preached much gossip, unnecessary junk, human laws, and legends, and we have said how we can through this or through that work become righteous and be saved, namely through infant baptism, vigils, masses, organs, pipes, ringing, indulgences, images, pilgrimages, brotherhoods, offerings, purgatory, masses, mumbling, growling, and bellowing. But all this is a small matter, if now we only confess and abstain from this trickery[64] and call to God with Paul, "O God, forgive us; we did it without knowing." The red whore of Babylon with her cup full of laws, school teachings, and fables has made us drunk, blinded, and deceived us. But henceforth our penance shall be never to do these things again. Therefore, dear sirs, brothers and sisters, wherever on earth you might be, be warned and admonished that henceforth you yourselves test the prophets and preachers and investigate their teachings as to whether it is written as they say or /158/ not. Search the Scriptures. They themselves will give the right witness about Christ and the Christian life. Do as the Thessalonians, Acts 17:11, and you will not go astray nor be deceived. And even if your pastors and preachers would offer to give their very souls for you, even that would not be enough. You must believe the Word of God and not them. God alone is truthful, but all human beings are deceitful. For Christ says: When a blind person leads a blind person, both fall into the ditch. It would be a little thing if the shepherd alone fell, but by the authority of the Word of Christ the sheep would fall also. But in summary, thus begins a Christian life.

First, when Christ begins to teach the Christian life, he says, "Repent, or change your lives and believe the gospel,"

---

[62] A play on words is lost here. Hubmaier is speaking of a new reign of prattle or babble. *Papazare* (*papazen* = to prattle mindlessly) refers also to *papa*, or the pope.

[63] At this point Hubmaier takes over the *Summa*. See above, text 9.

[64] Ger. *Larvenwerck*, lit. "masquerade."

Mark 1:15. Now, it belongs first to a change of life that we hear the law of God, and that in this we remember our deeds and our omissions. Thus, we find that from the top of our heads to the bottom of our feet there is no health in us. Instead, everything is poisoned, wounded, and impure, yes, we do that which God has forbidden us and we leave undone what he has commanded us to do, because we are conceived and born in sin. Thus Job, David, Jeremiah, John, and other God-fearing people have lamented. Furthermore, a person finds in himself neither help, comfort, nor medicine with which he could help himself. Therefore he must despair in himself and lose heart also like the man who had fallen into the hands of the killers. Such a miserable little worm is the person who looks into his own heart, who ponders on and recognizes himself.

Second, when the person lies there, wounded and beat unto death, and is unable to help himself, then the Samaritan must come, that is, Christ Jesus. He brings along medicine, namely, wine and oil, which he pours into the wounds of the sinner. Wine: he leads the person to repentance so that he is sorry for his sins. Oil: by which he softens his pain and drives it away, when he says, "Believe the gospel. It truly shows you that I have laid you on the beast of my humanity, that I have suffered death and martyrdom for you, and that through my sufferings I have registered you in the inn of the Christian church. I have commended you to the servant of the house, that is, to those who preach to you my gospel and proclaim to you the certain forgiveness of your sins, namely, that I /159/ am your physician who has come into this world to make the sinner just and righteous, that I am also your reconciler, intercessor, mediator, and peacemaker unto God, my Father, so that whoever believes in me will not be damned but have eternal life." Through such words of comfort the sinner is enlivened again, comes to himself, becomes joyful and henceforth surrenders himself entirely to this physician Christ. All his sicknesses he commits, submits, and entrusts to him. As much as it is possible for a wounded person he will also surrender to the will of the Lord. He calls upon him daily for healing and purification, so that what the wounded is not able to do out of his own capacity—as in fact he can do nothing—the physician counsels and helps him or does not blame him for his sickness or take it for evil, since he would gladly walk according to the word and will of the physician. But that he does not act accordingly is the fault of his sickness.

Of this he confesses himself guilty and desires grace, with the firm faith that God will not hold him to account for such weakness and sickness to eternal damnation because he has surrendered himself to this physician Jesus and has committed his sickness to him to be healed. Now, if God wanted to be angry and were to demand health from the wounded person and say: "I created you in my own image, healthy, pure, and perfect; thus I want you to be or I shall condemn you"—here now the physician steps forth, to whom you have entrusted yourself in faith. He pleads for you before God his Father with faithful intercession, that he may abstain from his anger, and also be gracious and favorable to you through the grace and favor which he has toward Christ. Here then the Father neither wants nor can deny anything to his most beloved Son but he grants him his request and thus forgives you your sin through Jesus Christ, our Lord. Now, dear Christian, all these teachings which reveal the sickness and point to the physician before they are believed are letter and they kill. But by faith the Spirit of God makes them alive so that they start to live, turn green, blossom, and bear fruit. Thus in faith the water becomes wine at the wedding. And we must first put on John's rough coat of camel hair before we may receive and touch the tender, gentle, and sweet little Lamb Christ Jesus. Now this person surrenders himself inwardly in his heart unto a new life according to the Rule of Christ, of this physician who has healed him, pleaded for him, and from whom he received life. Thus Paul confesses publicly that he does not live but Christ lives in him, is life for him, and outside of Christ he knows that he is empty, worthless, dead, and a lost sinner. /160/

Third, when a person now confesses himself to be a sinner, believes on the forgiveness of sins, and has committed himself to a new life, then he professes this also outwardly and publicly before the Christian church, into whose fellowship he lets himself be registered and counted according to the order and institution of Christ. Therefore he professes to the Christian church, that is, to all brothers and sisters who live in faith, that in his heart he has been thus inwardly instructed in the Word of Christ and so minded that he has surrendered himself already to live according to the Word, will, and Rule of Christ, to arrange and direct his doing and not doing according to him, and also to fight and strive under his banner until death. Then he lets himself be baptized with outward water in which he professes publicly his faith and his intention, namely, that he believes that he has a gracious, kind, and merciful God and Father in heaven through Jesus Christ, with whom he is well off and satisfied. He also has expressed his intention to him and committed himself already in his heart henceforth to change and amend his life. This he testifies publicly with the reception of water. And if he henceforth blackens or shames the faith and name of Christ with public or offensive sins, he herewith submits and surrenders to brotherly discipline according to the order of Christ, Matt. 18:15ff. Here everybody sees that infant baptism is a trick which is invented and introduced by human beings.

Fourth, since therefore the human being knows and confesses that he is by nature an evil, worm-eaten, and poisoned tree, who neither can nor wants to bring forth good fruit out of himself, thus this pledge, promise, and public testimony does not happen out of human powers or capacities, for that would be presumptuousness. But it takes place in the name of God, the Father, and the Son, and the Holy Spirit, or in the name of our Lord Jesus Christ, as has been shown sufficiently above in the first chapter and in other places. Here the Spirit of God begins to work and rejects the wisdom and the works of the world. The world does not like this, because it does not want to be a fool or an evil-doer, but to be wise, clever, righteous, just, and spiritual in its own works. It also establishes for itself laws, teachings, and rules by which it thinks it can be saved and consequently despises the unattractive, plain, and simple Rule of Christ. For its laws appear to be more beautiful, precious, and splendid in human eyes. But what is high before human beings is an abomination in the sight of God. Here the old Adam springs forth, /161/ that is, our poisoned nature in which we are conceived in our mother's womb and born. This old rascal bristles his hair, pricks up his ears, jumps up, and sneaks around everywhere. He expresses his inborn nature and resists the Spirit within the person, that is, he assails the newborn soul so much that the person does not do what he wants according to the Word of God. The flesh must daily be killed since it wants only to live and reign according to its own lusts. Here the Spirit of Christ prevails and gains the victory. Then the person brings forth good fruits which give testimony of a good tree. Day and night he practices all those things which concern the praise of God and brotherly love. By this the old Adam is martyred, killed, and carried to the grave. This is a summary and right order of a whole Christian life which begins in the Word of God. From this follows knowledge of sin and forgiveness of the same in faith. Faith is not idle but is industrious in good Christian works. But only those are good works which God himself has commanded us, and of which he will demand a reckoning from us at the last day, Matt. 25:34ff.

Fifth, after we have now recognized in faith the inestimable and inexpressible goodness of God clearly and plainly in the Word of God, then we should be thankful to God our heavenly Father who has loved the world so fervently that he did not spare his only begotten Son, but gave him for us even unto death, yes, unto death on the most shameful cross, so that we should not be lost. So that we do not forget his deed, Christ Jesus himself, our Savior, has ordained and instituted a beautiful memorial of his suffering in his Last Supper.

For when Jesus ate with his disciples, he took bread, blessed it (that is, he gave thanks to God his Father), broke it, gave it to his disciples, and said, "Take, eat, this is my body which is given for you. Do this in remembrance of me."

Likewise, he took the cup, gave thanks, gave it to them, and said, "Drink of it, all of you. This is my blood of the new testament which is shed for you and for many for the forgiveness of sins. Do this in my memory." /162/

Here everybody can see that bread is bread and wine is wine, like other bread and wine. But it is instituted by Christ as a reminder and memorial. For as often as we break it together, distribute it, and eat, we should remember his body broken for us on the cross and distributed to all those who eat and enjoy in faith, which derives from the words mentioned above. Here it is obvious that the bread is not the body of Christ but only a reminder thereof. Likewise, the wine is not the blood of Christ but also only a memorial that he shed his blood and distributed it on the cross to all believers for the washing away of our sins, as the hoop in front of the tavern is not wine, but a remembrance or reminder thereof. It is fitting that we should not forget his goodness but should proclaim, shout out, and be grateful for it to all eternity. Paul admonishes us very earnestly of this when he writes to the Corinthians in 1 Corinthians 11:26: "As often as you eat the bread (notice: he calls it bread, and it is bread) and drink the cup, that is, the wine (notice that it is wine which is drunk), you shall proclaim the death of the Lord until he comes." Notice: he says, "Until he comes." From this we hear that he is not present but will come only at the hour of the last judgment, in his great majesty and glory, shining visibly to everybody as the lightning from east to west.

From this it follows and is again seen clearly that the Supper is nothing other than a memorial of the suffering of Christ who offered his body for our sake and shed his crimson blood on the cross for the washing away of our sins. But up to the present we have turned this Supper into a bear's mass[65] with growling, mumbling, and bellowing—but not according to the will of God. We have sold the mass for huge uncountable amounts of property and money and, be it lamented to God, would gladly henceforth continue with it. The person who practices the Supper in that way and contemplates the suffering of Christ in a firm faith will also give thanks to God for this grace and goodness. He will surrender himself to the will of Christ, who wants that we also should do to our neighbor as he has done to us and give our body, life, honor, possessions, and blood for his sake. This is the will of Christ. But since this is impossible for us to do, we should call upon God diligently for grace and strength, so that he might give them to us and might not count our weakness and imperfection to eternal damnation, to make us able to fulfill his will as much as he gives us grace. For if he does not give us grace, /163/ we are already lost. We have been human, and we are human, and we will remain human until death.

Oh dear, pious Christians, take to heart what I have said to you and strive for the clear, plain, and pure Word of God

---

[65] Cf. above text 9, note 9, p. 88 above.

from which alone your faith comes. In it we must be saved, for the ax is already laid to the root of the tree. If there is no fruit at hand, the tree will be cut down. Truly I say to you, if you fear the frost here in this time, then the snow of eternal coldness will fall upon you. If you fear the coals, you even will fall into the fire. For Christ says with clear words, "He who confesses me before people, him will I confess before God, my Father. Whoever denies me before people, him I also will deny before God. Do not fear those who take the body from you, which is more than earthly goods, but fear him who can take both your body and soul and cast you into eternal damnation." Whoever has ears, let him hear the heavy and severe judgment of God over those who conceal, deny, and mutilate his Word. May the Lord God enlighten those who do not want to hear. Amen.

Finished on the eleventh day of July 1525.

Waldshût
Truth Is Immortal.

12

Recantation at Zurich

The increasing clarity and radicality of Waldshut's commitment to the Zwinglian Reformation made it only a matter of time until the most Catholic imperial government of Austria, which held sovereignty on the north bank of the Rhine, would take over the city and force the restoration of Catholic worship. The combined support of the Swiss neighbor cities might perhaps have prevented or postponed such a defeat; but since Waldshut had become Anabaptist, the Reformers of Zurich and Schaffhausen no longer wished to provide such assistance. Having returned after his first brief flight in late 1524, Hubmaier again found his way out of Waldshut just before it fell to the Austrians in December 1525 and took refuge in Zurich. By this time Anabaptism was a crime in Zurich.[1]

Hubmaier entered Zurich with the thought of hiding for a while with Anabaptist acquaintances until his health would improve and he could travel further.[2] On December 19 he was found and taken into the custody of the Council. He was held in the city hall rather than the prison, in order to keep him from stirring up other prisoners. His earlier request to be given an opportunity to dialogue with Zwingli was accepted. The meeting took place on December 19, with several of Zwingli's colleagues participating as well.

Hubmaier came from this meeting reporting that his mind had changed and that he was ready to renounce Anabaptism. He drafted a statement to that effect, which he was to read from the pulpit on Sunday, January 5, 1526. Although not dated, the first of the following texts would seem to be what he had prepared for that event. As befits a public statement, it begins with a confessional tone, as if addressed to everyone, and identifies the four theologians who had changed his mind.

---

[1] A fuller narrative of this troubled period is provided in the introduction to text 14 below, pp. 166ff.

[2] His protectors were especially Heinrich Aberli (cf. Harder 1965, p. 527) and Anna Widerker (ibid., p. 572).

Several references to "Your Wisdom" toward the end would indicate that as he went on writing he came to have the City Council in mind as addressee.

Once Hubmaier was in the pulpit of the Fraumünster, instead of reading his recantation, he began saying, "Oh how I have had great conflict and tribulation last night over what I had permitted myself to say. Now I must say that I am unable to recant." He then went on with an impromptu defense of adult baptism, until Zwingli interrupted him, saying that he had refuted him once and was ready to do it again.

Hubmaier was again led off to prison, where he was subjected to the torture rack. The official proceedings against him had to begin again. From the subsequent interrogations we reproduce only those fragments which throw light on the theological debate about his position and the interpretation of his readiness to recant. The paragraphs translated here in the second of four texts are selected from a longer text, omitting questions and answers concerning Hubmaier's earlier career, his income and tax payments, and his anti-Jewish preaching in Regensburg.[3]

Statement of Recantation[4]

I, Baldasar Huebmor from Fridberg, confess publicly in my own hand that [in the past] I could only understand all the Scriptures which deal with water baptism as saying that first one should preach, then one believes, and then one is baptized. I finally settled upon that conviction. Now, however, I have been shown by Master Huldrych Zwingli how the covenant of God, made with Abraham and his seed and [shown] circumcision as a covenant sign, and how baptism takes the place of circumcision. I have not been able to refute this. In addition I have been shown by Master Leo, Dr. Bastian and Myconius how love is to be the judge and referee in all Scriptures. This went to my heart. So I have meditated much about love, and have at last been moved to abandon my conviction that one should not baptize children, and [to con-

---

[3] Manuscript of translation by Henry C. Vedder at Colgate Rochester Library.

[4] vMS no. 147, pp. 148f. Cited in Vedder 1905, pp. 138ff.

clude] that in rebaptizing I have been in error.

Second, I am aware that I have been accused of rejecting government, and that I say a Christian cannot sit in a government. This report does me violence and injustice. Ever and always I have said that a Christian can be in government, and that the more Christian he is, the more honorably he would rule. That I have demonstrated with many Scriptures, which I do not just now have in mind.

Further, I am accused of wanting to have all things in common. That I have not done. I, rather, have designated it as "Christian community of goods" when one person has, and seeing his neighbor suffering need, that he shares alms with him so that the hungry, thirsty, naked, and imprisoned are helped. The more a person practices such works of mercy, the nearer he is to being Christian. /149/

I have not placed any weight on baptism. I have not boasted of any special feeling upon being baptized.[5] Nor was I the first who received baptism. Many did so before me, almost a quarter of the year [earlier]. Some others were baptized before me in Waldshût. Particularly in the territories and countryside belonging to you, My Lords, I have baptized no one, as has been falsely rumored on my account.

Further, I have never said that I am without sin, or am unable to sin anymore,[6] but have ever and always confessed that I am a poor sinner, conceived and born in sin, and will remain a sinner to the death. May God not count my sin against me to eternal damnation. Therefore no one should accuse me of such ideas, which I reject: no one should appeal to my name for support or use me as a cover.

Third, since Augustine and many others since his time, also in our time, have been wrong about baptism, therefore I beg Your Wisdom for God's sake, if I have ever angered or offended anyone in this connection, that he forgive me as we ask that God should forgive our sins. Would Your Wisdom take account of my great sickness, tribulation, banishment, and poverty. I have no coat of my own to wear. I escaped only

---

[5] Some of the Swiss Brethren were accused of claiming to have received when baptized an indubitable subjective experience of God's presence.

[6] Zwingli reported that the Swiss Brethren claimed to be sinless: below, p. 195, and Z 4, p. 230.

with the shirt on my back. Please take account as well of the
great wrath and fury which my adversaries have directed
against me; for God's sake be gracious to me. So that as much
as it depends on Your Wisdom I should not come or be turned
over into the hands of my enemies. For I am a weak person
and cannot escape bodily cares while in this weak body.

I will not forget my whole life long to pray to God for
Your Wisdom and for Christian government, nor shall I henceforth cause Your Wisdom or any other [government] any evil
either by my words or deeds. For that Your Wisdom can truly
trust me.

Fragment of an Interrogation[7]

He [Hubmaier] further says that Wilhelm from Witickon[8]
was the instigator of baptism, for when Wilhelm was at
Waldshūt he [Wilhelm] came sometimes to him [Hubmaier]
and he [Hubmaier] answered him as God led. Then Wilhelm
was able to attract some citizens to himself and went with
them out into a village and baptized them. After that they
came to him [Hubmaier] and asked why he would not also
take the matter in hand. He put them off and let the matter
wait until the Easter [week].[9] Whereas the custom had been
to consecrate the [water of] baptism, he omitted that
ceremony. Then Wilhelm came and baptized him, and at the
same time about /392/ 60 other people were baptized.

Following that he baptized about 300 people during the
day of Easter Monday. In response to the instruction provided
him by Master Ulrich, Master Leo, and Dr. Bastian[10] from
divine Scripture, he recognizes that he has erred and that he
will henceforth renounce his error, will cease rebaptism and
will perform a recantation however it is wished. He holds

---

[7] vMS no. 404, pp. 391ff.

[8] Wilhelm Reublin had been the priest of the village of Witikon since
1523. He was among the first Anabaptists expelled from Zurich following
the January 1525 disputation, and was the first actually to baptize and
form communities outside the canton of Zurich.

[9] The word for "Easter" is plural, i.e., Passion Week.

[10] We know of a meeting of Hubmaier with at least ten of the city
pastors, in the presence of four councilmen. The three men whom Hubmaier names here may have met with him more often.

infant baptism to be godly, right, and good. He said this and confesses this with heart and mouth.

Being further asked what then had driven him or what had strengthened him so that Friday he did not do what he had offered to do, he says as before that he doesn't know how it happened and how it came to pass that he didn't do it. He says also that no one had encouraged him in this but he did it of himself in a burst of contrariety, as has already been heard.

A councilman from Constance, namely Mr. von Allopfenn, had written him saying that the faithful Christians of Waldshût had come to Constance and were very worried about him, and that he should be patient and confident that God would help him in his time. That letter came to him at the town hall six or seven days before he was supposed to perform the recantation /393/.[11]

Concerning the letter and the sheet of notes, he answers that when someone had said that the imperial troops had arrived [at the gates of Waldshût] he imagined and fantasized all kinds of things. He had prepared for himself an outline, listing the points of what he thought he would have to say to the imperial authorities in order to defend himself against them [the representatives of the empire]—before Milords. He confesses now that in the pulpit he misused the points he had prepared for the imperial legates because he had been so upset and worked up, and his mind had been spinning, so far that he had come to think that as soon as he came out of the church the imperial police were going to seize him and lead him away. That bothered him so much, he confesses now, that he behaved wrongly and clumsily. He begs Milords for grace and mercy.

Zwingli's Letter to Capito

A valuable complement to the court documents concerning Hubmaier's time in Zurich is offered by our third and fourth texts, letters written by Huldrych Zwingli. One was immediately contemporaneous and one was much fuller, written eight months later. Wolfgang Capito, colleague of Martin Bucer

---

[11] Here we omit 21 lines of text concerning Hubmaier's time in Regensburg.

in the implementation of the Reformation at Strasbourg, was the most tolerant and flexible of the mainline Reformers.[12] *He had written to Zwingli on December 27, 1525, expressing concern about Hubmaier's treatment.*[13] *Zwingli answered him January 1, 1526.*[14]

"Balthasar of Waldshût has fallen into prison here—a man not merely irreverent and unlearned, but even empty. Learn the sum of the matter. When he came to Zurich our Council, fearing lest he should cause a commotion, ordered him to be taken into custody. Since, however, he had once in freakishness of disposition and fatuity, blurted out in Waldshut against our Council, of which place he, by the gods, was a guardian, until the stupid fellow disunited and destroyed everything, it was determined that I should discuss with him in a friendly manner the baptizing of infants and Catabaptists, as he earnestly begged first from prison and afterward from custody. I met the fellow and rendered him mute as a fish. The next day he recited a recantation in the presence of certain Councillors appointed to the purpose [which recantation when repeated to the /488/ Two Hundred it was ordered should be publicly made. Therefore having started to write it in the city, he gave it to the Council with his own hand, with all its silliness, as he promised.][15] At length he denied that he had changed his opinion, although he had done so before a Swiss tribunal, which with us is a capital offense, affirming that his signature had been extorted from him by terror, which was most untrue.

"The Council was so unwilling that force should be used on him that when the emperor or Ferdinand twice asked that the fellow be given to him, it refused the request. Indeed, he was not taken prisoner that he might suffer the penalty of his boldness in the baptismal matter, but to prevent his causing in secret some confusion, a thing he delighted to do. Then he

---

[12] Cf. Yoder 1973, pp. 18ff., 84ff.
[13] Z 8, No. 428, p. 475.
[14] Z 8, No. 434, pp. 487-88. Translation in Jackson 1900, pp. 249-50. The following from Zwingli is set in quotes to distinguish it from the writings of Hubmaier.
[15] The translation is partly conjectural at the point indicated by brackets because the manuscript is damaged.

angered the Council; for there was present most upright Councillors who had witnessed his most explicit and unconstrained withdrawal, and had refused to hand him over to the cruelty of the emperor, helping themselves with my aid. The next day he was thrust back into prison and tortured. It is clear that the man had become a sport for demons, so he recanted not frankly as he had promised, nay he said that he entertained no other opinions than those taught by me, execrated the error and obstinacy of the Catabaptists, repeated this three times when stretched on the rack, and bewailed his misery and the wrath of God which in this affair was so unkind.... Behold what wantonness! Than these men there is nothing more foolhardy, deceptive, infamous—for I cannot tell you what they devise in Abtzell—and shameless. Tomorrow or next day the case will come up."

Zwingli's Letter to Gynoräus[16]

Peter Gynoräus (Frabenberger), Alsatian humanist and friend of the Reformation, was expelled from Basel and lived in Augsburg until 1527. He wrote to Zwingli on August 22, 1526,[17] reporting Hubmaier's visit to Augsburg. Zwingli answered on August 31.

"That Balthazar of whom I wrote a few things in an epistle has acted as follows among us: He escaped secretly from the town of Waldshut and came to the home of a widow at Zurich. When the Council learned it they supposed that he was hatching out some monstrosity, as do the rest of the Catabaptists, and that for this purpose he had crept secretly into the city. So they gave orders that he be arrested and kept under guard in the courthouse. After the third or fourth day (I do not know exactly which), they suddenly ordered Engelhard, Leon [Jud], Myconius, Sebastian [Hofmeister], Megander [Grossmann], myself, and others to be present. When we had come, certain of the Council who had been appointed for the purpose told us that Balthasar had sent letters to them in which he promised that he would vanquish Zwingli on the

---

[16] Z 8, no. 524, pp. 700-706 (the part here excerpted, pp. 703 12ff.). Tr. Jackson 1900, p. 252.

[17] Z 8, no. 520, pp. 688-90.

subject of baptism by his own writings. We proceeded to business. Then the blind fellow adduced what I had written about teaching catechumens some years ago in the book on the Sixty-seven Articles.[18] /704/ For he did not know that it was our custom that the boys also, as in former times, were taught the rudiments of the faith. This he referred to baptism, rather indiscreetly; as if I had said that it was my counsel that the custom of not baptizing infants be brought back again, when I had spoken of imbuing children in the elements of faith. When he saw that he had erred in this matter he was charming. We proceeded after much debate, in which he was unwilling to recognize that perpetual covenant. We came to Acts 2, from which I proved that the children of Christians were in the beginning reckoned as of the church. When he had made many answers I was trying to bring him to a clear and definite reply to the question whether those children were in the church or not. But I made every effort in vain. Then I confess frankly when I came to 1 Corinthians 2, 'All our fathers were baptized unto Moses, etc.,' and was coming to the point of compelling him to acknowledge that children were included even though they were not expressly mentioned, and when he was unwilling to say whether or not they were—I confess that I went for the man rather vigorously. But yet only to the effect, that by his catabaptism he had drawn many wretched citizens into a revolt in which they had perished. But when he had endured this for a considerable time the man was confuted and overcome. He then took a new tack and demanded that he be granted an interview with Leon, Myconius, and Sebastian [Hofmeister] alone, in order that he might confer with them. The arrogant fellow hoped he would draw them over to his side by his soft-spoken ways. When he saw that this course did not succeed he made the demand a second time, and after many crafty tricks, he came to the point of saying that he would recant. The Council did not compel this, except in case he were unwilling to depart from the city.[19] For

---

[18] Hubmaier continues this argument in *Old and New Teachers*, below, p. 245ff. In other ways as well he claims support from the earlier Zwingli against infant baptism. Cf. p. 190.

[19] There are slight indications in the record that if Hubmaier had not renounced his recantation he might have stayed in Zurich as a minister; Yoder 1962, p. 83; Yoder 1959, pp. 14-16. Cf. below, p. 561, note 40.

it had made no severer provision against those who do not wish to desert the cause of catabaptism than that they should leave the city. Meanwhile the legates of the emperor came with a demand for the man to carry him to punishment. He was denied them on the basis of the law which provides that no citizen shall be put on his defense on any other charge than that for which he had been arrested. Such was the sin of the Council against that man, they defended him from the demand of Caesar just as though he were a citizen![20] And this aided, that he was in prison before he was in 'free guard.' However this /705/ may be, he was free when we came together and for some time after was guarded at the courthouse. Then a form of recantation was drawn up, not in accordance with any formula of the Council or of anyone, but by his own hand. And when he had read this in the church to which the name Abbey is given,[21] and the address which I delivered to the people had been finished, he straightway denied the recantation in the presence of the whole assembly.

"He did this supposing that he had an opportunity of speaking, and then adduced much against the baptism of infants and in favor of catabaptism. Hence there was a persistent rumor (but I think it is speculation) that he was secretly prompted to do this so that some commotion might result; for they hoped that I would go away when my speech was delivered. He was cast anew into prison and was held there for a month longer. Then he finally declared that he was entirely ignorant of saying anything to vitiate his recantation; and if he said anything else than what he had promised he must have been possessed by a demon. He put together a new recantation. I went around to my friends with the request that they would obtain a merciful judgment from the Council. This was granted. When he offered to make a final statement it was decreed through pity that he should make an express disavowal and then should depart immediately from the territory. I then personally besought Englehard, Leon, and Megander

---

[20] The protection against the still worse fate that would have befallen him in the hands of the Catholic iimperial authorities is probably an indication of some degree of support for Hubmaier within the Council.

[21] The Minster of Our Lady, Fraumünster, where Hofmeister shared pastoral duties with Heinrich Engelhard. There is in the court records no reference to Hubmaier's release.

[Grossmann], my fellow bishops, that they should intercede in company with me before the Council; for if he were driven out immediately after his disavowal, grave peril would threaten him both from our Swiss and from Caesar. The Council listened to our request, and after the recantation, which he pretended he made heartily, whereas there could have been nothing less hearty, a space of time was given him to stay until there should be found an opportunity of sending him first in safety. And this came about through a certain member of the Council who is most faithful in the cause of Christ, and he was secretly sent away so that the citizens did not know of his departure. See, my Peter, with how great generosity we treated the fellow and with what treachery he responded. For as soon as he reached Constance he so caluminated me before /706/ the ministers of the Word and boasted of his victory that I do not know but that he turned some of them against me. So unprepared are some for the detection of hypocrisy. We kept everything secret.[22] When he went away he so worked on those good men's feelings that they gave him ten gold pieces. And yet either he or his wife had more gold than they had silver. Thus do they abuse our simplemindedness who advance their own interests under the guise of piety. But that the man should so revile me is not to be wondered at, for he saw from the begining that I abhorred him and his practices. I give the man credit for cleverness and studious moderation; but still I see in him (I trust I am mistaken) nothing more than an immoderate thirst for money and notoriety. Accordingly, I am quite indifferent to what he may whisper about me into the ears of others. It is certain at any rate that he will act according to the saying in the comedy: 'It has not succeeded here, let us go elsewhere.' May the Omnipotent extinguish by celestial dew this desire for glory which glows in the hearts of some!"

---

[22] There is in the court records no reference to Hubmaier's release.

13

Interrogation and Release

*Once the expected recantation had not been performed it
was obvious that Hubmaier would be returned to prison. He is
next recorded on March 5 as requesting a new chance to speak
to someone from the Council.*

"Dr. Balthasar answers: As he previously answered to
Milords he is willing to forsake baptism, to be peaceable in
words and deeds and otherwise. He stands by that answer and
prays Milords, if he in any other way should have angered
them or acted against them that they for God's sake be willing
to forgive him.... He also begs the privilege of writing on four
subjects: on government, interest, tithes, and community. He
wants to be able to give an account of himself in such a way
that it is visible that he has been dealt with unjustly."[1]

*This request for a new chance to clear his name is on the
same sheet with other records of testimony taken from Felix
Mantz, Conrad Grebel, and Ulrich Hottinger, as well as several
men from Zollikon, who were all standing firmly by their commitment to adult baptism.*

*The following document demonstrates that ultimately the
authorities did give Hubmaier a chance to clear his name—that
is, to follow through with the recantation which had not been
properly performed in December. There is no record of any
actual public presentation of the recantation text, but circum-
stantially the fact of his release would indicate that he went
through with the form of words that was required of him. Our
text is the scribe's simultaneous record of Hubmaier's inter-
rogation by the Zürich Council (or a commission of the same).
The final paragraphs of the text record the Council's actions
taken in the same session.*[2]

Dr. Balthasar from Waldtshût answers as follows: he left
Waldtshût consciously and intentionally. He was deathly sick
under the attack and turmoil.

---

[1] vMS no. 170, p. 175, tr. Harder 1985, p. 445.
[2] Cf. also Sachsse 1914, p. 81, n. 4. Source: vMS, no. 179, p. 193f.

To demonstrate that, the apothecary Hartman sent him medicines for a value of 14 batzen. That got him on his feet again. While he was sick the people of Waldtshût went to the count and to [Eberhard] of Rischach[3] and negotiated /194/ in ways he could not know about. On one Wednesday[4] the entire city was called to the town hall and given the report, and told that whoever did not want to accept this could in God's name go wherever he wished.

Upon which he spoke:

Dear Friends,

You know how I have hitherto been your leader under the Word of God. Since, however, it has now been decided to accept the settlement, there will be mass again and the images will be brought back into the churches. That is something which I cannot tolerate or watch. Therefore in God's name I must take my leave of you and commend myself to God the Almighty. I am a deathly sick man and do not know what is to come with me. I beg you for God's sake, if I have angered any one of you, that you forgive me for that for God's sake."

With that he went into his house. Many people came to him who were very sorrowful that things were this way. At the same time he had to get out of his house quickly for many warnings were reaching him and he was just barely able to escape. He came into the home of another citizen with whom he and a boatman crossed the Rhine, going first toward Villingen. He didn't know where he should go. He had had in mind to go toward Basel and Strasbourg but Hapsburg troops were encamped there, so that he could not dare to go that way. So then he first came here and went into the home of Aberlin, with the thought that he would rest a day or two, because his feet were greatly swollen, and would get other clothing, because in his old clothing he was too recognizable and easily betrayed. He went from the home of Aberlin to that of Mrs. Widerker and had no other thought but that once he was rested he would travel on.

---

[3] Eberhard d.i. von Rischach was a Zurich citizen now living in Schaffhausen.

[4] According to vMS, p. 194, note 2, the actual date was Tuesday, December 5, 1525.

Concerning infant baptism he says that his conscience gave him no other certainty. My Lords know well how he wrote to Master Ulrich and always asked him to converse with him about it [baptism] and if he could be convinced of another opinion he would be glad to let himself be taught.

Conrad Grebel and Jacob Hottinger also came to him and they talked together about baptism.

Again Roggenacher and Hottinger were with him, at the time of the last disputation, and wanted him to go with them to the disputation.

When asked how he came to be against infant baptism he answered that the prior of Sion, [Sabastian] Ruggensberger, came to him and asked him to ride with him toward St. Gall for an early mass. He answered the prior, yes, if he would also ride with him to Zurich to Master Ulrich whom he wanted to see. The prior said yes. So they rode together to St. Gallen, stayed there about three days, and when they were ready to leave Dr. Joachim von Watt gave him a letter for Zwingli. /195/ When they arrived at Zurich and went to the inn Zur Linden, the prior sent Schwamberger[5] to find out where Master Ulrich was. They were told he was in Master Leo's house. They went there and found him. Then Master Ulrich invited him to breakfast the next morning. They accepted his invitation and when he wanted to leave after breakfast Master Ulrich said he didn't want him to leave. Then they went together to walk along the ditch. He had noted a number of matters on a little tablet, including specially one concerning infant baptism, concerning which he wanted to converse with Master Ulrich. At that time Master Ulrich gave him a good answer which immediately satisfied him.

From then on he frequently corresponded with Oecolampad, Leo, with Dr. Bastian at Schaffhausen and with others concerning baptism and they were all of the opinion that there is no clear Scripture in favor of infant baptism. Dr. Bastian especially wrote him that at Schaffhausen he had publicly stood before the Council and had said that Master Ulrich is wrong about infant baptism.[6] Said doctor did not

---

[5] Niclaus Swainberg appears in the early sources (Fast 1973, p. 380) among the radical Zwinglians. Later he became a councilman and then city treasurer.

[6] Cf. text 10 above, note 11, p. 91.

want to have his own child baptized either. That was what brought him as far as he has come with regard to baptism.

When he was asked whether he had conspired with Milords' men who had gone as volunteers to Waldshût and whether he had called upon them, he answered that he was not aware of any conspiracy nor of what their intention was, because at that time he was away at Schaffhausen. But the rumor was current at Schaffhausen that the company from Zurich had taken over the marketplace at Waldtshût.

As to persons from Zollikon having come to Waldtshût, he says that he never observed anything out of order on their part. He further had had no dealings with them, except that when they asked him about baptizing, he told them his opinion.

Asked concerning the people in the Klettgöw,[7] he had personally given them no allegiance nor supported them. All he did was always to preach the Word of God. How those of Waldshût negotiated with them he could not know, for they had never called him into that. However, it is true that he had sometime said that it would not be bad if people would help one another and thereby come to peace, rest, and a Christian order.

Further, he says concerning his recantation that he had no other intention when he went into the church and into the pulpit but that he had wanted to do what he had agreed to and carry out the intention and the judgment of Milords. He prepared the reasons for baptism ahead of time so that people would see and hear that he had not thought it up out of his own head. He was ready and disposed to read his recantation. Then, as God helps him,[8] he does not know what happened to him or how he came to that, so that he spoke differently from what he previously had had in mind to say. Thus he supposes that God wanted to test him most severely, in the midst of all his tribulation, of which he is so full. He is still /196/ disposed and willing once again to carry out the judgment of

---

[7] The Klettgau lies between Waldshut and Schaffhausen. It was the site of Wilhelm Reublin's first agitation after his expulsion from Zurich in late January and his entering Waldshut before Easter. The unruly peasants gathered in the Klettgau with relative freedom. Cf. Bergsten 1961, pp. 233ff., and Stayer 1975 and 1977b.

[8] An oath: "So help me God."

Milords, where and when and as often as is wanted. He prays Milords to forgive him his clumsiness for God's sake. He wants to perform his recantation and make everything right that he has dishonored. If he doesn't do it then he should be immediately thrown without grace into water or fire. He also says that no one encouraged him and no one else wrote anything, and he had not brought anything more with him than his clothing.

There was once a time when a chapel was being broken down just outside Waldtshût. He also went to see and while he was standing with some people Aberlin said that God does not live in any temples that are built with human hands. When he heard that he asked who it was that talked that way and he was told that this was Aberlin from Zürich. Then he greeted him and offered him his hand, for he had previously not known him. When they were done with the chapel they went together to Waldtshut. He led Aberlin toward the inn and he went together with the others to supper. Then Aberlin went to his home and spoke with him about baptism. He [Hubmaier] answered him [Aberlin] that he could not find anything in the Scripture except that first there should be preaching, teaching, and then baptism. Otherwise, he does not know anything about any conspiracy. At that same time Hottinger was with Aberlin.

Then his wife came to him at the town hall and said how it was going in Waldtshût and what people were doing with his things, even his clothing being sold, some of it auctioned off. She also brought him a greeting from Aberlin. Otherwise, she had said nothing to him nor had she brought support from anyone.

When he had to leave Waldtshût his wife gave him about 6 gulden worth of batzen in a neck purse. She herself also took about 3 gulden worth.

Concerning the bottles that are supposed to have been full of money he said that his wife had filled one full of rappis.[9] When he came to the lord of Mandach he put the bottle on the table and let them drink from it. There was no money in it.

---

[9] A wine concentrated by pouring old good wine over new grapes.

When he was asked about silverware he said that Master Augustin, the sculptor at Schaffhausen, had three silver cups and a golden ring, that is what it must be about, for he had entrusted that to him to keep a year and a day ago.[10]

When he then was again sent away from Schaffhausen, some men came to accompany him. It is well known that Master Steffan Zeller and Hans Hager had requested and warned him in a friendly way [what he should do] if he were clever. He is sorry that he did not do what they had advised.

Further, he acknowledges that he had the sheet of notes with him at the pulpit in a book.

As the dealings with the doctor are heard and read, Milords determined that this coming Friday he should now perform the first recantation which he had previously offered,[11] /197/ in the Fraümunster and on the following Sunday morning in the Grossmünster and afterward at St. Peter's. If that is done, then he shall swear an *urfehde*[12] to leave Milords' jurisdiction and lands and no longer bother Milords with his baptizing. If he should return and be caught he would then be dealt with according to his merits and his appeals.[13]

The letter should be written to the sculptor at Schaffhausen to send the silver goblets and a ring to Milords. When they have been received, Milords should take from their value the reimbursement of their costs and what is left over should be paid out to him and he should be let go. Determined Wednesday after Quasimodo [April 11] in the presence of Mayor Walder, Council, and citizens, 1526. [There follows an inventory of items received from the Schaffausen sculptor, which he had held for Hubmaier.]

---

[10] "A year and a day" means "a long time," not a precise date.

[11] This may mean rereading the actual text from January 5. Or it may merely mean following through with the same act.

[12] An oath of renunciation. If Hubmaier promised never to return he may not have had to acknowledge the rightness of infant baptism.

[13] "His appeals" refers to Hubmaier's stated willingness to be punished if proven wrong.

14

Dialogue with Zwingli's Baptism Book

The harsh lines of separation between the two former col-
leagues, Hubmaier and Zwingli, were clearly drawn after Hub-
maier's publication of Christian Baptism. *Certainly the Anabap-*
tist challenge was perceived by Zwingli as a growing threat
and was occupying much of his attention as church leader and
writer. His writings against the Radical Reformers were becom-
ing increasingly more extensive and frequent. In December
1524, he had written Those Who Give Cause for Rebellion[1]
followed in March 1525 by his Commentary on True and False
Religion *in which he addressed a major section to baptism and*
promised a treatise against the Anabaptists.[2] Zwingli's major
treatise against the Anabaptists, On Baptism, Rebaptism and
Infant Baptism,[3] *called the* Baptism Book *by Hubmaier,*
appeared in May. A further major theological attack against
the Anabaptists followed with The Preaching Office[4] *in June.*
By all counts it was an exhaustive publishing program directed
against the Anabaptists. If one places these writings against the
background of the six private and two public baptismal dis-
putations in the twelve months ending in March,[5] as well as the
actual outbreak of baptisms in January and the governmental
suppression which followed, one can understand the mounting
pressure under which Zwingli was laboring. Against this back-
drop came Hubmaier's major defense of believers baptism in
July, Christian Baptism. *Zwingli saw in this work a personal*
attack by a man he had counted among his friends.[6] In

---

[1] Z 3, pp. 374-412. Partial translation in Harder 1985, pp 315-21.

[2] Z 3, pp. 763-73, ZL 3, pp. 185-97.

[3] Z 4, pp. 206-337. Partial English translations in Bromiley 1953, pp. 129-75, and Harder 1985, pp. 363-74.

[4] Z 4, pp. 382-433, Pipkin 1984, pp. 150-85, and Harder 1985, pp. 385-409.

[5] See Harder 1985, p. 334, for a listing of the public and private discussions.

[6] The preface to Zwingli's response clearly shows Zwingli's reaction, Z 4, pp. 585-88.

October, Zwingli wrote to Vadian that he was soon to turn to writing against Hubmaier "... who stupidly treats the baptism of infants and the rebaptism of adults with much wresting and violence of the holy Scriptures."[7] The promised treatise was the less than moderate Answer to Balthasar Hubmaier's Baptism Book,[8] *published November 5, 1525, the day before the third disputation on infant baptism was convened in Zurich.*

The same time period was for Hubmaier hardly one of less tension. Indeed, he was about to enter into one of the most stressful periods of his life. The situation deteriorated rapidly for Waldshut in the course of the summer and fall. The Peasants' War in South Germany largely reached its climax in July with the defeat of the peasants. On November 4, the Klettgau peasants were defeated at Griessen. Hubmaier, attempting to reach Zurich for the baptismal discussions, was forced to turn back. As expected, the disputation was decided to the advantage of Zwingli.[9] As Bergsten observes, it was a "severe blow" for the Anabaptists, for the ... result was that the attitude of Zwingli and Zurich toward the Anabaptists became a model for other Swiss Reformers. Thus, Zurich's influence increased in the realm of religious policies. The gulf between Anabaptism and the Swiss Reformation could no longer be bridged. Hubmaier's attempts to achieve peace and unity on the baptismal question had completely failed. The religious isolation of the Anabaptist community in Waldshut was complete. At the same time its political situation had become hopeless.[10]

Matters moved swiftly. By the end of November it was clear that no military support was forthcoming from Zurich and that it was only a matter of time before the Hapsburg victory was accomplished. In this setting, only days before the capitulation of Waldshut and his own flight to Zurich, Hubmaier penned this Dialogue on Zwingli's Baptism Book, *though apparently without having read Zwingli's* Answer. *Cast in the form of a dialogue, it was Hubmaier's compensation for not having been able to participate in the Zurich disputation.*

---

[7] Harder 1985, p. 431.

[8] Z 4, pp. 585-641.

[9] See the statement of the Zurich Council to the Grüningen magistrates, November 15. Harder 1985, pp. 435-36.

[10] Bergsten 1978, p. 265.

Hubmaier allows Zwingli to speak by citing fragments from his writings, often verbatim. The main source is Zwingli's Baptism Book, *but occasionally Zwingli's* Exposition of the Conclusions, Those Who Give Cause for Rebellion, *and the* Commentary *are utilized. This treatise is thus closely bound to Zwingli texts and is consequently not as coherent a literary effort as his* Christian Baptism. *In every exchange Hubmaier has the last word; repetition is frequent.*

In general, the tone of Hubmaier's work is more moderate than Zwingli's Answer. *Although written in November it was not published until after Hubmaier had fled Waldshut and had spent·his time in Zurich. Because he was mistreated in Zurich, Hubmaier was understandably bitter in his remembrance of his former colleague. The preface and conclusion, penned in Nikolsburg before publication, have a distinctly sharper tone than the body of the treatise, though still not as belligerent as Zwingli's* Answer. *In the conclusion Hubmaier suggests that a public dialogue between the two should take place, perhaps in Regensburg, approximately halfway between Zurich and Nikolsburg. Unfortunately, the dialogue was never to take place. The distance between the two Reformers, so near in so many ways theologically if not in spirit, was never to be overcome.*[11]

---

[11] Partial translation in Hošek 1891, pp. 548-555. Quoted,in Vedder 1905, p. 180. Fragments cited by Klaassen, pp. 45, 233. Source: HS, pp. 167-214.

Title page of Zwingli's pamphlet: Authentic Grounded Answers Concerning Doctor Balthasar's Baptism Booklet

DIALOGUE
of Doctor Balthasar Huebmör
von Fridberg
with Master Ulrich Zwingli of Zurich's
Book on Infant Baptism.
Truth Is Immortal.
Earth, Earth, Earth, hear the Word
of the Lord, Jeremiah 22:2.
Nicolspurg
1526

To the Wellborn and Christian Lords, Leonard and Hans
von Liechtenstainn at Nicolspurg, etc., Cousins, his Gracious
Lords.

May the one who orders, creates, and works all in all
according to his best will, and without whom nothing may
happen, himself increase and strengthen your beginning faith,
hope, and love in Christ Jesus our Lord, and preserve you
from the serious errors which have forced their way in next to
his holy Word in these last days, in which Word alone we
shall be worthy of salvation. May he dispose Your Graces and
us all to bear his cross which is laid upon us with patience
and a happy disposition so that we will always do his will and
keep his commandments out of a truly heartfelt love and show
Christian, brotherly love to all the living saints as to our members—just as /168/ Christ himself has so paternally taught and
shown. That we show and demonstrate such as far as the
sacrifice of our goods and also the giving of body and life.
This I wish from my heart before Your Graces and also all the
church at Nicolspurg.

Gracious Lords. After the almighty eternal God so
strongly and earnestly commanded that one should set no
obstacle before the blind, Lev. 19:14, but fear him who is the
Lord, he also curses those who misdirect a blind person on
the way, Deut. 27:18. He powerfully orders one who
encounters the ox or ass of his enemy who is astray to lead

the same again into the way, Exod. 23:4. Now I see many
people more worthy than the ass and ox, who err in the way
of truth, namely on the subject of water baptism. Indeed, not
only the blind, but also those who want to be leaders of the
blind, a light to those who sit in darkness, teachers of the
ignorant and great master of the simple, who highly boast
never to have erred in any article—and even in the boasting is
their heart darkened and they become fools.[12] In Rom. 1:18-23
and 2:17-24 that is the punishment of God who cannot bear
such boasting or evil. Though in the power of the divine command I am to set such erring people again on the right
way—as much as God has given me grace, I am also obligated—and since to do such is impossible if I do not
beforehand throw the sticks, stones, and blocks from the way
over which for such a long time so many people have
stumbled and fallen to the ground, it is accordingly wholly
necessary that the seductive little book which Master Vlrich
Zwinnglen at Zürch has published on water baptism be struck
down with the staff of Jacob, that is, with the evangelical message, and cleared from the way. For till now this little book
has truly been a great stumbling block, before which many
devout Marys[13] and Christian souls have not been able to learn
or experience fundamentally the truth of the death and resurrection of Christ from the dead as signified in water baptism,
as Paul teaches in Romans 6:4. For this great stone has lain,
too heavily before the grave of the Holy Scriptures. And
although I would have gladly removed it a long time ago, I
have always been hindered by Satan in the printeries and
have also suffered at Zürch the great harshness and martyrdom of a difficult imprisonment, in spite of all offers to let
the case be decided in court and in spite of appeals to the
general confederates, to the Great Council at Zürch, and to

---

[12] With the assumed subject and predicate, "I see," carried over from the
previous sentence, this incomplete sentence is rendered as Hubmaier
wrote it.
[13] The phrase, *fromb Marien*, is rendered here literally, thereby preserv-
ing the possibililty that Hubmaier had in mind some allusion to a Mary
event in the Gospels. It may be, however, that a simpler translation,
"devout maids," would be what he had in mind.

the emperor himself."[14] There I would report on and testify to my reasons in the divine Scriptures that infant baptism is a work without any basis /169/ in the divine Word—and that in German, with bright, clear, and simple writing concerning baptism alone and without any additions. Then Master Huldrich Zwinnglen should show that one should baptize young children—and that also in German, with bright, clear, and simple writing, concerning baptism alone and without any additions.[b] When that had happened I offered to let his own books in Greek, Latin, and German be the proper judge between us both.[c] Where I am found wrong I should be simply judged in body and life with sword, fire, or water. If, however, Zwinglen was defeated, then I ask not that he be made to suffer any punishment, but only that he recognize his error and henceforth teach rightly.[15] But they did not want to allow my legitimate Christian and public offer at Zürch. Instead, they wanted to teach me—a sick man who had just gotten up out of his deathbed, hunted, pursued, who had lost everything—another belief through the executioner. Yea, according to the judgment of Zwingli, which he had announced from the public pulpit, that according to the power of the imperial law one should behead us as Anabaptists.[d] He preached this against me and many other godly people, namely Cùrad Grebel, Felix Mantz, George von Chur,[16] Anthony Kürßchner from Schwyz, Hainrich Aberli, baker at Zürich, Hanns Ackenfüeß, Karlen Bronnwald, Hansen Hottinger, Fridlen von Schweyz, Frau Mantzin and Frau Widerkerin, both widows at Zürch,[17] yes and many other

[14] The marginal notations given here may refer to writings of Hubmaier. See above, texts 3 and 8.
[15] This comment is reminiscent of the alleged testimony of Conrad Grebel, "and if Zwingli defeated him, they should burn Conrad Grebel, but if Conrad Grebel defeated him, they should not burn Zwingli" (cf. Harder 1985, p. 42).
[16] George Blaurock.
[17] Cf. vMS, nos. 170, 170a, and 170b, pp. 174-80 (tr. Harder 1985, pp. 444-48). These documents report the hearings of most of the prisoners whom Hubmaier names here.

[a] *Apellation* [appeal]; *Christian appeal.*
[b] *Ad kalendas grecas* [until the Greek calends], i.e., never.
[c] Judge.
[d] *Fides est opus dei* [faith is a work of God].

devout Christian men, women, and virgins.[a] That has been
his gospel, comforting word, and work of his mercy, by which
he has comforted and afflicted the captive Christians.[b] Yes,
he has preached strangely, and likewise Leo Jud, Sebastian
Hoffmaister, Caspar im Spital,[18] and the Johanitter priest,
Commander of Küßnach[19] (in whom truly there is nothing but
idle gossip and pomp), in which preaching they have not
alienated the government, so that they should certainly deal
with us hard enough. It led finally also to the point that all at
once they have miserably thrown more than twenty men,
widows, /170/ pregnant women, and virgins into dark
dungeons and pronounced over them the judgment that they
henceforth shall see neither sun nor moon their life long,[c]
that they reach their end on water and bread, and that in the
dark dungeons all the dead and living, until no more of them
remain, stay with one another, dying, suffocating, and rot-
ting.[d] Among them several did not taste one mouthful of
bread in three days, so that the others would have enough to
eat. O God, the hard, heavy, and harsh judgment[e] over
righteous and Christian people about whom no one can with
truth say anything evil, except only that they have received
water baptism according to the earnest command of Christ. At
the same time a cruel and frightful mandate has also gone out
from Zürch, and has been proclaimed throughout all the territory, a summary of which follows: Whoever henceforth in
these territories baptizes or lets oneself be baptized, as the
above-mentioned people have done, from this hour on such
persons shall be thrown into the water and drowned, and that
without any further judicial proceedings, self-defense, or
sentencing.[20] Those are the swords and pikes by which
Zwinglen has overcome the rebaptizers (as he wrongly names

[18] Caspar Megander.
[19] Konrad Schmid.
[20] Cf. vMS, no. 172, p. 180f., tr. Harder 1985, p. 448.

[a] Zwingli's judgment.
[b] *C. de virgine corr. Proles* [chapter on the improvement of young vir-
gins] and Exodus 22:16.
[c] An unheard-of judgment.
[d] Great lamentation and need.
[e] Strong arguments. Syllogism of Neptune.

them), although he boasts in his little book that he has done so with Scripture.* But he has not brought any into the light of day. He has himself confessed and attested even in public print that he is wrong, that those who baptize children have no clear word in Scripture by which they are commanded to baptize them—this on section E, page two, of the little book on the rebellious spirits published in 1525.[21] In addition to that, he permits himself to boast shamelessly that he has triumphed and been victorious with Scriptures, just as if the Germans had no brains so that they could judge writings in black and white against each other.

Yes, furthermore, in order to cause me enough distress and to deprive me of comfort, at that time they also took my dear wife who is without any guilt and put her into prison. For the present that is enough of that, unless it be the case that, for the protection of the truth I should be forced to speak more about it. May the merciful and good God forgive all /171/ those who are guilty of the imprisonment of the innocent so that the saying does not come to apply to them that if anyone leads into prison he will go into prison, Rev. 13:10. However, praise, honor, and glory in eternity be to God that now and always my great innocence, which I still offer daily and without ceasing to all people, has come to light. In my teaching the Holy Scripture shall be my judge; in worldly business, whatever Christian government at whose side God has hung the sword for the protection of the righteous and punishment of the evil. Therefore, Gracious Lords, I have had to

---

[21] Zwingli's treatise *Wer Ursache gebe zu Aufruhr* was published in December 1524. See Z 3, pp. 374-469. An abridged translation is Harder 1985, pp. 316-21. The reference given here by Hubmaier is Z 3, pp. 409,[16-19] tr. 1985, p. 319. Hubmaier makes liberal use of the writings of Zwingli in this treatise. Often he quotes Zwingli verbatim, though usually with minor changes as he adjusts Zwingli's regional language to his own. Sometimes he paraphrases Zwingli and often he collates or abridges Zwingli passages. In most cases he is judicious and fair in what he cites. We will note the Zwingli references cited by Hubmaier in available modern printed editions, including translations. In addition, we will note if the citation is paraphrased or abridged, but will not comment on exact Zwingli wording unless it is felt that Hubmaier has misquoted him.

---

* *Fune* [by rope]. *Fame* [by hunger]. *Siti* [by thirst]. *Aio* [I affirm]. *Nego* [I deny].

bring forth such matters, although against my own will, intention, and good judgment, not out of envy, hate, or vengefulness, as God is my witness—I would have preferred to remain silent—but only for the use, rebuilding, and edification of the Christian church according to the Word of God, to which no small offense and apostasy itself has taken place, owing to this Zwinglen. I offer to prove this in Scripture and in deed, as is right, and I am willing to let his own books be the judge between us both. I have already heard many, who had no other argument in their quiver for the protection of the godless children's baptism than to say: Aye, Zwingler[22] has proved it with Scripture. If one asks them which Scripture, they cannot point to any. Thus the shortsighted lead the blind, and both fall into one ditch. May God graciously pull them out again.

But let me come to the subject, gracious and Christian Lords. It is known that I wrote this dialogue book at Waldßhūt on about Saint Andrew's Day, 1525. Owing to the abovementioned causes I have been hindered until now. Since out of Christian duty I am bound not to hide the light under a bushel, but to lead the erring and blind into the right way of divine truth, in which we have failed on the present subjects so miserably for such a long time, even the past thousand years, Augustine being not a little responsible for this, I have accordingly first of all had to attack and root out the Zwinglian book, so that henceforth the true baptism of Christ again be implanted and established and practiced according to his order. For through this, as through a visible door, by the public confession of faith we must enter into the general Christian church, outside of which there is no salvation. For in water baptism* the church uses the key of admitting and loosing, but in the Supper the key of excluding, binding, and locking away, as Christ promises and gives to it the power of the forgiveness of sins, /172/ Matt. 16:19; 18:21ff.; John 20:23. God willing, on this matter four books will be published that have already been written. The first is a catechism or a textbook which teaches what a person should know before

---

[22] A play on words on the name of Zwingli: *Zwinger*, the forcer.

---

* Two keys.

being baptized in water. Next is an order of the Christian church, then what Christian water baptism is, and finally, an answer to the derisive dialogue of several preachers held at Basel. In the meantime I admonish* all Christ-believing people that they should turn away from the respecting of all the persons whom we have until now held to be sun, moon, and bright stars. For the last times are here of which Christ says, "The sun and the moon will lose their shine and the stars will fall from heaven," Matt. 24:29. Whoever now depends on these suns, moons, and stars and not on God, will lose the appearance of God's brightness and fall with them from the firmament of the heavenly Word. Without doubt Paul does not write in vain: "If an angel from heaven were to come and preach to us otherwise he will be accursed," Gal. 1:9. Thus Moses and all the prophets teach us that we should not look on their words but on the Word of God, saying: "Thus speaks the Lord, the one God of Israel; thus says the Lord of hosts." It is as if they wanted to say, "Do not look on Moses, Isaiah, Jeremiah, and Ezekiel. Note what God says to you."

Yet we now wholly and completely practice the opposite, may it be truly lamented to God! As soon as one speaks concerning a Christian subject no one says, "Christ teaches and commands us thus," but "The one writes this; the other, something else." Thus we look more to men than to God himself. Therefore there comes over us the penalty of blindness, indeed, the spirit of confusion, so that we do not know where we are. And the table of divine writings has been changed into a rope and net of confusion by the just judgment of God since we do not any longer look only to him so that no one may lead us astray. So it has happened also with us with Augustine, Jerome, Gregory, with papal law and with the Scholastics; therefore, we have wholly and completely fallen so far from the Word that nothing any longer remains with us which looks like a Christian church or a devout way of life.

Yea, truly, it is not without cause that God has so often truly and fatherly warned us in the Scriptures about the respecting of persons. We have not been obedient to him, however, but have blindly sailed after all human breezes and

---

* Christian admonition. Respect of persons.

winds, without any understanding and testing of the spirits. Therefore not without reason has God let us fall even in the purest and clearest matters. For, truly, if I be permitted to boast, in /173/ six years no subject has been opened up which is clearer, brighter, and more publicly testified to everywhere in Scriptures than that of water baptism, that one should apply it to believers and not to cradle babies. God has pronounced over us for a sentence such childishness and blindness since we have given water baptism to infants and minors, completely contrary to all baptismal Scriptures. But let us now henceforth abstain from this serious sin of respecting persons and run again to God, crying, believing, trusting, depending on, and following him. He will open our eyes again and wash the mud away in Siloam, will shake off the old scales, the ears will open, will loosen the tongue, and will show us the right way and path that goes into eternal life. May God help us all thereto. Herewith I want to have commended Your Graces together with other good-hearted people into the protection and care of the Holy Trinity. Praise be to God. Amen. Given at Nikolsburg, 1526.

Your Graces' obedient and willing servant,
Baltasar Hûbmör von Fridberg

Truth Is Immortal.

A Dialogue
On Master Ulrich Zwingli of Zurich's Book on Baptism
And of Doctor Balthasar Huebmör von Fridberg
Concerning Infant Baptism

The First Part

Zwingli   Balthasar

Zwingli: There are many in our time who not long before the beginning of baptism began to cry out to everyone: there is nothing in outward things, they are powerless for salvation, and no one should hope therein. Yes, we see the same ones now for the sake of the outward sign destroying all Christian peace, and whoever speaks against them they impugn as a heretic and antichrist.[23] /174/

Balthasar: My dear Zwingli. You know well·that there are two kinds of external ceremonies among Christians.[a] Several are not grounded in Scripture, such as palms, holy water, candles, salt, blessing, and the like, in which until now we placed the hope of salvation. We have cried out and written against these things, not without reason, for by them Christ is pushed out of the center. Some ceremonies, however, are grounded in the Scriptures, such as baptism and the Supper of Christ, by which we publicly testify outwardly before the people that we already inwardly believe and trust in Christ. We devote ourselves in the heart to what we have outwardly affirmed by these ceremonies, by virtue of their institution by Christ. For it is not enough that one should believe Christ with the heart.[b] One must confess him also externally in public so that one confesses oneself as a Christian. So then, these ceremonies are signs, as you yourself write in your *Commentary*.[24] "For whoever confesses me before people, the same I will confess before my Father," says Christ in Luke 12:8. Although these ceremonies, like any other good works, are not sufficient for salvation, and no one should also hope for that from them, nevertheless, since water baptism is an institution of Christ, which no one may deny, everyone who believes inwardly is also obligated to confess his faith outwardly with it before the Christian church.[c] Where now a Christian sees that these outward things, which Christ himself instituted, are being thrown to the ground, he is obligated to cry out without ceasing about that and not stop, even though the outward worldly peace among the godless is thereby shaken. For the order of God should always go upright and be confessed, even though the entire world thereby fall back. Christ is the sign that is contradicted. He is the cornerstone which the builders

---

[23] Z 4, pp. 206,[15-21] tr. Harder 1985, p. 363.
[24] Z 3, p. 761,[22] tr. ZL 3, p. 184. Zwingli's *Commentary on True and False Religion* was published in March 1525.

---

[a] Two kinds of ceremonies.
[b] External confession is necessary.
[c] Water baptism is an institution of Christ.

reject. He has sent the sword and not peace. Whoever now destroys his Word and institutions, whether they be outward or internal, should after sufficient instruction be properly esteemed as a destroyer of the indivisible cloak of Christ.[a] Concerning the ceremonies of the Old Testament, however, we clearly find that God himself has abolished them, Isa. 1:12-17; Jer. 6:20; Ezek. 20:39; Amos 5:21-24. But concerning the ceremonies of the New Testament we do not read that Christ has done away with them. These one should and must keep according to the institution of Christ, and make no misuse of them. /175/

Zwingli:[b] Baptism as they practice it is a heresy, that is, a sect and a faction.[25]

Balthasar: Think better, my Zwingli. For if baptism of those previously instructed and believing is a heresy, then Christ is the first archheretic. For he ordered that one should first preach, afterward believe, and third, baptize, Matt. 28:19; Mark 16:16. And the apostles must also be heretics who also practiced it thus, Acts 2:38,41; 8:12-13; 35-38; 10:44-48; 11:13-18; 16:14-15; 32-33; 19:5. Let every godly Christian read these chapters first and afterward judge.

Zwingli:[c] Yes, such people, who let themselves now be baptized, imagine they are gathering a church that is without sin.[26]

Balthasar: You do us violence and injustice. If we were to say that we were without sin we would be misleading ourselves and the truth would not be in us, 1 John 1:8.[d] O God, what disparagement that is! Do not say that to us, but to the guilty, from whom I shy away from no less than you.

Zwingli:[e] You overthrow infant baptism so that it may suit you to set up rebaptism.[27]

---

[25] Z 4, p. 206.[22-23]
[26] Z 4, p. 207,[1-2] abridged; cf. Harder 1985, loc. cit.
[27] Z 4, p. 207,[9-10] paraphrased; cf. Harder 1985, p. 364.

---

[a] Ceremonies of the Old Testament.
[b] An unchristian speech.
[c] An untruth.
[d] No one is without sin.
[e] An untruth.

Balthasar: You accuse us again and again of rebaptism and have, however, not proven with one single word that infant baptism is a baptism. You twist yourself, you bend back and forth, but no clear Scripture will come forth. Remember what you said against Faber[a] and published in the Article 15, that all truth stands clear in the Word of God.[28] If now infant baptism is truth, then point it out in the clear Word of God. Show it to us, for God's sake. Do it; do not forget.[b] Or the vicar will complain that you have used a sword against him that you now unbelt and that you cannot suffer to be stabbed with. That will be a great disadvantage to you, to your book, and the whole affair. Finally, you will have to strike down your *Theses* yourself. I also beseech you here, for the sake of the last judgment, drop your circuitous argument on circumcision out of the Old Testament. For you well know that circumcision is not a figure of water baptism.[c] You have no Scripture about that, but the /176/ ark of Noah is [a figure of water baptism], 1 Pet. 3:20f.[d] Look also at Cyril "Concerning John," book six, chapter fifteen.[29] Now just as no one went into the ark unless he had believed beforehand, so also in the power of this figure no one should receive water baptism unless he confess faith with the mouth beforehand.

Zwingli: Since the rebaptizers could not defeat us, they went out into the countryside and turned the hearts of the believers to nothing but quarreling over infant baptism.[30]

---

[28] Zwingli published 67 theses for the First Disputation in Zurich, January 29, 1523. He later published an exposition and defense of those theses in his "Exposition and Basis of the Theses or Articles," Z 2, p. 14-457, tr. Furcha 1984, in response to a published attack by Johann Faber after the disputation. Cited here: Z 2, p. 75,[11] tr. Furcha 1984, p. 61. Hubmaier claims to be using against Zwingli the same appeal to Scripture which Zwingli had then used against Faber.

[29] MPG 33, p. 433ff., tr. Schaff 1979, v. VII, pp. 14ff.

[30] Z 4, p. 208[1-4] abridged. Here Zwingli refers to the fact that after rebaptism was proscribed in the city, the Anabaptists scattered into the countryside, tr. Harder 1985, p. 364.

---

[a] Faber.
[b] Give proof.
[c] Circumcision.
[d] Ark of Noah.

Balthasar: He does not quarrel who teaches the truth, for love rejoices in the truth. However, the one who quarrels is the one who without any clear Scripture contradicts the truth. *Zwingli:* I know that they have been overcome with teaching and that even today stand overcome.[31] *Balthasar:* Tell me once, with which teaching? Or we will say to you as someone at Zürch said to Faber:[a] "Do not bring forth the sword by which the pastor of Fislisbach was captured at Constance and killed."[32] So also the pike with which you have overcome the baptizers does not want to come forth. Answer and fight with clear Scripture. Say: "There it stands written." It befits a scholar to defend his cause with clear Scripture. At that time you demanded the same also from Faber.[b]

Zwingli: If it should come to the point that everyone would like to begin whatever he wanted according to his own stubborn head, and not ask the church about it, then there would be more errors than Christians.[33]

Balthasar: One should ask the Scriptures and not the church, for God wants to have from us only his law and his will, not our stubborn heads or opinions. God is more interested in obedience to his words than in all our sacrifices and even the self-devised church practices, as we have it in all the divine writings of the prophets, the twelve apostles, and the saints, 1 Sam. 15:22; Eccles. 4:17. The greatest and right honor that we can offer to God is to keep his Word and live according to his will, not according to our laws and opinions. Now show us in the law and will of God where he wants children to be baptized with the water baptism of the New Testament. And do that with bold writing and not with the frivolous

---

[31] Z 4, p. 208[17], tr. Harder 1985, loc. cit.

[32] Hans Urban Wyß, the pastor of Fislisbach, a village in the canton of Aargau, was arrested by Swiss federal forces and delivered to the bishop of Constance in November 1522, because of his reformed preaching against Mary. The "someone" to whom Hubmaier here refers was Markus Röist, mayor of Zurich. Cf. Z 1, p. 568.[5-9]

[33] Z 4, p. 208,[18-20] tr. Harder 1985, loc. cit.

---

[a] Faber.
[b] Faber.

mocking words which belong to the cake venders[34] /177/ and to the women attendants in the baths, because of which devout Christians do not read your books anymore. That is the right behavior for a theologian, which, however, you do not do. You give counsel, but not from God, whose will is that one question him as to what one should do, and not the church, Isa. 30:2. The church is built on the Word and not the Word on the church, Matt. 16:18.

Zwingli The opponents of baptism are like Alexander Pseudomantes, who did not want to perform his magic trick where Christians or Epicureans were, for they saw through his game.[35] Thus they say first: no one should listen to Luther, Zwingli, and those who preach at Zurich.[36]

Balthasar: Paul says: "O, you unknowing Galatians, who has bewitched you that you do not believe the truth?" Gal. 3:1. Now let every devout Christian judge here whether you or we are doing magic. We have a clear word for baptizing believers and you have none for baptizing your children, except that you groundlessly drag in several shadows from the Old Testament. There are so many passages on water baptism that there would surely have been one on baptizing young children if that had been instituted. That we should listen neither to you, nor to Luther, nor to anyone else, God has himself commanded us, saying: "This is my beloved Son, in whom I am well pleased. To him should you listen," Luke 9:35. We should be taught by God, not taught by Zwingli with the false New Testament.[37] You note me well.[a] Otherwise we would have to learn a new faith as often as you let a New Testament be published. May God faithfully protect us from that.

---

[34] *Hipentragern. Hüppen,* a Zurich specialty, are long, round cakes filled with a sweet paste. Boys selling them were known to be rascals.

[35] Alexander the Paphlagonian was a second-century imposter and worker of false oracles who was opposed to the Epicureans and Christians.

[36] Z 4, p. 209,[6-10] tr. Harder 1985, p. 365. This was not a paraphrase but verbatim. The only exception: for "they" Hubmaier wrote "the opponents of baptism."

[37] The Zurich New Testament, in the text of which Zwingli entered some changes (cf. HS, p. 53f.) was published by Christoph Froschauer in Zurich in 1524.

---

[a] Note.

Zwingli: They ridicule me and say I have stirred up the fire so that the city and the countryside have been closed to them. There is no truth in that.[38]

Balthasar: That does happen and is true. How can you now deny that they punish them in body and goods. They capture them, they imprison them, they put them in dungeons, they throw them in the heretic's tower with bread and water, so that they see neither sun nor moon, /178/ and they send them forth into misery—men, women, widows, and virgins—and all on account of your teaching and outcries in the pulpit, saying: "Punish, punish, etc.[a] You do not want to punish them. According to imperial law one should cut the heads off such heretics." I think that is stirring the coals enough.

Zwingli: They agitate the simple with talk about community, saying, one must hold all things in common.[39]

Balthasar:[b] I have ever and always spoken thus of the community of goods: that one person should always look out for the other, so that the hungry are fed, the thirsty given drink, the naked clothed, etc. For we are not lords of our goods, but stewards and distributors. There are certainly none who say that one should take what belongs to the other and make it in common. Rather, much more that one should give the coat besides the mantle, Matt. 5:40.

Zwingli: You say that one should never add anything to God's Word, Deut. 4:12; 12:30; Gal. 3:15; Prov. 30:6. Now I ask you: Does it stand anywhere that one should not baptize children? If you say "No," you thereby add something to the Word.[40]

Balthasar:[c] O, the perfidious treachery which you perpetrate on the simple, my Zwingli! I am amazed that you are

---

[38] Z 4, p. 210.[8-10] Zwingli admitted that he had "stoked the fire that closed the city and canton against them" but claimed, nevertheless, to have pleaded their case before the Council (tr. Harder 1985, loc. cit.).

[39] Z 4, p. 210[27]-211,[2] tr. Harder 1985, loc. cit.

[40] Z 4, p. 211,[10-18] abridged and paraphrased, tr. Harder 1985, p. 366.

---

[a] Chapter on the improvement of young virgins and Exodus 22:16.

[b] Community of goods.

[c] A perfidious intrigue.

not ashamed of such farces. Or do you think that we do not understand? However, you have learned it from Faber,[a] where he says, "Whoever is not against you is with you, Luke 9:50. Now the customs and laws of the church which are created and instituted by people are not against God, etc."[41] At this point you answer him, "Lord Vicar, prove that!" and you lead him to the Word of Christ, Matt. 15:11, where he overthrows all teaching and human law which God the heavenly Father has not planted, and says that one serves him with these things in vain,[42] Isa. 29. If it does not say anywhere in Scripture that one should baptize children, then one should not baptize them, for that is in vain. Now, however, one should not take the three high names of God the Father and the Son and the Holy Spirit into one's mouth in vain.[b] Note here, Zwingle, it is not necessary that we point out a prohibition. For Christ does not say,[c] "All plants which my Heavenly father has forbidden should be uprooted," Matt. 15:13. Rather, he says, "All plants which my Heavenly Father has not planted should be uprooted." Here you must point out clearly the institution of infant baptism in the Scriptures, or it must be uprooted. One or the other must be, or God will not remain God. If, however, you want to practice infant baptism and do not prove the same as an institution of God, then you and not we are adding to the Word of God. For you make a water baptism where Christ /179/ has made none. To you is also not hidden the common rule of justice: *Affirmanti incumbit probatio. Tu affirmas baptisma infanticum, ergo, etc.* [The burden of proof falls to the affirming. You affirm infant baptism; therefore, etc.] Listen here to one more point. If the vicar had asked you at that time whether infant baptism was also contained clearly in the Word of God, what would you have answered?[d] *Da demonstrandi* [Give proof]; show it.[e] If

---

[41] Z 1, p. 549,[4-11] paraphrased, tr. Jackson 1901, p. 95.
[42] Z 1, pp. 549[16]-50,[7] paraphrased, tr. Jackson 1901, p. 96.

---

[a] Faber.
[b] Three high names.
[c] Plants of God.
[d] Faber.
[e] Give proof.

you say no, then it does not bind us, as you also at that time wanted to be free in all points which were not clearly expressed in the Word of God, as you set forth in your twenty-fourth thesis where you write that "every Christian is free of the works which God has not commanded."[43] You say yourself, "Not commanded." Therefore we beseech you for God's sake, let us remain by your own words. Give an answer.

Zwingli: It does not help, concerning things which should be forbidden, to say:[a] "Do not add anything to my word." But, as to what is supposed to be sin, one must point out a prohibitory law.[44]

Balthasar: What are you saying, my Zwingli? Why are you leading astray the whole world with such false teaching? If this, your teaching, were true, then it would be no sin to throw father and mother by their hair down the stairs, since you have no prohibiting law about that. You say, "I have one, however: 'You should honor father and mother.' " Answer: That is an affirmative and not a prohibitive law. Note what kind of misery you make of the Ten Commandments with this teaching, if with the prohibition "You shall not commit adultery," chastity were not also enjoined, and if with the prohibition "You shall not steal," acts of mercy and almsgiving were not commanded. On the other hand, the prohibitions are also included in the commandments. You write in your *Articles* book: "One should not believe in purgatory"[b] and you prove it on the basis of Mark 16:16, "Whoever believes and is baptized will be saved; whoever does not believe is condemned."[45] Here you cry overly loud and rightly: "The Scriptures know no purgatory, only hell and heaven."[46] Hey, my Zwingli. Would we not also like to have from you a prohibitory law not to believe in purgatory? Either by virtue of your

---

[43] Z 1, p. 461,[4-5] tr. Cochrane 1966, p. 39.
[44] Z 4, p. 221,[25-27] tr. Harder 1985, p. 366.
[45] Zwingli cites Mark 16:16 in a discussion on purgatory in Z 2, p. 436,[17ff.] tr. Furcha 1984, pp. 353-54. The sentence rendered by Hubmaier is not given in Zwingli, though the idea is there.
[46] This citation is from Zwingli's more lengthy fifty-seventh article on purgatory, Z 2, p. 414,[18] tr. Furcha 1984, p. 335.

---

[a] A false teaching of old and new papists.
[b] Purgatory.

teaching you must show us a forbidding word, or else you must again build up purgatory, introduce a new papacy, and remain by the speech of the vicar. Otherwise, your abovementioned teaching will be false. As in fact it is, as God is my witness.

Zwingli:[a] I have a clear word that circumcision refers to baptism.[47]

Balthasar: Where? /180/

Zwingli: Colossians 2:11ff.[48]

Balthasar: Oh, no. When Paul writes there on circumcision which is done without hand, and of baptism in which we are resurrected by faith, it refers to the inward baptism and not to the outward water baptism, as you say. I will let every Christian reader judge that for themselves after reading the text.

Zwingli:[b] Look to all directions, so that no one makes the gospel divisive.[49]

Balthasar: Aye, why do you have such vain concerns? It has already long before happened that five in a house will be divisive, Luke 12:52. But the holy gospel is not guilty of that, but our own pride, selfishness, and godless living.

Zwingli:[c] In baptism (let everyone forgive me), I cannot find anything other than that all teachers have erred, from the time of the apostles until this day.[50]

Balthasar: From this speech I note well that forever and always from apostolic times until today everyone has erred in the matter of baptism, around fourteen hundred years. What is left now of your pulpit outcry: "Children were baptized a thousand years ago.[d] God has not let the world err so long."

---

[47] Z 4, p. 212[8-10], paraphrased, tr. Harder 1985, loc. cit.
[48] The passages which Zwingli in this passage discusses in relating circumcision to baptism are Titus 1:14 and Gen. 17:23-27; 21:4. He only later turns to Colossians in a lengthy passage, Z 4, p. 327[21]-330.[5] But see also his earlier treatise, *Wer Ursache Gebe zu Aufruhr*, Z 3, p. 410,[11-19] tr. Harder 1985, p. 319.
[49] Z 4, p. 212,[23-24] tr. Harder 1985, p. 367.
[50] Z 4, p. 216,[14-16] tr. Bromiley 1953, p. 130.

---

[a] An untruth.
[b] The Gospel Divisive.
[c] Zwingli errs more than them all.
[d] Old practice.

Truly, Zwingle, if you are not a new papist, you speak like an old papist. Since then all the teachers have erred much in baptism, and yet have not been called heretical, as you call us. We beseech you in a most friendly and urgent fashion, that you let go of your anger and say with Gamaliel:[a] "If the matter is from God, then I may not suppress it. If it is from people, then it will itself fall to the ground," Acts 5:38f. Remember also that not long ago you were of this opinion with us, in the open pulpit and in print. You cannot deny it. At that time you spoke out of the Spirit of God against the vicar in your *Articles* book, as you boast. Now you are not speaking out of God, for God is not double-tongued.[b] Either you have a deception against Faber, or you are using one against us simple people. Look that you do justice to the matter. For with the innocent blood of Abel the incarcerated, imprisoned, hunted, and martyred blood of the innocent will cry out over you into heaven,[c] Gen. 4:10.

The Second Part

Zwingli: Christ left us two ceremonies, baptism and the Lord's Supper. With baptism we are dedicated[51] to God.[52] /181/

Balthasar: That is obscurely said. Who dedicates us to God? Godmothers or godfathers?[d] Who has given them this power? Show it in Scriptures. Is not having godparents just as much an additional and human trifle as renouncing the devil, mud, spit, oil, salt, fat, holy oil, baptismal shirt, and the like? Therefore they should properly all be rooted out together. Yea, how can one dedicate to God a child knows neither good nor evil, has no reason, says neither yes nor no, and of whom it is not known whether it will be a Christian or a heathen. Yes, you say, the child is born of Christian father and mother;

---

[51] *Verzaichnen*: to hand over by signature.
[52] Z 4, p. 217,[6.14-20] abridged, tr. Bromiley 1953, p. 131.

---

[a] Gamaliel.
[b] Faber.
[c] Abel.
[d] To have godmothers and godfathers is an addition.

therefore, it may well be, etc. Answer: "What is born of the flesh is flesh," John 3:6. To be or become a Christian does not come from the blood, nor from the will of the flesh or from the will of the man, but from God, who by his preached Word makes us to be reborn inwardly in faith, John 1:13; 1 Pet. 1:3. After which a person lets himself also be dedicated outwardly before the church and confesses that he is inwardly at peace with God through the death and resurrection of Christ Jesus, according to whose Word and rule he henceforth also wants to believe and live, as far as God the Father and the Son and the Holy Spirit give him grace and power. That is clear speech. However, we know well why you speak so obscurely.* You fear that the truth will come into the light, but to no avail. The day of the Lord will reveal all things.

Zwingli: Whoever is dedicated with baptism wants to hear what God says to him, learn his ordinances, and live according to them.[53]

Balthasar: Does such a child who is one hour old have such a will? You must confess: No. Why do you baptize it then? You say: The will only comes seven years later. Well said. So should one also put off baptism, until the time that the will is now here—on the authority of your own speech. Yes, the one who is baptized should know and believe beforehand the will and ordinance of Christ, Matt. 28:19-20 and Mark 16:15-16, and promise in water baptism to keep the same afterward.

Zwingli: Christ has changed circumcision and the Easter lamb into different, gracious symbols.[54]

Balthasar: Prove that with Scripture. We know that Christ has newly instituted baptism and the Lord's Supper and abolished the ceremonies, figures, and /182/ shadows of the Old Testament with his coming, as the epistles to the Colossians and the Hebrews clearly prove, Col. 2:16ff.; Heb. 8:13.

Zwingli: Baptism in Scripture is taken in four ways. First, for the dipping in water. Second, for the inward illumination.

---

[53] Z 4, p. 218,[9-10] tr. Bromiley 1953, loc. cit.
[54] Z 4, p. 219,[9-12] abridged, tr. Bromiley 1953, p. 132.

---

* Heraclitus, the obscure.

Third, for the outward teaching and for the dipping in outward water. Finally, for the outward baptism and internal faith.[55]

Balthasar:[a] What dark and obscure division that is, I will let every Christian reader decide. In the first place, for the dipping in water, in the third for dipping in the outward water, in the last for outward baptism. Is that one, two, or is it three? Item: Why don't you set the second, that is, the internal illumination before the first, namely before the dipping in water? Still you know also how the bread on the table of the Lord is death without prior faith in the heart. Thus the outward water baptism must also be nothing at all where the internal baptism of the Spirit has not preceded it. But it has to be done that way, so that the error does not come to light. Nevertheless, in summary:[b] Baptism is sometimes taken for the internal baptism of the Spirit, John 3:5-6, sometimes for the outward water baptism, Matt. 28:19. In the third place, sometimes it is taken for the subsequent suffering, when Christ says, "I must let myself be baptized beforehand with a baptism, and I am anxious until it has been completed," Luke 12:50. Whoever wants to point out another baptism to me with the whole Scripture, for I do not want to suffer patchwork, I will give faith to such Scripture.

Zwingli:[c] The outward baptism of John, Christ, and the disciples is always only one baptism.[56]

Balthasar: You say what you can never prove. It is certainly one kind of water, but not one baptism. For through the baptism of John the baptized testified themselves to be sinners and confessed their sins, Matt. 3:11. By the baptism of Christ the baptized testify to the forgiveness of their sins, which remission had already taken place in faith, before one

---

[55] Z 4, p. 219[26]-20,[3] abridged, tr. Bromiley 1953, loc. cit.
[56] Z 4, p. 220,[33-34] tr. Bromiley 1953, p. 133. The question of the baptism of John and whether it is the same baptism as that of Christ becomes one of the fundamental points in the disagreements between Hubmaier and Zwingli. For a theological study of the issues at stake, see Steinmetz 1979, Yoder 1968, pp. 33f.

---

[a] You fear the light.
[b] Baptizing.
[c] An unchristian untruth.

has come to water baptism, Acts 2:38; 8:12; 16:14-15; 31-33.
Do you say here, as you write to the king of France:[a] "I
understand, *quantum ad tinctionem adtinet quod perpetuo
inculcamus,*" [What is touched by liquid is what we
inculcate].[57] Answer: That is a pretty speech. Thus spoken
there is no difference between the Rhine and the Danube.

Zwingli: However, that "baptism" is taken for "teaching"
is found in John 3:22.[b] There it states how Christ baptizes.
Now it states likewise in John /183/ 4:2 how Jesus did not
baptize. So it cannot be denied that in John 3:22 baptism is
taken for teaching.[58]

Balthasar: My Zwingli, if I wanted to be a splitter of
hairs, I could prove with your words that Christ also did not
teach. For baptism is taken for teaching, as you say, John 3:22.
It states in John 4:2 that Christ did not baptize. So also he did
not teach, or here baptism must not be taken for teaching, as
you interpret it. However, what the right simple meaning of
this Scripture is, is pointed out in my book on baptism.[59]
Likewise, the text of Matthew 21:25, where Christ asked concerning water baptism, whether John practiced the same on
the authority of God or of people. We know well that water is
earthly. But baptism, as it happens, is heavenly, for John was
indeed sent by God to baptize, John 1:24ff.

Concerning Acts 19:1ff., I appeal to the German translation published at Zürch with your praise, which translation
you used in the dialogue before the vicar, with exalted
words.[c] You have also admonished the people in the public
pulpit to buy such books. Without doubt you did not pass off
poison for an antidote. Here I want every Christian reader to
judge according to the text read, Acts 19:1ff., whether or not
two kinds of baptism, that of John and of Christ, are described
here. Neither the previous nor the following word forces us to

---

[57] Z 3, p. 766,[8-9] tr. ZL 3, p. 189.
[58] Z 4, p. 221,[19-23] abridged, tr. Bromiley 1953, pp. 133-34.
[59] See above, "Christian Baptism," pp. 102.

---

[a] A subtle gloss.
[b] An intrigue.
[c] Faber.

take baptizing for teaching. Therefore such glosses are spun more out of your human brain than out of the Word of God.

Zwingli: The opponents of baptism have wanted sometimes to deny that a person can be saved without water baptism.[60]

Balthasar:[a] You do us an injustice. We know well that salvation is bound neither to baptism nor to works of mercy. Being unbaptized does not condemn us, nor do evil works, but only unfaith. However, whoever is believing lets himself be baptized and bring forth good fruits, Mark 16:16. Accordingly, if one wants to be a Christian and if he has a baptizer and water at hand, then he lets himself be baptized by virtue of the institution of Christ. If he does not do it, however, then he is not condemned because of his non-baptism, but because of his unfaith, from which his disobedience proceeds, Matt. 7:26. If he had been a true believer, then he would have taken the sign of Christ-believing onto himself, as Christ had instituted it with excellent words and the apostles had practiced it, Matt. 28:18-20; Acts 2:38-39; 8:35-38; 10:47-48; 11:16; 16:14-15; 30-31; 18:8; 22:16). /184/

Zwingli: The disciples gave water baptism without teaching and without the Spirit, John 3:22.[61]

Balthasar:[b] Too much said. You cannot show me one person in all of Scripture who has been water-baptized without prior teaching. Or show us one with clear Scripture, then we are already overcome.

Zwingli: However, that one was baptized in water before one believed one finds in John 6:66. For without doubt, of these disciples who turned away from Christ none was unbaptized.[c] Nevertheless, Christ pointed out their unbelief.[62]

Balthasar: Oh, the perfidious treachery: do you not fear God? Or do you think he does not know it, or we do not understand it? What do you have before you? I ask you also

---

[60] Z 4, p. 222,[13-16] tr. Bromiley 1953, p. 134.
[61] Z 4, p. 222,[23-24] tr. Bromiley 1953, p. 135.
[62] Z 4, p. 222,[28-32] paraphrased, tr. Bromiley 1953, loc. cit.

---

[a] An untruth.
[b] Say as much as you want.
[c] An intrigue.

something, whether Peter, John, Andrew, etc. on Holy Thursday or Maundy Thursday believed the Supper or not? If you say yes, as you must, then Christ did point to their unfaith on Easter day, Mark 16:14. O Zwingle, Zwingle, I note well where the shoe pinches you. I won't press the point any further.

Zwingli:[a] Baptism has also been accepted by those who have not believed beforehand. Like Simon Magus, Acts 8:13, where it states: "Simon also believed." There faith must be taken for "he listened" or for "he counted himself among the believers." Augustine somewhere also understands it the same way.[63]

Balthasar:[b] Whoever understands "faith" here differently than that he believed destroys the Scripture and violates it against their own understanding, whether it be Zwingli or Augustine, for it does not only state there that he believed, but that he also practiced the works of faith. He joined Philip, after that he sinned, and wanted to buy the Holy Spirit for money. Such happens to us all. However, when Peter admonished him, he confessed and desired that one pray for him so that his sins would be forgiven. That is again a deed of a believing person. If one were to introduce foreign glosses over clear words the entire Bible would be overturned and confused and nothing upright or constant would remain therein. O God, protect us from such glossers! The old pope has until now used the same glosses for such words as head, church, keys, rock, spiritual, etc., whereby he has overturned all things. /185/

Zwingli: Even nowadays we have some who let themselves be baptized and yet do not believe.[64]

Balthasar: We are not saying here how it is. Be it lamented to God, not all things go right, but we are saying how it should be according to the order of Christ.[c] *Quid iuris et legis non quid facti* [What is right and lawful, not what

---

[63] Z 4, p. 223,[7-12] tr. Bromiley 1953, loc. cit.

[64] Z 4, p. 223,[15-17] paraphrased, tr. Bromiley 1953, loc. cit.

---

[a] A misrepresentation of Scripture.

[b] Accusation of a lie.

[c] What is right, what is done.

is done]. Namely, that teaching and faith should precede water baptism. Woe to them who practice hypocrisy in this matter.

Zwingli: The baptism of the Spirit is given without the baptism of water.ᵃ Nicodemus, Joseph, and Gamaliel were believers, but secretly, and without doubt were never baptized.[65]

Balthasar: Secretly believing is something, but not enough. For, although one believes with the heart unto righteousness, one must confess with the mouth unto salvation, Rom. 10:10. Nicodemus afterward had to break out in words and works of faith, John 7:50f; 19:39; Joseph, in Matt. 27:59f.; Gamaliel, in Acts 5:34ff. I remember here several of those called Priscillians and Carpocratians.ᵇ Gerson and Eusebius write of them.[66] They thought it was enough to believe with the heart and thought it was unnecessary to confess such with the mouth and by fruits. But their opinion is against the Scripture, Rom. 10:10; Matt. 10:32: "Whoever confesses me before people, etc."

Zwingli: The thief on the crossᶜ believed and was on the same day with Christ in Paradise, and wholly not baptized with any outward baptism,[67] Luke 23:43.

Balthasar: With this counterargument you want to throw down wholly the water baptism of Christ. But I say to you: The person who has the excuse of the thief on the cross is wholly at peace with God although he has never had any water baptism. But wherever this excuse is lacking, there let each look to himself. For as the Word of Christ in its power says: "Whoever does not believe is condemned," so remains the other in the same authority in parallel to that: "Whoever

---

[65] Z 4, p. 224,¹⁻⁴ tr. Bromiley 1953, p. 136.
[66] The Carpocratians were a Gnostic sect which survived until the 4th century. See Eusebius, *Ecclesiastical History*, IV:7:9, tr. Schaff 1979, v. I, p. 179. Priscillianism, a sect characterized by a form of Manichean dualism, existed from the fourth to the mid-sixth century (after the time of Eusebius). See Sulpitius Severus, *Dialogus* XI, tr. Schaff 1979, v. XI, p. 50.
[67] Z 4, p. 224,¹⁴⁻¹⁷ tr. Bromiley 1953, loc. cit.

ᵃ Nicodemus, Joseph, Gamaliel.
ᵇ Priscillians. Carpocratians. Gerson. Eusebius.
ᶜ Thief.

believes and is baptized is saved," Mark 16:16. Here one must always leave faith and baptism together. Look at Theophilus;[68] on that text you will find something.[a]

Zwingli: This is now a hint, or a suggestion, not a foundation stone on which we build infant baptism.[69] /186/

Balthasar: You mock, Zwingle, and babble. May God be merciful. The truth does not need such hints, suggestions, and euphemisms at all. Paul has warned us against hints and colored words, Col. 2:8. Why did you not begin with the foundation stone? God forgive us all our vain words.

Zwingli: Many have said that signs are given for the strengthening of the faith that has been taught or promised us.[70]

Balthasar: Say that to those who speak thus, but we must have done everything.[71]

Zwingli: Many years ago this error misled me too so that I thought it would be better if one baptized children only when they had come to a good age.[72]

Balthasar: Yes, you have held thus, written, and preached in the open pulpit; several hundred people have heard that from your own mouth. But now all those who say that of you must be liars. Yes, you speak outrageously when you say that such an opinion has never your lifelong entered your heart, and something else on which I will now remain silent. I still ask you one more thing: How many years ago was this your opinion? Please remember that you had Johann Faber, vicar at Constance,[b] under your hand, in 1523 when you boasted that you "had preached the gospel purely, clearly, and brightly for five years."[73] And after that in the same year, about Philip's and James' day,[74] I conferred with you personally on the

---

[68] Theophilus, bishop of Antioch in the second century, was an early apologist.
[69] Z 4, p. 226,[27-28] tr. Bromiley 1953, p. 138.
[70] Z 4, p. 226,[31-32] tr. Bromiley 1953, *loc. cit.*
[71] I.e., we are the scapegoats for everything.
[72] Z 4, p. 228,[24-26] tr. Bromiley 1953, p. 139.
[73] Z 1, p. 487,[25-26] tr. Jackson 1901, p. 48.
[74] May 1, 1523.

---

[a] Theophilus.
[b] Faber.

Zurich Graben about the Scriptures concerning baptism.[75] There you said to me, rightly, that one should not baptize children before they have been instructed in the faith. That is the reason why in prior times they were also called catechumens.[a] But in your *Articles* book you intended also to state that, as you then did it in the eighteenth article on confirmation.[76] Whoever would read that, will clearly find your judgment. Sebastian Ruckensperger from St. Gall, at that time prior at Sion in Klingau, was also there. You also publicly confessed the same thing in another book on the riotous spirits, published in 1525, before you even came to the second page, that those who baptize infants have "no clear word" in Scripture, /187/ that one is commanded to baptize them.[77] Evaluate here, my Zwingli, how your word, writing, and preaching fits together. But may God illumine you and us all so that you abstain from your violent treatment of many righteous folk.

Zwingli: Here the opponents of baptism say that baptism is a sign that no one should take unless he knows that he can live without sin.[b] This makes God deceitful and reintroduces again the hypocrisy of justification by the law.[78]

Balthasar: Ah, my Zwingli, tell it to those who do it. Do not blame the innocent together with the guilty. That is Christian; therefore, I beseech you for God's sake.

Zwingli: I will prove that we are all sinners.[79]

Balthasar: Be still. There does not need to be any proof. We know that from the first epistle of John 1:8 and 5:16ff., also from Psalms 14:3; 51:7; 16:7.

Zwingli: Still, the opponents of baptism maintain simply that they can and do live without sin.[80]

---

[75] The present-day name of the street in Zurich where the meeting took place is the Hirschengraben.

[76] Z 2, p. 122[19]-125,[25] tr. Furcha 1984, pp. 100-02.

[77] Z 3, p. 409,[16-19] tr. Harder 1985, p. 319. Cf. note 6, above.

[78] Z 4, p. 229,[10-14] tr. Bromiley 1953, p. 139.

[79] Zwingli sets out to do this, that is, to prove that we are all sinners, though he does not say so in exactly these words. Cf. Z 4, p. 229,[13-14] tr. Bromiley 1953, loc. cit.

[80] Z 4, p. 230,[19-23] abridged, tr. Bromiley 1953, p. 140.

---

[a] Catechumens.

[b] An untruth.

Balthasar: You speak again where it would be better to be silent. Do not accuse Peter, John, and Andrew of having sold Christ as Judas Iscariot did.[a]

Zwingli: Baptism is such a sign of commitment that he who accepts it[b] shows that he wants to better his life and follow Christ.[81]

Balthasar: *Deo gratias* [Thanks be to God]. The truth must once come to light.[c] If baptism is truly a sign of commitment, then one must have expressed the commitment before the sign is attached to him.[d] Likewise, before someone expresses the commitment one should teach him beforehand with words or in Scripture. Or it would be a blind commitment, which would mean nothing. He must also agree to it with express words or one does not attach the sign to him. Now tell us something without any addition, my Zwinngle: Where, when, and how does the cradle baby express such commitment? You say the father and the mother, the godmothers or godfathers do that for the child. Did you not just say that baptism is a sign of commitment by which the one who takes it shows that he wants to improve his life and follow Christ? Pay attention. You said: the one who takes it, *he*, not another on his behalf. For it is not a secret to you that it would be an addition not grounded in the Word of God. Look, my Zwingle, how your self-confessed truth has taken away the ground from children's baptism.[e] Judge here for yourself, O Christian reader, consider it and you will see how the commitment or promise has remained with us since the first Christian water baptism, which one mumbled to the child in Latin,[f] /188/ and even though one now does it in German—they understand the German as well as the Latin, for one is like the other to them—and the water priest asks, *Credis in deum patrem omnipotentem, creatorem celi et terre* [Do you believe

---

[81] Z 4, p. 231,[24-26] tr. Bromiley 1953, p. 141.

---

[a] An untruth.
[b] Here the truth triumphs.
[c] Yes, yes.
[d] Baptism is a sign of commitment.
[e] Note: him, who, he.
[f] Baptism question.

in God the Father, omnipotent, Creator of heaven and earth?"].ᵃ "Say, 'I believe.' " Is it now grounded in the Word of God that the godmothers or godfathers should answer: "I believe?" If so, then prove it with clear Scripture. Item: Were it so, then why does the priest not say to the godmothers and godfathers: "You godparents say, 'We believe' "? But the truth is not hidden; it is as follows: What they answer is what the children themselves should do and say, "I believe in God the father, etc., and in Jesus Christ, who has forgiven me all my sins through his death, burial, and resurrection, Rom. 6:4. Therefore I commit myself, vow, and promiseᵇ that I will improve my life, renouncing the devil and his demons, and henceforth will follow Christ as much as God the Father, and the Son, and the Holy Spirit gives grace and power," Matt. 28:19f. That is the true baptismal vow, above which none can be higher; and if we had followed it until now and had practiced it in the churches, then the vows and commitments of all monks, priests, and nuns would have been unnecessary. Since, however, the true Christian baptismal commitment has been pushed out of the center point, Satan has insinuated himself with his cloister commitments.ᶜ I am certain Zwingli, in the Word, that you will never be able to throw down this cornerstone for eternity. Whoever wills, can consider here the word of Peter, 1 Pet. 3:21f. and Eusebius, how one questioned children in prior times, *Ecclesiastical History*, Book Ten, Chapter Fourteen.ᵈ⁸²

Zwingli: Water baptism is an initiatory sign, ceremony, or *Teleta*ᵉ (in Greek), just as when young people are pushed into the orders.ᶠ One has the cowls measured out for them, yet they have still not learned the law and the statutes, but they only learn them in the cowls.⁸³

---

⁸² See below, text 17, p. 253.
⁸³ Z 4, p. 231,²⁷⁻³⁰ tr. Bromiley 1953, loc. cit.

ᵃ Do you believe in God?
ᵇ Baptismal vow.
ᶜ Cloister commitment.
ᵈ Eusebius.
ᵉ *Teleta.*
ᶠ Baptism has become a cowl.

Balthasar: Just as such a child pushed (yes, well said: pushed) into the cloister is a monk or a nun, so is infant baptism baptism, and the little child an external Christian without knowledge of the law and without faith. A good example; they rhyme well.[84]

The Third Part

Zwingli: With the word, Matt. 28:19, where Christ says, "Go, teach all people, baptizing them in the name, etc., teaching them to observe all things I have commanded you,"[a] the opponents of baptism mislead themselves and /189/ others badly. For they do not want to see that just after that stands, "teaching them to observe all things that I have commanded you."[85]

Balthasar: Well then, Zwingle, let us make a pact with one another. I will allow you the teaching after water baptism and you allow me the teaching before water baptism. If you do that then we are already agreed. But that preceding teaching will empty out your water baptism. If you will not grant me that, it is nevertheless permitted by Christ. His Word, Matt. 28:19-20 and Mark 16:15-16, stands firm like Greek marble. However, that teaching is commanded before and after water baptism by Christ in Matthew 28:19-20 is the reason why it is not enough to drown the Pharaoh in the Red Sea,[b] Exod. 14:23ff. There are still the Amalekites, Amorites, Jebusites, and other enemies at hand whom one must also resist and destroy with teaching, after water baptism.

Zwingli: You have well "teaching all peoples and baptizing them," Matt. 28:19f. You do not have what one should teach. But we have clearly,[c] "teaching them to observe all things I have commanded you" and that stands after baptism.[86]

---

[84] I.e., they go well together
[85] Z 4, p. 231[33]-232,[5-7] tr. Bromiley, loc. cit.
[86] Z 4, p. 232,[17-19] tr. Bromiley 1953, loc. cit.

---

[a] See the preceding.
[b] Pharaoh.
[c] Is an escape.

Balthasar: You neglect the fact that Christ commands teaching before baptism and does not say what they should teach to all peoples. Look how careful you are. Would not a subtle person answer you here: Zwingle, you have well "teaching them to observe all things I have commanded you," yes, after baptism. However, you do not have what those "all things" are. But if you have, so do we, for to you and to us the Scripture has been equally given for teaching, comfort, and guidance, Rom. 15:4; 2 Tim. 3:15ff.; John 20:21ff. See, the whole world would be astonished at such a strong argument. But you wanted also to make a little book.

Zwingli: The word "teaching," in Greek *Matheteusate*, means just as well making disciples as teaching,[87] Matt. 28:19.

Balthasar: Making disciples does not take place without teaching. Young students know that well.

Zwingli: This is the right natural sense:[a] "going forth, making all peoples into my disciples" (only now follows the beginning as to how one should make them disciples), "baptizing them in the name of the Father, etc." (only now follows the teaching), "teaching them to hold all things I have given you."[88]

Balthasar: You do violence and are unjust to the Scriptures if the beginning takes place in making disciples, as you call it. One makes disciples only with teaching. In the second place, those who accept the teaching believe and want henceforth to be disciples of Christ. These one should baptize, and with water baptism they obligate themselves henceforth to improve their lives and to follow Christ /190/, as you have above confessed yourself. Third, since, however, there is a gap in faith and [it] remains until death, then it is necessary also after baptism always to teach so that faith increases and grows like a mustard seed. That is the natural true sense, understanding, and order of this Scripture, no matter how much you try to force it. Therefore I will let every Christian assembly judge for itself.

---

[87] Z 4, p. 232,[23-25] tr. Bromiley, pp. 141-42.
[88] Z 4, p. 232,[26-30] tr. Bromiley 1953, p. 142.

---

[a] A false teaching.

Zwingli: Baptism is not instituted[a] in Matthew 28:18ff.[89]

Balthasar: Where then is the general water baptism of all believers, be they Jews or heathen, a law? Aye, show us in the Scripture.[90] If you will gladly, then show us also Theophylact.[b91]

Zwingli: There Christ says, "Going forth, teaching all peoples, baptizing them in the name, etc.," Matt. 28:19. Since the Greek has no "and" so that they would say, "teaching and baptizing," but "teaching, baptizing them."[c] In this order we clearly note that Christ here has not accentuated the sequence of the words, for this Word, "baptizing them," is not bound into a clause, but hangs free.[92]

Balthasar: Ah, what a childish counterargument. I learned the same arguments in Latin school. I also know from logic what are explicit and implicit copulatives.[d] If you want to hear this mandate still more explicitly, you will find it in Mark 16:15: "Whoever believes and is baptized." Also Acts 2:38: "Repent and be baptized." Cornelius with his household believed and was baptized, Acts 10:47f.; 11:5ff.[93] I think that you have the little word "and" here explicitly so that the sequence is testified as teaching, believing, and after that baptizing. Baptism does not hang free, as you force the Scripture.

Zwingli: Baptizing[e] in the name of the Father, Son, and Holy Spirit is nothing other than handing over, giving, and

----

[89] Z 4, p. 233,[19-20] tr. Bromiley 1953, loc. cit.

[90] In this response Hubmaier does not speak to the issue about which Zwingli is writing. In his preceding comment Zwingli was addressing the issue of an overly literal interpretation of Scripture, especially in regard to Matthew 28:18ff. In speaking only to the issue of whether baptism is instituted in Matthew 28:18ff., Hubmaier fails to respond to the hermeneutical question.

[91] See below, text 17, p. 253.

[92] That is, "baptizing" is a participle and "hangs free." Z 4, p. 234[29]-235,[1] tr. Bromiley 1953, p. 143.

[93] Acts 11 continues the report of Peter concerning Cornelius, but does not, as such, refer to Cornelius's water baptism, but to the baptism of the Holy Spirit.

----

[a] Institution of baptism.
[b] Theophylactus.
[c] And.
[d] Copulative.
[e] Baptism.

leading to God the Father, Son, and Holy Spirit, the true God, those who previously had erred like wayward sheep who have no shepherd, that is, God.[94]

Balthasar: Where have the little children erred beforehand who know neither good nor evil? But here you give to all the world to recognize that you still do not know what baptism is in or [that it is] in the authority of God the Father, Son, etc. We want to set "authority" here for "name" so that you do not eternally delay us with your "in the name" and "for the name of." For water baptism is handing over, leading, and giving oneself to God so that no theologian, whom you here and there scold, /191/ may give any more to baptism than you. But I must show you once more what it is. (Forgive me that I so oft and clearly do it; there is a reason.) Baptism in water is in, for, over, or into the power of God, as the person is led through the law into the knowledge of his sins.[*] After that he learns from the gospel and believes unto the forgiveness of sins through the merciful promise of Christ. In the third place he promises in response to Christ that he henceforth wants to believe and live according to his salutary teaching as much as God the Father, and Son, and Holy Spirit gives him grace and power. Or such a baptismal vow would only be a human conjecture and presumption.

Zwingli: The apostles baptized into the name of Jesus Christ, Acts 2:38. For this reason we are also called Christians.[95]

Balthasar: It is one thing in itself to baptize in or into the name of the Father and Son and Holy Spirit, as the power of God the Father and our Lord Jesus Christ is one power. What do we need then of the sophistic word battles? In addition the believers were first called Christians at Antioch, Acts 1.[96]

Zwingli: Since no person on earth achieves perfection of faith, you must admit that if the person is beginning to be taught, then one should baptize him in water.[97]

---

[94] Z 4, p. 235²⁹-236,² tr. Bromiley 1953, p. 144.
[95] Z 4, p. 237,¹²⁻¹³ tr. Bromiley 1953, p. 145.
[96] The reference should be Acts 11:26.
[97] Z 4, p. 238,¹⁻⁶ paraphrased; tr. Bromiley 1953, loc. cit.

---

[*] Baptism in water.

Balthasar: Yes, we are content with this speech. Still "to be taught incipiently" means that the person recognizes his sin through the law and believes to the remission of the same through Christ Jesus. If you understand it otherwise, then you are purposely speaking obscurely so that you will not be understood.

Zwingli: The opponents of baptism cry out over the Word, Matt. 3:1, 6: "Do you not see that John first preached and after that baptized?" Certainly we say it; we do not only see it. We do it also thus, for no one brings his child to baptism unless he is taught beforehand.[98]

Balthasar: If you were blind, you would have no sin, John 9:41. But because you say that you see, therefore your sin will remain. For Matthew 3 says nothing about bringing a child. It says, "John preaches and whoever accepts his word, these he baptizes." Note: *these*, not their children.

Zwingli: We confess firmly that John first taught and afterward baptized.[a] No one can, however, deny that after that those who were taught also let their untaught children be baptized.[99] /192/

Balthasar:[b] O my Zwingle. How dare you say that John baptized young untaught children, this against the bright and clear text, Matt. 3:6, which clearly points out that those who were baptized by John confessed their sins? Ah, God, where does the truth force you? You would gladly like to flee, but do not know the way out. O reader, consider here the text itself and judge, for it is a notable error before which you know to protect yourself.

Zwingli: Matthew 3:5 says: "And all the Judean countryside and the territory around Jordan and Jerusalem went to him and were baptized by him in the Jordan." Here one would like to say, "If thus the whole multitude went out to him, then it is easy to presume that children also went out."[100]

---

[98] Z 4, p. 238,[22-24] tr. Bromiley 1953, loc. cit.
[99] Z 4, p. 238,[28-31] tr. Bromiley 1953, loc. cit.
[100] Z 4, p. 239,[2-7] tr. Bromiley 1953, pp. 146-47.

---

[a] A public untruth.
[b] John did not baptize children. O blindness.

Balthasar: Would one also not like to say, "It is also easy to see that Annas, Caiaphas, Pilate, and Herod also went out and let themselves be baptized." It is not, however, enough to think or to presume. Only *knowing* suffices in the Scripture of God.

Zwingli: Here I would like to say, although children were there and were baptized, which we do not claim clearly to bring forth, it would still be no less correct:ª they confessed their sin.[101]

Balthasar: You now say that you do not claim clearly to have brought forth that children were there and were baptized, and yet you said above that no one can deny John baptized our children.ᵇ

Zwingli: The opponents of baptism say that one should baptize no one unless he has the Holy Spirit. Who can now tell us how God dwells in children?[102]

Balthasar: We say that whoever is instructed in the Word of God, Matt. 16:16, so that he confesses publicly that he believes that Jesus Christ is the Son of the living God him one should baptize, for this confession is necessary before baptism, Acts 8:37. But how God dwells in young children, whether they have the Holy Spirit or whether they belong to God, does not belong to us to ask. It is a frivolous and arbitrary serpent question.ᶜ It is not fitting that we should pass judgment, since God knows whom he has chosen from all eternity, for we have no clear Scripture on that. For everything that is written is written for our insruction and not for the children, until the old Adam and the image of God in them also begins to function, 2 Tim. 2:23; Titus 3:9ff.; Rom. 15:4. But /193/ then some exclaim,ᵈ "Children are of God, children are of God; why do you not then want to baptize them?" These people intervene in God's secret judgment. For to be children of God is not a matter of blood or of the will of the flesh or of the will of

---

[101] Z 4, p. 239,[14-17] tr. Bromiley 1953, p. 147.
[102] Z 4, p. 242,[9-16] abridged; tr. Bromiley 1953, p. 149.

ª Is, is. No, no.
ᵇ O inconsistency.
ᶜ Serpent question.
ᵈ To be children of God.

man, but God has given it to all those to become his children who believe in his name, John 1:12f.; 6:29. Believing is a work of God and not of a human being. This is why we are not born as children of God from our fathers and mothers, but rather are children of wrath, Eph. 2:3; Ps. 51:7; Job 3:3; Jer. 20:14. Now whether God saves little children or how he deals with them, I leave to him. I commend them into his hands. I have no Scripture about it and therefore I do not want to know, as I have written more fully in my baptism booklet.[103] It follows that the proper ground for baptizing someone with water is

The oral confession of faith before the church,

and not their being born of a Christian father and mother.* Flesh and blood will not reveal that to us, but the Father who is in heaven. The rebirth to which water baptism testifies is not from the earthly father, Matt. 16:17. Still you would like to say here [that] we are not speaking of the spiritual childhood in which salvation lies; we are speaking of the outward one. Thus the children of God are such that they should outwardly be counted among the people of God; therefore one should not hold back the outward sign. Answer: You can say what you want. So the speeches come to the point that the children of Christ-believers are of God, have the Holy Spirit, and are saved. Christ has called them to himself. And some even want to make them believers through infused faith, which has no basis in Scripture. To this they cry: One should not exclude the little children from the general salvation of Christians—"Who now wants to forbid water?"—according to the words of Peter, Acts 10:47. Thus you write in your book to the king of France. The Jews had an explicit command from God to circumcise their boys on the eighth day and if they circumcised one on the seventh day, they would have acted against God, Gen. 17:9ff. So we have also a clear mandate to baptize people, whether they be young or old. Yes, those who publicly testify their faith orally before the church. There you

---

[103] See above, text 11.

---

* On that stands the church.

say: "Yes, I confess that it is written that one should baptize believers. The children, however, are not excluded anywhere." Answer: As soon as Christ commanded baptizing believers in water, from that hour on all people were already excluded who were not yet instructed in faith.[a] Parable: As soon as God in the Old Testament commanded /194/ to circumcise boys, from that hour on the girls were already excluded. As soon as he designated and set the eighth day, from that hour on it was forbidden to circumcise on the fourth or seventh day, although God did not explicitly say that.

Zwingli: If it were thus to come to pass, then Christian children would be at a disadvantage compared to Jewish children, whom one registered among the people of God on the eighth day.[104]

Balthasar:[b] Zwingle, I have something to say to you. There was a rich man who had two debtors, both of which were indebted to him for one hundred pounds. Since they did not have it, he waited eight days for one and for the other eight years and even longer. I ask you: to which of these was he more gracious?

Zwingli: Without doubt, to the one for whom he waited eight years and longer.[105]

Balthasar: You have judged rightly. So judge also to whom God is the more gracious, Jewish or Christian children, then you will have answered yourself.

Zwingli: Jeremiah was sanctified in his mother's womb. John recognized our Savior in the womb of his mother—and the like.[106]

Balthasar: For that you have Scripture, but not for our children—although I would not refuse them salvation: I commend it into the hand of God, Rom. 11:33. May his will take

---

[104] This is not a verbatim quotation from Zwingli, but the ideas are found in his writings. Cf. Z 4, p. 317;[18-20] Z 4, p. 330;[5-6] Z 4, p. 773,[20] tr. ZL 3, p. 197.

[105] This is not a quotation from Zwingli. It is what he might say in response to the question put here in the dialogue, based on Luke 8:40-43.

[106] Z 4, p. 242,[17-19] tr. Bromiley 1953, loc. cit.

---

[a] Command, prohibition.
[b] Parable.

place with them and with us all. For deep are the riches of the wisdom and knowledge of God, quite inscrutable are his judgments and unsearchable his ways.

Zwingli: Now comes the strongest place which teaches us that water baptism is an initial sign by which we obligate our selves to God to live a new life and also accept water baptism along with common Christians as a testimony. So states Romans 6:4.[107]

Balthasar: It is precisely the strongest passage against you, which I will demonstrate with your words and Paul's. You confess yourself that baptism is a sign with which we obligate ourselves to God to live a new life. Note, you say: "We, We, We,"[a] not someone else on our behalf, and "We accept water baptism as a testimony." The crying child in the cradle knows nothing at all about signs, obligation, baptism, new life, nor testimony. Second, Paul describes the significance of outward baptism in that passage, namely, that it means, as the outwardly baptized person should inwardly have died with Christ to vices and be buried, that as Christ was resurrected from the dead by the glory of the Father, so also will the baptized person rise up from sin and walk in newness of life. Now whichever child knows this significance of water baptism and wants thereby to make public commitment and testimony by affirmation of faith and by requesting water baptism before the church, whereby it is incorporated into the church, this same child one should baptize. If, however, it neither can, /195/ nor will, nor request the same, then wait with it until it is drawn by God. Here one should read the text of Paul in the above-mentioned passage and one will see whether Paul had written to cradle babies. Of such request[b] for water baptism before the church flows the custom here which the water priests[c] still hold, that they question the little child in Latin: *Vis baptizari?* [Do you want to be baptized?]"[d] Say: "I want it." Oh, the great foolishness whereby a child one hour old is

---

[107] Z 4, p. 243,[6-9] tr. Bromiley 1953, p. 150.

---

[a] We, We, We.
[b] Requesting water baptism.
[c] Water priests.
[d] Do you want to be baptized?

asked in Latin and it should answer to that in German, just as if it had learned two languages in the mother's womb. Should not all Jews and heathen simply laugh at us in that we perform such play-acting?ª[108] Still some masters want to force us with rope, fire, and water to believe and obey their trickery.[b] But their forcing will bring them to shame before God and his angels.

Zwingli: It says in Matthew 28:19, "baptizing them into the name of the Father, etc." and not "in the name." "Into" means, when one uses it, that one comes from the outside into, such as when one says, "he goes into the house."[c] "In" means, when one uses it, that one is already inside, such as when one says, "he walks around in the house."[109]

Balthasar: Yes, Zwingli, so it is with "into" and "in." I have learned once in Alexander:[d] *in campo curro, bene dicis si sis in illo. Si sis exterius, in campum sit tibi cursus* [I am running in the field. If you are outside, the running should be into the field for you].[110] Since we, however, know here basically what water baptism in the name of the Father, Son, and Holy Spirit is, we do not want to fight word battles. The person who needs defense resorts to unusual weapons.

Zwingli: Whoever lets himself be baptized among you must say: You are without sin and thus live and dress as you say they should, all of which is a sect and a faction.[e] You must not force baptism as if it were a monastic vow.[111]

Balthasar: You are unfair and unjust to us in all that. We force no one. God loves a joyous giver, 2 Cor. 9:7. Each one should eat and drink what God gives, though moderately and

---

[108] The word used is *Larvenspil*, illusions, trickery, etc. The masks of the wandering illusionists and actors were *Larven*.
[109] Z 4, p. 243,²⁷⁻³² tr. Bromiley 1953, loc. cit.
[110] The source of this grammar lesson on the difference between *in* and *into* is the thirteenth-century grammarian Alexander of Villa Dei, not Alexander of Hales as noted by Bergsten HS, p. 195. Thanks to Dennis D. Martin for identifying the correct Alexander.
[111] Z 4, p. 245,²⁷⁻³⁰ abridged; tr. Bromiley 1953, p. 152.

ª Foolishness.
[b] Hangmen became theologians.
[c] In the name.
[d] Alexander.
[e] An untruth.

with thanksgiving, 1 Tim. 4:4. Each one should dress as he wants, though the clothing should not be offensive. God forgive you and us all.

Zwingli: A person can shape himself according to the form of Christ, even if he is never rebaptized.[112] /196/

Balthasar: You accuse us without ceasing of rebaptism, but have, however, never proven that the children's bath is a baptism.[*] Prove that first and then it will be legitimate for you to write it.

Zwingli:[b] I cannot understand the opponents of baptism in any other way than that they ascribe much to water baptism.[113]

Balthasar: We do not make anything of it at all, inasmuch as it is an institution of Christ through which a person is inducted into the outward Christian church, which every person who believes accepts when he has a baptizer and water at hand. So did Christ institute it, the apostles practice it, and the Christ-believers accept it. On this matter I always appeal to the Scriptures, which should judge.

Zwingli:[c] Here the opponents of baptism say that the baptisms of John and of Christ are not the same thing. Not only they do it, all theologians whom I have read speak thus.[114]

Balthasar: God be praised that we are not the only crazy stubborn heads, as you call us, but all theologians with us, except for you.

Zwingli:[d] If John had begun another baptism than Christ, then he would not have begun to prepare the way of the Lord.[115]

Balthasar: If John had practiced the teaching and water baptism of Christ, then he would not have been a forerunner of Christ, Matt. 3:11; Luke 3:16. For the forerunning consisted

[112] Z 4, p. 246,[5-9] tr. Bromiley 1953, loc. cit.
[113] Z 4, p. 252,[21-23] tr. Bromiley 1953, p. 156.
[114] Z 4, p. 258,[19-22] tr. Bromiley 1953, p. 161.
[115] Z 4, p. 259,[14-15] tr. Bromiley 1953, pp. 161-62.

[*] Children's bath.
[b] An untruth.
[c] Whether the baptism of John and of Christ are one baptism.
[d] A great error.

originally in the word by which one points out to a person his sin, Isa. 40:3ff. Therefore John says, John 1:23, "I am a voice of one crying in the wilderness: 'Prepare the way of the Lord.' " He would have had to spill water a long time before preparing the way of the Lord, if he had not preached beforehand. Recognition of sins and not the pouring of water leads to Christ who is the way, truth, and life, John 14:6; Matt. 9:12. Now, however, the sick and not the healthy need the doctor. John points to this doctor and says, "Now, then, I have led you into the recognition of sins and into hell. If you would then now rid yourself of the same, then behold the lamb of God who takes away the sin of the world, John 1:36. Run to him, beseech him, your sins will be forgiven and you will be led back out into heaven." Now you hear that the baptism of John[a] is nothing other than a public testimony before people in water that a person recognizes himself a sinner before God, Matt. 3:13-15.[b] On the other hand, the baptism of Christ is a public and outward confession or oath of faith, that is, that the person inwardly believes the forgiveness of his sins through Christ, for which reason he lets himself be enrolled and outwardly dedicated among Christians, and that he wants to live according to the Rule of Christ. Thus you yourself write to the king of France on pages 201, 204, and 205.[116] Here you must yourself /197/ confess that the outward water baptism of John signifies an internal cooling down of the conscience on account of the recognition of sin.[c] But the outward water baptism of Christ signifies an inward comfort which precedes the water in faith through the recognition of the forgiveness of sins. The meaning of the water baptism of John is that it cools, freezes, frightens, kills, and leads into hell. There one sees and recognizes nothing but sin. The water baptism of Christ in this sense means heating, quickening, comforting, making alive, leading again out of hell.[d] For

---

[116] As Hubmaier himself notes here, he collates several references from Zwingli's *Commentary*. Cf. Z 3, p. 761,[13-15] tr. ZL 3, p. 183; Z 3, p. 761,[23-24] paraphrased; tr. ZL 3, p. 184; Z 3, p. 761,[34-35] tr. ZL 3, p. 184.

---

[a] Baptism of John.
[b] Baptism of Christ.
[c] The difference between the baptism of John and of Christ.
[d] The meaning of the water baptism of Christ.

there one sees and recognizes nothing but the forgiveness of sins through the blood of Christ. Do you see that these two baptisms are so far from one another as cold and heat, fear and comfort, spirit and devil, hell and heaven, death and life? How can you then so unashamedly make one baptism out of these? Yes, you say, I understand it *essentialiter* [essentially].[a] Understand it, if you will please, also *accidentaliter* [accidentally] for that is the basis and difference between the two baptisms.[117] For this I refer to the Scriptures in Acts 18:24ff. and 19:1ff. There you will find brightly and clearly that before Paul baptized them, Apollos and the twelve men of Ephesus knew nothing of the baptism of Christ, but only of the baptism of John in which they had been baptized. The disciples of John murmured also because of the baptism of Christ with which Christ made more disciples and gathered, set up, and dedicated a greater church than John. So it must not have been one baptism, John 3:22ff.; 4:1-2. I testify also to the judgment of the old and new teachers.[b] Read Origen on the epistles of Paul, and on Romans 6, page 179; Cyril on John, Book 2, chapters 57-60;[118] Theophylact on Matthew 3 and John 3;[119] Chrysostom, Book 1, page 51, Book 2, page 47; Jerome Against the Luciferians, Book 3, folio 63a-b, and the others altogether.[120] I know not one teacher on earth, new or old, who stands by you in this serious, strange, and misleading error which you speak, preach, and write, to wit, that the baptism of John and the baptism of Christ are one baptism.[c] Likewise, that John bap-

---

[117] Hubmaier shows that he understands Zwingli's claim that all baptisms (whether by John or by Jesus, whether of believers or of infants) have the same "essence" (i.e., the same meaning), as pointing to the covenant of grace (cf. Yoder 1968, p. 33). But, Hubmaier responds, all reality also has an outward dimension. If the outward ("accidental") components differ, that suffices to make Hubmaier's point that the (outward) meanings are different.

[118] The reference to Cyril may be incorrect. See below, text 17, pp. 268-269.

[119] MPG 123, p. 171ff., 1202ff.

[120] The reference to Jerome is given in Hubmaier's treatise "Old and New Teachers." See below, text 17, p. 252 and 267.

---

[a] A mocking gloss.
[b] Origen, Cyril, Theophylactus, Chrysostom, Jerome.
[c] A misleading error.

tized children. But it is just the same as Paul writes in Romans 1. If God graciously grants it, I will write a special book on these two kinds of baptism.[121] In the meantime I warn all people to protect themselves from this gruesome error.

Zwingli:[a] Here we must note two small tricks.[122]

Balthasar: You always used a lot of tricks with the words: "Wherein are you baptized" or "Where into are you baptized," Acts 19:3. Similarly, "baptizing" for "teaching," and whether Apollos baptized or not, Acts 18:25. Likewise with "into the name" and "in the name."[b] However, you have used tricks so long that you don't know anything else to do than to obscure the baptism Scriptures. /198/ The truth is too powerful for you. Especially do you do us violence and an injustice in saying that we base rebaptism, as you call it, on Acts 19:4.[c] But may God give you the recognition and bestow right mind and thoughts upon us all.

Zwingli: This rebaptism brought many battles 1,300 years ago, but nonetheless it was laid to rest.[123]

Balthasar: Rebaptism is easily refuted, but not proper baptism.

Zwingli:[d] Our rebaptizers have found a reason so that they can be rebaptized. They say: Either we have been baptized previously in the baptism of the papists, or we do not know whether we have been baptized or not, etc.[124]

Balthasar:[e] Once more you do violence to us. We have not been baptized, whereas the believer should be baptized. Or else he is a destroyer of the Word of Christ, Matt. 28:19; Mark 16:16; Acts 2:38-39; Heb. 10:22; Matt. 5:17ff. That is the reason which forces us.

---

[121] In his later writings Hubmaier treats this theme only cursorily. He had already written on it in "On Christian Baptism." See above, pp. 97ff.
[122] Z 4, p. 271,[2] tr. Bromiley 1953, p. 170.
[123] Z 4, p. 277,[15-18] tr. Harder 1985, p. 367.
[124] Z 4, p. 278,[18-21] tr. Harder 1985, p. 368.

---

[a] Strange tricks.
[b] Obscurer of Scripture.
[c] An untruth.
[d] An untruth.
[e] An untruth.

Zwingli:[a] You have falsely maintained to the simple that infant baptism was first begun under Pope Nicholas II.[125]

Balthasar: I have never said that; furthermore, what does it concern me, when it began? No one who has read the Decretals says that. As to many other fantasies, I do not take the responsibility for them.

Zwingli: Baptism is a ceremony in the New Testament, given as a general sign to the people of God, etc.[126]

Balthasar: There must be wine in the cellar before one hangs out the sign or the hoop of the keg, or it is a falsehood. Thus one must believe before one hangs out the sign of faith, or it will be hypocrisy.

Zwingli:[b] They sin seriously, despising also the death and resurrection of Christ, who kill themselves again with their rebaptism.[127]

Balthasar: Yes, that is true. Therefore Novatus and Novatian acted badly when they thought that as often as one sins one must let oneself be rebaptized.[c] We know no rebaptism. Nor are we hemero-baptists.[128]

Zwingli: Although they threaten, I nonetheless want to present the truth to them, God willing, and do not want to remain silent.[129]

---

[125] Z 4, p. 279,[7-9] tr. Harder 1985, loc. cit. Pope Nicholas II, 1059-1061, is best known for issuing the electoral decree that established the College of Cardinals as the legal body responsible for the election of the popes. Closely allied to Hildebrand, Nicholas is associated with the papal revolution of the High Middles Ages. Some Anabaptists did apparently ascribe to Nicholas I (A.D. 858-867)—not to be confused with Nicholas II—a role in the beginning of infant baptism (cf. Yoder 1968, pp. 66ff.).

[126] Z 4, p. 282,[14] tr. Harder 1985, p. 370.

[127] Z 4, p. 284,[21-26] paraphrased; tr. Harder 1985, p. 371. Hubmaier either misquotes or changes the meaning of Zwingli here. Zwingli says they kill Christ, not themselves. He then relates the despising of the resurrection to a failure to live without sin after baptism: "They despise also his resurrection. He has risen only once; thus we should be drawn out of the baptismal water only once and henceforth all our life long sin no more, just as Christ dies no more." Z 4, p. 284.[26-29]

[128] Hemero-baptists: persons who had themselves rebaptized, even on a daily basis. See below, p. 391, note 14.

[129] Z 4, p. 285,[19-20] tr. Harder 1985, p. 372.

---

[a] An untruth.

[b] Rebaptism is unjust.

[c] Novatus. Novatianists. Hemero-baptists.

Balthasar: How do you want to present the truth if you have no clear word, as you /199/ yourself publicly confess in print. You are presenting your illusion but not your faith. You have never believed that one should baptize children, but have only fancied and expressed your opinion as such.

Zwingli: Concerning the origin of infant baptism: neither I nor anyone else can say anything from a clear word than that there is no other baptism than the one true baptism of Christk.[a] Just as many other things which are not distinguished by words, and still are not sins against God, but are with God, etc.[130]

Balthasar: Be still, be still, my Zwingle.[b] Faber of Constance hears it. That was also his opinion at Zürch during the dialogue, but you would not let him have it. You required clear Scriptures from him and not without reason.[131]

Zwingli:[c] We let the women also go to the Lord's Supper, but do not read that women were at the Supper of Christ.[132]

Balthasar:[d] You remind me of something I had almost forgotten. I must whisper it in your ear, my Zwingli. All arguments which you use that one should baptize children will also force you to let them come to the Supper. For they are of God and theirs is the kingdom of heaven, as you say, Acts 2:43. Since also children were among the three thousand and were baptized according to your speech, so were they also with them in the breaking of bread, Acts 2:46. Likewise, it is not forbidden anywhere by Christ that the Bohemians take their children to the Supper.[133] Note what a new carnival of misery your unfounded contradiction sets up.[134]

---

[130] Z 4, p. 296.[1-5]
[131] Cf. Z 3, p. 549.[5-10]
[132] Z 4, p. 296.[5-7]
[133] The Czech Brethren or Utraquists admitted children to communion.
[134] There is a play on words in which Hubmaier substitutes *Jamermarckt*, carnival of misery, for *Jahrmarkt*, annual fair.

---

[a] An untruth.
[b] Faber hears it.
[c] A trick.
[d] A Christian warning.

The Fourth Part

Zwingli:[a] What I have always said, I will say until death and no one will ever find that I contradict myself.[135]

Balthasar: I offer to prove publicly with your own printed books that you have spoken this way and that way many times.

Zwingli: Then speak of infant baptism, for God's sake. If God commanded to baptize, then do not immediately say, "but not the children."[136]

Balthasar: Then permit us on this matter for God's sake to speak thus: God commanded to baptize, but believers and those instructed in his Word. Now look, where is infant baptism left? /200/

Zwingli:[b] Why do you differentiate between persons? Are children people or not? If they are persons or people, then you must let them be baptized.[137]

Balthasar: This far-out argument does as much for the Turkish as for the Christian children. Turks are also people. But we want to give you a short piece of information. Christ commands that one should baptize believing people. Now we call those people believing who testify to their faith outwardly with their mouth and with their works. However, how it stands with the heart we want to leave with God. Now faith comes from hearing through the Word of God, which is shown by the preacher in Romans 10:17. One cannot preach to the young children. Therefore, we cannot scripturally ascribe any faith to them.

Zwingli: Thus we demand of the opponents of baptism that they show us a clear word which forbids one's baptizing children.[138]

Balthasar: Then I will demand of you that you show me a clear word that forbids purgatory, monks, nuns, cowls, tonsures, and says that the mass is not a sacrifice. You say, the

---

[135] Z 4, p. 296.[21-23]
[136] Z 4, p. 297.[12-13]
[137] Z 4, p. 297.[14-16]
[138] Z 4, p. 297.[21-23]

---

[a] An untruth.
[b] An argument to the point.

mass is a memorial; therefore it is no sacrifice. Answer: Baptism is instituted for the faithful; therefore one should not baptize them who do not yet believe. Do you see here who is setting up a new popery and begins a new episcopal masquerade?[a]

Zwingli: How much teaching must precede baptism? Here they stutter like the stammerers, for what they say here they cannot make true with the Scriptures.[139]

Balthasar:[b] Before baptism we should learn the gospel, which is such a comforting teaching, through which we are certain and sure that we have a gracious Father in heaven who forgives us all our sins through the death and resurrection of his most beloved Son, our Lord Jesus Christ. I prove that with the Scripture, Mark 16:16. There it is mandated to the disciples first to preach the gospel out of which comes faith, and after that to baptize believers. In the power of this mandate we are and should be obligated to know that preached gospel before we are baptized. The second Scripture we will read is 1 Peter 3:21. I beseech you, Christian reader, to look at the same and then judge for yourself.

Zwingli:[c] That we must demand instructed faith only in the Supper of Christ stands in 1 Corinthians 11:28: The person must examine himself before he eats of the bread, etc. But of baptism it is nowhere written that one must test oneself beforehand or remember.[140] /201/

Balthazar:[d] As you have: "The person examines himself and after that he eats from the bread," so we have, Mark 16:16: "Go forth, preach, whoever believes and is baptized." See, you have "examine" and we have "believe." Philip also demands faith from the treasurer of Candace, Acts 8:37.

Zwingli:[e] Although infant baptism is not written down with definite or explicit words, it can well be discerned from

---

[139] Z 4, p. 297[32]-298.[2]
[140] Z 4, p. 298.[6-11] This is an allusion to the fact that the Supper is a memorial and therefore requires a certain ability to "remember," whereas baptism, since it is not a memorial, does not.

---

[a] New papacy.
[b] What the person should know before baptism.
[c] The Supper.
[d] To examine oneself.
[e] You lack Scripture.

the testimonies of the divine Word, for the infants were no less baptized with the common multitude who were baptized.[141]

Balthasar: One time you say that infant baptism is written in the Word of God but another time you say it is not written or expressed with words but that it is to be seen. That is a real confusion and treachery in the Scripture. For it is not enough to measure, to be of the opinion, or to think; there must be knowing and believing.

Zwingli: The children and the women were also fed in the common multitude, but one did not count them, Matt. 14:21.[142]

Balthasar: The food was ordered by God for the woman and the child, also for the young ravens; but baptism was for the faithful and the Supper for the self-examined. Baptized men and women were also reported in Acts 8:12, but not young children.

Zwingli: Christ said in Matthew 16 [Matt. 19:13ff.]; Luke 18:15ff.; and Mark 10:17ff: "Let the children come to me and forbid them not, for of such is the kingdom of God."[a] Truly I say to you, whoever does not receive the kingdom of God as a child will not enter it. We must first become as a child or we will not be capable of the kingdom of God.[b] Much more is the kingdom of God of children like whom we must first become.[143]

Balthasar: First I say that I cannot say whether the young children are saved or damned. I leave it to the judgment of God. Yes, if your argument were just, then all people who were baptized in their childhood would have to be of God and be saved. For no one can tear these out of the hand of God. Then, whence come the spiritual and worldly thieves, murderers, and tyrants, all of whom before their infant baptism, according to your speech, were also of the kingdom of God. Second, Christ has taken a bodily thing as a reason to speak, as the well of Jacob in John 4:13ff. and the five barley rolls in

---

[141] Z 4, p. 299.[2-6]
[142] Z 4, p. 299.[6-7]
[143] Z 4, p. 299,[9-16] abridged.

---

[a] Let them.
[b] Of the children is the kingdom of God.

John 6:26ff., and after that given them a spiritual meaning. So he has taught us humility here and taken the parable of the children. So the speech renders this much and no more: "Let the humble /202/ come to me, for of such is the kingdom of God," Deut. 1:39. But to speak about it more exactly, children are neither humble nor proud, since they know neither good nor evil, nor do they come to the knowledge of the Pythagorean theorem.[a] So also Origen understands these words as Christ himself says: "Whoever humbles himself will be exalted,"[144] Luke 14:11. In the third place, whether children are more or less receptive of the kingdom of God than we are, I leave to God himself. It is not given to me to judge; it is too high for me. For it is none of Peter's business as to what Christ wants to do with John, John 21:22. That one wants to draw such meaning out of the Scripture accomplishes nothing, for I find likewise in another place two Scriptures which say we should not be like children, Eph. 4:14; 1 Cor. 14:20, or he will close his kingdom before us. Therefore it is necessary that one is careful about what is written in a parable, to use it according to the purpose of the parable and not further, for all parables limp. Or it would also come to that afterward that we also had to ride on sticks like children if we wanted to enter the kingdom of God.[b]

In the fourth place, even if we allow that children are saved and that they are of the kingdom of God, it is still not proven that one should baptize them before they confess faith itself outwardly before the church and commit themselves henceforth to adapt their life according to the Rule of Christ with the help of God. However, in that you twist the word of Peter, "Who will forbid them water, etc.," Acts 16 [Acts 10:47], you misuse the Scripture. Peter used the word for the believers who had accepted the Word of God. You use it for those who do not yet know what the Word or God is. Pay attention here, Zwingle. We want to prove this article with your own writing to the king of France. There you write:

---

[144] Origen, "On First Principles," MPG 11, p. 250f., tr. ANF 4, p. 302.

---

[a] Origen.
[b] Goal of the comparison.

"Baptism is a sign with which the person shows himself to the church as a vassal or knight of Christ,[a] with which sign he makes the church certain of his faith more than he himself."[145] "For with outward baptism as with an oath or commitment, the baptized person binds himself to the change and improvement of his life."[146] Thus you have yourself written on pages 201 and 205 things that can never be ascribed to any child. In the fifth place, so it is a blind consequence or result which you thus introduce:[b] Whoever does not receive the kingdom of God like a child does not enter it. For we must first become like children or we are not receptive to the kingdom of God, for the kingdom of God belongs much more to children. For I want to set a similar speech: /203/ "Truly I say to you," says Christ, "if you will have faith like a mustard seed, etc.," Matt. 17:20; Luke 17:6. Therefore, much more is the mustard seed faithful, like which we must first become.

Zwingli: The children of Christians are certainly, undoubtedly children of God.[147]

Balthasar: Here you interfere in the judgment of God and ascribe to the fleshly birth what belongs alone to the Spirit and the Word of God. For to be children of God is a work of God,[c] John 1:13. For children are of sin and of wrath. We receive that and inherit it from father and mother, whether they be Christian or unchristian, so we are all conceived and born in sin as David himself laments in Psalms 51:7. Job curses therefore his day of birth, Job 3:1. So also Jeremiah 20:14. Paul writes the same, that we are all children of wrath by nature, Eph. 2:3. Christ also particularly does not like to allow that you give and ascribe something to the fleshly birth, as you obviously see and grasp in this statement, "Woman, what do I have to do with you?" John 2:4. "For whoever does God's will is my brother and my sister and my mother." Stop speaking thus, my Zwingli, or Christ will give the same answer

---

[145] Z 4, p. 761,[22] tr. ZL 3, p. 184.
[146] Z 3, p. 763[35]-764,[1] tr. ZL 3, p. 186
[147] Z 4, p. 301.[21-22]

---

[a] Baptism. Rightly spoken and badly done.
[b] Argument from the greater.
[c] Not out of the blood.

to you as to the woman who raised her voice in the crowd and said to him, "Blessed is the womb which has borne you and the breast which has given you to suck." He said, however, "Blessed are those who hear and keep the Word of God," Luke 11:27f. But I am really amazed, my Ulrich, who has be witched you so strongly that you do not hear at all and note the truth as it has been presented to you for two years. Nevertheless, I think I have found it out and I risk whispering it secretly in your ear. Thus you also know that in one hour, twins can be born, of whom one is elected and the other rejected, like Cain and Abel and Esau and Jacob, Gen. 4:1-2; 25:24-26. The hand of God is free and unshortened, Isa. 50:2; 59:16.

Zwingli: Where do we read that the pure mother[a] of Jesus Christ was baptized?[148]

Balthasar: Where do you read that she was at the Supper? What do you intend by such crafty and cunning snake's questions?

Zwingli: Where does it say that the apostles[b] were baptized?[149]

Balthasar: There is so much written that we know what baptism is, what it testifies, what belongs to it, and why one should receive it. Furthermore, the one who searches the Scriptures, Acts 10:47-48 and 11:15-17, will point it out to you from the words of Peter.

Zwingli: It is much more believable that in the time of the apostles, the children also /204/ were baptized; and for example, in 1 Corinthians 1:16, Paul says "I have baptized Stephen's household." Now it is clearly to be seen that in so great a household, children were more likely included than not.[150]

Balthasar: You speak about it, Zwingli, as if you had doubts concerning the matter. However, we want to say to you

---

[148] Z 4, p. 301.[28-29]
[149] Z 4, p. 301.[31]
[150] Z 4, p. 312.[5-10]

---

[a] Mary.
[b] Apostles.
[c] The household of Stephen.

what believable or more believable really means. "Believable" is what we have a clear Word of God for.[a] "More believable" is that for which we have an even clearer word. Show us now one single word of your faith. Now as concerns the household of Stephen it was as follows: There were many who boasted about their baptizer. Therefore Paul was thankful that he did not baptize many people other than Crispus, Gaius, and the household of Stephen, so that they could not boast about him.[b] Now the children could not boast about either Paul or Apollos; therefore, the text cannot be understood as applying to children. Therefore, it is only your illusion and your opinion that children were there, but not faith. You are not certain of it with the Word. Herewith we want to have answered the case of the households of Lydia and the jailer, Acts 16:15, 33, when the believers of the household were baptized, which I testify to openly with the Scripture.[c]

Zwingli: It is also well to think that all believers had cared for their children and committed them to that God and treasure into whose recognition they had come.[151]

Balthasar:[d] This care and commitment is just as meaningful as that of the foolish women who dedicated their children to God while still in their womb or in their childhood to God and said, "Aye, God, give me a healthy child and I will give him to you and offer him so that you can make a monk, priest, or nun out of him." What do you think, my Zwingle? Are not cradle monks, cradle priests, cradle nuns, and cradle Christians all the same thing? They are all together ignorant about what a monk, priest, nun, Christ, God, faith, or baptism is.

Zwingli: I speak here only of the children of Christians, who are the children of God, not that I want to exclude the children of unbelievers. I leave them to the judgment of God, for they are creatures of God, whom he may turn to chaste or honorable use, or unchaste, as it pleases him.[152]

---

[151] Z 4, p. 313.[17-19]
[152] Z 4, p. 313[23]-314,[2] abridged.

---

[a] Believable, more believable.
[b] Crispus, Gaius.
[c] Believing household.
[d] Cradle Christians.

Balthasar: Speak also thus of the children of the believers, then you will do justice to God. For you may not apply the secret judgments of God outside of Scripture as to how he will use his creatures, any more to unbelievers than to believers. His judgments are deep, Rom. 9:8; 10:7ff.; 11:17ff. /205/

Zwingli:[a] Paul admonishes the Corinthians in 1 Corinthians 7:14 that where one spouse is faithful and the other unfaithful, the believer should not dismiss the unbeliever, for otherwise, he says, "your children will be unpure; now, however, they are holy."[b] It is well known that "holy" was taken by Paul and the old Christians for a believer, for so called they the servants of God "saints."[153]

Balthasar: Here you want, Zwingle, that one should baptize the children of believers on the basis that they are "holy." Now you write further that it is well-known that "holy" is taken for "believing." Thus it follows that young children are believers, which you until now have always denied. In the second place, since on this basis, that Paul calls children of believers holy (assuming now that the word "holy" may be taken for "believing" or "pure"), you want to prove that Paul calls the children of believers holy and want to set the foundation of infant baptism on that, then you must also baptize the unbelieving husband of a believing woman, for Paul says that he is as holy as the child. If now "holy" is "faithful" here, then the unbelieving man is believing. Note, reader, what results when we spin glosses out of our own heads. For certainly "holy" must not be taken here for "believing," as *you* say.

Zwingli:[c] Our opponents of baptism initially stubbornly condemned children, in the power of this Word. ("Whoever does not believe is condemned," Mark 16:16.)[154]

Balthasar: No one should say such concerning us. You are unfair and unjust to us. We have not been content with Saint

---

[153] Z 4, p. 314.[2-8]
[154] Z 4, p. 315,[28-31] paraphrased.

---

[a] A false understanding.
[b] Holy for faithful.
[c] An untruth.

Augustine[a] in his canon "Firmissime" De Consec., distinction 4 [Canon "Most Firmly, "On Consecration, Distinction 4].[155]

Zwingli: I cannot prove the faith of children. Although some try to do that, it is in vain.[156]

Balthasar:[b] Have you not above, according to your own view, proven and said that Paul calls the children of Christians "holy"; and since "holy" means "believing," therefore they are believers? Remember what you have said. Look at your book. I am not unfair to you.

Zwingli: There one sees exactly that Christ only speaks of those who hear the Gospel preached and thereafter believe or not, Mark 16:16. Now, however, the children of Christians, who are still incapable of the word, do not hear the gospel. Therefore, they are neither believing nor unbelieving.[c] So the word does not apply to them.[157]

Balthasar:[d] Oh, you wonderful God, you are so powerful that you cry out and testify to your truth through just those people who want to kill it /206/ and you stab them with just those words with which they with Caiaphas want to kill you. Well we also say that the words, Mark 16:16, apply only to those who hear the gospel preached and not to young children. That is just the understanding of Saint Jerome on the word concerning water baptism, Matt. 28:19. There he writes as follows: "In the first place, they teach all the people. After that they dip the taught ones into the water. For it should not be that the body receive the sacrament of baptism unless the soul has received the truth of faith beforehand." So speaks Jerome, the holy teacher. If I also speak this way, I am an archheretic. If these words do not apply to young children, then the baptism of these words also do not apply. Then there

---

[155] CIC I:1362 (canon 3).
[156] Z 4, p. 316.[14-15]
[157] Z 4, p. 316.[26-31]

---

[a] Augustine, De Consec. di. 4 c. "firmissime." ["On Consecration," Distinction 4, Canon: "Most Firmly."]
[b] Oecolampad.
[c] The truth must break out.
[d] O right, right. Yes, yes.

must be another baptism for cradle children, of which baptism there is no report here nor in Matthew 28:19, for here and there is a history which no one can deny. Well, my Zwingle, please tell us, for God's sake, where in Scripture water baptism is instituted by Christ for those who have not yet heard the gospel, are not yet accountable and do not believe. If you can point out this baptism with a clear word, then, truly, truly, we are rightly defeated by you and should justly be punished in honor, goods, body, and life. If you cannot do that, then we beseech you for the sake of the last judgment, confess your error and henceforth be at peace with us.[a] Here I demand by the living God from you an account of your faith and of baptism, which is another baptism than this one to which the Word of Christ applies, Mark 16:16 and Matt. 28:19, as you yourself have confessed. Give answer. Give an account, for God's sake. Show us where infant baptism is grounded in the bright and clear Word of God, since the Word of Christ in Mark and Matthew does not apply to infant baptism. For the spirit of man does not become peaceful except through a clear Word of God, without which there is neither faith nor peace, Rom. 10:5. The same we desire from you. You are obligated to point that out to us, 1 Pet. 3:15.[b] Or else we will not stop crying out over you: "Word, word, word, Scripture, Scripture, Scripture." However, I counsel you faithfully: surrender. You have caught and bound yourself with your own words where you say: The words of Mark 16 do not apply to young children. Look, my Zwingle, how you have made so much trouble in vain above with the words "into the name" and "in the name," also with the preceding and following teaching, by which you force the same words on the young children, 1 Pet. 1:25. And now you confess openly: They do not apply to them. O truth, truth, you are immortal.[158]

Zwingli: When one studies the nature of baptism, one sees that it is proper for children.[159] /207/

---

[158] This is one of the rare occasions in which Hubmaier cites his epigram, "Truth Is Immortal," within the context of an argument.
[159] Z 4, p. 317.[13-14]

---

[a] Account of faith.
[b] Word. Word. Scripture. Scripture. Note.

Balthasar: First of all, you said the opposite in Mark and Matthew. Then look also at the significance of water baptism in Romans 6:3-4 and how the apostles practiced it in Acts. Likewise, in Hebrews 10:22 and 1 Peter 3:21, you find that it is not suitable for them. The Holy Scripture itself shall be the judge, Rom. 6:4; Acts 8:12; 10:47; 16:15; 31-33; 18:8; Ezek. 44; Deut. 17:11, 20; Exod. 18, 28; John 12:48.

Zwingli: That is now the whole sum of this point that it is more believable that infant baptism began also in the time of Christ.[160]

Balthasar: Nobody says believable or more believable, except in the Word of God.

Zwingli: How would it come about that the Christian church in part should be baptized and in part be unbaptized? There is only one sheep's stall and one shepherd,[161] John 10:7ff.; Acts 10:34ff.; Mark 16; Gen. 15:2-6; Acts 16:25-34.

Balthasar: How does the one church come out of Cornelius and the thief, as well as Abraham and the jailer? Most certainly, when you find three kinds of baptism in the Scripture, through which the person testifies as a Christian. Where one cannot be had, then there are still the two others, together with faith, if necessary.

The Fifth Part

Zwingli: Augustine[a] writes against the Donatists concerning baptism in Book 4, Chapters 23 and 24,[162] that the universal church holds that one should baptize young children.[163]

Balthasar: Augustine also writes that the children of Christians who die either in the mother's womb or outside without water baptism are not only robbed of the divine countenance, but are also tortured with eternal fire. However, he says this without any basis; therefore, we do not believe

---

[160] Z 4, p. 318.[3-4]
[161] Z 4, p. 318.[10-13]
[162] MPL 43, p. 174, tr. Schaff 1956, v. IV, p. 461f.
[163] Z 4, p. 321.[6-13]

---

[a] Augustine. An ungrounded judgment.

him in this matter. For I interpret from his own words, that if one had asked Augustine, where infant baptism is founded in the Scriptures, he would have answered, it has not been established in the councils, but it has always been practiced. Therefore one should simply believe that it was ordered by the apostles. Had Augustine known a Scripture here wherein infant baptism had been founded, then he would not have had to consult the councils, and finding nothing therein, finally to run to the old custom and tradition like the papists. For he well knows that also at the time of the apostles many errors entered in, which cannot be justified by the passage of time. But what God calls right and good, that is right and good.

Zwingli:[a] From the words of Augustine one sees well that in his time the greater part of the general church baptized their unknowing children. /208/ How then can infant baptism only have begun under Pope Nicholas?[164]

Balthasar: The universal Christian church and its majority are not the same, but one sees that there was always a part against it, Exod. 23:2. Whether they are more or less, the majority does not count here. The point on Pope Nicholas is answered above.[165]

Zwingli: We read the words of Augustine to the opponents of baptism. Nevertheless, they have told everybody that infant baptism is popish.[166]

Balthasar: Whether it is popish or abbotish it is still not Christian. Read to us the Word of Christ, not of Augustine.[b] Or we read to you the above-mentioned word of Jerome on the last chapter of Matthew.

Zwingli: Where do we read in the New Testament as to how close relations we may marry? Nowhere. Therefore we must look in Leviticus 18:6-18.[167]

Balthasar:[c] Here you take the argument from Faber of Constance;[168] give it back to him. For marriage has nothing to

---

[164] Z 4, p. 322.[5-8]
[165] See above, p. 212 and below, p. 270.
[166] Z 4, p. 327.[19-20]
[167] Z 4, p. 326.[4-6]
[168] Z 1, p. 566.[4-5]

---

[a] The majority does not make faith.
[b] A trick.
[c] Faber.

do with faith. It is also present among the heathen. But water baptism is a public testimony of faith before the church.

Zwingli:[a] Where do we have in the New Testament concerning restitution? Nowhere. Therefore we must run to and look in Exodus, chapters 22 and 23.[169]

Balthasar: Oh, the lightheaded arguments. Do you have nothing in the New Testament about theft, stealing, and avarice, Matt. 15:5ff.; Mark 8:36-37; Rom. 2:22; 1 Cor. 6:10; Eph. 4:28? Not to give back goods acquired unjustly is stealing. Where stealing is forbidden, there restitution is already commanded. Or all theology must fail.

Zwingli: In infant baptism there is no misdirected worship.[170]

Balthasar: But on the other hand, an idolatry. For not to be obedient to the Word of the Lord, says Samuel to Saul, is like the vice of idolatry, 1 Kings 15 [1 Sam. 15:23]. Not to say that by this infant baptism we are robbed of the true baptism of Christ and use the high name of God the Father, Son, and Holy Spirit in vain over the children, which words, as you confess, do not apply to them. /209/

Zwingli:[b] The reason for godfathers and godmothers is as follows: if the father and mother have died, they guarantee that the doctrine of salvation is taught to the child. Therefore one incorporates them in presenting the child and they are witnesses that the child has been baptized.[171]

Balthasar: Baptism is a public testimony of faith which the baptized one himself makes before the church, not godmothers or godfathers. In that each believing person has three witnesses in heaven: Father, Son, and Holy Spirit, in whose name and power he inwardly surrenders to God and outwardly has obligated himself to lead a new life according to the Rule of Christ.[c] He also has three witnesses on earth: spirit, water, and blood, 1 John 5:6ff. The Spirit leads, the water

---

[169] Z 4, p. 326.[7-9]
[170] Z 4, p. 328.[20-21]
[171] Z 4, p. 332,[19-26] abridged.

---

[a] A trick.
[b] To have godmothers and godfathers is a work without faith.
[c] Three witnesses.

makes the breakthrough, the blood gains advantage in the power of God and finally is victorious. Whoever has ears to hear, let him hear. These are the true godfathers and godmothers.

Zwingli: No one should know too much, but one should know the right measure,[172] Rom. 12:3.

Balthasar: Yes, therefore, you know too much. You know an infant baptism which Christ himself did not know.

Zwingli:[a] It is as fitting for a Christian person to have witnesses at the beginning as it is in the admonishment of Matthew 18:15ff., where it is necessary and the order calls for it.[173]

Balthasar: Here Scripture, there no Scripture. Or Christ must have forgotten godmothers and godfathers. But here I ask all child-baptizers together: "Under what form of the word do you baptize young children?" Answer: "In the name of the Father and the Son, and the Holy Spirit." I ask further: "Who taught you the form?" You answer: "Christ, in Matthew 28:19." Oh, what are you saying?[b] These words still do not apply to young children, also according to the understanding of Jerome, Erasmus, and Zwingli, yea, the old and new teachers.[174]

Balthasar Fridberger's Theses

which he wants to defend against everyone with the help of God. For he knows that infant baptism robs the true baptism of Christ and that God will let it fade away and the true baptism rise again./210/ '

On Baptism in General

1. No element or outward thing in this world can cleanse the soul. Only faith purifies the hearts of people, 1 Cor. 2:5.

---

[172] Z 4, p. 332.[27-28]
[173] Z 4, p. 333.[6-8]
[174] See below, text 17.

---

[a] Form of baptism.
[b] Jerome, Erasmus, Zwingli.

2. It follows that baptism can wash away no sin.

3. If it does not wash away sin and still is of God, then it must be a public testimony, Rom. 6:4 of internal faith and an outward sign of commitment to a new life henceforth to be led according to the Word of Christ, as much as God gives grace.

4. Whether the children of Christians and the children of the Old Testament are children of God, we want only to leave to him who knows all things and will not make any judgment.

5. The ark of Noah is a figure of water baptism; therefore, we have a clear Scripture, Gen. 8:1ff.; 1 Pet. 3:20. However, for the outward circumcision we have no Scripture.

6. Baptism with which believers are water baptized has teaching and example in the clear Word of God and no one can ever call it a rebaptism in truth, Matt. 28:19; Mark 16:15-16; Acts 2:38, 41; 8:12, 38; 10:47-48; 11:16; 16:15, 33; 18:8; Heb. 10:22. But infant baptism has no basis; therefore, it is not of God.

Zwingli:[a] Now follows the form of baptism as it is now practiced at Zürch and all additions which have no basis in the Word of God are left out.[175]

Balthasar: Look out that no one asks you, Zwingle, where it is written that one should take godmothers and godfathers and ask them instead of the child whether it believes.[b] And they speak in place of the child, I believe, and yet the child neither believes nor disbelieves for itself, as you confessed above. Tell us one more thing: Where is the baptismal shirt based in the Word of God? For you did not allow Faber[c] the smallest letter outside of the clear Word of God, and you were right and just.[176] If you do the same for yourself, then we are at peace.

Zwingli:[d] The following is from Mark 10:13ff.: "It happened once that that they brought the children to the Lord

---

[175] Z 4, p. 334.[12-14]
[176] Z 3, p. 552.[14-15]

---

[a] How one baptizes at Zurich.
[b] To have godparents is an addition.
[c] Faber.
[d] Here you slander Christ and Mark.

Jesus so that he might lay his hand on them. But the disciples scolded those who brought them to him. When Jesus saw that, he was incensed and said to them: 'Let the children come to me and do not forbid them, for of them[a] is the kingdom of God.' "[177]

Balthasar: You know, Zwingle, that the Holy Scripture is such a whole, consistent, genuine, infallible, eternal, immortal Word that cannot wear away nor can the smallest letter or the smallest point be changed, Luke 21:33. Heaven and earth must first break apart, as /211/ Paul also writes to the Galatians: "Dear brothers, one does not despise a human testament, when it is confirmed, nor does one add anything to it. Much less should one do little or more to Christ's testament. He has confirmed it with his bitter death," Gal. 3:15; Deut. 4:2; 12:30; Heb. 12:24, 30; Rev. 22:18f. God cannot suffer it either; he is a consuming fire. Cursed is he who adds to or detracts from it. How beautiful is the friend of God that is the Holy Scripture, in which Christ dwells, lives, and rests; and there is no flaw in it. However, disregarding all of this you make one, Zwingle, and say publicly in print: "The following is from the Gospel of Mark 10," in which you do injustice to the evangelist Mark and do violence to his Scripture.[b] You reject Christ's Word and against all justice tear apart his speech and in human sacrilege set out another word in its place, through which the whole meaning and understanding of Christ is falsified. For through the addition of one single letter you make Christ's whole gospel invalid, blameworthy, impotent, and imperfect, as much as is in you.[c] To make it true you add out of your head, "Of theirs is the kingdom of God." That is directly against the clear word, sense, and understanding of Christ, as well as hinders and discards his teaching which he taught at that time. All this I offer to prove here publicly and to show how divine justice is to be accomplished even with your own books. I will let them serve as witnesses

---

[177] Z 4, p. 335.[26-31]

---

[a] Of them.
[b] Accusation of a lie.
[c] An unspeakable error.

between you and me, whether they be Greek, German, or Latin. After one has seen and read these words in the foundation of Scriptures, I will let every Christian congregation judge in the power of the read and heard Word whether it says "theirs" is the kingdom of God or "of such" is the kingdom of God.[a] However, you would like here to cover yourself with a fig leaf, excuse yourself, and say, "I know it myself well and have above translated it into German thus: 'Of such is the kingdom of God.' " Answer: This is all the worse; it is our greatest complaint that you know a thing well and truly, and yet write and act against it, in order to protect and confirm your useless speech all the better. Why do you write "of theirs" and not "of such?"[b] Truly you hold upright your pillar on which you build infant baptism, so your quarreling and your honor do not go under. But the pillar is worm-eaten and therefore your infantile infant baptism will lose hands, feet, and head like Dagon, 1 Sam. 5:1ff.

Remember, my Zwingle, how you used above a sophistry with "into the name" and "in the name of," etc.[c] We do not mind letting you do that, but stay in the right natural meaning of the words of Christ. But here word, sense, meaning, faith, and work are all together smashed down and falsified. /212/ Therefore, we as Christians who see into your game do not want to permit such any longer.[d] Christ says these words to adults, who should be children in humility. So you then apply them by force onto the young minor children whom Christ does not teach nor to whom does he preach, they being incapable of his Word. Rather, he points to them only as a bodily example of his teaching from which one should learn spiritual humility. Therefore it ill befits a scholar to force Scripture into an alien understanding. One must always imagine that he does the same with other Scriptures. Therefore I beseech and admonish you, dear Zwingle, for the sake of God, that you henceforth keep back such glosses and worthless speeches as you used, for example, in the words of Christ concerning the Supper where you unnecessarily replaced an "est" for a

---

[a] Theirs, of such.
[b] Theirs, of such.
[c] Into. In. Accusation of a lie.
[d] Scripture falsifier, ripper, abuser.

"significat."[a][178] I said it several years ago to several special friends: "*Judicium Zwingli de pane et vino placet. Modus iudicandi non placet*," [The judgment of Zwingli about bread and wine is pleasing. The manner of his judging is not pleasing.] Doctor Sebastian knows it well, and Clivanus.[179] However, I did not make much of an outcry about it since in the main we were one. Both my good brothers, Jörg Joachim von Bregentz and Sebastian Hauenschild von Waldshut, know that. Had you left it with the simple understanding of the words which Christ had spoken, then much mischief would have been avoided. For truly with such words about a metamorphosis which you use here in Mark, you confuse and bring down the entire Bible (I say peacefully). Particularly you tear apart thereby also the Scriptures—Matthew 19:14; Luke 18:16; and Mark 10:14—which always have there "of such" and not "of theirs."[b] Now, however, "of such" and "of theirs" are as far apart as you and I. You also thereby give reason to the godless to slander Christian teachings so that they now say: "Watch. They bend and gloss the Scriptures according to their pleasure." Why do you accuse the poor brothers and sisters, fighting so grimly against them with such ungrounded weapons, leading them into misery and need? Why do you reject your poor conscience which shows you otherwise? Why do you reject Christ so that you push his Word out of the center and set your own invented and composed words in place of his? Only for the reason that it serves your water bath better than his.[c] Look, do not be one of the builders who reject the cornerstone /213/ and set in its place a sandstone which cannot bear the building.

---

[178] Zwingli first developed the argument that *is* should be interpreted as *signifies* in the *Letter to Matthew Alber*, Z 3, p. 345,[5ff.] tr. Pipkin 1984, p. 138f.
[179] Sebastian Hofmeister, 1476-1533, was the Reformer of Schaffhausen, cf. above, pp. 36ff., 78, and below, p. 258. Rudolf Clivanus, 1499-1578, schoolteacher and ambassador, was a close friend and co-worker of Zwingli. He often took political missions to Waldshut on behalf of Zwingli and Zurich.

---

[a] Is, signifies.
[b] Of theirs.
[c] Water bath.

One gets the impression, my dear Zwingli, that you have also treated the Scriptures in this way above when you take "baptism" for "teaching," an "into" for an "in," a "holy" for a "faithful," a "whereinto" for a "wherein," etc. You may not blame such error on the laziness of the publisher, for it is now once more published and spread abroad throughout the whole of Christendom.[180] Truly, it has been badly handled.[a] Now all of Christendom sees the great error which you deal with daily, as often and much as you baptize at Zürch. Also, in addition, you have misled many priests, who also practice it as you do, who think in their mind that they have done well to have followed you. Look into yourself, my dear Zwingle, for the sake of the last judgment, confess that you are guilty, leave off your word battles, give God the glory, confess the truth. You are its prisoner; truly you will not be able to extract yourself from it. Confess it openly and freely and speak about it as you did two years ago.[b] Protect yourself and your city from shame. You know that the truth will finally prevail and be victorious, Gal. 2:11ff. Remember that Peter also stumbled and at one time did not walk according to the truth of the gospel. Paul and Barnabas became estranged, Acts 15:39.

Your fall has happened for the best, for you and for us all, so that you may not raise yourself up so high, so that we do not look onto the person, yea, and that we humble ourselves under the powerful Word of God and not go forth any more according to our own brain, Luke 22:24ff.; Gal. 2:6. Stop also the miserable imprisoning and banning of pious brothers, the exiling out of the territory, imprisoning, throwing into the dungeons, putting in stocks and blocks, drowning, and the like, all of which [stopping] you may do easily, if you only give way to the clear truth of God again.[c] If you had preached and yourself baptized according to the order of Christ or had ordered others to do that baptism, then others would not have been able to begin, Luke 19:40. But since you

[180] Zwingli's *Antwort über Dr. Balthasars Taufbüchlein* was published in Zurich, Nov. 14, 1525. Cf. Z 4, pp. 577-647.

[a] A daily error. A misleading of many priests.
[b] You cannot retain it.
[c] Imprisonment.

remain silent and the others with you, then at last the stones had to cry out and restore the true water baptism of Christ. Aye, my dear Zwingle, do so for the sake of God and the truth, then the cause will soon come right everywhere. May God give you his grace and help you so that you again grasp his bright, clear, limpid Word as before /214/ and walk according to the same. May the dear merciful God the Father in heaven through Jesus Christ his most dear Son, our only Savior, grant that to you and to us all. Amen.

Dear Zwingli. You see that I have quoted your words, as you have spoken in public print. I do you no injustice. Accordingly, if you want to, answer; then you will be answered by me again faithfully by Scripture with the help of God. For you know how you and your city of Zürch have held yourself in this matter. It would not be a miracle if the stones were to speak out about it. However, if you would prefer to have an oral public dialogue with me, I suggest to you herewith, though certainly with the approval of the government, the old and imperial city of Regensburg in Bavaria, for the same way, place, and safe conduct.* Recognize yourself and live well in Christ. Given at Nicolspurg.

1526
Printed by Simprecht Sorg,
called Froschauer.
Nicolspurg

---

* Regenspurg.

15

Twelve Articles in Prayer Form

When Waldshut fell and Hubmaier took refuge in Zurich, he was held in a kind of protective custody until he retracted his proffered recantation; then he was a bonafide prisoner from December 29, 1525, until the middle of the next April, when he was released. The prison used for Anabaptists was the Wellenberg, a tower on an island in the middle of the Limmat River. Hubmaier calls it the Watertower.

Sometime during his imprisonment he wrote this text. He was able to publish it only when he had reached Nikolsburg the next year. Though there is little originality in the doctrinal content, the form is original in that the affirmations of the Apostles' Creed are transformed into a prayer and expanded into a description of Christian experience. This makes it one of his more "confessional" or "pastoral" writings. Along the way we discern Hubmaier's view of the fate of the truth under persecution.[1]

---

[1] First-draft translation by Elizabeth Horsch Bender. Earlier translation in Davidson 1939, pp. 208-26. Fragments in Vedder 1905, p. 130, and Klaassen 1981, pp. 25, 74, 102, 320. Manuscript of translation by Henry C. Vedder at Colgate Rochester Library. Source: HS 10, pp. 216-220.

The Twelve
Articles of Christian
Faith
Phrased in the form of a
Prayer at Zürich
In the Watertower

Doctor Balthasar
Hůebmör
Nicolspurg
1527

The Twelve Articles of the Christian Faith

I believe in God, the Almighty Father, Creator of the heavens and earth, yea in thee,[2] my most gracious Lord and most merciful Father, thou who for my sake hast created heaven and earth and all that is in them. Furthermore, thou hast in fatherly grace made me, as thy beloved child, a lord and an heir, to dwell and live therein eternally. Yet, I confess, we humans have lost this gracious sonship, dignity, and heritage, through the disobedience of Adam. Nonetheless I place in thee, in my most gracious Father, all my consolation, hope, and confidence, and know surely and certainly that this Fall will be harmless and no source of condemnation for me.

I also believe in Jesus Christ, his only begotten Son our Lord; that he has atoned for me for this Fall before thee my Father, has made peace between thee and me, a poor sinner, and through his obedience has again won the inheritance for me. Further, he has restored to me, by his holy Word which he has sent, the power to become thy child in faith. I hope and trust in him completely. May he not let his saving and

---

[2] To render the second person direct address, which makes of the creed a prayer, this translation will use traditional English thou/thy forms, despite the fact that in Hubmaier's time there was nothing archaic about the *Du* usage.

consoling name of Jesus, of whom I believe that he is Christ, true God and Man, be lost on me miserable sinner, but may he redeem me from all my sins.

I also believe and confess, my Lord Jesus Christ, that thou wast conceived of the Holy Spirit, without any seed of man, born of Mary, the pure and eternally chaste virgin, that thou mightest restore me and all believers and mightest win from thy heavenly Father the grace of the Holy Spirit, which had been withdrawn from me because of my sins. I believe and trust that the Holy Spirit has come into me, and that the power of the most high God has overshadowed my soul like that of Mary, so that I might be conceived a new man and be born again in thy living, indestructible Word, and in the Spirit, and that I might /217/ see the kingdom of God. For that thou, Son of the living God, didst become man to that end, that we miserable men might through thee become children of God.

I also believe and confess that thou hast suffered under the judge Pontius Pilate, wast crucified, dead, and buried, and all of that for the sake of my sins, that thou mightest release and redeem me from the eternal cross, torture, suffering, and death through thy cross, suffering, anxiety and distress, torture, and bitter dying, and through the shedding of thy rose-red blood. Thy greatest and highest love toward us poor humans is made known therein, that thou has transformed thy heavy cross into an easy yoke, thy bitter suffering into imperishable joy, and thy grim death into eternal life. Therefore I give thee praise and thanksgiving, my gracious Lord Jesus Christ, always and forever.

I also believe and confess, my merciful Christ, that in the Spirit, thou didst go and didst preach the gospel to the spirits that were in prison, namely the holy patriarchs, proclaiming to them also the new and joyous message. Namely how according to the prediction of the holy prophets thou hadst become man, suffered torture and death, paid and done satisfaction for the sins of all men, as they had long been desiring with great earnestness, devotion, and fervent zeal, and then led them mightily out of captivity. And on the third day thou didst reunite spirit, soul, and body in the grave, and as a strong and mighty Victor over death, hell, and the devil, and riṣe again from the dead for our sake, so that all those who believe in thee might not perish but in thee should also overcome sin, death, hell, and the devil, and might also attain to eternal life, as thy brothers and fellow heirs with thee.

I also believe and confess, my Lord Jesus Christ, that after forty days, during which thou didst walk on earth as a testimony to thy joyous resurrection, didst ascend into the heavens and seat thyself at the right hand of thy heavenly Father with authority, glory, and majesty equal to the Father as our sole intercessor, mediator, and advocate before the Father, who has given thee all authority over all his possessions in heaven and on earth. There thou dost sit mighty and strong to help all believers who place their trust, consolation, and hope in thee and call upon thee in all their needs. Thou dost command all those who are burdened to come to thee, for thou willst give them rest. It is therefore needless, my meek Christ, to worship thee either here or there, yea neither in bread nor in wine, for thou art to be found sitting at the right of thy heavenly Father, just as also the holy Stephen saw thee and worshiped thee. It is also vain to seek another intercessor.[3] Thou art alone and dost will to be alone [our intercessor]. Whoever believes otherwise is a liar. /218/

I also believe and confess that thou shallst come from there to judge the living and the dead on the day of the last judgment, which for every godly man will be a special, elect, and joyful day. Then we shall see our God and Savior face-to-face in his great glory and majesty, coming in the clouds of heaven. Then our carnal, sinful, and godless life will come to an end. Then each will receive the recompense for his works. They who have worked well will enter into eternal life, those [who have worked] evil, into eternal fire. O my Lord Jesus Christ, shorten the days and come down to us soon; yet give us grace and strength meanwhile so to lead our life that we might be worthy then to hear with joy thy gracious and sweet voice, when thou shalt say, "Come hither, ye blessed of my Father, inherit the kingdom which was prepared for you from the beginning of the world, for I was hungry and you have fed me. I was thirsty and you have given me drink. I was a

---

[3] A clear anti-Catholic polemic with regard to the saints' intercession; probably anti-Lutheran (i.e., pro-Zwinglian) as well, regarding the Eucharist.

stranger and you gave me hospitality. I was naked and you clothed me. I was sick and you visited me. I was a prisoner and you came to me. Verily I say to you, what you did to one among these, the least of my brethren, that you did to me." But as for the fearful and unbelieving, accursed, unchaste, adulterers, gluttons, blasphemers, proud, envious, covetous, robbers, enraged, sorcerers, idolators, and liars, their lot will fall in the lake which burns with fire and brimstone. From this preserve us at all time, O gracious and good Lord Jesus Christ.

I also believe in the Holy Spirit,[4] which proceeds from the Father and Son and yet is with them one true God, who sanctifies all things, without whom nothing is holy, in whom I place all my trust, that he will teach me all truth, increase my faith, and stir up the fire of his love in my heart with his holy breathing and kindle it right properly that it might burn in genuine, unadulterated, and Christian love toward God and my neighbor. This I pray heartily, my God, my Lord, my Comforter.

I also believe and confess one holy universal Christian church, that is, a communion of saints and a brotherhood of many righteous and believing men, who unanimously confess one Lord, one God, one faith, and one baptism, which is gathered, established, and governed on earth by the one living divine Word. Yea, fully beautiful, without blemish, infallible, pure, without wrinkle, and blameless. I also confess publicly that thou, my Lord Jesus Christ /219/, hast thyself sanctified the church unto thyself through thy rose-red blood. Thou art her head and bridegroom and shalt also be with her unto the end of the world. O my God, may I and all Christ-believing men be finally found in this church. May we in concord with her believe, teach, and hold all that thou dost command us through thy Word, and also root out everything contrary that thou hast not planted,[5] so that we might not be led into error by any kind of respect of persons, human dogmas, or doctrine

---

[4] Instead of the second-person address, which transformed the first two articles of the creed into a prayer, Hubmaiaer here reverts to the credal form: "I believe."

[5] The imagery of uprooting what the Father did not plant (Matt. 15:13) is the standard phrase of Zwingli and Hubmaier for thoroughgoing reformation. Cf. above, p. 53, note 9.

of the ancient fathers, popes, councils, universities, or old customs. O my Lord Jesus Christ, institute once again the two bands, namely water baptism and the Supper, with which thou has outwardly girded and bound thy bride.[6] For unless these two elements are again established and practiced according to thy institution and ordering, there is among us neither faith, love, church covenant, fraternal admonition, ban, nor exclusion, without which it can never again be well with thy church.

I also believe and confess the remission of sins. Thus this Christian church has received keys, command, and authorization from thee, Christ, to open the doors of heaven to the sinner as often and frequently as he repents and regrets his sins, and to receive him again into the holy fellowship of Christ's believers like the prodigal son and the repentant Corinthian. But if after threefold fraternal admonition he is unwilling to abandon his sins, I believe assuredly that this church also has authority to exclude the same and to hold him for a publican and pagan. Here I believe and confess publicly, my Lord Jesus Christ, that whomever the Christian church thus looses on earth, the same is certainly loosed and freed from his sins also in heaven. And contrariwise whom even the church binds and excludes from her fellowship on earth, the same also stands bound before God in heaven and excluded from the universal Christian church (outside which there is no salvation), since Christ himself did hang both keys at the side of his spouse and dear bride, turned them over and committed them to her, as he was still on earth.[7]

I believe and confess the resurrection of the body. Yea of this very body which now clothes me. Even if it should be consumed by worms, drowned, decomposed, burned; yea and even if my temporal honor, property, body, and life are taken away, I will still first receive the true honor which is valid

---

[6] Baptism and the Supper are in a very functional way the bands which hold the church together. They have, according to this, not yet been effectively "re-instituted." Hubmaier thus considers neither the broader Anabaptist movement nor his own Waldshut effort as yet having achieved a successful Reformation.

[7] This phrasing is reproduced later in Hubmaier's "On The Ban" (below p. 411ff.). It is significant that fraternal discipline for Hubmaier is rooted in the creedal affirmation of the remission of sins.

before God, imperishable possessions, an impassable, trans-figured, immortal body, and eternal life on the day of the joyous resurrection of my flesh. O my mild Lord Jesus Christ, strengthen and preserve me in faith.

I also believe and confess eternal life that thou, my God and Lord /220/, shalt give to thy believers and elect ones after this miserable life, endowing them with certain, bright, and joyous contemplation of thy divine countenance, and satisfy all their desires with eternal rest, eternal peace, and eternal blessedness, which joy, rapture and delight no man can express or conceive here on earth. For no eye has seen, no ear has heard, and it has never entered into the heart of man, what God has prepared for those who love him.

O holy God, O mighty God, O unkillable God. This is my faith, which I confess with heart and mouth and have testified to publicly before the church in water baptism. I pray thee faithfully, wilt thou preserve me therein graciously until my end. And if through human fear and weakness, through tyranny, torture,[8] sword, fire, or water I should even be driven away from it, even so I herewith appeal to thee, O my merciful Father, restore me again with the grace of thy Holy Spirit and let me not depart in death without this faith.[9] This I pray thee from the depth of my heart, through Jesus Christ thy most beloved Son, our Lord and Savior. For in thee, Father, I hope; let me not be ashamed in eternity. Amen.

---

[8] This perspective is a concrete possibility for Hubmaier as he writes. Hubmaier was in fact tortured: cf. Zwingli to Capito, text 12 above, p. 150, HS, p. 215, Bergsten 1978, p. 307.

[9] As he writes, Hubmaier looks forward to another formal recantation, which was in fact needed to get out of prison (Yoder 1957, p. 16, note 42), but prays that thereafter he may again return to his (Anabaptist) confession before dying.

16

A Brief "Our Father"

There is no definite basis for dating the writing of this brief devotional text. Its content leads to the surmise that it, like the preceding one, may have been written during Hubmaier's incarceration in Zurich. It was printed in late 1526, soon after his arrival in Nikolsburg. The original has no marginal notes and no Scripture references.[1]

A Brief
Our Father
Dr. Balthasar
Huebmör of Fridberg
Ask, and you will
receive. John
Chap. 16
Nikolspurg
1526 /222/

Our Father. O gracious Father, I am not worthy that I should be called thy child, or that I should call thee my Father. I have not fulfilled thy fatherly will but rather the will of the father of liars. Pardon me, O merciful Father, and make me thy child in faith.

Thou who art in heaven. O gracious Father, behold how we are here in this miserable valley of suffering. Now children are never better off than when they are with their beloved

---

[1] Following current usage, Hubmaier identifies by its first words what Americans call the "Lord's Prayer." Thus his title is literally "A Brief Our Father." As in the previous text, in an effort to render the literary form of prayer, the translation will use thee/thou language. First draft by Elizabeth Horsch Bender. Source: HS 11, pp. 221-223.

Father, who feeds, gives drink, clothes, protects, and shelters them according to all their need. O gracious Father, take us as thy miserable children to thee in the heavens.

Thy name be hallowed. O merciful Father, we confess that we have often and frequently dishonored thy holy name in words and in deeds. And that we have made the sufferings of Christ, that should have been for us medication unto eternal life, into an eternal malediction by cursing and scolding.[2] Forgive us, Father, and henceforth give us grace that we may not speak thy name in vain, that we might set aside all blasphemy and swearing, so that thy holy name might be exalted, magnified, and praised eternally.

Thy kingdom come. O gracious Father, we once again confess ourselves captive[3] that we are in the kingdom of sin, of the devil, hell, and eternal death; but Father, we shout and call unto thee as to our most beloved Father, that Thou mightest soon come to us with thy kingdom of grace, peace, joy, and eternal blessedness. Come to our help, O gracious Father; for without thee, we are completely miserable, troubled, and forsaken.

Thy will be done on earth as in heaven. O loving Father, we publicly confess that thy fatherly will is not being done in us earthly humans, for our will is fully and completely in contradiction to thy divine will. We pray thee to send us thy Holy Spirit, that he might work in us genuine faith, constant hope, and fervent love, that we might make our will in all things to be subject to thy fatherly will.

Give us today our daily bread. O tender Father, because man lives not alone from bread, but from every word that proceeds from thy holy mouth, so we pray thee humbly that thou wouldest nourish us with the bread of thy holy Word, which comes down from heaven, whereof he who eats will never hunger.[4]

---

[2] For his time, Hubmaier was especially sensitive to the sins of the tongue. Cf. text 23 below, p. 375.

[3] In the idiom of the time, *gefangen* meant not only literally "captured" but also "convicted" or "guilty." "We confess ourselves to be guilty" would be a correct rendering. Yet at the same time the other meaning remains in the link to the following phrase. Guilt is moral servitude as much as forensic culpability.

[4] Allusion to the imagery of John 6. There, however, the phrase (vv. 27, 33, 50f.) is "shall not die" more often than "not hunger" (only 6:35). This entire text has no marginal notes or other biblical references.

Bring it to life in our soul, that it might burgeon, grow up, and bear fruit for eternal life. Give us also Christian and industrious workers, who will divide the same to us[5] pure, clear, and undefiled and distribute it faithfully, so that thy fatherly will, which can be known only from thy Word, might be fulfilled. /223/

Forgive us our debts as we forgive our debtors. O tender-hearted Father, we again confess ourselves guilty, that we have sinned much with words, works, and evil thoughts, so that we do not even know the number, the measure, nor the size of our sins. O Father, forgive us and give us strength henceforth to improve our lives, as we forgive all those who have ever done us harm. Father, forgive them; they know not what they do. Illuminate all those who are in error concerning thy holy Word, which they persecute and outlaw, that they might come to the true way which leads to eternal life.

Lead us not into temptation. O heavenly Father! Behold the great anxiety, desolation, misery, persecution, and tribulation which is inflicted upon us here on earth. Consider also our human weakness. Therefore, O sweet Father, we pray thee for the sake of thy fatherly love that thou mightest not abandon us in our pain and suffering and that we might not be overcome, nor fall away from thy holy Word. Let us not be tested harder than we are able to bear.[6] We are weak and impotent, and our enemies are strong, powerful, and cruel. Thou knowest that, O merciful Father.

But deliver us from evil. From sin, from the devil, from our own body, which is our greatest enemy, and also from everything which hinders our access to thee. Likewise, grant to us everything which furthers us toward thee, *for thine is the authority and the power and the glory in eternity.*

O eternal Father, as we now have prayed to thee, fulfill it unto us according to thy fatherly good pleasure. This we pray thee for the sake of the multitude of thy mercifulness, and for the sake of thy gracious promise which thou hast spoken to us

---

[5] 2 Tim. 2:15. To "divide the word," i.e., to make significant distinctions, is seen positively as an interpretative ministry. There may also be an allusion to Jesus' breaking bread for his disciples.

[6] Bergsten (HS, p. 221) correctly sees in this passage a parallel to the recognition of Hubmaier's possible weakness in the face of coming persecution, as in his "Twelve Articles" (above, p. 241).

244 / *Balthasar Hubmaier*

always and again through Moses, the prophets and the apostles. Especially we pray thee thus, and cry unto thee through thy most beloved Son, our Lord Jesus Christ, who has assuredly promised to us and certified by his bitter death that whatever we pray thee in his name, that thou wouldst give us. Father; into thy hand we commend our body, life, honor, goods, soul, and spirit. All that which we receive from thee we in return will consecrate unto thee. Thou dost give and thou dost take, may thy name be praised. Amen, so be it.

Nicolspurg /224/

17

Old and New Teachers
on Believers Baptism

The third major work on baptism by Hubmaier was dedicated on July 21, 1526, to Martin Göschl, who was the leading evangelical pastor in Nikolsburg when Hubmaier arrived there. Perhaps thereby Hubmaier hoped to win him and the church in Nikolsburg to the Anabaptists. It was probably the first work of Hubmaier printed by Simprecht Sorg.

Hubmaier's previous works were based on the interpretation of Scripture. This one turned to the "old and new teachers," to make the point that Hubmaier was neither schismatic nor heretical. The citations from the fathers were to prove that the original practice of the early church had in fact been believers' baptism. The numerous citations from contemporaries give the reader to understand that the questioning of infant baptism had been widespread and that the practice of believers' baptism need not have been schismatic. To accept the quotations at face value is to conclude that the failure of several of Hubmaier's contemporaries to practice believers baptism was the result of inconsistency, stubbornness, or failure of nerve.

There are two editions of the work; the second is longer. We translate the first in its entirety, followed by the material added in the second. The treatise comprises two parts: the first part a group of citations from early church sources, primarily the fathers, the second from contemporaries of Hubmaier. The citations are not always fully correct and many references are inaccurate. Many of the dates, for example, are incorrect. Citations from contemporary printed sources are generally correct.[1]

---

[1] The basic work of checking the citations was done by Sachsse 1914: 33-40. Unfortunately, his references are outdated, since many modern editions of works cited have been published since Sachsse did his work. The failure of Westin and Bergsten (HS) to provide adequate annotations for the present treatise is an unfortunate lapse for a critical edition. Armour 1966: 157-58, can be used as a supplement. We have filled in the missing references as possible but have not made publication await our locating them all. Important assistance in identifying some references was received from Dr. William L. Petersen.

Bergsten concludes that Hubmaier began the work on this treatise when he was in Waldshut and that he finished it only in Nikolsburg.[2] The treatise reveals that Hubmaier, the doctor of theology, was determined to bring all his resources and capabilities to bear on the issue of believers baptism.[3]

The Opinion of the Ancient and New Teachers that One Should Not Baptize Young Children until They Have Been Instructed in the Faith. 1526

Dr. Balthasar Huebmör von Fridberg There must be Divisions Among You in order that those who are true May be revealed among you. 1 Cor. 1:19. Nicolspurg

To the most venerable in God, Martin, former Bishop at Nicopol, now Provost at Khůonitz, his gracious lord.

Grace and peace from God the heavenly Father, through Jesus Christ our Lord. Most reverend in God, gracious lord. Your Grace is well knowledgeable about the ancient error which many from the time of Cyprian[a] until today have practiced out of ignorance. Namely, that they led young children also to the sacrament (as they called it)[b] of bread and wine, which nevertheless has no basis in the Word of God. These bring forward no other justification or excuse for their deeds than that we Germans also baptize our children. On such a basis they think it fitting to give their children to eat

---

[2] HS, 225-226.

[3] The best studies of this treatise are Armour 1966, pp. 49-52; and Windhorst 1976, pp. 108-112. Partial translation in Hošek 1892, pp. 131f.; Davidson 1939, pp. 226-253. Source: HS 12, pp. 227-255.

---

[a] Cyprian.
[b] Leading the children to the Supper.

and to drink of the sacrament since baptism and the breaking of bread are two like ceremonies, having been instituted in the New Testament by Christ.ᵃ Although we have already set over against them the statement of Paul from 1 Corinthians 11:28 that a person examine oneself before going to the Supper, /228/ which young children cannot do, from that hour on they cite against us numerous passages on water baptism, Matt. 28:19f.; Mark 16:16; Acts 2:38, 41; 8:12, 38; 10:47-48; 11:16; 16:15, 33; 18:8; 22:16; Heb. 10:22; 1 Pet. 3:21. Yet all these passages clearly show that one should also believe beforehand and confess faith with the mouth before one receives water baptism. Which just as well is impossible for young children to do. And here, although màny in our midst highly boast of infused faith,ᵇ wanting to ascribe the same to children, they do it without any basis in the Scriptures, which point to no other faith than that which comes from hearing, from hearing the Word of God, Rom. 10:17. On the other hand, the others would also like on the same authority to put forward an infused testing and examination for their children. Although they have for the same as little basis in Scripture as we have for infused faith, so we, like those who are uncertain of their affairs, fall from infused faith and flee to the foreign faith of church, father, mother, or godparents.ᶜ That does not help us at all. For the church is built on our own faith and affirmation, not we on the faith of the church. Faith is the foundation and the church is the building, whatever Augustineᵈ says with his proverb: "*Euangelio non crederem* [I would not believe the gospel], etc."⁴ For if I did not believe the gospel I would never believe the church, since the church is built on the gospel and not the gospel on the church. Thus Paul says, "No other foundation can anyone lay except that which is laid who is Christ Jesus," 1 Cor. 3:11. Thus also Christ says, "You are Peter and on the rock (which you believe and confess) I will

---

⁴ MPL 34:97-98, tr. Schaff 1956, v. IV:131.

ᵃ Baptism. Supper.
ᵇ Infused faith.
ᶜ Foreign faith.
ᵈ Augustine: 1. gospel; 2. faith; 3. church.

build my church," Matt. 16:18. Therefore in the first place we must be instructed in the Word of God that Jesus is Christ, Son of the living God.

In the second place, to believe and to confess is to build on that foundation of gold, silver, and precious stone, 1 Cor. 3:12. In the third place, the church is built on our faith and confession, and not our faith on the church, but on the preached Word of God, which is God himself and which has become human, John 1:1, 14. To that Christ said: "Whoever believes himself and is baptized, etc." He does not say, for whomever father, mother, or godparents believe. Indeed, a child whose salvation should depend on the faith of his father, mother, or godparents, would often suffer from heartbreak. Where would Paul be, where Saint Barbara and Catherine?[5] Accordingly, gracious Lord, so that we give offense to no one in this article on infant baptism, and also that no one be able to use us to cover his error, I have set together the opinion of the very ancient and wholly new teachers on infant baptism. Although I do not need the testimony of human beings /229/ since I have previously published a little book on the witness of Scripture concerning this matter,[6] wherein I proved clearly with divine Scripture that infant baptism is a work without any basis in the divine Word or in faith.* I will leave it at that even if many rail and shout unduly loud: Christ has not forbidden infant baptism; therefore one can safely baptize. To the same I give the following reply to their popish assertion: Whatever Christ has not commanded in those things which concern the honor of God and salvation is already forbidden, Luke 11:45-52. He is the way, truth, and life, John 14:6. He cannot suffer that we turn to the right or left, Deut. 5:29. He rejects all false teaching. Peter calls these same teachers

---

[5] Hubmaier is making the point that the people would be left out if they were dependent on the confession of their parents. The reference to Saints Paul, Barbara, and Catherine is to early Christians who grew up in non-Christian settings and were converted and baptized only after they reached adulthood. See Englebert 1951, pp. 250f., 448f., 461f.

[6] See above, text 11.

---

* An old and new papal argument.

deceitful masters, 2 Pet. 2:1.⁷ Christ says further: "Everything my heavenly father has not planted will be uprooted," Matt. 15:13. He does not say, "Everything that he has forbidden will be uprooted." From that hour on in which Christ commands us to preach the gospel, Mark 16:15, everything is forbidden to be preached that is not the gospel. *Locus enim arguendi ab autoritate negatiue in Theologia est vrgentissimus* [in theology it is most urgent to argue a proof from negative authority] which Paul also uses in the epistle to the Hebrews 1:5, where he says, "To which angel has God ever said, 'You are my Son, etc.,' " Ps. 2:7. It is as if he wanted to say: "Since we do not find that in Scripture, then he said it to no one except to his dear Son, etc." So also, as soon as Christ said to his disciples, "Go forth, teach all people and baptize, etc.," Matt. 28:19, it is already forbidden to baptize those who have not yet been instructed in the faith. Hereupon, gracious Lord, I beseech, that Your Grace graciously accept from me this unworthy little book at this time, that you take this matter to heart, thereto counseling and helping as a Christian bishop, so that everything he has commanded may be established in the power of God and, conversely, that what he has not planted may be uprooted. For Your Grace is still the only bishop I have experienced who has surrendered himself on earth so powerfully and faithfully to God and his holy Word in doctrine and works, and this in a wholly valiant and manly fashion. God be praised in the heavens. Herewith I commend Your Grace and your Christian housewife to the protection of God. Given at Nicolspurg, in Herr Oswald's room, July 21, 1526.

Your Grace's obedient servant,
Balthasar Huebmör von Fridberg /230/

---

⁷ Hubmaier cites Rev. 3 in a marginal note. The citation does not fit a particular sentence from the text and may be a general reference for the paragraph.

The Witness and Opinion of the Old and New Teachers on Infant Baptism

Origen[8]

"The person who stops sinning receives baptism for the forgiveness of sins. Therefore I beseech you that you do not come to baptism without thoughtfulness and without diligent prior consideration, but that in the first place you demonstrate fruits worthy of the renewal of your life. Spend some time living a good life."[9] Thus writes Origen about Luke 3:8. Concerning the word of Paul in Romans 6:3, he says, "Here Paul points out that baptism was not practiced the same way in the time of the apostles as it is in our time. For at that time those who were knowledgeable and instructed in the death of Christ were baptized; they were also buried with him through baptism into death. For as Christ was resurrected from the dead through the glory of the father, so shall those who are baptized walk in newness of life."[10] He writes further concerning Exodus 8, Homily 8, folio 43, E:[a] "When we come to the grace of baptism, we deny all idols and lords. We confess God the Father, the Son, and the Holy Spirit alone."[11]

Basil the Great[12]

" 'Go forth,' says Christ, 'baptize in the name of the Father, the Son, and the Holy Spirit,' Matt. 28:19. For baptism is a seal of faith, faith an affirmation of divinity. For one must

---

[8] Origen, ca. 185-ca.254., was the great theologian and biblical exegete of Alexandria.

[9] MPG 13:1858. In noting Hubmaier's use of sources we will utilize quotation marks only where a fairly literal translation is made. Otherwise, the references should be understood as paraphrasing the sense of a passage.

[10] MPG 14:1003ff.

[11] MPG 12:354f.

[12] One of the Cappadocian fathers, Basil, ca. 330-379, was the successor to Eusebius as bishop of Caesarea.

---

[a] Homily on Exod. Eight.

first of all believe and afterward be marked with baptism,"[13] Book 3, *Contra eunomium* [Against Eunomius], folio 44.*

He also compares water baptism with the flood from which no one was saved except whoever entered the ark in faith, as Peter also reports in 1 Peter, chapter 3, at the end (v. 21). Thus look at Psalm 28, at the end, Ps. 29:10.[14] Likewise: where a ready will is, there is nothing to hinder baptism. He testifies to that with the treasurer, Acts 8:36f. Look at the same in the *Exhortatione ad Baptismum* [Exhortation to Baptism], folio 142f.[15] Look also at the treatise *Quid instruendi monedique sint ad Baptismum venientes* [What Is to Be Taught and Instructed to Those Coming to Baptism].[16]

Athanasius[17]

On the change of life in baptism: First of all, we should be sorry for our previous life. After that we are washed in baptism. Thus he writes about this word from Hebrews 6:6.[18]

Concerning 1 Corinthians 15:29, where he speaks of the baptism of the dead he says, "Whoever wanted to accept baptism spoke the articles[19] in entire faith, etc." One should also read what he has to say about 1 Corinthians 1:13. /231/

He says concerning Hebrews 6:2: If we are baptized it is signified to us by a symbol that as we are drawn out of the water so will we see the resurrection in order to profess and confess that the dead will rise.

---

[13] MPG 29:666.
[14] Cf. MPG 29:303, 30:82. ET in Basil 1963, p. 210.
[15] MPG 31:438.
[16] Basil's treatise on baptism (Basil 1950, p. 339) supports Hubmaier's argument but does not include this particular phrase.
[17] Athanasius, ca. 296-373, bishop of Alexandria, was the great defender of orthodoxy against Arius.
[18] A similar assertion is made by Athanasius in his fourth letter to Serapion, paragraph nine. MPG 26:650.
[19] "The Articles" here means the so-called Apostles' Creed.

---

* Book 3, *Against Eunomius.*

Tertullian[20]

Baptism is a sealing of the faith which is given and begun in the faith of repentance. Therefore we are not baptized because we want to stop sinning, but because we have already stopped, for we have now already been baptized in the heart. That is his judgment in *lib. de Poenitentia[21]* [On Repentance], folio 440.[*]

In the book *De corona militis* [Of the Garland of the Soldier], folio 416, he writes thus: "Now I come to speak about baptism. Those of us who want to come to baptism will testify some time before in the church under the bishop's hand that we renounce the devil and his spirits and angels. After that we are immersed three times."[22]

Jerome[23]

Those on whom the bishop lays his hands are those who have been baptized in right belief, who have believed in the Father and Son and Holy Spirit, three persons and one nature. Jerome, "Against the Luciferians."[24]

Likewise, concerning Matthew 28:19, he writes thus: "In the first place, teach all peoples. After they have been taught, baptize them in water. For it may not happen that the body receive the sacrament of baptism unless the soul beforehand has received the truth of faith."[25]

---

[20] Tertullian, ca. 160-ca. 220, the first Christian theologian to write in Latin, is often classified as second only to Augustine as a Western theologian from the patristic period.

[21] MPL 2:1351f., tr. Roberts 1981, v. III:662.

[22] MPL 2:79, tr. Roberts 1981, v. III:94.

[23] Jerome, ca. 342-420, was an outstanding biblical exegete, best known for his translation of the Bible into Latin (the Vulgate).

[24] CIC I:384f. (canon 75). Numerous of the citations by Hubmaier in this treatise are to be found in the canon law of Gratian. We will simplify the references by referring to the volume, page, and canon number of the modern Friedberg edition. The Jerome text is also in Schaff 1979, 6.[324]

[25] MPL 26:226. This text is Jerome's translation of Origen's homily on Luke 3.

---

[*] Book, *On Repentance*.

Cyril[26]

Those who are being instructed in faith should not immediately be taken to baptism. Thus he writes about John, Book 2, chapter 36.[27] He describes also the figures of water baptism from the Old and New Testaments, all of which fit believers. On John, Book 6, Chapter 15.[28]

Theophylact[29]

About the Word of Christ in Mark 16:16, *Qui crediderit* [Whoever Will Believe], he writes thus: "It is not enough that one believes, he must also be baptized. For whoever believes and is not baptized, but is a catechumen, is not now saved."[30] Also pay attention to him in any case, dear reader, concerning Matthew 28:19 on /232/ the text: "Go forth, teach all peoples." There he testifies what one should teach before and after baptism, and how a common institution of baptism has come about through Christ which applies to Jews and heathen.[31]

Eusebius[32]

Eusebius, Book 10, Chapter 14, *Ecclesiastical History*,[33] writes a wonderful story of a bishop in Alexandria and of several children who baptized one another in the sea.* From

[26] Cyril of Jerusalem, ca. 315-86, was bishop of Jerusalem after 349. What lies behind the reference (note 79, below) to Basel is unknown.

[27] The reference to John cannot be found and must be incorrect. Sachsse 1914: 36n.3 suggests the correct source is Cyril's *Catechetical Lectures*, specifically Lecture XVII, "On the Holy Spirit." See MPG 33:1009, tr. Schaff 1979, v. VII:132.

[28] Cf. MPG 33:433ff., tr. Schaff 1979, v. VII:14ff.

[29] Theophylact was an eleventh-century exegete, best known for his commentaries of the Old and New Testaments.

[30] MPG 123:679f.

[31] MPG 123:485f.

[32] Eusebius, ca. 260-ca. 340, known as the "Father of Church History" for his many historical writings was the bishop of Caesarea.

[33] The reference to Eusebius is incorrect. See Sozomen, *Ecclesiastical History*, Bk II, chap. 17, MPG 67:217ff., tr. Schaff 1979, v. II:269.

* Book Ten, Chapter Fourteen, *Ecclesiastical History*.

254 / Balthasar Hubmaier

this it is clearly understandable what and how one questioned those in the first churches who wanted to be baptized. For reasons of space I have not cited this story.[34]

De Consecr., [On Consecration]/[a] Distinction 4, Canon *Queris* [You ask]/ In verbo: *Difficillimam* [at the word: *Difficult*][35]

Pope Boniface has conflict with Bishop Augustine. The pope says[b] that godparents, when they bring the child to baptism, may not truthfully answer in place of the child that it renounces the devil or that it believes. For they do not know whether that child will be chaste or not, pious or a thief. To that Augustine gives a blue answer.[36]

Likewise, the canon *Prima* [First][37] points to the article of faith about which one should question before one baptizes a person.[c] The canons *baptizandi* [those to be baptized][38] and *ante baptismum* [before baptism][39] teach how those who are to be baptized should present themselves several days before to their bishop.[d] Also they should hold themselves back several days from wine and meat. All this cannot apply to children. For water baptism, one's own confession of faith is necessary and foreign faith is not sufficient.[e] Christ

---

[34] See below, pp. 268, where Hubmaier does tell the story.
[35] The first word of the fourth paragraph of the letter of Augustine begins with *"Difficilimam."* Thus Hubmaier is able to refer the reader to a specific portion of this long canon.
[36] In the letter to Boniface, paragraph four, Augustine justifies the bringing of an infant by the parents to baptism, even though it is not known of what sort the child will be when grown. CIC I:1402 (canon 129), tr. Schopp 1962, 18.[135] Hubmaier calls this a "blue answer," meaning "a lie."
[37] CIC I:1386f. (canon 73).
[38] CIC I:1383 (canon 60).
[39] CIC I:1383 (canon 59).

---

[a] Spiritual law.
[b] *De consec.* Di. 4, canon *queris* ["On Consecration," Distinction 4, canon, "You ask"].
[c] Canon *Prima* [First].
[d] Canons *Baptizandi* [Those to be baptized] and *Ante Baptismum* [Before baptism].
[e] Foreign faith.

testifies to that when he says, "Whoever believes himself and is baptized, etc.," Mark 16:16. He does not say, "For whom the godparents believe." Thus Philip demanded from the treasurer his own faith when he wanted to be baptized, and said to him, "If you believe with the whole heart, then it is appropriate." The treasurer answered, "I believe that Jesus is the Christ, Son of the living God," Acts 8:37. Then Philip baptizes him on the basis of his own faith. It is like having a useless tool to have godparents at a baptism, as are salt, oil, dirt, spittle, and the like.* Therefore, if one wants to preserve the one, then the other must also let stand. However, nothing is better than tearing out everything that God has not planted, Matt. 15:13. It must all be broken, whether it has been standing a short or a long time. If I wanted to believe for another person, then I would also want to be baptized for another. Faith is more than the sign of water baptism. /233/

Erasmus of Rotterdam on baptism in Matt. 8:18ff.

He recounts all the articles of faith as they are contained in the *Symbolo Apostolorum*, [The Apostles' Creed] and adds these words: "After you have taught the people these things and they believe what you have taught them, have repented of their prior life, and are ready henceforth to walk according to evangelical doctrine, then immerse them in water in the name of the Father and the Son and the Holy Spirit."[40] Here Erasmus publicly points out that baptism was instituted by Christ for those instructed in faith and not for young children.

He writes further on the second chapter of Acts (2:38): "The Lord commanded the evangelical shepherds: Go forth and teach all peoples, baptize them, teach them to hold all things which I have commanded you," Matt. 28:19. Teach those who are to be baptized the basic elements of evangelical wisdom. Unless one believes the same, then he is immersed in

---

[40] The quotation is from Erasmus' 1523 paraphrase of the Gospel of Matthew. Erasmus 1961, VII:146.

---

* To have godparents is a human trifle.

water in vain.[41] Consider him also, dear reader, on the eighth chapter of Acts[42] and many other places.*

Martin Luther

Luther wrote a sermon six years ago on the mass, wherein he points out in the seventeenth article how symbols like baptism and the Supper mean nothing without prior faith.[43] They are like a sheath without a knife, a case without a jewel, a hoop before an inn without wine. /234/

Johannes Oecolampadius

"Until now we have encountered no passages in the Scriptures which cause us to confess the baptism of small children, as far as we are humbly able to see it."[44] I have this in his own handwriting.[45]

He writes further concerning Romans 6:3: "The Lord, who in the last chapter of Mark says, 'Whoever believes and is baptized,' Mark 16:16, forces us with this word 'baptism' to confession and demands from us a perfect faith. Whoever does not want to be baptized, the same does not want to confess Christ."[46] From this judgment it follows that every Christian should first confess Christ and afterward be baptized with outward baptism. About the words, *In mortem* [into the death],

---

[41] See the 1524 paraphrase of Acts by Erasmus. Erasmus 1961, VII:674.

[42] Erasmus 1961, VII:697ff. Likely it is Acts 8:12 which is meant.

[43] In the section to which Hubmaier alludes, Luther writes: "...in every promise of God there are two things which one must consider: the word and the sign." It is the words and the promise of God that Luther considers as important, not faith. Without them "...the sacraments are dead and are nothing at all, like a body without a soul, a cask without wine...a sheath without a knife, and the like." WA 6:363, tr. LW 35:91. Hubmaier does not remember the Luther passage correctly and thus incorrectly cites a passage that does not in fact support his view.

[44] Stahelin 1927: 355f. Oecolampadius continues: "*Attamen non video, quid prohibeat*" [Neither do I see any which would forbid it].

[45] Cf. above, text 6, pp. 67ff., esp. p. 72, the actual correspondence between Oekolampad and Hubmaier.

[46] Oecolampadius 1525: 52/v.

---

* Vain water.

Rom. 6:4: The mystery of baptism is that we are baptized into the death of Christ and learn how Christ Jesus has died and thus provided satisfaction for our sin. To learn such is not possible for a cradle baby.[47] Also read what he has to say about verse 11, and other places.

Zwingli in his Article Book
On the 18th Article, On Confirmation*

"From its practice and from the fact that the name is still asked today I have come to the conclusion that confirmation only came into use when it became the common practice to baptize children in childhood, indeed, as soon as they were born, so that when older they would not ignore the faith which the father and mother had affirmed for them through the godfather and godmother.[b] I know well, as the fathers pointed out, that from the ancient time until today children sometimes have been baptized, but that it has not been so commonly practiced as in our time. Rather, one taught them publicly with each other, when they had come to the understanding of the word of salvation, which is why they have been called "catechumens," that is, the instructed.[c] When they have given themselves to a firm faith in the heart and have confessed such with the mouth, they were baptized."[48] Thus did he also often publicly preach at /235/ Zürich and he confessed the same against me before Sebastian Rückensperger. God is not two-tongued, however. He writes further in the fifteenth article against Faber:[d] "All things are expressed brightly and clearly in the Word of God."[49] In the 24th thesis: "Every Christian is unbound toward those

---

[47] Oecolampadius 1525: 54/b
[48] Z 2, p. 123.[4-16] Cf. Furcha 1984, p. 100.
[49] This sentence is rendered as a quotation by Hubmaier, but it does not occur as such in the place cited. It is, however, a fair summary of what Zwingli says. Cf Z 2, p. 74,[7ff.] tr. Furcha 1984, pp. 60-61.

---

* Zwingli on confirmation.
[b] Those are evil, heathen words.
[c] Catechumens.
[d] Faber.

works which God has not commanded."[50] In the little book on the rebellious spirits, page E, second side, recently published in 1525: "Those who baptize children have no clear word in which they are commanded to baptize."[51] From these three theses every Christian may basically conclude that since children's baptism has no clear word in Scripture, one is not bound to baptize them. Answer!

Master Leo Jud[52] of Zurich.[*]

"One has no clear Word of God on the baptism of children." I have that in his own handwriting.

Doctor Bastian Hoffmayster of Schaffhausen,[53] now at Zürich

"First, I beseech you through Christ, that you not harbor resentment against me that I had to be admonished so often by you, as I have delayed to disclose to you my opinion on baptism. I did not want to spur you—as one who is already easily heated in this matter—lest disunity result from that, when you would see that we are also inclined in your direction. However, it has so also pleased the heavenly Father that the matter has come into debate without me, so much so that by now it has even creeped up to us; so God has willed it. Therefore, /236/ we have not been ashamed of the truth, but publicly we have confessed before the Council at Schaffhausen[b] that our brother Zwingli, if he would want that children must be baptized, errs from the goal and does not walk according to the truth the gospel. Truly I could

[50] Z 1, p. 461.[4-6] Cf. Furcha 1984, p. 197.
[51] Z 3, p. 409.[18-19] Zwingli also says in this passage, "...those who refuse to baptize them have no clear prohibition against baptizing infants." Z 3, p. 409,[14-15] tr. Harder 1985, p. 319.
[52] Leo Jud, 1482-1542, was a close confidant of Zwingli and pastor of St. Peter's in Zurich during the Reformation.
[53] Sebastian Hofmeister, 1476-1533, was the Reformer of Schaffhausen.

[*] Leo Jud of Zurich.
[b] He also preached that publicly.

not be forced to baptize my child. Accordingly, you act in a Christian fashion when you again bring forth the true baptism of Christ which has long lain neglected.· We would also undertake such. May God give grace to your and our enterprise, that it come out well." This opinion I have in his own handwriting.[54]

The Preachers at Strassburg.
Wolfgang Capito, Capar Hedio, Matthew Zell, Simpor Pollio, Theobald Niger, Joannes Latomus, Anthony Firn, Martin Hackh, Martin Bützer, in their little book, "Basis and Reason."

"As in the beginning of the church no one was baptized and taken into the Christian church unless he had given himself wholly to the Word of Christ," folio K, page one.[55] They point out from Scripture their "basis and reason" and write that "the beginning of the Christian life" lies in the confession that all our deeds are sin. "Therefore John the Baptist, Christ, and the apostles started with this: 'Repent.' And in the congregations of God repentance of sin, that is, confession prior to baptism was the first thing with the ancients. For generally only the understanding ones, not children, were baptized." That is the published opinion of all of them, folio K, pages two and three.[56]

Likewise, they write further that without the baptism of the Spirit, water baptism is an illusion, folio M, page two. Now if baptism without faith is an illusion, then infant baptism is not from God, for God has not instituted an illusion.[57]

---

[54] There is no reason to doubt that Hubmaier had such a letter. Cf. Fast 1973, 11, p. 13.
[55] Stupperich 1960, p. 245. Bucer's "Basis and Reason" was published in 1524.
[56] Stupperich 1960, p. 247.
[57] Stupperich 1960, pp. 257-58.

· Zachariah is his name.

Christoph Hegendorf[58] on 1 Pet. 3:21

"There you hear that faith is prior to baptism for no other reason /237/ than that it is not baptism but the faith of baptism that saves us. That is the faith of baptism that we believe we have received the remission of all sins through Jesus Christ and thereto with firm words we commit ourselves to God and say that we believe in God the Father Almighty and in Jesus Christ, etc." Whether a cradle baby can do that I leave to the judgment of every Christian reader.

Ludwig Hätzer[59]

"You despise godless infant baptism according to the integrity of your intention. Stand like a firm rock.* For it is certain that all the masters of this world and of high thoughts[60] must therein be brought to shame. What is it then that they call us revolutionaries? Was not the same thing said about Christ, etc?" This I have in his own handwriting with his seal pressed on it, and much more besides.

Cellarius[61]

"Since you urge me to tell you our opinions on baptism and the Supper of the Lord, I will please you heartily and in brief. /238/ In the first place, it is a horror in the sight of God that one baptizes young children, which baptism is neither testified through Scripture nor through the example of

---

[58] Christoph Hegendorf, 1500-1540, was a humanist theologian and jurist and follower of Luther.

[59] Ludwig Hätzer, ca. 1500-1529, an early radical supporter of Zwingli, has been called a "marginal figure in early Anabaptism" (ME II, pp. 621-626).

[60] High thoughts: "hohen synnen," meaning the Scholastics. It is a term that both Hätzer and Hubmaier use to refer pejoratively to the Scholastics. See also HS, pp. 295, 309, 389.

[61] Martin Cellarius, 1499-1565, a humanist and temporary sympathizer with the Anabaptist cause, left Zurich before the January baptismal disputation of 1525.

---

* Marpesian rocks.

the apostles. Against that cry out the judgments and opinions[62] which can be illustrated by the example of the distribution of the created things by God: 'For in the beginning the earth was void, etc.' " On that I have his own handwriting.

Balthasar

I point out these opinions, not because I need human witnesses, but so that it may be seen how we have been paper Christians and mouth Christians.[a] Yes, one testifies the truth with Scripture and mouth, but one does not touch the same with the least finger, which the devil appreciates very much. However, Christ says, "The servant who knows the will of his Lord and does not do it will be struck with many blows." Yes, the words, teaching, practice, and example of Christ and the apostles, also the people and our own consciences will bear witness against us at the last day before Christ the Judge. Christ will say, "I have set up baptism in the church for the Jews and heathen (as also your own sentences write),[b] and said, 'All power is given me in heaven and on earth. Go forth, teaching all people, and baptize them in the name of the Father and the Son and Holy Spirit,' " Matt. 28:18f. "Do you hear," Christ will say, "that one should first teach faith, and after that baptize in water?" I have said to you even clearer through my official scribe, Mark 16:16, "Go forth into the whole world and preach the gospel to all creatures. Whoever believes and is baptized will be saved. Whoever does not believe, is condemned." You see here even more clearly how one should first preach; second, believe; third, be baptized; fourth follows salvation. Peter the apostle will stand against us with the three thousand persons, Acts 2:41, and with Cornelius and his household, Acts 10-11, and testify, "I have taught that one should first repent and after that be baptized in the name of our Lord Jesus Christ." Yes, the three thousand persons, also Cornelius and his household,

---

[62] The second edition adds here, "of God."

---

[a] Paper Christians. Mouth Christians.
[b] Sentences, Distinction 3.

will testify for him publicly and say, "We first of all heard the
Word of God; after that believed; third, were baptized with
water; and fourth, broke bread and gave ourselves to prayer."
Likewise, the man and wife in Samaria and also Simon the
magician will bear witness against us before the final judgment and will say, "Philip first of all preached to us, we
believed the Word and were lastly also baptized," Acts 8:12.
The treasurer of Queen Candace of Egypt will say the same
thing: "Philip /239/ instructed me in faith in the chariot.
After that I desired water baptism according to the order of
Christ. But Philip did not want to baptize me before I had
publicly affirmed faith with my mouth. As soon as I did that
and confessed that Jesus is Christ, Son of the living God, only
then did Philip command the chariot to stop and baptize me
in water," Acts 8:38. See, if we had no other Scriptures than
these, they would be enough to prove that baptism should be
given to believers and not to young children—until they also
have been instructed in the Word of God and faith, confessing
and expressing the same with the mouth. Paul will also stand
up and testify powerfully against us with his example, teaching, and practice of baptism. "See, you know well and cannot
deny that the Word of God was first preached to me by
Ananias; then second the old scales fell from my eyes; third I
received eyesight in faith; fourth, I arose and let myself be
baptized, Acts 9:1-19; 22:1-16. So has my most dear co-worker
in the gospel, Luke, whose praise is great in the church, written to you faithfully how I first preached to Lydia the seller
of purple and the jailer, Acts 16:14-15, 31; the Corinthians,
Acts 18:5; and the twelve men at Ephesus, Acts 19:1-7. Then
they accepted the Word and believed and not until then were
they baptized. Search the Scripture for they also bear witness
of me," John 5:39. You will find this order so bright and clear
in Heb. 10:22 that no excuse at all will help you.

Thus, let us go forth to Christ, first of all with a true
heart in perfection of faith; second, purified in our heart of
an evil conscience, that is, with internal baptism, and third,
after that, the body washed with pure water. The outward baptism only comes then, for without the internal baptism it is
only hypocrisy. For as I wrote to the Corinthians in 1
Corinthians 11:28, that they should examine themselves before
they eat of the bread and drink from the chalice, or else they
thereby eat and drink judgment on themselves, thus I say,

indeed, not I but Christ himself, that one should have faith before one receives baptism—or else one acts against his Word, teaching, and institution, which is a horrible idolatry, not obedience to the words of the Lord, Matt. 28:19; Mark 16:16; 1 Sam. 15:22. To say nothing of the fact that through such infant baptism people are robbed of the true baptism of Christ, imagining that they are baptized, and yet are anything less than baptized. Also Noah, along with Ham, Shem, Japheth, and their wives, Gen. 6:1ff., will testify against us and say: "Look. We were a figure of water baptism with our ark in the Flood, as Saint Peter has written to you in his epistle," 1 Pet. 3:20. Now, however, no one went into the ark /240/ unless beforehand he believed the Word of God. Thus you should properly baptize no one unless he believes beforehand. However, whether everyone has been a believer who until now has been baptized, I leave to God in his judgment. For what matters is not how it is, but how it should be according to the order of Christ.[a] For without doubt there have also been many who have gone to the Supper of Christ who should have examined themselves beforehand and it did not happen so. Nevertheless, the Word in its power remains. The person should examine himself beforehand, 1 Cor. 11:28.

O, you dear pious Christians.[b] Since we have so many stronger words, works, teaching, example, and Scriptures against us, which we cannot dissolve, or heaven and earth must first break apart, then let us first take up the matter with word and teaching, and point out the same faithfully, peacefully, and virtuously to the people, as we have hitherto done in other matters. And if the churches are instructed rightly in the Word and thoroughly, they will themselves beseech and desire that everything be uprooted and abolished that is against God and which he has not planted, so that we not take in our mouth in vain these three highest names: God the Father, Son, and Holy Spirit,[c] using them against the institution of Christ, who always said, "Whoever is not with me is against me," Luke 11:23, so that also his holy baptism, which he instituted with such great earnestness after his

---

[a] What is right, not what is done.
[b] Faithful admonition.
[c] Father. Son. Spirit.

praiseworthy resurrection, so that it will be rightly given and practiced by us. For whoever does not practice something according to the Word, will, and pleasure of God, misuses it. May the omnipotent, merciful God bestow grace and power on us so that we renounce all human care, fear, respect of persons, and old customs, and henceforth adhere to and follow only his pure, clear, and true Word: or else it will go worse for us than for Sodom and Gomorrah, Matt. 10:15. Whoever has ears to hear should hear, for no lack of knowledge will henceforth excuse us in this matter. May God grant us his eternal peace. Amen.

Truth Is Immortal.
1526.
Printed by Simprecht Sorg,
called Froschauer.
Nicolspurg
/241/ Second Edition[63]
/243/ True Witness and Proofs from the Chronicles,
Decretals and Ancient Fathers and Teachers,
as to how long the
First Practice of Baptism persisted, against this
Contemnptible Practice of New Baptism.[64]

Clement,[65] the first of this name,* a disciple of the apostle Peter, sets out in the 29th Article, among other places,

---

[63] Only those parts of the second edition that were changed will be translated. The letter of dedication is the same in both editions, save for three misprints which would produce no difference in the translation. The last eleven items, from Erasmus through Balthasar, are likewise the same. The first part of the main body of the treatise, i.e., the section on the "ancient teachers," was rearranged and enlarged in the new edition, adding twelve new authorities. We here reproduce the whole first part of the main body of the second edition.

[64] This heading is considerably expanded over that of the first edition.

[65] In order to demonstrate graphically the growth and change of the second edition, the first 21 items are here listed, noting in the case of the "old" items their placing in the first edition as well: (1) Clement, (2) Donatus, (3/7) Theophylactus, (4/4) Tertullian, (5/1) Origen, (6) Cyprian, (7/3) Athanasius, (8/5) Jerome, (9) Augustine, (10/8) Eusebius, (11/6) Cyril, (12) Pelagius, (13) Ambrose, (14) Pope Siritius, (15) Pope Boniface, (16) Pope Leo I, (17/2) Pope Basil the Great, (18) Pope Nicholas I, (19) Beatus Romanus, (20/9) Canon Law, (21) Councils and Decretals.

---

* 91 years after the birth of Christ.

that the baptism of heretics should be neither recognized nor accepted. Therefore, according to the truth of the church, whoever has received baptism should not be baptized again. Whoever does not again baptize those stained and those baptized by the godless or the heretics /244/ should be cut off as one who mocks the cross of Christ and his death and does not differentiate the false priests from true.[66]

Donatus,[a] learned bishop at Carthage, teaches that one should baptize no child who does not confess faith.[67] Therefore, they were all educated and experienced people, powerful and mighty in virtue, art, and riches.

Theophylact, the teacher,[b] concerning the Word of Christ in Mark 16:16, *qui crediderit* [whoever will believe] writes the following: "It is not enough that one believes, but he must also be baptized; for whoever believes and is not baptized, but is a catechumen, is not yet saved." Always consider him also, dear reader, on the text of Matthew 28:19: "Go forth, teach all people." There he testifies as to what one should teach before and after baptism and how there was one common institution of baptism by Christ, belonging to Jews and heathen.[68]

Tertullian[c] teaches in the *Libro de Corona Milites* [Book on the Garland of the Soldier][69] that those who go to baptism should make a confession beforehand and also be taught a certain time before in the congregation or church and before the bishop so that they renounce the pomp and angels of the devil. After that they are immersed three times

---

[66] Clement I of Rome was in Hubmaier's time mistakenly identified as the compiler of the two actually much younger *Constitutions of the Holy Apostles* (MPG I:947ff., Roberts 1981, VII 391ff.). Section VI,15 (Roberts 456) and Canon 47 (Roberts 503) call for rebaptism of those heretically baptized.

[67] Donatus, incorrectly dated 137 by Hubmaier, was the early fourth-century rigorist bishop who gave his name to the Donatist schism. See Frend 1952 for a study of the movement. The writing to which Hubmaier refers has not been found.

[68] See above, p. 253.

[69] Should be *Liber de Corona Militis*. Roberts 1981, 4, p.378.

---

[a] The year 137.
[b] The year 189.
[c] The year 208.

and baptized in the name of the Father, Son, and the Holy Spirit.[70]

Origen,[a] the teacher, says that the person who ceases sinning receives baptism for the forgiveness of sins. "Therefore I beseech you that you do not come to baptism without consideration and thoughtful preparation, but that you come so as to show first worthy fruits of the renewal of your life. Practice some time in a good life," Luke 3:8. Such he writes concerning the preaching of repentance of John. About the word of Paul in Romans 6:3: here Paul points out that baptism in the time of the apostles was not practiced as in our time. For at that time the understanding and instructed in the death of Christ were baptized and they were also buried through baptism with him into death. For as Christ was raised from the dead through the glory of the Father, so should the baptized walk in newness of life. He further writes in the "Homilies on Exodus Eight," Folio 43e: "If we come to the grace of baptism, we deny all idols and lords, we confess God the Father, Son, and Holy Spirit alone."[71]

Cyprian,[b] bishop at Carthage, concluded with an entire council that heretical baptism was no baptism, having neither God, Spirit, gospel, sacrament, and grace—nor having the ability or capability of giving any of the above. Therefore, /245/ all those who return from the heretics to the church of Christ should be baptized again or, better said, should be baptized for the first time—since what had been done previously is not to be regarded as baptism.[72]

Athanasius, bishop,[c] writes concerning Hebrews 6:6: "For the change of life in baptism, first of all we should be sorry for our previous life, and afterward be washed with bap-

---

[70] See above, p. 252.

[71] See above, p. 250.

[72] In 255, Cyprian wrote to Stephen a report concerning the fourth synod of Carthage during his tenure, "... that those who have been dipped abroad outside the church, and have been stained among heretics and schismatics with the taint of profane water, when they come to us and to the church which is one, ought to be baptized...." Roberts 1981, 5, p.378.

---

[a] The year 230.

[b] The year 240.

[c] The year 348.

tism." Concerning the epistle of Paul, 1 Cor. 15:29 on the baptism of the dead, he says the following: "Whoever wanted to accept baptism said the articles in complete faith."[73] One should read in the epistle of Paul, 1 Cor. 1:13. Look further at Hebrews 6:2. If we are baptized, something is signified to us through a figure: as we are drawn out of the water, etc., so will we see the resurrection, in order to affirm and confess that the dead will rise again.[74]

Jerome[a] the teacher, writes, "When the bishop lays on his hands, he lays them on those who are baptized in a true faith in the name of the Father, the Son, and the Holy Spirit: on those believing the names of the divinity." From *Against the Sect of the Luciferians*. Further, concerning Matthew 28:19, he writes the following: "In the first place, teach them, yes, all the peoples. After they have been taught, baptize them in water. For the body cannot receive the sacrament of baptism unless the soul has first received the truth of faith."[75]

Augustine,[b] in Canon One on the Tiophiles, writes concerning baptism what is too long to relate here. Likewise, in Distinction Four, *Agunt Homines* [Men act], Augustine says that persons should repent before baptism, as it stands in Acts 2:38: "Repent and all of you be baptized in the name of Jesus, then you will receive the gift of the Holy Spirit. For to you and to your children is that promise given that belongs to believers."[76] Likewise, Augustine in Canon *Nihil* [Nothing] says, "The baptized members of Christ should also participate in the body and blood of Christ. For he wants that only the believers receive, desire, and seek the sacrament, for only they belong to the confessors and followers of Christ—for without a true acknowledged faith all sacraments are powerless and nothing."[77] *Ibi* [There].

---

[73] That is, the baptizand must first be able to recite the Apostles' Creed. This requirement, of course, excludes infants.
[74] See above, p. 251.
[75] See above, p. 252.
[76] CIC I:1393 (canon 97).
[77] CIC I:1404-05 (canon 131).

---

[a] The year 370.
[b] The year 370.

Eusebius the teacher,[a] writes a story in Book 10, Chapter 14, *Ecclesiastical History*, "Once upon a time in the time of Alexander, the bishop of Alexandria, /246/ several schoolchildren went for a walk at the sea. As they now wanted to amuse themselves for a short while, they also read through their lessons, for many of them had learned the baptism catechism. When they now had examined one another, one among them, called Athanasius, said, "Why do we not now ourselves baptize one another since we know well what baptism is, for we all together know well the Christian faith. In the church we are embarrassed before the adults: it would suit us better here." Thus they elected him as deacon. He baptized them all, just as they had seen it done in the church. Meanwhile, their teacher came and observed the thing they had done. He reported it immediately to the bishop, priests, deacons, and clerics. After a long disputation on this affair, they came to the following conclusion regarding it: Since they know what baptism is and have seen how one practices it and have desired it from the heart, knowing and confessing faith, one should bring them before the congregation, then question and proceed otherwise, but not baptize them again. Rather, one should give them a baptismal gift and consider them as baptized members. This is the story in short.[78]

Cyril,[b] bishop at Basel, writes, "Those who are in the instruction of faith one should not take soon to baptism." So he writes on John, Book 2, Ch. 36. He also describes the figures of water baptism from the Old and New Testaments which all serve the faithful. They are too long to tell here. See Book 6, Ch. 15, on John.[79]

Pelagianus, the disciple of Augustine, a bishop,[c] says that children are without original sin; therefore, baptism for them is in vain. Young children, if they are not baptized, are nonetheless saved. On the other hand, the rich cannot be saved

---

[78] See above, p. 253-254.
[79] See above, note 26.

---

[a] The year 371.
[b] The year 373.
[c] The year 380.

even if they are baptized if they do not deny all that which they have.[80]

Ambrose, bishop of Milan,[a] among other subjects teaches on baptism as follows: namely, that baptism of apostates and unbelievers does not heal and the baptism of those who do not come near to the Lord through the flood does not make whole or pure, but makes impure. For, as it is said by the apostle Paul, "What does not come out of faith is sin," Rom. 14:23, and it is both for those who practice or do it and for those who receive it not only useless but even for judgment. For the chief intention and real basis of every sacrament is in word and deed, not in the external ceremony or in human repetition, but in the heart and the confession of faith. /247/

Pope Siricius, number forty in the list,[b] orders and confirms this also, namely that baptism is to be practiced only twice in the year, that is, at Easter and Pentecost, unless there is a special need for baptizing.[81]

Pope Boniface, number forty-four in the list,[c] had a quarrel against Augustine, who often wavered, who wanted unknowing children to be baptized and wanted to confirm godparenthood.[82] The pope answered him that godparents who hold the children at baptism can never with truth answer in place of the child that it renounces the devil or that it believes, since they do not know whether the child will be chaste or unchaste, godly or a thief. For that reason, Augustine gave him a silly answer.[83]

---

[80] The reference is to Pelagius, the early fifth-century opponent of Augustine, founder of the Pelagian heresy. He was not a bishop and not Augustine's disciple.

[81] CIC I:1364 (canon 11). Siricius, thirty-eighth in the Roman list, was pope from 384-399. Hubmaier's numbering of the popes differs from the current Roman listing.

[82] According to the Roman listing, Boniface(418-19) was number forty-two.

[83] See above, p. 254.

---

[a] The year 383.

[b] The year 384.

[c] The year 420.

Pope Leo I,[a] forty-eight in order,[84] explicitly set forth in his decretals that baptism was to take place only twice a year, at Easter and Pentecost, except in the case of greatest emergency.[85]

Pope Basil the Great,[86b] number twenty-two, in Book III, *Contra Eunomium* [Against Eunomius], Folio 44: " 'Go forth,' says Christ, 'baptize in the name of the Father, of the Son, and of the Holy Spirit,' Matt. 28:19. For baptism is a seal of faith, an affirmation of the divinity. For one must first of all believe and after that be marked with baptism." Likewise, where one has a ready will, nothing is to hinder baptism and he underlines this with the story of the treasurer from the land of the Moors, Acts 8:37. See the *exhortatione ad pabtissmus* [Exhortation to baptism], folio 142ff. See also *intract quid instruendi memendi que sunt ad baptissmus venientes libro* [Book on what those are to be taught and instructed who are coming to baptism]. He compares water baptism with the Flood from which no one was saved except those who entered into the ark in faith, as Peter also reports it, Gen. 7:7, 17; 1 Pet. 3:20f. He also writes thus concerning Psalm 29.

Pope Nicholas I, number ninety in order,[c] writes and makes himself his own catechism as to how the teacher should instruct and hold the baptizands and pupils in the faith. *Ex baptissmo fidei*) [From the baptism of faith].[87]

Beatus Romanus[d] says that the old practice has been that adults have been baptized and washed with the bath of the rebirth, which custom was kept until the time of emperors Charlemagne and Louis. The laws, set up and sanctioned by

[84] Pope Leo I was pope 440-461 and is numbered forty-five.
[85] CIC I:1365 (canon 12).
[86] In the first edition, Basil is not identified as a pope, which he was not. The date cited in the margin is incorrect: Basil died in 379. See above, page 251, note 16.
[87] Pope Nicholas I, 858-867, was 105 in the Roman list. Nicolas had a special role in the Anabaptists' understanding of the origins of infant baptism. Cf. Yoder 1968, pp. 66-69. Cf. above, pp. 212 and 225.

[a] The year 836.
[b] The year 490.
[c] The year 863.
[d] The year 1315.

them, point this out in which it was forbidden that the priest should baptize even one person except in the case of the threat of death, other than at Easter and Pentecost.[88] /248/

Decrees and Order of the Old Popes and Teachers

Boniface, forty-fourth pope,[*] published a decree in *De Consecreti* Book Four, Chapter Nine, "verus in verbo difficilimam scribetur" [truly written at the word 'difficult']. Likewise, in the canon *Prima ea diserit* [First, this he will have said][89] he cites the articles of faith which one should ask about before one baptizes the person. The chapters *baptizandi* [those to be baptized] and *ante Baptinavea*, [before baptism] teach how the ones who shall be baptized should present themselves several days beforehand to the bishop, also how they should refrain several days from wine and meat, all of which cannot apply to young children.[90] In *De consec.* [On Consecration] Distinction 4, *Ante Pabtisti* [Before Baptism], Rabanus, bishop of Metz, says, "The catechism should precede baptism so that the individual may be previously instructed in the doctrine of faith. Therefore Christ first covered the eyes of the blind man with mud and spittle and sent him to the water Siloam. John 9:6f. It is in the same way that the baptizand is instructed in faith beforehand and thus brought believing to baptism, so that he may know what grace he receives therein and to whom he afterward owes obedience." Likewise, in the canon *Postquam*, [After] Rabanus says, "After now the baptizand by faith has given and done obeisance to another, namely, to Christ, and through renunciation has withdrawn himself from the servitude of his prior lord, the devil,

---

[88] Hubmaier is referring to the German humanist Beatus Rhenanus (1485-1547). The marginal notation is incorrectly given as 1315.

[89] Again Hubmaier cites a canon incorrectly, meaning the canon *Prima igitur* [First, therefore]: CIC I:1386f. (canon 73). See above, p. 254, note 37.

[90] See the reference above to canons 60 and 59, p. 254. In the following discussion, Hubmaier expands his treatment of canon 59 ("Before Baptism"), even though the spelling and manner of referring is slightly changed.

---

[*] The year 425.

the evil spirit is exorcized by the office of a devout servant of God and place and room is prepared for the Spirit of the Lord."[91] Read further at the same place. What this learner in faith has undertaken beforehand is too long to relate here.

Councils and Decrees of the Ancients
As to What was Decided on Baptism
Which Luther and Those of the Present Day Turn All Around

The Fourth Council at Carthage[a] decided that those who were not absolutely sure that they had not been baptized should be baptized.[92]

The Council at Arles in Gaul,[b] held in the time of Emperor Constantine the Great and Pope Silvester, decreed that those who returned from the churches of the heretics should be baptized in the name of the Trinity.[93] At the Council at Nicea[c] it was decided that heretics or those baptized by heretics should be baptized again if they wanted to return to the true church.[94]

The Council at Laodicea in Syria[d] decided that the catechumens one wants to baptize should be taught the Creed and on Maundy Thursday should recite and speak before the priest or bishop.[95]

The Sixth Council at Carthage[e] under Emperor Honorius decided that those who want to receive baptism should be tested and examined a long time beforehand, /249/ should abstain from wine and meat a certain time, and be examined thoroughly and be baptized with the laying on of

---

[91] CIC I:1383 (canon 61).

[92] It was the fifth synod at Carthage under Aurelius (401) that published such a canon, CIC I:1396 (canon 111).

[93] The council (314) decided in fact that only those should be rebaptized who had not been baptized in the name of the Trinity, CIC I:1395 (canon 109).

[94] CIC I:378 (canon 52). 325 is the correct date.

[95] CIC I:1383 (canon 58).

---

[a] The year 311.
[b] The year 315.
[c] The year 323.
[d] The year 368.
[e] The year 406.

hands.[96] A definite time was also designated when the catechumens should be admitted to baptism, when they had confessed faith beforehand, so that they could answer the minister, and how they should live after baptism and avoid the ban. *De Consec.* Distinction 4, *Pabtismi Ex Concilio laoidensis,*[a] ["On Consecration," Distinction 4. Of the Baptized, from the Council of Laodicea] decided that the baptizands should learn faith beforehand and give account of the same to the bishop on Maundy Thursday.[97]

One article among others of the Seventh Council at Carthage,[b] held by the Latins, Africans, Europeans, and others, provided that the widows and nuns, who were endowed for that reason, were elected to the office and ministry of women. They should teach the women the art of writing and in addition should instruct the uneducated farmers' wives as to the time at which the girl catechumens should be admitted to baptism, how they should answer the baptismal minister, and then how they should live after baptism.[98]

The Council of Gerona[c] decided that the catechumens, that is, the learners in the faith, should only be baptized at Eastertime and Pentecost, except in cases of the threat of death, otherwise no one.[99]

The Second Council of Braga[d] decreed that it was necessary for baptism to be offered to children. Moreover the catechumens should be taught for twenty days and instructed in the faith before baptism.[100]

In this council it was decided that if a pregnant woman was baptized, then nothing of her baptism affected the child

---

[96] It is in fact the fourth Aurelian synod of Carthage, dated 398, about which Hubmaier has already written.
[97] Here Hubmaier refers again to the Council of Laodicea, to which he has just referred above. See note 95.
[98] This was really the fourth Carthaginian synod under Aurelius (398). Mansi: 952 (canon 12).
[99] CIC I:1366 (canon 15). The synod took place in 517.
[100] CIC I:1382 (canon 55). The council took place in 572.

---

[a] The year 438.
[b] The year 490, and several years after.
[c] The year 700.
[d] The year 710.

that is in her. Therefore, the confession of each individual must be made by his own faith.[101]

---

[101] This canon does not come from the council, but from a list of old Greek canons which Archbishop Martin of Braga collected. See CIC I:1397 (canon 116). The section beginning with Erasmus which comes at this point in Edition II is the beginning of the concluding section common to both editions.

18

On Infant Baptism Against Oecolampad

The dialogue treatise On Infant Baptism, *similar in style, format, and content to the* Dialogue with Zwingli's Baptism Book, *signaled the end of friendly relations between Oecolampad and Hubmaier.*

A dialogue between the Reformed pastors of Basel and several Anabaptist leaders, including Lorenz Hochrütiner, formerly of Zurich and St. Gall, took place in August 1525 in the residence of Oecolampad.[1] After the discussion it was rumored in the city that the Anabaptists had silenced Oecolampad and his colleagues. In order to lay that rumor to rest, Oecolampad produced by September 1 his report on the conversations, A Dialogue of Several Preachers at Basel, Held with Several Confessors of Rebaptism. *Although a valuable report, in fact, the first such published account of the course of a dialogue between mainline Reformers and Anabaptists, it was not a complete record. Oecolampad drew up the* Dialogue *a few weeks after the encounter, based on his memory of the event and incomplete notes. The Anabaptist statements were brief, mostly given in only a few words, whereas the speeches of the Reformed participants often occupy a complete page.*

This reply by Hubmaier, prepared in 1525, could not be printed until 1527 in Nikolsburg. In the preface to his earlier Dialogue *Hubmaier had mentioned four books that he had written and which were waiting to be published, among them this response to the report of Oecolampad.[2] In July 1527 Oecolampad wrote to Zwingli that he had received a writing of Hubmaier on pedobaptism.[3] The treatise made enough of an*

---

[1] A summary of the dialogue and the publications resulting from it is found in Yoder 1962, pp. 63-69.

[2] See above, p. 175.

[3] Z 9, p. 176.[14ff.]

impact on the Basel Reformer that he felt compelled to reply in his Answer to Balthasar Hubmaier's Booklet.[4]

The main purpose of the treatise is to continue the dialogue with Oecolampad, though Hubmaier furthers the polemic against Zwingli as well, especially Zwingli's doctrine of original sin as contained in his 1526 treatise on that subject.[5]

On Infant Baptism
Ecolampadius,
Thomas, the Augustinian Novice Master,
M. Jacob Immelen,
M. Vuolffg[ang] Weissenburger.
Balthasar Hubmör
von Fridberg.
Nicolspurg 1527.
A dialogue
between the preachers of Basel and Balthasar
Hùebmör von Fridberg
on infant Baptism.

Oecolampad: Let us begin in the name of the Lord.[6] The rebaptizers have boasted here and there as to how in the recent dialogue between us /259/ held in the parsonage at Saint Martin at Basel, they were honorably victorious and silenced us.[*] Therefore I want to point out in writing what

---

[4] *Antwort auff Balthasar Huobmeiers büchlein wider der Predicanten gespräch zu Basel,* September 1527.

[5] Z 5, pp. 359-96, tr. ZL II, pp. 1-32. Fragmentary translation in Hošek 1891, pp. 532-544; and Vedder 1905, pp. 120f. Manuscript of translation by Henry C. Vedder at Colgate Rochester Library. Source: HS 13, pp. 258-269.

[6] The *Dialogue* by Oecolampad is a small treatise of 14 pages, numbered ai to biiii. For the most part Hubmaier follows the treatise carefully, omitting few arguments and editing little, so that there is limited distortion. We will note the pages in the Basel edition from which Hubmaier took his comments from Oecolampad and his colleagues. The significant arguments which were omitted and the few misrepresentations will be noted.

---

[*] Basel.

both sides at that time presented so that their glory is further praised and proclaimed, and so that everybody may see of what kind of spirit these skillful fellows are, and where they are hurting.[7]

Balthasar: It is quite right, my Oecolampad, that you now want to bring forth the rebaptizers into the light. However, do such with bright and clear Scripture, or you will truly come to shame in the matter, however scholarly you are. For truth is immortal.[8] It can be overcome neither through the respect of persons, nor with high-blown rhetoric or flowery speech, although it can be spoken in all simplicity by Balaam's donkey, Tobith's dog, or David's mule.

Oecolampad: What I have said, preached, and written I would henceforth also do and prayerfully command others also to do, for your teaching[a] is a wholly new fantasy, begun here and elsewhere in the past two years. Therefore it is suspect.[9]

Balthasar: I beseech you for the sake of God, my Oecolampad, let these devious arguments be stuck under the bench and deal with clear Scripture. For you know that the teaching of Christ always suffered this blow on the cheeks, i.e., that it was called a new teaching, Mark 1:27. And to Paul it was said: "What does this slanderer want? He is a proclaimer of new devils. May we also learn what kind of new teaching it is which is preached by you. You put new teaching in our ears," Acts 17:18. We have not invented it, but Christ has thus commanded it, and the apostles practiced it. Therefore we have wanted to present ourselves against you and everyone before the judgment chair of Holy Scripture.[b] If we are right in this and other articles, why are we beaten? If, however, we are not wrong, then give witness with the Scripture concerning the evil and then punish us afterward in life and limb.

---

[7] *Dialogue*: ai/v.
[8] One of the few occasions when Hubmaier inserts his epigram into the course of an argument, as above, text 3, p. 42.
[9] *Dialogue*: aii/r.

---

[a] New teaching.
[b] A legitimate offer.

Oecolampad: If this teaching is tested it will be found that it is directly against true love.[10]

Balthasar: If in the testing of the Scriptures it is found that water baptism was instituted for the instructed and believers and not for cradle babies, then it is the truth. But Paul writes that love rejoices in the truth, 1 Cor. 13:6. How now is truth against love? But you speak perhaps of worldly love,[11] which cannot suffer the divine truth, for its works are evil. Therefore it hates the light, John 3:20. /260/

Oecolampad: It is also disgraceful to the Christian community that we should have erred so long.[12]

Balthasar: That is a light-headed argument. The godless also make it. It is certainly necessary that you defend yourself, that you have drawn this straw-sword with which, if it were sharp, the papists would have stabbed you to death long ago.

Oecolampad:[a] This teaching, however, is directed toward separation and sectarianism, which cannot be of the Spirit of God.[13]

Balthasar: Are you amazed? Christ himself is a sign that will be spoken against, Luke 2:34. He sent a sword and not peace, Matt. 10:34. Five in a house will be contentious, the father against the son and the son against the father, the mother against the daughter and the daughter against the mother, Luke 12:52f. Oh, that is a blessed sectarianism and separation, says Chrysostom. And if Paul had been well-pleasing to the world he would not have been a servant of Christ, Gal. 1:10. However, that the truth gives birth to rebellion is not its fault but the fault of our wickedness, as the murderer Herod, not the newborn Christ, was guilty of the grim murder of the innocent children.

Oecolampad: Tell me, who has thus taught till now, or when has one kept such a custom?[14]

---

[10] *Dialogue*: aii/r.

[11] Cf. Yoder 1968, pp. 44ff., 49ff., 90ff., concerning the concept of "love."

[12] *Dialogue*: aii/r. Hubmaier divides this sentence of Oecolampad from the next so as to address the question of error. Oecolampad, however, was concerned not with error in his statement, but with schism.

[13] *Dialogue*: aii/r.

[14] *Dialogue*: aii/r.

---

[a] Sectarianism.

Balthasar: Christ so taught us when he instituted water baptism in the church, Matt. 28:19; Mark 16:16.[a] And the apostles have written and practiced thus, 1 Pet. 3:21; Heb. 6:2;[15] 10:22; Acts 2:38; 8:12; 37f.; 9:18; 10:47-48; 11:16; 16:15, 33; 18:8; 19:5; 22:16. Examine the Scripture rightly, then you will explicitly find that in seven years no argument has come into the way that is more clearly expressed than that Christ instituted his water baptism for believers and not for unknowing children.[b]

Oecolampad:[c] I know enough of the histories that children's baptism has never been forbidden from the time of the apostles until now.[16]

Balthasar: But it was before the time of the apostles. Search the Scripture, says Christ, not the histories.

Oecolampad:[d] It has also been the custom of the mothers in the church to baptize children.[17]

Balthasar: Yes, of the papist but not of the Christian mothers in the church, nor of their Father, who is in heaven. He would have instituted it otherwise through his Son Christ Jesus, whom he also commanded us to hear, Matt. 15:10; 17:5. He, not custom, is the way, truth, and life, John 14:6.

Oecolampad: Infant baptism was also treated in the Council of Milevis over which Saint Augustine presided.[18] /261/

Balthasar: Let Augustine or a council say what they may, Augustine greatly erred in his canon *Firmissime*, De Con., dist. 4 [Canon "Most Firmly," "On Consecration," Distinction 4].[19] If he had written *Impijssime* [Most impiously] for that he would have been better off.[e] If you can justify Augustine, I will praise you.

[15] It is not clear whether the allusion of Hebrews 6:2 to plural *baptisms*, rendered *ablutions* in the RSV, actually refers directly to water baptism or to Jewish ablutions in general.
[16] *Dialogue:* aii/r.
[17] *Dialogue:* aii/r.
[18] *Dialogue:* aii/r. The Synod of Milevis, an anti-Pelegian synod, was held in 416.
[19] CIC I:1362 (canon 3).

[a] Note this.
[b] History.
[c] History.
[d] Church, a mother.
[e] Augustine.

Oecolampad: Oh, it would have been a good support for the Pelagians if they had been able to invent the idea that infant baptism was forbidden by the apostles.[20]

Balthasar:[a] What is not commanded in Scripture is already forbidden in those matters concerning the honor of God and the salvation of our souls.[b] For Christ does not say: "What God my heavenly Father has forbidden must be rooted out." Rather, he says: "All plants which God my heavenly Father has not planted must be rooted out," Matt. 15:13. Paul calls all teachings which are not contained in the Holy Gospel a curse, even if an angel were to bring them down from heaven, Gal. 1:8f. Peter calls them false teachings of the lying masters, 2 Pet. 2:1.[c] So Christ earnestly commands that we should teach all things which he has commanded us to teach, Matt. 28:20. Or the apocalyptic plagues will come over us, Rev. 22:18.[d] Do you see, Oecolampad? Either you must point out with a clear Scripture where God has instituted infant baptism or it must be rooted out. One of these must be or God will not remain God. How does this Scotistic argument please you?

Oecolampad:[e] Now the Pelagians were also highly learned in the Scripture. Likewise, Cyprian and the Council of Carthage have not been able to reject infant baptism.[21]

Balthasar: I will trust Cyprian, councils, and other teachings just as far as they use the Holy Scripture, and not more.[22] They themselves also desire nothing more than that from me. With this I let it lie.

Oecolampad:[f] Origen was approximately fifty years before Cyprian. He points out clearly in the epistle to the

---

[20] *Dialogue:* aii/r.

[21] *Dialogue:* aii/r-v.

[22] In *Old and New Teachers,* Hubmaier had argued from Cyprian's recommendation for the baptism of those who had been "baptized" by heretics, but who now returned "from the heretics to the church of Christ." See above, text 17, p. 266.

---

[a] Prohibition.
[b] Command.
[c] False teaching.
[d] Scotistic argument.
[e] Pelagians. Cyprian. Council.
[f] Origen.

Romans that such a custom came from the apostles. Origen is also in no way to be judged that he might have failed in this matter, although otherwise he certainly erred badly in much.[23]

Balthasar: You should look at Origen more carefully on the word of Paul "to the ignorant" in Romans, also on Luke 3 and Homily 8 on Exodus 8, page 43.[24] There you will find much that is different. And although Origen wrote such, since he erred badly in many other things, then he could also have erred in that.

Oecolampad: Now you do not want to consider the many hundreds of thousands who up till now have been baptized in childhood as Christian brothers. How can you make Christ's kingdom so narrow?[25]

Balthasar: Now you will not consider as Christian brothers the many hundreds of thousands who up till now have honored and worshiped the bread and wine in the mass for the flesh and blood of Christ. How can you make Christ's kingdom so narrow? /262/

Oecolampad:[*] If you are only introducing a new sect, then you are grafting yourself to the devil.[26]

Balthasar: Blasphemy. Give testimony with the Scripture, Scripture, Scripture, that baptizing according to the indisputable order of Christ is grafting oneself to the devil. If you look to the only master in the heavens and to truth itself with a gentle and eager-to-learn heart, then you will avoid such scolding and shameful words. But you have spoken out of anger and evil. May God, who thereby gives us to recognize that you can also fall like a human being, forgive you this.

Oecolampad: I know and want not to teach such schism. I must teach faith and love.[27]

---

[23] *Dialogue*: aii/v. Oecolampad argues that Origen was sufficiently close to apostolic times, so that if he had lied concerning infant baptism, he would have been answered or corrected by his contemporaries. The reference to Origen's having erred is to Origen's use of allegorical interpretation.

[24] See above, text 17, pp. 250 and 266.

[25] *Dialogue*: aii/v.

[26] *Dialogue*: aii/v.

[27] *Dialogue*: aii/v.

---

[*] New sect.

Balthasar:[a] Whoever rightly teaches baptism and the Supper rightly teaches faith and love. On this matter I appeal to the baptismal vow and pledge of love. If you teach faith, then you teach that all works that do not flow out of faith are sin, Rom. 14:23. Now, however, infant baptism is a work without faith, or prove it with the Word from which faith flows, Rom. 10:17. There the hare is caught again in the hedge.

Oecolampad: Papal abuses and infant baptism are two different things. The abuses are against the Scripture, and they have never been accepted everywhere.[28]

Balthasar: Infant baptism is against the Scripture, for what is not with the Scripture is against the Scripture. Or point out where the Scripture commands baptizing children. Then the Word of Christ is also such a teaching which is contradicted everywhere, Acts 28:22.

Oecolampad:[b] Here, however, in the case of infant baptism it is another matter deliberately to overthrow a practice which is not forbidden in Scripture.[29]

Balthasar: To overthrow a practice which is not instituted in Scripture is not an abuse but a command of Christ, Matt. 15:13. The Spirit of God speaks also through Isaiah: "Woe to you, children, who leave me, who take counsel, but not from

---

[28] *Dialogue:* aiii/r. Oecolampad is prepared to use the canon of Vincent of Lerins, whereby "catholic" is that which is always accepted everywhere by everybody, (*quod ubique, quod semper, quod ab omnibus creditum est*). He believes that all the abuses which Protestants denounce are later and local accretions. Hubmaier omits an argument of Oecolampad to the effect that although many doctrines and practices of Roman Catholicism had been opposed throughout history, the matter of infant baptism was never seriously questioned. Several examples of questionable practices were given, e.g., the power of the pope, marriage of priests, the mass as sacrifice, images in the church, living in monasteries, and the intercession of saints. All these were questioned, but infant baptism was not. Hubmaier ignores this argument.

[29] *Dialogue:* aiii/r. Oecolampad goes on to argue that infant baptism does not harm love and faith, suggesting thereby that the Anabaptists by their rejection of infant baptism do injure love and faith. For the specific hermeneutic role of "faith" and "love" cf. Heinrich Bullinger, "How to Deal with Anabaptists," MQR XXXIII, April 1959, pp. 83-95.

---

[a] Faith. Love.
[b] Practice.

me," Isa. 30:1.[a] Here you yourself write concerning these words: "Whoever makes something from out of himself although God has not forbidden the same with a particular command, the same does what is forbidden by God, for he does something not out of God."

Oecolampad:[b] I do not want to occupy myself with strange ceremonies such as exorcising devils, salting, burning candles, spittle, breathing on, and others, for I myself have no praise for them, etc.[30]

Balthasar: If you want to praise the one, you must glorify the other. One Satan came in with the other.

Oecolampad:[c] If the apostles baptized whole households, then presumably among these numbers there were also children.[31] /263/

Balthasar: Explain the term *whole households* correctly according to the way of Scripture, or you must confess that also unbelieving men were baptized with the believing women and fools. Thinking, having opinions, and imagining do not count in Scripture; knowing counts. Also, you have not believed all your lifelong that any young child was baptized. Show me one in Scripture; then I will be defeated.

Oecolampad: You have the burden of proof that infant baptism is forbidden.[32]

Balthasar: The burden of proof lies with you that God has instituted infant baptism,[d] for the need to prove stands with the affirming and not with the denying. Or it will become a self-chosen worship, that is, a church law created out of human will and fantasy.

Oecolampad: I want to do it.[33]

---

[30] *Dialogue:* aiii/r. In this passage, Oecolampad does not condemn the "strange ceremonies" as such, for there may be some value in them—although they are ceremonies which Christians can freely dispose of if desired.

[31] *Dialogue:* aiii/r.

[32] *Dialogue:* aiii/v.

[33] This sentence is not in the *Dialogue.* It is inserted here by Hubmaier simply to advance the flow of the argument.

---

[a] A Christian teaching.

[b] Ceremonies.

[c] Whole households.

[d] Legal rule. Self-chosen worship.

Balthasar: Ad kalendas grecas [at the Greek calends].[34]

Thomas: Where, however, is a woman mentioned by name who was baptized?[35]

Balthasar: Bene veneritis [You may have arrived at something],[36] dear teacher of the Augustinians. Have you never heard read at the table the 8th[37] and 16th chapters of the Acts of the Apostles (16:14-15) of the Samarian women and Lydia, the seller of purple? In fact you are a teacher in name only. Pfui, be ashamed in your heart that you are said to be a preacher, teacher, and knowedgeable person in Christian discussions and have never read so much in Scripture whether the apostles also have baptized women, and moreover you yourself let such mockery go out in public print. Who has so entirely bewitched you that you do not look to the truth?

Oecolampad: We confess that one should baptize no adult who has reason, without instruction. However, it is different with children who are without all sin and are unspotted.[38]

Balthasar:[*] If the children are without sin and unspotted why would Job and Jeremiah curse the day of their birth, Job 3:3; Jer. 20:14f. Why does David complain that he was conceived in sin and that his mother gave birth to him in evil, Ps. 51:5. Why does Paul testify that we are all by nature children of wrath, Eph. 2:3, and all have sinned in Adam, 1 Cor. 15:22.

---

[34] Since the calends were Latin, not Greek, to wait for the Greek calends was to wait for what would never transpire. Oecolampad will never deliver the promised proof.

[35] *Dialogue*: aiii/v. The question by Thomas is in response to a question raised in the Basel dialogue, but not noted by Hubmaier, as to where one might find Scripture passages in support of infant baptism.

[36] By referring to Thomas Geyerfalk by his full academic title Hubmaier echoes, perhaps ironically, the manners of the disputation. He compliments Geyerfalk ironically for advancing the conversation by asking a rhetorical question to which there is in fact an answer.

[37] Acts 8:3 speaks of men and women in Jerusalem, but not directly of women in Samaria. However, Acts 8:1-4 implies that Christians of both sexes were scattered throughout the region of Judea and Samaria and verse 16 refers to their baptism.

[38] *Dialogue*: aiii/v. Oecolampad does not say "all sin," but that children do not have their "own sin." By making this editorial change, Hubmaier can accuse Oecolampad in the next paragraph of not accepting original sin, an assertion contrary to the intention of Oecolampad.

---

[*] Whether children are without sin.

I must simply think, Ecolampad, that you do not speak such out of yourself, but from Ulrich Zwingli, Master at Zürich,[39] who first fell into the error, so that he fights for godless infant baptism with pen, teaching, and executioner against recognized truth.[a][40] When he protects such untruth, God punishes him so that he falls into the second error and publicly says that original sin is no sin.[41] /264/ So now the scholarly Doctor Verbanus Regius[42] has pointed out to him such with sufficient conviction of Scriptures, Rom.7 and other passages.[b] Soon he falls into the third error and writes, "Paul did not speak properly and with careful rhetoric about sin," but he [Zwingli] speaks properly about it.[43] As if Paul had not spoken by the Holy Spirit or had not known what sin actually was.[c] From this error he falls immediately into the fourth and says with unclean mouth that Almighty God, the highest workman, made the woman Eve from a rib of the sleeping Adam into a most unhappy symbol.[d][44] Those are four strong

---

[39] Here Hubmaier repeats a charge made by the Anabaptists in the Basel dialogue against Oecolampad that he is a follower of Zwingli, who is accused of denying original sin. On Zwingli's view of original sin, cf. Yoder 1968, p. 20.

[40] This is likely a reference to Zwingli's *Von der Taufe*, Z IV, pp. 206-337, as well as to his preaching at Zurich and his oppressive leadership against the fledgling Anabaptist movement including, of course, his treatment of Hubmaier.

[41] In his earlier treatise, Zwingli prefers the term *erbprest* (hereditary weakness or sickness, in Latin: *morbus*) to *erbsünd*, original sin. *Erbprest* does not condemn, Z 4, p. 309,[26] for guilt only comes when one transgresses the law, Z 4, p. 308.[28-29] Much attacked for this, Zwingli refined his position in the reply to Rhegius. In fact, all human beings do sin, for the *prest* is an irresistible compulsion to do so. In the letter to Rhegius, he asserts, "Original sin damns, to be sure. . . ." Z 5, p. 381,[15-16] tr. ZL 2, p. 15.

[42] Urbanus Rhegius (1489-1541) was the Lutheran reformer of Augsburg, author of anti-Anabaptist tracts. Rhegius wrote Zwingli a personal letter on baptism during the last half of June 1526. It has not been preserved.

[43] In fact, Zwingli does not make such an assertion about Paul in the writing to Urbanus Rhegius. It is perhaps implied in Zwingli's interpreting at length Paul's understanding of sin.

[44] Z 5, p. 374,[7] tr. ZL 2, p. 7.

---

[a] Zwingle. The first error. The second error.
[b] The third error.
[c] The fourth error.
[d] Before the fifth page.

and intolerable errors which Zwingli has sown publicly in print in the letter on original sin to Doctor Vrbanus Regius.* But it goes this way, that if we want to protect an untruth then God lets us fall into others, so that whoever is wicked becomes even more wicked. May God graciously help him [Zwingli] to recognize such blasphemy and mercifully help him out of it again. He has indeed fallen seriously.

Immelen: We have it that God loves children and that they have the promise. Why then should one not baptize them?[45]

Balthasar: Well then, let God love the children, still you have not proved that one should baptize them. For baptismal Scriptures do not apply to them but to those who now believe and confess their faith orally. On this confession Christ built his church, Matt. 16:18. And this is the order:[b] (1) Christ, (2) word, (3) faith, (4) confession, (5) water baptism, (6) church. If you understand that, then you should be satisfied. When you say, however, that the children have the promise, you imply that they also have their own faith. For promises are given in vain to those who are without faith. What need then do the children have of the alien faith of their fathers, mothers, godparents, or the church, as you argue, wholly without any basis in the Scriptures.

Immelen:[c] It is written in Mark 10:14 that "of these is the kingdom of heaven."[46]

Balthasar: Immelen, I love you from the heart but love the truth more. Therefore I must instruct you better in the Scripture. Show me where you have ever read in Scripture that Christ has said to the children: "Of these is the kingdom of heaven." You do violence and injustice to Christ and the

---

[45] *Dialogue*: aiii/v.
[46] *Dialogue*: aiii/v. Immelen then says that he is aware that this passage refers to adults who become like children. In the paragraph which follows, Hubmaier accuses Immelen of not being aware of this. Immelen goes on to say that although the passage speaks of adults, it does not thereby remove the "promise" from the children.

---

* Dr. Vrban[us] Regius.
b Order of the church.
c Of these is the kingdom of heaven.

Scripture.ª It is written "of such" and not "of these."⁴⁷ Now "of such" and "of these" are so far from one another as heaven and earth.ᵇ But the false baptism book of Zürich has seduced you.ᶜ Look at the Scriptures yourself, Matt. 19:14; Mark 10:14; Luke 18:16, then you will find it. /265/

Immelen: What should then hinder our taking them into the Christian church and society with baptism?⁴⁸

*Balthasar:*ᵈ This hinders, that they do not yet themselves believe. Christ says: "Whoever believes and is baptized." Not for vicarious faith; for if I believe for another, then I should also be baptized for him, for faith is always more than baptism.ᵉ Although some highly boast here of an infused faith, there is no basis for that in Scripture.⁴⁹

Immelen: Peter says: "Who may then deny water that these be baptized who have received the Holy Spirit even as we also?"⁵⁰

Balthasar: Paul uses this saying for the believing Cornelius and his household, Acts 10:47. You misuse it then for those who have not reason. That is called torturing the Scripture.

The Second Part

Oecolampad: There are two kinds of baptism: of adults and of the children of believers.⁵¹

---

⁴⁷ Hubmaier treated this issue at length in his *Dialogue with Zwingli's Baptism Book.* See above, text 14, pp. 230ff.

⁴⁸ *Dialogue:* aiiii/r.

⁴⁹ Hubmaier briefly addressed the question of infused faith in *Christian Baptism.* See above, text 11, p. 141.

⁵⁰ *Dialogue:* aiiii/r. At this point Hubmaier omits a discussion over Mark 16 and whether baptism is therein instituted.

⁵¹ *Dialogue:* aiiii/r. Here Oecolampad argues that on the basis of Romans 10 one should preach to unbelieving, unbaptized adults so that they might believe and be baptized, but differently to children, meaning children of believing parents. He then proceeds to argue the appropriateness of baptizing children on the basis of the inclusion of children in the Mosaic covenant.

ª Of such.
ᵇ Of these.
ᶜ The baptism book of Zurich.
ᵈ One's own fault.
ᵉ Infused faith.

Balthasar: That is rightly said. For the first is based in Scripture, the second not at all; therefore there are indeed two kinds.

Oecolampad: I want to point it out from the book of Exodus and ask first of all whether the children of the Jews also belonged to the people or not.[52]

Balthasar: Water baptism is a ceremony of the New Testament. Therefore I demand from you a clear word out of the New Testament with which you bring to us this infant baptism.[a] The word, the word, the word belongs to the species of the night owl and hates the light; it will not come forth into the sun. But you prove infant baptism from Exodus just as Zwingli his "Est" for "Significat" from Genesis.[b53]

Oecolampad: Whoever is inwardly baptized cannot be condemned, for God would have to condemn himself in them.[54]

Balthasar: Those who are inwardly baptized will let themselves truly be also outwardly baptized, and they do not despise the command of Christ, where they otherwise are able to have baptizer and water. The three thousand people, Acts 2:41; the treasurer, Acts 8:36f.; Paul Acts 9:18; Cornelius, Acts 10-11; Lydia and the jailer, Acts 16:15, 33, testify to that—also the twelve Ephesians, Acts 19:5. With this argument then, as it appears, you want to throw over and pour out Christ's water baptism entirely.

Oecolampad: There are many who are baptized who do not have faith and deceive us Christians regarding the water.[55]

Balthasar: We are discussing how it ought to be and not how it is. Without doubt many also sit down at the Supper of Christ who have never examined themselves. /266/ Nevertheless, the truth of the Word remains: the person should examine himself, 1 Cor. 11:28.

---

[51] Dialogue: aiiii/r-v.

[53] Zwingli first presented his argument for interpreting *est* for *significat* in the *Letter to Matthew Alber*, November 1524. He argued from Genesis by referring to Joseph's interpretation of Pharaoh's dream. Z 3, p. 345,[5-9] Pipkin 1984, p. 138.

[54] *Dialogue*: aiiii/v-bi/r.

[55] *Dialogue*: bi/r.

---

[a] Word. Word. Word.

[b] Zwinglen. *Est* /is/. *Significat* /signifies/.

Oecolampad: The fact is, baptism is for the sake of the person.[56]

Balthasar: *Deo gratias* [Thanks be to God]. Therefore the believing person will recognize the obligation of water baptism by virtue of the command of Christ, and not dispute further.

Oecolampad: Yes, the parents see also with joy that their children are killed in the name of Christ.[57]

Balthasar: My Ecolampad. What kind of death do the children die in water baptism? If physical death, then drown the baby. If you are speaking of spiritual death, which is the death of the old Adam, then I hear you saying that cradle children can also sin and resist sin, which is against the clear Word of God, Deut. 1:39. O God, where does the truth force you to go?

Oecolampad: What need is there for schism for the sake of water?[58]

Balthasar:* It is not for the sake of water, but for the sake of the high command and the baptism of Christ. Water is not baptism. Just as the making of idols is not about stone and wood, but for the sake of idolatry, which is practiced thereby against the earnest command of God, Exod. 20:23; Deut. 5:7ff.

Wolfgang: Well, then, in baptism it is not your father's faith that is appealed to but rather the Christian church's.[59]

Balthasar: Some of you speak to me of the foreign faith of father and mother, others of the faith of the godparents, while

---

[56] *Dialogue*: bi/r. Hubmaier makes a small editorial change here. Oecolampad does not say baptism is for the sake of the person, but for the sake of the neighbor, i.e., baptism is confession.

[57] *Dialogue*: bi/v. The reference to children being killed is an allusion to the "confession of martyrdom," one kind of confession among many about which Oecolampad had spoken in the preceding paragraph, but which was not noted by Hubmaier. Oecolampad does not say that the children are killed in baptism, but that as children do not understand what happens in baptism, they do not grasp what happens in martyrdom either. Hubmaier omits the reference to martyrdom in the following response.

[58] *Dialogue*: bi/v.

[59] *Dialogue*: bi/v. Wolfgang's statement is an answer to an assertion by a Basel Anabaptist that he did not know whether or not his father was a believer, even though he had been baptized.

---

* Water is not baptism.

others speak of the faith of the church, and that without any basis in Scripture. For if the children are baptized in the faith of their father and mother, why then are fathers and mothers forbidden to sponsor their children for baptism? If it is done by virtue of the faith of the godparents or the church, then people would be saved by the faith of another. All of which is totally contradictory to the Scripture.[a] For the righteous one will live by his own faith, Hab. 2:4; Rom. 1:17. Whoever himself believes and is baptized is saved, not the one for whom one believes, Mark 16:16. Philip demands from the treasurer his own faith, Acts 8:37. On the confession of its own faith is the Christian church built, Matt. 16:18.

Thomas: Do you also know that you had a father?[60]

Balthasar: Yes, and also a mother. Forgive me, Thomas, if I sometimes speak ironically with you. You almost provoke me because you speak empty words here and there without any Scripture. We desire Scripture, not masquerade.

Oecolampad:[b] Baptism is more a testimony than a covenant between Christians.[c] We testify in baptism that we are bound to Christ.[61] /267/

Balthasar: I am quite satisfied with this statement. But tell me one thing for God's sake: Can a cradle baby give such witness and unite itself thus to Christ? If you say no, then why do you baptize it? If you say other people act on its behalf, that is an invented addition introduced without any scriptural basis.

Oecolampad: I will show you a place in Tertullian where baptism is not a covenant.[62]

Balthasar: You speak to me much of Tertullian, Origen, Cyprian, Augustine, councils, histories, and old customs. I must somehow think that you lack the Scriptures, which do

---

[60] *Dialogue*: bi/v. Thomas asks this polemical question here in response to the Anabaptist who asserted several times in the Basel debate that he did not know if his father was a Christian.

[61] *Dialogue*: bii/r. Here Oecolampad answers an Anabaptist assertion that baptism is a covenant between Christians.

[62] *Dialogue*: bii/r.

---

[a] One's own fault.
[b] Witness.
[c] Covenant.

not want to come out of the quiver.[a] Dear Ecolampad, set your Scriptures together on infant baptism as I have done Scriptures on the baptism of believers in my baptism book printed at Straßburg.[b] Then we will both consider them against each other and will soon agree. Do it; do not forget.

Wolfgang: How can you say that you have not been rebaptized? For just as you are now baptized, so also were you then.[63]

Balthasar: If you with clear Scripture bring forth that infant baptism is a baptism, or is worthy of the name baptism, then we are in fact guilty of rebaptism. However, before you prove such, heaven and earth will first fall apart.[c]

Immelen: Tell me, did you have a true faith before baptism[64] or not? If you had a right faith, then you are justified by faith and rebaptism is not necessary for you for salvation.[65]

Balthasar: Hold on, Master Jacob, so that you do not fall. For I can also well make you such a false argument thus: faith makes us righteous before God, therefore water baptism and the Supper of Christ are in vain. If you, however, know thoroughly what baptism is by definition and why one needs it, you would be most ashamed of such a counter-argument.[d] Nevertheless, tell me one thing, my dear schoolmate, were the young children already baptized whom the Lord commanded to be brought to him or not? You again bring them up and say how Christ loved, blessed, and embraced them. If you say "Yes," then it is against you, for you think that you thereby fight for not depriving unbaptized children of water baptism, since the Lord commanded leading the unbaptized to him. If you say, however, "No, they were not baptized," then I hear clearly that Christ also blesses unbaptized children, calls them to himself, embraces, and loves them. Then, what need do they have of baptism, since the general institution of water

---

[63] *Dialogue:* bii/v.
[64] In the *Dialogue* Immelen says "rebaptism."
[65] *Dialogue:* bii/v.

---

[a] Scripture, Scripture.
[b] Straßburg.
[c] A corrupt argument.
[d] Practice of baptism.

baptism does not apply to them, also according to the understanding of Origen, Basil the Great, Athanasius, Tertullian, Jerome, Erasmus, and Zwingli? I want to let their own books be my witnesses.[66] Answer from Scripture. /268/

Oecolampad:[a] I confess that we do not consider believers as Christians, so long as they do not accept the Christian symbols, no matter how holy they are otherwise. For in this way Christ wanted to gather a people to himself by the sacramental symbols.[67]

Balthasar: God be praised. Therefore all those who want to be considered Christians should let themselves be baptized according to the command of Christ and confess Christian faith publicly before the church with mouth and water, or they are looseners of his words. For whoever now loosens the smallest of his commandments will be called the smallest in the kingdom of God, Matt. 5:19. Also, whoever keeps all the commandments and falls in one is guilty of all, James 2:10.

Oecolampad: Concerning Christian children I am of good hope that God has sanctified them, indeed, from their mother's womb on.[68]

Balthasar: Hope flows from faith, faith from the Word.[b] Show me a word which says that God sanctifies Christian children in the mother's womb. You will truly not find it but certainly the opposite as said above, and also as John writes: "As many as received him, to them he gave power to become children of God, who were not out of blood, nor out of the will of the flesh, nor out of the will of man, but were born out of God," John 1:12f.

Oecolampad:[c] What does it matter if even the children receive the symbol?[69]

---

[66] See *Old and New Teachers*, text 17.

[67] *Dialogue*: biii/v. Preceding this paragraph Oecolampad distinguishes two views of the church. Only God can surely see who has true faith and who has the Spirit. Such judgment is beyond human capability. Thus, to look at the church from the human perspective, one must be willing to call a person a Christian who accepts the sacraments of the church as a Christian.

[68] *Dialogue*: biii/v.

[69] *Dialogue*: biii/v.

---

[a] O right, right.

[b] Word. Faith. Hope.

[c] Baptism of Christ falls to the ground.

Balthasar: It does not matter to me. I do not grudge them milk, puree, indeed, wine and water. But it matters to the earnest command and baptism of Christ, which thereby falls to the ground when a fictitious and false baptism is additionally introduced by the false masters. Christ can simply not endure that. You again all together raise your voice and say: "Whoever believes is saved."

What need do we have of water baptism? Answer: thus speaks Christ: "Whoever believes and is baptized is saved," Mark 16:16. Likewise Peter: "Mend your ways, and each of you be baptized in the name of our Lord Jesus Christ for the forgiveness of sins," Acts 2:38.[a] If now faith alone would be enough, then Christ and Peter would have added baptism in vain. Here now you claim authority to lead Christ into school, to reprimand him for his vain words, and to teach him to speak correctly.

In summary, to conclude.[b] Dear friends, you cry so strongly and so much about custom, old practices, holy fathers, councils, and the long traditions of the mother, the Christian church, that everyone must note how you are lacking in Scriptures.[c] And there is, however, no Christian church or mother, other than the one conceived in the Word of Christ, born out of the Word of Christ and married through the Word to Christ. And yes, just you, my Ecolampad, know, to whom you, in answer to his manifold desire, gave account of your /269/ convictions concerning infant baptism thus:[d] "We did not until now find any places in the Scriptures which cause us to affirm the baptism of young children, so far as my humble self sees, etc."[e] So you write this opinion also concerning the epistle of Paul, Rom. 6:3.[70] However, the Lord, in the last chapter of Mark, by saying "Whoever believes and is baptized," Mark 16:16, forces us with this name "baptism" to the

---

[70] Hubmaier makes this point concerning Oecolampad in *Old and New Teachers*. See above, text 17, p. 256.

---

[a] Everyone. No one excluded.
[b] Summary.
[c] Christian church.
[d] The judgment of Ecolampadij.
[e] One's own handwriting.

294 / *Balthasar Hubmaier*

confession and demands from us a perfect faith.[a] For whoever does not want to be baptized also does not want to confess Christ. From this it follows that every Christian is obligated to let himself be marked with the outward water baptism of which Christ speaks in that place, "in the name of God the Father and the Son and the Holy Spirit for the forgiveness of his sins." Further, you write concerning the Word: *In mortem Christi, etc.*, [Into the death of Christ, Rom. 6:3] that the secret of baptism is that we are baptized into the death of Christ and learn how Christ Jesus died and thus did enough for our sin so that we also die to sins. Again: such learning and dying to sins cannot be said of a child one day old. Further, concerning the Word: *Ita et vos., etc.* [So you also, etc.] [verse 11], you write thus: "As far as concerns baptism each is obligated to experience for himself as if he had died to the world and that he may say to himself in temptations: 'Since you have died, what business do you have with the world.' " Young children can neither feel nor say this of themselves in the same way.

Now you hear the reason, my dear Ecolampad, why I have beseeched, admonished, and warned you in my writing so much and so diligently that you should not let such ungrounded and shameful speaking come into print. So by this, because of the reputation of your great teaching and your blameless life you would become a stumbling stone to many people, as it unfortunately has already happened, which people stumble over you or are even crushed. Accordingly, I beseech and admonish you for God's sake and on account of evangelical holiness and truth, recognize your error, return, give God the glory, and become a prisoner of the Word of Christ.[b] For you may hope for no more honorable victory than that you confess yourself to be overcome by Christ.

In short.[c] I let all of you be highly educated, and you are; but I have spoken in simplicity. My speech should be thus and will be thus and must be thus because the carpenter's Son, who never went to any school, has commanded me to

---

[a] Public print.
[b] The most honorable victory of all.
[c] Final conclusion.

speak in this way and to write such with the pen he himself
cut with his carpenter's ax. God be gracious to us all. Amen.

Printed by Simprecht Sorg,
called Froschauer
1527

19

A Brief Apologia

Released from Zurich in the spring of 1526, Hubmaier first went to Augsburg, where he met Hans Denck, and may have baptized him.[1] The end of July found him in the Moravian town of Nikolsburg, whose Lords, the brothers Leonard and Hans of Liechtenstein, were willing to give him asylum and even support his kind of Reformation.

Yet Hubmaier was by now a notorious refugee, having been condemned by the Catholic authorities of Austria and imprisoned by Protestant Zurich. It may well have been, as Bergsten suggests, that it was the princes von Liechtenstein themselves who urged Hubmaier to clear his name with this apologia, probably the first writing he did after arriving in Nikolsburg. The argument in favor of religious liberty and the call for a fair chance to confront his detractors' accusations are reminiscent of Hubmaier's earliest defensive writing in Schaffhausen; but this time we see in addition the whole gamut of Reformation doctrine, exposited with a view to demonstrating its biblical basis and Hubmaier's own good faith.[2]

---

[1] That Hubmaier baptized Denck at Augsburg was the standard tradition, thereby constituting a "succession" linking South German Anabaptism to the Swiss Brethren origins. Bergsten 1978, p. 354, assumes this tradition's accuracy. As indicated above, p. 17, note 4, it has been questioned by Packull 1973.

[2] A first translation draft was prepared by Elizabeth Horsch Bender. Fragmentary translation in Hošek 1892, pp. 28-32. Fragments in Vedder 1905, pp. 97, 141, 214; Davidson 1939, pp. 533-537; Armour 1966, p. 53; and Klaassen 1981, p. 166. Manuscript of translation by Henry C. Vedder at Colgate Rochester Library. Original in HS 14, pp. 272-83.

A Brief Apologia
Dr. Balthasar Huebmor von Fridberg
to all believers in Christ,
that they may not be offended by
the fabricated untruths with which
his detractors charge him
1526
Truth Is Immortal.
Nicolspurg
Our law judges no person
unless it has heard him first
and found out what he does. John 7:51

A Brief Apologia

I wish grace and peace from God the Father through his beloved Son Jesus Christ, our Lord and Redeemer, to all godly and devout people. Beloved brethren and sisters in God, Christ Jesus our Savior and Redeemer has said, "Blessed are you when people revile you and persecute you and utter all kinds of evil against you falsely on my account. Rejoice and be glad, for your reward is great in heaven," Matt. 5:11. My situation is no less. For four years my detractors have spoken so much evil of me that if it were true I would have had to pass upon myself a sentence of death by sword, fire, or water. But I have until now patiently borne these fabricated untruths as much as God granted me grace, and I have always thought: It is simply a part of my cross which Christ has laid on me; I will not cast it away from me. It is a draft from my cup which he has offered me; I will not pour it out. I would truly have been of a mind to endure such things even longer and to keep silent about them, because my Christ also did not justify himself by replying to all the public /273/ untruths ascribed to him by false people. Nevertheless, now that I hear that a stumbling block or offense may arise thereby among the weak (who have not yet experienced how things must go for a Christian) I am induced to make my innocence known. Since I am everywhere decried and denounced[a] as a proclaimer of new teachings, alleging that I desecrate the mother of God, reject the saints, destroy prayer, fasting, Sabbaths, confession, that I despise the holy fathers, councils, and human teachings, attach no value to monasteries and priestly vows, nor to singing and reading in church. I make a mockery of extreme unction, which is also called the last baptism, and set up a new rebaptism. I break down the altars and deny the flesh and blood in the mass. I am a revolutionary and a seducer of the people; I preach that one should not obey the government, nor pay interest or tithes. I secretly fled Regensburg.[3] In sum: I am the very worst Lutheran archheretic that one could find.

Listen, O you dear pious Christians, what great things these witnesses say against me. Yea, they say unduly loud that I am possessed, that I have seven devils with me who speak out from me. That I am a Mammaluke,[4] that I have crosses branded on my heels and have goat's feet. Thus absolutely nothing is too much for these godless people to say; they do not notice that they thereby become liars, come to mockery and shame and also will be eternally damned. Thus ignorance of God's Word, self-interest, hatred, and pride delude them. But truly as I shall want to and must give account to God on the last day, I want very briefly to reveal to you my innocence.[b]

---

[3] There seems to be no basis for the accusation that Hubmaier had been forced to flee Regensburg when he moved to Waldshut, either in 1521 or in 1523. He seems, rather, to have had the blessing of the authorities. Bergsten 1978, pp. 94, 106. At that time he was still a friend of his later adversary, Johannes Faber, and must have had the authorization of the bishop of Constance to make the move.

[4] The Mamelukes were the military caste dominating Egypt since the thirteenth century. Through some indirect derivation presumably related to the crusades, the name had become a familiar term for "infidel" or "apostate," with a meaning more exotic and perhaps less threatening than "Turk."

---

[a] Accusation.
[b] Answer.

To the point: I know nothing of any new teaching; I preach Christ crucified.[a] But the holy gospel had to suffer this very slap on the cheek also in the time of Christ, Mark 1:27. And for the sake of the gospel Paul was denounced as a proclaimer of new devils, Acts 7.[5] So I confess the pure Virgin Mary[b] to be a chaste maiden before and after the birth.[6] I believe her to be a true mother of God, and with Elizabeth, I call her blessed because she believed, Matt. 1:20; Luke 1:42; John 19:27; Isa. 7:14; 9:6. The dear saints I honor in God as his instruments in whom he worked many miracles,[c] as Paul writes, Gal. 1. But that they should be called upon as our mediators with God and as our helpers in distress, I deny. We have one intercessor and helper in distress, Christ Jesus, Matt. 11:25-27; 1 John 2:1; 1 Tim. 2:5; John 14:14. I teach praying without ceasing,[d] as Christ taught his disciples; but I hate much mumbling with the lips while the heart is nowhere in it, Luke 18:11, 1 Thess. 5:17; Matt. 6:5ff.; Luke 11:1-13. One ought to fast daily[e] and refrain from excess in food and drink; bread, meat, fish, eggs, milk, /274/ and wine should be accepted in moderation and with thanksgiving at all times without differentiation. For what goes into the mouth does not defile a person, Rom. 13:13; 1 Tim. 1 and 4:3ff.; Col. 2:16; Rom. 14:14; 1 Cor. 10:23-31; 8:8; Acts 10; 11; 15:29; Luke 10:7; Mark 15. I teach the Sabbath faithfully, resting, and abstaining from all sins on all days which is the true Sabbath, Exod. 20:8-11; Deut. 5:12-15; Isa. 58:13; 66:23.[f] One should continually confess and lament one's sins against God with David, with the prodigal son, and with the publican.[g] But the auricular confessional[7] I consider to be in vain, 2 Sam. 12:13;

---

[5] It is not clear which text is meant by the reference to Paul; perhaps Acts 17:18.

[6] In contrast to later Protestant polemics, some of the early Reformers affirmed the perpetual virginity of Mary.

[7] *Klapperbeicht*: noise-making confession.

---

[a] New teaching.
[b] Mary a virgin.
[c] Honoring the saints.
[d] Praying.
[e] Fasting.
[f] Sabbath.
[g] Confessing.

Psalm 51; Luke 15:21; 18:13; Matt. 15:8. I test the holy fathers, councils, and human teachings by the touchstone of Holy Scripture, 1 John 4:1.[a] If they measure up with it, then I am believing the Scripture. If they do not conform to it, I command them to get behind me, as Christ did to Peter when he was not minded according to the will of God, Matt. 16:23. This is also what Augustine desires, as well as Jerome,[b] and also it is included in the papal laws that one should not believeae any person beyond what one can prove with the Word of God, however holy one may seem to be. Paul also teaches us the very same. Even if an angel were to come down from heaven and preach to us another gospel, it should be accursed, Gal. 1:8. For one honors God in vain with human teachings, Isa. 29:13; Matt. 15:9.

Yes, I confess that I attach no value to the vows of monks, priests, and nuns.[c] For if we lived according to the baptismal vows we would have enough to do day and night;[d] however, we would still have to confess ourselves as unprofitable servants and would not lay on ourselves additional burdens. But since we did not know what water baptism means, and what the baptismal vow requires, Satan introduced monastic vows and other false vows regarding food, drink, days, clothing, and pilgrimages.[e] I am well satisfied with singing and reading in the church,[f] but not as it has hitherto been practiced—only if it is done in the spirit and from the heart and with understanding of the words and for the edifying of the church, as Paul teaches, 1 Cor. 14:26; Col. 3:16; Eph. 5:19. Elsewhere God rejects it repeatedly and does not want our Baalite shouting at all, Mal. 2:8; Ezek. 33:31f.; Amos 5:23. Extreme unction,[g] or as it is called in some countries, "last baptism," I consider not only a mockery, yea also an idolatry, for to it is ascribed forgiveness for sins; and he who receives it may not go to the baths nor dance nor gamble for a certain time. But any one who receives the sacrament of the altar,

---

[a] Councils.
[b] Augustine in *On Nature and Grace* and Jerome's *Foundations*.
[c] Monastic vows.
[d] Baptismal vows.
[e] False vows.
[f] Singing, reading.
[g] Unction.

which according to papal belief is the flesh and blood of Christ, may indeed bathe, gamble, dance, and from that hour on sit at tables with a prostitute and give her the offering and money, for which the priest or bishop has sold Christ or the chrism. Note, dear Christian, how we /275/ have elevated above God the stinking oil (which the bishops have greeted probably a hundred thousand times on Maundy Thursday, and it has never yet thanked them). However, the spiritual anointing which Christ announced to us, Luke 10:34 and also James 5:14, I esteem highly and am quite satisfied to have it called the last baptism. For I confess three kinds of baptism:[a] that of the Spirit, which takes place inwardly in faith; the second, of water, which takes place outwardly by oral affirmation of faith before the church; and the third, of blood in martyrdom or on the deathbed, of which Christ also speaks, Luke 12:50, for which we are indeed in need of the spiritual wine and oil which the Samaritan poured into the wounds of the injured man, Luke 10:34. John calls these three baptisms, with which all Christians must be baptized, the three witnesses on earth, 1 John 5:7.[b] For whoever wants to cry with Christ to God: "Abba, pater, dear Father," must do so in faith, and must also be cobaptized in water with Christ and suffer jointly with him in blood. Then he will be a son and heir of God, fellow heir with Christ, and will be jointly glorified with Christ, Rom. 8:17. Therefore no one should be terrified of persecution or suffering, for Christ had to suffer and thus enter into his glory, Luke 24:26. And also Paul writes: "All who desire to live so devoutly in Christ Jesus will be persecuted," 2 Tim. 3:12. This is indeed precisely the third baptism or last baptism in which people should indeed be anointed with the oil of the holy and comforting gospel (in order that we may be meek and ready to suffer). Thus the illness is lightened for us, and we receive forgiveness of sins, James 5:14ff. But those whom James calls priests, whom the sick person should have to minister over himself, Christ calls servants, that is, preachers and pastors, who attend to the sick sinner with the Word of God. For that purpose Christ has placed into the hand the two coins of the Old and New Testaments, Luke 10:35. So much

---

[a] Three kinds of baptism.
[b] Three witnesses on earth.

for the present on spiritual anointing.

To proceed: I have never taught rebaptism.[a] Nor do I know of any except the one in Acts 19:3ff. But I do teach the true baptism of Christ, which teaching and oral confession of faith precedes; and I say that infant baptism[b] is a robbing of the true baptism of Christ and a misuse of the lofty names of God the Father and the Son and the Holy Spirit, and completely contrary to Christ's institution and the usage of the apostles, Matt. 28:19; Mark 16:15-16; Acts 2:38, 41; 8:12, 38; 9:18; 10:47-48; 11:16; 16:15, 33; 18:8; 19:4-5; 22:16; 1 Pet. 3:21; Heb. 10:22. Nevertheless, it is correctly and well called infant baptism. For what on earth could be thought of as more infantile than asking an infant two hours old, in Latin, whether it renounces the devil and expecting it to answer in German that it does /276/ renounce, as if it had learned two languages in its mother's womb. O childishness! O blindness! When one wants to restore and properly observe the Supper of Christ, I indeed demand tearing down the altars[c] on which we, as far as it concerned us, have till now crucified and killed Christ Jesus again. For the table of the Lord has no communion with the tables of devils. Nor can Dagon stand side by side with the ark of God, 1 Cor. 10:21; 1 Sam. 5:2ff. The word *mass*[d] I do not recognize in the Scripture at all, except as much as Daniel writes about it that Maoz is an idol set up by the antichrist, "which must be honored with gold, silver, precious stones, and everything costly," Daniel 11:38.[8] Consequently I attach to the priest's mass just as much value as I do to the Frankfurt fair, for there is nothing there but daily buying and selling, only that in the priest's mass this takes place spiritually. Yea, O Christ, who drove the Gadarene swine into the lake, come with your whip and drive such

---

[8] In this and the following sentences, Hubmaier composed a three-way pun on the word *mass*. Daniel 11:38 refers to an idol named "god of fortresses"—*eloah ma'uzzim*, Vulgate *maozim*. A second pun has changed "idol" (*Abgott*) into "Abbot's god" (*Abtgott*). Then the next sentence compares the mass to a fair (*Messe*).

---

[a] Rebaptism.
[b] Infant baptism.
[c] Altar.
[d] Mass.

simoniacal merchants out of thy temple!

For Simon has so badly injured their righteous ears that they cannot hear your righteous Word.[9] Throw over their money changers' tables on which they put up for auction and daily sell your grace, indulgences, heaven, baptism, marriage, yourself, and your crimson blood under the guise of bread and wine. They know, however, that you are not there, but sit at the right hand of your heavenly Father. Yea, Christ, as far as they are concerned they raise you in the air, they make three pieces out of you, they drown you in wine, and finally crunch you with their teeth for the sake of money,[a] and thus show you their gratitude as the cuckoo does to his feeding father and his brooding mother.[b]

But as to the charge that I am a revolutionary, praise be to God for that! That is the same name that was also given to Christ, my Savior. He was also supposed to be an agitator who stirred up the people from Galilee to Jerusalem, and he was especially the one who forbade paying taxes to the emperor, Luke 23:2.[c] Jeremiah was accused of being a divider of the soldiers in Israel, who did not desire peace but agitation, Jer. 38:4. King Ahab railed at Elijah as a troubler of his country.[d] But Elijah answered and said, "I do not make a rebellion against you; but you do so and your father's house, who have abandoned the commandments of the Lord and followed the Baals," 1 Kings 18:17-18. Note that if Ahab had not attached himself to Baalish bishops, monks, and priests, there would have been a lasting peace in the land. Paul was also accused /277/ by Tertullus of being a stirrer-up of the people, a cause of sects, a pestilent fellow, Acts 24:5. Therefore I am not at all surprised that it is happening to me, who am not worthy to loosen the thongs of their shoes. Nevertheless, this I affirm with God and with several thousand people that no preacher in the areas where I have been[e] has gone to more trouble

---

[9] The "Simon" reference is to Simon Magus of Acts 8:9ff. His name had become the code word for financial profiteering through religious office.

---

[a] Mass priests torture Christ as a thief and murderer.
[b] Cuckoo Eucharist.
[c] Revolutionary.
[d] Cause of the rebellions.
[e] Public protestation.

and labor in writing and preaching than I in order that people should be obedient to the government.* Since it is of God, who hung the sword at its side, one should without contradiction render to it tolls, duties, tribute, honor, and respect. Of this I have written and preached in Latin and in German so earnestly that many people became ill-disposed toward me, fled from my preaching, and, yes, some even interrupted me openly in church on this point, defaming me as a blood sucker[b] who does nothing but defend the governmental sword. On the other hand I have also told the government to wield the sword according to the order of God for the protection of the righteous and punishment of the evil, or God will take away its mandate and mete out to it with the same measure.

In sum: for affirming with such high diligence the authority of the government I have had to suffer much, often and heavily. But never in my life have I taught that subjects should not fulfill the duty and obedience due to their government. Rather, when even heavier burdens are imposed upon them that are not contrary to God (whom one should obey more than people), they are to take them up willingly and carry them with patience as their cross. On the other hand I have also never taught that it is proper for the government, bishops, abbots, monks, nuns, and priests to overload their poor people, more than is godly and just, with unprecedented unchristian impositions, and to tear them away by force from the Word of God. For God will not, as truly as he is God, leave this unavenged. Waldshût must bear me the same witness.[c] Before long I will also have my writings published[10] and thus bring into the open what I then preached publicly. But so shall it come to pass. Someone else breaks the fence, and I must suffer the blow on the mouth.[11] Concerning

---

[10] These lines may indicate that the *Apologia* is the first to be printed of the 1526 publications.

[11] The image is that of striking a bovine on the muzzle to drive it back into the pen.

---

* Government is from God.
[b] Blood tippler.
[c] Waldßhût.

interest and tithes[a] I have said and still say: A Christian does not quarrel or fight, rather he gives a fifth or a third, not to mention a tenth of his goods. Yes, he also lets his coat go with the cloak, Matt. 5:40. But if there were genuine brotherly love among us, it would indeed teach us to give and take interest, Luke 6.[12] Yet among us not the least word has been spoken against either interest or tithes.

Nevertheless, they have tried in violence and contrary to all laws to drive us away from God's Word; this has been our only complaint.[b] Here I assert, in spite of all people on earth and all the devils of hell,[c] that they had no other cause for a charge against Waldßhůt excepting only, only, only the Word /278/ of God. God give them all to understand and enlighten those who have maligned us to the contrary before the Princely Majesty. What I have now said I would like to convey to his Princely Majesty himself. When they were at Breysach in Breißgau, the people of Waldßhůt presented this their request to his Princely Majesty both orally and in writing. Also with other princes and lords who were personally involved in this, and especially with the Christian city of Constentz,[13] where the last diet was, the people of Waldßhůt[d] publicly offered that they would continue to do for his Princely Majesty and the others everything just as they had done hitherto, what their forefathers had done and, far beyond this, to hand over and shed their body, life, honor, possessions, and blood for

---

[12] In mid-1523 Zwingli had attacked tithes and interests (Yoder 1962, p. 118f.) but then had accepted their legal retention. Hubmaier gives the word "love" his special meaning (Yoder 1962, pp. 44-52). It is the motivation for retaining voluntarily what is no longer obligation. The lender should no longer demand interest on his loan; but the borrower will nonetheless pay it, out of love. Most of the Swiss Brethren taught that one should give but not receive interest payment. Hubmaier slips here from "I" to "us." It is not clear to whom (besides himself) the plural refers.

[13] In January 1525 efforts had been made in Constance by agents of several Swabian and Swiss cities to mediate between Waldshut and Austria (Bergsten 1961, pp. 217ff., Bergsten 1978, p. 278). At that time Hubmaier and Waldshůt were not Anabaptist but Zwinglian.

---

[a] Interest. Tithes.
[b] Note.
[c] In spite of.
[d] Constentz, Waldßhůt.

the sake of the praiseworthy house of Austria.[a] And if there were one stone buried sixty feet under the earth at Waldßhůt that were not good Austrian, then they would scratch it out with their fingernails and throw it into the Rhine. They also have always and ever been the first to pay obeisance and tribute to his Princely Majesty. Only for God's sake have they always and ever begged with tears in their eyes that they be left with the pure and clear Word of God. Then this answer was given them at Constentz by the Councillors of his Princely Majesty, that they would simply not allow it,[b] for if it were allowed them it would be the same as extinguishing one fire while kindling four. Other cities would afterward also want to have the same.

I know all those who gave this answer, but at the present time I do not want to name them.[14] When this answer was given the delegations of the cities of Zürch, Basel, and Schaffhausen[c] were present.[15] So there rode against me to Schaffhausen the Councillors of his Princely Majesty, namely Veit Suter[d] along with several members of the Confederacy and Mr. Tegen Fuchs[e] of Zürch, who accused me in both towns unnecessarily high and hard in the years 1524, '25 and '26; and they finally demanded in the name of his Princely Majesty to turn me over into their hands.[16] Both cities did not want to do that, but it was proposed to them to take all legal proceedings against me.[f] This is why I am now still daily

---

[14] I.e., the imperial representatives in this process were people Hubmaier knew from his earlier career.

[15] Hubmaier being in protective custody in Zurich since early December, Austria was demanding his extradition in order to try him, whether for heresy or for insurrection. Bergsten 1978, p. 278, n. 25 reports one negotiating session, in Constance January 22-26. This was referred to in the preceding paragraph. Hubmaier refers here to Schaffhausen, as to a different event.

[16] The appeal of Austria for the deliverance of Hubmaier into their hands was dated December 14, 1525. vMS, p. 390.

---

[a] Austria.
[b] Note what a Christian answer.
[c] Zürch, Basel, Schaffhausen.
[d] Veit Suter.
[e] Tegen Fuchs.
[f] Justice, justice, justice.

appealing: they ought to accuse me. If I /279/ had been justly convicted, Zürch and Schaffhausen[a] would have stick, sword, fire, and water, and would not let me go unpunished. This was never accepted by my accusers, who only pressed that I be handed over to them without being called to court, unheard and unconvicted,[b] as I have also shown in public print in 1524.[17] But how I left Ingolstat and Regenspurg[c] is known to the illustrious and highborn Prince and Lord, Lord John, Count Palatine,[d] etc., and Administrator of Regenspurg,[18] my very gracious Lord, also to the noble, strict, honorable and wise Lords, the Captain,[e] City Treasurer, and the Council of Regenspurg; likewise the university[f] and an honorable Councillor of Ingolstat, who all will give me a special written certificate of my innocence against such made-up and false lies. And also Wilhalm Wyelannd,[g] citizen and Councillor of Regenspurg publicly put me and my household on his iron ship and brought me in the middle of the day from Regenspurg to Ulm. Also at all the toll and custom stations I was allowed to pass freely owing to the written papers my gracious Lord of Regenspurg had given to me. But truly, such lies do not concern me as to my person at all. I have two ears to hear and the slanderer has only one mouth to speak. I know also that to be defamed by evil people is an honor.

But that nobody may be bothered or offended by my teaching (which is not mine but Christ's) good lords and friends prevailed on me to publish a short apology, although I would much more have preferred to be silent so that no one might think that I am seeking my own glory with this. But that in the end my ungracious detractors accuse me publicly to be the most evil of all Lutheran archheretics,[h] I let them judge,

---

[17] See above, items numbered 2 and 3.
[18] Hubmaier's references here reach back before his Waldshut time. He left Ingolstadt in 1515 and Regensburg in 1523.

---

[a] Zürch, Schaffhausen.
[b] Kill. Crucify.
[c] Ingolstat, Regenspurg.
[d] Johann Count Palatine.
[e] Thomas Fuchs.
[f] University, Council.
[g] Wyelannd, ship's captain at Regennsburg.
[h] Lutheran heretic.

since these Triackers[19] have never heard me,[a] nor instructed
me, nor overcome me. Paul teaches us not to associate with
heretics like that, Titus 3:10. I may err, I am a human
being—but a heretic I cannot be, for I constantly ask instruction in the Word of God.[20] But nobody has yet come forth who
has showed me a different word, save one sole man with his
party, and that contrary to his own prior preaching, word, and
publications. His name I will protect on account of the divine
Word. He wanted to teach me the faith by means of public
law[b] and trial before his own government, before the confederates, also before the emperor himself, /280/ by means of
capturing, imprisoning, torture, and the executioner.[21] But
faith is a work of God and not of the Heretics' Tower,[22] in
which one sees neither sun nor moon and lives on nothing but
bread and water. But praise be to God, who protected me
from this lions' pit in which dead and living people remain
lying next to each other and must thus perish.[c] O God, forgive me my weakness.[23] "It is good for me," as David says,
"that you have humbled me. The son whom you love, you
chasten. I am well satisfied with you. You have given and
taken, praised be your name. You know what I say."

Here is now, O dear pious Christians, a short apology, in
which I have truly shown my innocence.[d] Whoever accepts it
accepts the truth; but whoever thinks that it is not so, the

---

[19] Derived from the Latin word *theriacus*, an herb or drug used as an
antidote. The word here is used as a term of opprobium, meaning in effect
"drug peddlers."

[20] This phrase was often repeated by dissenters asking for a hearing.

[21] This unnamed person who tried to debate Scripture with Hubmaier
with the state's power behind him was obviously Zwingli himself. That
Hubmaier was tortured is in the records. That he was threatened with
death is not. The first execution of an Anabaptist by Zurich was that of
Felix Mantz a year later. The Council action establishing the penalty of
death by drowning was issued March 7, 1526, while Hubmaier was in
prison there.

[22] The reference is to a specific building in Zurich, the *Ketzerturm*.

[23] The allusion to weakness is probably to Hubmaier's recantation. See
above, text 12.

---

[a] Triackers.
[b] Public law.
[c] A severe sentence.
[d] First admonition.

same may call me to account for it. Over my teaching let the
Word of God be the sole judge, John 12:48; over me every
Christian authority who bears the sword in the place of God,
Rom. 13:4. I do not want anything other than with Paul: a
hearing, judgment, and justice. I want that come weal or woe.
But where there exists nothing but grim violence and tyranny,
there I will use the basket of Paul at Damascus and will not
wait for the attack by the forty men, but will flee and give
way, as Christ bade, Matt. 10:23, as long as it is God's will, so
that I do not tempt him and give others cause for their anger
and wrath. Yes, where all that may take place without viola-
tion of the divine Word and without vexation of the believers.
But when the hour of our dying is at hand, which only God
knows, then no fleeing will help us.

Yet I ask, admonish, and warn in the name of Jesus Christ
and his final judgment, all those at whose side God has hung
the sword, that they not use it against innocent blood, neither
through capturing, chasing, beating, putting in .the blocks,
hanging, drowning, or burning.ª For truly, truly, I say to
them, the martyred and shed blood will cry up to God in the
heavens together with the innocent blood of the pious Abel
against such Cains,ᵇ murderers, and blood spillers. He will
demand it at their hands and will pour out his revenge over
them and their children. For whoever sheds human blood
(understand: against the order of divine justice) that one's
blood, says God, shall itself also be shed, Gen. 9:6. Whoever
takes the sword and uses it shall himself be destroyed by the
sword, Matt. 26:52. Therefore, you government,ᶜ watch what
you do (so speaks King Jehosaphat by the Spirit of God to his
judges, 2 Chron. 19:6-7). You do not wield a human office but
one from God, and what /281/ you judge will come over you.
Watch that the fear of God be with you and do everything
with diligence. With God there is no malice, nor respect of
persons, nor covetousness for bribes or gifts. Take heed, take
heed, O government, that you not stain your hands and wash
them in the blood of the innocent. You know how it fared
with the murderer Herod, with that whited wall, the chief

ª Second admonition.
ᵇ Cains.
ᶜ Government is an office of God.

priest Ananias,[24] and the blood-judge Pontius Pilate. Remember that you also have a judge above you in the heavens, who will measure you with the measure of Adoni-bezek, Judg. 1:7, with which you have measured others. You cannot escape his judgment. Nor will it help you to say: "Well, I had to do it. My gracious Lord told me to; he wants to have it that way." No, that won't do. One has to obey God more than people. Pilate preferred to be a friend of the emperor than of the poor innocent Christ and feared the loss of his office and of his properties. What help is the emperor to him now? Where is his office? What use is his property? Yes, the emperor with all his might, power, offices, and properties could not come to your help with a single, cool drop of water. So it also happened to the rich man, Luke 16:24. And to conclude, in short, so that we come to an end, God will not graciously accept anything from an unjust government. Yes, even if it would make foundations and build into heaven, and move mountains and distribute all its goods among the poor, as the Spirit of God testifies through Isaiah and says to the government: "Hear the Word of the Lord, you princes of Sodom; hear the law of your God, you people of Gomorrah. What shall I do with your many food offerings?" says the Lord. "I am fed up with burnt offerings of rams and the fat of the animals and the blood of the oxen and the lambs and the he-goats I have not desired. When you come before my face and enter my courts, who has asked that from your hands? Do not henceforth offer me any offerings in vain. Your burnt offering is a horror to me. I do not like the malice and assemblies of the new moon and of the Sabbaths. My soul hates your days of the new moon and the particular festival days; they weary me. I am tired of enduring it. And if you stretch out your hands I shall hide my eyes from you. And even if you make many prayers I will not hear them, for your hands are full of blood. Wash yourselves, cleanse yourselves, put away from my face the evil of your plots, stop oppressing. Learn to do good, practice justice, help the oppressed, judge for the orphan, render assistance to the widows. Come here, I ask you, /282/ we shall be reconciled, says the Lord. Though your sins be like a red

---

[24] Here Hubmaier designates Ananias with the contemporary term *pfaffen Bischoff.*

thread, they will become as white snow. Though they be like red-colored wool, they will be as white wool. If you desire it and if you listen, you will eat the goods of the earth. If you are not willing and if you provoke me still more, you will be consumed with the sword. For the mouth of the Lord has spoken this. But how the faithful city, full of justice, has turned into a whore. Righteousness lived in it, but now murderers.[a] Your silver has changed into foam, your wine is mixed in water. Your princes do not fear God and keep company with thieves;[b] they all love bribes and follow after gifts. They speak no justice to the orphan; the cause of the widows does not come up before them."[25]

Observe here, O pious Christian, how severely God accuses the unjust government. Truly, a hard punishment will befall it afterward. God will take revenge on it as on his enemies. He will make it like a fir tree without needles and like a garden without water, that is, mockery and shame. Its strength will be like stubble and the workman like a little spark of fire; both will burn together, and nobody will extinguish it.[c] These are the words of God.

Herewith I admonish all emperors, kings, princes, lords,[d] all governments and rulers, as Moses also commanded his judges, Deut. 1:17, that they hear everybody and do not sentence and condemn anyone uncharged, unheard, yes even unseen, only on the basis of false witness. For many a person nowadays is being accused of being a heretic and an agitator, into whose heart never entered any heresy and discord. But Satan attempts to give the gospel a full blow on the cheek and to make it hateful to all governments.[e] The Spirit of God says further through Moses: And judge what is right between everybody and his brother and strangers. You should respect

[25] The Scripture which Hubmaier quotes but does not cite is Isaiah 1:10-23.

[a] Murderers.
[b] Princes.
[c] A prince is wild game in heaven. Observe whether this punishment is not before our eyes with the Turks.
[d] Third admonition.
[e] Woe to his legates with their blood lists.

no person in court, but you should hear the small as well as the great and not shrink back from any person, for the judgment is of God. Here you hear once again that the judges sit in the place of God;[a] therefore it is necessary that they not judge against God. Thus Paul calls them also servants of God. But God is angry with the guilty and protects the righteous. Consequently the servant should also do the will of his lord or he will be punished with many blows. God also descended to Sodom and Gomorrah and saw whether they had thus sinned, as the outcry against them went, Gen. 18:21.[b] Thus government should first find out for sure, whether the evil outcries are true which are now being spoken against many people by their detractors. But if a case /283/ is too difficult for you, says Moses, then let them come to me that I may hear them. It would be fair if it would happen thus in our time. If a cause were too difficult for the worldly government and would concern the faith of the Christian church, then one should immediately refer it to Moses, that is, to the Scripture. That is the right judge for matters touching the faith, as it is written in Isaiah 8:20; Ezekiel 44:5; Deuteronomy 18:15; 28:1; John 5:39; 12:48. And Christ says in the parable: They have Moses and the prophets, Luke 16:29. There one will find true discernment to make peace and concord. For rage, fury, and the shedding of innocent blood will not help. Since this advice is from God, it cannot be suppressed, and even if you should all reach an agreement, dear lords, against the innocent Christ and his members, it will still be in vain. The Lord in the heavens laughs at you. You dig a ditch and will fall into it yourselves. Therefore leave off from your anger, give glory to God and honor to his mighty Word. It is too hard for you to kick against this sharp point. You will and must give in to it. Shout with your heart to him as did Paul: "Lord, what do you want that we should do?" and he will without doubt send you an Ananias who is just and truthful, not merchants greedy for money or benefices, but preachers who will open up to you clearly and brightly his holy, living, and eternal Word. That Word will penetrate and pierce your hearts; and then you will recognize yourselves, change your life, and call to God:

---

[a] Judges sit in the place of God.
[b] Interrogate the other part as well: that is divine.

"Father, forgive us, we did not know what we did." Thereafter God will mercifully accept you again and will bring you after this ephemeral life into eternal happiness. May God the Father, Son, and Holy Spirit grant this to you and to all of us. Amen. Turn to God, dear lords and friends, and he will graciously remove his iron scourge from us again.

Truth Is Immortal.
Nicolspurg
1526
Printed by Simprecht Sorg,
called Froschauer

20

A Simple Instruction

A Simple Instruction *is one of three writings of Hubmaier in which the Lord's Supper is the main subject of concern.*[1] *Written in late 1526 at about the same time as his* Brief Apologia, *it came at a time when the issue of the Supper was under discussion. The appearance of two separate editions of the work suggest that it touched upon an important issue and that it met a need in the Moravian debates. Hubmaier wrote the treatise at the height of his influence as an Anabaptist.*

The treatise is colored by a strong polemical tone. Hubmaier begins with listing fifteen different erroneous opinions on the Eucharist, thereby thoroughly distancing himself not only from Catholic opinion but also, by the clear denial of the real physical presence of Christ, from the Lutheran. He also separates himself from the Carlstadtian and Zwinglian interpretations of the words of institution while nonetheless articulating a view that was close to that of Zwingli.[2]

---

[1] See above, number 7 and below, number 25.
[2] Source: HS 15, 286-304. Partially translated in Hošek 1892, pp. 134-141.

A Simple Instruction
on the Words:
This is My Body
in the Supper of Christ.
Dr. Balthasar Huebmör
von Fridberg.
Nicolspurg
1526.
Truth Is Immortal.
To the highborn Lord,
Lord Leonhard von Lichtenstein
at Nicolspurg, etc., to his gracious Lord.

Grace and peace in Christ Jesus our Savior. God, our heavenly Father, changed the names of many people in the Old Testament and gave them a new one, such as Abram into Abraham, Sarai into Sarah, Jacob into Israel,[a] Gen. 17:5, 15; Gen. 32:29. Also Christ in the New Testament called Simon Bar Jonah, Peter, so that the name and the work matched one another, Matt. 16:18. Thus Gideon was called by Christ, Jerubbaal, Judg. 6:32; likewise, James and John: Boanerges, that is, sons of thunder, by Christ, Mark 3:17. Thereby such people were reminded how to direct their words, teachings, and life henceforth /287/ so that they not bear their name in vain before people.[b] Would to God that all people would also be well aware of our high, noble, and blessed name, which comes to us from Christ, and through this to be faithfully admonished and challenged to follow in a manly way our Head, Christ Jesus, in his Word, fighting under his banner, sacrificing and pouring out our body, life, honor, goods, flesh, and blood for his name's sake. For if we want to be Christians and confess this name genuinely, then it is necessary that we

---

[a] Giving of name.
[b] Being Christian a high name.

risk all we have, or we will be unworthy to be called his disciples. Since, however, gracious Lord, I have this time inquired after Your Grace's name also, I learn that Your Grace's name is Leonhard von Lichtenstein auff Nicolspurg, of which I am not a little amazed that such a high and powerful name is gathered together in one person. Without doubt God has given and will also daily give more and more grace and power together with the names. For Leonhard is a name indicating such strength, manhood, and toughness of a person that the same is not even frightened by the angry lions of this world; but in the power of the Spirit of God, without any weapon he will with his hands tear them apart like lambs, as Samson also did when he went down into Timnath, so that at that time one could truly say, Samson has become a Leonhard,[a] Judg. 14:5; 15:15. Likewise, David also became a Leonhard and Bernhard since he strangled a lion and bear, 1 Sam. 17:34-36. Yes, and although initially it was gruesome and frightening for Samson to attack the lion, in the end it became a honeycomb and sweet food for him. This figure teaches that the beginning of a Christian life always looks frightening to our flesh and blood, like an angry lion, rough like the camel shirt of John, and fearsome like the great giant Goliath, Matt. 3:4. However, when the Spirit of God comes, then it all becomes sweet like honey, mild like the little Lamb Christ, and quite easy as the Lord himself has told us in Matthew chapter 11, Matt. 11:29f. Thus, a Christian Leonhard will overcome all lions, werewolves, auerochs,[3] dragons, snakes, and basilisks in the power and strength of the Spirit of God. However, what a select, spendid, noble name Lichtenstein[b] is, I offer for everyone's consideration. Even though Christ is the true light[4] that has come into this world, John 1:9, still he illumines all those who run to him and desire his light in firm faith, so that it not be hidden under a bushel, Matt. 5:15, but

---

[3] An extinct type of bison.
[4] Hubmaier's first concern in considering the etymology of the name *Lichtenstein* is to note the reference to *Licht*, or light. He will consider below *Stein*, stone.

---

[a] Samson was a Leonhard.
[b] Liechtenstain.

that, lit, it may /288/ burn and shine before all people, so that God the Father will thereby be praised in the heavens, John 3:19. For that is the judgment, that the light has come into the world, but people have loved darkness more than light. For their works were evil; and everyone who is evil hates the light and comes not to the light, so that his works will not be punished. But whoever deals with truth and righteousness comes to the light and is not ashamed of his works for they have taken place in God.

Thus, gracious Lord, I speak truly without any hypocrisy. Since so much Christian preaching and business are being practiced in Your Grace's territory, and in particular by the chosen Christian servants of God,[a] John Spitalmayer[5] and Oswald Glaitt,[6] who so valiantly and comfortingly show the bright light of the gospel and set it on the candlestick, the like of which I have neither yet known nor seen in any place on earth, I observe that God has so inflamed Your Grace in a Christian fashion and especially blessed you not only with the external name of light, but also internally in the soul. May this God henceforth also protect you and all lovers of the light, of his living Word, so that we are never more seized by darkness, John 1:5. Likewise, there is no less comfort indicated by the word *stone* in the name Lichtenstein, for as the light has its luminescence in the Word of God, so also the stone, as Christ himself said,[b] "Whoever hears my Word and does it is like a wise man who builds his house on a stone or rock. Although the rain and the floods come and the winds blow and fall on the house, nevertheless the house does not fail for it is built on a firm stone," Matt. 7:24ff. In this, gracious Lord, I see also that the divine Word is not only preached and heard in Your Grace's court and territory, but also that it is lived out in many regards. God will also grant grace so that it may increase from day to day and even if rain, floods, wind, light-

---

[5] Hans Spittelmaier, a minister in the Nikolsburg congregation, became a supporter of Hubmaier. ME IV:599.
[6] Oswald Glaidt was an early minister in the Nikolsburg Anabaptist congregation. He was martyred in Vienna in 1546. ME II:522f.

---

[a] John Spitalmayr and Oswald Glaytt.
[b] Stone.

ning, and thunder were to rise against Your Grace, Your Grace
need not fear. Samson slew a thousand men with the jawbone
of an ass, Judg. 15:16. Jael, the wife of Abner the Kenite,
killed Prince Sisera with a hammer and stake, Judg. 4:21.
Judith, a single woman, killed the very mighty Holophernes,
Jth. 13:9. For the house is light and built on a solid stone who
is Christ; therefore, the attacks and waves of this world cannot damage it, 1 Cor. 10:4.

Finally, the name of this house is Nicolspurg.[a] Gracious
Lord, when I think of it now and then I cannot find anything
else but that Nicolspurg is Nicopolis, although there are other
cities of this name. Now, however, Nicolspurg /289/ and
Nicopolis are also called Emmaus by the map-makers.[b]
Hence it is well worth thinking about how Christ appeared to
the two disciples Luke and Cleophas on the way when they
went to Emmaus. They beseeched him to stay with them, for it
was evening and the day was spent, Luke 24:29. Thus, just as
Christ, after the joyful resurrection of his living Word in
recent years, which initially manifested itself in the beginning
through Dr. Martin Luther among the most Christian of the
princes and lords, Lord Frederick, duke of Saxony, etc.,[c]
after that he subsequently continued his pilgrimage on to
Emmaus, that is, Nicolspurg. There he was beseeched by his
servants to remain, for it had almost become night and the last
days were coming. Then he was recognized graciously by them
in the breaking of bread. Just as at that time the two disciples
soon made their way to Jerusalem in order to proclaim also to
the other disciples the living resurrected Christ, so shall Your
Grace assist and advise by the given grace of God the princes,
lords, regents, and subjects in your territory and everywhere.
Thus may the Word of Christ peaceably and amicably be
proclaimed, and may the truth in which we alone must be
saved come to the light of day clearly, brightly, and purely by
Your Grace's preachers and with others. Whatever I, as an
unworthy pilgrim of Christ, decried as a seducer, rebel, and
archheretic (although innocently, God be praised, as I now
and always have offered to be called to trial, justice, and an

---

[a] Nicolspurg.
[b] Emmaus.
[c] Duke Fridreich of Saxony.

accounting)[a] whatever I can do to help so that the honor of God and his holy Word are witnessed to, I am ready, willing, and able to do with great diligence, as much as God gives me grace at any time. I hereby commit and surrender myself to Your Grace obediently, wholly, and completely to serve. Long live Your Grace, with your blessed spouse and your dear cousin,[7] Lord Hans von Lichtenstein,[b] my especially gracious lord, also with all the Christian servants of the court, in Christ Jesus our only Savior. Amen.

Your Grace's subject
Balthasar Huebmör von Fridberg.

Truth Is Immortal. /290/

A simple instruction on the words: This is my body, in the Supper of Christ.
1526

In ancient times there has always been great disunity on the sacrament (as they called it) of the altar.[c] Thus many said and believed that the bread is only a sign and memorial of the body of Christ. Others, that it is not only a sign but also the thing itself that is being signified in it. The third [group], that the bread is flesh, and the wine is blood. The fourth, that the bread is not flesh nor the wine blood, but that the flesh and blood are hidden under the form of the bread and wine. The fifth, that the bread in its essence is transformed into the flesh through the words and the wine in its essence into the blood. The sixth, that the bread is not changed into the flesh or the wine into the blood essentially but the bread and wine cease to be essentially bread and wine. The seventh, that bread and wine do not cease, but that the nature and matter of the bread and wine are become com-

---

[7] Hans von Liechtenstein was not the cousin, but the nephew, of Leonhard.

---

[a] Justice, Justice, Justice.
[b] F. Katharina von Tschernahor. Lord Hanns von Liechtenstain.
[c] Many kinds of opinions of the teachers.

pletely nothing, are annihilated, and disappear. Thus neither the matter nor the essential form of the bread or wine remain, but only the two kinds of forms. The eighth say, yes, it is so; as often as one holds the mass a miracle happens daily, that the attributes or the accidents remain without the matter. The ninth say that such happens not through daily miracles, for that would oblige God to act miraculously whenever any mass-priest wanted, but it happens out of an old miracle which lasts for ever and ever. The tenth want that the word of consecration, as they call it, to be taken *personaliter*, that is, essentially. The eleventh say no to that, but that these words are used materially and unessentially, so that the masspriest's body is not changed into the bread when he says the bread is his body. The twelfth have not been able to and still do not agree as to whether the body of Christ is present when the priest says the first word *Hoc*, or the second *est*, or the third *corpus*, or the fourth *meum*. I will be silent about the fact that they, by their own power, have added to the words of Christ with the little words *enim* and *aeterni*. The thirteenth are of the opinion that the body of Christ is not at all there after the speaking of these words, "Hoc est corpus meum," this is my body, until the masspriest has also breathed or aspirated these words over the chalice, so that the body not be on the altar without blood, and dead. The fourteenth say that Christ is here as he hung on the cross. The fifteenth say no, not thus, but as he entered through closed doors to his disciples. These and still many more opinions and conjectures one finds in the papal rules /291/ and school teachings of Guiellelmo Altisiodore,[8] one of the fathers, among the commentators of the Sentences, up to Holcott, Gabriel Biel, and Major[9] who have lived in our times. Note here, dear Christian, I have therefore pointed out these disagreements and differences of opinion so that no one is angry or takes offense in our times when one hears that there are also disunities concerning this matter between the present-day preachers and teachers, as

[8] Archbishop Isidore of Seville, c. 560-636.
[9] The commentators to whom Hubmaier is referring are: Robert Holcot, OP, d. 1349, an English nominalist theologian; Gabriel Biel, ca. 1420-95, a German nominalist; and John Major, 1496-1550, a Scottish theologian in the Ockhamist (nominalistic) tradition.

one already hears our masspriests crying out overly loud and saying to the hindrance of the divine truth: "Look, look:ᵃ the present-day preachers themselves disagree. One says black, the other white." I have seen that already, good man. Do you not see that you are even less united. But to a pious Christian such disunity brings no harm. By that his faith is tested and he recognizes that he depends on no person nor holds to the respecting of persons, but only looks to God, beseeches him for understanding, judges for himself according to his simple Word, and looks about himself so that he is not misled by anyone whereby the blind together with the blind leaders would fall into the ditch. That is rightly done, Matt. 24:11; 15:14.

Second, since indeed also with the present-day teachers who write on the Supper of Christ are to be found disagreements and arguments about the word of Christ, "This is my body," many write that the trope or type of this Word lies hidden in the little word *hoc* or *this*.ᵇ That is, that this little word *hoc* does not point to the bread but to the body of Christ.¹⁰ The others use the little word *est* for *significat*, that is, *is* for *signifies*, thus: "The bread signifies my body."ᶜ Which opinion can never be forced with clear and orderly Scriptures nor conquered, for the proof with the seeds, Luke 8:4-15, and with the seven oxen, Gen. 41:2-3, 26-27, is too outlandish, strange, and wide-ranging. It does not satisfy the human conscience; it gives more cause for erring and confusing the entire Bible than to satisfying or overcoming the adversaries.¹¹ For if this is the practice then no one would be certain as to where *est* /is/ stands in the Scripture for *significat* /signifies/ or for itself. And in the end there would be so many fights over words as there are *ests* and *ises* in the

---

¹⁰ Hubmaier refers to the distinctive view of Carlstadt, wherein he said that Jesus was pointing to his own body and not to the bread when he said, "This is my body which is given for you." See Hertzsch 1957, pp. 15-17.

¹¹ Hubmaier is countering the position of Zwingli that was argued in the *Letter to Matthew Alber*. See Pipkin 1984: 204ff.

ᵃ The cry of the masspriest.
ᵇ *Hoc* [This].
ᶜ *Est* [Is].

Bible.[a] So I would maintain just with the same authority and with the same arguments that this bread must be the body of Christ and thus *is* is taken in the Old Testament for *is*, Genesis 1:3: "God said let there be light and /292/ there was light." Likewise in the New Testament: "And the word became flesh,"[12] John, chapter 1, John 1:14. Therefore, in this saying, "This is my body," the *is* must also be used in this way. Now the papists have proven their *is* just as well as these opinionists their *signifies*.[b] But one must not play with the Scriptures arrogantly in this fashion, or we would well let the ark of God soon fall into the mud with the willful oxen, 2 Sam. 6:6. One has to look up, up, up. The third group makes out of the corpus or body a figurative body[c] and the like, although they all come together in the main point and unanimously confess, "God be praised," that the bread is bread and the wine, wine. Since, however, just as every Christian is obligated to give account of his faith as often as he is requested, I too am obligated to do such to all those who have desired the same from me by the grace of God, I therefore present this rule[d] which should be used everywhere in Scripture as follows: Where several sayings of the Scriptures are dark or presented very briefly, from which disagreement may follow, one should resolve these with other Scriptures which are clearer or brighter—though on the same matter—setting them next to the dark or shortened sayings as much as one can have them at hand. One should ignite them and let them burn like many wax candles bound together so that a bright and clear light of the Scriptures breaks forth. Now everyone must confess that Matthew and Mark, in these words which Christ used when he took the bread in hand, were *micrologi*, that is, they indicated his words in the shortest way.[e] But Luke and Paul, by the special providence of God, presented these words of the Supper much more richly. Therefore we want to take all four

---

[12] In English the phrase would read "has become flesh."

---

[a] Word battles.
[b] The opinionists.
[c] Body.
[d] A rule.
[e] *Micrologi* [Little words].

sayings of them and set them together and after that draw a perfect conclusion from them.[a] Matthew writes thus: "When they were eating, Jesus took the bread, gave thanks, broke it, and gave it to the disciples and said, 'Take, eat, this is my body,' Matt. 26:26ff. And he took the chalice, gave thanks, gave it to them, and said, 'Drink all of it, this is my blood of the New Testament which is poured out for many for the forgiveness of sins. I say to you from now on I will not drink of the fruit of the vine till the day that I drink it anew with you in my father's kingdom.' "

Mark says the following: "And when they were eating, Jesus took the bread and praised God, broke it, gave it to them and said: 'Take, eat, this is my body.' And taking the chalice, gave thanks, gave it to them, and they all drank from it and he said to them, 'This is my blood of the New Testament which is poured out for many,' " Mark 14:22ff. Luke writes further, Luke 22:19ff., "He took the bread, /293/ gave thanks, broke it, gave it to them, and said: 'This is my body which is given for you. Do this in my memory.' In the same way he took the chalice after they had eaten supper and said, 'This is the cup of the New Testament in my blood that is poured out for you.' "

Paul, however, writes to the Corinthians this meaning, 1 Cor. 11:23ff.: "I have received from the Lord what I have given to you. For the Lord Jesus, in the night in which he was betrayed, took bread, gave thanks, and said, 'Take, eat, this is my body which is broken for you. Do this in my memory.' Likewise, he took also the cup after the evening meal and said: 'This cup is the New Testament in my blood. Do this, as often as you drink it, in my memory. For as often as you eat of this bread and drink from this cup you shall proclaim the death of the Lord until he comes.' " These are now the words on the Supper written by these four witnesses and in summary, so much do they all say together in what they report.[b] Christ took the bread, broke it and gave it to his disciples, and said, "Take and eat. This is my body which is given for you. Do this in my memory. As often as you eat the bread and drink the drink, you proclaim the death of the Lord until he

---

[a] Augustine.
[b] Summary of the Word.

comes." From all these words follows the final conclusion that the bread offered, broken, taken, and eaten is the body of Christ in remembrance. Thus also the cup taken, distributed, and drunk is the blood of Christ in remembrance. Now the general true thesis or maxim is known: *Talia sunt subiecta qualia permittuntur ab eorum predicatis*, that is: The preceding words should be understood according to the following words.[a] In the power of this saying everyone must confess and say that this baked bread is the body of Christ who was crucified for us. Now, however, this bread in itself is not the body, for this bread was not crucified and did not die for us, so the bread must be the body of Christ in remembrance, so that all the words of Christ can remain in their plain and simple sense, for he always spoke in the most simple fashion, so that it would be understood clearly as his parting word by his disciples.[b] So much is said that the bread in itself is not the body of Christ, but is, however, an admonition of the body of Christ and that from the institution of Christ. For these words, "in my memory," testify in the entire previous saying that the breaking, distribution, and eating of the bread is not a breaking, distribution, and eating of the body of Christ, who is sitting at the right hand of God the Father in the heavens, but all that is a remembrance of his being broken and distributed in suffering.[c] It is also an eating in faith, that he was thus taken, broken, and divided for us, that is, captured, /294/ martyred, and died for us, so that we remember this and be aware of his death.[d]

In the third place, one may understand from similar sayings that these words, "in my memory," are of the type and character to draw all previous words to the memory. If I say, "That is Emperor Julius in memory, that is my father in my memory," then it is not Emperor Julius or my father himself, but something else that reminds me of them.[e] We have the same manner of speaking in daily use when we say to the wooden images: "That is Our Lady, St. Peter, or St. John," and

---

[a] Thesis.
[b] Christ spoke simply.
[c] In my memory.
[d] In my memory.
[e] Emperor Julius.

it is not they, but only the memory of them by the institution of human beings, whereas the former is by the institution of Christ. So should we rightly speak here also and understand in all simplicity, since Christ himself clearly drew the whole matter into the memory and did not speak another parable.

The first counterargument[a] which takes place here: When Christ says, "Do this in my memory," he points to the custom by which we also should thus take, break, distribute, and eat the bread. He does not want this bread to be his body in memory. Answer: It pleases me well that one confesses how the taking, breaking, and eating takes place in the memory of Christ Jesus. Now, however, nothing is taken into the hands, broken, distributed, and eaten except the bread. If now the bread is the body of Christ, then Christ must be touched with the hands, grasped, broken, divided, and eaten with the teeth. That is, however, to all Christians a very difficult saying. Who can hear it? Accordingly, it must now be bread used this way in memory of Christ. Therefore the simple meaning and understanding of these words, "Do this in my memory," is as follows: "Take the bread, break it, distribute it among yourselves, eat it, and remember that as truly as you eat the bread, so truly have I given my body for you into death and shared it, with you and made all those who believe this and trust me participants in my suffering." That is the simple and right understanding of Christ. "See that you do the same among yourselves also. Then you are my disciples," John 13:12ff.

You say: "Yes, Christ is not broken and eaten and also not the bread, but the form of the bread under which the body of Christ is hidden." Answer: Pope Nicholas forced Berengarius[b] to speak otherwise. *De Consec.* di. II c. *Ego* ["On Consecration" Distinction II, canon "I"].[13] However, I leave such a /295/ speech to be an Anaxagorean but not a theological issue.[c] Therewith the word and meaning of Christ is ripped apart and violated, since he says of the bread, "This is my

---

[13] CIC I:1328 (canon 42)

---

[a] Counterarguments.
[b] Pope Nicolaus. Berengarius.
[c] Under the form.

body," and does not say, "Under the form of the bread is my body," as the dream and Thomistic addition of these miserable people states.[14] If you had forever, you could not prove this with the Scripture. For according to such expositions created out of their own brain, the little word *hoc*, "this" does not point to the bread which has already gone away and has disappeared according to their speech, but only to the form of the bread. Thus must the body of Christ be there before the mass priests begin to speak the first little word of consecration over the bread, which they then themselves must deny. You say: "Such things are difficult to understand." Answer: In themselves the words of Christ are very easy and understandable. For what is more understandable than to say, "The bread is the body of Christ in active, practiced, or held memory," so that justice is done to the little word *facite* or "do." But the Sophists and the Scholastics have made the same words difficult again for us, so that now we must root again from out of the way their weed, thornbushes, sticks, and rocks which they have thrown in here, so that three times as much work has become necessary before one can plant and build what has long lain waste, deserted, and fallow.

Fourth: the second counterargument.[*] Everything which Christ said is so. Now, Christ said concerning the bread, "This is my body," therefore it must be so. Answer: I can also well make such an argument, which is worth nothing, as follows: Everything that Christ said is so. Now Christ said: "Whoever does not hate father and mother cannot be my disciple." Therefore it is so that the human being should hate father and mother, Luke 14:26. Yes, you say, this saying of Christ is illumined through another even better, Mark chapter 10, where he says, Mark 10:29: "Whoever does not hate father and mother for my sake and the sake of the gospel when they depart from it." *Deo gratias* [Thanks be to God]. Thus also here it is not enough to say, "This is my body," in order to

---

[14] Hubmaier is referring to the view of Thomas Aquinas, whereby the substance of the bread has been transformed (transubstantiated) into the body of Christ, but the form (or accidents) of the bread remain as bread. See Q. 75, art. 6 of *Summa Theologica*, Blackfriars 1914: XVII:275ff.

---

[*] Counterarguments.

prove that the body of Christ is there. Rather, we must set the words together which have been spoken in the whole speech by Christ and which belong together, as follows:[a] "He took the bread, praised God, broke the same, and gave it to his disciples and said, 'This is my body which is given for you. Do this in my memory,' " Luke 22:19; 1 Cor. 11:24. Here you see clearly, where one wants to determine a right conclusion out of the Scriptures, that one does not make patchwork and present half Scriptures,[b] but sets all the Scriptures of one kind of matter wholly and completely together, and after that, to introduce a perfect final judgment.

A parable.[c] If I have given someone a book and I see he has it and say, "That is my book," immediately the person interrupts me and says, /296/ not so. I say, "Let me finish; that is my book, which I have given you." Now he is well satisfied. Another parable: I see an image of Emperor Nero and say that is Emperor Nero.[d] The speech is false in itself. If, however, I say, that is Emperor Nero in memory, then it is now true. Thus also if one says of a statue of Maximilian, that is Emperor Maximilian, then the speech is false, for he is no longer here.[e] But if one says that is Emperor Maximilian of praiseworthy remembrance, then now one sees apparently that these words, *praiseworthy memory* have the character, type, and nature of directing the entire speech and previous words to the late Maximilian.[f] Lest anyone think that such speaking is a subtlety or sophistry I want also to give an example in Scripture. One might truly say, of the dead body of Christ lying in the grave on Good Friday, "That is the dead Christ," and still it could not in truth be said at that time, "That is Christ." One single little word of an entire statement gives and takes so much. So it is also here, with the adjoining clause, "Do this in my memory," as also especially the right and true dialecticians take good account of these words:[g] "Memory, remember, remembrance," and the like. Now we

---

[a] Consult the Greek.
[b] Tailor work.
[c] Parable.
[d] Emperor Nero.
[e] Maximilian.
[f] Praiseworthy memory.
[g] Dialectics.

Christians are obligated according to yet another rule to speak with sober and clear words, since particularly in teaching, simplicity and dialectical or skillful characteristics of speaking are necessary, and not empty speaking or figures of rhetorical persuasion, as Augustine* teaches us in *De doctrina Christiana.*[15] But that is enough on this matter for the time being.

In the fifth place. However, in order that we also bring to bear our above-mentioned understanding to work and use in Scripture, we should consider well the Word of Christ, when he said immediately after Supper to his disciples, Mark 14:25. "Truly I say to you that I will not henceforth drink from the fruit of the vine until the day that I drink it anew in the kingdom of God," Mark 14:25, that is, "after my resurrection, when I will have overcome sin, devil, and death." Now we read how Christ appeared to the two disciples on the way to Emmaus, pointed out to them their unbelief and the hardness of their hearts, also explained the Scriptures to them, so that their hearts were enflamed. Still, they did not recognize him until he ate the supper with them, Luke 24:13ff. Then he took bread, praised God, broke it, /297/ and gave it to them. Only at that time did they recognize him in the breaking of the bread, as in the memorial sign or in the last penny,[16] which he had left to them for a special memorial and thereby had commanded them to remember him. Then the two disciples immediately got up and ran to the other disciples at Jerusalem, proclaiming to them how the dead Christ was risen again, had eaten the Supper with them, and how they had recognized him in the breaking of the bread. Just so did Paul also teach us to proclaim the death of the Lord as often as we eat the bread and drink the drink in his exalted Supper according to the order of the institution by Christ in his exalted Supper, 1 Cor. 11:26.

---

[15] Augustine writes throughout *Christian Doctrine* of the need for the Christian teacher to utilize the arts of dialectic and rhetoric in understanding and explaining Scripture. See especially Book IV, chapter 17ff. MPL 34:97-98, tr. NPNF/1, p. 2[586ff.]

[16] The reference is to the spending of money for the holding of a departure meal.

---

* Augustine, *On Christian Doctrine.*

Now follow the Scriptures, according to which Christ does not bodily come to us until the hour of the last judgment, and then we will see him as he ascended.

Matthew 26:26ff.

"However, (a) as they were eating, (b) Jesus took the bread, (c) gave thanks, broke it, gave it to the disciples, and said, (d) 'Take, (e) eat; (f) this is my body.' And he took the cup and gave thanks, gave it, and said, (g) 'Drink from it all of you; (h) this is my blood of the New Testament which is shed for many for the forgiveness of sins. I say to you, from now on I will no longer drink from the fruit of the vine until the day that I drink it anew with you in my Father's kingdom.'"

Consider here, every Christian, the words of Christ.

(a)[17] "As they were eating": Here one notes that one person alone cannot celebrate the Supper of Christ, whether he is sick or well. There must be others there.

(b) "The bread": Christ took bread, broke it, and gave it to his disciples to eat, not the form of bread, as the high schools say.

(c) "Gave thanks": Note that blessing and thanksgiving are one thing, for what Matthew and Mark call *benedixit* [he blessed] and *benedicens* [blessing] is called by Luke and Paul *gratias egisset* [he gave thanks] and *gratias agens* [giving thanks]. Therefore it is not adequately translated into German as *gesegnet* [blessed] unless *Segnen* [to bless] is understood as praising God, as in Luke 2:28, where Simeon blesses Jesus, that is, praises God. It follows that one cannot make a "consecration" out of the blessing, as our mass priests say.[18]

---

[17] Beginning at this point, Hubmaier (or his printer) begins to put the letter notations in the margin. We shall, however, continue to insert them in the text, as in the preceding paragraphs.

[18] Hubmaier, though knowledgeable of Greek to some degree, is more comfortable arguing in Latin. The word *benedicere* may mean "to bless," as it is here translated, and as it was in fact translated, for example, in the King James version, which is in many ways the English version closest to Hubmaier's German. Another meaning of the word, as Hubmaier notes, is "to commend, praise, or adore."

(d) "Take": He gives to the disciples and not they to him. Therefore we have wrongly and without any basis made out of taking a giving and sacrificing. Here /298/ you see that the mass is not a sacrifice, for Christ did not say "sacrifice," but receive it from me.[a]

(e) "Eat":[b] He commands them to eat the bread, not to lift it into the air, divide it into three parts, drown it in wine, not to walk around carrying it against floods, fire, and storms, or to lock it in stone and iron, etc.

(f) "This is my body": Understand, it is not in itself that the bread-eating is the body of Christ really, but only in the celebrated remembrance. That is not our gloss, but the clear words of Christ which Luke and Paul witness to us, as pointed out above. For that is all one passage without a paragraph break.

(g) "Drink from it all of you": Here Christ commands that they all drink from the cup—before he spoke the words over it. Take note of that.

(h) "This is my blood": As the bread is the body of Christ in enacted remembrance, so also is the drink the blood of Christ in the enacted remembrance. For it is not the wine poured out in the Supper that is for the forgiveness of sins, but his crimson blood on the cross afterward on Good Friday. Only then did it become the blood of the new testament through his death. For where there is a testament, the death of the one who makes the testament must have taken place. For a testament comes into effect through the death. Otherwise, it has no power when the one who made it still lives, Hebrews chapter 9, Heb. 9:16f. From this it follows that the blood of Christ in the Supper on High Thursday or Maundy Thursday has not yet become blood of the new testament. Rather, it only became that on the cross on Good Friday after the ninth hour.

"From the fruit of the vine, etc.":[c] Note once again, Christian reader, how, after the words of consecration, the drink is here called a fruit of the vine by Christ in Matthew. That it was thus also called by him a fruit of the vine before

---

[a] Sacrifice.
[b] Mass priests are hangmen.
[c] A fruit of the vine.

these words in Luke is without doubt not without the special provision of God, lest we let ourselves be deceived by anyone, that this drink is something other than wine before and after the words. Therefore Christ clearly called it a fruit of the vine and not blood, to prevent future error.

Mark 14:22ff.

"While they were eating, Jesus took bread, praised God, broke it, gave it to them, and said, 'Take, eat, this is my body,' and took the cup, gave thanks, gave it to them, and they all drank from it. He said to them, 'This is my blood of the new testament which is poured out for many.' " /299/ Here we note, that as Mark describes the words of Christ, so also are they stated by Matthew. Only this fact should be considered: that Christ commanded his disciples that they should all drink before he spoke the words of consecration over the cup in Matthew. Thus, Mark testifies that they all drank from it and only afterward did Christ say, "This is my blood." Now then, on the basis of these words how could the wine be trans-formed into blood as our sacrificers and consecrators pretend, forcing us to believe such against the clear words of Christ by means of sword, fire, and water, since faith is a work of God and not of the hangman? However, let them rage and rave thus so that the Scriptures be fulfilled in them.

Luke 22:19ff.: "Jesus took the bread, gave thanks, broke it, gave it to them, and said, 'This is my body which is given for you. Do this in my memory.' Likewise he took the cup af-ter they had eaten the evening meal and said, 'This is the cup, the new testament in my blood, which is poured out for you.'"

(a) "Which is given for you:" As the bread did not suffer for us nor was given for us, but the living true body of Christ, so must the bread not be the body of Christ, except in remem-brance, on the authority of the institution of Christ.

(b) "Do this in my memory": Oh, how much our papists would give if Luke and Paul would never have thought of these words, for by them all their counterarguments are thwarted and thrown back. However, it pleased the heavenly Father who knew from the beginning of the world the error of this gruesome idolatry, namely, that we not only would wor-ship a Ceres, that is, an idol of bread, as the heathen, or an idol of wine, Bacchus, or a water god, Neptune, but that we would make out of these three idols a whole trinity—honoring and worshiping bread, wine, and water at the same time in the mass, which is the greatest abomination on earth before the face of God.[a] Christ truly warned us about this when he said that the bread and wine is his body and blood in the enacted remembrance and not otherwise. Let whoever has eyes see and who has ears hear. Whoever does not want to see and hear wants by all means to be blind and deaf. May God open our ears and eyes and loosen our tongues, so that we henceforth hear, see, and speak rightly, so that such idolatry may no longer grow and this trine idol and abomination be thrown down from the holy throne. Amen. /300/

(c) "In my blood": The cup is called here the new testament, as circumcision is called the covenant, Genesis 17,[b] Gen. 17:10. That is a symbol of the word of Christ or of the covenant of God. For the testament in itself is nothing other than the word of the gracious promise of Christ in the forgiveness of our sins. The blood is the payment and satisfaction. The cup or the drink is the memorial sign. Therefore Christ actually said, "This is the cup in my blood."

Paul, 1 Corinthians 11:23ff.

(a) "I received from the Lord what I have given you, for the Lord Jesus in the night in which he was betrayed, took bread, gave thanks, broke it, and said, 'Take, eat, this is my body which is broken for you. (b) Do this in my memory.' Likewise he also took the cup after the evening meal and said, 'This cup is the new testament in my blood. Do this as often as you drink it in my memory.' (c) For as often as you eat of this bread and drink from this cup you proclaim the death of the Lord (d) until he comes. (e) Whoever now eats from this bread and drinks from this cup of the Lord unworthily is guilty of the body and blood of the Lord. (f) Let the person, however, examine himself and thus eat from the bread and drink from the cup, for whoever eats and drinks unworthily eats and drinks judgment on himself, (g) because he does not discern the body of the Lord."

---

[a] Ceres, Bacchus and Neptune. The mass priests' trinity.
[b] Testament. Blood. Cup.

(a) "I have received from the Lord": Paul cannot and does not want to say anything unless he has a certain basis from the Lord, as he also writes in Romans 15:18.

(b) "Do this in my memory": After Christ said, "This is my body," lest his disciples fall on the visible body, as if he were speaking of that, and he caused to stumble, as many had also done in John 6:41, he added immediately, "Do this in my memory," so that he lead them away from his natural body, which profits nothing, John 6:63.

(c) "For so often as you eat of this bread, etc.": The sum and final cause of the Supper is briefly summarized in these words. Namely, that the Supper is a remembrance, a memorial sign, and a reminder of the suffering of Christ, and not a sacrifice.

(d) "Until he comes": It follows that he is not present. For if he were present, then we would hold the Supper in vain and against the words of Christ and Paul. For where a person is essentially and bodily present, there a remembrance is not necessary. However, where he is not bodily present, then one celebrates his remembrance until he comes.

(e) See how bright and clear Paul writes, "Whoever now eats of this bread and drinks from the cup of the Lord unworthily is guilty of the body and blood of the Lord." See here, who wants to see, how Christ above called the drink a fruit of the vine before and after the words of /301/ consecration. Thus Paul also calls the bread bread and the cup a drink, and whoever eats of this bread and drinks of this drink unworthily is guilty of the body and blood of the Lord, and he does not say guilty of the bread and wine.[a] Therefore it does not have to be one thing, or it would be *nugatio*, that is, empty speech. But let the person examine himself, however, etc., as to whether he has real internal and intensive hunger and thirst for this bread and drink, as Christ also had when he said, "With fervor have I desired to eat the supper with you." And all this in faith, so that he wholly believes that his sins are remitted[b] through the death of Christ. Likewise, in love, in which he obligates himself now, and with this breaking of the bread and drinking of the cup publicly before the church

---

[a] Bread, bread. Drink, drink.
[b] What is the content of the examination.

commits himself and promises that for the sake of his neighbor he is also willing to let his flesh and blood be broken and sacrificed, with which he has now become one bread and one drink. It is also in thanksgiving to God our heavenly Father and his only begotten Son our Lord Jesus Christ whom he has given even unto death for our salvation. Thus the three thousand people in the Acts of the Apostles first recognized themselves as sinners, believed in the forgiveness of sins through Christ, let themselves be baptized, remained constant in the apostolic teaching, in communion and the breaking of bread, and in prayer, Acts 2:41. That is true self-examination according to the teaching of Paul.

(g) "That he does not discern the body of the Lord": O dear pious Christians, although the bread is not the body of Christ nor the wine his blood, nevertheless, since we are concerned about the true body and blood of Christ, even so shall we be concerned about the Supper of Christ, so that the same is not held with mockery or carelessness, but with great earnestness, devotion, and fervor according to the order of the institution of Christ. Or truly, where we do not differentiate the Supper of Christ from other eating and drinking we eat and drink judgment on ourselves as also Paul therefore chastised the Corinthians harshly. Let every one look to himself here and consider the sacred earnest institution of the Supper of Christ, for it is not child's play. For whoever despises or abuses the ceremonies of the New Testament, despises and abuses Christ himself. Yet I do not speak here of church practices invented by people, but of the two ceremonies of Christ, that is of baptism and the Supper. No others are necessary to us.

Acts 1:9ff.

"When Jesus said this he was visibly lifted up and a cloud took him up before their eyes. And when they looked after him ascending into the heavens, behold, there stepped beside them two men in white clothing who also said, 'You men of Galilee, why do you stand and look into heaven? This Jesus /302/ who has been taken from you into heaven will come as you have seen him ascend into heaven.' "

Note: Luke writes, "As you have seen him." Thus we do not want to seek him either in the bread or in the wine.

That One Cannot Enclose Christ in the Little Stone-houses or in the Monstrances. In Acts 7:48ff. Stephen speaks thus:

"But the Most High does not live in temples made with hands. As he says through the prophet, 'Heaven is my throne and the earth my footstool, what kind of house do you want to build me?' says the Lord, 'or what is the place of my rest? Has not my hand made all that?' " Isa. 66:1-2. Here you thoroughly hear that one cannot make for Christ either wooden, stone, silver, or golden houses. Therefore it is all useless costs that one has invested until now in such precious minsters and monstrances.[19] However, they are well called monsters and monstrances,[a] from monstrosity, from the sea monster that comes up out of the sea, as John writes in Revelation,[b] Rev. 13:1. For how can a gruesome monster or sea monster be made and be shown to us so that we see and worship an earthly thing for a heavenly good, a perishable thing for an eternal, a creature for the creator and for God himself in the monsters and monstrances. *O monstra, monstra, monstrastis nobis monstruosa monstra* [O monster, monster, show us the monstrous monsters].

In Acts 17:24f. Paul says,

"God who made the world and all that is in it, since he is a Lord of heaven and of earth, (a) he does not dwell in temples made with hands, (b) he is not cared for with human hands as one who needs anyone, since he himself as he always gives everyone life and breath, etc."

(a) "In temples built with hands, etc.": Here you see once more that God does not want to live in temples made by hand,

---

[19] In this whole paragraph Hubmaier makes several plays on words between "minster," "monstrance," and "monster."

---

[a] Monster. Monstrances.
[b] Sea monster.

but in those made out of living stones. As Paul writes, "Do you not know that you are the temple of God?"

(b) "He is also not cared for with human hands": As we have till now practiced a puppet's play in the mass when we have lifted up the bread and placed it here and there as children do their puppets in the sun. These who have done it and seen it testify to this.[a]

Whoever now wants to have more Scriptures will find them quite useful in regard to this matter. Matthew 24:5ff.; Luke 17:22ff.: "Here is Christ." Matthew 26:64: "Henceforth you will /303/ not see me. You will not always have me."[20] John 16:28: "I leave the world." 1 Corinthians 15: "Sit at my right etc."[21] Matthew 24:27; Luke 17:24: "As the lightning, etc.," and the like. All of these together and thoroughly testify that Christ Jesus ascended into heaven, sits at the right hand of God his heavenly Father, and also will not come from there until the time of the last day when he will come to judge the living and the dead. Just there he sits according to his humanity. Just there Stephen saw him, Acts 7:55. There we want to seek, honor, and worship him.

The conclusion[b]

O you dear good Christians. Since you see that this matter of the Supper is so high and weighty, we can neither comprehend nor grasp it with human reason. For we have so deeply waded into the water of human teachings and are so much drowned and stuck in the mud of the long-practiced usage that we can no more reach solid ground and to the recognition of the divine Word in this matter without a special measure of the grace of God our heavenly father. For such stupidity and awkwardness is not only in the common people but also in many who should go before and lead us with works and with teaching. Therefore I beseech and

---

[20] The rendering of Matt. 26:64 is not correct, though it is likely that this passage is the basis of Hubmaier's argument.
[21] There is no such statement in 1 Cor. 15. Cf. Matt. 22:44; Mark 12:36.

---

[a] Puppet play.
[b] Christian admonishment.

admonish all Christ-believing people for God's sake that with
high diligence they earnestly and without ceasing cry and sigh
to God in a right faith and firm trust, doubting nothing, Luke
1:13, and beseech him as Christ himself and Saint James in his
beautiful and useful letter taught us, James 1:5, so that the
Lord of the harvest, Matt. 9:38, God our heavenly Father, will
send us right, true, and God-fearing workers and preachers
who will diligently proclaim to us his will and faithfully feed
us with our daily bread without any mixture of human yeast
and without any leaven, so that also the merciful God should
impart and increase in us such reason, wisdom, and faith
through Jesus Christ his beloved Son, so that we do not only
speak his holy eternal Word with the mouth or hear with the
ears, but that he make it also alive in our /304/ hearts, so that
it might turn green, grow, blossom, and bring forth fruit in us
unto eternal life. Therefore let us diligently cry to God, dear
pious Christians, and say: "Our Father, give us today our daily
bread, lead us into the knowledge of your fatherly will. Give
us grace and power to walk according to the same, now and
always and in eternity," 1 Kings 3:5ff. Thus also Solomon
prayed and was heard overabundantly by God. Without doubt,
God will also hear us. He has promised us and told us through
his beloved Son, Matt. 7:7: "Pray, so you will receive. Knock,
and it will be opened to you. Seek, and you will find." Here
one notes very well that not only those who teach are
responsible for the error and blindness which lifts itself up in
our miserable and lamentable times. Yes, all of us, since we
are all so careless, lazy, and slothful, should pray to God that
he henceforth grant us right-minded, truthful, and pious
pastors who show us the true ladder of Jacob to the heavens,
Gen. 28:12, on which we are again in the power of God
helped out of the mire of this human error and may climb into
eternal life.

Therefore, O dear brothers and sisters in God, let us
without ceasing call to God with the apostles of Christ, Luke
11:1: "Lord, teach us to pray." With Paul, Acts 9:6: "Lord,
what do you want that I do?" With Philip, John 14:8: "Lord,
show us the Father." With the blind man, Matt. 9:27: "Jesus,
Son of David, be merciful to us, we want to see." With the
disciples, Luke 17:5: "Lord, increase our faith." And with the
father of the moon-struck son, Matt. 17:20 [but cf. Mark 9:24]:

"Lord, help our unbelief." If we do this with true hearts and with untainted devotion, God will without doubt send us also a Philip who will sit with us on the chariot, Acts 8:29. Or perhaps will call a Peter out of the tanner's house, Acts 10:21ff., who will proclaim the will of God to us as Peter did to Cornelius, so that with the blind in the water of Siloam, John 9:7, the spittle and mud of our ignorance and blindness will be washed away from our eyes, John 9:6-7, and we will henceforth see, so that we pay attention to the one alone and follow without any delay him who said, "I am the way, truth, and life," John 14:6, and never take our eyes from him. May God the Father, Son, and Holy Spirit help us to that end. The peace of God be with us all. Amen.

Truth Is Immortal.
Nicolspurg
1526
Printed by Simprecht Sorg,
called Froschauer

21

A Christian Catechism

With this catechism our collection moves from materials testifying to beginnings in Waldshut and Zurich (although some were published after Hubmaier left there) to the mature products of his work in Moravia. Here he found a refuge not yet directly under the sovereignty either of archcatholic Austria or of the official Protestant parties. Nikolsburg (Mikulov) lay along the route from Vienna to the Moravian capital of Brün (Brno). Although for a century the province had already been the scene of far-reaching Hussite and Brethren Reformation movements, those were effective mostly among the slavic population; Nikolsburg was a predominantly German town.[1] The way for reformation had already been opened in 1524 by one Hans Spittelmaier, joined in 1525 by Oswald Glaidt. In Nikolsburg Hubmaier could once again project a solid ministry as "established" churchman. The senior priest, Martin Göschl, became an Anabaptist and married. The Lord of the place, Leonhard von Liechtenstein, was baptized sometime in the fall of 1526. Hubmaier could most appropriately proceed to publish his corpus of basic writings on church order.

A catechism has a double function. As everywhere in the Reformation, a catechism pursues the goal of simplicity and coherence in the exposition of true doctrine, as its author understands it recently to have been clarified. We shall thus see Hubmaier putting together his thoughts on all important questions; not only on those immediately in dispute. For the antipedobaptist, in addition, catechesis links formally with the commitment of water baptism (cf. the subtitle of this text).

The literary form of the dialogue, whereby neither party demonstrates personality or argues, was a standard pedagogical artifice of the time. The two speakers represent the Lords von Liechtenstein—Leonhard and his nephew Hans, the latter per-

---

[1] For a full view of the importance of Nikolsburg/Mikulov, cf. Zeman 1967, Vol. XLI, item 101, p. 118, and ME III, p. 883.

haps not yet baptized. The preface was begun December 10, 1526; printing was completed early in 1527.[2]

A *Christian Catechism*
which everyone should know
before he is baptized
in water
Dr. *Balthasar Huebmör*
of Fridberg
The Truth Is Unkillable.
Nicolspurg
1526 /307/

To the Most Venerable Martin, former bishop of Nicopol, but now a rightful married resident[3] in the Christian community at Nicolspurg, his gracious Lord.

Grace and peace in Christ Jesus, our only Savior, to whom be praise, thanks, honor, and glory for ever and ever, that he so graciously, without any merit on our part, entered our tossing boat with us poor miserable and powerless humans, and by his saving, living, and eternal Word admonished and instructed us and so clearly taught us that we henceforth know thoroughly how to navigate only by the glow and star of his holy Word, and how we are to cast our nets into the water that we may fish with benefit and salvation, catching the souls

---

[2] Previously published in an independent English translation, without notes, by Denis Janz. See Janz 1982, pp. 133-78. Earlier translation: Hošek 1892, pp. 251-268; Vedder 1905, p. 192; and Davidson 1939, pp. 254-328. Fragments in Klaassen 1981, p. 87f., 167, 195, 214. Manuscript of translation by Henry C. Vedder at Colgate Rochester Library. The source for this translation: HS 16, pp. 306-26.

[3] Marriage was often part of a priest's move to Protestantism. No longer enjoying sacerdotal status, Martin Göschl had needed to assure his civil status in the town. "Resident" (*mitwoner*) is less than "citizen" (*bürger*), yet is a position with defined rights. By addressing Martin as "Lord" and later as "brother," Hubmaier avoids seeming to take over ecclesiastical prerogatives such as he had had in Waldshut. He even uses the honorific "E.G." (Your Grace) normally reserved for rulers. Hubmaier functions here only as teacher.

of men with the hook of his divine teaching and be able to pull them out of the briny, stormy syrenian sea[4] of this world. Unless all this takes place in his name, it is in vain, even though we toil all night long.

Gracious Lord and brother! We have long known well that a Christian life must begin with the teaching from which faith flows, and that accordingly water baptism follows afterward in accord with its institution by Christ, by which a person in a public confession of his faith makes his first entry and initiation into the holy, universal Christian church (outside of which there is no salvation) for the forgiveness of his sins. Now, by the first key which Christ promised and gave his church, Matt. 16:19, 18:18, John 20:23, he is admitted and accepted into the community of the saints. But since Your Grace knows and recognizes that it is not enough to know *that* one must be taught and instructed before receiving baptism, as I previously proved in the booklet[5] which was sent to you, but that it is also necessary to say *what* it is that one should first learn and know. Therefore Your Grace as a faithful, zealous, and careful shepherd and bishop earnestly encouraged, urged, and requested me to draw up a catechism or list of those articles that should be previously taught, in order that the youth (to whom we indeed owe a great responsibility) may be instructed in a proper and orderly way and from childhood on given food and drink and brought up with the teachings of Christ, especially since we clearly 'see that, being outdated and congealed in the mire and mud puddles of human precepts, /308/ of partiality to persons, of ancient practices and old customs, the Word of God is able to effect so very little on account of their unbelief and is so poorly applied that we must bewail it before God.

Although, gracious Lord, I would prefer properly to excuse myself, on the grounds of ignorance and other reasons, nevertheless, since this invitation is so honorable, useful, and Christian, I have no right to refuse such a wholesome request. Accordingly, with the grace of God's Holy Spirit I shall and will heartily and gladly comply with Your Grace's wish, not

---

[4] *Syrenisch* probably refers to the tempting calls of the legendary sirens.
[5] The *Opinion of Old and New Teachers*, text 17 above, p. 245. Its foreword of July 21, 1526, is also addressed to Martin Göschl.

only so that inexperienced youth may be helped but also because both of us previously were captive to many errors, hypocricies, and evil abominations. We have planted them and industriously (although ignorantly; we did not know any better at that time) built them up. Indeed, we ran all around the sea until, with teaching, persuading, cowls, tonsures, and with oil and chrism, we had made a priest or a fellow monk. But the almighty and merciful God in his divine mercy opened our eyes so graciously that both of us see, acknowledge, and confess ourselves guilty of our error, have desisted from it, and have consented, in the strength of our Lord Jesus Christ, henceforth to direct our lives according to his rule.[6] We also know with certainty that he has forgiven us our sins. To him be eternal praise. We therefore desire wholly and sincerely, in writing, in teaching, and in deed, to give to all those who through us fell into the same darkness and pit cause to open their eyes, to cry to God for enlightenment, to arise from the fall, and to reform their lives. To this end may the power of God help them. Amen.

As examiners, questioners, and assessors we have created a good number of priests and monks who, taken all together, were unable to translate the least of Paul's epistles into German, or even read it correctly. Nevertheless, they were all supposed to *Digni sunt Justi sunt*, i.e., to be righteous, worthy and capable priests. Oh, the great untruth and foolishness! Indeed, it is in many cases manifest what incompetent shepherds and pastors have been forced upon us by popes, bishops, provosts, abbots, and also by secular emperors, kings, princes, and nobles, by their bulls and mandates, such as courtisans,[7] donkey curriers, fornicators, adulterers, procurers, gamblers, drunkards, and foolish rogues, whom we would in truth not have trusted to herd our pigs and goats, but still we had to accept them /309/ as our souls' shepherds. They have become nothing but thieves and murderers, for they did not enter through the right door of Christian election, John 10:9.[8]

---

[6] "Rule" here is *Regel*, a technical term referring to Matt. 18:15ff.

[7] Bergsten/Westin translates *cortisanen* as "benefice-chasers." It probably means more broadly persons currying favor at court.

[8] The reference to "thieves and murderers" for clergy who entered office unworthily, with reference to John 10:9, goes back at least to Zwingli.

But in order to confess my own ignorance with my own blushes, I say without subterfuge, and God knows I am not lying, that I became a doctor in the Holy Scriptures (as this sophistry was called),[9] and still did not understand the Christian articles contained here in this booklet. Yes, and at that time I had never read a Gospel,[10] or an epistle by Paul, from beginning to end. What kind of a Holy Word could I then teach others or preach to them? Of course: Thomas, Scotus, Gabriel, Occam, decree, decretals, legends[11] of the saints and other scholastics. These were previously our hellish scriptures.

But gracious Lord, in order that no one may be too greatly surprised by our blindness and foolishness, be it known that the pure, clear, and unadulterated Word of God has from the beginning until now never come into our German nation, already entire, seven times purged and unmixed; but as our shepherds and bishops have always and ever been from the beginning, thus they pastured their sheep. They were, however, papists from the outset: namely monks and priests, sent out into the field of Christ by the popes from Rome, Scotland, and England, as I can prove by all the chronicles, to sow their tares, trifles, laws, and doctrines. People were asleep[12] and did not test and try their teachings by the plumb line of the Bible. Meanwhile these tares took root, grew up, and multiplied to such an extent that they cannot possibly be eradicated until the time of harvest, until the Lord himself comes. No matter that some incompetent Maozites and Maospriests[13] boast and shout: We have always and ever heard, learned, and even preached the gospel. Answer: Dear friends, I grant that this is your claim and cry, but not that it is the truth. For even if some bits and patches have been drawn forth from the gospel, so much chaff and grit of human comments and additions are mixed with them that we have not

---

[9] Hubmaier had earned the Doctorate in Theology at Ingolstadt in 1512.
[10] Literally "evangelist."
[11] Pun: Hubmaier has *Lügend* (lying) for *legend*, and *höllisch* (hellish) for *heilig* (holy).
[12] The parable of the tares (Matt. 13) is transformed. In German Europe there never was a good crop in a good field; the message, having been brought by a fallen church, was fallen from the beginning.
[13] Cf. text 19, note 8, p. 302, concerning the Mass/Maos pun.

tasted the sweetness of the real wheat and kernel. We /310/
were led so far astray from the spring of living water that we
have been drinking nothing but muddy, filthy, and poisoned
cistern water sullied by human feet. How then could health
and salvation have been there? All who have read the history
of the German nation can bear me witness of this, how it is
said to have come to Christian faith.[14] But when we say such
things now and warn people of these empty hulls and filthy
mud puddles, just as Augustine, Jerome and the papists themselves do, we must be [decried] as heretics, defamers of the
saints, seditionaries, perjurors, sectarians, and seducers.
Nevertheless, we should not allow ourselves to be led astray
by this, but shall rejoice the more because God has counted us
worthy to suffer disgrace, shame, mockery, and injury, banishment, poverty, misery, dungeon, torture, and all manner of
grief for the sake of his holy Word. May he alone grant us
patience that we may endure everything willingly and with
joy. For this is indeed the right way which leads to eternal
life. Christ himself also had to walk this road to enter into his
glory. Anyone who seeks another path by way of temporal
honor, sensuality, worldly pleasures, or by way of devilish possessions and money will miss the portals of heaven.

But to come to the point, gracious Lord, according to the
Christian wish of Your Grace I have composed a brief dialogue
or conversation in which I used two persons, Leonhart and
Hans, who converse with each other as brothers on the articles that pertain to the Christian faith. I was moved to use
these two names in preference to others by the special
inclination and affection that we both feel toward the noble
and Christian Lords, Lord Leonart and Lord Hans von
Liechtennstain at Nicolspurg, particular lovers of the holy
gospel, our gracious Lords. May the merciful and loving God
preserve them to their end in his shelter, in his protection,
and in a genuine, unadulterated, and Christian faith against all
the onslaughts of sin, world, devil, and hell. May he who for
our salvation died and rose again, Jesus Christ, our Savior,
grant this to them and to all of us. May Your Grace live well
in the Lord together with your Christian wife. Written at

---

[14] "Nation" here means no one political unit, but the entire Germanic
cultural world.

Nicolsburg on December 10, 1526.

Your Grace's docile Balthasar
Hüebmör of Fridberg /311/

A Christian Catechism
that every person before he is baptized in water should previously know, in the form of a dialogue.

Leonhart questions, Hanns replies[15]
Leonhart: What is your name?
Hans: My name is Hans.
Leonhart: Who gave you this name?
Hans: My father and mother.
Leonhart: For what purpose?
Hans: To tell me apart from other people.
Leonhart: What are you?
Hans: A corporeal reasonable creature, in body, soul, and spirit, created thus by God in his image.
Leonhart: What is God?
Hans: He is the highest good, almighty, all-wise, and all-merciful.
Leonhart: How do you recognize his omnipotence?
Hans: From the marvelous creation of the heaven, the earth, and all that is therein.
Leonhart: How his all-wisdom?
Hans: By the ingenious ordering and governing of all creatures.
Leonhart: How his all-mercifulness?
Hans: By his sending his only-begotten Son, our Lord Jesus Christ, into this world that it may not be lost because of sin, but through him attain to eternal life.
Leonhart: What is sin?
Hans: It is every movement or desire contrary to the will of God, whether in thought, in word, or in deed.
Leonhart: How do you recognize sin?
Hans: By the commandments of the Law.
Leonhart: How many commandments are there?

---

[15] The original text is run on like prose. Here it is set as dialogue for the sake of clarity.

Hans: Ten.

Leonhart: Recite them.

Hans: "I am the Lord your God, who brought you out of the land of Egypt, out of the house of bondage to sin.

"You shall have no other gods before me.

"You shall not make for yourself a graven image, or any likeness of anything that is in heaven above, or that is in the earth beneath, or that is in the water under the earth; you shall not worship them or serve them; for I the Lord your God am a jealous God, visiting the iniquity of the fathers upon the children to the third and fourth generation of those who hate me, but showing steadfast love to thousands of those who love me and keep my commandments.

"You shall not take the name of the Lord your God in vain; for the Lord will not hold him guiltless who takes his name in vain.

"Remember the sabbath day, to keep it holy. Six days you shall labor, and do all your work; but the seventh day is a sabbath to the Lord your God; in it you shall not do any work, you, or your son, or your daughter, your manservant, or your maidservant, or your cattle, or the sojourner who is within your city's gates; for in six days the Lord made heaven and earth, the sea, and all that is in them, and rested on the seventh day; therefore the Lord blessed the sabbath day and hallowed it.

"Honor your father and your mother, that your days may be long in the land which the Lord your God shall give you. /312/

"You shall not kill.

"You shall not commit adultery.

"You shall not steal.

"You shall not bear false witness against your neighbor.

"You shall not covet your neighbor's house; you shall not covet your neighbor's wife, or his manservant, or his maidservant, or his ox, or his ass, or anything that is your neighbor's."

Leonhart: But if you have fallen into sin, how do you get rid of it?

Hans: By repentance and prayer to God.

Leonhart: What is repentance?

Hans: Accusing oneself of sin before God, asking, him for forgiveness, and thenceforth never again committing it; that is

the highest form of repentance,[16] namely, to guard oneself
from sin and to walk henceforth according to God's Word.

Leonhart: What is prayer?

Hans: It is lifting up the mind to God in spirit and in
truth.

Leonhart: How do you pray?

Hans: As Christ taught his disciples, Matt. 6; Luke 11.

Leonhart: What did he teach them to say?

Hans: Thus: Our Father who art in heaven,
Hallowed be thy name.
Thy kingdom come,
Thy will be done,
    On earth as it is in heaven.
Give us this day our daily bread;
    Forgive us our debts,
    As we also forgive our debtors;
    Lead us not into temptation,
    But deliver us from evil. Amen.

Leonhart: How do you know that God hears your prayer?

Hans: From God's promises and from the gospel.

Leonhart: What is the difference between the two?

Hans: The promises comfort and preserve the confessing
sinner, that he may not despair in his sins, for a Messiah will
come to atone for the sins, to release the debtors from prison,
and to lead them with him into the promised fatherland. It is
as if one directed the sick man to a good physician who will
surely make him well, but he is not yet well. The gospel, on
the other hand, completely calms the person, helps him to rest
in his conscience and makes him completely well, for it shows
that the Law is now fulfilled in Christ, who has paid the debt
of sin for us and has already vanquished death, devil, and hell.
Thus the patriarchs of old had the benefit of the promises of
God as in Abraham's bosom; where they were preserved until
the time of Christ's descent into hell. When the gospel was
proclaimed to them there by the Spirit of Christ, only then
did they really live in the Christ who had been given them
and obtain redemption and eternal joy through the joyful message that he has vanquished sin, death, devil, and hell. Only

---

[16] "Ceasing to sin is the best repentance" is a current proverb.

then were the holy fathers freed of their pains in hell which they (but not the soul of Christ) had suffered there for a long time. Now the words of Peter are clearly understood, Acts 2:24; 1 Pet. 3:19ff.; 4:6. /313/

Leonhart: Point out to me a promise in the Bible.

Hans: The seed of the woman shall crush your head, serpent, Gen. 3:15. Likewise, through your seed, Abraham, shall all the peoples of the earth be blessed, Gen. 22:18.

Leonhart: Show me also a message of the gospel.

Hans: Christ died for the sake of our sins, and arose for the sake of our justification, Rom. 4:25.

Leonhart: What follows from this message?

Hans: Faith.

Leonhart: What is faith?

Hans: Faith is the realization of the unspeakable mercy of God, his gracious favor and goodwill, which he bears to us through his most beloved Son Jesus Christ, whom he did not spare and delivered him to death for our sakes that sin might be paid for, and we might be reconciled to him and with the assurance of our hearts cry to him: Abba, Father, our Father who are in heaven.

Leonhart: How many kinds of faith are there?

Hans: Two kinds, namely a dead one and a living one.

Leonhart: What is dead faith?

Hans: One that is unfruitful and without the works of love, James 2:17.

Leonhart: What is living faith?

Hans: One that produces the fruits of the Spirit and works through love, Gal. 5.

Leonhart: What are the fruits of the Spirit?

Hans: Love, joy, peace, patience, kindness, goodness, faith, gentleness, self-control, and the like.

Leonhart: What are the works of the flesh?

Hans: Adultery, whoring, impurity, licentiousness, idolatry, sorcery, enmity, strife, jealousy, anger, quarreling, dissension, party spirit, hatred, murder, drunkenness, gluttony, and the like.

Leonhart: How many articles of the Christian faith are there?

Hans: Twelve.

Leonhart: What are they?

Hans: I believe in God the Father Almighty, Maker of heaven and earth. I believe in Jesus Christ, his only Son our Lord, who was conceived by the Holy Spirit, born of the Virgin Mary. I believe he suffered under Pontius Pilate, was crucified, died, and was buried. He descended into hell; the third day he arose again from the dead. He ascended into heaven, where he sits at the right hand of God his Almighty Father, from whence he shall come to judge the quick and the dead. I believe in the Holy Spirit. I believe and confess the holy universal church, which is the fellowship of all holy and Christ-believing persons. I believe that by the command of Christ it has authority to forgive sins. I believe the resurrection of the body and the life everlasting.

Leonhart: After faith what do you desire?

Hans: Water baptism.

Leonhart: How many kinds of baptism are there?

Hans: Three kinds.

Leonhart: What are they?

Hans: A baptism of the Spirit, a baptism of water, and a baptism of blood.

Leonhart: What is the baptism of the Spirit?

Hans: It is an inner illumination of our hearts that takes place by the Holy Spirit, through the living Word of God.

Leonhart: What is water baptism?

Hans: It is an outward and public testimony of the inner baptism in the Spirit, which a person gives by receiving water, with which one confesses one's sins before all people. One also testifies thereby that one believes in the forgiveness of his sins through the death and resurrection of our Lord Jesus Christ. Thereupon one also /314/ has himself outwardly enrolled, inscribed, and by water baptism incorporated into the fellowship of the church according to the institution of Christ, before which church the person also publicly and orally vows to God and agrees in the strength of God the Father, Son, and Holy Spirit that he will henceforth believe and live according to his divine Word. And if he should trespass herein he will accept brotherly admonition, according to Christ's order, Matt. 18:15ff. This precisely is the true baptismal vow, which we have lost for a thousand years; meanwhile Satan has forced his way in with his monastic vows and priestly vows and established them in the holy place.

Leonhart: What is the baptism of blood?

Hans: It is a daily mortification of the flesh until death.

Leonhart: Where did Christ mention these baptisms?

Hans: Concerning Spirit baptism in John 3:5, concerning water baptism in Matt. 28:18ff.; Mark 16:15f., and concerning the baptism of blood in Luke 12:50.

Leonhart: Why were you not baptized in infancy?[17]

Hans: Because then I did not yet believe nor know what faith, Christ, or baptism is.

Leonhart: What is your opinion of the infant baptism which the water-priests use?

Hans: Nothing other than that the adult child gives a bath to the young child, thereby depriving it of the real water baptism of Christ.

Leonhart: If only believers are to be baptized who publicly confess with their mouth, as Christ instituted water baptism for believers alone, Matt. 28; Mark 16, must we submit to rebaptism? What seems right to you?

Hans: Our approving, supposing, and thinking are of no importance; we must ask advice of the mouth of the Lord who said: Go therefore and teach all nations and baptize them; he who believes and is baptized will be saved. Since Christ commanded his disciples to preach and baptize, that very command orders us to hear the preaching and to be baptized. For whoever then loosens one of the least of these commandments shall be called least in the kingdom of heaven, Matt. 5:19; James 2. But now water baptism is a very earnest command; it has been proclaimed to be performed in the name of the Father, the Son, and the Holy Spirit. If we accept this baptism, even though we were one hundred years old, it would still not be a rebaptism, because infant baptism is no baptism and is unworthy of being called baptism. For the infant knows neither good nor evil and cannot consent or vow either to the church or to God.

Leonhart: What is the baptismal pledge?

Hans: It is a commitment made to God publicly and orally before the congregation in which the baptized person

---

[17] Note that the question assumes the nonvalidity of infant baptism. It is not that Hans *should* not have been baptized at birth. It is that the ritual performed in his infancy was not baptism.

renounces Satan /315/ and all his imaginations and works. He
also vows that he will henceforth set his faith, hope, and trust
solely in God and regulate his life according to the divine
Word, in the strength of Jesus Christ our Lord, and if he
should fail to do so, he thereby promises the church that he
would dutifully accept brotherly discipline from it and its
members, as has been said above.[18]

Leonhart: Which of the articles of the creed deal with
baptism?

Hans: The ninth and tenth articles, where we confess the
universal Christian church, the fellowship of the saints and
forgiveness of sins, just as the Lord's Supper is also included
there. For with outward baptism the church opens her doors
to all believers who confess their faith orally before her and
receives them into her bosom, fellowship, and communion of
saints for the forgiveness of their sins. Therefore, as one cares
about the forgiveness of his sins and the fellowship of the
saints outside of which there is no salvation, just so much
should one value water baptism, whereby one enters and is
incorporated into the universal Christian church. This is the
understanding and decision Christianly issued by the Nicene
Council, in these words: I acknowledge one unique baptism
for the remission of sins. Peter gives it the same meaning: Be
baptized every one of you in the name of Jesus Christ for the
forgiveness of your sins, Acts 2:38.

Leonhart: Now that you have assured the church of your
faith by your baptism, tell me, what is the church?

Hans: The church is sometimes understood to include all
the people who are gathered and united in one God, one
Lord, one faith, and one baptism, and have confessed this
faith with their mouths, wherever they may be on earth. This,
then, is the universal Christian corporeal church and fellowship of the saints, assembled only in the Spirit of God, as we
confess in the ninth article of our creed. At other times the
church is understood to mean each separate and outward
meeting assembly or parish membership that is under one

---

[18] This interlocking of baptism and fraternal admonition is a favorite
theme, which recurs below, pp. 381, 384, 389, 416. It was a part of the
earliest Swiss Brethren questioning of infant baptism; cf. Harder 1985, p.
290.

shepherd or bishop and assembles bodily for instruction, for baptism and the Lord's Supper. The church as daughter has the same power to bind and to loose on earth as the universal church, her mother, when she uses the keys according to the command of Christ, her spouse and husband.

Leonhart: What is the difference between these two churches?

Hans: The particular congregation may err, as the papist church has erred in many respects. But the universal church cannot err. She is without spot, without wrinkle, is controlled by the Holy Spirit, and Christ is with her until the end of the world, Matt. 28:20. And God will through all time preserve to himself seven thousand who will not bend their knee to the idol Baal, 1 Kings 19:18; Rom. 11.

Leonhart: On what is the Christian church built?

Hans: On the oral confession of faith that Jesus is the Christ, /316/ the Son of the living God. This outward confession is what makes a church, and not faith alone; for the church that has the power to bind and to loose is outward and corporeal, not theoretical,[19] and faith is inward. And although faith alone makes righteous, it does not alone give salvation, for it must be accompanied by public confession. Of this we have good testimony, Matt. 16:18. There Christ says, "You are Peter, and on this rock (meaning: which you confess) I will build my church." Likewise, he also says, "Everyone who acknowledges me before men, I will also acknowledge before my Father who is in heaven; but whoever denies me and is ashamed of my words before men I also will deny and be ashamed of him before my Father," Matt. 10:32; Luke 9:26; 12:5f. And Paul says, "For one believes with the heart and so is justified; but one confesses with the mouth and so is saved, Rom. 10:10.

Leonhart: What authority do those in the church have over one another?

Hans: The power of fraternal admonition.

Leonhart: What is fraternal admonition?

Hans: One who sees his brother sin goes to him in love and admonishes him fraternally and quietly to abandon such

---

[19] Hubmaier's adjective is "mathematica."

sin. If he desists, he has won his soul. If he does not, then he takes two or three other witnesses with him and admonishes him once again. If he obeys him, all is well; if not he tells the church. The church calls him forward and admonishes him the third time. If he now leaves off his sin the church has won his soul, Matt. 18:15ff.

Leonhart: Whence does the church have this authority?

Hans: From Christ's command when he said to his disciples: Whatever you bind on earth shall be bound in heaven, and whatever you loose on earth shall be loosed in heaven, Matt. 18:18; John 20:23.

Leonhart: But what right has one brother to use this power against another?

Hans: From the baptismal pledge, in which one has made himself subject to the church and all her members, according to the Word of Christ.[20]

Leonhart: What if the admonished sinner refuses to reform?

Hans: In that case the church has the power and the right to excommunicate and ban him as a perjurer and perfidious.

Leonhart: What is the ban?

Hans: It is an exclusion and separation of such a nature that henceforth Christians may have no fellowship with such a person, either in word, eating, drinking, grinding, baking, or any other form, but treat him as a heathen and publican, i.e., as an offensive, disorderly, and poisonous person, who is bound and handed over to the devil. He must be avoided and shunned so that the whole outward church may not be ill spoken of, shamed, and disgraced by fellowship with him or be corrupted by his evil example, but rather that it will be frightened and filled with fear by this punishment and henceforth die to sin. For as truly as God lives, what the church admits or excludes on earth /317/ is also admitted, or excluded in heaven.

Leonhart: What are the causes for excommunication?

Hans: Refusal to be reconciled to the brother or to desist from sin.

Leonhart: Why is one excommunicated?

---

[20] Cf. above, note 16.

Hans: Not for petty offenses[21] as our papists have been doing, but for an offensive sin; and it is done for the good of the sinner, that he may examine himself, know himself, and desist from the sin.

Leonhart: If he desists from his sin, avoids the ways and paths that might cause him to fall again, and reforms, what attitude does the church take toward him?

Hans: She receives him again with joy, as the father did his prodigal son, and as Paul did the Corinthians, Luke 15:20; 2 Cor. 2:10. She opens the door to heaven for him and lets him return to the communion of the Lord's Supper. In sum: Where water baptism in accord with Christ's institution is not reestablished and practiced one does not know who is a brother or sister, there is no church, no brotherly discipline or reproof, no ban, no Supper, nor anything that resembles the Christian stance and nature. God lives. So it must be, or heaven and earth must shatter.

Second Part of the Dialogue

Leonhart: What is the Lord's Supper?

Hans: It is a public sign and testimonial of the love in which one brother obligates himself to another before the congregation that just as they now break and eat the bread with each other and share and drink the cup, likewise they wish now to sacrifice and shed their body and blood for one another; this they will do in the strength of our Lord Jesus Christ, whose suffering they are now commemorating in the Supper with the breaking of bread and the sharing of the wine, and proclaiming his death until he comes. Precisely this is the pledge of love in Christ's Supper that one Christian performs toward the other, in order that every brother may know what good deed to expect from the other.

Leonhart: Is the bread not the body of Christ and the wine his crimson blood, as the Maoz-priests have been telling us?

Hans: By no means; the bread and wine are nothing but memorial symbols of Christ's suffering and death for the for-

---

[21] Literally "not for a shillings' worth of hazelnuts." Cf. HS, p. 317, n. 43, for other criticisms of the use of excommunication for minor offenses.

giveness of our sins. This on the basis of the institution by Christ on Maundy Thursday when he was about to go out and show us the greatest of all signs of love, on the next day giving his flesh and blood unto death on our account, which our forefathers consequently called Good Friday (*Karfreitag*) from *caritate*, i.e., from love. Indeed, to state it bluntly, /318/ the Lord's Supper is a sign of the obligation to brotherly love just as water baptism is a symbol of the vow of faith. The water concerns God, the Supper our neighbor; therein lie all the Law and the Prophets. No other ceremonies were instituted by Christ and left behind on earth, and whoever correctly teaches these two signs teaches faith and love correctly.

Leonhart: Where do you worship Christ?

Hans: Not at any one particular place. Even though someone says: "Look; there on the altar is Christ! There in the stone or silver tabernacle he sits!" I do not believe it. I worship him seated at the right hand of his heavenly Father; there he is my only intercessor, mediator, and reconciler to God, as I have confessed above in the sixth article of the creed. There he remains seated, on the strength of the Scriptures, until the judgment day; and then he will come in his great majesty and judge the quick and the dead. Then we shall see him descend as he ascended; for this we wait and will not seek him in bread or wine.

Leonhart: Just what is the mass?

Hans: It is the very idol and abomination, spoken of by the Prophet Daniel in his prophecy, Daniel 11:31, to whom Christ so faithfully and earnestly directed us, that we read him and take heed, Matt. 24:15. This idol stands in the holy place and is honored with gold, silver, gems, and all that is costly. By his honor[22] he is recognized as the kind of God he is to the papists, maozites, mass-priests, sophists, and all belly-Christians.

Leonhart: Do you also confess your sins?

Hans: Yes, I confess them to God but not to a monk or priest.

Leonhart: How do you confess?

---

[22] I.e., by the costliness of the symbols of veneration of the sacrament.

Hans: Thus: Father, I have sinned against heaven and before you; I am not worthy to be called your son, because I have not fulfilled your fatherly wish. But speak a word of comfort and my soul will be healed. God, be merciful to me a sinner. Amen; may this be true.

Leonhart: Do you also fast?

Hans: I ought to fast daily, using food and drink in moderation, so that I do not overfeed the old Adam and he become insolent and cast the ark of the divine commands into the mud together with the stubborn ox.[23]

Leonhart: Do you also bless the food and drink before you partake of them?

Hans: No. God blessed it long ago and created all things very good. It is not what goes into the mouth that defiles a man, but the evil that comes from it, that defiles him; and to the pure all things are pure. Therefore I eat all kinds of food without any difference whether it be fish or meat, but, as Christ and Paul teach me, with propriety and thankfulness.

Leonhart: How do you thank God before your meal?

Hans: Thus: Praise and honor be to you, God, Creator of the heaven and earth, who have created all things good and well, particularly food and drink, /319/ and ordained that we shall accept it with thanksgiving. Glory and honor be to God the Father and to the Son and to the Holy Spirit. As he was from the beginning, is now and ever shall be, world without end, God be praised in the heavens. Amen, so be it.

Leonhart: What do you do at the table?

Hans: I eat and drink with my household what God has given me. I speak to them about God's Word. I restrain myself in order not to eat human flesh or drink human blood.

Leonhart: Who then eats human flesh and drinks human blood?

Hans: All who while eating swear, rave, and curse by the flesh, blood, pains, wounds, and suffering of Christ, take the name of God in vain, slander their neighbor's honor and good reputation, and speak ill of him, eat and drink the flesh and blood of men.[24]

---

[23] Perhaps an allusion to 2 Sam. 6.

[24] Hubmaier is especially concerned for the sins of the tongue. His form for discipline also uses this example: cf. p. 381.

Leonhart: How do you thank God after the meal?

Hans: Thus: We thank and praise thee, Lord God, Creator of heaven and earth, for all the kindness thou hast shown unto us; especially since thou hast in this meal so graciously fed us in body and soul with our daily bread. Glory and honor be to God the Father, the Son, and the Holy Spirit, as he was in the beginning, is now, and ever shall be, world without end. May the almighty and merciful God grant us his eternal peace. Amen, may this come to pass.

Leonhart: Do you observe the Sabbath?

Hans: Yes. Man has an eternal Sabbath; this he should celebrate daily and without ceasing, keep himself from sin, and allow God to work in him.

Leonhart: What do you believe regarding Our Lady?

Hans: I believe that she was a pure, chaste, and spotless Virgin before, during, and after the birth; a mother of God, and blessed, because she believed those things that were told her by God. I can give her no greater title, name, or praise than that.

Leonhart: Would you call on her or the other saints to pray to God for you that he would be gracious to you and save you from all your troubles?

Hans: At the marriage feast at Cana in Galilee, Mary said, "Do whatever my Son tells you," John 2:5. Her Son commanded us that when we are oppressed or in need of something we should all come to him and he will give us rest; he is the door, the way, the truth, and the life; no one comes to the Father except through him, Matt. 11:20; John 10:9; 14:6. Anyone who does not do this dishonors Christ, and whoever dishonors Christ and does not follow his command dishonors Mary, his dear mother, also. Such a man does not follow her teaching when she said, "Do whatever my Son tells you." Therefore, if you want to obey and honor Mary, do not call upon her or the other saints, but alone upon her Son, Christ Jesus, giving him the glory and honor, for he is the most gracious, kindest, and most merciful, unspeakably more than his own mother and all the saints. Whoever runs to the saints and cries to them that they should ask Christ for them that he be gracious to him blasphemes Christ, for he does not believe that Christ is the most merciful /320/ and most gracious one in the heavens, our only intercessor, mediator, gracious one with the Father. That is a blasphemy against God contrary to all the Scriptures, 1 Tim. 2:5; 1 John 2:1, whereby Christ and Mary are accused of lying as if they had not properly indicated to us the way to the heavenly Father.

Leonhart: Do you believe that the saints can perform wondrous signs and miracles?

Hans: No. God alone performs miracles through them. I find that in Mark 16:17f.; Acts 3:1ff.; 14:18ff., about the two cripples.

Leonhart: Do you also make and honor images of Christ, Mary, and the dear saints?

Hans: By no means. For images have been seriously forbidden by God and are of no benefit, Exod. 20:4; Deut. 5:8; 7:25; Baruch 6:6; Gal. 4:8; 5:1ff.; 1 Pet. 4; 1 John 5; Acts 19:23ff. But one should above all uproot such idols and images out of human hearts with the Word of God, or the outward destruction of idols is futile.

Leonhart: Whom, then, do you honor?

Hans: God alone, and no one else in heaven or on earth, except inasmuch as God is in his creatures.

Leonhart: What is the highest honor to God?

Hans: To hear and believe his Word.

Leonhart: Do you hear his Word in the church?

Hans: Yes.

Leonhart: Why?

Hans: That my faith may constantly grow day by day as a mustard seed grows to the skies, and that I may perform my works in true faith, lest they lead to eternal damnation: for it is not enough to do something with good intentions; one must also be assured and convinced from God's Word that God will accept from us the work done with good intentions. Peter, with truly good intentions, was unwilling to let Jesus wash his feet. But Christ wanted none of his good intentions, but said: "Peter, if I do not wash you, you have no part of me," John 13:8. Likewise, Uzzah, no doubt with good intentions, seized and held the ark of God which contained the Commandments to keep it from being thrown into the mud by the stumbling oxen; but God was angry with him and smote him, and he died there beside the ark, 2 Sam. 6:6f. He will never accept anything except only what he has commanded us; of his mouth we must ask for counsel. "Woe," he says, "to the same children who forsake me, who carry out a plan, but not mine," Isa. 30:1.

Leonhart: In what does the sum of all preaching lie?

Hans: In love.

Leonhart: In what way?

Hans: That I love the Lord my God with my whole heart, my whole soul, and all my strength, and my neighbor as myself. If I do that, I have fulfilled all the Law and the Prophets.

Leonhart: Do you sing in church?

Hans: Yes, /321/ with my mouth I sing understandable words, and with my spirit I reflect on the words, so that I do not honor my God with my lips while my heart is far from it, as the Pharisees did. It is also better to speak or sing five words understandably before the church than ten thousand that cannot be understood, Mark 7; 1 Cor. 14:19.

Leonhart: Can you do good works of your own strength?

Hans: God alone is good, and he works in us to will and to do the good, Matt. 19:17; Phil. 2:13.

Leonhart: Since man cannot do anything good, why does God condemn him?

Hans: God does not condemn him for doing, but for not doing, as a schoolmaster does not strike the boy for learning, but for not learning. Nor does a man strike his wife for doing, but for doing nothing. Likewise, God does not condemn a man on account of his works, but because he has neglected to do them or has not done them according to God's will and pleasure.

Leonhart: But after all, the Scriptures contain many verses that clearly indicate that doing good or evil is in our power and will, as Christ says, "If thou wilt enter into life, keep the Commandments," Matt. 19:17.

Hans: Yes, that is true. But these Scriptures do nothing more than to reveal how man was created by God in the first place, how he lost his freedom through sin, and how he is reborn through the Word sent to him. There is a vast difference between being and having been. We were, to be sure, free before sinning; but after sin we were not free until we were made truly free by the death and resurrection of Christ. One who falls and is crippled was straight before, but he is no longer straight until the physician helps him so that his lameness no longer handicaps him. Likewise, although there is indeed still something in us of God's likeness in which we were initially made, Gen. 1:27, still this likeness has been dimmed, captured, and bound by Adam's disobedience. We are thus mired there until Christ makes us free; that is, he renders flesh, sin, death, devil, and hell harmless. Here there is need to pray earnestly and to cry without ceasing to Christ with the apostles: Lord, help us! Lord, we are perishing! Lord, increase our faith! On the other hand, we find just as many Scriptures that reveal to us our human weaknesses, incapabilities, and lameness so that we—yes, in spite of our best performance of the divine commands—are unprofitable servants, and so that all our righteousness can be likened to the garment of a defiled woman, Luke 17; Isaiah 64:6. Wherefore one must ruminate these Scriptures, to make an exact distinction between human nature before the Fall, after the Fall, and after the restoration from the Fall through Christ, carefully judging each and making distinctions; /322/ thereby one also very easily acquires a true distinction between the free will and the bound will. If before the Fall God's likeness was free and unbound in us, since the Fall it is held captive and the sin of the Fall is damning. After the restoration of the Fall through Christ, this likeness is made free again, although captive in the sinful and poisoned body; but the curse has been removed from the sin of the Fall insofar as we do not by our own wickedness make it damning again by rebelliously walking in it. Thus Paul teaches us in Romans 8:13. Here you see clearly that the image or inbreathing of God is still in us all, although captive and as a live spark covered with cold ashes is still alive and will steam if heavenly water is poured on it. It also lights up and burns if one blows on it. That is the source of the conscience in the Jews, pagans, and Christians, as Paul writes about it, Rom. 2:15. But Christ restored the quenched spark of flame on Easter Day when he breathed upon his disciples and said, Receive the Holy Spirit, John 20:22. Now Christ has ordered his servants to inbreathe and blow by the proclaiming his holy Word, that the wounded soul may be reawakened from sleep.

From this you will note: If one says there is nothing good in man, that is saying too much. As Paul also said too much when he said, I know that nothing good dwells within me. But he hastens to explain this by adding to this concept: I know that nothing good dwells within me, that is, in my flesh, Rom. 7:18. Likewise all the other Scriptures must be understood that indicate that there is nothing good in man, that is, in his flesh, for God's image has never yet been completely obliterated in us. How can it be evil, for (like the law) it shows and teaches us the good. Far be it from us then to call it evil. For we know that it is holy, makes us righteous and is wholly good. Notice the Trinity in those three phrases. In sum: First God made us good and free in soul, body, and spirit. This goodness and freedom were through Adam's disobedience taken captive in our spirit, wounded in our soul, and completely corrupted in our flesh; therefore we are all conceived and born in sin and are by nature the children of wrath. If we are now again to become free in the spirit and healthy in the soul, and if this Fall is to be made completely harmless in the flesh, then this must take place through a rebirth, as Christ said, or we /323/ shall not enter into the kingdom of God, John 3:5. But now God has given birth to us of his own will, as James writes, James 1:18, and Peter, 1 Pet. 1:3, by the word of his power in which we are really made whole and free again. Christ likewise says, the truth will make you truly free, John 8:22, and David, he sent forth his Word and healed us, Ps. 106 [Ps 107:20]. Yes, to the present day through the Word God sent, our souls are just as free in themselves to will good and evil as was Adam's soul in Paradise.

Leonhart: How does it happen then that God at many places in the Scriptures promises a reward for our works?

Hans: That is due to his gracious kindness. He ascribes these to us as if we had done him a great favor out of ourselves and of our own [strength], whereas he, of course, has no need whatever of us and does not wish our service except for our own benefit. Then let God call it a reward, but woe to you if you should consider it a payment. Consider all God's dealing with you as pure grace. There is nothing that God's grace cannot tolerate or observe less than presumptuous merits of our own, as Paul teaches in Romans 3 and 4.

Leonhart: Give me a parable that I may know that you understand it correctly.

Hans: Yes, very gladly. If a serf performs a day's statute

362 / *Balthasar Hubmaier*

labor or socage[25] for his lord, what can he expect from him except what is given out of mercy? A good son does not serve his father for pay, but out of love, even though the father wants to call the good he does for his son a payment. But if the son were to demand pay, it would rightly grieve the father. Therefore we should not conclude from these Scriptures that they indicate earnings or wages.

Leonhart: Why then do the Holy Scriptures attribute doing good and keeping God's commands to our will, as several passages seem to say, if we after all can do nothing good without him?

Hans: God wants to awaken us from sleep with them and give us the heart to resolve to do good and to accomplish this with the hope of divine help, because he asks it of us. Otherwise, we would not dare to be presumptuous in this, for it would be impossible for us in ourselves, without God's drawing which comes through his Word. Therefore we must first beg him and say, "O Lord, give us what you command of us." We would not even dare to say "Our Father," if he had not commanded us to do so.

Leonhart: How does God draw or call a person?

Hans: In two forms, outwardly and inwardly. The outward drawing occurs through the public proclamation of his holy gospel, that Christ has commanded to preach to all creatures in the whole world, which is now proclaimed everywhere, Mark 16:15. The inward drawing is this, /324/ that God also illuminates the person's soul inwardly, so that it understands the incontrovertible truth, convinced by the Spirit and the preached Word in such a way that one must in one's own conscience confess that this is the case and it cannot be otherwise.

Leonhart: Explain this by an example.

Hans: Gladly. Just as one hears outwardly with his ears and inwardly understands: All that enters into the mouth does not make one unclean. He knows too that Christ said this, Matt. 15:17. In his conscience he is now convinced that this must be true, and he cannot oppose it at all with clear Scrip-

---

[25] Hubmaier uses two technical terms: *Frontag* and *Robat*. The two terms differ as to the legal base of the serf's obligations. *Fron* describes the basic duty of the serf. *Robat* pays the rent for a particular piece of land.

ture. That is the outward and inward drawing of God, which everyone can safely believe and trust. But if he does not do this, God will abandon him and with just judgment give him over to a perverted mind, blind, harden, and strike him with a deceiving mind like Babylon, the Jews, and the Romans, Jer. 51:7; Matt. 13:15ff.; Rom. 1:18ff.

Leonhart: No doubt many people hear God's Word outwardly but do not understand it inwardly. What must they do?

Hans: Then they have to pray and in faith ask wisdom of God like Solomon, nothing doubting, and cry: Father, give us today our daily bread. Or like David, Lord, give me understanding that I may learn thy justification and thy commandments. One who prays thus is certain that God will enlighten him, even if he has to order a Peter from Joppa on the sea,[26] or an angel from heaven. Here you can hear that the very highest theology is fervent unceasing prayer to God. He will give us a mouth and wisdom .[27]

Leonhart: Some people do not want to hear the Word of God. Some hear but do not comprehend. Some comprehend and do not obey. Some persecute the truth vehemently. What happens to them?

Hans: As one is saved in his own faith and not in that of someone else, so also are such people condemned in their own unbelief, for which condemnation they themselves are guilty and not God. For God has often desired to gather them with his Word like a hen her chicks, but they of their own volition have freely and wickedly refused, nor do they recognize the day of their visitation. Therefore they cannot blame it on God, as he himself says, The condemnation is thine, O Israel; only in me lies your salvation, Hos. 13:9.

Leonhart: Tell me what are the genuine good works.

Hans: The works of mercy, for which Christ will demand an account.

Leonhart: When?

Hans: On the day of judgment.

Leonhart: With what words?

Hans: With these: Come here, blessed of my Father, inherit the kingdom prepared for you from the foundation of

---

[26] Acts 10:5.
[27] Luke 21:15.

the world; for I was hungry and you fed me, I was thirsty and you gave me drink, I was a pilgrim and you took me in, I was naked and you clothed me, I was sick and you visited me, /325/ I was in prison and you came to me, Matt. 25:34-36.

Leonhart: What are the evil works?

Hans: Those that Christ will reproach us for on the judgment day.

Leonhart: With what words?

Hans: Depart from me, you cursed, into the eternal fire prepared for the devil and his angels; for I was hungry and you did not feed me, I was thirsty and you gave me no drink, I was a pilgrim and you did not take me in, naked and you did not clothe me, sick and in prison and you did not visit me.

Leonhart: You mentioned the judgment day. What is the judgment day?

Hans: It is the day on which the Lord shall come down from heaven with a battle cry and the voice of the archangel and the trumpets of God, and the dead in Christ will first be raised; that is, body, soul, and spirit will be reunited; then we who are living and surviving will immediately be snatched up into the clouds with them to meet the Lord in the air and will be with the Lord forever in everlasting life, yea, those who have done good. But those who have done evil will go forth to the resurrection of the judgment, 1 Thess. 4:13ff.; John 5:29.

Leonhart: What is eternal life?

Hans: It is an eternal, sure, and joyful vision of God's face, prepared from the foundation of the world for all believers in Christ who have performed works of mercy toward their neighbor, where there is nothing but bliss, joy, peace, rest, and all security throughout eternity.

Leonhart: Which is the shortest path of all to eternal life?

Hans: Through fear, distress, suffering, grief, persecution, and death for the sake of the name of Christ Jesus, who himself had to suffer and thus enter into his glory, Luke 24:26. St. Paul also says: All who desire to live a godly life in Christ Jesus will be persecuted, 2 Tim. 3:12. For where Christ is and dwells, there he brings the cross with him on his back from which he gives every Christian his own small cross to carry and to follow after him. We are to expect this small cross and if it comes accept it with joy and patience, and not pick and choose our own chips and bits of wood in false spirituality, selecting and gathering them up without divine understanding.

Leonhart: Who are these people?[28]

Hans: The poor in spirit. Those that mourn. Those who are meek. Those who hunger and thirst after righteousness. The merciful. The pure in heart. The peacemakers. Those who are persecuted for righteousness' sake. Those who are reviled and despised on account of Christ's name. Also those against whom much evil is spoken falsely for Christ's sake, Matt. 5:3ff.

/326/

Leonhart: What is hell?

Hans: Hell is the eternally painful and unending deprivation of the contemplation of God's face; it has been prepared for the devil, his angels, and all unbelievers who have not performed deeds of mercy for their neighbor. There is nothing there but everlasting fire, outer darkness, weeping and gnashing of teeth, from which may the almighty kind and merciful Father in heaven graciously preserve us throughout eternity through Jesus Christ, his only begotten Son, our Lord, to whom be glory, praise, honor, and majesty always and forever.

Leonhart: Amen. The peace of God be with us all.

Hans: Amen. So be it.

Truth Is Unkillable.
Printed by Simprecht Sorg, called Froschauer.
Nicolspurg
1527

---

[28] The antecedent is not clear. It may refer back to the persons mentioned in the 2 Tim. quotation.

22

The Ground and Reason

With the exception of only a few changes the main part of this treatise is a reprinting from text 11 above, Christian Baptism of the Believer, *of the ten reasons for the necessity of baptism according to the order of Christ. One paragraph is added at the end of the fourth reason, and four sentences are omitted at the end of the paragraph concerning the seventh reason. Finally, in Nikolsburg, Hubmaier added reasons eleven through thirteen. Only the new portions are printed here.*

The treatise is dedicated to Johann von Pernstein, a leading adherent of the Utraquists and a sympathizer to the evangelical movements. Bergsten concludes that by dedicating this treatise to von Pernstein he hoped to gain his support for the Anabaptist movement.[1] Apparently von Pernstein did later provide asylum for Anabaptists.

The preface notes that there are many people who do not know whether they should have themselves baptized as adult believers or not, thereby reflecting Hubmaier's awareness that the Anabaptist message was making something of an impact. The publication of the several reasons why one should be baptized was intended to further the Anabaptist movement. As such it was a missionary tract. Written in 1526, it was published in 1527.[2]

---

[1] Bergsten 1978, p. 338.
[2] Fragments translated in Hošek 1892, pp. 127-130; Vedder 1905, pp. 181, 203-204; Armour 1966, p. 46; and Klaassen 1981, p. 213. Source: HS 17, pp. 328-336.

*The Ground and
Reason
why every person
even if he has been baptized
in his childhood
is responsible
to have himself baptized rightly
according to
order of Christ,
even if he were
a hundred years old.
Dr. Balthasar Hubmör
von Fridberg.
Nicolspurg
1527*

To the wellborn and Christian Lord H. Jan von Bernstain of Helffenstain, highest governor of the Margraviate of Moravia, my gracious Lord. Grace and salvation in God.

Highborn Gracious Lord

I know many godly people who publicly confess that infant baptism has no basis at all in Scripture. However, whether those who in their childish ignorance were until now baptized are obligated to let themselves be baptized anew, as they say, or not, there are still many people hanging like Absalom on the oak tree between heaven and earth, 2 Sam. 18:9, not knowing what they should do. On the one hand they see the serious baptismal command of Christ, Matt. 28:19; Mark 16:15; Acts 2, but on the other they fear the stigma of rebaptism, since there are none in their own circle of acquaintances.[3] So that they may be helped out of this confu-

---

[3]This awkward sentence is rendered as Hubmaier wrote it. He indicates that he is aware that there are those who would like to follow the command of Christ for believers baptism, but that since they know no one who practices it, they fear being charged with the stigma of rebaptism if they do.

sion, I have brought together in writing, for the praise of God and the use of all people, the ground and reasons* so that it be thereby indisputably proven that every believing person who has available water and a baptizer is responsible for [the sake of] his soul to have himself also baptized in water according to the order of Christ, regardless of his having been bathed in water in his childhood. Herewith I call /329/ on heaven and earth to testify that I have said it faithfully, Deut. 27:26. Cursed be the one who dissolves the smallest Word of God. Whoever cannot say "Amen" is still under the law. To him it would be better if he did not speak of baptism at all. Herewith I want to recommend myself to your grace that you also graciously accept this my little book.

Your Grace's subject
Balthasar Hûebmör

Here Hubmaier takes over verbatim from Christian Baptism *several paragraphs, namely, reasons one through four. See above, pp. 121-123. The following paragraph is added to reason four:*

/330/ But notice by this, dear ecclesiastics. You have till now so diligently grasped the pleasing verse of Paul where he says, "Because of harlotry each man should have his own wife and each woman her own husband," 1 Cor. 7:2, and this verse you have often called out with high voice and loudly for the justification of priestly marriage. When Paul says, "each man," no one is excluded. Why then do you not give the same weight to the words, "each one, each one" in this verse of Peter where he says with the same authority, let "each one" of you be baptized in the name of Jesus Christ for the forgiveness of sins? I warn you by the righteous judgment of God that you do not push away the earnest word of Peter, which serves the souls for the forgiveness of sins, Acts 2:38. Or God will truly abolish for you with punishment the word of Paul /331/ to you, which pleases your flesh. Watch out, O brothers, see that you do not deny what you have, so that there not be

---

* Thesis of this booklet.

given to you what you would rather do without, and that it be
taken from you what you do not now want to have. Therefore
let the Scriptures of both Peter and Paul remain in equal
weight teaching, truth, power, and effect. For just this way
has it pleased God.

Here follow reasons five through ten. See above, pp. 123-127.

/334/ The eleventh reason.* We read of Cyprian and
many other bishops who decided in the Council of Carthage
that all those who were ever baptized by heretics must again
be baptized rightly by Christians.⁴ That is also yet today the
practice of the brothers who are called the Picards.⁵ For those
who have received the baptism of heretics have no baptism,
for the heretics (they say) are outside the church. Therefore
they can let no one into the community of Christians, nor can
they open the doors of the Christian church with the keys
given by Christ Matt. 18:18; John 20:23; Matt. 7:15; John 10:8.
Since, however, almost all preachers till now have publicly
cried out that the papists are idolators, false prophets,
seducers, antichrists, heretics, yes thieves and murderers of
the soul, how can they regard or judge the silly infant baptism
received from them to be good and right?

The twelfth reason. It is certain and undeniable that John
was sent by God to baptize, John 1:26; 3:26-28. Accordingly
he also made disciples and baptized them according to the divine command. Therefore all those who were baptized by him
could have said: "John, who was sent by God to baptize in
water, has baptized us. We need no further baptism, Luke
1:13ff.; Matt. 3:1ff.; Luke 3:3; John 1:6. He recognized Christ
in his mother's womb. He was a forerunner of Christ on earth

⁴Hubmaier referred to this Council in *Old and New Teachers*. See above,
text 17, p. 266 and 273.
⁵ "Picards" was a standard designation for Czech Waldenses or Brethren.
Dutch historians (ME IV, p. 168) believe it comes from the Beghards.
Zeman 1969 (p. 162) has better documentation for its derivation from
Picardie, the French province just south of Flanders (also a Waldensian
center) from which refugees had come to Bohemia. Hubmaier's awareness
of their existence and their (alleged) practice of rebaptism was formed
prior to his coming to Moravia. Zeman documents thoroughly the sources
of this awareness.

* Cyprian, *On the Baptising of Heretics*.

and a revealer of the Lamb of God. He could not err, etc." However, regardless of all this, those whom John had already baptized were obliged to be baptized again /335/ with the baptism of Christ. Thus, the Scripture testifies sufficiently in the Acts of the Apostles, reading as follows: "It happened, however, when Apollos was at Corinth, that Paul traveled through the upper territories and came to Ephesus and found several disciples there. To them he said, 'Did you receive the Holy Spirit when you became believers?' They said to him, 'We have never even heard whether there is a Holy Spirit.' And he asked, 'In what name were you then baptized?' They answered, 'In the baptism of John.' Paul then said, 'John baptized with the baptism of repentance and said to the people that they should believe in him who is to come after, that is, in Jesus who is the Christ.' When they heard that they had themselves baptized in the name of the Lord Jesus." Dear Christian, what do you think moved and pushed these twelve men to the baptism of Christ after only the baptism of John? Without doubt, without doubt, nothing other than the high and earnest mandate of Christ, Matt. 28:19; Mark 16:16; Acts 2:38, 41. It follows from that that we who have all been baptized in childhood are much more obligated to let ourselves be baptized rightly according to the institution of Christ than these Ephesians, because we can point out no letter, basis, or mandate at all for our foolish infant baptism in Scripture. It is written in the very Christian epistle of James, "Whoever keeps all the commandments but fails in one point, is guilty of all," James 2:10.

The thirteenth reason. Water baptism is given for the forgiveness of sins, Acts 2:38; 1 Pet. 3:21. It is also understood in the ninth and tenth article of the Christian faith, wherein we confess the general Christian church, communion of saints, and remission of sins.[6] All of this is also the understanding and conclusion of the Council of Nicea, which ended in a Christian manner with these words: "I confess one baptism only for the remission of sins."[7] Therefore, as much as the communion of God the Father, and of the Son, and of the

---

[6] The reference is to the articles of the Apostles' Creed, as numbered by universal tradition and as assumed by Hubmaier in text 21 above, pp. 344.
[7] Schaff 1931:59.

Holy Spirit, yea, also the communion of all the heavenly host and the entire Christian church, and also as much as the forgiveness of sins is important to a person, so much also is water baptism through which he enters and which is embodied in the universal Christian church, outside of which there is no salvation. It is not that forgiveness of sins is a characteristic of the water, but of the power of the keys, which Christ on the authority of his Word commanded in his bodily absence and hung at the side of his bride and immaculate spouse, the Christian church, when he said to her, "Receive the Holy Spirit. To whomever you remit sins, then to these are they remitted, and to whomever you hold them they are kept," John 20:22f. So also Christ says in another place to the church, "Truly I say to you that whatever you bind on earth shall also be bound in heaven, and whatever you release on earth shall also be released in heaven, Matt. 18:18. /336/

Here one notes exactly that the universal church has the power to remit or to bind sins now on earth, which Christ had held previously as a bodily man on earth. Whoever now believes in the Word of God enters into the ark of Noah, which is a proper figure of water baptism, so that he not drown outside of this ark in the flood of sins, 1 Pet. 3:21. However, whoever resists here does not resist me (I am not my own) but the Lord with the winnowing shovel, whose message I have announced. Whoever does not want to unite here with the truth shall indeed be a liar and sometimes speaks a truth without truth.[8]

Pay attention, people, to these thirteen landmarks,[9] which are set forth for you. You see them, and if you trip or fall over them you are guilty and not God. He has done his part, Matt. 18:15-18. The gospel has been preached to you for a testimony. Follow or you will be beaten with many strokes, Luke 12:47. May God grant to us his grace. Amen.

Truth Is Immortal.
Printed at Nicolspurg by
Simprecht Sorg, called Froschauer.
1527

---

[8] I.e., even if he says true things, their meaning in the context of resisting a larger truth cannot be true.

[9] Ger. *zeügnuβtain*, lit. "witness stones."

23

On Fraternal Admonition

Very early in the development of Reformation antipedobaptism, a connection was made between the baptismal pledge and the practice of pastoral admonition. "Without Christ's rule of binding and loosing, even an adult should not be baptized," Conrad Grebel had written to Thomas Müntzer in September 1524.[1]

Hubmaier's "Theses Against Eck" had referred to Matthew 18:15ff. as the churches' reason to be heard "in matters concerning offense or brotherly love."[2] His early "Summa of the Entire Christian Life" had made the pledge to participate in fraternal reconciliation a part of the baptismal commitment.

It is a fitting expansion of that initial vision, that the practice of "the Rule of Christ" should have developed into an independent liturgical entity, a third regular congregational practice to be discharged according to the mandate of Christ, beside baptism and the Supper.[3] Hubmaier's provision of a form for the practice worthily rounds out his liturgical trilogy.[4]

---

[1] Harder, 1985, p. 290.
[2] Above, p. 53.
[3] Cf. Schlabach 1977 and Jess Yoder 1968, pp. 111ff.
[4] There is no way to determine in what time sequence the three companion texts, here numbered 23, 24, and 25, were written and printed. It is likely that all three had been drafted earlier, and were ready for print as soon as Hubmaier had settled into Nikolsburg. Earlier translations in Hošek 1892, pp. 189-193; Davidson 1939, pp. 328ff.; in Vedder 1905, pp. 189ff., and 206f.; and in *Concern: A Pamphlet Series*, number 14 (February 1967), pp. 33ff. An independent translation is that of Durnbaugh: Durnbaugh 1974, pp. 28ff. Source for this translation: HS 18, pp. 338-46.

On Fraternal Admonition
"Where this is lacking,
there is certainly also no church,
even if Water Baptism
and the Supper of Christ
are practiced."
Dr. Balthasar
Hůebmör of Fridberg,
The Truth Is Invincible.
Nikolspurg, 1527.

On Fraternal Admonition

When the people had heard the Word of God, accepted it, believed it, committed itself in water baptism to God publicly before the church:[5]

—henceforth to live according to the command of Christ, and has promised God to be subject to him and in the power of God, Father and Son and Holy Spirit, Matt. 28:10; Mark 16:15; Acts 2:38, to work and to suffer, in fortune and misfortune, in joy and suffering, in living and dying, yea however God may dispose;

—that it desires to accept all things willingly and with Christ to suffer, die, and be buried, Rom. 6:4, in the hope and confidence also to rise again with him by the glory of the Father;

—to walk in newness of life and henceforth not to permit sin to rule in the mortal body nor to be obedient to its desires, but rather to abandon one's members in obedience to God the Lord to be weapons and /339/ an instrument of righteousness that they might become holy and might reach that goal which is eternal life, a gift of God in Christ Jesus our Lord;

---

[5] This following page composition is not in the original; it has been resorted to in order to enable the reader to find the way through the very complex construction of Hubmaier's first sentences.

—and that they would in eternity jubilate "Holy, Holy, Holy!" Rev. 4:8, and sing to him praise, honor and adoration in eternity;

Yea and when, in public confession of Christian faith, and with the receiving of water baptism, the people has let [committing themselves] to do and to complete the same, itself be counted, marked, and incorporated in the fellowship of the holy universal Christian church—outside which there is no salvation, as outside the ark of Noah, Gen. 6; 7; 1 Pet. 3:21; now out of this people a particular visible congregation has been brought into being. A new daughter has been born to her mother, the universal Christian church,[6] which daughter* now fittingly must do the will of her mother, as the mother, i.e., the general Christian church, does the will of her spouse and bridegroom, who is Christ Jesus the Son of the living God, Matt. 16:16; 26:63, whose will he in turn did unto the death. So that thereby the will of God the Father will be done on earth as it is in heaven, Matt. 6:10; Luke 11:2, in like fashion by the beloved Son, mother and daughter.

Whereupon, O you believing Christians, it is always necessary, since human beings are by nature children of wrath, Eph. 2:13; Ps. 14:3; 1 Cor. 15, evil and vicious, to treat them with wholesome medication and in fact sometimes completely to cut off the corrupt and stinking flesh together with the poisoned and unclean members, so that the entire body might not thereby be deformed, shamed, and destroyed, but rather that Christian people progress and persevere in their newly Christian life once begun and not fall back like a wild sow into the mudholes of sin, 2 Pet. 2:22, back again into the wrath of God. All of which cannot be better achieved otherwise than by means of fraternal admonition according to the institution and order of Christ, Matt. 18:15-20.

---

[6] Hubmaier's use of a Latin technical term in the margin shows his concern to hold a consistent systematic understanding of the relation of church universal and local congregation. The mother/daughter imagery is used frequently.

---

* *Ecclesia particularis.*

Yea, God lives and testifies that I tell the truth.[7] Unless fraternal admonition is again restored,[*] accepted, and used according to the earnest behest of Christ, it is not possible that things might proceed aright and stand well[8] among Christians on earth. Even if we should all shout, write, and hear the gospel until we are hoarse and tired, still all our shouting, effort, and industry is in vain and useless. Yes, even water baptism and the breaking of bread are vain, pointless, and fruitless, if fraternal admonition and the Christian ban do not accompany them, admonition belonging to baptism as the ban belongs to communion and fellowship.

This we have clearly seen and manifestly experienced in many places within a few years. In which time people had learned no more than two points, without any amelioration of life.[b] The one point, that they could say: "We believe. Faith saves us." Second: "We can do nothing good of ourselves." Now both of these are true. But under the mantle /340/ of these half truths all kinds of iniquity, unfaithfulness, and injustice have completely taken over, and fraternal love has meanwhile become colder among many, Matt. 24:12, more than in many thousand years. Yea, the common proverb is true and is fulfilled:[c] The older, the more evil. It is getting better; it is getting worse.[9] The older, the colder. The longer the world stands, the more evil it becomes. And we must accept this slap in the face from the godless.

But before God let us lament it—we suffer this through our own fault. For we all want to be Christians and good Protestants by taking wives and eating meat, no longer sacrificing, no more fasting, no more praying, yet apart from

---

[7] Hubmaier is less thorough in avoiding oathlike language than were the Swiss Brethren.

[8] The phrase is a proverbial one: *recht zugehen und wohl stehen.*

[9] Probably these four sentences are all understood as proverbs or as a variation of one proverb. The second couplet is a word play: *bessert* (improve) is aurally near to *bösert* (worsen). The third couplet is also a rhyme.

---

[*] The sum of a Christian life. Where there is no fraternal admonition, there is no church either.

[b] The people have learned two things.

[c] Proverb.

this one sees nothing but tippling, gluttony, blaspheming, usury, lying, deceit, skinning and scraping, coercing, pressing, stealing, robbing, burning, gambling, dancing, flattery, loafing, fornication, adultery, rape, tyranny, strangling, murder. Here all the frivolity and insolence of the flesh finds free play; here the luxury of this world has the place of honor, rules, jubilates, and triumphs in all things.

Here no Christian deeds shine forth from anyone. Brotherly love and faithfulness is utterly extinct. Yet all of this (as painful as it is to say it) comes to pass behind the facade of the gospel. For as soon as you say to such "evangelical" people: "Brother, it stands written, forsake evil and do good," immediately he answers, "It stands written, we can do no good. Everything comes to pass according to the providence of God and necessarily." They think that thereby sin is permitted them. If you say further, "It stands written, they who do evil shall go into eternal fire," John 5:29, immediately they reach for a fan of fig leaves, Gen. 3:7, to cover their vice with, and say, "But it stands written: faith alone saves us and not our works."

Thanks to such devious argument we are after all good evangelicals, and know how skillfully and masterfully to cite, decorate, and embroider holy Scripture, like the friends of Job and like the devil, Matt. 4,[10] to cover over the self-willed license and shamelessness of our flesh.[*]

But if fraternal admonition were to be restored among us, such excuses and counterfeit embellishment of our sins and vices would soon be uncovered and made an end to. Let us with the help of God undertake fraternal admonition not only in teaching but also with the hand and in deed. May God graciously accord us his grace and the strength to achieve the same. /341/ Then the old Adam will just begin to raise his ears, to grumble, to buck, to snort, and to kick out before and behind.

For he can absolutely not accept such admonition. He wants to be a Christian and yet above being reproached. But

---

[10] The reference to the temptation account of Matt. 4 is in the text.

---

[*] Good and evangelical with the mouth. In words whatever you wish; in deeds nothing but chaff [the latter couplet in Latin].

in the power of the Holy Spirit we will show him something quite different and we beg of his inborn pride that he give us a gracious hearing. But in case he should not want to accept this now, he will have to let it happen at the last judgment. Hereby we will have preserved our honor and conscience toward everyone.

Christ Jesus our Lord and Savior always and in every way brought forth great effort and earnestness in order to uproot and to suppress the vices among his people, by which many are offended, made more evil, and robbed of eternal life. He says, "Woe, woe to the world because of scandal! Woe, woe to him through whom scandal comes. It were better for him that a millstone were hanged around his neck and he were thrown into the sea than that he should offend one of these little ones. Watch out," Matt. 18:7; Luke 17:2. "But if your brother sins against you, go and admonish him between yourself and him alone. If he hears you, you have won your brother. If he does not hear you, take with you one or two others, so that every case be determined by the mouth of two or three witnesses. If he does not hear them either, tell it to the congregation. If he does not hear the congregation, consider him as a heathen and a tax gatherer. Verily I tell you, what you shall bind on earth shall be bound in heaven, and what you shall loose on earth shall be loosed in heaven," Matt. 18.

Here Christian reader, in the words "against thee" or "into thee" should be noticed that there are two kinds of sin, public and secret. Public: Those which are committed shamelessly before all men.ᵃ These sins should be reprimanded also publicly and immediately, so that no one else among the pious and simple people may be misled nor seduced and might say, "If it's all right for him, then it's also all right for me"—as the common people have done and lived until now in fornication and all adultery, because they saw that their maos priests[11] and rulers led the same kind of life.

Similarly, as soon as the pope had allowed the spiritless crowd and foundations to take five gulden (and a little more)

---

[11] For the pun mass/maos cf. above texts 19 note 8, p. 302, 21 note 13, p. 343, and below 26 note 12, p. 422.

ᵃ Open sin.

per hundred, counter to the bright and clear word of Christ, Luke 6:30, then others as well have done the same and in fact made a respectable business out of it. Scandal is such an evil sin, it eats away all around itself like cancer and leprosy, if it is not hastily uprooted through fraternal admonition.[12] Wherefore Paul teaches us, writing: "They who sin publicly, reprove them before all, so that the others might fear," 1 Tim. 5:20. /342/

Likewise Christ reprimanded Peter in a humane and well-intentioned way, when he had pleaded with him in just a few words that he should take care of himself and not go to Jerusalem, so that no evil might befall him. Immediately Christ said to him, "Get away from me, Satan, you are a stumbling block to me, for you think not what is godly but what is human," Matt. 16:23. Similarly Peter reproved Simon, because he wanted to buy the Holy Spirit from the apostles with money, and said, "May you be damned with your money, because you think God's gift can be obtained with money. You shall have no part or share in this word, for your heart is not sincere before God; so repent of this thy wrongness and pray to God." Acts 8:20.

Yet let every Christian take heed to himself that such remonstrance and sharpness of the word might flow forth out of love and not from envy, hate, or wrath, as we see in the words of Peter, when he desires the correction of Simon and says, "Repent." In just the same way Paul also reproached Peter, when he saw that he was not behaving according to the truth of the gospel, and said, "If you, who are a Jew, live as a Gentile, and not Jewishly, why then do you force the Gentiles to live as Jews?" Gal. 2:14. Yes, Paul withstood Peter publicly to the face, because he was reprehensible.

But some sins are private, which are committed in stillness and hiddenness.* Such sins should also be reproved privately according to the command of Christ. Thus Nathan the prophet reproved King David, and Christ reproved Judas the

---

[12] The quality of "scandal" is independent of the particular deed. What is wrong is that there is offense, a bad example.

---

* Secret sin.

betrayer, in front of the disciples it is true, but by a hidden manner of speech, 2 Sam. 12:7; Matt. 26:24. If your brother then hears you, obeys your admonition, and forsakes the sin, then with one act you have profited more than all the merchants of Venice in their whole life.[a]

Should he not hear you, then take one or two with you for the sake of testimony. If he will not hear them either, then tell it to the congregation. Thereby you are doing the will and following the earnest command of Christ, who in one commandment has bound together two salutary commands. Namely, that he first has commanded you to admonish your brother or else you are participant in his sins; but with these same words he has commanded your brother to accept fraternal admonition from you meekly and honorably. If he does this, it is unto salvation; if he does not, then you are from this point on innocent before God of his sin.

At this point carnal wisdom (to which all words of God are poison and gall)[b] grumbles and says, "This does not seem right to me, that my brother should make manifest my private sins. He would not want me to do that to him; accordingly he should reasonably also spare me the same and much rather help me to cover over my sins."

Answer: This is why he reprimanded you between himself and yourself alone so that your sin would not become manifest. But you did not want to hear him, therefore according to the command of Christ he had to bring with him two or three, once again hoping to be able to win your soul, so that you might not need to be ashamed /343/ before the whole congregation. When you refused to accept the same, only then did he have to go on and bring it before the church. For the command of Christ and the salvation of your soul were of deeper concern to him than your temporal, false, and hypocritical honor and piety, wishing that you might be considered righteous when you were unrighteous. For it is still much better for you to be shamed in front of a particular congregation than before the church universal and all the heavenly hosts at the last judgment. For what is ever so pri-

---

[a] "Hear" means "obey."
[b] Admonition tastes bad to the flesh.

vate will be made public and especially all sin must absolutely be put to shame, Matt. 10:26.

Since then you did not want to hear the church either, then it was better for you that you should be excluded and considered as a pagan, rather than that you would bring to shame the whole church through scandal, and that you might have seduced other members with yourself into sin and eternal perdition. It was also more profitable for you, for the reason that you might come to awareness, recognize your misery, abstain from sins, and then be received again by the church with great joy and admitted into her Christian fellowship.

You see, righteous Christian, how useful and salutary is brotherly admonition to him who recognizes its wholesomeness and who honestly accepts it.[a] Yet flesh, blood, and the soulish man[13] cannot grasp this. He wants ever to be looked on as pious and be reprimanded by no one. But he who is spiritual judges all things, 1 Cor. 2:15. But such admonition and exclusion is not only good for one according to the nature of the case, but it would also be much better for him that a millstone be hung around his neck and he be thrown into the sea than that he should give the very least offense or scandal in the church and pile sin upon sin, Matt. 18:6.

Now since fraternal admonition and the Christian ban proceed from such inner, heartfelt and fervent love, which one Christian should have daily toward another in true faithfulness, therefore he must be a most ignorant, wild and godless monster, yea a grim Herod, Mark 6:14ff.; Matt. 14:1ff., who would not accept such admonition from his brethren in a friendly and kind way, and with thanksgiving.

One thing more you must know, faithful reader. That in these matters there are two kinds of commandment.[b] The first orders each Christian in particular to admonish his sinning brother according to the order of Christ, Matt. 18:15f. The other commands the admonisher, that he must first take

[13] *Seelisch*, i.e., driven by the vitality of the natural *anima*.

[a] Fraternal admonition is a healing poultice.
[b] Two kinds of command about admonition.

the plank out of his own eye in order to be able to see to
remove the splinter which is in the eye of his brother, Matt.
7:4f; Luke 6:42.

This now is the true order of Christ, which should be
practiced just in this way. But the first commandment is not
done away with by the second. For it is better to fulfill one
commandment than to neglect them both. /344/ Therefore no
one can be excused who would fail to admonish his brother
simply because he himself is a sinner,[a] for in this way
brotherly admonition would completely collapse. Rather, the
greatest sinner of all is obligated to admonish his brother, or
else through his silence he makes himself also a participant in
the guilt of another.

This is what Isaiah called being companions of thieves, Is.
1:22. David calls it consorting with thieves and partaking with
adulterers, Ps. 50:18. I say this for this reason: under the
appearance of recognizing that we are all sinners, no one was
willing anymore to admonish others, nor to accept admonition,
and thus fraternal admonition was completely smothered and
turned to ashes.

How to Admonish One Another

According to Scripture it shall proceed as follows:[b]

Brother! It stands written that everyone must give an
account on the judgment day for every vain word that they
have spoken, Matt. 12:36. Now dear brother, you made a baptismal vow to Christ Jesus our Lord. You committed yourself
to him in such way, and publicly pledged it before the church,
that you would henceforth desire to direct and rule your life
according to his Holy Word (to which Scripture testifies); and
that if you should not do so, you would willingly let yourself
be admonished according to the command of Christ. Thereupon you received water baptism and were numbered in the
membership of the Christian community.

Now you are using much vain language and frivolous
speech, whereby good morals are seriously destroyed, as is not

---

[a] We are all sinners.
[b] The form of admonition.

fitting for a Christian man, 1 Cor. 15:33.[14] I therefore remind
you of your baptismal vow, my very dearest brother, that you
would call to memory what you promised to God, and I beg
you for the sake of God and of the salvation of your soul
henceforth to avoid such frivolous talk and to improve your
life. Thereby you are doing the will of God.

If now your brother ceases to sin, you have won a precious jewel. If he does not, then take two or three witnesses
with you and try once more in the same words. If he will not
hear them either, then say it to the parish[15] congregation,
which will know how to proceed. Deal in the same way with
all other sins.

If further you notice, Christian man, that one brother has
something against another, be it envy, hate or any other kind
of enmity, bring them together and hold before them the
teaching of Christ, who says, Matt. 5:23f.: "If you are offering
your gift on the altar and there you become aware that your
brother has something against you, leave the gift at the altar
and go, reconcile yourself first with your brother, then come
and offer your gift." For God does not wish to receive or
accept graciously anything from us, so long as we still bear
enmity against our neighbor. Thus reconcile them between
/345/ yourself and both of them. But if they will not hear you,
then proceed as was indicated above with fraternal admonition.

Verily, verily, where this happens, here God will stand
powerfully and wonderfully by his Word in such a way that
the Christian brethren and the fellowship will be able to
reconcile and conciliate such great causes and disunities, as
could not have been judged in many years at great cost and
with great damage.* The party which refuses, the same God
will punish with such measure that for ten gulden he will lose
one hundred, yea even body and life. God is so strong that he
is peaceful with the peaceable and contentious with the contentious. He can punish contention with contention.

---

[14] It is noteworthy that the specimen sin Hubmaier chooses is that of the
tongue.

[15] *Pfarr Kirche.* I.e., the institutional or "parish" church.

---

* Here the jurists will have an excuse.

Such exhortation and admonition, Christian brethren, cannot occur in a better way than according to the precedent of the Word of God, that is with the Ten Commandments, Exod. 10; Deut. 5, and other Christian teachings, Matt. 5; 6; 7; Rom. 12. For these things are written, as Paul says, for our exhortation, upon whom the end of the world has come, 1 Cor. 10:11. And elsewhere: All scripture given by God is useful for teaching, for admonition, for betterment, for discipline in righteousness, that a man of God might be unchanging, apt for every good work, 2 Tim. 3:16.

Now we see clearly whence the authority arises that one brother has the power and the right to admonish another.[a] Namely from the baptismal commitment, which a person gave before receiving water baptism, in which he subjected himself, according to the order of Christ, to the church and all her members. This is something which the antichrist and his troop cannot stand.[b] He would[16] be fully infallible, free and blameless, even if he daily leads a great crowd of souls into hell. Yet let no one say to him: Why do you do thus? For this reason he has overturned the proper baptismal pledge and water baptism itself, because they were unreconcilable with his pride, pomp, and avarice. But still he wants to be counted as a baptized Christian in the church, yes in fact to be a head of the church, and cannot accept that anyone would say to him: "Brother Pope, Brother Bishop, Brother Kaiser, King, Prince, or Lord, you are in error and sinning against God."

This is why the antichrist has day and night put forth such a remarkable effort in order to empty out Christ's water baptism for him and replace it with his counterfeit, miserable anti-Christian infant baptism. So that, if someone would faithfully remind him of his sacramental baptismal confession and commitment, he could easily excuse himself by saying, "But I was a child, I didn't understand Latin, I didn't promise anything, nor did I even know then what a pledge, faith, Christ, baptism, or fraternal admonition are."[c] But, you anti-

---

[16] I.e., he makes the claim to be.

---

[a] Whence comes the authority for one to admonish another.
[b] Why the antichrist emptied out Christian baptism, *Dist. 40; si papa.*
[c] A miserable excuse.

Christian crowd, such an excuse will not help you, for the gospel has been preached in all the world as a testimony to you, Matt. 24:14. No one can talk himself out of it.

He who then will loosen the smallest of the commandments of Christ, he will be the least in the kingdom of heaven, Matt. 5:19. Woe, woe, woe to all those /346/ who have dissolved and abused the water baptism of Christ, fraternal admonition, the Lord's Supper, and the Christian ban. They who rightly practice and teach the commands of Christ, blessed, blessed, blessed are they for they will be called great, great in the kingdom of heaven.

So all of those who cry: "Well, what about water baptism? Why, all the fuss about the Lord's Supper? They are after all just outward signs! They're nothing but water, bread, and wine! Why fight about that?"[a] They have not in their whole life learned enough to know why the signs were instituted by Christ, what they seek to achieve òr toward what they should finally be directed, namely to gather a church, to commit oneself ·publicly to live according to the Word of Christ in faith and brotherly love, and because of sin to subject oneself to fraternal admonition and the Christian ban, and to do all of this with a sacramental oath before the Christian church and all her members, assembled partly in body and completely in spirit, testifying publicly, in the power of God, Father and Holy Spirit, or in the power of our Lord Jesus Christ (which is all the same power), and yielding oneself to her in hand-pledged fidelity. Look to this, dear brethren, and not to water, bread or wine, lest our water baptism and breaking bread might also be only an appearance and a sleight of hand, nothing better than what the stupid child baptism and baby feeding[17] have been before, if fraternal admonition and the Christian ban do not constantly accompany them.[b]

---

[17] *Pappen*; the way one feeds soft food to an infant, deprecatory reference to the eucharistic communicating of children.

---

[a] The complaint is not about water, bread, and wine, but about Christ's command. *The use of signs.* What is the ultimate goal of baptism and the Supper [italics indicate Latin original].

[b] Fraternal admonition must be reinstated, or everything is hypocrisy and in vain.

In sum: Where water baptism is not given according to the order of Christ, there it is impossible to accept fraternal admonition from one another in a good spirit. For no one knows either who is in the church and who is outside. No one has authority over another, we are scattered to the winds, like sheep without shepherds, without a pasture, without markings, neither knowing nor being able to recognize who has let himself be marked as a sheep of Christ, or who chooses to remain as a wild buck outside the flock of Christ. May God help us all, that we might enter into the sheepfold of Christ through the right door, John. 10:2, and not climb in elsewhere against the express ordering of Christ. Amen.

Truth Is Unkillable.
1527

24

A Form for Water Baptism

As with On Fraternal Admonition, *we have here to do with the ripe fruit of both Hubmaier's thought and his experience. He publishes as a model for ecclesiastical practice forms which he has already been using in Nikolsburg, after having evolved them ever since his early days in Waldshut.[1] The reference to usage in Nikolsburg suggests final redaction in the fall of 1526.[2]*

A Form for Baptism in Water
of Those who have been Instructed in Faith
Dr. Balthasar Hubmor of Fridberg
Nicolspurg
Truth Is Unkillable.
1527

Preface
To the noble, firm
Lord Jan Dubschanskij of Zdenyn
and from Habrowan.[3]
Grace, joy, and peace in God,
Noble Christian Lord,

---

[1] That he prepared his own liturgical form was already indicated in his January letter to Oekclampad (text 6, p. 69 above).

[2] Excerpts in Hošek 1892, pp. 132-134; Vedder 1905, pp. 202, 211; Armour 1966, pp. 43, 143f., 243f.; Klaassen 1981, p. 121, 168. Source: HS 19, pp. 348-352.

[3] Dubcansky was a nobleman of Zwinglian leanings, who since 1520 had been attempting like Zinzendorf two centuries later to unite the several streams of the Reformation. After Hubmaier's death Dubcansky founded his own small church. Zeman 1969, pp. 102ff. and 165ff., draws out the meaning of the several dedications of Hubmaier texts to noblemen.

I send Your Majesty the form for water baptism as we practice the same in Nicolsburg and elsewhere. Might Your Majesty discuss and confer about it with Milords John Sylvanus, Christian Entfelder, churchmen in Ewantzig,[4] and with other Christian brethren, whether this form is found conformed to Scripture. Not that we have any doubt /349/ of this, but so that all might see that we have thus far not been running in vain, and that our deeds have been right, appropriate, and fitting, by virtue of Scripture. We also ask the right hereby[a] to give account of the same publicly with the Word of God.[5] If, however, violence should be done to us despite this offer and counter to justice, may the will of God be done, we wish to live and die unto him.[6] But woe to all those who would wash their rapacious[7] hands in our innocent blood. Herewith we commit Your Grace to God.

Your Majesty's willing [servant]
Balthasar Hubmor of Fridberg.

Whoever Desires Water Baptism[8]

should first present himself to his bishop, that he may be questioned,[b] whether he is sufficiently instructed in the articles of the law, gospel, faith, and the doctrines which concern a new Christian life. Also how he can pray and speak with understanding the articles of the Christian faith,[9] all of which must necessarily be known first if one wishes to be in-

---

[4] Jan Silvan was a Slovakian poet and preacher with Protestant sympathies. He remained in the Czech country and may have died Catholic. Entfelder was later an active dissenter at Strasbourg, 1529-33. Cf. Seguenny 1980, 37ff. This reference by Hubmaier is the only indication that they were both once ecclesiastics at Ewantzig/Eibenschitz/Ivancice.
[5] The phrase in the margin is the same as the title to our text 1 above.
[6] An unidentified allusion to Rom. 14:8.
[7] Literally "flesh-lusting."
[8] The words set as subtitle are at the same time the beginning of the following sentence.
[9] I.e., specifically the Apostles' Creed.

---

[a] Christian challenge [*erbiettung*].
[b] Testing.

corporated into the congregation of Christians through outward baptism for the forgiveness of his sins. If he can do this, the bishop presents him to the church, calling on all brothers and sisters to fall to their knees, to call upon God with fervent devotion, that he might graciously impart to this person the grace and the power of his Holy Spirit and complete in him what he has begun through his Holy Spirit and divine Word.

Thus:

"Come, Holy Spirit, fill the hearts of thy believers, kindle the fire of thy love in them, thou who hast assembled by manifold tongues, the peoples into the unity of faith. Hallelujah, hallelujah. God be praised. God be praised."

Here the bishop holds forth the baptismal pledge* thus:

"Jan.[10] Do you believe in God the Father Almighty, Creator of heaven and earth? If so, speak publicly":

"I believe."

"Do you believe in Jesus Christ his only begotten Son our Lord, who was conceived of the Holy Spirit, born of the Virgin Mary, suffered under Pontius Pilate, crucified, /350/ dead and buried, that he went in the Spirit and preached the gospel to the spirits which were in prison, 1 Pet. 3:19; 4:6, that on the third day he again united with the body in the grave and powerfully arose from the dead, 1 Cor. 15:4; Acts 2:32, and after forty days ascended into heaven. There he sits at the right hand of his almighty Father, whence he will come to judge the living and the dead? if so speak":

"I believe."

"Do you also believe in the Holy Spirit, and do you believe a holy universal Christian church, a fellowship of the saints, that the same possesses the keys for the remission of sins. Do you believe also the resurrection of the flesh and eternal life? If so, speak":

"I believe."

"Will you in the power of Christ renounce the devil, all his works, machinations, and vanities, then speak":

---

[10] Literally, the text of each of these vows is stated conditionally: "If you believe ... then speak."

---

* The baptismal pledge.

"I will."

"Will you henceforth lead your life and walk according to the Word of Christ, as he gives you grace: So speak":

"I will."

"If now you should sin and your brother knows it, will you let him admonish you once, twice, and the third time before the church, and willingly and obediently accept fraternal admonition, if so speak":

"I will."

"Do you desire now upon this faith and pledge to be baptized in water according to the institution of Christ, incorporated and thereby counted in the visible Christian church, for the forgiveness of your sins, if so speak":

"I desire it in the power of God."

"I baptize you in the name of the Father and the Son and Holy Spirit for the forgiveness of your sins, Matt. 18:19; Acts 2:38. Amen, so be it."

Now let the bishop again exhort his church to pray for the baptized neophyte, that God will increase his faith and that of all Christian men and give to us all strength and constance, that we might all persevere and be found at the end in Christian faith.

After the church has completed this prayer,[11] the bishop lays his hands on the head of the new member[a] and says:

"I testify to you and give you authority that henceforth you shall be counted among the Christian community, as a member participating in the use of her keys, breaking bread and praying with other Christian sisters and brothers. God be with you and your spirit. Amen."

The first error,[b] O Christian reader, which you recognize here, is that hitherto all of us in all of Europe, with the only exception (as I hear) of the Picards, the Russians, the Moscovites, and the Walachians,[12] have missed the path of truth

---

[11] It seems that this congregational prayer was silent.

[12] Walachia is a southern province of Romania. "Picard" was a current popular designation for the Czech Brethren. Cf. above, text 22, p. 369, note 5.

---

[a] Laying on of hands.

[b] The first error. Picards, Russians, Muscovites, Wallachians.

most crude, in that we have baptized children, although it was no baptism, since they did not yet know what God, Christ, baptism, faith, or vow is. But so it is; the great, red, seven-headed /351/ ten-horned dragon[a] stands unceasingly before the pregnant woman, who is in travail of childbirth, waiting, when she gives birth, hastily to swallow up the infant. But if he is not able to succeed in this, then the serpent shoots a torrent of water from its mouth at the woman to drown her.

The second error;[b] that nearly everywhere the Supper of Christ has been restored and (so-called) communion given to people "in both kinds," and yet there was preceding this no baptism, which is counter to clear Scripture, which indicates this sequence: first preaching, second faith, third confession, fourth water baptism,[c] fifth the breaking of bread, Acts 2:42 and other texts. But Satan can well stand to have us build something up today and break it down again after a short time, for thereby many persons are seriously weakened, confused, and scandalized,[d] so that they no longer know at all what they are supposed to believe or practice.

Yes indeed, says our carnal wisdom, which in such matter above all does not want to look like a fool: "We must have forbearance[e] with the weak.[13] Right now it is not fitting to preach that. In a while it will be fitting. Now I preach what, if I had preached it a year ago, I would long ago have been chased out. But now I am still with my sheep." O you of little faith, you are speaking as if it was through your own counsel that the people have stood by the Word of God, and that God would not have been able to sustain it.[f] Here you rob the divine Word of its power and of the efficacy which is ascribed to it everywhere in Scripture, Isa. 40:8; 55:11; Gen. 1; Jer. 6; 23:29; Heb. 4:12; Rom. 1. But so that one can tell when to

---

[13] For the specific meaning of "forbearance" as compromise, cf. J. Yoder, 1968, pp. 52, 141, 193.

---

[a] Antichrist; Rev. 12:3.
[b] The second error.
[c] Which is to build a house without a foundation.
[d] Offense [i.e., scandal, cause of stumbling].
[e] Forbearing, going slow, creeping.
[f] Preach the word and then let God act.

exercise forbearance and when not, let me this time establish this rule.[*]

In those things which have to do with human practices, such as eating meat or not eating meat, holding or not holding holidays, etc., one may well forbear and do or admit something for the sake of the weak, but only for a time until our neighbor is better instructed in the Word of God, and so that Christian freedom should not be made into a new human law. But in true doctrine and in Christian deeds, one must freely proclaim and do what God has commanded us and not otherwise, and trust again to the Word of God for its efficacy, even if the whole world were to fall away again. For it is much better that a person should fall than that the Word should fall, for by the Word it will be very easy for him, as with Jacob's ladder, to be helped up again. Thus Christ himself did with the teaching on food, Matt. 15:17ff. and with the eating of his flesh, John 6:53ff. He does not ask whether the Jews and the disciples are offended but speaks out freely the Word of truth, whoever might fall away from him or toward him. /352/

The third error:[b] That we have called the water of baptism, like the bread and the wine of the altar, a "sacrament";[c] and held it to be such, although not the water, bread, or wine, but in the fact that the baptismal commitment or the pledge of love is really and truly "sacrament" in the Latin; i.e., a commitment by oath and a pledge given by the hand which the one baptized makes to Christ, our invincible Prince and Head, that he is willing to fight bravely unto the death in Christian faith under his flag and banner.

But since this oath is made to Christ himself, who abides in all eternity, one who has been once baptized should not be baptized again,[d] as did the Novatians and Hemerobaptists.[14]

---

[14] The historiography of the time regularly referred to "hemerobaptists," who were supposed to have repeated baptism daily. It is not clear whether such a group existed. It may have been a mental construct arising from the notion that each sin destroys the effect of one's previous baptism.

---

[*] Rule for forbearance.
[b] The third error.
[c] Sacrament.
[d] Rebaptism is wrong.

But since the counterfeit infant baptism is no baptism, those who now receive water baptism according to the order of Christ cannot be accused of rebaptism, even if in their childhood and in the blindness of their fathers they were washed in water before. May Christ Jesus open our eyes with the salve of mud and spittle, and send us again to the right baptism in the water of Siloa, that henceforth we might attend only to his Word and walk after him. To this end may God help us all. Amen.

25

A Form for Christ's Supper

A Form for Christ's Supper completes the trilogy of Hubmaier's mature liturgical writings, published during the few months' respite at Nikolsburg when there was a context for properly structuring congregational life and practice. These three texts and the preceding catechism constitute a rounded picture of Anabaptist church life, unique among the documents of that century. They capsule and concretize the import of the earlier polemic texts.

The value of this text was recognized early in the course of the modern rediscovery of Anabaptism. It was one of the first old texts to be reprinted,[1] to be translated,[2] and one of the still fewer to be adapted for contemporary use.[3]

Form
of the Supper
of Christ
Dr. Balthasar Hübmör of Fridberg
Truth Is Unkillable.
1527
A Form of the Supper of Christ

1. The brethren and sisters who wish to hold the table of the Lord according to the institution of Christ, Matt. 26:26ff.; Luke 22:19ff.; Mark 14:22ff.; 1 Cor. 11:23ff., shall gather at a

---

[1] Reprint in *Mittheilungen dem Antiquariate von S.* Calvary & Co., Berlin, 1870, pp. 112ff.

[2] Hošek 1892, pp. 142-147. McGlothlin 1906.

[3] Early excerpts of the present translation were adapted and published by C. J. Dyck, "Teaching Anabaptist History and Theology," in *The Mennonite*, April 21, 1981, p. 247. Fragments in Vedder 1905, p. 202. Source: HS 20, pp. 355-365.

suitable place and time, so there may be no division, so that one does not come early and another late and that thereby evangelical teaching is neglected. Such the apostles desired when they asked Christ, "Master, where wilt thou that we prepare the passover lamb?" Then he set for them a certain place. Paul writes, "When you come together ... etc.," 1 Cor. 11:20ff. Then they should prepare the table with ordinary bread and wine. Whether the cups are silver, wood, or pewter, makes no difference. But those who eat should be respectably dressed and should sit together in an orderly way without light talk and contention, 1 Pet. 3:3; Eph. 4:29; Heb. 12.[4]

2. Since everyone should begin by accusing himself and confessing his sins and recognizing his guilt before God, it is not inappropriate that the priest first of all should fall on his knees with the church and with heart and mouth say the following words:

"Father we have sinned against heaven and against thee Luke 15:21.[5] We are not worthy to be called thy children. But speak a word of consolation and our souls will be made whole. God be gracious to us sinners, Luke 19:1ff. May the almighty, eternal and gracious God have mercy on all our sins and forgive us graciously, and when he has forgiven us, lead us into eternal life without blemish or impurity, through Jesus Christ our Lord and Savior. Amen.

3. Now let the priest sit down with the people and open his mouth, explaining the Scriptures concerning Christ, Luke 24:31,[6] so that the eyes of those who are gathered together may be opened, which were still somewhat darkened or closed /356/, so that they may recognize Christ, who was a man, a prophet, mighty in works and teaching before God and all people, and how the highest bishops among the priests and princes gave him over to condemnation to death and how they

---

[4] The verse intended in Hebrews is not clear; perhaps 10:25 is meant.

[5] In his liturgical texts Hubmaier refers to the presiding person sometimes as "priest" and sometimes as "bishop." No distinction is intended.

[6] That the "priest" is seated "with the people" may represent an intentional innovation in liturgical form. He is not standing at the pulpit, but at the table. Or it may only mean that as he had previously knelt "with the church," now they take their seats at the same time. The following lines allude again to the Emmaus road story, thus placing this teaching in a resurrection context.

crucified him, and how he has redeemed Israel, that is, all
believers. The priest shall also rebuke those who are foolish
and slow to believe all the things that Moses and the prophets
have spoken, that he may kindle and make fervent and warm
the hearts of those at the table, that they may be afire in fervent meditation of his bitter suffering and death in contemplation, love, and thanksgiving, so that the congregation
with its whole heart, soul, and strength calls out to him:[7]

Stay with us, O Christ! It is toward evening and the day is
now far spent. Abide with us, O Jesus, abide with us. For
where thou art not, there everything is darkness, night, and
shadow, but thou art the true Sun, light, and shining brightness, John 8:12. He to whom thou dost light the way, cannot
go astray.

On another day the servant of the Word may take the
10th or 11th chapter of Paul's First Epistle to the Corinthians,
or the 13th, 14th, 15th, 16th, or 17th chapter of John. Or
Matthew 3 or Luke 3 on changing one's life, Sirach 2 on the
fear of God, or something else according to the opportuneness
of the time and persons.[8] No one shall be coerced herein, but
each should be left free to the judgment of his spirit. But
there must be diligence so that the death of the Lord is
earnestly proclaimed, so that the people have a picture of the
boundless goodness of Christ, and the church may be
instructed, edified, and led, in heartfelt fervent and fraternal
love, so that on the last day we may stand before the judgment seat of Christ with the accounts of our stewardship,
Luke 16:8, and shepherd and sheep may be held together.

4. Now that the death of Christ has been proclaimed,
those who are present have the opportunity and the authority
to ask, if at any point they should have some misunderstanding or some lack, 1 Cor. 14:26ff;[9] but not with frivolous,

---

[7] Indentation by the editors.

[8] That these alternative passages suggested for the homily may include
the apocryphal Sirach is significant. As McGlothlin points out, great freedom is left to the local leader. Cf. McGlothlin 1906, p. 96.

[9] The term *mangel* (literally "lack") may mean either a gap in one's
knowledge or an offense/dissatisfaction. This reference to the congregational reconciliation process points us back to Hubmaier's earliest works;
cf. above, texts 3,4, and 5.

unprofitable, or argumentative chatter, nor concerning
heavenly matters having to do with the omnipotence or the
mystery of God or future things, which we have no need to
know, but concerning proper, necessary, and Christian items,
having to do with Christian faith and brotherly love. Then one
to whom something is revealed should teach, and the former
should be quiet without any argument and quarreling. For it is
not customary to have conflict in the church.[10] Let women
keep silence in the congregation. If they want to learn anything, they should ask their husbands at home, so that everything takes place in orderly fashion, 1 Cor. 11; 14.

5. Let the priest take up for himself the words of Paul, 1
Cor. 11, and say:*

> Let every one test and examine himself, and let him thus
> eat /357/ of the bread and drink of the drink.[11] For whoever
> eats and drinks unworthily, eats and drinks a judgment upon
> himself, as he does not discern the body of the Lord. And if
> we thus judged ourselves, we would not be condemned by
> the Lord.

Now such examination comprises the following: First, that
one believes, Matt. 26:26ff.; Mark 14:22ff.; Luke 22:19f.; 1
Cor. 11:24ff., utterly and absolutely that Christ gave his body
and shed his crimson blood for him on the cross in the power
of his words, as he said: "This is my body, which is given for
you, and this is my blood, which is shed for you for the forgiveness of your sins."

Second: Let a person test himself, whether he has a
proper inward and fervent hunger for the bread which comes
down from heaven, from which one truly lives, and thirst for

---

[10] McGlothlin writes that the meaning of the phrase, "it is not customary
to have conflict in the church," is not clear. The above paragraph is a
digest of the procedural guidance of 1 Cor. 11 and 14, and this particular
sentence alludes to 11:16.

[11] Hubmaier seems intentionally to avoid the term *kelch* (cup or chalice).
He says either *trank* (drink, as here) or *trinkgeschirr* (vessel), depending
on the context. A smoother English would render both by "cup"; we retain
here the more literal, clumsier terms. He uses *kelch* only when citing the
words of Jesus.

---

* How one should examine onself.

the drink which flows into eternal life, to eat and drink both in the spirit, faith, and truth, as Christ teaches us in John 4; 6; and 7. If the spiritual eating and drinking does not first take place, then the outward breaking of bread, eating and drinking is a killing letter, 2 Cor. 3:6; 1 Cor. 11:29, hypocrisy, and the kind of food and drink whereby one eats condemnation and drinks death, as Adam did with the forbidden fruit of the tree in Paradise, Gen. 3:6.

Third: Let one also confirm himself in gratitude, so as to be thankful in words and deeds toward God for the great, overabundant, and unspeakable love and goodness that he has shown him through his most beloved Son, our Lord Jesus Christ, John 3:16; Rom. 8:32. Namely that he now gives praise and thanks from the heart to God. Further, that he be of an attitude and ready will to do for Christ his God and Lord in turn as he had done for him. But since Christ does not need our good deeds, is not hungry, is not thirsty, is not naked or in prison, but heaven and earth are his and all that is in them, therefore he points us toward our neighbor, first of all to the members of the household of faith, Matt. 25:34ff.; Gal. 6:10; 1 Tim. 5, that we might fulfill the works of this our gratitude toward them physically and spiritually, feeding the hungry, giving drink to the thirsty, clothing the naked, consoling the prisoner, sheltering the needy. Then he will be ready to accept these works of mercy from us in such a way as if we had done them unto him. Yea, he will say at the last judgment, "I was hungry and you fed me. I was thirsty and you gave me drink. I was naked, in prison, and homeless, and you clothed me, visited me, and housed me," Matt. 25. He says I, I, I, me, me, me.* From this it is certain and sure that all the good that we do to the very least of his, that we do to Christ himself. Yea, he will not let a single drink of cool water go unrewarded, Matt. 10:42. If one is thus inclined /358/ toward his neighbor, he is now in the true fellowship of Christ, a member of his body, and a fellow member with all godly persons, Col. 1:4.

Fourth: So that the church might also be fully aware of a person's attitude and will, one holds fellowship with her in

---

* I, I, I, me, me, me.

the breaking of bread, thereby saying, testifying, and publicly assuring her, yea, making to her a sacrament or a sworn pledge[a] and giving one's hand on the commitment that one is willing henceforth to offer one's body and to shed one's blood thus for one's fellow believers. This one does not out of human daring, like Peter, Matt. 26:33, but in the grace and power of the suffering and the blood shed by our Lord Jesus Christ, his (i.e., meaning Peter's) only Savior, of whose suffering and death the human being is now celebrating a living commemoration in the breaking of bread and the sharing of the chalice.

This is the true fellowship of saints, 1 Cor. 10:16. It is not a fellowship for the reason that bread is broken, but rather the bread is broken because the fellowship has already taken place and has been concluded inward in the spirit, since Christ has come into flesh, John 4:27. For not all who break bread are participants in the body and blood of Christ, which I can prove by the traitor Judas, Matt. 26:25. But those who are partakers inwardly and of the spirit, the same may also worthily partake outwardly of this bread and wine.

A parable: We do not believe because we have been baptized in water, but we are baptized in water because we first believe. So David says: "I have believed, therefore I have spoken," Ps. 116:10; Matt. 16:16; Acts 8:30. So every Christian speaks equally: "I have believed, therefore I have publicly confessed that Jesus is Christ, Son of the living God, and have thereafter had myself baptized according to the order of Christ, the high priest who lives in eternity." Or: "I have fellowship with Christ and all his members, 1 Cor. 10:16, therefore I break bread with all believers in Christ according to the institution of Christ." Without this inner communion in the spirit and in truth, the outward breaking of bread is nothing but an Iscariotic and damnable hypocrisy. It is precisely to this fellowship and commitment of love that the Supper of Christ points,[b] as a living memorial of his suffering and death for us, spiritually signified and pointed to by the breaking of bread, the pouring out of the wine, that each one should also sacrifice and pour out his flesh and blood for

---

[a] Sacrament.
[b] Supper.

the other. Herein will people recognize that we are truly disciples of Christ, John 13; 14; 15; 16; 17. All of the words which Christ spoke about the Last Supper tend toward this. For just as water baptism is a public testimony of the Christian /359/ faith, so is the Supper a public testimony of Christian love. Now he who does not want to be baptized* or to observe the Supper, he does not desire to believe in Christ nor to practice Christian love and does not desire to be a Christian. How much someone cares about the flesh and blood, that is about the suffering and death of Christ Jesus, about the shedding of his crimson blood, about the forgiveness of sins, about brotherly love and communion in God the Father, the Son, and the Holy Ghost, yea the communion of the whole heavenly host and the universal Christian church outside of which there is no salvation, just this much he should care about the bread and the wine of God's table. Not that here bread and wine are anything other than bread and wine; but according to the memorial and the significant mysteries for the sake of which Christ thus instituted it.ᵇ If now one had no other word or Scripture, but only the correct understanding of water baptism and the Supper of Christ, one would have God and all his creatures, faith and love, the law and all the prophets. So whoever makes a mockery of the Supper of Christ, the Son of Man will mock before God and his angels. So much for self-examination.

6. Since now these ceremonies and signs have to do completely and exclusively with fraternal love,ᶜ and since one who loves his neighbor like himself is a rare bird,ᵈ yea even an Indian phoenix on earth, who can sit at the supper table with a good conscience? Answer: One who has thus taken to heart and has thus shaped himself in mind and heart and senses inwardly that he truly and sincerely can say, "The love of God which he has shown to me through the sacrifice of his only begotten and most beloved Son for the payment of my sins, John 3:16; 1 John 4:9; Rom. 8:32, of which I have heard and been certainly assured through his holy Word, has so

---

* *Nota bene*: note this [n both Latin and German].
ᵇ Baptism and Supper are faith and love.
ᶜ Love, love.
ᵈ Phoenix.

moved, softened, and penetrated my spirit and soul that I am so minded and ready to offer my flesh and blood, furthermore so to rule over and so to master it, that it must obey me against its own will, and henceforth not take advantage of, deceive, injure, or harm my neighbor in any way in body, soul, honor, goods, wife, or child, but rather go into the fire for him and die, as Paul also desired to be accursed for his brethren and Moses to be stricken out of the book of life for the sake of his people," Rom. 9:3; Exod. 32:32. Such a person may with good conscience and worthiness sit at the Supper of Christ.

You say: "This is humanly impossible." Answer: Certainly for the Adamic human nature. But all things /360/ are possible to the Christian, Mark 9:23, not as persons, but as believers, who are one with God and all creatures, and are (except for the flesh) free and independent of themselves.[12] For God works such willing and doing in his believers, Phil. 2:14, through the inward anointing of his Holy Spirit, so that one stands in complete freedom to will and to do good or evil. The good one can do is through the anointing of God. The evil comes from one's own innate nature and impulse, which evil will one can, however, master and tame through the grace given by God, Deut. 30:1ff.; Gen. 4:17; Rom. 10; Matt 19; John 1:12.

It is not sufficient that sin be recognized through the law, nor that we know what is good or evil. We must bind the commandments on our hand, grasp them and fulfill them in deeds, Deut. 6:8; Matt. 11:30; John 3. To do this is easy and a small thing to the believer, but to those who walk according to the flesh, all things are impossible. Yet the believing and newly born person under the gospel is still also [a person] under the law. He has just as many trials as before, or even more. He finds (however holy he may be) nothing good in his own flesh, just as Saint Paul laments the same with great seriousness regarding the conflict and the resistance of the flesh, Rom. 7:18. Nevertheless the believer rejoices and praises God that the trial is not and cannot be so great in him, but that the power of God in him, which he has received through the living Word which God has sent is stronger and mightier (1

---

[12] The mix of singular and plural in this sentence is in the original.

Cor. 10:13; Rom. 8:11. He also knows certainly that such resistances, evil desires, and sinful lusts of his flesh are not damning for him if he confesses the same to God, regrets them, and does not follow after them, but reigns and rules mightily over the restless devil of his flesh, 1 Cor. 9:27, strangles, crucifies, and torments him without letup; holds in his rein, does not do his will, cares little that that breaks his neck, Exod. 34:20.ᵃ So every one who is a Christian acts and behaves so that he may worthily eat and drink at the table of the Lord.

Know thou further, righteous Christian, that to fulfill the law it is not enough to avoid sins and die to them. Yea, one must also do good to the neighbor, Ps. 37. For Christ not only broke the bread, he also distributed it and gave it to his disciples. Yea, not only the bread, but also even his own flesh and blood. So we must not only speak the word of brotherly love, hear it, confess ourselves to be sinners, and abstain from sin, we must also fulfill it in deeds,ᵇ as Scripture everywhere teaches us:[13]

Forsake evil and do good, Ps. 37.

Brethren, work out your salvation, Phil. 2:12.

While we have time let us do good, for the night comes when no man can work, Gal. 6:9.

Wilt thou enter into life, keep the commandments, Matt. 19:17.

For not those who hear the word are righteous before God, but those who do the law will be justified, Rom. 2:7.

Not all those who say to me, Lord, Lord, will enter into the kingdom of the heavens but he who does the will of my Father who is in heaven, will enter into the kingdom of

---

[13] In the text the following quotations are run together in a single prose paragraph, with the sources in the margin as usual.

ᵃ God teaches us to break the donkey's neck; Exod. 34:20.
ᵇ Mouth Christians, ear Christians, hand Christians.

heaven, says Christ, /361/ and adds: Everyone who hears my words and does them, he shall be likened unto a wise man who built his house upon a rock. But everyone who hears my word and does it not shall be likened to a fool who built his house on sand, Matt. 7:21-27.

In sum: God requires of us the will, the word, and the works of brotherly love, and he will not let himself be paid off or dismissed with words, Matt. 14; Luke 8:21; Rom. 8:1; Luke 17; Isa. 64:5ff.; Col. 2:10; Ps. 32:1f.; Rom. 4:5; 5; 7; 8. But what innate weaknesses and imperfections constantly are intermingled with our acts of commission and omission because of our flesh, God—thanks to the grace of our Lord Jesus Christ—will not reckon to our eternal condemnation; for in Christ we have all attained perfection, and in him we are already blessed. What more do we lack?

7. Since now believers have inwardly surrendered themselves utterly to serve their fellow members in Christ at the cost of honor, goods, body, and life, yea even to offer their souls for them to the point of hell with the help of God; therefore, it is all the more needful sincerely to groan and pray to God that he may cause the faith of these new persons to grow, also that he may more deeply kindle in them the fire of brotherly love, so that in these two matters, signified by water baptism and the Lord's Supper, they might continually grow, mature, and persevere unto the end.

Here shall now be held a time of common silence, so that each one who desires to approach the table of God can meditate upon the suffering of Christ and thus with Saint John rest on the breast of the Lord. After such silence the "Our Father" shall be spoken publicly by the church, reverently, and with hearts desirous of grace as follows, Matt. 6:9ff.; Luke 11:2ff.:

Our Father who art in heaven,
Hallowed be thy name,
Thy kingdom come,
Thy will be done on earth as in heaven.
Give us today our daily bread.
Forgive us our debts as we forgive our debtors.
Lead us not into temptation but deliver us from evil.
Amen.

8. Now the priest shall point out clearly and expressly[a] that the bread is bread and the wine wine and not flesh and blood, as has long been believed.

Whoever now desires to eat of this bread and drink of the drink of the Lord's Supper, let him rise and repeat with heart and mouth the following pledge of love:

The Pledge of Love[b]

Brothers and sisters, if you will to love God before, in, and above all things, in the power of his holy and living Word, serve him alone, Deut. 5; 6; Exod. 20, honor and adore him and henceforth sanctify his name, subject your carnal /362/ and sinful will to his divine will which he has worked in you by his living Word, in life and death, then let each say individually:

I will.

If you will love your neighbor and serve him with deeds of brotherly love, Matt. 25; Eph. 6; Col. 3; Rom. 13:1; 1 Pet. 2:13f., lay down and shed for him your life and blood, be obedient to father, mother, and all authorities[14] according to the will of God, and this in the power of our Lord Jesus Christ, who laid down and shed his flesh and blood for us, then let each say individually:

I will.

If you will practice fraternal admonition toward your brethren and sisters, Matt. 18:15ff.; Luke 6; Matt. 5:44; Rom. 12:10, make peace and unity among them, and reconcile yourselves with all those whom you have offended, abandon all envy, hate, and evil will toward everyone, willingly cease all action and behavior which causes harm, disadvantage, or offense to your neighbor, [if you will] also love your enemies and do good to them, and exclude according to the Rule of

[14] McGlothlin suggests that here Hubmaier is taking his distance from other Anabaptists regarding magistracy. Cf. McGlothlin 1906, p. 96.

[a] On this there is a special booklet. [Hubmaier refers to his "Simple instruction" on the Eucharist (text 20, above, p. 314).]
[b] The pledge [or duty] of love.

Christ, Matt. 18, all those who refuse to do so, then let each
say individually:

I will.

If you desire publicly to confirm before the church this
pledge of love which you have now made, through the Lord's
Supper of Christ, by eating bread and drinking wine, and to
testify to it in the power of the living memorial of the suffering and death of Jesus Christ our Lord, then let each say individually:

I desire it in the power of God.

So eat and drink with one another in the name of God the
Father the Son and the Holy Spirit. May God himself accord
to all of us the power and the strength that we may worthily
carry it out and bring it to its saving conclusion according to
his divine will. May the Lord impart to us his grace. Amen.

9. The bishop takes the bread and with the church lifts
his eyes to heaven, praises God and says:

We praise and thank thee, Lord God, Creator of the
heavens and earth, for all thy goodness toward us. Especially hast thou so sincerely loved us that thou didst give
thy most beloved Son for us unto death so that each one
who believes in him may not be lost but have eternal life,
John 3:16; 1 John 4:9; Rom. 8:32. Be thou honored, praised
and magnified now, forever, always and eternally. Amen.

Now the priest takes the bread, breaks it, and offers it to
the hands of those present, saying:

The Lord Jesus, in the night in which he was betrayed, took
the bread, give thanks, and broke it, and said: "Take, eat.
This is my body, which is broken for you. Do this in my
memory." Therefore, take and eat also, dear brothers and
sisters, this bread in the memory of the body of our Lord
Jesus Christ, which he gave unto death for us.

Now when everyone has been fed, the priest likewise
takes the cup with the wine and speaks with lifted eyes:

"God! Praise be to thee!"

and offers it into their hands, saying:

Likewise the Lord Jesus took the vessel after the /363/ Supper and spoke: "This cup is a new testament in my blood. Do this, as often as you drink, in memory of me." Take therefore also the vessel and all drink from it in the memory of the blood of our Lord Jesus Christ, which was shed for us for the forgiveness of our sins.

When they have all drunk, the priest says:

As often as you eat the bread and drink of the drink, you shall proclaim the death of the Lord, until he comes, 1 Cor. 11:26.

Now the church is seated to hear the conclusion.

10. Most dearly beloved brethren and sisters in the Lord. As we now, by thus eating the bread and drinking the drink in memory of the suffering and shed blood of our Lord Jesus Christ for the remission of our sins have had fellowship one with another, 1 Cor. 10:17; 12:12; Eph. 4:4; Col. 1:3; Eph. 1; 4; 5, and have all become one loaf and one body, and our Head is Christ, we should properly become conformed to our Head and as his members follow after him, love one another, do good, give counsel, and be helpful to one another, each offering up his flesh and blood for the other. Under our Head Christ we should all also live, speak, and act honorably and circumspectly, so that we give no offense or provocation to anyone, Matt. 18; Mark 9; Luke 17; 1 Cor. 8. Rom. 14. So that also those who are outside the church might not have reason to blaspheme our head, our faith, and church, and to say: "Does your head Christ teach you such an evil life? Is that your faith? Is that your baptism? Is that your Christian church, Supper, and gospel, that you should lead such an ungodly and shameful life in gluttony, drunkenness, gambling, dancing, usury, gossip, reviling, cursing, blasphemy, pride, avarice, envy, hate and wrath, unchastity, luxury, laziness, and frivolity? Matt. 18:6. Woe, woe to him who gives offense! It would be better for him that a millstone should be hung around his neck and he should be cast into the depth of the sea. Let us rather take upon ourselves a righteous, honorable, and serious life, through which God our Father who is in heaven may be praised.

Since our brotherly love requires that one member of the body be also concerned for the other, therefore we have the earnest behest of Christ, Matt. 18:14ff., that whenever henceforth a brother sees another erring or sinning, that he once and again should fraternally admonish him in brotherly love. Should he not be willing to reform nor to desist from his sin, he shall be reported to the church. The church shall then exhort him a third time. When this also does no good, she shall exclude him from her fellowship. Unless it should be the case that the sin is quite public and scandalous; then he should be admonished also publicly and before all, so that the others may fear, 1 Cor. 5:1; 1 Tim. 5:20; Gal. 2:11.

Whereupon I pray and exhort you once more, most dearly beloved in Christ, /364/ that henceforth as table companions of Christ Jesus, Luke 22:15, you henceforth lead a Christian walk before God and before men. Be mindful of your baptismal commitment and of your pledge of love* which you made to God and the church publicly and certainly not unwittingly when receiving the water and in breaking bread. See to it that you bear fruit worthy of the baptism and the Supper of Christ, that you may in the power of God satisfy your pledge, promise, sacrament, and sworn commitment, Matt. 3:8; Luke 3:8.[15] God sees it and knows your hearts. May our Lord Jesus Christ, ever and eternally praised, grant us the same. Amen.

Dear brothers and sisters, watch and pray lest you wander away and fall into temptation, Matt. 24:42; 25:13; Luke 16. You know neither the day nor the hour when the Lord is coming and will demand of you an accounting of your life. Therefore watch and pray. I commend you to God. May each of you say to himself, "Praise, praise, praise to the Lord eternally!" Amen.

Arise and go forth in the peace of Christ Jesus. The grace of God be with us all.

Amen.

---

[15] The reference to "sworn commitment" (*aydspflicht*) as synonym for the pledge of love is not a basis to know whether Hubmaier differed from other Anabaptists about the civil oath as he did about government. He seems to have used the word "oath" only in this figurative sense to describe baptism or the Supper.

---

* Remember and hold.

Truth Is Unkillable.

To the noble Lord Buriano of Cornitz, my gracious sovereign.[16]
Grace and peace in Christ, noble and Christian Lord.
Although the majority of people who stand by the gospel
recognize that bread is bread and wine wine in the Lord's
Supper, and not Christ,[a] Acts 1:9; Mark 16:19; Heb. 1:3;
12:2;, Matt. 22:44; Ps. 110.[17] For the same ascended into
heaven and is sitting at the right hand of God his Father,
whence he will come again to judge the living and the dead.
Precisely that is our foundation, according to which we must
deduce and exposit all of the Scriptures having to do with
eating and drinking. Thus Christ cannot be eaten or drunk by
us otherwise than spiritually and in faith.[b] So then he cannot
be bodily the bread either but rather in the memorial which is
held, as he himself and Paul explained these Scriptures, Luke
22; 1 Cor. 11. Whoever understands them otherwise does
violence to the articles of our Christian faith.[18] Yet the restless Satan has invented another intrigue to hold us in his
snare.[c] Namely, that such a Lord's Supper should be established without a prior water baptism, something which again
Scripture cannot suffer. When the three thousand men and
Paul had been instructed in the Word and believed, only
thereafter did they break bread with the brethren, Acts 2:41f.;
Acts 9. For as faith precedes love, so water baptism must
precede the Lord's Supper. So that Your Grace may know in
what form the Lord's Supper is celebrated in Nicolspurg, I
have had it printed, for the praise of God, the honor of Your

[16] Burian Sobek of Kornice, nobleman, student at Wittenberg, admirer,
and translator of Luther, admirer as well of Thomas Müntzer, was elected
Chancellor of Prag in 1523 and briefly jailed in 1525 for his Protestant
sympathies. Later he associated with the Czech Brethren and wrote their
history.
[17] The thought left dangling with "although" will be picked up with the
"yet" five sentences later.
[18] The "articles" means the Apostles' Creed.

[a] Bedrock.
[b] How Christ is eaten or drunk.
[c] A new error.

Grace, and the salvation of all believers in Christ. So that no one might think that we fear the /365/ light or that we are unable to give reasons for our teaching and actions. May Your Grace be commended to God and graciously accept from me this written token of respect, through my dear brother Jan Zeysinger,[19]

Your Grace's willing [servant]
Balthasar Hûebmör, etc.

---

[19] Jan Cizek (germanized Zeising) had been a monk at Wroclaw. He had been moving gradually through the positions of Luther, the Czech Brethren, and Zwingli. Hubmaier probably baptized him since he is here called "brother." He was burned at the stake at Brno in April 1528.

26

On the Christian Ban

The treatise On Fraternal Admonition *(text 23 above) provides the rationale and a form of words for the exercise of that moral correction without which, according to common Anabaptist conviction, a congregational order cannot be faithful.*

The present text fills out the disciplinary pattern with reference to the case in which the person admonished has refused to repent and must accordingly be excluded from the fellowship.

Unlike Hubmaier's major writings, this pamphlet neither begins nor ends with a greeting to some prominent person. There are allusions in the closing paragraph of this text to the season of nativity. This supports the supposition that the text may have been written, or finally prepared for print, in the last weeks of 1526, as part of Hubmaier's constructive pastoral program at Nikolsburg. Its substance extends directly the logic of the preceding treatise, concluding the series of pastoral tracts.[1]

[1] Previously translated in Hošek 1892, pp. 193-209. Source: HS 21, pp. 367-378.

Of the Christian Ban
Where the same
is not instituted and used
according to the orderly
and earnest command
of Christ, there
nothing reigns
but sin, shame,
and vice.
Dr. Balthasar Hubmör
of Fridberg
Truth Is Unkillable.
Nicolspurg
1527

On the Ban

Now after a sinner has been first exhorted and admonished by his brother in secret, then in the presence of two or
three witnesses, and finally, before the whole church according to the order of Christ, Matt. 18:15ff., which is the first
office and authority of the keys, and still he does not desire to
better his life, nor to abstain from this sin, then he shall be
bound according to the command of Christ, excluded, and
banned. It is therefore necessary, useful, and most helpful to
know what the Christian ban is, whence the church has this
power, how to ban, and in what way one should deal with one
who is banned.

1.ª It is to be noted that the ban is a public separation
and exclusion of a person from the fellowship of the Christian
church because of an offensive sin, from which this person
will not refrain, recognized according to the earnest and

ª What the ban is.

express command of Christ, decided by a Christian congregation, and publicly proclaimed, so that the Word of God and the whole Christian church might not be shamed, calumnied, and despised, and so that the novices and the weak might not be caused to stumble by his evil example or to be corrupted, /368/ but rather that because of this punishment they might be startled, afraid, and might know henceforth better how to protect themselves from sins and vices. For the Christian church bans no one unless he has first been found guilty of a scandalous sin or public vice. The same takes place also for the sake of the sinner,[a] 1 Cor. 5:2, so that he might become aware of his misery, and willingly forsake sin and thereby escape from the eternal ban and exclusion, which the master of the house, Christ Jesus himself, will apply saying: "Get hence from me, ye cursed ones, into eternal fire, which is ready for the devil and his messengers," Matt. 25:41. O the miserable, O the fearful, O the terrible ban! O my God and Lord, we pray thee with weeping hearts, to preserve us graciously from this horrible ban.

2.[b] It is known and is evident that this authority is given to the Christian church and comes from Christ Jesus her spouse and bridegroom, as his heavenly Father has given the same to him, in heaven and on earth, and as Christ used the same in teaching and in deed, as he walked among us bodily. But when he was to ascend into heaven and to sit at the right hand of his almighty Father, no longer remaining bodily with us on earth, just then he hung this power and these keys at the side of his most beloved spouse and bride, Matt. 28:20; Mark 16:19; John 20:23; Acts 1:9 (whom he had prepared, purified, and restored for himself with his precious crimson blood), and recommended and commanded to use the same faithfully according to his word, as he then promised to her, Matt. 16:16ff. and 18:18, when he said to Peter. "You are a

---

[2] It is not clear, according to Hubmaier's account, whether sins which are not publicly offensive need to be disciplined in the same public way. Other Anabaptists did not to the same degree link the imperative of discipline to the dimension of scandal.

---

[a] 1 Cor 5:2: "The ban occurs for the sinner's good."
[b] Whence the ban came.

stony one, and on the rock, which you openly confess as you say fearlessly that I am the Christ, Son of the living God, I shall build my church, my gathering, my congregation, and the gates of hell cannot stand against her, and I will give to you[*] [3] the keys of the kingdom of Heaven. Verily I say to you: All that you shall bind on earth will be bound also in heaven, and what you loose on earth shall be loosed in heaven."

When Christ says, "To you," he signifies the unity of the church. But when he says, "You," he indicates that many men shall be gathered together in this unity of faith and Christian love. This same power and these keys Christ gave and commended to the church after his blessed resurrection, Matt. 28:19f.; Mark 16:15f. Namely, to preach the gospel, thereby to create a believing congregation, to baptize the same in water, thus with the first key opening to her the door the portals of the Christian church, admitting her to the forgiveness of sins John 20:22f. /369/

The church never had this power before the resurrection of Christ, for although John and the disciples of Christ preached and baptized with water before the resurrection of Christ, Matt. 3; Luke 3; John 3, 4, they never pointed those who were baptized to the church for the forgiveness of their sins. For at that time the church had received no keys from Christ, but rather they pointed, drove, and brought to Christ the newly born and baptized disciples (whom they had led to an awareness of their sins). He himself received them, forgave them their sins, opened up to them the gates of Christian fellowship, and took them into his holy communion. So he dealt with the sinful woman in the house of Simon the Pharisee, as he said to her, "Your sins are forgiven," Luke 7:47, and with the criminal on his right hand hanging on the cross, "Today shalt thou be with me in Paradise," Luke 23:43. Thereafter with regard to the keys there was a great difference between water baptism before the resurrection of Christ and water baptism after the resurrection,[b] even though both ultimately

---

[3] Hubmaier accents the shift of number in Jesus' saying from singular (Peter) to plural (church) with two marginal notes.

---

[*] To thee, to thee; to you, to you, to you.
[b] Difference between water baptism before and after Christ's resurrection.

point to Christ. But as I said concerning the keys, first Christ himself used the keys, loosed and bound the sinners according to the command of his heavenly Father. Thereafter he turned the same over to the Christian church and let her deal, practice, dispose, and authorize, as she possesses [this authority] and will possess it and use it until the coming of the Lord. This we can show much more clearly than the sun and demonstrate with his own command, as he says, "Receive the Holy Spirit, John 20:22. Before, you saw him come upon me visibly, by the Jordan as John baptized me Acts 2:1ff. Soon you will see him coming down upon yourselves on the day of Pentecost. I now give to you the key and all authority,ª just as I myself received the same before from my Father, for the forgiving of sins, and hereby promise you verily and assuredly that all, to whom you forgive their sins, to them they shall be forgiven," John 20:23.

Whoever now says that Christ is bodily present in the bread and the wine, according to the words of Christ, "This is my body, etc.," is not saying the whole truth.ᵇ Our faith cannot tolerate his, "etc."[4] He thereby unbuckles the keys from the side of the Christian church, which Christ with serious words attached to her side gave her and commended to her until he come again, as Paul writes to the Corinthians, 1 Cor. 11. Whoever then understands correctly and fully the authority of the use of the Christian keys, the same will also know well and properly how to speak and to write of water baptism and of the Supper of Christ, namely, that the water does not save us, nor is Christ bodily inside the bread or the wine. But hitherto we had for a long time lost the keys, the belt, the church, water, wine, and bread. /370/ Then, when we read it in the Bible, our Christian house got a roofᶜ over it.[5] And so

---

[4] By "etc." Hubmaier designates the medieval doctrine of the sacramental presence of Christ. If Christ is among us, then his having given the church the keys when he ascended to heaven is nullified.

[5] What proverb or folk dictum is meant is unclear; it turns on the rhyme between *Bibel* and *Gibel* (gable, roof).

ª The first key.
ᵇ A half-truth: etc.
ᶜ Proverb.

we went on. And although some pious persons already have learned an understanding of the genuine truth by God's grace in these matters, there are still everywhere contrary, vain babblers and seducers who with their groundless and quarrelsome complaints seek to tear the truth once understood back out of their hands (before God we truly lament it). A few years ago they were wading around very deep in the mud puddles of this error with booklets; and now rather than being willing to return and to give God the glory and confess his truth openly, they would rather continue to wade and even to drown in the pits of this abominable idolatry. May the good and merciful God graciously help them out. They are stuck in it up to the ears.

Christ, rather, gives to his church a second key,* namely the authority to exclude again persons who had been received and admitted into the Christian congregation if they should not will to behave in a right and Christian way, and to close her doors before them, as he says, "Whose sins you retain, to them they shall stand retained," Matt. 18:18 [John 20:23]. This command and authority Christ strengthened with an oath which he spoke in his own name[b] as he said, "Verily I say to you, all that you will bind on earth shall be bound in heaven, and what you will loose on earth shall also be loosed in heaven."

It follows that the Christian church now has this authority to forgive and to retain sins here on earth until the second coming of the Lord, just as the same Christ also possessed when bodily upon earth.[c6] So great and mighty is the authority of the particular and visible church, gathered together in part bodily and yet completely in the Spirit, even though only two or three are together in the name of the Lord Jesus and all of the others on the other hand are in error. For he is with her himself by his grace until the end of the world, Matt.

---

[6] In the marginal in fn. c, "mother" is the church universal, "daughter" the local congregation.

---

* The second key.
[b] Christ's oath.
[c] The church truly has Christ's power. The daughter has her mother's power.

28:20, although bodily he has ascended into heaven where he sits at the right hand of his heavenly Father there in heaven, Mark 16:19; Acts 1:9. Yea, it was in heaven that Stephen saw him; there he sits bodily according to his humanity. He has a particular place "in heaven, in heaven" and not everywhere, as deity is omnipresent.[a][7] Yea, neither in the bread nor in the wine nor in other creatures.

In sum: God the Father had all authority and used it in heaven and on earth until the incarnation of Christ.[b] After his Son had become man he fully gave to him this authority to him and /371/ commanded the people to listen until his death. After his resurrection, just as he was to ascend into heaven, Christ assigned all his authority to the holy Christian church and hung the promised keys at her side, that she should use the same for the loosing and binding of sins according to his command in his bodily absence, until his second bodily coming, John 20:23; Matt. 16:19. Then with a battle cry and the voice of the archangel and with the trumpet of God he will come down again from heaven; the dead in Christ will first rise, 1 Thess. 4:16f. After them we who live and survive will at the same time with them be seized up into the clouds to meet the Lord in the air. There and then the church will return her authority and keys to Christ her spouse, for her authority will have come to an end, since she is no longer on earth.[c] Now she is with Christ in the air and will be with him forever. Thus her power is given to her only on earth as Christ precisely spoke to her, "All that you loose or bind on earth," Matt. 18:18. Now that Christ has taken back the keys, he will judge the living and the dead, and give to each what he has earned, John 5:29. When that has all happened, then Christ will again render and give back

---

[7] The "fly cupboards" of fn. a were places to store food, protected from the flies by netting. Hubmaier uses the term as mocking designation for the tabernacle in which the consecrated host was reserved, cf. above p. 347. Hubmaier is with Zwingli, against Luther and the Catholics, in reading the Ascension and *sessio ad dextram* as argument against the real presence of Christ in the Eucharist.

---

[a] Christ is seated in heaven and not in the fly cupboards.
[b] Christ has precisely the power of the Father.
[c] Christ will hold the last judgment in Heaven.

his authority and keys to God his heavenly Father. Now God will be all in all, 1 Cor 15:28. If that is not said in simple clear German, then I neither can nor know how to talk German. He who has ears let him hear.

3. When I previously described some particular forms for how to celebrate baptism and the Supper of Christ, I by no means did so in order to take away the freedom of others. I did it only so that nothing might be introduced and established by anyone counter to or besides the Word of God. I want to do just the same here, namely, to describe a form for the ban in the simplest possible way and thereby to leave every person of goodwill free in his reasonableness and judgment.

The Form of the Ban Before the Church

Brother N. You are not unaware of your baptismal commitment and of the pledge of love which you made on receiving water baptism and in the breaking of bread, which you made to God the Father, Son, and Holy Spirit, and also to the general Christian church, publicly in the presence of many witnesses,[a] thereby then knowingly, willingly, and with afore-thought pledging and promising to God and the Christian church, giving your hand in the pledge, that you would henceforth give yourself to the almighty God and to our Lord Jesus Christ in faith and to your /372/ neighbor in brotherly love, and that you would henceforth rule and lead your life in the power of God according to his divine will. And where you might not do the same, you would then accept fraternal admonition according to the earnest and authoritative command of Christ Jesus, Matt. 18:15ff., would accept the same admonition virtuously and in a friendly way from your brethren and improve your life, or else be subject to the Christian ban. Now, brother, you have sinned against heaven and against God. You have therefore been admonished by your brother M between you and him alone first of all, and then again in the presence of these two or three witnesses, A, B, and C, and the third time publicly according to Christian

---

[a] One whose heart this exclusion does not touch has a heart of stone, and does not give heed to eternal separation from Christ.

order before our Christian congregation, which faithfully, benevolently, and fraternally, yea for God's sake and for the sake of your soul's salvation, with weeping eyes exhorted, pleaded with you and admonished, that you desist from this offensive sin,[a] Ps. 76, and change your life in the power of your baptismal promise and pledge of love. So that the Word of God might not thus be blasphemed through you, nor your neighbor harmed, and so that the general holy Christian church might not by your sin and haughtiness be so deeply shamed, despised, and mocked. All of which (we lament it truly before God) has until now continued to be ignored and despised on your part. Now since the particular church as an obedient daughter properly should fulfill the will of her mother the general Christian church, Matt. 18; 1 Cor. 5, as the mother, does the will of her spouse Christ Jesus, and the spouse does the will of his Father who is in heaven:[b] Therefore, our Christian congregation and assembly has reason, is moved and obliged by the earnest command of God and our Lord Jesus Christ to behave toward you according to his divine command, of which we far more than you must keep reminding ourselves of, so that we might not become participants of your sins and might not be eternally punished and damned together with you.[c]

Therefore in our congregation we conclude unanimously with our spirit concerning you who have thus behaved, in the name and in the authority of our Lord Jesus Christ, and give you over to the devil for the destruction of the flesh so that the spirit might be saved on the day of the Lord Jesus, 1 Cor. 5:1ff.

How to Behave Toward One Who Has Been Banned

4. It should be clear that with a banned person one should have no fellowship, not in eating, drinking, greeting, nor have dealings with him in any other way, 2 John 10; Matt. 18:17. Otherwise we make ourselves /373/ participants of his

---

[a] Make promises and fulfill them [in Latin].
[b] Particular church: Universal church; Christ the spouse, God the Heavenly Father [in Latin].
[c] O dear Christian! take note of Paul's severe verdict, and beware.

evil works. Rather we should consider him a pagan and a publican, i.e., a disorderly, offensive, and leprous person, who is
captive and bound by sin and given over to Satan, so that no
one might be defiled and poisoned by the leprosy of his vices.
All of this shall be done for the honor of God, for the welfare
of the church, and for his own admonition and welfare, that
he might be ashamed, might renounce his sin, and better his
life. Yet we should not consider him an enemy. We should
neither strike him nor drive him away, nor kill him, but should
rather avoid him, flee from him, stay out of his company. This
is not said to disarm orderly government of its sword,[8] Rom.
13:4; 1 Pet. 2:14. This is briefly the will of God for the sake
of which we want to hear the witness of Scripture.

Paul writes to the Corinthians thus: There is a common
report[a9] that there is fornication among you, and such a
fornication that even the heathen do not know what to say
about it; that a man has his father's wife, and you are puffed
up, and are not rather suffering in such a way that he who has
done such a deed would be put away from you, 1 Cor. 5:1ff. I
therefore, although absent in body, still am present in spirit,
and have come to a decision as if I were present concerning
him who had done such a thing; in the name of our Lord Jesus
Christ, in your own meeting with my spirit and in the power
of our Lord Jesus Christ, to turn him over to the devil for the
destruction of the flesh so that the spirit might be saved on
the day of the Lord Jesus.

Your boasting is not seemly; do you not know that a little
leaven sours the entire dough?[b] Therefore sweep out the old
leaven that you might be a new dough, that you might be
unleavened, for we have an Easter Lamb, namely Christ,

---

[8] Hubmaier does not want the statement that the banned one is not to be
harmed to be mistaken as interfering with the sword of government.

[9] As the marginal note indicates, Hubmaier differs from other Anabaptists
in holding that public offense justifies telescoping the three stages of
Matt. 18.

---

[a] Paul banned the fornicator without previously admonishing him.
Reason: the sin was public, not fitting for secret reprimand.

[b] Here is clearly seen that there is no excuse. Where there is a church,
one must simply throw out the leaven of malice, or one is a bad
housekeeper.

which was sacrificed for us. Therefore let us celebrate Easter not with the old leaven, nor with the leaven of malice and ill will, but in the sweet loaf of purity and truth. Put away from yourselves whoever is evil.

I wrote in the letter that you should have nothing to do with fornicators. By that I do not mean the fornicators of this world, or the avaricious or robbers or idolaters; otherwise, you would have to leave the world. Now I wrote to you that you should have nothing[a] to do with them, namely, if there is someone who lets himself be called a brother (i.e., who carries the name of a Christian) and is a fornicator or avaricious or idolatrous or abusive or drunken, or a robber; with such a person you should not eat.

Here observe carefully and well the following, oh Christian reader. Since it is forbidden to eat together with one who has been banned, now much more are other kinds of fellowship and association forbidden which are less necessary than eating, such as all works of friendship, but not the works of necessity. /374/ The same shall and may well be shared with one who had been banned, such as the need to give food, to give drink, to give shelter, as likewise the works of necessity should be shared with enemies, Jews, and pagans. Yes, in fact I should show friendship toward Jews and heathen, but not toward persons who have been banned, because they have fallen away from the knowledge of the truth, whereas the former have not yet come to it. [I should show friendship] so that they might be drawn by a Christian example to Christian faith (which issues in such friendly works, Gal. 5:23). With a banned person [in contrast to the Jew or pagan] one cannot behave according to the ordinary rule of our Christian faith[b] which says that whenever the works of love cannot be shown toward our neighbor without doing damage to faith (as is true in this case), then love must cease and faith must go on. Thus God commanded the Israelites to borrow silver and golden ornaments from the Egyptians, Exod. 11:2; Ps. 105:37 and, counter to love,[c] to carry them away with them, so that the

---

[a] Nothing excludes everything. Fornication is everything which is dearer to us than God. It may be life, goods, wife, child, meadows, fields, house, farm, government, princes, lords, and the like.

[b] A Christian rule.

[c] A good example.

420 / Balthasar Hubmaier

omnipotence of God might be known thereby. The borrowed goods had to testify to the powerful hand of God, in that the Egyptians could not ask for their own goods back from the Israelites, whom they previously had in many ways oppressed, but had to let them depart freely therewith according to the divine command.

Paul writes further, what do they who are without have to do with me, that I should judge them? You should not judge those who are way out there.[a] That is: those who through water baptism and the public confession of faith have committed themselves to your churches, let themselves be listed, incorporated, and taken for Christians. But God will judge those who are outside. As if Paul wanted to say: We have no authority over them to admonish them. They have not been counted in our congregation by water baptism through their own oral consent. They are not our brethren, nor do they let themselves be called brethren. But now Christ says: "If your brother sins, admonish him." Yea, although Christian faith in the heart is the beginning and the source of spiritual brotherhood, still the same cannot be recognized by people unless there be a public affirmation of faith, Matt. 16:16 (upon which Christ built his church), for only God knows the hearts. He then who confesses Christian faith, accepts the sign of water baptism according to the institution of Christ, and argues no more, Matt. 28; Mark 16; Acts 2. Here we see once again most evidently that, where the water baptism of Christ has not been restored according to the order of Christ, then it is impossible to know who is in the church or who outside, whom we have authority to admonish or not, who are brothers or sisters.

Just so Paul writes further to the Thessalonians saying, "We hear that some of you are walking in a disorderly way, not working, but /375/ frivolous, 1 Thess. 3:11ff. Such persons we command, admonishing them through our Lord Jesus Christ, that they should quietly work and eat their own bread. But you, dear brethren, not be weary of well doing. But if someone is not obedient to our word, identify him by letter,[b]

---

[a] We want to condemn and drive out the Turks; yet we have not yet driven from our midst the evil ones.

[b] Loafers, lazy, rumor mongers. Those who are idle are to be listed.

have nothing to do with him, that he might be ashamed, yet do not consider him an enemy, but admonish him as a brother. That means: tell him why he is being shunned and we are having no fellowship with him.

Thus once again you see full well that the admonition and ban does not take place out of hatred, nor to harm anyone, but out of Christian love,ª and for the welfare of the sinner, so that he might renounce his sins and that together with soul and body his spirit might be saved.

St. John writes thus: "If someone comes to you and does not bring this doctrine, do not accept him in your house, do not even greet him. For whoever greets him has fellowship with his evil works," 2 John 10.ᵇ¹⁰ Further, Paul writes to Titus, "Avoid a disputatious person, if he has been admonished once and again, and be aware that such a person is perverse and is sinning as one who has condemned himself," Titus 3:10-11.

In sum: All these texts concerning the ban together testify that evil persons should be promptly excluded and banned: those who become unfaithful, who dishonor the sacraments and perjure,ᶜ¹¹ who have not held to their pledge, duty, faithfulness, honor, or faith in the Almighty God and his only begotten Son, our Lord Jesus Christ, also to his most beloved bride the holy general and Christian church, but have made shipwreck of their faith, who with their offensive and godless works have fallen into the judgment of the blasphemer and still will not accept admonition or change their ways. Such were then Hymeneus, Alexander, 1 Tim. 1:20 and the fornicator at Corinth, 1 Cor. 5:1. All, all, all of them shall be expelled, writes Paul, who counter to the rule of Christ, Gal. 6:12, to which they had pledged themselves are leading a dis-

---

¹⁰ Heinold Fast suggests that the marginal note means "even three letters are too much greeting for such a person," Titus 3:10.

¹¹ Hubmaier understands "sacrament" according to the Zwinglian definition as "oath." Thus both baptism and the Supper represent promises which the excommunicated person has broken.

ª The ban does not occur out of envy or hatred.

ᵇ *Ave* [greetings] has only three letters.

ᶜ Those who truly dishonor the sacraments are those who do not honor their baptismal vow and love pledge to the church.

orderly life, such as loafers, loiterers, gamblers, blasphemers, gluttons, drunkards, usuers, and other such vicious persons. If I should say it still more clearly, such offensive persons should be listed and [their names] sent to other churches, that they too may know to defend themselves against them. Thus Paul named Phigelus, Hermogenes, Demas, and Alexander the coopersmith, 2 Tim. 1:15, 4:10, 14.

O God, how many years have we shoved this Christian ban under the bench! How long has it been completely lost! Yea, even though much /376/ has now been written about the ban, I let every Christian judge for himself how it has been encountered. I know full well that our popes, bishops, monks, nuns, and Maoz-Priests[12] have completely made a tyranny out of this wholesome ban (counter to their own rules which call it a medicine for the souls).[a] Then they have also used it so hard and rigidly in temporal matters that hitherto Caesars, kings, princes, lords, and all men have feared this invisible sword. Yea, as soon as one did not promptly believe and do the same as was commanded by their canon law,[b] that is, their kitchen rules,[13] decrees, decretals, sext, and clementine commands, or as soon as one did not hurriedly turn over to the abbot, the provost, the vicar, or the official the chicken for carnival, or to every sheep shearer[14] his simony, absence,[15] pension, and usury in a hurry. Yea, even for five shillings of hazel nuts, you would have to be struck immediately by the power of the invisible air-sword of their ban, that they had placed in the holy place of the Christian ban, up on the pulpit and on every holiday to hack, beat, stab, strangle, curse, shoot, ring out,[16] stone, anathematize. Then there was nothing but

---

[12] "Maozpfaffen," cf. above texts 19, note 8, p. 302, and 21, note 13, p. 343.

[13] Hubmaier puns: in the margin (see fn b) *Virus Canonicum* for *jus canonicum* and in the text *Kuchenrecht* ("kitchen") for *Kirchenrecht*.

[14] Usurer.

[15] The authorization for a priest to draw the money from a benefice where he does not serve.

[16] All of these verbs describe the Roman ban. Ringing churchbells was part of the excommunication ritual.

---

[a] *De Sen. ex. com.; Cum medicinalis*, book 6.

[b] Canonical law.

"the heavens have revealed," "God my praise,"[17] disobedience, disobedience, heretic, heretic, bang, bang, come, devil, and take the evil man. He did not properly give the small goose tithe or the offering penny. He spoke against the grace and indulgence of the pope. He called the abbot's concubine a harlot. Briefly: what has to do with the purses, the cakes, the money chests and the cellars of the religious, there the false ban, claiming to look like the wholesome ban of Christ, counter to the clear teaching of Christ and Paul, has to become doorman, judge, hangman, and executioner. Meanwhile, however, the holy belly fathers[a][18] sat around in full freedom and luxury of the flesh. The body was taking good care of itself, however the soul might be faring.

Paul, on the contrary, teaches and commands earnestly that such persons should be excluded. Such as have a high view of themselves, avaricious, ambitious, proud, blasphemers, disobedient to parents, ungrateful, unspiritual, unfriendly, stiffnecks, defamers, unchaste, ungenerous, wild, traitors, sacrilegious, abominable, puffed up, those who love the pleasure of this world more than God, those who have the appearance of righteous behavior but deny its power, those who run around from house to house and mislead young women, those who are laden with sin and those /377/ who resist the truth, 1 Tim. 3:2ff. These are men of degenerate senses, incapable of faith, unable to carry it out.

How to Deal with the Returning Sinner

Finally: Once the banned person recognizes himself[b] and his misery, 2 Cor. 2:1ff., renounces sin in deed, returns, repents, prays God for grace and ameliorates his life, immediately the church shall accept him again with great joy and with the authority of the keys given to her open up again

---

[17] Phrases from the ritual of excommunication; some are cited and some mocked by punning.

[18] The pun substitutes belly (*bauch*) for *beicht* (confession), i.e., belly-father for confessor.

---

[a] Bellyfather.

[b] Know thyself [in Greek].

to him the kingdom of Christ, according to the command of Christ: "What you shall loose on earth shall stand loosed in heaven as well," Matt. 18:18. This should happen not just seven times but seventy times seven times, Luke 17:4, i.e., four-hundred-ninety times, a number which points to the weeks of years of Daniel, Dan. 9:24. This is to give us to understand that as often as a sinner genuinely finds remorse and sorrow for his sin, it is forgiven him through the suffering of Christ. That is proper repentance and remorse over sin:[a] that one renounces that same sin in deed and henceforth flees, sets aside, and avoids everything whereby he might again be attracted and drawn again into sin, such as gluttony, drunkenness, gambling, wrath, fornication, evil company. Whoever does not do that, such a person's contrition is not from the heart, whatever the mouth might say. For he who says he is sorry about his sins but does not avoid the causes of sins is a liar. He is behaving like someone who says he doesn't want to get dirty and yet spends all his time with coal and old kettles.

Yea the father accepts the prodigal son with great joy when he returns with his whole heart and confesses that he has sinned against heaven and against his father, Luke 15:20f. He says he is not worthy to be named his son but he asks to be forgiven. He will never do it again, which is the greatest repentance.[b]

This is also the way Paul deals with the Corinthian, 2 Cor. 2:1ff. He writes the church there that he shall be forgiven and consoled so that he might not despair, and that they should work the works of love toward him.

Therefore, O faithful Christian, now that the mighty, great, and[c] powerful Lords, cities and countrysides, do not want to accept and will not suffer this order of fraternal admonition and the Christian ban, it is very difficult that a Christian order should be established among them. If then it cannot take place among them, then the small despised manger in Bethlehem should be far preferable to us, together with Christ, Mary, and Joseph, Matt. 1; 2; Luke 2, than the

---

[a] Authentic remorse and repentance.
[b] Never do [it again] is the greatest repentance.
[c] A Christian admonition.

great and majestic church of the Pharisees and the scribes in the venerable city of Jerusalem. We should prefer Corinth to Athens, Acts 18. /378/ Yea much rather the fellowship of the fisherman Peter, John 1, the tentmaker, Paul, Acts 18, the tanner Simon, Acts 10, the public sinner Zacchaeus (Luke 19) and the customs collector Matthew, rather than the high and spiritual princes and bishops Herod, Pilate, Annas, Caiaphas, Luke 3; Matt. 2, and the painted wall Ananias, Acts 23. Yea among them one would lose from sight the star of Christ, but among these others one will see it before him and walk after it. This the royal prophet David desired, saying: "I would rather be despised and rejected in the house of my God than high and majestic in the tabernacles of the godless," Ps. 84:10.

It has thus pleased the heavenly Father to hide his mystery from the kings and the wise men of this world and to reveal them to the humble (Matt. 13 [11:25-26]; Luke 10:21. Therefore, I have spoken thus, Christian reader, so that people might be drawn away from their respect for the high churches of the popes, bishops, councils, cathedral chapters, and high schools,* and might look only at the bright clear stars of the Word of God which itself will show them the way to find a true church near Christ, Gal. 1:10, 2:6; Rom. 2:11; Eph. 6:7; Col. 3:23; Acts 10:34; 1 Pet. 1:17. Only this star should we perceive and follow. It will lead us most directly to Christ. And [if we] have no respect of the height or the number or the holiness of persons, we will not be led astray. May the almighty benevolent and merciful God let us be illuminated by the star of his Holy Word always and forever. Amen.

Truth Is Unkillable.
1527

---

* What is exalted among men is an abomination before God.

27

Freedom of the Will, I

*With his two treatises on the freedom of the human will,
Hubmaier entered into one of the hotly debated contests of the
Reformation era. The two primary contestants in the debate
were Erasmus with his 1524* De libero arbitrio *and Luther with
his answer to Erasmus of 1525,* De servo arbitrio.[1] *Hubmaier
himself first addressed the issue in his* Christian Catechism.[2]
*Bergsten suggests that it was the pastoral concern of Hubmaier
that caused him to address the issue.[3]*

*The denial of the freedom of the will had led to the devel-
opment of tensions in Nikolsburg which he felt were based
ultimately on half-truths deriving from a perversion of the biblical perspective. The result was that one might conclude that
since it is God who works in us the willing and the doing, there
is no reason for Christians to attempt to live the disciplined
Christian life. In the course of both treatises Hubmaier makes a
study of an unusually large selection of biblical passages in
order to prove the freedom of the human will, without at the
same time denying the role of grace.*

*The first treatise, dated April 1, 1527, is dedicated to
Count George of Brandenburg-Ansbach, a follower of Luther.
Not only influential in support of evangelical causes in Upper
Silesia and Brandenburg, he was as Bergsten notes "an influen-
tial protector of the Reformation in Hungary, Bohemia, and
Moravia."[4]*

*This treatise is not only one in which typical Anabaptist
concerns surface, but it is also one of Hubmaier's most
theological. His theological anthropology, doctrine of God, and
doctrine of salvation all play important roles. As Moore 1981
and Windhorst 1976 indicate, what some might call "typical*

---

[1] Rupp 1959 contains complete translations of both treatises.

[2] See above, pp. 359ff.

[3] HS, p. 379. At about the same time Hans Denck was writing on the
same theme in his "Whether God Is the Cause of Evil" (Williams 1957, pp.
88ff.).

[4] HS, pp. 379-380.

*Anabaptist concerns" could be spoken of by others as closer to
Catholic traditions.*[5]

> ## On the Freedom of the Will
> ### which God through His Sent Word
> ### offers to all people
> ### and thereby gives them the power to become His
> ### Children
> ### and also the choice
> ### to will
> ### and to do good.
> ### or else to let them remain
> ### Children of Wrath
> ### which they are by nature
> ### Dr. Balthasar Hubmör
> ### von Fridberg
> ### Nicolspurg.

To the majestic, highborn prince and lord, Lord George,
Margrave at Branndenburg, Duke of Stetin, Pomerania, of the
Kashubes and the Wends, Burgrave at Nüremberg and Prince
at Rügen, my very gracious lord, grace, joy, and peace in
God./381/

Most majestic Prince, gracious lord. Although for several
years great earnestness and diligence has been expended so
that the gospel was preached to all creatures, I, nevertheless,
unfortunately, find many people who to this point have
learned and grasped no more than two pieces from all the
preaching. First, one says: "We believe; faith saves us." Second, "We can do nothing good. God works in us the desire
and the doing. We have no free will." Now, however, such

---

[5] An earlier partial English translation was published by George Hunston
Williams in the *Library of Christian Classics*: Williams 1957, pp. 114ff.,
and in Davidson 1939, pp. 603-636. Fragmentary quote in Hošek 1892, p.
232; more in Hošek 1892, pp. 148-155. Also quoted in Vedder 1905, pp.
182-195. The source of this translation: HS 22, pp. 380-397.

remarks are only half-truths from which one can conclude no more than half-judgments.[a] Whoever makes a whole judgment and does not lay the counter-Scriptures on the same scale next to it, to him a half-truth is more damaging than a whole lie. For when the half-truth is believed and sold under the appearance of a whole truth, then all sects, quarrels, and heresies result.[b] They are only doing patchwork with the Scripture, not comparing opposing Scriptures and uniting both into a whole judgment. Whoever does not divide the judgment in the Scripture in such a way eats of the unclean animals who do not part their hooves, Lev. 11:4.[6] Indeed, under the cover of these aforementioned half-truths all kinds of evil, disloyalty, and unrighteousness have fully and totally gotten the upper hand. Now all carelessness and impudence hang in the balance. There sit unfaithfulness and falsehood in their splendid throne, ruling and triumphing mightily in all things. No longer does any Christian work shine forth among all people. Brotherly love is extinguished in all hearts; and it has come to pass, as the prophet says, that truth has fallen to the ground in the streets and righteousness cannot enter anywhere, Isa. 59:14. Wisdom calls aloud and no one wants to hear her, Prov. 1:20. For it has come about (may it be faithfully lamented to God) that the world is now more evil than a thousand years ago, as all histories prove. All this happens, as painful as it is to say it, under the appearance of the gospel. For as soon as one says to them, "It is written: leave evil and do good," Ps. 37:27, they answer: "We can do no good. Everything happens out of the providence of God and from necessity." They imagine that by that they are permitted to sin. If one says further: "It is written: 'Whoever does evil will go into the eternal fire,' " John 5:29; Matt. 25:41, immediately they find a fan of fig leaves with which to cover their vices and they say: "Faith alone saves us and not our works." Yes, I

---

[6] The "cloven hoof" metaphor was the standard designation for the notion that proper understanding of the Scriptures depends on "solving" apparent contradictions. Cf. Deppermann 1979, pp. 214ff. Cf. also Hubmaier's use of paradoxes in text 29, p. 514ff. and note 13.

---

[a] Half-truth. Half-judgment.
[b] All quarreling originates from half-judgments.

have heard of many people who have not prayed, fasted, nor given alms for a long time, for their priests say that their works are of no value before God, wherefore they straightway neglect them. These are the half-truths under which we, as under the form of angels, protect all license /382/ of the flesh and blame all our sin and guilt on God, as Adam did on his Eve and Eve on the snake, Gen. 3:12. Yes, God must be responsible for all our vices, which is the greatest blasphemy on earth.

To uproot such tares, gracious Lord, I have written a small booklet for Your Princely Grace and summarized in short therein who and what is the human being in and outside of the grace of God, and what he is capable of. I will also as soon as possible make another book wherein I will testify incontrovertibly and still more powerfully with the Holy Scriptures to the freedom of the human being to do good and evil. I will also thereby thoroughly resolve the contrary passages concerning Pharaoh, Esau, Jacob, the potter and the like, Exod. 9:33; Mal. 1:2f.; Isa. 45:7; Jer. 18:6; Wisdom 15:7; Rom. 9:21. Your Princely Grace, I request in all humility that you accept this little book from me graciously. Herewith, may Your Princely Grace be commended unto God. Given at Nicolspurg, on the first day of April, 1527.

> Your Princely Grace's subject,
> Balthasar Hûbmör von Fridberg

The human being is a corporal and rational creature, created by God as body, spirit, and soul, Gen. 2:7. These three elements are found essentially and in varying ways in every human being, as the Scripture thoroughly proves. When the Lord God made the human being out of the dust from the earth, he blew a living breath into his face and thus the human being became a living soul, Gen. 2:7. Here Moses points to three things with distinct names. First, the flesh or the body is made out of the earth, which clod of earth or lump of clay, *aphar* and *erets* in the Hebrew, is translated in German as "dust," "ashes," or "mud taken from the earth." Second, notice the living breath, *neshamah* in the Hebrew, translated as "blowing on," "breathing on," "blowing upon," or "spirit." Third, the soul, called *nephesh*, is expressed separately; it is that which makes the body alive. Saint Paul mentioned these three essential substances quite clearly also with special and distinctive Greek names in writing to the Thessalonians: *pneuma, psyche,* and *soma*; in Latin: *spiritus, anima, corpus*; in German: *Geist, Seel, Leib*.[a] He said: "May he, the God of peace, sanctify you through and through and preserve your whole spirit, soul, and body without fault until our Lord Jesus Christ returns," 1 Thess. 5:23. Likewise, we read in Hebrews the distinction between the soul and /383/ the spirit thus: "The Word of God is lively and active and sharper than any two-edged sword and cuts until it separates soul and spirit and also joints and marrow and is a judge of the thoughts and feelings of the heart," Heb. 4:12. Likewise, Mary, the perpetually pure and chaste Virgin, noted this difference when she said to Elizabeth: "My soul magnifies the Lord and my spirit rejoices in God my Savior. For he has looked upon the misery of his servant," Luke 1:46ff. Here once again stand explicitly: soul, spirit, and misery, which means the flesh. For *Tapeinosis* in the Greek is misery or lowness of the human. *Tapeinophrosyne* is the humility of the mind. Christ also made this distinction more than apparent when he said to his disciples on the Mount of Olives: "My soul is distressed exceedingly, unto death. The spirit truly is willing, but the flesh is weak," Matt. 26:41.[b] Therefore the saddened soul of Christ cried out according to the will of the flesh: "My father, if it is possible, then remove this cup from me," but according to the Spirit the soul adds, "Nevertheless, not what I want, but as you want" [Matt. 26:41f]. Here, Christian reader, you see bright and clear that these three special and essential substances—soul, spirit, and body—are made and unified in every human being according to the image of the Holy Trinity.

Now since with scriptural authority no one can deny these three essential things, substances, or essences, it follows that one must confess also three kinds of will in human beings, namely, the will of the flesh, the will of the soul, and the will of the spirit.[c] However, so that I might teach in clear writing the different divisions of these three wills, the Spirit of God

---

[a] Spirit, Soul, Body.
[b] Soul, Spirit, Flesh.
[c] Three kinds of will in the human being.

speaks in John 1:13 of the will of the flesh, which does not want to suffer; the will of the soul, willing to suffer, but due to the flesh seeks not to; and the will of the spirit which strongly desires to suffer (cf. John 1:13). In order that I might teach with clear writing the different divisions of these three wills, the Spirit of God through the disciple whom Christ especially loved, speaks these words of the true and eternal light which became human and came to his own and his own did not accept him. To as many as accepted him, he gave the power to become God's children. Yes, to those who believe in his name, who are born not of blood, nor out of the will of the flesh nor out of the will of man (thus is the soul called in Scripture) but out of God, John 1:13; 1 Sam. 10. Now we are once born, but in original sin and wrath, as Paul laments to the Romans and Ephesians, also David, Job and Jeremiah, Rom. 7:5; Eph. 2:3; Ps. 51:7; Job 3:1. Accordingly we must be born again or we cannot see the kingdom of God, nor enter it. We must be born of water and Spirit, that is, through the Word /384/ of God, which is water to all who thirst for salvation, which Word is made alive in us through the Spirit of God, without whose working it is a killing letter, Jer. 20:14; John 3:5, 4:14, 7:48; 2 Cor. 3:6; Rom. 8:13; Ps. 51:12; Deut. 8:3; Matt. 4:4. The same helps our spirit, bears witness to it, and strengthens it in the battle and strife against the flesh, sin, world, death, devil, and hell. To this end every word that proceeds out of the mouth of God helps the spirit so that the flesh with its evil will and lusts can nowhere flee, hide, or cover itself. It finds outwardly neither rest nor respite before the preached Word of God whose sound goes throughout the whole world, nor internally in the spirit for it is everywhere convicted Ps. 19:5; Mark 16:15; Acts 1:8; Rom. 10:18; Rom. 2:15. Since all testimony is proved in the mouth of two or three witnesses, thence comes the conscience and the gnawing worm into the heart of the human being.

That is the true rebirth of which Christ speaks in John 3:3, whereby our Adam, who had become a woman and an Eve through the Fall, now again becomes a man; and the soul, which had become flesh, now again becomes spirit. Thus quite properly Saint Peter writes about this rebirth and says, "Make pure your souls through the obedience of truth in the spirit to sincere, brotherly love. Have fervent love for one another, out of a pure heart, as those who are reborn, not out of a perishable, but out of an imperishable seed, namely from the living Word of God which remains forever. Since all flesh is like grass and the glory of humanity is like a flower of the grass. The grass has withered and the flower fallen away, but the Word of the Lord remains for eternity," 1 Pet. 1:22-25; Isa. 40:6; Ecclus. 14:17f.; James 1:10. Note here, dear Christian, how the soul, which has become flesh through the disobedience of Adam, must through the Spirit of God and his living Word be reborn to a new spirit and become spirit, for what is born of the Spirit is spirit, John 3:6. I remain silent here as to why Peter only speaks concerning the soul and says, "Make pure your souls," and does not add to that, "your spirit and flesh." But he knows that the spirit from the beginning is entirely a divine creation and needs no rebirth, Gen. 1. Therefore, he says, "by the obedience of truth in the spirit," Gen. 3:19. Nor does the rebirth help the flesh, for the judgment has already been made and enacted by God that the flesh must wither like the grass and become ashes. Otherwise it cannot possess the kingdom of God, 1 Cor. 15:50; Matt. 16:17-19.

Second, it is to be noted that the human being should be considered in three states or forms: first, how he had been before the Fall of Adam; second, how he became after the Fall; third, how he is after the restoration.*

How the Human Being Was Before the Fall of Adam

Before the transgression of Adam all three substances in the human being—flesh, soul, and spirit—were good, Gen. 1:31. For God considered all the things which he /385/ had made and they were very good—indeed, especially the human being made in the image of God, Gen. 1:31. The three substances were also wholly free to choose good or evil, life or death, heaven or hell. Thus they were originally made good and free also in the recognition, in the capability, and performance of good and evil by God, as the Scripture itself testifies and says: "God made the human being from the

---

* How one should consider the human being.

beginning and left him free in the power of his own counsel,"
Ecclus. 15:14ff. He gave him the commandments and the law
and said: "If you will to keep the commandments" (God says:
If you, man, will, it is given to you to keep the commandments), "then they will preserve you."[a] He has set water and
fire before you (note: you); you have only to stretch out your
hand to the one you want. Before the human being are life
and death, good and evil; whatever pleases him (yes, him) is
given to him.[b] Here the Scripture clearly and plainly shows
us that the human being originally, in body, soul, and spirit,
was given a free will to will and to perform good or evil.
However, after the transgression of Adam, it has become
otherwise for him.

How the Human Being Has Become
After the Fall of Adam
Concerning the Flesh

After our first father Adam transgressed the commandment of God by his disobedience, he lost this freedom for
himself and all his descendants. Likewise, if a nobleman
receives a fief from a king and if he acts against the king, the
king will take this fief from the nobleman and all his heirs, for
they must all carry the guilt of their forefather. Thus the flesh
has irretrievably lost its goodness and freedom through the
Fall of Adam and has become entirely and wholly worthless
and hopeless unto death. It is not able or capable of anything
other than sin, striving against God and being the enemy of
his commandments. Whence springs forth the fearsome complaint which Paul utters to the Romans against his miserable
and ill-fated flesh (Rom. 7 and 8). Therefore it must, according to the curse of God, return to the earth from which it has
come, or it cannot possess the kingdom of heaven, Gal. 5,
Gen. 3. So is it also with the blood, for the two are of one
will, as Paul writes 1 Cor. 15:50; Matt. 16:17; 1 Cor. 11:11f.;
Ps. 51:7. Flesh and blood cannot possess the kingdom of God.
And Christ says to Peter: "Simon Bar Jona, flesh and blood
have not revealed this to you," Matt. 16:17. When Eve, who is

---

[a] You, you. To you, to you.
[b] Him, him.

a figure of our flesh, desired to eat and did eat of the forbidden fruit, she thereby lost the knowledge of good and evil, indeed of wanting and doing the good, and had to pay for this loss with death, so that as soon as a person is conceived and born, he is conceived and born in sin. From the first moment already he is up to his ears in sin and from that moment on when he receives life /386/ he begins to die and become earth again Gen. 2; 3. As God said: "On the same day you eat of the tree of the knowledge of good and evil you will die," Gen. 2:17. Therefore Job curses the day of his birth and so does Jeremiah. For the same reason King David heatedly laments the day of his conception and birth, complaining to God how he has been conceived in evil, and in sin his mother has borne him, as reported above, Job 3:1; Jer. 20:14; Ps. 51:7. And Paul in a few words says that we have all died in Adam, and God calls it returning to the earth and becoming ashes, 1 Cor. 15:22; Gen. 3:19.

Concerning the Spirit

The spirit of the human being, however, has before, during, and after the Fall remained upright, whole, and good. For it has neither with counsel nor deed, will nor action, been disobedient in any way in allowing the flesh to eat the forbidden fruit. Indeed, like a prisoner in the body, it had to eat against its will. However, the guilt was not its own, but that of the flesh and the soul, which also became flesh. This wholeness and uprightness of the spirit Saint Paul already demonstrates clearly in writing to the Thessalonians: "And may your whole spirit and soul and body be held blameless until the coming of our Lord Jesus Christ," 1 Thess. 5:23. He says, "Your whole spirit" and not "your whole soul," or "your whole body." For what has once disintegrated and been shattered is no longer whole. King David laments also because of the Fall and cries to God, "I have become like a broken cask, etc.," Ps. 31:12. In the same way also, so that the spirit might be saved, Paul gives the fornicator to the devil for the destruction of the flesh in the power of our Lord Jesus Christ, that is, in the power of the keys, which Christ has given to his bride, the Christian church, to bind and to loose on earth after him, 1 Cor. 5:5; Matt. 16:19; 18:18; John 20:23. It is as if he were to say, "If the flesh wants to be ruined and of the devil, then we give it to him; but the spirit remains saved and whole for the day of the Lord. Then will God act and deal with it according to his pleasure. It is unnecessary for us to know more.

Concerning the Soul

However, the soul, the third part of the human being, has through this disobedience of Adam been wounded in the will in such a way and become sick unto death so that it can on its own choose nothing good. Nor can it refuse evil since it has lost the knowledge of good and evil, Gen. 2; 3. There is nothing left to it but to sin and to die. Yes, as far as doing good goes, the soul has become entirely powerless and ineffective, Rom. 7. Only the flesh can act, without which the soul is outwardly able to do nothing, for the flesh is its instrument. Since, however, the instrument is incapable of doing anything, how can anything good be done with it, even if the soul /387/ gladly wanted to and made every effort. Nevertheless this Fall of the soul is reparable through the Word of God, Ps. 119:7; which teaches us again what it is to will or not will good or evil, and that after this life through the resurrection of the flesh, the body will become a heavenly, imperishable, noble, and spiritual one for action and fulfillment, 1 Cor. 15:44. Yes, it is the body of these people born again of the water and the Spirit, as the first human Adam was created into the natural life and the last Adam into the spiritual life. The first human is of the earth and is earthly; the second is from heaven and is heavenly.

That, however, this Fall of the soul is also reparable and harmless here on earth, while that of the flesh irreparable and even deadly, is due to the following: Adam, a figure of the soul—as Eve is a figure of the flesh—would have preferred not to eat of the forbidden tree, 1 Tim. 2:14. He was not seduced by the snake but Eve was, Gen. 3:6. Adam knew well that the word of the serpent contradicted the Word of God. Nevertheless, he willed to eat of this fruit against his own conscience in order not to grieve or anger his rib and flesh, Eve. He would have preferred not to do it. Thus, since he was more obedient to his Eve than to God, he lost the knowledge of good and evil. So he cannot will or choose good, nor can he not will or flee something evil, for he does not know what is truly good or evil before God, Ps. 14:3; 32:5; 53:2. Nothing tastes good to him but that which tastes and seems good to his Eve, that is, his flesh. For he has lost the right sense of taste.

A parable:*(i) a wounded or feverish person neither wants nor likes to eat or drink something good and healthy. Only cold water and harmful food taste good to him. That happens because his healthy nature and whole constitution have been disordered by sickness, for he has lost the right and healthy taste of knowledge. He has an embittered tongue so that he judges to be good what is harmful to him and to be evil what is useful. Just so is it with our soul after the transgression of Adam. As soon as he ate from the tree of the knowledge of good and evil, from that hour on he lost the taste of the knowledge of good and evil so that he can neither know nor judge what is right, good, or evil before God, what righteousness is sufficient before God, or what works are pleasing to God; all this even though he would gladly do right according to the spirit. This desire is still present today in all people, in Jews and heathen, as Paul writes to the Romans, Rom. 2:14. Indeed, if one is blind, he would gladly see.

If one is lame, then he would gladly /388/ go upright. Has one fallen among murderers, wounded and half dead, then he would gladly be whole again. However, as to the right way, truth, and means for coming to this health of the soul, all err who are not instructed by the Word of God. From this now follow all deviations, false doctrine, error, idolatry, and heresy, Ps. 119:11.

Here are to be excluded all those people who have sinned against the Holy Spirit, Matt. 12:32; Luke 12:10; 1 John 5:16ff.; Heb. 6:6; Rom. 1:18ff. In these all willing and desiring has been perverted. This is a judgment of the righteous God on account of their own wilfull, wanton, and unrepentant evil, because they fight against the known and recognized truth. Yes, they turn their backs on God and say that he will not let himself be seen. They stop up their ears so that they do not have to hear his voice. If they were to hear his voice they think they would have to die, even though it is in that way

---

* A good parable.

that one must and should become alive. They turn their eyes away from God and blame him for not wanting to know them. They close off their hearts and hide themselves and yet complain that he does not knock at their heart's door nor seek them. And if he knocks, they do not want to open the door; if he seeks them, they do not want to let themselves be found. That which they have, they deny; therefore God gives them what they do not want to have. Thus it happens in all those who deny the freedom of the will in the newborn human beings. Nevertheless, the time is coming when they will seek God, but will not be able to find him.

Also, as they flee from him, they will fall into his hands, for he will encounter them and act toward them according to their faith. Therefore, their sin will not be forgiven, neither here nor there, for the Spirit of God will be taken from them, without which Spirit our spirit is quite helpless. Therefore it is necessary to pray earnestly with David that God not take his Holy Spirit away from us, Ps. 51:13.

On the other hand, God will also fill all those with good things who hunger and thirst after righteousness and want gladly to do good, desiring and asking such from God who has created heaven and earth, who perceive his invisible nature, that is, his eternal power and divinity as they observe the works of the creation of the world. The same he will not let go away empty and without instruction, but he will fill them with good things and will also send ambassadors and epistles by which they will be led on the right way of truth. He did this for the treasurer of Queen Candace in Egypt by Philip and for Cornelius by Peter. Indeed, before God will forsake such a spirit-hungry person all the angels must come down from heaven and through them he will proclaim and announce all the glory of God, which he wants from us, in the highest, right peace on earth and goodwill to the people, as to the shepherds in the field in the /389/ night of Christ's birth, Luke 2:8ff. Therefore in the Scripture God commonly calls his Word bread, water, drink, meat or blood, for he wants all those who hunger and thirst after it to eat and drink, and that no one be left to suffer want.

Whether now such a power for willing what is right and good is in us, it is not in us as if it were from us,' for it is originally from God and his image, in which he created us

originally, 2 Cor. 3:18; Gen. 1:27; which the old serpent
almost blacked out and darkened through sin, Gen. 3:1ff.
Nevertheless, it was not possible to extinguish entirely this
breath of God in us, and it still cannot be done, for God lets
no one be more seriously tempted beyond that which he can
bear, 1 Cor. 10:13. But God can extinguish it as a punishment
so that a person can have eyes, ears and heart and still not
see, hear, nor understand, Matt. 13:9; Mark 4:9; Luke 8:8.

Here one sees truly how the flesh after the Fall can do
wholly and completely nothing; and how, as far as good is
concerned, it is completely unprofitable and dead, in all its
powers incapable of doing good, and is impotent, an enemy of
the law, to whom it does not want to be subservient even unto
the grave, John 12:40; Rom. 7:5; Gal. 5:17; Gen. 6:3; Rom.
8:1ff.; 1 John 2:16f. Thus did King David so bitterly complain
and cry that no health was in his flesh, Ps. 38:4. On that Paul
says: "I know truly that nothing good dwells in me, that is, in
my flesh," Rom. 7:18; 8:26. The spirit, however, even if it
gladly wanted to will and to do right, is imprisoned. It can
accomplish nothing other than bear internal witness to
righteousness against evil and cry as a captive to God without
ceasing, with unspeakable sighs. Thus the soul has fallen
among murderers, has been badly wounded by them and lies
there half-dead, Luke 10:30. It has no taste or knowledge any
more of either good or evil. Thus Paul speaks of the matter
and says: "The psychic person[7] grasps nothing of the Spirit of
God," 1 Cor. 2:14. It is foolishness to him and he cannot
recognize it for it must be discerned in spiritual ways. The
spiritual person, however, judges all things and is judged by
no one. Here you note again, dear Christian, the wholeness of
the spirit in the human being which rightly judges all things
and the wounds of the soul, which in itself is of no value for
judging. Both flesh and soul are damaged and seriously
wounded. Only the spirit has retained its original righteousness in which it was first created. This is the way things are
among the three substances in the human being before and
after the transgression of Adam, our first father, whatever the
scholastics say about the upper and lower parts of the human

---

[7] Ger. *seelisch mensch.*

being. Aristotle, the pagan, seduced them because he knew and ascribed nothing to the human being, save body and soul.* The spirit was too heavenly for him. He was not able to grasp this breath of the living God with his natural and pagan understanding. /390/

How the Human Being Is After the Restoration

If the human being after the restoration by Christ is considered, one finds clearly that the flesh is still good for nothing and wholly ruined, as all the Scriptures lament. The spirit is happy, willing, and ready to do all good. The soul, sad and troubled, standing between the spirit and the flesh, knowing not what to do, is in its natural powers blind and ignorant of heavenly things. However, since it has been awakened by the heavenly Father through words of comfort, threats, promises, good things, punishment, and in other ways prodded, admonished, and drawn, as well as made whole by his dear Son, and enlightened by the Holy Spirit—as the three main articles of our Christian faith concerning God the Father and the Son and the Holy Spirit show—by this the soul now again knows what is good and evil. Now it has again obtained its lost freedom. It can now freely and willingly be obedient to the spirit, can will and choose good, as well as it was able in Paradise. It can also reject evil and flee it. It is the sent Word of God that works such in the soul, as David says: "He has sent his Word and made them whole," Ps. 107:20. Thus Christ says also: "If you remain in my Word, then you are my true disciples and will recognize the truth and the truth will make you free. If the Son makes you free, then you are truly free," John 8:31ff. Here note and let hear whoever has ears, that we are again made free through the sent Word and truth of God, through his only begotten Son, Jesus Christ. Therefore there must be true health and freedom in humanity again after the restoration, for God works always in us the willing and the doing, according to the good resolution of the heart, Phil. 2:13. Although the flesh does not afterward want to do so, it must against its own will do what the soul, which is united

---

* Aristotle.

with the spirit, wants. Thus David calls to God: "Lord, my soul clings to ashes (that is, the flesh), but make me alive, according to your Word," Ps. 119:25. On this basis, true health and freedom must be in humanity after the restoration, or these Scriptures must fall to the ground, which God forbid. Therefore Christ and Paul ascribe this freedom to humanity and say, "If you will enter into life, then keep the commandments. If you live after the flesh, then you will die. If you will walk according to the Spirit, then you will live," Matt. 19:17; Rom. 8:13. Here is confirmed that ancient proverb: "Man, help yourself; then I also will help you." Yes, God speaks first and gives power through his Word. /391/ Now the human being can also help himself through the power of the Word or he can willfully neglect; that is up to him. Therefore one says: God has created you without your help, but without your help he will not save you. Since God first created the light, whoever wants to accept it will do so on the basis of the commandment of God; whoever despises it falls into darkness because of the just judgment of God, John 1:5ff.; 3:19. And the talent which he has and does not want to use, but hides in the handkerchief, will therefore be simply taken from him.

The soul stands between the spirit and the flesh, as Adam stood between God, who tells him he should not eat of the tree of the knowledge of good and evil, and his Evē, who tells him he should eat of the tree, Gen. 2; 3. The soul is now free and may follow the spirit or the flesh. However, if it follows Eve, that is, the flesh, then it becomes an Eve and flesh. If it is obedient to the spirit, then it becomes a spirit. The soul should beware that it not linger too long at this oak of human choice and first at length consider whether it will follow the flesh or the spirit, lest it, like Absalom, who also hung between heaven and earth, 2 Sam. 18:9, be stabbed to death by the slave of sin, that is, by the flesh, with three wounds: of consent, word, and deed. Therefore David says, "I have hurried and neglected nothing to hold to your commandments," Ps. 119:4. And in another place: "If you today hear the voice of the Lord, do not stop your ears," Ps. 95:7f. "Today," he says, "Not *Cras, cras,* tomorrow, tomorrow, as the ravens cry."[a]

---

[a] Tomorrow, tomorrow.

Accordingly, after the restoration the soul is now made healthy and truly free through the sent Word. Now it can will and do good, as much as depends on it, for it can command the flesh in such a way that it tames and masters it, so that against its own inclination it must go into the fire with the spirit and with the soul on account of the name of Christ. Although there remain imperfection, weakness, and defect in all action and omission, for we are all unprofitable servants, such is not grounds for rebuke or injurious to the soul, but to the body which is the evil instrument and worthless tool.

A parable: A carpenter gladly wants to make a clean and smooth table, but his plane is bent and notched. Now, to make such is impossible for the worker, even though not he but the plane is responsible. /392/ Likewise such a defect is not damnable to the soul, since it is sorry for it and confesses its impotence before God. However, for the flesh it is destructive; therefore it must pay the penalty, suffer, and return again to the earth. Nevertheless, the soul is again so free after the restoration that it can will evil and perform it, for in evil it has a competent and useful instrument in the flesh, which by nature is quick to do evil and is inclined to do so.

For this reason it is said: Sin is done willingly; if it were not, it would not be sin. This willfulness is the theme of those Scriptures in which God rebukes us because we do not want to hear, know, or accept the good. As when Christ says: "Jerusalem, Jerusalem, how oft have I wanted to gather you as a hen gathers its chicks under its wings, and you were not willing," Matt.23:37. Thus he says to the young man who asks what good things he should do in order to inherit eternal life: "He answers him: 'If you want to enter into life, then keep the commandments.' " Willing and keeping must have been in the power of the young man, for he said: "I have kept them from youth on," Matt. 19:17ff. Without doubt he spoke the truth. For Jesus looked at him and loved him, Mark 10:21. He does not, however, love liars. Nevertheless, Christ shows him his inborn imperfection, which is in every person, and tells him to sell everything that he has and give it to poor people. Therefore he was moved with sadness. However, the same is unharmful to him, for it is fulfilled through Christ, who is the Alpha and Omega, the beginning and the end of the fulfillment of divine commandments. In him is our perfection. If the commandments of God are fulfilled, says Augustine, those other things not fulfilled by us are forgiven us. John also has written more than clearly concerning this power, when he says that God has given over and entrusted us with the power to become children of God.

Here you sée clearly, Christian reader, how to will the good belongs to us to whom the Word is sent, but we do not find it in ourselves to fulfill. That happens because of our wretched body in which nothing but sin dwells, Rom. 7:18.

To summarize: The spirit is whole also after the restoration. The flesh can do nothing at all. The soul, however, can sin or not sin. But the soul which sins will die, Ezek. 18:20. Accordingly, it can well and rightfully say, *propter me orta est haec tempestas*, that is, "it has to do with me." The flesh has received its judgment. The spirit keeps its wholeness. If I now will, then I will be saved by the grace of God; if I do not will, then I will be damned, and that on the basis of my own obstinacy and willfulness. Thus speaks the Spirit of God through Hosea: "The condemnation is yours, Israel; only in me is your salvation," Hos. 13:9. /393/

From this passage it is easy to note how the law is given in different ways:[a] to the flesh for the recognition of its sins; to the spirit as an aid and witness against sin; to the soul for a light whereby it can see and learn the way of righteousness and flee sin and evil.[b] Thus, when the flesh hears the law, it is frightened and its hair stands on end in terror. The spirit leaps for joy. The believing soul thanks God and praises him for the lamp and light to his feet, Ps. 119:105. For as the devil neither wishes to nor can do good, but is stuck in his evil, so likewise our flesh, since it has sinned out of willfulness when it saw that the forbidden fruit was good to eat and was appealing to the eyes and lovely to the sight. However, the soul did not sin out of its own willfulness but out of weakness and the impulse of the flesh since Adam did not want to grieve Eve, who was his flesh. As he then excused himself and said: "The woman, whom you gave me for a mate, gave me from the tree and I ate," Gen. 3:6. Only the spirit has

---

[a] Law.
[b] Therefore to the blessed is the law not a law but a guide.

remained upright in this Fall; therefore it will return to the Lord, who gave it, Eccles. 12:7.

In summary: Here you see, reader, how God created the human being so free that he was at first able without new grace to remain in his inborn innocence and righteousness unto eternal life.[a] He could also forfeit this grace through disobedience, which is what happened. As a result, through the Fall, grace and freedom have been darkened and lost to such a degree that the human being does not know any longer what is good or evil without a special and new grace of God. How can one will to do good and avoid evil if one cannot will anything good, unless one has recognized it beforehand. However, after the restoration, the human being has acquired and again received such grace, health, and freedom through the merits of our Lord Jesus Christ that one can now again will the good and do it, indeed against the nature and will of the flesh in which there is nothing good.[b]

In the third place: since free will in the human being is nothing other than a power, force, energy, or adroitness of the soul to will or not will something, to choose or flee, to accept or to reject good or evil, according to the will of God, or according to the will of the flesh, which fleshly will and potentiality should more exactly be called an impotence rather than a power or energy. But the soul, through the eating of the forbidden tree lost the recognition of good and evil in the sight of God, which knowledge it certainly had before the Fall, as far as it was necessary and sufficient for a human creature to know. Therefore that same tree was called a tree of the knowledge of good and evil from which God forbade Adam to eat, Gen. 2:17, that is, to desire, know, and /394/ experience more than is necessary for a human being. For Eve wanted also to know everything that God knows, as promised to her by the crafty serpent. "On the day they eat thereof, their eyes will open and they will become as gods, knowing good and evil," Gen. 3:5. Accordingly they were rightly removed and robbed of this knowledge of good and evil by God and have become as a horse and a mule in whom there is no understanding.

---

[a] The human being is created free.
[b] Free will.

For whichever person does not accept a divine gift from God with thankfulness or who does not want it, from the same will also justifiably be taken that which he has. So has it happened also to humanity in this case. Now a person can no longer will something good nor flee evil unless he knows beforehand what is good or evil in the eyes of God. Therefore this recognition and power of knowledge, willing, and working must happen and be attained by a new grace and drawing of the heavenly Father, who now looks at humanity anew by the merit of Jesus Christ our Lord, blesses and draws him with his life-giving Word which he speaks into the heart of a person. This drawing and call is like an invitation to a marriage or to an evening meal. Through it God gives power and authority to all people insofar as they themselves want to come; the free choice is left to them. It is a new birth, a beginning of his creatures, like humanity in Paradise first had been, excepting only the flesh; indeed, it is truly becoming children of God.

But whoever does not want to come, like Jerusalem and those who have bought oxen and houses and have taken wives—these he leaves out as unworthy of this Supper. He wants to have uncoerced, willing, and joyous guests and donors; these he loves. For God does not force anyone except through the sending and calling of his Word, as also the two disciples at Emmaus did not force Christ to remain with them otherwise than by request and good words, Luke 24:29. In the same way Lot was not compelled by the two angels in Sodom, Gen. 19:2f. For the divine Word is so powerful, authoritative, and strong in the believers that the person (though not the godless one) can will and do everything that said Word commands him to want and to do. For the gospel is the power of God to the salvation of all believers, Rom. 1:16. Likewise the sick man, who had lain thirty-eight years in the portico by the pool at Bethesda, heard the Word of Jesus, saying: "Stand up, take your bed, and go forth," John 5:9. In the power of these words of Christ he freely stood up, took his bed, and went forth. He could have refused, saying to the Lord in unbelief, "It is impossible," or "I prefer rather to lie here." As also Christ could not do many wonders in /395/ his fatherland because of their lack of faith, Matt. 13:57-58. However, as soon as this sick man heard the Word and believed, he was whole, stood up, and walked. Thus as soon as Christ says to a person: "Keep my commandments. Leave evil and do good," from that hour on the person in faith receives power and strength to will and to do such. Yes, all things are now possible to the believer in the one who strengthens him, Christ Jesus. Here can be introduced all the writings which testify to the power and effect of the divine Word.

Now we surely know that originally God made all things good and especially the human being in spirit, soul, and body. However, by the disobedience of Adam this goodness in us has been wounded in the soul, it has been held captive and obscured in the spirit by the darkness of the body, and has been completely ruined in the flesh. If we would again be free in the spirit, be healed in the soul, and also that this Fall be unharmful to us in the flesh, then such must, must, must take place through a new birth, as Christ himself says, or we will not enter into the Kingdom of God.ᵃ Now God, however, as James writes, gives birth to us willingly with the Word of his power, so that we become a new a beginning of his creatures, James 1:18. In this Word, which Peter calls an indestructible seed, 1 Pet. 1:23, we become free and whole again by a new law so that absolutely nothing damning is any longer in us, Rom. 8:1. Thus says Christ: "The truth will make you truly free," John 8:36. Also David: "He has sent his Word and has made us healthy," Ps. 107:20. And in another place: "Lord, make me alive according to your Word," Ps. 119:107. Now it follows incontrovertibly that through the power of the divine Word there must be in the believer right freedom, true health, and real life, or we will have to abolish half the Bible. Far be that from us.ᵇ

From the things said above one notes clearly and surely that the human being received two wounds by the Fall of Adam.ᶜ The first is an inner one which is ignorance of good and evil; therefore Adam was more obedient to the voice of his Eve than to the voice of God. The second wound is external, in doing and acting. Thus the human being cannot wholly complete and hold the commandments of God on account of

---

ᵃ Must, must, must.
ᵇ Freedom of the will is in the human being, or half the Bible must be false.
ᶜ Two wounds.

the inborn evil of his flesh; rather, in all his works he is a useless servant, Luke 17:10. This weakness or lack originates from the fact that Adam has not rightly mastered his rib Eve according to the command of God, but against the same has also eaten of the tree which was forbidden him on penalty of death.

The first wound is healed by the wine poured on it by the Samaritan Christ, Luke 10:34, that is, through the law in which the human being by a new grace is again taught anew what is truly good and evil before God. The second wound is healed by the oil, that is, /396/ with the gospel. Thus this sin or weakness no longer has anything poisonous or damning in it, if we do not follow it wantonly. Therefore in the New Testament Christ, the true physician, mixed together both wine and oil, that is, the law and the gospel, and made out of them a healing plaster for our souls. Thereby our souls became righteous and healthy again.

Here one grasps with both hands how Christ has made the Fall of Adam wholly innocuous for us and incapable of condemning, and how he crushed the head of the old serpent through the seed of the woman, Gen. 3:15, how he took away the sting and made its poison no longer lethal to us, 1 Cor. 15:30f. Thus, henceforth, no one may decry Adam or Eve nor excuse or gloss over his sins with Adam's Fall since everything which had been lost, wounded, and had died in Adam has been· sufficiently restored, healed, and made healthy. For Christ with his Spirit has acquired for our spirit from the heavenly Father that the prison is not harmful to our spirit.* And with his soul he has acquired for our soul that through his divine Word it is again taught and enlightened as to what good and evil is. Yes, also by his flesh he earns for our flesh that after it has become ashes it may again be resurrected in honor and be immortal, 1 Cor. 15:22. Accordingly, henceforth every soul that sins will bear its sin itself since it is willingly responsible for its own sin and not Adam, not Eve, not the flesh, sin, death or the devil, for all these things are already captured, bound, and overcome in Christ. To him we say, with Paul, be praise, honor, and thanks for eternity.

---

* What Christ has acquired for us.

Finally, we see here thoroughly and clearly what great rubbish all those have produced and introduced into Christendom to this point who deny the freedom of the will in people and say how this freedom is an empty and idle name and is nothing in itself. For thereby our God is shamed and blaspheméd as if he like a tyrant penalized and condemned humanity for something which it was impossible for them to will or to do. Thereby is also lifted and overthrown the justifiable charge which Christ will use against all the godless on the last day when he says, "I was hungry and you did not feed me," Matt. 25:42. For then they could all too easily excuse themselves and answer: "It was, however, impossible for us, for you have robbed us of willing and working the good because of Adam. For we were also foreseen from eternity in your unchanging wisdom and thereto ordained that we should not feed you."* Likewise: Judas Iscariot, when he betrayed you, /397/ and Pilate when he had to sentence you even though you were innocent. "What do you now accuse us of, since we are not guilty, but you yourself who hast made and used us as an unworthy vessel, and now so that your eternal wisdom and providence remáin true and just, we must go as damned ones into the eternal fire with the devil and confirm your foreknowledge."

Through this denial of the free will manifold cause is given to the malevolent to lay all their sins and evil deeds on God, saying, "That I practice harlotry and adultery is the will of God. What God wills must take place. Yes, who can counter his will? Were it not his will, then I would not sin. If it is his will, then I will stop sinning." Not to mention that by this erroneous opinion many people are misled into laziness and great despair, so as to think that since I cannot will or do anything good, and since all things happen out of necessity, I will thus remain therein. If God wants to have me, then he will freely draw me. If he does not, then my will is in vain and unfruitful. Yes, such people are waiting also for a special, unusual, and miraculous drawing of God which he would use with them, as if the sending of his holy Word were not enough to draw and summon them. All of which is the work of

---

* Foreknowledge. Predestination.

such an evil, crafty, and blasphemous devil, that I do not know whether a more harmful Satan for the hindrance of all righteousness and godliness could rise up on earth among Christians. Through this false opinion a great part of the Holy Scriptures is overthrown and made powerless. May the all powerful, good, and merciful God graciously aid us against such serious error and crush it with the breath of his mouth, through Jesus Christ our Lord. Amen.

**Printed by Simprecht
Sorg, called Froschauer.
Nicolspurg
1527**

28

Freedom of the Will, II

In the preface to his previous treatise on the subject of the freedom of the will, Hubmaier promised another writing on the subject. This is that treatise, dated May 20, 1527.

The references by Hubmaier to his "dear friends" who "heatedly" deny the freedom of the will points to the reality of a controversy on the subject at Nikolsburg.[1] With this and the preceding treatise he sets about to settle the issue by a study of the relevant scriptural passages, more extensively so in this second treatise.

Freedom of the Will, II *is dedicated to Duke Friedrich II of Liegnitz, Brieg, and Wohlau, in Silesia, who had been won to the evangelical faith by Caspar Schwenckfeld. Duke Friedrich was later to provide a place of refuge for many Anabaptists, including Hubmaier's printer, Simprecht Sorg.[2]*

The treatise was evidently influenced by Erasmus and bears similarities to many concerns of Hans Denck.[3], For all of that, it is a thorough presentation of an important theme familiar to Anabaptists.[4]

---

[1] Also, at the beginning of "The Third Part" Hubmaier refers to "opponents who come to me daily." See below, p. 471.

[2] Cf. Zeman 1969, p. 168.

[3] See the discussion of Hubmaier's use of Erasmus and Denck in Bergsten 1978, pp. 352-358. The influence of Erasmus is more obvious, but even here Hubmaier maintains his own perspective. The clearest dependency of Hubmaier on Erasmus is in the selection of Scriptures to be used in the treatise. The notes to the treatise below will suggest the extent of the usage of Erasmus by Hubmaier. For a study of the probable influence of Erasmus on Hubmaier and Denck, see Hall 1961. Walter Moore finds a more likely dependence by Hubmaier on his teacher, John Eck, concluding that "Hubmaier maintained throughout his theological pilgrimage the position that he learned as a student of John Eck at Freiburg and especially at Ingolstadt." Moore 1981, p. 95. Rollin Armour's analysis of the Catholic roots of Hubmaier's doctrine of the will is also worth noting, Armour 1966, pp. 33-34.

[4] Translation in Davidson 1939, pp. 639-689. A fragment in Williams 1957, pp. 131-135; and Vedder 1905, pp. 197-200. See also Estep 1967, pp. 107ff. Source: HS 23, pp. 400-431.

The Second Book
On the Freedom of the Will
Of the Human Being
In Which it is Testified
With Scriptures that
God by Means of His Sent Word
Gives Power to All People
To Become His Children and
Freely Entrusts to Them
the Choice to Will and to Do Good.
Also Thereby Are the Counter Scriptures
Of the Opposition Dissolved.[5]
Balthasar Hûbmör
von Fridberg

To the majestic highborn Prince and Lord, Duke Frederichen von Lignitz, Brickh, etc., Sovereign of Lower Schlesien, my Gracious Lord.

Your serene highness. Gracious Lord. Christ our Savior was led by Satan to the top of the temple at Jerusalem and to the top of the very high mountain, so that he might visibly throw himself down from it, or, secondly, that he might worship the devil, Matt. 4:5f.; Luke 4:9ff. So also is every person

---

[5] Hubmaier's use of Scripture citations in this treatise is especially problematic. As elsewhere he seeks to appeal to Scripture whenever possible, occasionally citing a passage which does not contain clear support for what is being discussed. He is not alone among sixteenth-century writers in this regard. In this particular treatise, Hubmaier's wish to support his position with overwhelming use of Scripture often leads him to passages that are marginally related at best. Where the editors have left a chapter reference without verses, it is for one of two reasons: either the whole chapter could be taken as applying, or it has not been possible to find an applicable verse in that chapter. All Scriptures cited by Hubmaier have been given. Only by reproducing all Hubmaier's references, even those hard to identify, can it become graphically clear as to how deeply grounded in Scripture Hubmaier's approach was. We continue the practice of taking over the scriptural citations from the marginal notes into the text.

led to the heights of his feelings, and Luciferian and Eve-like thoughts rise in his heart, as to how he might acquire temporal power, glory, praise, skills, honor, fame, and riches of this world here on earth, Isa. 14:12ff.; Gen. 3:6. Immediately the devil whispers in one ear, "Cast yourself down from the temple, risk a dangerous and sacrilegious act, do not care whether it is against God." He uses then a half-truth: "It is written: God has commanded his angels to bear you in their hands so that you do not /401/ injure a foot on a stone," Ps. 91:11f. The Spirit of God, however, says in his other ear: "It is written: 'You should not tempt the Lord your God' " Deut. 6:16. Satan further shows the person the riches of this world and says on the one side: "Look at the land, the people, wife, child, meadows, acres, and all the splendor of this world. All this I will give you if you serve and worship me. However, if you leave me and follow the gospel, then you will miss all that." The Spirit of God stands against that on the other side and says, "It is written: 'You should worship the Lord your God and serve him alone.' " Now the person hangs freely in the balance and hovers between heaven and earth. One may freely choose—for the choice is given to one—blessing or curse, fire or water, good or evil, life or death, and one is free to be obedient to God or to Satan. Freedom of the will is freely given to him, like a cut-down tree, to fall on the one side or the other, which freedom until now several of my friends have very heatedly denied.

Since, however, I see that their error results in great dishonor for our God and Lord, who planted us to be a good vineyard. When we do not bring forth good grapes, but bitter and sour unripened grapes,[6] it is our fault, not God's, Isa. 5:4. For if all things happened from necessity, as my friends say, and God effected good and evil in us, he would no longer have the right to condemn people because of sin. He would have to condemn himself. Adam and Eve could have so easily excused themselves before God with the words, "Lord, that we have transgressed your commandment happened out of your providence and necessity. You made and ordered us to be so. Therefore, it had to happen." Such is far from God. He

---

[6] *Winttertrollen: Herblinge*, grapes that do not ripen, due to late blossoming.

was, is, and remains righteous in all his works, Isa. 1, 5; Ps. 51:1-8; John 8:51; Matt. 19:17. Therefore he wants us to judge and decide ourselves and asks us to do that. For truly the one saying of Christ, "If you will enter into life, keep the commandments," is more powerful in every single Christian heart as a testimony to the freedom of the human will than a big ship full of human glosses imported from foreign lands of carnal wisdom.

Accordingly, Gracious Prince and Lord, in order to maintain with the Holy Scripture such freedom of the will in the human being, to whom God has sent his Word, I now dedicate the second book to Your Princely Grace in which first of all I introduce Scriptures to testify to the truth. Second, I set forth several theses which are very useful in this matter. Lastly, I have dissolved the arguments and objections of my friends so that no one be deceived and sophistrated[7] by half-truths under the appearance of whole truths.[*] Finally, I desire for God's sake that the testimony of both sides be heard /402/ and that afterwards, every Christian reader judge for oneself according to the plumb line of Holy Scripture. If then I have erred, then one should point it out to me with the Scripture. If, however, I am right, then do not believe me, but God himself. To him be given all glory and honor. Please let your Princely Grace accept this book from me graciously, and herewith let me be commended to your Princely Grace, to serve in all submissiveness. Nicolspurg, May 20, 1527.

> To Your Princely Grace
> Your Obedient Servant,
> Balthasar Hûbmōr

The Scriptures concerning

the human being, how he was first made by God and how he was before the Fall, namely, completely free to do good and

---

[7] A neologism alluding to the sophists.

---

[*] More than that I cannot claim to do.

so graced so that in the said grace of God he could have kept his commandments, live eternally, and be saved.[8]

Ecclesiasticus Chapter 15[9]

In the beginning God set the human being in Paradise and left him in[a] the power of his own counsel, Gen. 2:15. He gave him[b] commandments and laws and said: "If you[c] will keep the commandments, they will maintain you[d] and hold you in acceptable faith for eternity ." He has set before you[e] water and fire to which you[f] have only to stretch out your hand.[g] Before the person is life and death, good and evil. Whichever pleases him will be given to him.[h]

Here you see, Christian reader, how God originally made the human being so free and highly graced that he could remain in his created innocence and original righteousness without any new grace, keeping the commandments of God and living eternally in rest, ecstasy, and joy, Gen. 2:8-17. Yes, freedom and choice were left to him. He could stretch out his hand to water or fire, life or death, to good or evil. Whatever the human being wanted, God wanted to give him. First of all

---

[8] The clearest indication of the dependence of Hubmaier on Erasmus is that Hubmaier tends to use the same Scriptures as Erasmus in the order in which Erasmus used them. As a rule, however, the arguments are not those of Erasmus, but of Hubmaier, who develops his own exegesis and interpretations. He does not use all of the Scriptures which Erasmus uses. Occasionally he adds a Scripture which Erasmus did not use. We will note here only the broad outline of the Erasmian citations which were used, as well as citing those Scriptures which were added anew. We will note as well those few places where the dependence of Hubmaier on Erasmus' wording is apparent.

[9] Both Erasmus and Hubmaier begin with this citation and, in general, Hubmaier follows the order of Old Testament references used by Erasmus in his *De libero arbitrio* sections II.a.1-II.a.18, DLA: 36-72, tr. Rupp 1959, pp. 47-58.

---

[a] In, in, in.
[b] Him, him.
[c] You, you.
[d] You, you.
[e] Before you, before you.
[f] You, you.
[g] Your hand, your hand.
[h] To him, to him.

God created him in such great honor and high dignity[a] (Ps. 32:8f.). However, he did not consider it nor did he embrace it in his heart but became like an unreasoning animal, in whom is no understanding; and he stretched out his hand to fire, evil, and death, Gen. 3. Therefore God has given him the same, so that he is henceforth a child of fire, of evil, and of death. Of which the human being himself and not God is guilty. /403/ Henceforth, without a special and new grace of God, the person may neither know nor recognize, not to say achieve, what fire, water, good, evil, life, or death is. How can he then will and choose the good or flee the evil, since he does not recognize such? Thus the person has wholly and completely lost the knowledge of good and evil in the flesh and in the soul by the eating of the forbidden tree in Paradise, Gen. 3:6ff. If now God the heavenly Father had not come to our help with a new and special grace through Jesus Christ, his most beloved Son, our Lord, we would all have to remain in this blindness, die, and be eternally lost, John 3:16.

Yet, it should be exactly and well noted here that everything which we possess in this time of grace from the gospel through the given Christ, the same had the patriarchs and fathers of the old marriage possessed from the prophecies—through the promised Christ in this case,[b] 1 Cor. 10:1ff. For as the Christian church of the New Testament has received the eternal Son of God as her own spouse and husband through his holy and bodily incarnation, so also was Jesus Christ, Son of the living God, espoused, promised, and assured to the church of the Old Testament for a future spouse and bridegroom by God himself in the book of creation and through the holy prophets again and again, Gen. 3:15; 22:18; 26:4; 28:14.

It is for this reason that our ancestors called the books of the Old Testament the old marriage, and the books of the New Testament the new marriage. Nevertheless, there is only one marriage and only one church of the only bridegroom and Head, Christ Jesus, Deut. 18:15; Isa. 7:14; 9:5f.; Heb. 1:2. This marriage is just the mystery of which Paul wrote: "The

---

[a] The will and the choice is freely given to the human being.
[b] It is one and the same faith unto old and new marriage.

mystery is great. (We have till now called it a sacrament.) I speak, however, of Christ and the church," Eph. 5:32.

The Scriptures concerning the human being,

how he lost his freedom through the Fall of Adam and how he became a child of sin, wrath, and death. Also how without a special and new grace of God he cannot keep the commandments nor be saved.

God said, in Genesis 6:3:

"My spirit will not always be judge among people since they are flesh." And soon thereafter in the eighth chapter the Lord says, Gen. 8:21: "The judgment of the human heart is evil from youth on." /404/

Job also earnestly laments
concerning sin in Job 3:3ff., saying:

"Let the day be lost wherein I was born and the night wherein one said: 'A boy is conceived.'*(e) The same day must be dark and God from above must not ask after it. Let no brightness shine over it, darkness must stay in it, and may darkness remain above it with clouds, etc."[10]

He indicates the reason and says: "I know that no person is justified before the face of God," Job 9:2f. For if he were to litigate with us we would not be able to answer him one time in a thousand, Job 15:14. For not even the heavens nor the stars are pure before God, Job 25:5. Therefore all creatures sigh and call to God for redemption, Rom. 8:19.

Jeremiah makes a similar complaint
about sin in Jeremiah 20:14f.:

---

[10] This Scripture and the following two passages on Jeremiah and Ps. 51 are taken up independently by Hubmaier, in order to argue about original sin, an argument missing in Erasmus.

---

* Note what complaint the holy men make about their first birth.

456 / Balthasar Hubmaier

"Cursed be the day in which I was born; may the day in which I was brought forth by my mother not be blessed. Cursed be the man who announced to my father saying, 'Born to you is a son, etc.,' " Jer. 20:14.

Likewise David also grieves about the day of his birth, Psalm 51:5:

"Notice, O God, in evil was I conceived and in sin did my mother give birth to me," Ps. 51:5.

Paul

In particular Saint Paul also wholeheartedly laments everywhere in his epistles. Namely, how through one person, that is, through Adam, sin has come into the world and death through sin and thus death has come to all people and the judgment from one sin unto condemnation has come over all people,* Rom. 5:12. He also confesses openly that there is nothing good in him, that is, in his flesh. Therefore he calls out very loud: "Miserable person that I am, who will relieve me from the body of this death?" Rom. 7:24. We have all died once in Adam and have all become children of wrath by nature, 1 Cor. 15:22; Eph. 2:3.

Here you hear, O reader, what heavy accusations these holy men bring against themselves as they regard themselves and recognize what they are like according to the first birth, from Adam, Ps. 38:4. For there is no health at all in their flesh. /405/

The Scriptures concerning the human being,

how after the restoration by Jesus Christ he received again his freedom and a new grace to will and to be able to do good through the sent Word of God—except for the flesh alone which before its resurrection does not and cannot do anything at all but sin and fight against the spirit, Rom. 7:25; Gal. 5:17;

---

* Therefore the young children must also die.

Rom. 8:1. Yet such sin of the flesh does not condemn the human being because he does not will it nor walk according to it.[11]

God said to Cain, Genesis 4:5ff:

"Why are you angry? And why does your face change?[a] Is it not so, that if you were righteous it would be a sacrifice? If, however, you are not righteous, then sin is waiting to be revealed. But let it, that is, the sin, bow before you and be master over it."[b]

If now Cain was a lord and master over his sin, yes, over all his anger and rage, then, as God himself says, he would have been able to master, suppress, and knock it to the ground, John 20:22-23. So that the sin, if he had wanted otherwise, would have had to be subject to him and bow before him. It follows that we also can be lords and masters of our sins, which lordship and mastery comes to us out of the new grace of the sending of the divine Word by which God breathes on us newness, awakens us, gives us birth anew, and gives us the choice and the power to become his children, John 3:3; John 1:12. For Cain was born only after the Fall, like us, coming from Adam and Eve. That is the simple and right understanding of this Scripture. I will not let myself err with any different or strange glosses and additions, for "smoothly forged is soon polished."

In Deuteronomy 11:26ff. Moses says:

"Behold, today I lay before you[c] a blessing and a curse. The blessing if you[d] will be obedient to the commandments

---

[11] Erasmus also has a passage on the restoration of the human being, sections II.a.2.-II.a.3. DLA: 38-43, tr. Rupp 1959, pp. 48-49. The similarity of the argument is in the attention to grace; the major difference is that Hubmaier characteristically emphasizes the Word of God.

---

[a] You, You.
[b] Before you, Before You.
[c] You, you, you.
[d] You, you, you.

of the Lord your God which I command you today. The curse, however, if you are not obedient to the commandments of the Lord your God, and diverge from the way, which I command to you today, so that you walk after other gods whom you do not know."[12] Note, Christian reader, and judge for yourself in your conscience whether anything more sacrilegious could ever be ascribed to our God than that his divine majesty /406/ said such high words to the children of Israel through Moses just for fun and not with earnest concern, as some mumble in their dreams. Judge and decide, dear Christian, 1 John 4:1; Gal. 2; Eph. 6:14; Col. 3. The judgment is given to you. Do not look at the character of a person, even if he were like an angel from heaven, Gal. 1:8.

Moses speaks further to the people, Deuteronomy 30:11ff.:

"The commandment which I give to you[a] today is not too strange to you,[b] nor too far, nor in heaven, so that you could say: who will go into heaven and fetch it for us so that we hear and do it. Neither is it on the other side of the sea, so that you[c] could say: who will sail over the sea and fetch it for us so that we hear and do it. For the word is very close to you, in your mouth and in your heart, so that you do it. See I have laid before you today life and good, death and evil, I who command give you today that you[d] love the Lord your God and walk according to his ways, keeping his commandments, practices, and justice, so that you might live and multiply and that the Lord your God may bless you in the land to which you are going in order to conquer it.

"If, however, you[e] turn your heart and do not obey but fall away so that you worship other gods and serve them, then I proclaim to you today that you will die and not live long in

---

[12] This passage is not paralleled in Erasmus.

---

[a] To you, to you.
[b] You, you.
[c] To you, to you.
[d] You, you.
[e] You, you.

the land which you are crossing the Jordan to inhabit and conquer.

"I here call heaven and earth to witness over against you.[a] I have laid before you life and death, blessing and curse, so that you choose life and so that you[b] and your off-spring may live, that you love the Lord your God, obey his voice and follow it."

See here, Christian reader, how bright and clear this Scripture shows us that God has freely entrusted to the human being anew also after the Fall the choice of evil and good, blessing and curse, life and death. So that even if the whole world said otherwise, heaven and earth would stand against it and testify openly on the last day before the judgment throne of Christ against all people that not God, but we ourselves, out of free will, are responsible for our sins and eternal damnation. /407/

Jeremiah 21:8:[13]

"Behold the things, says the Lord God, which I give you for the way of life and the way of death."[c]

Why did God need to present two ways if we had to go the one way by necessity, as many say?

Isaiah 1:19:

"If you will and listen then you[d] will eat the goodness of the earth. And if you do not want and if you oppose me, then you will be torn apart with the sword, for the mouth of the Lord has spoken it."

Aye, what could be more clearly spoken by the mouth of the Lord, who cannot lie, than that the willing or the not will-

---

[13] Erasmus makes the same argument in this place with a different, though very similar passage, Deut. 30:15-19. See section II.a.14, DLA: 60, tr. Rupp 1959, p. 54.

---

[a] Heaven and earth testify against the deniers of freedom of the will.
[b] You, you, you.
[c] Life and death are in our hands.
[d] You, you, you.

ing stands in our own free choice? Some, however, say that
God was mocking us when he commanded us to will something
good. In that case almost the whole Scripture would be a
mockery and God the very mocking-bird.ᵃ That is far from
him. Yes, what kind of God would that be who would want
from us what we cannot give?

Psalm 34:13:

"Whoever wants to see good days must hold his tongue
from evil,"ᵇ Ps. 34:13.
David would have sung a song in vain here if we were not
strong enough to keep back and protect our tongues from evil
speaking.

Jeremiah 18:8, 10:

"If the people will repent of their evil, which I have
spoken against them, then I too will repent of the evil which I
intended to do to them.ᶜ If, however, they do evil before my
eyes and do not hear my voice, then I will also repent of the
good that I have said I would do to them."
O, what useless words those would be if we had to do
good or evil out of necessity. Although I know ánd confess
that we cannot will and do such of ourselves. But God gives it
to us through his sent word, where he now gives it to us
beforehand. The same he knows well as to where he can
demand it again. /408/

Matthew 19:17:[14]

"If youᵈ want to enter into life, keep the commandments."

---

[14] The New Testament passages in the following section are largely taken
from Erasmus, sections II.b.1-II.b.8, DLA: 72-91, tr. Rupp 1959, pp. 59-64.

ᵃ God is no mocking-bird.
ᵇ The choice lies with us.
ᶜ God wants to accommodate himself to the people.
ᵈ You, you.

"If anyone wants to come after me, then let him deny himself,[a] take up his cross and follow me," Luke 9:23.

John 14:15:

"If you love me, keep my commandments."[b]

Matthew 11:28:

"Come to me, all you who are heavy-laden."[c] With what right would Christ use such and several thousand similar speeches against us, if no freedom at all or the possibility of willing and doing lay in our power? Would not that be singing a song to the dead?

Matthew 23:37:

"Jerusalem, Jerusalem, you kill the prophets and stone those who are sent to you. How often I[d] would have gathered your children, like a hen gathers its chicks under its wings, but you[e] did not want it."

If all things happened by necessity, then Jerusalem could have said with good reason: "O, Lord, why are you weeping in vain? That we have killed the prophets, stoned those sent to us, and have not let ourselves be gathered under your holy Word, is not our, but your fault, since all such things had to happen and had to be according to your eternal providence, will, and necessity." That of course is to accuse God and, in short, not to want to be among the people whom Christ oft wants to gather as a hen gathers her chicks under its wings, but they did not want it.[15] That is, in my opinion, to slap Christ in the face. But such people's sin, O /409/ reader, is

---

[15] The argument in this paragraph is part verbatim quotation, part paraphrase of Erasmus, section II.b.1, DLA: 74, tr. Rupp 1959, p. 59.

---

[a] Himself, himself.
[b] You, you, you.
[c] Whoever says all, excludes no one.
[d] I, I.
[e] You, you.

more serious than the sin of Adam and Eve. For Adam lays his guilt on Eve, Eve on the snake, and these folks lay it on God himself who is innocent of all sins, Gen. 3:12f. He hates sin. He has forbidden it with eternal punishment. His will is to do justice and not to do injustice.

Romans 7:18f:

Although I have the desire, I am not able to accomplish the good, for the good that I want, I do not do, but the evil I do not want to do, that I do.[a] Here one sees clearly the desire to do good in a human being, which is a good work.[16]

Luke 2:14:[17]

"Glory to God in the heights, peace on earth, and to humankind a good will."

As glory is glory and peace is peace, so also is a good will a good will for humankind.[b]

Philippians 2:13:

"It is God who works in you the willing and the doing according to good will."[c]

Listen: Paul says, "God works in you the willing and the doing." He does not say God wants and does in you, though both sayings are also true if you regard the problem as a whole.[18]

---

[16] The argument is taken in part verbatim from Erasmus, section II.b.5, DLA: 86, tr. Rupp 1959, p. 63.

[17] This Scripture not used by Erasmus.

[18] The argument appears to be based on Erasmus, section III.c.6, DLA: 144, tr. Rupp 1959, p. 81.

---

[a] I, I.

[b] A short and powerful Scripture.

[c] In you, in you.

2 Corinthians 9:7:[19]

"Everyone should give his alms according to how he has chosen previously in his heart, not out of pity or necessity.[a] For God loves the joyful giver."

If now almsgiving is not out of necessity or out of pity, but out of joy, then not all things must happen out of necessity.[b] For a forced and a joyful giver do not fit together.

To Philemon, Paul writes:

"I wanted to keep Onesimus with me so that he might serve me in your place in the bonds of the gospel. However, without your will I did not want to do anything /410/ so that your goodness might not be forced but voluntary,"[c] Philem. 13-14. Whoever wants should look at Jerome concerning these words, though in themselves they testify more than clearly about the free will of the human being.

John 1:11f.:

"He came to his own and his own did not accept him. As many as accepted him, however, he gave the power to become the children of God."[d]

Here you learn once more, dear Christian, that God freely gives power and strength to all those to whom he sends his living Word, and gives them the free choice—if they desire it—in the power of the sent Word to become children of God. Whoever now is a child of God can will and do good, also not will and flee evil according to the will and pleasure of his Father.

---

[19] This Scripture and the next are not used by Erasmus.

---

[a] The choice lies with a person.
[b] Good works should happen out of good will and be uncoerced.
[c] Note reader, voluntary (literally: self-willing).
[d] The power is given to us.

John 6:67:

Christ says to his disciples, "Do you also want to go away?"[a]

It follows that going away or remaining with him must be in the power of the disciples.

John 8:31f.:[20]

"If you remain in my words, then you are my true disciples and will recognize the truth and the truth will make you free."[b]

If now the son makes you free, then you are truly free.[c]

Whoever now denies true freedom in the believers denies Christ himself and the power of his Word through which we can come to God. Whoever has ears, let him hear. Whoever cannot hear, let Christ shout "Ephphatha!" in his ears, Mark 7:34. Amen.

The Second Part
Several Very Useful Theses in This Matter, Set up in the Manner of a Disputation.

Whomever God commands to break his bread with the poor and does not believe that with the words "break your bread with the hungry," God now gives him the power and strength to will and do such, and still lets the inborn /411/ stinginess of the flesh remain as it is, does not recognize the power of the mouth of God, Isa. 58:7.

That is the power of the mouth of God, that through his spoken word he again offers anew to the human being his originally created wholeness which was lost in Adam, Isa. 55:11; John 1:12. Thus the human being, now free as in Paradise, can will, choose, and do good, although against the will of his own flesh, Gen. 3.

---

[20] This Scripture is not used by Erasmus.

---

[a] You, you, you.
[b] You, you, you.
[c] You, you, you.

Such power of his Word God revealed in manifold ways in the Old and New Testaments with signs and wonders.

Whoever looks at Adam after the Fall, before God challenges him and speaks with him, sees him naked and bare, Gen. 3:7.

Whoever looks at him after the comforting Word of God, sees well that he wears a fur garment so that the cold may not harm him.˙ If he should want gladly and willfully to unclothe himself and to freeze anew, then the harm is his own.

Whoever knows what the new birth is will not deny the freedom of the will in the human being, John 3:5; 1 Pet. 1:23; James 1:18; Mark 2:14.

As often as Christ said to a person, "Stand up and walk. See. Hear. Stretch out your hand. Be cleansed," he gave to the same the power to stand up, to see, to hear, to stretch out his hand, and to be cleansed. That must be or his Word will be like a human word, John 5:8; Luke 18:42; Mark 6:56; Matt. 8:4; .12:13; Mark 3:5; Luke 6:10. Whoever says that the flesh need not desire against his natural will, to do the will of the soul, which has been awakened by the Word of God, taps at the wall in the bright sunshine,[21] Matt. 7; John 7; Gen. 4; Rom. 8:13.

A foolish lord it is who sets a goal for his people and says: "Go to it, run so that you win," when he knows all along that they are forged into chains and cannot run, 1 Cor. 9:24.[22]

Whoever says that wives cannot be obedient and subject to their husbands, servants and subjects to their lords, and that sin cannot be obedient to evil Cain, calls God and his saints liars. You are no less than Cain, O you of little faith, Gen. 4:7; Rom. 13:1; Eph. 5:22; 6:5f.; Col. 3:22; 1 Pet. 2:13f.; 3:1.

That would be a perfidious God who would invite all people to a supper, offer his mercy to everyone with exalted earnestness, and would yet not want them to come, Luke

---

[21] That is, like a blind person.
[22] A similar motif is found in Erasmus, section IV.5, DLA: 62, tr. Rupp 1959, p. 55.

˙ Their seed will, etc.

14:16ff.; Matt. 22:2ff. That would be a false God who would say with the mouth, "Come here," but would think secretly in the heart, "Stay there," Isa. 55:1; Matt. 11:28; John 1:12; Luke 15:22.

That would be a disloyal God who would give a human being grace publicly, and clothe him in a new garment, but secretly would take it back again from him and prepare hell for him. /412/

It is a curse to say that God commanded us to do impossible things, Matt. 19:17. For everything that is impossible in our strength is made possible to the believer through his sent Word, Luke 18:27; Mark 9:23; 13:11. Thus it was possible for Mary, the pure virgin, to give birth to a child, she who had never known any man, Luke 1:31. So much power does the sent Word of God have.

The reason that the commandments of God are commonly written in describing and not in commanding ways, *indicative* and not *imperative*, is that one does not have to force the righteous person, but only to show him the way, which he then follows freely, joyfully, and without compulsion, Exod. 20:7-17; Deut. 5:6-21; 1 Tim. 1:9; 2 Cor. 9:6ff.

We should work like a man and know that our work is not worthless to the Lord, Josh. 1:7; Pss. 27; 31; 1 Cor. 15:58. Nevertheless, it still stands in the general judgment that we are useless servants, Luke 17:10. But one should refrain from patchwork in the Scriptures.

As the eyes are ours and yet are not made by us, so is the work of willing and working the good also ours, but not from us.

As the eye of the human being has the ability to see the light and yet cannot see unless the light enters beforehand into the eye, so does the human being have the ability to see the light of faith through the Word of God, which he cannot see unless the light enters beforehand into his soul by heavenly illumination.[23]

As now the bodily seeing is a quality of the bodily light, where that is not, there is nothing but darkness, so also is the inner and spiritual seeing a grace of God, John 6:19-21.

---

[23] These two paragraphs on the eye are similarly treated by Erasmus in section IV.9, DLA: 172-174, tr. Rupp 1959, p. 91.

Where that is, there is seeing, willing, and working. Where it is not, there is eternal darkness, John 12:35. Brothers, since we have the light let us walk so that the darkness does not seize us.

All things happen according to the will of God: the good in the power of his Word, the evil for punishment.

God wants the human being to do good. He also wants the one who does not want to do good to be the master of his own works, and to do evil, so that his separation from the good is thus punished, as sin with sin, John 13:27; Ps. 80; Deut. 29:18-28; Rom. 1:18ff.

Evil is evil to no one except to the one who does it. Therefore, what is evil to the evil one, is good before God and before all believers.

No one may resist the will of God where God does not himself graciously offer freedom of will, Ps. 76:8; Rom. 9:19. However, where he offers the same to a person, /413/ his will once again takes place, either for good or for punishment, which is also good to the one who recognizes its goodness, Heb. 12:6; Prov. 3:12.

Whoever recognizes that for him sin is a punishment, to him is sin not sin, but he will henceforth protect himself from the punishment, so that the punishment does not again become sin for him and condemning, Rev. 3:19; Rom. 8:1.

Whomever God has chosen and selected by his special choice, in order to keep them, concerns the secret God, whose mind we do not know. For deep are his judgments and unfathomable are his reasons, 1 Cor. 2:7; Rom. 11:33.

Nevertheless, it is certain and sure that the crucified Christ wants all people to be saved and come to the recognition of the truth, 1 Tim. 2:4.

We should listen to the incarnated God—thus speaks the voice of the heavenly Father out of the clouds—and not concern ourselves with researching and investigating further God's omnipotence, omniscience, and eternal foreknowledge, predestination, providence, or reprobation, lest like we become gods like Adam and Eve, Matt. 17:5; 2 Pet. 1:17; Luke 9:35; Rom. 11:33; Gen. 3:5.

It is a crazy foolishness of ours that we desire to know the secret will of God, and we despise his known will.

Yes, it is thus, that God knows all things truly, necessarily, and unchangeably from eternity. Which one of two opposites he knows, however, is still unknown to us.[24]

It is a great blasphemy in us to suggest that we want to sin so that we do not make the eternal providence and unchangeable truth of God into a lie, Rom. 6:1.

In the articles concerning faith and love we are sure and certain which choice God wants to have from us, John 20:27-29.

For the person who does not bring together the will and the works, that is a sign that his will is not just and not yet truly united with the divine will, Matt. 7:15-20; Rom. 2:7; James 1:22; 2:8-10; Rom. 8:1-10. The true and simple will of God is that we hold his beloved Son Christ Jesus before our eyes and follow his life and teaching wherein lie all the law and the prophets, Matt. 17:12.

Just as much as the death of the flesh lies in us and is recognized, so much is the love of God in us and nothing is greater. It is recognized in the works, Song of Sol. 8:7; Matt. 7:26.

For that is the grace and favor of God which he bears to us and with which he embraces us: that power which he offers us through his preached Word, so that we—it lies now in our power—can become children of God, also desire and complete his fatherly will and please him, John 1:12; Rev. 3:20.

Grace comes to us, not out of us, so that no one boasts in himself but /414/ in the merits of our Lord Jesus Christ, 1 Cor. 1:4. For our flesh and blood cannot reach such sonship out of their own power, John 1:12; Matt. 16:17; 1 Cor. 15:50.

Since, however, this sonship is offered to all people equally, for the seed of the divine Word falls equally in four kinds of earth, it follows that we have the equal power to accept the seed and to bear fruit, John 1:12; Matt. 28:19; Mark 16:15; Matt. 13:3ff.; Mark 4:3ff. If we do not do that, then it is not God who is guilty, or his seed, but the evil of the earth, that is, we ourselves.

Thus Peter hears Christ, accepts his Word, and brings forth fruit, John 1:42. Herod also hears it, however, does not

---

[24] Meaning that which one of two possibilities will come true, we do not know because we cannot know the future, but God does.

accept his Word, and does not bear fruit. Now that is the fault of the wickedness of Herod.

Since, however, Peter and Herod are alike sinners and evil, the reason why his inborn evil does not harm Peter and yet harms Herod is that Herod follows his inborn evil and walks according to it, but not Peter, Eph. 3; 1 Cor. 15:45ff.; Rom. 8:5-9.

In addition, the fact that God looks at Peter and moves him to lament his sins has to do with the mercy of God, Matt. 26:75. That he does not look at Judas is the fault of the traitor who sold innocent blood for thirty pennies. He had to sentence himself and say, "I have sinned in that I have betrayed innocent blood," Matt. 27:4.

Whoever is not satisfied with this answer, namely, that the mercy of God is the cause of our salvation and our wickedness the cause of our damnation, must ask God himself,* Rom. 11:11-12. I was not his adviser, nor was I with him in his council.

Whoever says that God wills sin does not know what God or sin is. For sinning is always to do or to omit something against the will of God, 1 John 2:5-6.

Yes, as one says: "If God does not want it, I will not sin." I say the opposite. Because God does not want such, we sin, for we resist his revealed will, 1 John 3:9-10.

The will of God turned toward us is a will of love; his will turned from us a will of punishment,[25] Isa. 55:6-7; Jer. 51:1.

---

[25] Hubmaier's concern with the nature of the will of God is a typical later medieval nominalist concern, perhaps learned from John Eck. Cf. Moore 1981. He typically discusses the hidden, or absolute will of God (*voluntas absoluta*) which is the will of God in his being as God. Thus it is essentially beyond our capacity to know and understand. He also considers the revealed or ordained will (*voluntas ordinata*), which is the will of God we as humans can discern insofar as God reveals himself. At this point in his discussion, Hubmaier introduces two further concepts, the will of God as *zukerennder will*, the will turned toward us, and the *abkherender will*, the will of God turned away from us. He later uses the Latin terms *voluntas conversiva* (the conversive will, or the will of God turning toward us) and *voluntas aversiva* (the aversive will, or the will of God turning away from us). We will translate the terms as "conversive" and "aversive" only when Hubmaier uses the Latin.

---

* *Causa et Culpa differunt* [Cause and guilt are different things].

We should not seek higher things than we are, Eccles. 3. Nor should we search more powerful things than we. Rather, we should always have before our eyes what God has commanded us, and in many other works should not be curious, for it is not necessary to see the hidden and heavenly things here on this earth with our eyes, Deut. 4; 5. As it is not good to eat too much honey, so also the one who wants to be a searcher of divine majesty will be thrown down by the splendor of God, Prov. 25:16. To want to know outside of Scripture which people God wants to save or condemn is the worst serpent himself who counsels us so that we become gods, that is, naked and bare, Mark 16:16; Gen. 3:7. /415/

Christ could never suffer the impertinence of his disciples when they asked him about the last day and the reestablishment of the kingdom of Israel, Acts 1:7. Nor could he bear Peter when he asked what John would do, John 21:22.

We should let drop all speech concerning the secret judgments of God and take care of faith and love so that we do not, by looking at heaven, at the same time lose the earth.[*]

If God were to give us today everything that he gave Adam in Paradise, with this manner of acting, we would not long keep it, Gen. 1:29; 2:15; Heb. 2:8.

Whoever cries out concerning Adam that it was through him that death entered into the world sings exactly that same song about himself, Rom. 5:12; 1 Cor. 15:22. He does not do injustice to Adam himself.

As death before the Fall could do no harm to Adam, indeed there was no death, so has it become harmless for the entire world through Christ, unless the world does not want something else, as in fact it does not, 1 Cor. 15:21; 2 Tim. 1:10; 1 Pet. 3. Therefore it will carry its burden itself, Gal. 6:5.

It follows that if not all people are saved, then it is not God but we who are guilty of that, for he gave his most beloved Son into death for us all, John 3:16.

The mercy of God is much more richly recognized after the Fall of Adam than if he had remained in his innocence. For to make a God-blessed person out of a godless person is

---

[*] Thales Milesius.

much greater than creating a God-blessed person out of nothing, or maintaining a God-blessed person in his blessedness.

We should not for that reason sin so that the mercy of God be more greatly recognized, Rom. 6:1. Rather, for that reason we should not sin so that we do not make ourselves unworthy of this mercy and fall under the judgment of God, from which also the angels are not exempted, 2 Pet. 2:4.

Therefore there should be no dispute concerning the omnipotence of God, as to what and how much is possible to God, but of his known will which he has revealed to us by the Scripture,[26] or we will in the last analysis make a special god out of every single cherry pit, Rom. 12:2.

Whoever denies the freedom of the will in the human being to whom God sends his Word and who has not sinned against the Holy Spirit, denies, overthrows, and rejects more than half the Holy Bible, Matt. 12:32; Luke 12:10; Heb. 6:6; 10:31.

Whichever soul is now living shall stand up and walk. Whichever does not stand up, to the same Christ calls, "Talitha cumi," I tell you once more, Mark 5:41. Amen.

The Third Part

After that my opponents who come to me daily introduced here many Scriptures by which they hope to eradicate completely the freedom of the will of the human being.[27] /416/ It has become necessary to remove such stumbling blocks and contrary arguments from the way and to smite them with the sword of the divine Word so that no one fall over them or be injured by them, Eph. 6:17. Now their contrary arguments follow one after the other.

God is merciful to whomever he will.
Whomever he wants, he hardens, Romans 9:18.*

---

[26] A similar argument is made by Erasmus, section III.a.8, DLA: 100-102, tr. Rupp 1959, p. 57f.

[27] Contrary Scriptures are treated by Erasmus in sections III.a.1-III.c.8, DLA: 90-147, tr. Rupp 1959, pp. 64-82.

---

* The first argument.

Here my dear friends cry out against me, as Job's friends did also against him: "Do you see how everything stands with God and nothing in our power? What God wants should and must happen." Answer: That is a statement about the omnipotent and hidden will of God who owes no one anything. Therefore he can without any injustice be merciful to whomever he wills or harden the same, save, or condemn.[a] This power or will the schools have called the omnipotent power or will of God, which no one, as Paul writes, may stand against.[b] Yes, God has the right, power, and authority to make of us what he will, a vessel of honor or dishonor, as the potter has power over his clay and we cannot rightly say, "Why do you do that?"

Now, however, one also finds a revealed will of God according to which he wants all people to be saved and to come to the recognition of the truth.[c] Christ clearly presented the same to us when he said, "God has so loved the world so that he gave his only begotten Son, that whoever believes in him would not be lost but have eternal life," John 3:16. He suffered for our sin and not only for our sin but for the sin of the whole world, 1 John 2:2. He gave himself for redemption of all people, 1 Tim. 2:6. He is also the true light that illumines all people who come into this world, John 1:9. And all those who accept him he gave power to become children of God, after that he also commanded them to preach the gospel to all creatures, so that all those who accept it, believe, and are baptized will be saved, Mark 16:15; John 1:12. From this it is easy to conclude that according to his preached and revealed will God does not want to harden, darken, or damn anyone except those who want to be hardened, blinded, and damned out of their own evil and freedom of will.[d] These are exactly the people who, when Christ comes to his own, do not want to accept him, nor recognize the time of their visitation, nor let him in when he knocks, John 1:11; Luke 19:44. The Scripture that says no one may

---

[a] Two wills of God. An omnipotent will.
[b] *Voluntas absoluta* [Absolute will].
[c] A revealed will.
[d] God is not guilty of the hardening.

resist his will does not refer to the revealed will of God, /417/ but it refers to the hidden will. Where one now confuses and mixes the two wills with one another there soon follows out of that a notable misunderstanding, error, and confusion of Scriptures.ᵃ Therefore one should wisely divide the judgments in the Scriptures and ruminate truly on them in order to. know which Scriptures point to the secret will of God or to the preached.ᵇ

The schools[28] call the revealed power and will of God an ordered power and will.ᶜ Not that the first will is unordered for everything that God wills and does is orderly and good. He is not subject to any rule. His will is itself a rule of all things. Therefore they call the will "ordered" since it occurs according to the preached Word of the Holy Scriptures in which he revealed to us his will. From that now comes the division wherein one speaks of the hidden and the revealed will of God. Not that there are two wills in God, but thus the Scripture serves us and accommodates itself to speak according to our human ignorance so that we know that although God is almighty and can do all things omnipotently, nevertheless, he wills not to act toward us poor people according to his omnipotence, but according to his mercy, as he has sufficiently testified the same to us through his most beloved Son and through all those who point to him in the Old and New Testaments.

Paul speaks of this difference of the two wills very brightly and clearly, saying: "Who has recognized the mind of the Lord? We, however, have Christ's mind," 1 Cor. 2:16. When Paul writes, "Who has recognized the mind of the Lord?" he is pointing to the hidden will of God, on the basis of which Isaiah also calls our God a hidden God, Isa. 45:15. When Paul says, "We have the mind of Christ," he points to the revealed and preached will of God, which is God himself and which has become human and we have seen his glory, a

---

[28] Erasmus makes a similar definition based on what the scholastics say in section III.a.8, DLA: 102, tr. Rupp 1959, p. 68.

ᵃ Equivocation.
ᵇ Divide the judgment.
ᶜ *Voluntas ordinata* [Ordained will].

glory as of the only begotten Son of the Father, full of grace and truth, John 1:14.

Well then, let us treat the division of the two wills with an example.[a] According to his secret will the almighty and hidden God could set Peter in hell and, contrariwise Judas or Caiaphas into heaven and do injustice to no one. We are in his hand. But according to his revealed will he cannot send the embattled Jacob away from him without the blessing, Gen. 32:29. He must be merciful also to the weeping David and has to forgive him his sins, so that he be found to be just in his speaking when he is judged,[b] Ps. 51. He also could not dispatch the heathen woman from him unheard, Matt. 15:28. So great and mightiful is the power and dignity of the prophecies of God who has become human and been revealed through his Word, who cannot deny himself, or heaven and earth must first fall into pieces, Luke 21:33. Not that /418/ our will, word, or work are so high and valuable in themselves, but so powerful and forceful are the divine prophecies in all the believers. Therefore God is captured, bound, and overcome with his own Word by the believers, Rom. 8; Mark 9:23; Matt. 18:18. In the Scriptures that is called "God being in our midst."

God wants all people to be saved, 1 Timothy 2:4.
Who will now resist his will, Romans 9:19.[c]

There once again my friends Eliphas, Bildad, and Zophar say: "Do you hear that God wants all people to be saved. Therefore, it must happen according to his will. Therefore neither to will nor not to will lies in us." Answer: Here, however, an equating and mixing of the wills is going on. For the first Scripture refers to the revealed will of God, the second to his hidden will. Therefore, since these are half-truths, one must divide the judgment and thus not swallow them undivided or unchewed, Lev. 11, or one will eat death therein, as is said above.

---

[a] An example.
[b] Must, must.
[c] The second argument.

Now we will let the secret will of God, which is unnecessary for us to explore, remain in its dignity, Rom. 11:4ff. We want to take the revealed in hand and divide the same according to the order of the Scriptures into a facing and withdrawing will. The facing will of God is that God wants all people to be saved.[a] Therefore he turns himself to all people with the offer of his grace and mercy, not saving even his only begotten Son, but giving him for us all into death so that we are not lost, but receive eternal life, Rom. 8:32; John 3:16.

God bears this salvation toward us and offers it to us joyfully when he says: "Come here, buy wine and milk without silver and without any money, Isa. 55:1. For you are already bought and paid for with a great price, 1 Cor. 6:20. Come here, all you who are laden, and I will unburden you," Matt. 11:28. As soon as now God turns to us, calls, and admonishes us to follow after him, and we leave wife and child, ship and tools, also everything that hinders us on the way to him, we are already helped, John 1:35ff. That is called his facing and drawing will with which he wants and draws all people so that they be saved. Nevertheless, the choice lies with them for God wants them, unpressed, unforced, and without coercion.

Whichever people do not accept, hear, or follow after him, the same he turns himself away from and withdraws from[b] and lets them remain as they /419/ themselves want to be. That is now called the withdrawing will of God, concerning which David gives information when he says, "O God, do not turn your face from me," Ps. 51:11. So just in this way is God holy with the holy, and withdrawing with the withdrawn. The first will can be called in the Scripture *Voluntas conversiva a convertendo* [The conversive will in relation to the one to be converted].[c] The second, *Voluntas aversiva ab avertendo* [The aversive will in relation to the one to be turned away from], not that there are two wills in God, as also said above, for there is one single will in God, but one must speak about God humanly and with human words, as if he had eyes and ears, face and back, turned to and away from, and

---

[a] The facing will.
[b] A withdrawing will.
[c] *Voluntas Conversiva. Aversiva* [Conversive, aversive will].

that because of our small understanding. Nevertheless, he does not for this reason have eyes, ears, hands, or feet, as the anthropomorphites say. The Scripture which says "God wants all people to be saved," 1 Tim. 2:4, refers to the first revealed will of God. The second part of the Scriptures, "that God wants to harden the godless and damn them," Exod. 4:21 refers to the second. The hidden will of God still remains upright and omnipotent, according to which he can do what he wants and no one need question, "Why do you do that?" Rom. 9:20. His facing will is a will of mercy. His withdrawing will is a will of his justice and punishments, of which we are guilty with our vices, and not God.

The Scripture says to Pharaoh: For this reason have I awakened you, that I may demonstrate my power in you, so that my name shall be proclaimed in all countries, Rom. 9:17.ᵃ

Here, however, the friends of Job cry out overly loud: "Do you see how God hardened Pharaoh's heart and awakened him so that he might show his power in him. Therefore, Pharaoh had to sin and pursue the children of Israel, Exod. 1:15ff. Where remains the freedom of his will?" Answer: We know that Pharaoh acted unjustly, when he loaded the Israelites with unbearable work and let their children be drowned against the law of nature and his own conscience. Therefore he was justly abandoned by God because of his own guilt and was hardened in his sins.ᵇ For just so does God punish sin with sin as he gave also the Romans a wrong mind and blinded their hearts, because they changed the honor of the indestructible God into an image of a destructible human and bird and a four-footed and crawling animal.²⁹ Accordingly, it was never possible for Pharaoh and the Romans to will and work anything but evil, just as if falling by necessity from one vice into another, though it does not come from God but from their own guilt. For it is fair and just that all those be

---

²⁹ To this point Hubmaier follows the same argument as Erasmus, section III.a.10, DLA: 104, tr. Rupp 1959, p. 69.

ᵃ The third argument.
ᵇ There pharaoh died and was awakened by God, that is, he held him for punishment until the given time.

abandoned by God who first already have left God. Thus God speaks through Jeremiah: "We have healed Babylon but it did not become whole; we will leave it," Jer. 51:9. /420/ Thus Christ also says to Jerusalem: "How often I wanted to gather you and you did not want it," Matt. 23:37. Thus Paul says to the Jews: "The Word of God had first to be preached to you, but since you reject it, we now turn to the heathen," Acts 13:46.

Therefore we confess with you, dear friends, that in those people whom God has abandoned there is no freedom of will, Heb. 6:4-6; 10:38. However, we set the same freedom of the will in those people drawn, illumined, and reborn by God, for to them the power is offered and given to become children of God in the power of his Word, 2 Pet. 2; John 1:12. For although no one comes to Christ unless the Father draws him, it, nevertheless, does not follow from this speech that all those come to Christ who have been drawn by the Father, John 6:44. As also not all those accept the light to whom Christ came to enlighten, John 1:9, 11. However, it does not follow that God is without power, for it is just his revealed will that he in the beginning sends to all people his Word and after that gives them the power, freedom, and choice so that they can accept or reject the same, as has been said sufficiently above, Mark 16:15; John 1:16. Now God could have strangled Pharaoh from that moment on because of the infanticide, Exod. 1:15ff. But he kept him in the mildness of his disposition as a tool of wrath so that he might show in him his power for our good even more powerfully at the right time, Rom. 9:17; Exod. 9:16. Therefore the text says, "For that reason I have awakened you" and not "For that reason I have created you"—"that I might show through you my power."[30] But Pharaoh made himself thus through his infanticide and God let him remain thus and used him as his instrument insofar as he was useful.

A parable.[*] If a lord has a murderer in his dungeon, he could justly kill him from that moment on. However, he lets

---

[30] This argument is a near verbatim quotation of Erasmus, section III.a.3, DLA: 94, tr. Rupp 1959, p. 65f. Erasmus is actually quoting Origen's *Commentary on Romans*, MPG 14: 1146.

---

[*] A parable.

him lie there for a longer time until many people come together so that he demonstrates his power and justice still more powerfully in the punishment, and that to the use and fear of his people, to guard themselves against such evil deeds. As now the lord is not guilty of the death, he, nevertheless, calls the murderer before the court, wakes him up, lets him be broken on the wheel and uses thus his evil and shameful death as an example to other persons and to his people for good. Just so did God act with Pharaoh. Whoever is not purposefully blind in his will understands it well, for the text is not so difficult as was thought until now.

The words of God are further presented here when he says: "I will harden his heart and he will not hear you,"[a] Exod. 4:21. Answer: In short, God, according to his revealed will does not want simply to harden anybody or to give him a wrong mind, except for the one who out of his innate evil wants himself to be hardened and wrong, no matter what one says to him. Yet he thus resists /421/ the recognized truth against his own conscience. Thus Pharaoh acted against the words and signs of Moses. Therefore God wanted to harden his heart because he himself wanted to be hardened.

Jacob have I loved, but Esau I have hated. Malachi 1:2f.; Romans 9:13.[b]

My good friend Eliphaz raises up the Scripture on Esau so powerfully, that he thinks he can prove that we are all from eternity and originally already predestined, and already foreordained to good or evil by God. Therefore we cannot do other than how and what God has made us to do. Esau had to sell his birthright for a pot of lentils, Gen. 25:33; Heb. 12:16; Pharaoh had to pursue the children of Israel, Exod. 14:8; Judas had to betray Christ, Matt. 26:48; Pilate had to condemn him innocently, Matt. 27. Answer: The Scripture on Esau touches the article of divine foreknowledge, in which the divine majesty gives us to recognize that God knows all things before they happen.[c] For Paul teaches us four points in the

---

[a] Whom God hardens.
[b] The fourth argument.
[c] Note.

Epistle to the Romans, Rom. 9; 10; 11: The omnipotence of
God in Pharaoh, his divine foreknowledge of all things in Esau
and Jacob, his full power of the will with the clay and the potter, his mercy to the heathen, Rom. 11:32. The first three
things are inconceivable to us. The fourth, God has revealed
to us through the incarnation of his only begotten Son, Jesus
Christ, our Lord.

That Paul, however, quotes this passage on Esau from the
prophet Malachi, Mal. 1:3, happens not so that we fall back on
the foreknowledge and say: Aye, why is it that I have much
effort and work? It is in vain.[a] If God hates me from eternity
then my works do not help. If, however, he has loved me, then
I do not need them. It had already been decided in eternity
in the council of the Holy Trinity as to what should happen to
me. But, therefore, Paul introduces this saying so that he sup-
presses the pride of the Jews who thought and boasted that
the grace of God was turned to them because of the Jewish
inherited righteousness since they were of the family of
Abraham,[31] John 8:33. Such pride and boasting Paul knocks
down and says: "Esau was a Jew and Jacob was also a Jew."
Still, God hates the one and loves the other, Rom. 9:13.
Therefore the favor and grace of God must never come from
the blood-inheritance. /422/ That is the mind and proof of
Paul. Enough of that. Whoever wants to suck more out of this
honeysuckle must watch out that he not get poison for honey.

The Scripture would be clear, simple, and understandable
in itself if only our fleshly hairsplitting would not seek more
out of it than its simple sense could bear. Without doubt God
knew from eternity that Esau and other people would sin. He
did not, however, order them to sin, as Fulgentius[32] already
wrote in his first book to Monimo.[b]

However, that we want out of great impertinence to find
out and know the causes of divine foreknowledge, omnipotence, future things, and his hidden will, as, for example, why

[31] This is a partially verbatim quotation of Erasmus, section III.a.12,
DLA: 106-108, tr. Rupp 1959, p. 70.
[32] Fulgentius of Ruspe, died 532.

[a] A fleshly argument.
[b] Fulgentius.

God hated Esau and not Jacob, why God punished Pharaoh for the infanticide more strictly than the other infant-murderer Herod, why God permitted so long the idolatry in the worship of the bronze snake, that is lifting the mouth into heaven,[33] searching the divine hiddenness, and wanting to be like gods, knowing good and evil, Gen. 3:5. That is highly forbidden us, as said above in the theses. Christ says: "Let the dead bury their dead and follow after me," Luke 9:60. Yes, although he hates Esau, he still wants that you freely and willingly follow him and keep his commandments. However, with such arguments we want to load our guilt gladly on God so that we can go out unburdened.[a] But it will not help us. Whether he hates Esau or loves him his Word remains upright and firm like a wall. If you want to enter into life, then keep the commandments, Matt. 19:17. If you, yourself, says the Lord.[b] He does not say: "Look at Esau."

Further, that Pharaoh, Judas, and Pilate are cited by my friend Eliphas I answer thus:[c] Pharaoh could have pursued the Israelites according to the command of God who said to him through Moses: "I want to use you to show my power," Exod. 9:16. Also Judas could have given Christ into death according to the word of Christ: "Whoever dips with me in the dish will betray me," Matt. 26:23. And Pilate could have condemned Christ according to the word of Christ: "You would have no power over me if it were not given from above," John 19:11. And all this without sin, insofar as they had only sought herein the command, will, and glory of God and also the salvation of people and not their own advantage—as they did not do. Pharaoh sought his /423/ kingdom, Judas the thirty pennies, Pilate feared the displeasure of the emperor and the loss of his office. Therefore, they sinned. If Abraham could innocently have killed his son according to the command of God, Gen. 22:1-14, why could Pilate not have condemned the Son of God according to the same command if

---

[33] Probably a figure of speech suggesting presumptuousness.

---

[a] We want gladly to wash our hands.
[b] You, you, you.
[c] Pharaoh, Judas, Pilate.

he had thought thus: "My God and Lord. Since your command always applies to me, that I am your instrument and should do such, so that the Scripture and the salvation of humanity be completed according to your divine will, I am ready and willing not only to condemn your beloved son but also to hang him myself and to tear him with my teeth if I have your public command about that. Otherwise I would not take the whole world; indeed, I would rather lose my body and life. But let your will be done and not mine." In the same way Pharaoh and Iscariot could have spoken and acted. But their own advantage and not the consideration of the command of God brought them into this fall and sin.

Here you see, dear Christian, why God punishes us.[a] Namely because we do not want to submit our will finally to his divine will, so that he could use us as whatever tool he wishes. Yes also because we keep before our eyes our own advantage more than his command and seek ourselves more than him in all our deeds and actions. Therefore he lets us go as punishment into the Egyptian darkness. Thereby once again several people's counter-arguments are dissolved when they say: "Aye, so Christ had to suffer. Yes, the Scripture had to be fulfilled in that way. Judas and Pilate had to be guilty of that." As if the Scripture could not be fulfilled without sin.[b] That is far from it. It would be a great blasphemy against God to say that his will cannot happen without sin.

Yes, dear man, who are you that you want to dispute with God? Does a tool speak to its master: Why do you make me so? Does not a potter have the power to make out of a lump of clay a pot of honor and out of another, one of dishonor? Romans 9:20f.[c]

Note, good friend. I know very well that, like a lump of clay in the hand of the potter, [I] cannot say to the potter, "Why do you make me thus?" so also are we thus in the hand of God, who can make of us without any injustice a vessel of life or of death, Jer. 18:6; Isa. 45:9; Rom. 9:21. Since now he already made us into vessels of honor by his grace and by the infusion of the taste of his most sweet Word, which we have

---

[a] Why does God punish us?
[b] A blasphemy against God.
[c] The fifth argument.

all heard, it is right and just that we not dirty these vessels with the impurity of sins, but rather we should clean them, 2 Tim. 2:21. Or God will with his just judgment say against us: "The human being, /424/ while he was in honor did not think, but became like a horse and a mule in which there is no understanding," Ps. 32:9.

Do you see here how seriously all those err who say: "Aye, whatever I do, whether it be good or evil, is the will of God, for we are his lump of clay. He makes of us what he wants." Yes, he has made of you a vessel of honor by pouring his holy Word into you and has given you the free power and choice to become his child, John 1:12. Since, however, you do not will, you make of yourself out of your own wantonness a vessel of dishonor. Yes, according to his revealed will God also wants to be justified by us.[a] One might say: "Why have you made me thus?" As God himself commands us and says: "Come, I beseech you, and we will reason together," Isa. 1:18. "And you my inhabitant of Jerusalem and you, man of Judah, judge, I beseech you between me and my vineyard," Isa. 5:3. David also says to God: "Lord, be merciful to me so that you will be called just in your speaking, when you are judged," Ps. 51:1. Christ also says to the evil Jews: "Which of you will condemn me of sin?" John 8:46. But Paul writes here about the hidden will of God, according to which nobody may say: "Why do you make me thus?" For in this chapter he teaches the killing of the flesh in order that it not raise itself above God out of its own power.

It depends not on the willing nor on the running but on the mercy of God, Romans 9:16.[b]

Now once again my good friends cry out over the housetops against me: "Do you hear, do you hear? It is not of willing. It is also not of running." Answer: Yes, for once you are right, if you understand it well as a half-judgment. For it does not depend on the willing nor on the running of their own strength. But if God is merciful to us and has offered us mercy through his divine Word, then we can well will and

---

[a] So just is God in all things.
[b] The sixth argument.

run.[34] Paul testifies to that and says: "The willing is in me,"[a] Rom. 7:18. And in another place: "Thus you have to run in order to obtain."[b] "I did not run in vain," Phil. 2:16. "Thus I run and not with uncertainty.[c] I fight thus, not as one who strikes the air, but I tame and castigate my body so that I do not preach to others and be guilty myself," 1 Cor. 9:26f. Note here once more how Paul wills, runs, fights, strikes, tames his body, and preaches. Dear friends, let these Scriptures stand besides yours, I beseech you, or you will finally have to. /425/

Here, however, they introduce strange glosses and say: "Paul ran," means that God ran in Paul.[d] Samson strangled the lion, that is, God strangled the lion in Samson. Stretch out your hand, that is, God stretches out the hand. The young man kept God's commandment from youth on, that is, God has kept the commandments of God in the young man. All of that, in short, amounts to knocking down half of the Scriptures and to darkening and confusing them in nearly all words with strange glosses.[e] For as the tree, tree, tree in the garden brings forth fruit out of the power of the divine Word when God said: "Every tree shall bear fruit according to its kind," thus shall man, man, man, in the power of the sent Word of God also will and do good,[f] Gen. 1:11.

We are not sufficient in ourselves to claim something

for ourselves, but our sufficiency is in God, 2 Corinthians 3:5.[g]

Yes, dear friends. I say also that of ourselves we are not able to think good. For we do not know what is good; we have lost the knowledge, Gen. 2:17; 3:5. But out of the power of the divine sent Word, which is a power to salvation for all

---

[34] A similar argument is advanced by Erasmus in section III.a.4, DLA: 96, tr. Rupp 1959, p. 66.

---

[a] Me, me.
[b] You, you, you.
[c] I, I, I.
[d] Ridiculing glosses.
[e] Half of the Bible would have to be glossed.
[f] Tree, tree. Man, man.
[g] The seventh argument.

believers; thence is all our sufficiency, John 1:14; Rom. 1:16. For Christ did not speak as a human being or as the scribes and Pharisees, but as an authority, Matt. 7:29; John 7:14ff.; Luke 1:32. Therefore we are again often admonished in the Scripture to remember, observe, and pay attention to those things which pertain to God, Prov. 3:3; Ecclus. 3:21; Phil. 4:8.

It is God who works in you what you will and what you do according to good will. Philippians 2:13[a]

Dear Bildad, the Scripture is clearly with us and against you. For it says: God works in us the willing and the doing. Without doubt this happens through his Word. Thus it follows that we are able to will and do good. Yes: we, we.

But then we do a work according to good will if we will something according to the will of God, and also do the same in deed, against the will of our own flesh, Rom. 7:18. Just as if I took myself a wife even though my fleshly lust would much prefer to be free to have one prostitute today and tomorrow another. Paul calls that *perficere pro bono animi proposito* [to perform for the good purpose of the soul].[b] Now the two texts to Romans and Philippians can be joined together into a whole judgment. /426/ For one says: "Though I desire it, I do not act." The other assigns to us the desire and the doing, Phil. 2:13.

I know, Lord, that it is not the way of a human being,
nor of man,
that he walks and directs his footsteps, Jeremiah 10:23.[c]

Here my friend Zophar cries out overly loud: You see, neither the way nor the path is in the power of the human being. Yes, everything is in God alone: knowledge, willing, and walking. To that I answer: The prophet speaks here of those things which concern the salvation of the soul in which the human being, outside of the divine Word and leading, is

---

[a] The eighth argument.
[b] To perform.
[c] The ninth argument.

completely helpless and wholly ignorant. How then could he will the good or walk rightly?[35] Therefore without ceasing he calls to God with the prophet: "Lord, my God, direct my ways before your face, Pss. 5:8; Ps. 106. For your word is a light to my feet," Ps. 119:105. If now God sends his Word, then the human being is able to know, desire, and walk the way of the divine footsteps, as the counter scriptures show clearly, Prov. 16:9. It is up to the human being to prepare the heart, but up to God to govern the tongue. Jeremiah says also: "Let every person turn away from his evil way and direct your ways and thoughts," Jer. 18:11. It follows that it now lies in our power to prepare the heart, to turn, to lead our ways and deeds according to the sent Word of God, to guide and direct ourselves according to these Scriptures, which you, dear friend, also must accept besides your own in a whole judgment.[36]

God has made everything for its purpose, also the godless for the evil day, Proverbs 16:4.[a]

Whatever my opposition shouts, the simple understanding of this verse is: God does not want to kill the godless immediately, but out of the mercifulness of his heart he tolerates them longer until the evil day, which is not evil in itself, but it will be evil to the godless because of the punishment,[b] Rom. 9:22. On that day God will carry out the punishment of the godless to demonstrate his glory and for the sake of our salvation and will give him the wages of his sin as he deserves it. However, that God has made the godless person evil is not so. For he has made everything very good, even Lucifer, Gen. 1:31. But out of his free wantonness he himself turned away from the eternal God /427/ and good. Therefore

[35] A similar argument is made by Erasmus, section III.b.5, DLA: 130, tr. Rupp 1959, p. 77.
[36] A whole judgment for Hubmaier is a judgment based on the whole of Scriptures and on the whole of a context within which a passage of Scripture occurs. He contrasts such a whole judgment often with "patchwork" or a "half-judgment."

[a] The tenth argument.
[b] All days are good.

God perserves him until the evil day, that is, to the day of punishment, when he will give him all the more to the punishment of eternal pain?[37] The devil and his gang fear that day highly. Therefore he says to Christ: "Jesus, Son of the Highest, why did you come before the time to cause us pain." See the Scriptures on that in Matthew, Peter, and Jude, Matt. 8:29; 2 Pet. 2:4ff.; Jude 5ff.

Like the division of the water,[38] so is the heart of the king in the hand of the Lord, Proverbs 21:1.[a]

Here my friend Zophar is of the opinion that what the king does he does out of necessity, for his heart is not in his own power but in the hand of the Lord. I am most amazed that he and others of my friends cite such Scriptures which do not serve them at all. For it is well known that Solomon here masters and kills the wrath and anger of the queen, teaching her to be merciful and mild, for, as the general proverb states, if they want to tyrannize too strongly then Jesus will appear to them on the way and knock them down himself, as it happened also to Paul and the prophet Balaam,[b] Acts 9:4; Num. 22:21ff. Therefore, however, freedom of the will is not taken away from all people or in all things. For the exceptional case does not rob the general truth of the Scriptures.[c]

Without me you can do nothing, John 15:5.[d]

Yes, it is so, dear friend, that without God we do not know what is good; how then could we do it without him, for our spirit is imprisoned, our soul wounded, our body killed, Gen. 2; 3. But if we remain in the vine, that is, in the knowledge of his divine Word, the same will teach us what we will,

---

[37] The three preceding sentences are largely a paraphrase of Erasmus, section III.b.6, DLA: 132, tr. Rupp 1959, p. 77.

[38] The RSV translates this verse: "stream of water."

---

[a] The eleventh argument.
[b] Proverb.
[c] A useful rule.
[d] The twelfth argument.

should do, and are able to do, John 15:5ff. Whoever understands the verse otherwise than about doing good has to confess finally that we cannot sin without Christ.[39] That is far from him.

However, not I, but the grace of God which is in me, 1 Corinthians 15:10.[a]

My dear Eliphas, as you think that not I but the grace of God is working, so I think: with me and not without me.[b] For the Scripture does not say, /428/ "I without the grace" nor "the grace without me." But it says: "The grace of God with me."[40] Therefore also the saying of Paul should be understood: "I can/ do all things in him who strengthens me," Phil. 4:13. Farewell: you have good counsel.

Why have you, Lord, made us go astray from your ways and hardened our hearts, so that we do not fear you, Isaiah 63:17.[c]

To that God answers, not I: "Therefore, Israel, because you wanted to err, be blinded and be hardened, because you wanted to follow your dreams and human laws, not hearing me, but doing that which was good in your eyes, and because you despised my commandments, therefore, this happened to you as also to the Romans, for thus I punish sins with sins,"[d] Rom. 1:18ff. Christ also says: "Jerusalem, Jerusalem, how often did I want to gather you like a hen gathers its chicks under its wings, but you did not want to," Matt. 23:37. Therefore, your house will be waste. For God does not want to make anyone err or be hardened, except the one who himself wants to err wantonly and be hardened. Thus the doctor abandons the sick one who does not obey him nor take his medicine.

---

[39] Cf. Erasmus, section III.b.8, DLA: 136, tr. Rupp 1959, p. 79.
[40] Hubmaier takes over the argument of Erasmus, section III.c.7, DLA: 146, tr. Rupp 1959, p. 82.

---

[a] The thirteenth argument.
[b] I see with the sun, not without the sun, nor the sun without me.
[c] The fourteenth argument.
[d] Why God hardens us and makes us err.

> **God makes the light and creates darkness.**[a]
> **He makes peace and creates evil.**
> **I am the Lord who makes all things.**
> **Isaiah 45:7**[41]

Here my friends fight with hands and feet in order to bring God even more into the stew, laying our wickedness on him, for since he creates the darkness, therefore God is a cause of evil. They are truly engaging there in a great word battle. Answer: There are two kinds of bad things or evils.[b] One evil is that of sin. Of this evil God is the punisher and not the cause, creator, or effector. For it is written: "Whoever commits a sin, does evil, for sin is evil," 1 John 3:4. Since, now, there is no evil in God, it is not of God either. For God is faithful, in whom is no evil, Deut. 32:4.

The other evil is an evil of punishment. That evil God wills and does out of his justice. For where the justice of God does not act, there his goodness would be a cause of sins. Of that evil the prophet speaks here. For as he opposes the darkness to the light, thus he also sets against peace the evil, that is, rebellion, discord, penalty, and pain. For thus he wants to punish the first evil with the second, so that in his works he also in his works may be found to be a just God, for he wants to be found fair /429/ according to his judgments. Bad or evil is also understood thus in the Gospel where Christ says: "Sufficient to the day is its evil," Matt. 6:34. Yes, to speak about it simply: We will not confess that God is a doer or creator of sin. According to what Augustine writes against Julian Pelagius:[c] "Of what God is not the planter he is neither the maker nor effector." Now in eternity it can never be proven that God planted sin. The devil, however, is the father of lies, John 8:44. God has no fellowship with the same, 1 Cor. 10:20-21; 2 Cor. 6:17.

---

[41] This Scripture is not used by Erasmus.

---

[a] The fifteenth argument.
[b] Two kinds of evil.
[c] Augustine, Book Three, Chapter Eight.

God works all things in all things.[a]

Here my dear friends introduce their strongest Hercules and say: "If no other Scripture testifies that God effects or works good and evil in us, and we work nothing, this one would be enough to bring forth such and knock down all willing and working of people." Answer: Dear friends, at last remember three things. First, that one has to recognize two things in every deed of a human being.[b] On the one hand, the deed as it is in itself. On the other, the disorder, lack, weakness, imperfection, vice, sin or blame of the deed. Now God is the preeminent agent of the deed itself, but not of the blame of the deed, which comes out of the vice of co-worker or instrument. For God commands the goodness of work and not the blame.

Second, it is to be noted that the Holy Scripture takes up two kinds of role. Sometimes it puts on the role of God when it takes the completion of all things from the human being and gives it alone to God, as it is shown in the Scripture above.[c] Sometimes it puts on the role himself and ascribes everything to the human being as if God did nothing at all, as one will see clearly in the following Scriptures. And all this occurs out of the rich grace and goodness of God, who ascribes to us what he does. For there the Scripture says: "The poor will take us into the eternal tabernacle," Luke 16:9. And in another place: "Blessed are the servants whom the Lord finds awake." On the other hand we should ascribe all glory and working to God and recognize ourselves as useless servants and say, "not to us, Lord, not to us, but to your name shall the glory be given, for the pains of this time are not worthy of the splendor which will be revealed in us," Luke 17:7-10; Ps. 115:1. Whoever cannot accommodate himself to the two divisions of Scripture will often stumble. May God keep him from falling. For he will judge many half-truths to be full truths, which is the biggest error in dealing with Scripture. /430/

---

[a] The last argument.
[b] Two things in the deed.
[c] The Scriptures speak, sometimes like God, sometimes like man.

In the third place, note, dear friends, the counter-Scriptures and add them here and there besides yours, forming a whole judgment. Do not make rubble out of the Scripture, then you will learn to recognize the truth rightly. Now follow the Scriptures which attribute to us the working and doing.

Abstain from evil and do good, Ps. 37:27. Brothers, work out your salvation, Phil. 2:12.

While we have time, let us do good for the night comes in which nobody can work anymore, Gal. 6:10. If you want to enter life, keep the commandments, Matt. 19:17.

For it is not those who hear the commandments that are righteous before God, but those who fulfill the law that will be justified, Rom. 2:13. My mother and my brothers are those who hear the Word of God and do it, Luke 8:21.

Not everyone who says to me, "Lord, Lord," will enter into the kingdom of heaven, but the one who does the will of my father who is in the heavens. Whoever hears my words and does them, the same is compared with a wise man who builds his house on a rock, Matt. 7:21, 24.

Those who have done good will enter into eternal life, John 5:29.

God will reward everyone according to his deeds, Rom. 2:6.

Glory and honor and peace be with everyone who does good, Rom. 2:7.

If you are the children of Abraham, do his works, John 8:39.

Be fruitful in all good works and grow up in the knowledge of God, Col. 1:10.

Be doers of the Word and not hearers only, so that you deceive yourselves. For if one is a hearer of the Word and not a doer he is like a man who looks at his physical face in a mirror and after he has seen himself he leaves and forgets how he looks, James 1:22ff.

What does it help, dear brothers, if someone says he has faith but not works? Can faith also save him? If, however, a brother or a sister should be naked and had lack of daily food, and one among you were to say to them: "God bless you, warm yourself and be full" and you do not give to them what is necessary for the body, what use would that be? Thus also faith, if it has no deeds, is dead in itself. But one may say, you have faith and I have works. Show me your faith with your works and I will also show you my faith with my works. You believe there is one God. You do well. The devils believe also and tremble, James 2:14ff. /431/

Conclusion

Now, dear friends, you have the resolution and dissolution of your Scriptures, which you have introduced against the freedom of the will of the human being in its whole understanding and for its complete judgment, and yet they are only half-truths, as you have heard clearly and sufficiently.[*] Accordingly, I beseech you to go forth and henceforth to be at peace with God, so that you do not sadden his Spirit, for I, unworthy servant of God, will henceforth give you little answer. Unless it be the case that I have to speak "Amen" concerning you a third time, which I would prefer not to do. Praise, honor, and glory be to God for eternity. His peace be with us at all times. Thus it was, is, will be, will become, and remain for eternity.

Truth Is Immortal.
Nicolspurg
1527

---

[*] Whoever dissolves these arguments has also dissolved all others.

29

On the Sword

Radical Zwinglianism raised three formal challenges to the mainstream Reformation proceeding under the guidance of Zwingli and the governments friendly to him: whether the authority to implement the Reformation belonged to the civil government,[1] whether infants should be baptized, and whether Christians should wield the sword.[2] As dissent developed in Zurich, but especially as it scattered beginning in early 1525, finding support from other quarters as well, these three themes did not propagate themselves with the same frequency nor win the same constituencies. It was thus possible that in other places than Zurich, especially in smaller centers whose distant sovereigns were doing little about the Reformation, local Reformation initiatives would arise where the first issue (the authority to reform) was crucial. Later historians call this development "congregationalism." In such a setting the implementation of adult baptism was secondary, and the questioning of "the sword" could easily not arise.

Hubmaier's Waldshut had been one such place; there were others.[3] The changes made at Waldshut in 1525 had the approval of the city authorities, and Hubmaier retained an advisory relationship to the Council not very different from

---

[1] This is in fact two questions. One is geographic; central government versus the local city or town. The other is the tension between the extant civil authorities and someone else (clergy? voluntary association?) who might claim the right to act as "church."

[2] This concept too raises more than one issue; a) there is the participation of the Christian in the ordered life of the civil magistracy (*obrigkeit*); b) there is defensive war; c) there is aggressive war for dynastic, real political, or religious reasons. Hubmaier's argument is traditional in assuming that forms (a) and (b) held together, so that advocacy of (b) is subsumed in the argument for (a), and ignoring the reality of (c). Cf. Goertz 1980, pp. 116ff.

[3] Cf. Stayer 1975 and 1977. The ambiguity noted in note 1 above applied in these cases. These "congregations" made an issue of local autonomy. If they had survived it is not clear whether there would have come into being a "church" made up of the baptized, structured independently of the "state."

that of Zwingli at Zurich. Thus it was natural that on the issue
of "the sword" early Anabaptism should be quite varied. This
text by Hubmaier is our best evidence to that effect, the only
early Anabaptist writing sustaining this view.

In Zwingli's realm the nonpacifist view lost ground after
the strong statement of the pacifist alternative at Schleitheim
in February 1527.[4] In the territories under Austrian rule it
ended when Hubmaier's protectors turned him over to the
authorities. In the Netherlands the debate was to last another
dozen years.

The view Hubmaier represents does not claim to be
original. It is close to what Luther and Zwingli were saying. It
was rather the pacifist alternative which at this time was not
very coherently stated. The arguments (including the specific
choice of Scripture texts) of Hubmaier's interlocutors as he
plays them back are significantly different from those of Article
VI of the Schleitheim "Brotherly Union," different again from
those of the original Zurich group,[5] different again from the
Erasmian and patriotic pacifism of the young Zwingli.

In Nikolsburg Hubmaier's work had had the active support
of the ruling von Liechtenstein family. Many of his treatises
were dedicated to nobles.[6] Clearly he did not have the negative
understanding of civil government which many other Anabaptists had. This finally brought him problems. A group of
opponents emerged in Nikolsburg, especially under the leadership of Hans Hut.[7] Hubmaier's intention to express his own
viewpoint on this issue led him to the occasion of writing on
government—not against mainline Reformers, but against his
own "dear brothers." On the Sword is not only directed against
Hut and the Nikolsburg Stäblers, however. He knows that there
is an older nonviolent stance widely held among the "Brethren." His treatise is not merely polemical. Clearly, one impor-

---

[4] Cf. Yoder 1973, p. 39. Word of the Schleitheim event could have
reached Nikolsburg before June 1527 but there is no indication that Hubmaier was aware of it.

[5] First stated in September 1524, in Harder 1985.

[6] For example, treatises number 14, 20, 22, 24, 25, 27, 28, 29, and 30.
Cf. Zeman 1969, pp. 165ff., for the interpretation of these dedications.

[7] For a brief account of the story of the conflict between Hubmaier and
Hut, see Bergsten 1978, pp. 361-77. The "Sword" was not the main difference between them, but later Hubmaier made it seem central. See
below, p. 560ff.

tant purpose of the treatise is to set forth Hubmaier's positive attitudes toward government.

Not surprisingly, the treatise is dedicated to a nobleman: Arkleb von Boskovic und Cerna Hora auf Vranov, member of one of the leading families of Moravia.[8] Dated June 24, 1527, On the Sword is Hubmaier's last Nikolsburg treatise. Ironically enough, only a few weeks after he had written the treatise, he was arrested and taken to Kreuzenstein Castle, and this with the acquiescence of his protector Leonhard von Liechtenstein.[9]

On The Sword

A Christian explication
Of the Scriptures
which are often quoted earnestly
by many brethren
against the government,
that is, that the Christian
should not sit in authority nor wield the sword.
Dr. Balthasar
Hüebmör von Fridberg
1527

To the noble and Christian lord, Lord Arkleb of Boskovic and Erna Hora at Vranoy, First Secretary of the treasury of the Margraviate of Moravia: to my Gracious Lord, grace and peace in God.

Noble and gracious sir. Your Grace, you are well aware that during these recent dangerous times all those who have

---

[8] Cf. Zeman 1969, p. 160.

[9] A digest was offered in Hošek 1892, pp. 379-386 and 435-445. A fuller English translation was published by Vedder and reprinted by Estep. See Vedder 1905, pp. 174, 279-310; Estep 1976, pp. 108-25; and Davidson 1939, pp. 717ff. Fragment in Klaassen 1981, pp. 248, 271f. Goertz 1980, pp. 116ff., provides an excellent analysis of the text. Source: HS 24, pp. 434-457.

accepted the holy gospel and who love and preach it not only
have to suffer damage to their property and be martyred in
their body, but indeed also are hurt in their honor (which
indeed is the highest treasure to human beings on earth) and
violated by the godless. For these are the weapons of the
infernal Satan, by which he undertakes without ceasing to suppress, exterminate, and hinder evangelical teaching and truth.
He will not succeed; his head will be crushed thereby. Furthermore, now all Christian preachers are being decried by
such servants of the devil as being rebels, seducers, and
heretics—as those who reject the government and teach disobedience. However, one should not be surprised by this. The
same thing also happened to Christ, although he taught
publicly that one should give the emperor what belongs to the
emperor, for example, when /435/ he let taxes be paid for him
and Peter. Nevertheless, he had to endure the slap in the face
by the blasphemers when they called him a rebel and accused
him of being an agitator of the people whom he supposedly
forbade to pay the tax to the emperor. When now the same
happens to us, what does it matter? The servant is no more
than the lord, and the disciple not more than his master. If
they have now blasphemed the head of the house in this manner, how much more they will do such things also to us. But
therefore, so that Your Grace might recognize and know of
what conviction and opinion I have always been concerning
the government, what I have also preached publicly from the
pulpit at Waldshut and elsewhere, written, and numerous
times taught, and for which I have also suffered a great deal
(I do not boast) although my opponents (only with distorting
the truth) have said many other things about me, I have put
together a little book, in which I make known my judgment to
Your Grace and to everyone. I also disprove in general all
writings which so far my adversaries have introduced and used
against me concerning the rejection of government among
Christians.*

    May Your Grace graciously accept this little book from me
and reflect on my theses concerning the Christian magistracy

---

* I have more earnestly than any preacher within twenty miles treated
Scripture concerning the righteous government. However, I have also
shown the tyrants their vices; therefore there comes envy, hate and
enmity.

according to the contents of the Scriptures, for in this and all my other teachings and deeds I always ask for justice and right. If I err, I will then gladly let myself be corrected and punished.* One should, however, give evidence beforehand with the Scripture of what is wrong. But if I do not err, why then am I attacked, why am I accused? But if my detractors (of which I have as many as the old snake has scales) can demonstrate in all this that I am not right, then I am not myself. If my God and Lord can suffer his Word to be blasphemed and violated, then I have to endure it also, nevertheless, praise God, not as an evildoer. Let everyone judge here as he wants to be judged by the Lord. Well then, it is the will of God because of our sins; therefore it shall and must also please my will against my will.

Herewith I commend myself to Your Grace in humility, to my very gracious lord, in all servitude at all times. May Your Grace live well in Christ Jesus. Given at Nicolspurg, June 24, 1527.

To Your Grace   Sincerely, Balthasar
                                          Hůebmör von Fridberg /436/

On The Sword
The First Passage

> Christ says to Pilate, "My kingdom is not of this world. If it were of this world, my servants without doubt would fight for me so that I not be handed over to the Jews," John 18:36.

On the basis of this Scripture passage many brethren say that a Christian should not carry the sword, because the kingdom of Christians is not of this world. Answer: If these people would just open their eyes, they would have to think much differently, namely, that our kingdom should not be of this world. But, unfortunately, be it lamented unto God, it is of this world, as we ourselves confess in the Lord's Prayer where we pray, "Father, thy kingdom come, Matt. 6:10; Luke 11:2, for we are in the kingdom of the world, which is a kingdom of

---

* A legitimate offer.

sin, death, and hell. But Father, help us out of this kingdom, we are stuck in it right up to our ears, and we will not be able to be free from it here on earth. It clings to us until death. Lord, deliver us from this evil and help us home into thy kingdom."[10] Now these brethren see the truth and must confess that our kingdom is of this world, about which we are sincerely sorry. However, Christ alone can say in truth, "My kingdom is not of this world," because he was conceived and born without sin, an innocent little lamb, in whom there is no deception, without sin or blemish. He alone could say in truth, "The prince of this world has come, but in me he found nothing," John 14:30, which we here on earth could never truthfully say. For as often as that prince, the devil, comes, he finds in us evil lusts, evil desires, evil inclinations. Therefore also St. Paul, while filled with the Holy Spirit, calls himself wretched, Rom. 7:24. Likewise the most righteous and pious Christians must also confess their wretchedness until death, no matter what we make of ourselves.

The Second Passage

Jesus says to Peter, "Put your sword into its place, for whoever takes up the sword shall perish by the sword. Or do you think that I could not ask my Father to send me more than twelve legions of angels. But how would the Scripture be fulfilled? In that way it must come to pass," Matt. 26:52-54.

Consider well here, dear Christian, the words of Christ; then you already have an answer to the accusation of the brethren. First, Christ says, "Put the sword in its place. It is not proper for you to carry it. You are not in authority. That is not commanded you. You are neither called nor chosen for it. For, whoever takes the sword will perish by the sword." They take up the sword who use it without calling, unorderly, and on their own authority.[a] No one /437/ should take up the

---

[10] The exegesis of the Lord's Prayer is a familiar theme in Hubmaier. See above, text 16, pp. 241ff.

---

[a] What is taking the sword.

sword himself, except where one is chosen and ordered for
that purpose. For he does not take it up of himself; rather, it
is put before him and given to him. Now he can say, "I have
not taken the sword. I rather wanted to go without it, because
I am myself still very culpable. Since, however, I am called to
it, I pray to God, that he give me grace and wisdom to carry it
and to rule according to his Word and will." Thus did
Solomon pray, and great wisdom was given to him by God to
carry the sword justly, 1 Kings 3:6ff.

In addition, you hear here that Christ says to Peter, "Put
your sword back into the sheath." He does not say, "Untie it
and throw it away." It is because he drew it that Christ
rebukes him and not because he had it hanging at his side. He
would have rebuked him long before if it had been wrong. It
follows further, "Whoever takes up the sword shall perish by
the sword," that is, he has fallen under the judgment of the
sword, although he will not always for good reasons be judged
by the sword. Do you realize how Christ here confirms the
sword, that one should punish those with it who practice by it
their own violence and sacrilege. And those shall do that who
are chosen for it, whoever they might be. Yet, it is certain
that the more righteous they are the better and more orderly
they will carry the sword according to God's will for the protection of the innocent and the fear of evildoers. For it is for
that purpose that it has been instituted and ordered by God,
Rom. 13:1.

Third, Christ spoke to his disciples when they tried to
hinder his going to Jerusalem, because the Jews wanted to
stone him. Christ says, "Are there not twelve hours in a day?"
John 11:9. It is as if he wanted to say, "They will not kill me
until the twelfth hour comes, that is, the one which is ordered
by God for my death," Luke 22:53, which Christ also calls an
hour of darkness. But when this twelfth hour had come Christ
himself said to his disciples at the Mount of Olives, "Get up
and let us go to them. The hour has come that I shall be given
into death in order that the Scriptures be fulfilled," Matt.
26:46. Notice: Peter heard that the hour determined and
ordered by God had come. Yet he wanted to prevent it and
drew the sword on his own authority. That was the greatest
mistake. That is why Christ said, "Protecting and guarding
does not help any longer. The hour chosen by God has come

and even if twelve legions of angels were present, they would not be able to help me against the will of God, my heavenly Father. Therefore, put it back. It is of no use. I have told you before that the hour has come. The Scriptures shall and must be fulfilled."

From this every Christian learns that one should not stop protecting and guarding all righteous and innocent people as long as one does not know with certainty that the hour of their death has now come. When, however, the hour comes, /438/ whether you know it or not, no protecting and guarding will help anymore. Therefore the rulers are obliged for the sake of the salvation of their souls to protect and guard all innocent and peaceful people until a sure voice of God comes and is heard surely to say, "Now you should no longer protect this person," just as Abraham also heard a voice saying, contrary to the commandment, "You shall not kill," Exod. 20:13, that he should kill his son, Gen. 22:2. Therefore the government is obliged to shield and to free all oppressed and subjugated people, widows, orphans, friends, and strangers without regard to persons according to the will and earnest command of God, according to Isaiah 1:17; Jeremiah 21:12; 22:3; Romans 13:4, and many other passages, until ordered otherwise by God. For this it will have to wait a long time, Rom. 13:4. Therefore God has hung the sword at the government's side and has made it to be his servant.

The Third Passage

Lord, if you want, we will call fire from heaven to fall and consume them, as Elijah did. Jesus turned to them, rebuked them and said, "You do not know of what spirit you are. The Son of Man has not come to destroy human souls, but to preserve them," Luke 9:54-56.

Here, however, my brothers make a lot of noise, though there is little wool here, and say, "Here you see, Balthasar, that Christ did not want to punish by fire. Now then, we should also not do it and use neither fire, water, sword, nor gallows." Answer: Consider, dear brothers, why Christ came to earth, what the office and mandate given him by God was. Consider along with this also what the office of the superiors is. If you do that you already have received the answer. Christ came, as he himself says, not to judge, condemn, or punish people with fire, water, or sword. He did not become human for this reason. Rather, his mandate and office was to save people by the Word. This office he fulfilled, for which he had become human. He says so himself in Luke 12:14, "Who has chosen me to be a judge between you and your brother?" It is as if he wanted to say, "Surely you can find other judges. I am not here to interfere in the office and mandate of others. On the contrary, the office and orderly mandate has been given by God to the government to protect and guard the godly and to punish and kill the evil ones, Rom. 13:4. For this he hung the sword on its side. For what reason should it hang there if one were not permitted to use it?" Now sometimes God punishes the evil ones by hail, floods, and illnesses, also by /439/ special people who are chosen and elected for that end. For that reason Paul calls the government a servant of God. For what God wants to do himself he often wants to do through creatures as his tools.

Yes, and although in Scripture sometimes the devil, Nebuchadnezzar, and other evil people are also called servants of God, it is quite another thing with the true government when it punishes the evil ones according to the mandate of God for the benefit of the godly and the innocent. But the devil and his cohorts do nothing for the benefit and the peace of the people, but only to their disadvantage and injury with a jealous and vindictive mind. The government, however, has a special compassion for those who have erred. It wholeheartedly wishes that it had not happened. The devil and his followers want all people to be miserable. You see here, brothers, how far these two servitudes—of the devil and of the true government—are separated from one another. Just as Christ wanted to do justice to his office on earth, likewise we should fulfill our office and calling, be it in government or in obedience, for we shall have to give account of it to God on the last day.

The Fourth Passage

One of the people spoke to the Lord, "Master, tell my brother that he should share the inheritance with me." But he said to him, "Man, who has put me as a judge or divider of inheritances over you," Luke 12:13f.

Here, these my brothers cry out overly loud into the clouds and say, "Do you hear it, Fridberger, Christ wants neither to be a judge nor a divider of inheritances. The court and the council are rejected by Christ. Therefore Christians should simply not be judges, never sit in a council, nor carry the sword, for Christ did not want to decide or judge between the two brothers." Answer: Stop shouting, dear brothers. You do not know the Scriptures; therefore, you err and you do not realize what you are shouting. Christ says, "Who has put me as judge over you?" He wanted to say thereby, "I am neither chosen nor appointed to be judge. It is not my office. It belongs to others." Realize that Christ does not here reject the office of the judge, because it is not to be rejected, as will be shown immediately below. Rather, he points out that nobody should set himself up as a judge, unless he is called or chosen for it. That is why we have the election of the burgomasters, village mayors, and judges. Christ lets all of those stand to rule and judge with God and a good conscience over temporal and physical matters. However, he did not want to concern himself with them. He had not become human for that purpose; nor was he appointed to that end. /440/ In like manner, nobody should use the sword unless he be elected properly to it, or called by God in another way, like Moses had been between the Israelites and the Egyptians, or Abraham in the deliverance of his brother Lot and Phineas against the unchaste, Exod. 2:12; Gen. 14:14ff.; Num. 25:7f.

The Fifth Passage

If somebody wants to fight with you before the court and wants to take your garment, then let him also have the coat, Matt. 5:40.

The Sixth Passage

It is already a fault among you that you go to court against one another. Why do you not rather allow injustice to be done to you? Why do you not rather prefer to be harmed and cheated? But instead, you do injustice and you cheat, and you do this to the brothers, 1 Cor. 6:7f.

These two passages are so highly and anxiously esteemed by the brothers that they think, and would even dare to go into the fire for it, that "a Christian may not be a judge."

Now then, let us examine the Scriptures and we shall find a good answer. First, we confess that disputing, quarreling, arguing, and debating before a council or court about temporal matters insofar as one seeks one's own, is not right, as the two above-mentioned passages brightly and clearly show.[a] However, it is not so that wherever the parties want to go to court, a Christian could not be a judge and administer justice between them without sin. Let us therefore leave the judgment to the sixth chapter of the first epistle of Paul to the Corinthians. Paul writes the following: "How dare anybody among you, if he has a dispute with somebody else, let himself be judged before the unrighteous and not before the saints, that is, before Christians.[b] Do you not know that the saints will judge the world? If then the world will be judged by you, are you then not good enough to judge over minor things? Do you not know that you will judge over the angels, how much more over matters of temporal nourishment. When you now have a dispute because of nourishment, then take the most despised in your community, and set them as judges. I say this to your shame. Is there no wise person among you, or not even one who could judge between /441/ brother and brother? But instead, one brother lets himself be judged with the other, and that before the unbelievers."

Here, here listen to Paul, you dear brothers and see. If ever the Christians want to bring suit against each other over nourishment, that is, for temporal goods, which already is wrong, then it should nonetheless happen before a Christian and not before an unbelieving judge. Note here, brothers. This you have skipped, that if Christians ever want to dispute with each other and are not at peace with one another, that they sin even more, yes indeed they sin in a twofold way if they carry out such dispute before an unbelieving judge and not before a Christian. That is why Paul mocks the Corinthians and says that if they ever want to bring suit against each other, they should take the most despised ones among themselves as judges. That he said to their shame, as if they had no righteous and wise Christians among themselves who might

---

[a] Quarreling before the court is not right.
[b] A Christian may well be a judge.

judge between them, but they have to run to get an unbelieving judge. For that they should really be ashamed.

Here even a blind person can see that a Christian may very well and with good conscience sit in court and council and may judge and decide also in temporal matters. Although the wranglers and quarrelers are sinning, they would sin even more if they would carry out their cases before unbelieving judges. If then, a Christian, by power of the divine Word, may and should be a judge with the mouth, he may also be a protector with the hand of the one who wins justice and may punish the unjust. For of what use would the law, court, and judge be if one were not allowed to carry out and enforce the punishment on the evildoers? Of what use would a shoe be if one were not allowed to put it on? See, dear brothers, that council, court, and law are not wrong. That also the judge may and should be a Christian, although the quarreling parties are sinning because they do not prefer to be taken advantage of. Consequently, a Christian may also, according to God's order, carry the sword in God's place over the evildoer and punish him. Because of the evil ones it is ordered in this way by God for protection and shielding of the godly, Rom. 13:3. That is what the Scripture means when it says, "You judges, watch out what you are doing. You are not carrying out an office of human beings but of God. What you judge shall come over you. Therefore, the fear of God should be with you and you should act with diligence because God does not like to see nor endure injustice," 2 Chron. 19:15-17. This Scripture is given to us as well as to those of old because it concerns brotherly love.

You say, "But is it not so that one should not judge?" Matt. 7:1. Yes. Nor should one do injustice to anyone. But should it ever happen among Christians, a Christian judge should be appointed immediately who will administer justice for residents and foreigners. This must happen or Scripture must break to pieces. As far as I am concerned, no human being can ever overthrow that. /442/

The Seventh Passage

If your brother sins against you, then go to him and admonish him in private. If he listens to you, then you have won

your brother. If he does not hear you, then take one or two
with you so that the whole matter be established on the basis of two or three witnesses. If he does not hear them, then
tell it to the congregation. If he does not hear the congregation, then consider him as a heathen and tax collector,
Matt. 18:15 ff.

On the basis of this text the brothers again level a serious
accusation against me and say: "If there should be government
among Christians, then the Christian ban would be worthless
and in vain. For where one punishes evil doers with the sword
the church does not need the ban."[11] Answer: The ban and
punishing with the sword are two different commands given
by God.[*] The first is promised and given to the church by
Christ, Matt. 10:34; 18:15ff.; John 20:23, to be used according
to his will for the purpose of admitting the godly into her holy
communion and in the exclusion of the unworthy. Thus,
whomever the Christian church forgives sins on earth, the
same are already also forgiven in the heavens, and whomever
she does not forgive their sins here on earth, the same are
also not remitted in the heavens.

For Christ has assigned, entrusted, and handed over to his
bride the Christian church for the time of his bodily absence
his mandate to loosen and to bind in all measure as he
received it from his Father. Thus the Christian church can
and should in the meantime teach to the peoples everything
that Christ has commanded her to teach. She also has the
power and authority to seal with water baptism all people who
want to accept, believe, and henceforth direct and lead their
lives according to such teaching; also to enlist and include the
same in her holy communion. For everything that she governs
and directs here on earth, the same is already made and done,
included and excluded also in the heavens until Christ her

---

[11] In the 1524 letter addressed by Conrad Grebel to Thomas Müntzer the
ban is described as sufficient for the church and, indeed, replaces the
sword of the government. See Harder 1985, pp. 289-290. The opposition
between the ban and the sword was further developed by the nonresistant
Anabaptists; cf. Schleitheim article VI (Yoder 1973, p. 39) and Yoder 1968,
pp. 114ff.

---

[*] The ban is an office of the church.

bridegroom descends again bodily and visibly to her in his glory and majesty and himself bodily assumes that kingdom again. He will then immediately return and submit it to his heavenly Father so that God, as Paul writes, may be all in all, 1 Cor. 15:28. Just that is the mystery of Christ and his church according to the content of the Letter to the Ephesians 5:32.

The second command* concerns the outward and temporal authority and government which originally was given by God to Adam after the Fall, when God said to Eve: "You will be under the authority of the man and he will rule over you," Gen. 3:16. If Adam has now been set as a ruler by God over his Eve, then he has also received authority over all blood and /443/ flesh, which has been born in pain by Eve. Thus God also afterward empowered and gave the sword to other special and God-fearing people, namely, Abraham, Moses, Joshua, Gideon, and Samuel. However, after that, the evil of humankind increased even more and became overabundant, indeed took the upper hand in such a measure that the people at that time demanded a king from Samuel and rejected God, 1 Sam. 8:5. Samuel in fact, on the basis of divine command, gave them that king, but earnestly pointed out to them thereby the royal rights, obligations, and services which they were committed henceforth to do for the king on account of their sins because they had despised and rejected God and had demanded from Samuel a king like the other nations and not from God. We must and should still today obediently and willingly bear, suffer, and endure such services and troubles, also give and hand over tribute to whom tribute is due, taxes to whom taxes are due, respect to whom respect is due, honor to whom honor is due. Rom. 13:7. For our sins are to blame for that, as the sin of Eve that she must give birth in pain and the sin of Adam that he must eat his bread in the sweat of his brow, Gen. 3:16f. For if we had remained obedient to God and righteous, then neither law, sword, fire, rod, nor gallows would have been necessary. However, since we have sinned it must and will be thus. Therefore, neither rebellion nor anything else on earth can help us. For God's words are "yes"

---

* Carrying the sword is the office of the government.

and not "no," 2 Cor. 1:20. If we, however, pile up disobedience on disobedience and increase sin with sins, God in his wrath will give us kings and children for princes. Yea, he will also let the suffragans rule over us and if we want to flee Rheoboam we will run into the hands of Jeroboam. All of this happens on account of our sins, according to the common and true proverb: as the people, so the king. A stork fell on the frogs who did not want to recognize nor accept the Aesopic and harmless log as their king. Accordingly, it is of great necessity, O you dear Christians, to pray to the all powerful God with high diligence and with earnest devotion for a pious, righteous, and Christian government on earth so that we can lead a peaceful and still life among one another in all blessedness and honesty. Where now God gives us these, we ought to accept the same with special thanksgiving. If he does not give them to us, then it is surely and certainly true because of our sins that we are not worthy of any other or better. In this matter the Bible of the Old Testament will give us many stories for example and testimony. /444/

Now you see, dear brothers, that these two offices and mandates of the ban and external sword are not against each other since they are both from God. For the Christian ban is often used for good reason, for example in many secret sins where the sword can not always be used. For the punishment should be according to the character of the sins. Christ clearly teaches us this when he asks the adulterous woman: "Woman, has no one judged you?" She says: "No one, Lord." He says: "Then I will also not judge you. Go forth and henceforth you should not sin," John 8:10ff.

Note: Christ asks, "Woman, has no one judged you?" It is as if he wanted to say: "If a judgment had been spoken over you according to the law of God concerning adultery, then I would not interfere with the judges, for it is the command of God my Father that one should stone adulterers. Since, however, no one has judged you, I will also not judge you, for it is not my office. I have also not been set up as a judge but as a Savior. Therefore, go forth and sin no more. That is my office: to forgive sins and to order that one from now on abstain from sins." Do you hear here, dear brothers, how Christ uses his office so properly and nevertheless lets the judicial office remain in its own dignity? Thus can also the church with its ban and the government with its sword go along with each other and neither interfere in the office of the other.

The Eighth Passage

You have heard that it is said: an eye for an eye and a tooth for a tooth. But I say to you, that you should not resist evil. If someone strikes you on your right cheek, then offer him the other also, Matt. 5:38f.; Luke 6:27ff.

This passage is so highly valued by the brethren that they are of the opinion that by it they unbuckle the sword of the government which wants to be Christian. But take it easy, do not hurry so much, dear friends, and listen. We want to treat the passage correctly. You have heard that it was said in the Old Testament, "an eye for an eye and a tooth for a tooth," Lev. 24:20; Deut. 19:21. Thus if one were to come and accuse another before the judge to the effect that he had knocked out an eye or a tooth (for such accusations were permitted to the ancients as you find in Deuteronomy 1). If now then the judge heard the complaint and testimony, he must judge an eye for an eye and a tooth for a tooth according to the law of God. But in the New Testament it must not happen this way; but where one hits you on the right cheek, then do not accuse him, do not run to the judge, do not demand vengeance like the ancients to whom it was permitted /445/ to accuse, but offer the other cheek also, Matt. 5:39. For suing is always forbidden Christians, as you have heard, 1 Cor. 6:1. Now if you thus suffer and do not resist, you do the right thing, for so has Christ taught every single individual to do. However, thereby the government's sword is not yet unbuckled. Yes, it is much more commanded to protect the righteous and to punish the evil with the sword, where it notices such wantonness or sacrilege by itself or it is pointed out by others. Therefore, it is ordered to be a servant of God, insuring peace for the good and terror for the evil. Thereby it does the will of God.

A parable: Although the two who quarrel about temporal goods sin before the judge, the Christian judge does not sin when he judges the quarrel rightly. But even if no one sues and the government knows that someone violates and does injustice to the other, it should nonetheless discharge its mandated office and judge rightly and also punish the evildoer. For it does not carry the sword in vain. In this matter there is now a higher stage in the New Testament than in the Old: the slandered and injured do not sue, but still the government punishes. In the Old Testament the injured one sues and the judge punishes. Do you see, dear brothers, how you must let the thirteenth chapter of Romans stand upright by the above mentioned words of Christ, for the two strings thus resonate together and one wheel runs well with the other.

The Ninth Passage

So now, stand, your loins girt with the belt of truth, and dressed with the breastplate of righteousness and your feet shod with the preparation of the Gospel of peace. But in all things grasp the shield of faith with which you are able to extinguish all the fiery darts of the evil one. And take the helmet of salvation to yourself and the sword of the Spirit which is the Word of God, Eph. 6:14ff.

The Tenth Passage

The weapons of our knighthood are not carnal but mighty before God for destroying the fortifications so that we destroy the ambush and all height which lifts itself against the knowledge of God, 2 Cor. 10:4f.

Here the brothers run to and fro, crying overly loud: "Here you see what the Christian breastplate and defense should be, not made of iron or long wood, but of the gospel, the gospel. /446/ The faith, the faith. The Word of God, the Word of God should be our sword and weapon. Truly Paul tells us to polish the breastplate and to clean our Christian weapons well for the other weapons are all from the devil." Answer: Stop running about, dear brothers, and note what I want to say to you in good peace.

First, I find in this passage that Paul points out one sword to us with these words to the Ephesians and a second in Romans, Chapter 13 [v. 4]. Now tell me whether here and there one sword is written about or two.[a] You cannot say

---

[a] Two kinds of sword in the Scripture.

with truth, dear brothers, that only one sword is written about. For to the Ephesians and to the Corinthians Paul speaks of a spiritual sword and says himself it is the Word of God with which one destroys that which lifts itself against the knowledge of God, while he writes there to the Romans of a physical sword which one wears at the side and with which to frighten the evil persons who do not let themselves be frightened nor punished by the Word of God. If there are now then two different kinds of swords, of which one belongs to the soul and the other to the body, then, dear brothers, you must let both of them remain in their dignity.

On the other hand, I beseech you, for the sake of divine love, that you start to read eleven lines above the verse to the Ephesians which you introduce. Then you will clearly see and hear that Paul there describes the breastplate, sword, and armor which one should use against the devil for the protection of the soul and not of the sword which one uses against evil people here on earth who injure the innocent in property, body, and life. Now begin to read, then the truth from that hour on will be revealed to you in which the text says, "Finally, my brothers," writes Paul, "strengthen yourself in the Lord and in the power of his strength, putting on the breast plate of God that you can withstand the perfidious attacks of the devil. For we do not have to fight with flesh and blood, but with principalities and powers, with the universal rulers of darkness in this world, with the spirits of evil under the heavens, etc." Note here, dear friends, if your mind were fair, then you would speak as follows: There are two kinds of sword in the Scripture. There is a spiritual one which is used against the perfidious attacks of the devil, such as Christ also used against Satan, Matt. 4:1-11.[a] And that is the Word of God. Indeed, Paul speaks here to the Ephesians and the Corinthians about this sword concerning which Christ also says, "I have not come to bring peace but the sword," Matt. 10:34.[b] In addition to that there is also an external sword which one uses for the protection of the righteous and for the /447/ terror of the evil persons here on earth. That is given to the government in order to maintain a common ter-

---

[a] A spiritual sword.
[b] An external sword.

ritorial peace with it. It is also called a spiritual sword, when one uses it according to the will of God. These two swords are not in opposition to each other.

In the third place, Paul teaches after that that we should pray for the government so that we can lead a peaceful and quiet life in all blessedness and honesty among one another, 1 Tim. 2:1. I ask you all together, brothers, whether a believing or unbelieving government is more useful and effective in maintaining the people in such a peaceful, restful, quiet, blessed, and honest life. You must, must, must all confess that a Christian government can perform and will do such much better and more earnestly than an unchristian one, which takes to heart neither Christ, God, nor blessedness, but only thinks and plans thereby to remain in its power, pomp, and circumstance. You have examples in David, Hezekiah, Josiah, and also counter-examples in Saul, Rehoboam, and Jeroboam. Therefore, get behind me, you Satan, and stop misleading the simple people under the appearance of great patience and spirituality. We recognize you by your old tricks.

The Eleventh Passage

You have heard that it was said: "You should love your neighbor and hate your enemy." But I say to·you: "Love your enemy, speak well to those who speak evil about you. Do well to them who hate you, pray for those who slander and persecute you, that you may be children of your Father in heaven. For he lets his sun rise over the evil and over the good and lets it rain over the just and the unjust. For if you love those who love you, what reward will you have? Do not the tax collectors also do the same? And if you are only friendly to your brothers, what do you do special that the tax collectors do not also do? Therefore you should be perfect as your father in heaven is perfect," Matthew 5:43ff.

Here once again the brothers cry out, "Murder!" over the government and say: "Do you not see here that the government which wants to be Christian should not attack at all with the sword, but love its enemies, do well to them and pray for them." Answer: Well, then, we want to consider and weigh these words of Christ /448/ so that we do not err. Christ says: "You have heard that it was said: 'You should love your neighbor and hate your enemy.' " Note here clearly who is an enemy, namely, the one whom one hates and envies. Now, however, a Christian should neither hate nor envy anyone, but love everyone. Therefore, a Christian government has no enemy, for it hates and envies no one. For what it does with the sword, it does not out of envy or hate, but from the mandate of God. Therefore, punishing the evil is not hating, envying, or being an enemy. For, otherwise, God would also be hateful, envious, and an enemy to people. However, he is not that. Even though he punishes evil persons, he does so not out of envy or hate, but out of righteousness. Thus a just and Christian government does not hate those whom it punishes. It is wholeheartedly sorry that such culpable people have not watched themselves. Yes, what it does it does because of the order and the earnest mandate of God, who has made it into a servant; and the sword has been hung at its side for the execution of righteousness. Therefore it will also have to give serious account at the last day as to how it has used the sword. For the sword is nothing other than a good rod and whip of God, which he commanded to use over evil people. For what God calls good is good. If he commanded you to butcher your son, then it would be a good work. For God thus wants to do many things through his creatures as his instruments which he could well do alone and without them. But he wants to use us so that we serve one another and are not idle, but that everyone fulfill his office to which he has been called by God. One should preach, the other protect, the third cultivate his field, the fourth do his work in another way so that we all eat our bread in the sweat of our brow. Truly, truly whoever rules rightly and in a Christian way has enough to sweat. He is not idle.

Now we once again see clearly how the above-mentioned words of Christ and the sword remain so dearly and amicably together. Thus one does not need to unbuckle the sword on account of brotherly love. Yes, and if I were a Christian and right-minded and I fell into sin, I should want and desire that the government punish me soon so that I not pile more sin upon sin. Therefore, it follows that the government not only out of righteousness, but also out of great love, which it bears to the evildoer but not to his evil deed, can and should punish his sin, for it is good and useful to the sinner that one soon ties a millstone around his neck and throws him into the water, Matt. 18:6. /449/

The Twelfth Passage

You have heard that it was said to the ancients that you should not kill, but whoever kills will be worthy of judgment, Matt. 5:21.

Dear brothers, what is it that you shout out here and cry out overly loud into the heavens: It is written, you should not kill. You should not kill. Now those in the Old Testament had the commandment just as we do, and still they killed. But you say, yes, but God commanded them to kill. Against this I answer also the following: God has also commanded the government that they should kill and strangle the unpeaceful. Therefore he gave them the sword and not in vain, as Paul writes in Romans 13:4. If you ask, dear Christian, how can killing and not killing go together, I answer: Very well, Matt. 19:10ff.

Like being chaste and getting married, 1 Cor. 7:9, 29.

Like having a wife and not having one, John 5:32.

Like my witness is true and not true, John 8:14.

Like having all things and having nothing, 2 Cor. 6:10.

Like being rich and being poor, Matt. 5:3.

Like preaching the gospel to all creatures and not casting pearls before the swine, Matt. 16:15; 7:6.

Like loving father and mother and hating them, Exod. 20:12; Luke 14:26.

Like seeing God and not seeing him, Gen. 32:31; John 1:18.

Like all people being saved and those who do not believe being damned, 1 Tim. 2:4; Mark 16:16.

Like swearing by the name of God, and not swearing, Deut. 5:11; 6:13.

Like not sinning, and yet having sin, 1 John 1:8, 10; 5:18.

Like selling everything that we have and giving it to poor people, and giving what we have to spare so that we do not fall into poverty, Matt. 19:21, 2 Cor. 8:2.

Like being poor and like its being more blessed to give than to receive, Matt. 5:3; Acts 20:35.

As Christ always being with us until the end of the world and yet not always having him with us, Matt. 28:20; Matt. 26:11.

As God punishes the evil of the fathers unto the sons of the third and fourth generation and yet the son does not carry the evil of the father, Exod. 29:28; Ezek. 18:20.

As we should not do good works before people and yet should do them so that people see our good works, Matt. 5:16; Matt. 23:5.

Like not knowing the mind of the Lord and yet the secret of his will has been revealed to us, Rom. 11:34; 1 Cor. 2:16; Eph. 1:17.

As we pray and receive from God all things; we also pray and do not receive, Matt. 7:8; James 4:3.

Like melting the swords into plowshares and the lances into sickles and yet breaking the plow for swords and the hoes for lances, Isa. 2:4; Joel 3:10.

As we should not judge and yet should install judges who judge among us, Luke 6:37; 1 Cor. 6:4. /450/

Like Abraham, justified by faith and yet by works, Rom. 4:5; James 2:21; Heb. 11:17.

Like pleasing our neighbor and yet not pleasing people, Rom. 15:2; Gal. 1:10.

Like hating wicked people and yet wishing well to those who persecute us, Ps. 119:113; Rom. 12:14.

As we should become children and yet not be children, Matt. 18:3; Matt. 19:14; 1 Cor. 14:20; Eph. 4:14.

As God wants to save all people and yet he is merciful to whom he wants, and he hardens whom he wants, 1 Tim. 2:4; Rom. 9:18.

Like the yoke of Christ is sweet and yet impossible with people, Matt. 11:30; Matt. 19:26.

Like the angels want to see the face of God, and yet they are satisfied if his glory appears, 1 Pet. 1:12; Ps. 17:15.

As the law of God is good and yet God has given a law that is not good, Rom. 7:12.

As the king should not have many wives and yet Rehoboam had fourteen,[12] Abijah just as many, David also

---

[12] According to 2 Chronicles 11:21 Rehoboam had eighteen wives.

many, and Solomon seven hundred wives and three hundred concubines, Deut. 17:17; 2 Chron. 11:21; 13:21; 2 Sam. 12:8; 1 Kings 11:3.

As God will not be eternally wrathful and yet the damned must go into the eternal fire, Jer. 3:12; Matt. 25:41.

As no law is given to the righteous and yet Christ has given us a new commandment, 1 Tim. 1:9; John 13:34.

Like God tempts no one and yet tempted Abraham, James 1:13; Gen. 22:1ff.

As the Father and Christ are one and yet the Father is more than Christ, John 10:30; John 14:10, and many other passages which let themselves appear contradictory on the surface, like the winged cherubim, and yet they all come together in Christ. Therefore one should divide the hooves of the Scriptures, Lev. 11:3,[13] and chew them well before one swallows them, that is, believe or one will eat death therein and through half-truths and half-judgments deviate far, far from the whole truth and seriously go astray. A parable: When Christ says, "This is my body," that is a half-truth, Matt. 26:26; Mark 14:22; Luke 22:19; 1 Cor. 11:24. However, if he says, "This is my body which is given for you, do this in my memory," that is now a whole truth. Whoever now judges on the basis of the half-truth says that the bread is the body of Christ, and errs.[*] However, whoever judges on the basis of the whole truth says that the bread is the body of Christ given for us. He is not bodily or essentially in it himself, but is in the held memory in the power of the institution of Christ which took place at the Last Supper. And that is entirely true and not otherwise. Whoever understands that also, understands well how not killing and killing can stand very well by one another in whole truth and should not be judged without discrimination.

---

[13] Hubmaier probably had his own collection of apparent antitheses in Scripture, as background to self-conscious theories about Scriptural interpretation. Hans Denck listed forty antitheses in his *Who Truly Loves the Truth* (Fellman 1956, pp. 67-74). The notion is also in Carlstadt, Müntzer, Tauler, and Hofmann.

---

[*] O Christian, learn to divide the judgment rightly.

Well then, we want to take the Word of Christ for us and see whether the government is forbidden to kill. Christ says, "You should not kill," and he goes beyond that also to rip out the roots of killing and says, "However, I say /451/ to you whoever is angry with his brother is guilty of judgment. Whoever says to his brother, 'Raca,' is guilty of the council. Whoever says 'You fool,' is guilty of hellfire, Matt. 5:21ff. Read that in addition, dear brothers, and you will see clearly which killing Christ has forbidden, namely, the killing that happens out of anger, mockery, or despising. However, the government—I speak of just government—does not kill out of anger or move out of mockery and despising words, but by the order of God, which commands it earnestly to do away with the evil ones and to hold the righteous in peace.

If now the government may kill the evildoer, and is obligated to do that by the order of God, but is not able to do that on its own, if it now commands and calls me or another to do that, then we are obligated to help it, and whoever resists is resisting the order of God and will receive over himself the eternal judgment.[*] Do not believe me here, dear brothers, but believe Paul, and there you will certainly find it so. Therefore those whom we now call executioners were in the Old Testament pious, honorable, and brave men. One called them "prefects," that is, executors of the order and law of God. For if it is honorable for the judge to sentence the guilty with the mouth, then how could it be unjust to kill the same with the sword and fulfill the word of the judge? For the executor of the law would not strike or kill with the sword if the judge had not commanded him. We read that Solomon gave the responsibility to the honorable Benaiah to kill Shimei, Adonijah, and Joab, 1 Kings 2:25, 31, 46. Saul commanded Doeg to kill the priests and David commanded his servant that he should also kill the murderer of Saul, 1 Sam. 22:18; 2 Sam. 1:15. For neither the judge nor the executioner kill the evildoer, but the law of God, 2 Chron. 19:6. Therefore the judges, governments, and executors of justice are called servants of God in the Scripture and not murderers, Rom. 13:4. God judges, sentences, and kills through them, and not

---

[*] The subjects are obligated to help the government in all justifiable things.

516 / *Balthasar Hubmaier*

they themselves. From this it follows that those who do not want to kill the evildoer but let them live, are acting and sinning against the commandment: "You should not kill."[a] For whoever does not protect the righteous kills him and is guilty of his death as much as the one who does not feed the hungry.

The Thirteenth Passage

The worldly kings rule, says Christ, and the powerful ones are called gracious lords, but you do not do that, Luke 22:25f.

I cannot sufficiently tell what great noise my brothers make here, particularly about the words "but you do not do that."[b] But I /452/ complain myself about you as above, that you do not want to see either the preceding or following words. For if you would look at them correctly we would soon be reconciled. Well then, we want to begin this passage three lines higher. Then the understanding will come forth by itself. The text goes as follows: A quarrel arose among the disciples as to which among them would be considered to be the greatest. Christ, however, said to them, "The worldly kings rule and the powerful ones are called gracious lords, but you do not do that. Rather, the greatest among you shall be as the youngest and the most prominent like the servant."

In the first place, it is clear that Christ is speaking here to those who would preach his Word. These should not let themselves be involved in alien roles nor enmeshed in worldly affairs as our pope and bishops have done until now in all worldly matters. Yes, also in matters of war they have been the first and the last.

Thus, when two roosters in France or Italy fought with one another on a dung heap, the pope and his cardinals supported one over against the other.[c] Christ does not want to bear that and says that the proclaimers of his holy Word

---

[a] If you do not defend, you kill [in Latin].
[b] But you not.
[c] The pope has forbidden battle between two men and has yet led 80,000 men into the field, let them be slaughtered, and also gave them grace and indulgences for that.

should realize and also fulfill their commission and calling and
stay away from other worldly affairs as also Paul writes to
Timothy, 2 Tim. 2:22-26.

In the second place, the text clearly points out that each
one among the disciples wanted the rule, and would gladly
have been superior. They also quarreled as to which among
them should be the greatest. Christ does not like to see such
quarrels. It is not appropriate to any Christian to desire the
rule of the government nor to strive after it, but rather one
should flee from it. For if there is a more dangerous position
that one can find on earth—excepting the preaching
office—then it is the office of the government and temporal
authority. To that Christ says, "The worldly kings dominate
and are called gracious lords. But a Christian, even if he is in
the government, does not dominate. He also does not desire to
be called gracious lord or prince."[14] But he considers himself
a servant of God and takes care that he acts according to the
order of God, so that the righteous are protected and the evil
punished. Also, he raises himself up over no one, but right
well takes to heart the Word of Christ that the most prominent should be like a servant.

Do you see, brothers, how Christ himself here points out
how the greatest should recognize and consider himself as the
youngest and the most prominent as a servant. So must be the
great and small, the prominent and those who are subjects
/453/ among Christians, or he would have given this rule in
vain. Therefore, dear brothers, do not make patchwork of the
Scripture, but place the preceding and the following words
together into a whole judgment, so that you then obtain a perfect understanding of the Scriptures, and see how the little
word, "but you do not do that," does not forbid the
government to Christians, but teaches us that we should not
quarrel, fight, and strive about it, nor conquer land and
people with the sword and with force. It is against God. Also
we should not desire to be "gracious lords" and princes as do
the worldly kings, princes, and lords.[a] For the government is

---

[14] *Junckher*, "nobleman."

---

[a] Herewith the honor of the government should also not be taken away.

not a domineering and a princely sovereignty, but a service according to the order of God, Rom. 13:1.

The Fourteenth Passage

Do not avenge yourselves, my beloved, but give place to wrath. For it is written, Vengeance is mine, I will repay, says the Lord. If now your enemy hungers, then feed him, if he thirsts, give him to drink, Rom. 12:19f.

Whoever has heard the tenth and eleventh passages above has it easy to answer. For as Christian government has no enemy, hates no one, envies no one, it also then does not desire to wreak vengeance on anyone. Rather, what it does it must do by the mandate of God, who intends through it as his instrument to punish wicked and harmful people. It does this not out of anger, but with a sad heart. Vengeance, however, follows from wrath, but if one wants to avenge oneself out of one's own wrath it is forbidden here, for the vengeance is God's, Deut. 32:35f.; Heb. 10:30. He wants to repay evil, Prov. 25:21-22. Therefore after the twelfth chapter Paul shows the reason in the thirteenth chapter why we should not avenge ourselves, for God has ordained the government as his servant to bring vengeance. It is the government's duty to protect, punish, and avenge.

The Fifteenth Passage

Christ is our head and we his members, Eph. 1:22-23; 4:15-16; 5:23; Col. 1:18; 2:9-10.

Here my patience is tried, for they cry out over me: "Do you not see that our Head, Christ, did not strive or fight? Therefore, we should also not fight but go patiently to death." In the first place, dear brothers, I fear that you do not know what is divine or Christian, for there is a great difference between them. In regard to that, if we look at ourselves, how we are by nature, then Christ is not our Head; also, we are not /454/ his members. For he is just and truthful. We are evil and deceitful. Christ is a child of grace; we are children of wrath. Christ never sinned; we are conceived and born in sin. Do you see how the members agree with the head?

In the second place, that Paul calls us members of Christ takes place in faith, or in other words: If we confess that we should be members of Christ and are not, then we confess ourselves to be guilty of that and ask God for forgiveness through Christ Jesus. For what we have now prayed, if we wholly believe, God has forgiven us our sin. Now we become members of Christ in faith, not in nature, that is, not in willing and doing as it concerns the flesh, which does not want to be subject to the law of God; but in faith the power is now given to us to become the children of God according to the spirit and the soul, also to will and work good, although all our works according to the flesh are still blameworthy, lazy, worthless, and not at all just before the face of God, Isa. 64:5.

In the third place, although we now know that we are children of God and members of Christ only in faith, nevertheless we do not all have the same office. Rather, one should go forth with teaching; the other protecting; the third cultivating the earth; the fourth making shoes and clothes—all these works flow here from faith and should be used to the advantage of our neighbor. Yes, also in outward and corporal things, as the worldly government has power over the flesh or body and over temporal goods alone, but not over the soul. Accordingly, the sword is commanded to it by divine order, not to fight, battle, make noise, brawl, strive, and tyrannize—as many cat-fighting names as there are—but to watch over the orphans, protect the widows, care for the righteous, and free all those who are threatened and oppressed by power.[*] That is the office of the government, as God himself indicates in manifold ways in Scripture, which cannot go forth without blood and killing. Therefore God has hung a sword at the side of the government and not a fox's tail.

The last passage for the confirmation of the government among Christians

Every person should be subject to the government and authority, for it is no authority if not from God. But the authority which is everywhere is ordered by God. Thus whoever sets himself against the authority resists the order

---

[*] Body and property is of the emperor, but the soul of God.

of God. But those who so resist will receive a judgment over themselves /455/ for the powerful do not frighten those who do good but evil. However, if you do not want to fear, then do good; then you will receive praise from the same. But if you do evil, then be afraid. For the authority does not bear the sword in vain. It is a servant of God, an avenger for punishment over the one who does evil. So now be subject out of necessity, not only for the sake of punishment but also for the sake of conscience. Therefore you must also pay taxes, for they are servants of God who are in charge of such protection, Rom. 13:1f.

This writing, dear brothers, is alone enough against all the gates of hell for the confirmation of the government. For Paul says clearly that everyone should be subject to the government. Believing or unbelieving, we should be obedient and subject to it. He points out the reason. For there is no government which does not come from God. Therefore obedience consists in all that which is not against God, for God has not ordered the government against himself. Now if the government wants to punish the evil ones—as it should for the sake of their souls' salvation—and is yet not strong enough to deal with the evil ones, then it is now to command its subjects through bells and various alarm signals, letters, or through other summons. Subjects are obligated for the sake of the salvation of their souls to sustain and help their superiors so that the evil ones are annihilated and rooted out according to the will of God.* Nevertheless, subjects should first test well the spirit of their governments, as to whether they are not moved and compelled more out of arrogance, pride, avarice, envy, hate, or for their own advantage, rather than out of love of the common good and territorial peace. For that would not be to use the sword according to the order of God. However, if you recognize that the government punishes the evil only so that the righteous remain at rest and unharmed, then help, counsel, and sustain it, as often and as much as you are commanded. Thereby, you fulfill the order of God and do his work and not a human work. However, if a government is childish or foolish, yea, perchance it is not competent at all to

---

* One should test the government to see whether it commands against God.

reign, then you may escape from it legitimately and accept another, if it is good. For on account of an evil government God has often punished an entire land. If the seeking of another cannot be done lawfully and peacefully, and not also without great damage and rebellion, then one must endure it, as the one which God has given us in his wrath, and as if he desires to chastise us on account of our sins, as those who deserve no better.

Whoever now does not want to help the government save widows, orphans, and other oppressed ones, as well as to punish vandals and tyrants, /456/ resists the order of God and will receive a judgment from him, for he acts against the mandate and order of God, who wants the righteous to be protected and the evil punished. However, if you are obedient you should truly know that you are obedient not to the government or to people but to God himself, and you have become a special servant of God just as the government itself also is nothing other than a servant of God.

However, Paul testifies openly that the government has the power and authority to kill the evil when he says: "The authority does not bear the sword in vain." If now the government did not have the authority to kill, why should the sword then hang at its side? It would then bear it in vain, which Paul cannot bear. He also explicitly adds that the authority is the servant of God. Where are now those who say a Christian cannot use the sword? For if a Christian could not be a servant of God, could not fulfill the mandate of God without sinning, then God would not be good. He would have made an order which a Christian could not fulfill without sin. That is a blasphemy.

Accordingly I counsel you faithfully, dear brothers, return and repent. You have stumbled badly and produced much trash everywhere against God and against brotherly love under the appearance of spirituality and the pretense of humility. God knows whom I mean. Concerning this it is written: if you had not run although no one had sent you, everything would be in a better state. For where one sees that a Christian government has consolidated itself with its subjects in a manly, brotherly, and Christian fashion, then many a tyrant, on account of his forcing and pushing against God and all that is right, would be summoned, removed, and have his sword sheathed according to the mandate of God. If, however, God wants that we should suffer, his will cannot be hindered by our protection. In short: That one should protect the righteous and punish the evil is the earnest mandate of God which remains until the last day. No one may deny it. Consult the passages, O Christian reader, in Isaiah 1:17; Jeremiah 21:12; 22:3; Psalms 62:11; Micah 6:8; Nahum 3:1ff.; Zepheniah 3:1ff.; Zechariah 7:9ff.; and all of Habbakuk. This mandate obligates the government just as much today as fifteen hundred years ago.

Paul writes further: "So therefore be subject out of necessity, not only because of punishment but also for the sake of conscience." What does that say? It is as much as to say: "The temporal power is ordered by God for the sake of temporal peace." /457/ Therefore even if there were no Scripture which made us subject to the government, our own consciences and scruples would nonetheless insist that we should help the government to protect, shelter, discipline, take care of, do statutory and compulsory labor, stand guard, and pay taxes so that we may abide together in temporal peace. For having temporal peace is not against the Christian life.* Otherwise Paul would not have rightly taught us in Timothy to pray for kings, princes, and governments, 1 Tim. 2:2. But to have peace with all people, as much as in us, that is right and Christian. If, however, God sends us any adversities, we should accept them also with patience, Rom. 2:4. Do you see now dear brother, that your own conscience forces you to be supportive and helpful, so that the evil are punished and the good are protected. That means in good German: the commonweal.[15] It is just to further and to sustain this territorial peace that we must, says Paul, pay taxes, tariffs, and tributes.

Note here, dear brothers. If government is so unchristian that a Christian cannot use the sword, why do we help and support it then with our taxes? Are we not obligated to our neighbor, as much as to ourselves, to prevent his injury? Why do we then choose a government? Or are those in the

---

[15] *Landesfrieden*, literally: "territorial peace."

---

* To have temporal peace is not unjust.

government not our neighbors? Yes, if we desire to live in peace under a heathen government, why not much more under a Christian one, since for the Christian the order of God goes more to the heart than with the heathen. What way out do we have, dear brothers?

Paul goes further and says: "The authority is a servant of God," which should take care of such protection, which occurs for the good of our neighbor, and to sustain the commonweal. Where does it now stand written that a Christian cannot be such a servant of God, who can perform the mandate of God for the well-being of all people? Or that he cannot execute such a divine work, as Paul himself calls it, according to the order of God? Well, then, may God impart his grace to us all, so that we again come onto the right path of his holy Word and so remain and abide in the same until the end, through Jesus Christ our Lord. The peace of God be with us all. Amen.

Truth Is Immortal.
1527

30

Apologia

In July 1527, at the orders of King Ferdinand, who had been trying to seize him since December 1525,[1] Hubmaier was taken from Nikolsburg to Vienna and imprisoned. From Vienna he was taken to Kreuzenstein Castle near Korneuburg, north of Vienna. This castle dates back to at least the eleventh century. By 1520 it was in ruins. On occasion it was used as a prison. Hubmaier's dedication testifies that life there was very hard. During the Thirty Years' War the ancient castle was demolished, and at the end of the nineteenth century a new one was built on the same site in medieval architectural style.[2] While in prison Hubmaier asked Ferdinand for an opportunity to talk to his friend and former fellow student, John Faber, who was later to become bishop of Vienna. This request was granted. The conversation, which took place toward the close of 1527 and at which two other prominent men were present,[3] lasted several days. Faber gave a detailed account of this debate with Hubmaier at Kreuzenstein in his Defense of the Orthodox Catholic Faith ... against Dr. Balthasar Friedberg, printed in 1528.[4] Hubmaier takes up in this Apologia most of the ideas that Faber says were discussed.

Hubmaier's concern to interpret his own convictions in a way that would be as acceptable as possible to the Catholic king was reinforced by his having heard from Faber, in the course of those conversations, that he had been accused of some association with the views of Hans Hut, whom he had in fact been denouncing throughout much of the past year. What those views of Hut are is not indicated, either in the preface or in the section on the sacraments, but the Apologia makes clear that he rejects both the views of Hut on one side, who may have taught that in some imminent apocalyptic future there

---

[1] Loserth 1891, pp. 130ff.
[2] ME III, p. 240.
[3] HS, p. 460.
[4] Full titles in ME II, p. 285f. The *Defense* was printed in 1537.

would be a violent revolution, and on the other hand those of the majority of the Swiss Brethren, who taught an obligation of nonviolence.

While obsequious and working hard to win the grace of the king, Hubmaier does not recant. As the annotation in Sachsse 1914, pp. 231ff., indicates in detail, everything he says here echoes earlier writings. He accentuates those points at which he had always been closer to Catholic tradition than to the Reformed, as, for instance, regarding freedom of the will, or to the Swiss Brethren, as regarding the state. The authorities, however, complained that this did not constitute a satisfactory recantation, and it did not prevent his execution.

The text is preserved only in a manuscript copy, which is not from Hubmaier's hand. The dedication of the document, dated Kreuzenstein, January 3, 1528, shows that it is a direct outcome of Hubmaier's discussion with Faber.[5]

Apologia

To His Most Majestic Highness and greatest Mightiest Ruler, Lord Ferdinand, King of Hungary and Bohemia, Archduke of Austria, etc., His Most gracious Sovereign, An apologia for his Faith, by Balthasar Huebmör of Frydtberg, in bonds, in twenty-seven articles, submitted on January 3, 1528.

Your Most Serene Highness, Greatest and Mightiest King, most gracious Sovereign. Your Royal Majesty is first of all the object of my poor prayers to God. Most gracious King; I thank and praise your Royal Majesty especially for sending to me, out of special grace and kindness, the Reverend Lord John Faber, Doctor, etc., who then in the presence of the procurator[6] and of the Lord Rector of [the University of] Vienna,[7] showed and kept himself kind and virtuous in all his dealings with me, whereby I learned that in many items of our holy faith I have been greatly and seriously maligned and slandered in the eyes of Your Royal Majesty. Accordingly

---

[5] Quoted in Vedder 1905, pp. 230-235. Fragments cited in Klaassen 1981, pp. 42-45, 250, 324f. Source: HS 25, pp. 460-491.

[6] Marcus Beckh of Leopoldsdorf. *Vitzthum* (for *vice-dominus*) was the title of the provincial administrator.

[7] Ambrosius Salzer, professor of theology, was in the second of his four terms as rector.

/461/ I have formulated my apologia on twenty-seven articles of faith, and submit them herewith to your Royal Majesty, asking for God's sake and most abjectly, that Your Majesty will graciously hear and consider these articles and again show to me your royal and Austrian kindness, grace and mercy. I am also, most merciful King, a prisoner in heavy bonds and have been for a long time, in severe sickness, cold, and wretchedness, without books, and in my head and memory am quite weak and clumsy. Accordingly, where I have overlooked anything in my writing I beg Your Royal Highness again for God's sake not to hold it against me. All my life I will be willing and zealous to merit this with my poor prayer for Your Royal Majesty, in all submissiveness; I herewith commend myself to Your Royal Highness as My Most Gracious Ruler.

> Given in bonds in Kreuzenstein, January 3, 1528.
> Your Royal Majesty's Most Submissive Prisoner
> Balthasar Huebmör of Frydtberg

In the Name of Jesus, Amen
The First Article, On Mere Faith

Mere faith alone is not sufficient for salvation. This article will first be proven from Paul. (1)[a] For man believes with his heart and so is justified, and he confesses with his lips and so is saved, Rom. 10:10.[8] But we must not be mere Mouth-christians, boasting and saying, "Look! we believe that Jesus Christ suffered torture and death for us," but we must also exercise our faith in works of love toward God and our neighbor. (2) This John teaches us when he says, "Little children, let us not love one another in word and with the tongue but in deed and in truth. By this we shall know that we are of the truth," 1 John 3:18f. (3) For faith shall be active through love, Gal. 5:6. Therefore mere faith is like a green fig tree without

---

[8] There are only two substantive marginal notes in the entire document. The rest of the margin bears in some but not all sections Arabic numerals designating each of the Scripture citations. These are reproduced here in the text with parentheses as at the beginning of this sentence.

---

[a] The first witness of Scripture.

fruit, like a cistern without water, like a cloud without rain. I have taught thus in my booklets. In them I bemoan with tears that people have in so many years not learned better than to say: "We believe, faith saves us"; while in this age brotherly love and loyalty have grown staler and colder /462/ in us than ever before. Indeed in the meantime[9] all vices have been gaining ground, and human audacity is seated in the highest seat of its violent dominion and [continuing] the practice of all vices and wantonness, which I have often and very sincerely bemoaned to God. We still claim to be Christians, truly evangelical, and boast of our great faith, and have never touched the works of the gospel and of faith with our little finger. We are, consequently, as said above, nothing but mouth-Christians, ear-Christians, paper Christians, but not hand-Christians. Concerning these, St. James speaks most rebukingly in his Christian and very profitable epistle when he writes: (4) "What does it profit, my brethren, if a man says he has faith but has not works? ... If a brother or sister is ill-clad and in lack of daily food, and one of you says to them, 'Go in peace, be warmed and filled,' without giving them the things needed for the body, what does it profit? So faith, by itself, if it has no works, is dead.... 'You have faith and I have works.' Show me your faith apart from your works, and I by my works will show you my faith. You believe that God is one; you do well. Even the devils believe—and shudder," James 2:14-19. Yea, I confess on the strength of this article that mere faith does not deserve to be called faith, for a true faith can never exist without deeds of love.

The Second Article, On Good Works

Since mere faith is not sufficient for salvation, good deeds must truly be added to the faith.

This article I stressed so earnestly and highly in my booklets on the Lord's Supper and the second one on the freedom of the human will[10] that my heart can be known from them well enough, by the vigor of my insistence on good works.

In both pamphlets I cited these verses of Scripture:

---

[9] I.e., while we say "we believe."
[10] See above, texts 7, 27, and 28, pp. 73ff., 426ff., and 449ff.

(1) Depart from evil and do good, Ps. 37:27.

(2) If you would enter into life, keep the commandments, Matt. 19:17.

(3) God will recompense every one according to his works, Rom. 2:6.

(4) As we have the time, let us do good, Gal. 5:10.

(5) Brethren ... work out your salvation, Phil. 2:12.

(6) My mother and my brothers are those who hear and do the word of God, Luke 8:21; Mark 3:25.

(7) It is not the hearers of the law who are righteous before God, but those who do the law who will be justified, Rom. 2:13.

(8) Everyone who hears my words and does them will be likened to a wise man who builds his house upon the rock, Matt. 7:24. /463/

(9) Each shall receive his own wages according to his labor, 1 Cor. 4:8.

(10) Not every one who says to me, "Lord, Lord," shall enter the kingdom of heaven, but he who does the will of my Father who is in heaven, Matt. 7:21.

(11) Glory and honor to every one who does good, Rom. 2:7.

(12) Be fruitful in every good work and increase in the knowledge of God. Col. 2 [1:10]. Col. 2 1:10

(13) If you are Abraham's children, then do his works. John 8:39.

(14) Be doers of the word, and not hearers only, deceiving yourselves. For if any one is a hearer of the word and not a doer, he is like a person who observes his bodily face in a mirror; after he has observed himself he goes away and at once forgets what he was like. James 1:22-24.

In sum: Just as a good tree cannot be without fruit at the proper season, so it is also impossible for true faith to be without good works. Those who say they can do nothing good deceive themselves and there is no true faith in them.

The Third Article, On Christian Liberty

Whoever lets his faith stand naked and does not clothe it in good works adulterates Christian liberty into carnal license. This article is right and true, as I have also shown in my booklets, citing Paul, who says, (1) "For you were called to freedom, brethren, but be careful not use your freedom as license for the flesh, but through the love of the Spirit serve one another. For the whole law is fulfilled in one word, 'Love your neighbor as yourself,' " Gal. 5:13f. Peter also writes: (2) "Brothers, you are free, but you should live as free men, yet not use your freedom as a pretext for evil, but you shall be as servants of God," 1 Pet. 2:16.

Granted that Christ has made us free, as John writes; (3) "Then you are free indeed, if the Son makes you free," John 8:36. Nevertheless, he has made us no less servants of the cross, which he has laid on our backs, saying, (4) "He who does not take up his cross and follow me is not worthy of me," Luke 9:23; Matt. 10:38. Here he tells us clearly that we are not flesh Christians but cross Christians, and we are not to follow the flesh but the Spirit, as I have also said in my catechism,[11] for if we act otherwise /464/ we turn evangelical truth into human laziness, living faith into a dead letter, the fruitful vine and fig tree of Christ into thistles and thornbushes, and indeed Christian freedom into a devilish servitude, effrontery, and wantonness, of which the Scripture has repeatedly warned us, as, for instance, when Paul says, (5) "Brethren, ... if you live according to the flesh you will die," for "the wisdom of the flesh is death but the wisdom of the Spirit is life and peace," Rom. 8:6, 13. God also says, (6) "My spirit shall not abide in man for ever, for he is flesh," Gen. 6:3. (7) "Therefore those who belong to Christ have crucified their flesh with its vices and desires. If we live by the Spirit, let us also walk by the Spirit," Gal. 5:24f.

Likewise the holy David laments, not without great cause, saying, (8) "There is no health in my flesh," and likewise Paul: (9) "For I know that nothing good dwells within me, that is, in my flesh.... O Wretched man that I am! Who will deliver me from this body of death?" Rom. 7:18, 24. Yea even though carnal Christians will cry loudly that no law has been laid down for the just, 1 Tim. 1:9, they must nevertheless for a full picture allow Christ's words to stand beside Paul's: (10) "I have not come to abolish the law but to fulfill it.... Whoever

---

[11] See above, text 21, pp. 344, 360f., and 363.

then relaxes one of the least of these my commandments ... shall be called least in the kingdom of heaven," Matt. 5:17ff. (11) Yes, whoever keeps all of God's commandments but transgresses in one is guilty of all of them, James 2:10.

The Fourth Article, On the Fear of God

In this wretched and dangerous life it is most needful to teach people this fear of God unceasingly in order that the people remain in this fear of God and in all their works keep God before their eyes. This point is repeatedly mentioned in the Scriptures, as, for example, when Moses said to the people, (1) "You shall fear the Lord your God and serve him alone," Deut. 10:12. We also read (2) that the fear of God was so great in Abraham that he did not spare his only son, Isaac, but at God's command he was willing to kill him and sacrifice him to God, Gen. 22. Therefore we should (3) carry the book of the law of Moses in our hands day and night and read in it every day of our lives that we may learn to fear the Lord our God and keep his words and practices that are found in the law, Deut. 17. Thus, the ruler Joshua subjected himself with his people to the servitude and fear of God, and on that occasion placed a very large stone under an oak which stood in the sanctuary of the Lord, and said to the people, (4) "Behold this stone shall be a testimony to you that you have heard all the words written in the book /465/ of the law of the Lord, so that if you fall away into disobedience and irreverence toward God you will not be able to deny it and lie to the Lord your God [saying] that you had not heard or known it," Josh. 24:27. For lack of fear of God is such an abomination that God will reprove us especially for it and say, (5) "If then I am a father, where is my honor? And if I am a lord, where is my fear?" says the Lord of hosts, Mal. 1:6. Likewise the pure and chaste virgin says in her Magnificat (6) that the mercy of God is from generation to generation to all who fear him, Luke 1:50.

Let those learn who sin in the name of Christian liberty and say: Well, Christ has by his death freed us from eternal death, and God is merciful, as Mary said, to those who fear him, as David also says, (7) "All the ways of the Lord are mercy and faithfulness, for those who keep before their eyes his covenant and his law," Ps. 25:10. Likewise, Christ also teaches us, (8) "Fear him who, after he has killed you, also has power to cast into hell," Luke 12:5. (9) The heathen Cornelius was a God-fearing man; therefore God sent him Peter from the city of Joppa to instruct him in the Christian faith, Acts 10:22. Concerning this fear of God I have until now preached so earnestly that many people hated me for it and said I was trying to make monks and nuns of them, as I can prove by hundreds of people.

The Fifth Article, On the Conscience

One should take heed to his thoughts, words, and works and zealously measure them by the plumb line of the divine Word, in order always and constantly to have a good conscience toward God. This point is very often mentioned in the Scriptures, as they very faithfully admonish us, saying, (1) "My son, if you aspire to enter into service of the Lord, stand fast in the righteousness and fear of the Lord and prepare your heart for testing, for those who keep God before their eyes perceive what is pleasing to God," Sirach 2:1, 16, that they may at all times (2) give to God an acceptable offering, Rom. 12:1, and (3) constantly stand in the uprightness of their hearts, Ps. 119. Nor should one act without faith, (4) for what is not of faith is contrary to conscience, and what is against the conscience is against God and is a sin, Rom. 14:23. When one man hears God's commandment, and then one obeys it or not, from that time on (5) it is his conscience which accuses or excuses him in his deed, Rom. 2:15. If he is guilty he forfeits the uprightness of his heart, as did (6) Adam when he had /466/ eaten the forbidden fruit, and (7) Cain, when he had slain his brother, so that for fear neither knew where he could hide or escape, Gen. 3, 4.

(8) Such consciences God calls trembling and pounding hearts, Deut. 28:67, which without ceasing knock at a person's door and show him that he is not upright toward God. I have usually called it a gnawing worm, which gnaws at man constantly and allows him no rest, or also St. Peter's cock[a] by which when he crowed Peter was reminded of his sin and

---

[a] St. Peter's cock.

began to weep bitterly. Likewise, as soon as St. Peter's cock crows also in us, and scratches in our conscience, we can be sure that we have overstepped the plumb line of the divine Word and have sinned. Then, like Peter, we must weep bitterly, repent, and show remorse, grief, and repentance for the sin and thus reconcile ourselves again to God and achieve peace through a good conscience. John calls this God dwelling in us and we in God, 1 John 3:24.

The Sixth Article, That Not Everything Occurs by Necessity

It is a harmful error, dishonoring to God and intolerable to the Christian faith, that everything must take place by necessity.

This error is so great and grave that it has resulted in much evil and mischief among both heathen and Christians. For the sake of brevity the stories of the damage cannot be recounted here. This error is also specifically against God and his highest honor, for since God created reasonable beings, in heaven as angels and on earth mankind, he desired to be supremely honored and praised by them. Now, there is no greater honor that man can render to God than to praise, honor and magnify him without compulsion and unforced, for God loves the cheerful givers (and not those who give by compulsion), 2 Cor. 9:7. He therefore gave both kinds of beings a free and unforced will, as the Scriptures testify and say: "In the beginning God placed man (in Paradise) and left him free to make his own decisions; he gave him his commandments and law, saying, "If you keep the commandments, they will preserve you and eternally keep your faith. He has set before you fire and water; reach out and take which you choose; before a man are life and death, good and evil, and whichever he prefers is his," Sirach 15:14-17. Here we see clearly that in the first place God made man that he could and should, without compulsion and without force, honor and praise him and keep his commandments; God gave a person this choice and entrusted to him the power to choose water or fire, good or evil, life or death. /467/

But that a person can choose, will, and work, not only before the Fall, but also since the Fall on the authority of the

divine Word in which God gives to those who will and believe
the power and might to do and to accomplish what he has
commanded them to do, I want to cite a number of
testimonies from the Scriptures, which I have, of course, also
taught and preached previously, and have published this particular doctrine in my second booklet on the freedom of the
human will.[12] The first Scripture follows:

"The Lord said to Cain, (1) 'Why are you angry and why
has your countenance fallen? Is it not true, that if you were
righteous, your sacrifice would be accepted? And if you do not
do well, sin is crouching to manifest itself; but make it (the
sin) bow before you and master it,' " Gen. 4:6f. It follows that
we have the mastery over sin and can master it. (2) "This
commandment" (says God, the Lord, through Moses) "which I
command you this day is not too hard for you, neither is it far
off. It is not in heaven, that you should say, 'Who will go up
for us to heaven, and bring it to us, that we may hear it and
do it?' Neither is it beyond the sea, that you should say, 'Who
will go over the sea for us, and bring it to us, that we may
hear it and do it?' But the word is very near you; it is in your
mouth, and in your heart, so that you can do it. See, I have set
before you this day life and goodness, death and evil, I who
today command you that you love the Lord your God and walk
in his ways, and that you keep his commandments, his statutes,
and his ordinances, so that you may live and multiply.... But if
you turn your heart away, and you will not obey, but fall away
... I declare to you this day, that you shall perish.... I call
heaven and earth to witness against you this day, that I have
set before you this day life and death, blessing and curse, that
you might choose life, that you and your seed may live, that
you love the Lord your God, obeying his voice, and cleaving
to him."[13] Here anyone who has ears can hear that we are able
to will, perform, keep and fulfill God's commands without
force and without compulsion.

(3) "Be attentive to these things, says the Lord God:
'Behold, I set before you the way of life and the way of
death,' " Jer. 21:8. It would be a false god that would offer

---

[12] See above, text 28, p. 457f.
[13] This long extract from Deut. 30:11-20 is one Scripture whose source
Hubmaier does not identify in his text.

two ways, knowing that we would necessarily have to take the one way. But he is faithful.

(4) "If you are willing and hear," God the Lord says further, "you shall eat the good of the land; but if you refuse and rebel against me, you shall be devoured by the sword; for the mouth of the Lord has spoken," Isa. 1:19a.

He would be an untruthful God if the willing, hearing, and eating were not in our power. But he is truthful, therefore the error is untruthful.

(5) "He came to his own," writes John, "and his own received /468/ him not. But to all who received him, who believed in his name, he gave power to become children of God," John 1:11f. Here we see again that God has given us the power and the choice to become his children, or by our own wickedness to remain children of wrath. If we then become children of God there is no doubt that we can serve, honor, and praise our Father out of love and without being compelled by necessity. Anyone who teaches differently misleads many people into indolence and despair through such ideas; for if all things happen by necessity, why should I do much praying, fasting, and giving of alms; if God will have me, it will take place by necessity, but if he does not want me, then all my works are vain. Here one sees now very clearly what great harm and evil have grown out of this false doctrine, as I have clearly set forth in my first booklet on the freedom of the will.[14] But as Adam put the guilt on Eve, and Eve on the serpent, so we would also like to make a fig leaf apron for our malice, put the blame on God, toss our sins off of ourselves and put them on him, which is a great blasphemy, which will not help us escape divine punishment. Let every one know how to direct himself accordingly.

The Seventh Article, On Free Will

He who denies the freedom of the human will, and says it is an empty and useless title in name only and is nothing in itself, calls God a tyrant, blames him for unrighteousness, and gives evildoers much reason to persist in their sins. Indeed he

---

[14] See above, text 27, p. 428, 436ff.

knocks down half of the Holy Bible. Proof of this article: If people were deprived of their free will God could never by just judgment condemn the sinner on account of his sins. For if he now were to condemn him for something that is impossible to do and to will, far be that from God. Also this would take away from Christ his legitimate charge that he will make against sinners on the judgment day saying: "I was hungry and you gave me no food, I was sick and in prison and you did not visit me," Matt. 25:42f.; then they could rightfully excuse themselves and say, "It was impossible for us to feed or visit you, we had no free will. Yea, it is on account of your eternal prescience and condemnation that we must now go with the devil into the everlasting fire to fulfill your eternal foreknowledge." From such a harmful doctrine it follows that every sinner could lay the guilt upon God and say, "That I stole /469/ and robbed was not my fault but the will of God whom no one can withstand," Rom. 9:19. Without his will I could not have done it. According to my will I had to do it, for it is captive and bound. Through this error also all the Scriptures would be knocked down that refer to willing and doing, which fill more than half of the Bible. I shall now cite a few of them; all the others are comprehended in these:

(1) If you would enter into life (says Christ), keep the commandments, Matt. 19.

(2) Let him who would see good days keep his tongue from evil, Ps. 33 [Ps. 34:12f].

(3) Glory to God in the highest, on earth peace, and a good will toward men, Luke 2:14.

(4) If anyone wills to follow me let him deny himself, take up his cross, and follow me, Matt. 10:13.

(5) I would have been glad to keep Onesimus with me, in order that he might serve me on your behalf during my imprisonment for the gospel; but I preferred to do nothing without your consent in order that your goodness might not be by compulsion but of your own free will, Paul to Philemon 13f.

(6) Will ye also go away? says Christ to his disciples, John 6:67.

(7) If you continue in my word, you are truly my disciples, and you will know the truth, and the truth will make you free. Now if the Son frees you, you are free indeed, John 8:31f.

(8) Jerusalem, Jerusalem, you who kill the prophets and stone those who are sent to you! How often would I have gathered your children together as a hen gathers her brood under her wings, and you would not! Matt. 23:37.

Many other Scripture passages in which the freedom to choose, to will and to do is presented to man by God have been cited in both of my booklets on this subject. But these will suffice for this time, for if I were to indicate all of them I would have to copy half the Bible.

The Eighth Article, On Remorse, Sorrow, and Repentance

Everyone ought to feel remorse and sorrow and to repent for his sin.

This article is rooted many fold in the Scriptures.

(1) First, God says through the prophet Jeremiah: "If that nation will repent of its evil concerning which I have spoken against it, I will repent of the evil that I intended to do to it.... And if it does evil in my sight and will not listen to my voice, then I will repent of the good which I had intended to do to it," Jer. 18:8, 10. /470/

(2) When the prophet Nathan reproved King David for his sins of adultery and the death of Uriah, David searched his soul and said, "I have sinned against the Lord," and because of the deep pains of remorse and sorrow for his sin he fell into the fear of death. Thereupon the prophet said, "The Lord has remitted your sin, you shall not die," 2 Sam. 12:13 .

(3) A broken and contrite heart God will not despise, Ps. 51:17.

(4) Repent, for the kingdom of heaven is at hand. Bear therefore fruit that befits repentance, for even now the axe is laid to the root of the tree; every tree therefore that does not bear good fruit is cut down and thrown into the fire," Matt. 3:2, 8, 10; Luke 3:8f.

(5) "Behold, Lord," said Zacchaeus, "the half of my goods I give to the poor; and if I have defrauded anyone of anything, I restore it fourfold," Luke 19:8.

(6) "Behold, a woman of the city, a sinner, when she learned that Jesus was sitting at table in the Pharisee's house, brought a flask of costly ointment, and standing behind the

Lord at his feet, she dried them with the locks of her hair, and kissed his feet, and anointed them with the ointment," Luke 7:37f.

Here one sees that as the woman has previously submitted her members—hands, feet, mouth, hair, and eyes—to servitude to sin, so she now submits the same members to servitude to Christ. These are the deeds of true Christian repentance. In sum: God is merciful; but he desires equally that if someone has sinned he make compensation, according to the nature of his sins, for his transgression against divine righteousness, by remorse, sorrow, and repentance; about this I have also written in my booklets on fraternal admonition and on the ban.[15]

The Ninth Article, On the Virginity of Mary

The Holy Scripture expresses clearly and plainly the virginity of Mary, and we read nowhere that any man had sexual intercourse with her. Accordingly we should obviously believe her to have been an eternally chaste virgin before, in, and after the birth. This article is proven thus: God told Eve that her seed would crush the serpent's head. At that time Eve was betrothed to Adam and was, however, a pure virgin, as the text clearly states that Adam knew her only after their expulsion from Paradise, Gen. 3; 4. Accordingly it cannot fail that Mary, the bearer of our Savior Jesus Christ, who has crushed the head of the hellish serpent, must /471/ have been a chaste virgin even after the birth, although she was betrothed to a man. This I shall also demonstrate with Scripture:

(1) "Therefore," says Isaiah, "the Lord himself shall give you a sign. Behold a maiden or virgin shall conceive and bear a son, and his name shall be called Immanuel, God with us," Isa. 7:14.

The fact that the Jews want to make a "young woman" of this "maid" or "virgin" changes nothing, for Eve is after all also called a "woman" by the Scriptures throughout her virginity, Gen. 3. Besides, the Jews have to grant that such a birth was to be a sign from God. But when a young wife bears a child, this is not a sign but the ordinary course of nature.

---

[15] See above, texts 23, pp. 372ff. and 26, pp. 409ff.

Therefore neither Jews, Helvidians, or Antidicomarians[16] can dethrone the pure and chaste Mary from her virginhood.

(2) Luke also writes thus: "The angel Gabriel was sent by God to a city of Galilee named Nazareth, to a virgin betrothed to a man whose name was Joseph, of the house of David; and the virgin's name was Mary," Luke 1:26f.

(3) The angel also spoke to Joseph: "Joseph, son of David, do not fear to take Mary your wife, for that which is conceived in her is of the Holy Spirit," Matt. 1:20. And thus I have always and everywhere confessed her to be an eternally pure and chaste virgin, as can be seen in my books of catechism, apologia, and the twelve articles of faith.[17] If anyone has reported anything contrary to this about me, may God forgive him, he has wronged me.

The Tenth Article, That Mary Is Mother of God

A Christian confesses that Mary is not only mother of Christ but also truly mother of God. It was an error of the Nestorians to say that Mary was *Christotokos*, mother of Christ, but not *theotokos*, mother of God, against which error I have always and in every way contended. In my booklets Apology and Catechism, I wrote the following: I confess that Mary is the mother of God and blessed, (1) for she believed the things that were told her by God, Luke 1:38. No higher titles and praise can I ascribe to her. Thus, Elizabeth said to Mary, (2) "Why is this granted me, that the mother of my Lord should come to me?" Luke 1:43. Mary is also called the mother of Jesus. (3) "Standing beneath the cross of Jesus /472/ were his mother ..." John 19:25. If Mary is the mother of Jesus, and the Lord Jesus is true God, it must follow that Mary was the mother of the true God. This logic cannot be refuted by any Christian; although she is not the mother of Christ according to his deity, she is according to his humanity. All my life I have spoken of Mary in this way, and I am sure and certain that no one can truthfully speak otherwise of me.

---

[16] Helvidius (4th century), known by Jerome's opposition to him, taught that after Jesus, Mary bore additional children to Joseph. "Antidicomarian" is the synthetic label coined by Epiphanius to designate challenges to the doctrine of Mary's perpetual virginity.

[17] See above, texts 21, pp. 339ff., 19, 296ff., and 15, pp. 234ff.

The Eleventh Article, Whether Christ Is True God

The confession of the foundation of the catholic Christian Church and of our salvation is comprehended in these few words, that with Peter we believe and confess Jesus, that he is Christ, the Son of the living God. Thereupon Jesus said to him, "Blessed are you, Simon Bar-Jonah! For flesh and blood has not revealed this to you, but my Father who is in heaven. And I tell you, you are Peter, and on this rock I will build my church." On this very confession stands the Christian church and our salvation, Matt. 16:17f.

Here three items ought by great necessity be introduced, but are omitted for the sake of brevity. The first: The Old Testament Scriptures indicate clearly that a man would be conceived on earth without the seed of man and be born of a virgin. The second: Old Testament Scripture clearly states that this man would be true God. The third: The Scriptures of the Old Testament as well as the New conclude unanimously and with one accord that this Man and God is Jesus Christ. Of these three items I have by God's grace in my bonds received so firm a foundation, whereby to maintain them against all Jews, bad Christians, etc., such as I have never in my life heard or read. Praise be to God. I also beseech here all well-intentioned Christians not to rest in this article, but to call without ceasing upon God for a thorough understanding, for it is to be considered that Jews, heathen, and bad Christians unite under the pretext of the gospel in this error that Christ is not God. There will be one shepherd and one sheepfold, John 10:16. In order to encounter them in wisdom and be able to withstand them through the spirit of understanding, if it should be God's will I would be most happy to debate on these three points and on the holy Trinity with a learned Jew and a heathen before my death.

In sum: I believe that Jesus is Christ, the only begotten Son of the living God, true God and Man, conceived of the Holy Spirit, born of Mary, the eternally chaste Virgin, who has crushed /473/ the serpent's head, and that in him all families of earth are blessed; that he is also Immanuel, Lord, and the Child who was to bear the government upon his shoulder, and whose name was to be called Wonderful, Mighty God, Ever-

lasting Father, Prince of Peace, of the increase of whose
government there shall be no end, Gen. 3; 22; 26; Isa. 7; 9;
Jer. 33; Luke 1; Matt. 1; 4; 8; 17; 22; 27; Mark 1; 3; 5; 12; 15;
John 1; 3; 5; 6; 10; 11; 20; 1 John 5; Heb. 1; Rom. 8; Col. 2.
Thus do I testify and confess in my booklet on the Twelve
Articles of the Christian faith.[18] Whoever has presented me
differently, may God forgive him once again. Amen.

The Twelfth Article, On Original Sin

Original sin is not only a weakness[19] or lack, as some write
of it, but it is a damnable sin of those who are not in Christ
and who walk according to the flesh, it is also the matrix and
root of all sins.

As testimony to this article it is written that King David
lamented very deeply this very same inherited sin and cried
out to God, (1) "Behold, I was conceived in iniquity, and in
sin did my mother hear me," Ps. 50 [51:5]. Likewise (2) Job
cursed the day when he was born and "the night in which was
said, 'A man-child is conceived,' " Job 3:3. Likewise Paul: (3)
"The willing depends on me, but to achieve the good, I cannot. For I do not do the good I will, but what I do not will,
evil, is what I do. Now, if I do what I do not want, it is now
not I who do it, but sin which dwells within me," Rom. 7:18-
20. (4) Through sin death came into the world, Rom. 5:12, (5)
and in Adam we all have sinned, 1 Cor. 15:46ff., and (6) have
by nature become the children of wrath, Eph. 2:3. Many other
Scriptures could be cited here, as Genesis 3; 8; Romans 8, etc.
I shall leave it at this for the present: Anyone who says that
inherited sin is no sin tries to give Paul a lesson and teach
him what sin is or is not; that is a sacrilegious presumption
against which I have also written in my debate booklet to the
clergy at Basel.[20]

---

[18] See above, text 15, p. 234ff.
[19] Weakness (*brest*) was the term preferred by Zwingli and Zwinglians to
describe hereditary sinfulness. The German term is inherited (*erb*) sin; not
as in English "original."
[20] See above, text 18, p. 275ff.

The Thirteenth Article, On Purgatory

Just as the heavenly kingdom is a place of joy for all persons who build on Christ with gold, silver, and precious stones, so the realm of hell is a purgatory for all who have built on Christ with wood, hay, and stubble./474/ But for those who are completely outside of Christ there will be an everlasting fire. But I know no basis in the Scripture that there is besides heaven and hell a special purgatory.

(1) This article is first proved by Paul when he writes: "According to the grace of God given to me, like a wise master builder I laid a foundation, and another is building upon it. Let each one give heed, what he builds on it. For no other foundation can any one lay than that which is laid, which is Christ Jesus. Now if any one builds on the foundation with gold, silver, precious stones, wood, hay, stubble, each one's work will be revealed for the day of the Lord will reveal it, for in the fire it will be revealed, and the fire will reveal what sort of work each one has done. If the work which any man has built on the foundation survives, he will receive a reward. If anyone's work is burned up, he will suffer loss, though he himself will be saved, but only as through fire," 1 Cor. 3:10ff.

(2) Likewise Christ also teaches: "Agree quickly with your accuser while you are going with him, lest your accuser hand you over to the judge and the judge to the guard, and you be put in prison; truly, I say to you, you will not get out until you have paid the last penny," Matt. 5:25f.; Luke 12:58.

(3) Furthermore, Christ points out two different kinds of sin and says: "Whoever says a word against the Son of man will be forgiven; but whoever speaks against the Holy Spirit will not be forgiven, neither in this age nor in the age to come," Matt. 12:32; Mark 3:29; Luke 12:10. It follows on the authority of the Word of Christ and of Paul that there is forgiveness of sins in the other world, or these three texts cannot be completely understood.

The Fourteenth Article, On the Last Day

Although Christ gave us many signs whereby we can tell how near at hand the day of his coming is, nevertheless, no one but God knows the exact day.

(1) The Gospel writers describe in some detail the signs that will precede the judgment day, Matt. 24; Luke 21; Mark 13; but concerning that time let us examine the Scripture.

(2) "Of that day and hour (says Christ) no one knows, not even the angels of heaven ... but only the Father," Matt. 24:36.

(3) Mark records Christ's words even more clearly: "Of that day or that hour no one knows, not even the angels in heaven, nor the Son, but only the Father. Therefore take heed, watch and pray; for you do not know when the time will come," Mark 13:32f.

Paul also writes: "As to the times and the seasons, brethren, you have no need that we write to you. /475/ For you yourselves know well that the day of the Lord will come like a thief in the night. When people say, "There is peace and security," then sudden destruction will come as travail comes upon a woman with child, and there will be no escape. But you are not in darkness, brethren, that that day should surprise you like a thief," 1 Thess. 4 [5:1ff]. Out of these words I have always and everywhere formulated the article as it is stated above, but said that the day of the Lord is closer than we know; therefore we should persist in daily contemplation, righteousness and the fear of God.

I was also very severe against Johann Hutt and his followers [because] they gave simple folk the idea of a definite time for the last day, namely now at this very next Pentecost,[21] and thereby induced them to sell their possessions and property, forsake wife and child, house and farm, thus depriving the simpleminded of work in order to persuade them to run after him. This seductive error arose out of a serious misunderstanding of the Scripture which indicates the four

---

[21] Hans Hut's presence at Nikolsburg overlapped with that of Hubmaier. Hut's leaving Nikolsburg after perhaps as little as two weeks was the result of Hubmaier's rejecting his message, with the support of the Lords. Hut's expecting the return of Christ for about Pentecost 1528 was only one of their many differences. See Seebass, 1972, Vol. I, pp. 252ff., 274ff., and ME II, p. 84. As Hubmaier says, Hut's reasoning about the end time was based on the "three and one-half years" of the apocalypse, counting from the first baptisms or from the beginning of the peasant wars in 1525. Cf. Seebass, op. cit. pp. 388ff.

years that Daniel calls "a time, two times, and half a time," Dan. 12:7. John in Revelation 13:5 calls the time forty-two weeks, which weeks constitute three and one-half years; this will be the period when the Antichrist (whom Paul calls a man of sin and a son of perdition, 2 Thess. 2:3), will become active and reign, and at the close of the period God will destroy him with the breath of his mouth without moving his hand, Isa. 11:4, Dan. 8. Out of these three and one-half years, which are solar and Danielic years, the ignorant Hutt made ordinary years. This is a great error. A solar year is the time in which the sun runs its own course of a circle once, which in an ordinary year occurs once, with a little left over. Therefore leap years were inserted, so that an ordinary year makes just one day of a solar year. It follows from this that where Hutt teaches about three and one-half years, as found in Daniel, or about forty-two weeks in Revelation, understanding them as three and one-half ordinary years, which in a correct understanding and truth of the Scriptures is three and one-half sun years, which make 1,277 ordinary years, his reckoning has erred to that extent, as I unambiguously told him openly and earnestly and rebuked him for exciting and misleading the simple populace without basis in the truth, as I can testify by the theses that I made against him.[22] Indeed, I could speak even more profoundly and clearly about the judgment day, by the grace and revelation of God which he made to me through his Word, but for the sake of brevity I cannot do it at this time. Thus, I conclude with Christ: "Take heed, watch and pray; for you know /476/ neither the day nor the hour," Mark 13:32; Matt. 25:13. "Behold," says James, "the Judge is already standing at the door," James 5:9.

---

[22] Concerning Hubmaier's "Theses against Hut," cf. Bergsten/Estep, pp. 361ff. If a specific text bore that name it has been lost. On the other hand, there exist several versions of a list of "Nikolsburg Articles," purporting to have been extracted, perhaps by Hubmaier, from Hut's writings. Hut denied teaching those things and said Hubmaier was falsely accusing him. Cf. Seebass, 1972, Vol I, pp. 261ff. and ME III, p. 886. It is evident that Hubmaier did not categorically reject Hut's drawing end-time predictions from Daniel and Revelation. They differed about the prophetic arithmetic and about the wisdom of announcing a date.

The Fifteenth Article, On Prayer

In these dangerous times it is very necessary for every Christian believer to pray without ceasing, for the prayer of a righteous person has great power before God.

This article is clear and plain; as God is righteous and good, we are unrighteous and evil. Out of his omnipotence he is able, and out of his mercy he is desirous to forgive our unrighteousness and wickedness, but he wants us beforehand to make some amends to his injured righteousness. This is done by prayer and by never repeating [our sin], which is the highest penitence.[23] Accordingly, as truly as God is just he will forgive no man his sins unless he has first prayed; he will give to those who ask, open to those who knock, let himself be found by those who seek him, Matt. 7:7; John 16. Therefore Christ teaches us to pray, Matt. 6; Luke 11. He also says that we should pray without ceasing and never stop, and gives a parable about a judge for this. Luke 18:1ff. Concerning prayer there would be much to say, what it is and how beneficial it is, but I shall simply cite the Scriptures: Genesis 20; Exodus 32; Numbers 11, 16; 1 Kings 8; 17; Daniel 9; Matthew 26; Luke 1; John 4; James 1; 5. Paul and Stephen teach us to pray on our knees, Acts 7; 20; 21, and with upraised hands, 1 Tim. 2:8. The publican teaches us to beat our breasts, Luke 18:13; Christ also teaches us to fall on our faces in prayer, Matt. 26; Hannah, the mother of Samuel, 1 Sam. 1 and Christ, Luke 11, teach us to pray with weeping hearts and eyes; Christ also teaches us to cry to God with a loud voice, Matt. 27; Luke 23. Prayer is that serious a matter.

Accordingly, I have faithfully and constantly admonished the populace to prayer, and in all my sermons I have led in praying the Mea Culpa or the Lord's Prayer or a psalm with a very loud voice and kneeling. Those who have heard me publicly in the temple must bear witness to this. I have also reinstated the ringing of bells for prayer, evening, morning, and noon, where it had previously been discontinued by other preachers, and have therefore designated to the people the

---

[23] Proverb: cf. above, p. 424, note b.

ninth hour as the hour of prayer,[24] Acts 3:1, at which hour
Cornelius also prayed when God answered his prayer, Acts
10:3. Pliny II, in a letter to Emperor Trajan, wrote that the
Christians arose before dawn, gathered, and prayed and
praised /477/ God in Psalms; of this Eusebius also writes in
book 3 (Ch. 33) of his History of the Church. But this praise
is the greatest reason for prayer, O most gracious King, this is
why I would like to be with my wife, although I am also with
her in spirit, for (without any boasting) I have never in my
life heard or seen a person more earnest and ardent in prayer.

The Sixteenth Article, On Confession

I have hitherto preached that the Scriptures designate
three kinds of confession. First, when one confesses to God,
as David did, 2 Sam. 12, likewise Azariah, Dan. 3, King
Manasses in his prayer, the publican, Luke 18, the prodigal
son, Luke 15. The second confession is that which one makes
to the person whom we have offended, as Christ teaches us:
"If you are offering your gift at the altar, and there remember
that your brother has something against you, leave your gift
there before the altar and go; first be reconciled to your
brother," Matt. 5:23f. The third confession is directed to the
church; as when someone by a mortal sin has grieved and
injured the church and offended its members and now
becomes reconciled to it again by confession, admission of
fault, and recognition of his sins, which church then has the
authority by Christ's command to forgive and remit the same
sins through its priests and dispensers of the Word of God, as
Christ promised such authority to the church, saying, "I will
give you the keys of the kingdom of heaven, and whatever you
bind on earth shall be bound in heaven, and whatever you
loose on earth shall be loosed in heaven," Matt. 16:19. This
promised power he also gave the church later once again,
saying: "Receive the Holy Spirit. If you forgive the sins of
any, they are forgiven; if you retain the sins of any, they are
retained," John 20:22f.

---

[24] There is little other evidence of Hubmaier's having retained or
restored Catholic worship forms which other Reformers had done away
with. There is, however, no reason to doubt the report.

This is the very power of the church about which I wrote similarly in my booklets on the sword and ban; i.e., that before the incarnation of Christ, God the Father dealt with all matters related to sin, as we find it in Moses and the Prophets. Afterward he transferred the authority to Christ. In the third place, Christ hung these keys at the side of the church, his bride, to teach, rebuke, bind, loose, admit, and exclude according to his word, John 20:23. This power the church on earth now possesses until Christ returns in the clouds, 1 Thess. 4. Then the bride will be drawn up into the clouds to meet her bridegroom Christ and will hand over these keys again to him, who will /478/ then judge the living and the dead and after this give all power back to his heavenly Father. For in this way God will become all in all, 1 Cor. 15:22ff.

The Seventeenth Article, On the Church

The church is an outward assembly and community of Christ-believers in one Lord, one faith and one baptism, Eph. 4:4f. It should be noted here that the word *church* is used in the Scriptures for two kinds of church: First, for the universal holy, Christian communion and assembly of all who believe in Christ, wherever on earth they be, in the whole circle of the world. And so we believe[25] in a holy Christian church, which is a community of the saints. Christ also speaks of the church in this sense, Matt. 16; 18. This church is the body of Christ. Christ is the head and we are the members of the body of Christ, 1 Cor. 12; Eph. 2; 4; Col. 1; 3. Second, the church is understood in the Scriptures as a particular community of some believers in Christ, such as the church of the Galatians, Gal. 1, the church of the Corinthians, 1 Cor. 1. This refers to each believing parish populace of a town, marketplace, or village, as one also finds in Ephesians 1. It is this specific congregation that is commonly called the daughter and the general church the mother. Now the daughter has equal authority with the mother, which is the general church, to bind and to loose sin according to Christ's command, as the Scripture testifies concerning the Corinthian church, 1 Cor. 5; 2 Cor. 2.

---

[25] I.e., in the Creed we say, "We believe."

This authority the particular church now commends and gives over to its chosen, established, and ordained minister and priest,[26] so that all things may be done in an orderly manner. Both of these churches are outward communities and not imaginary, conceivable, or logical essences, as I explained in my booklets on the catechism, on brotherly discipline, and on the ban.[27] Now whoever hears and is obedient to the priest is also obedient to the particular church as the daughter; whoever is obedient to the daughter is obedient to the mother; whoever is obedient to the mother is obedient to her bridegroom and husband Christ Jesus; whoever is obedient to Christ Jesus is obedient to his heavenly Father, who is the source of all authority, Matt. 28:18. Therefore Christ says: "He who hears you hears me, and he who rejects you rejects me," Luke 10:16; and at another place, "He however who refuses to listen even to the church, let him be to you as a gentile and a publican," Matt. 18:17. But just as Jesus said and did nothing unless he learned it from the Father /479/, John 5:19, 8:28, so shall the church and its ministers also teach and do nothing except in accord with the word and command of Christ, Matt. 28:20; Rom. 15.

The Eighteenth Article,
Of Virginity and Widowhood

Whoever retains her virginity has a precious treasure which surpasses the married state and widowhood, although both states are also pleasing to God, honorable and good, Gen. 1; 2; John 2; Heb. 13; 1 Tim. 4; 5.

That human state is higher which is nearer to its original source. Now, anyone existed first in a virginal state, then entered the married state, and third, after this followed the widowed state; therefore the state of virginity would be nearest to God, which I will prove with the clear testimony of Scripture.

---

[26] Hubmaier's use of the term *priest* may be partially an adjustment to his Catholic judges, but does not imply any significant commitment to a specific view of sacerdotal authority, any more than does his regular use of *bishop* in his liturgical texts. Interestingly, the question of priestly orders does not seem to have appeared to either party as needing to be debated.

[27] Cf. above, texts 21, pp. 339ff., 23, pp. 372ff., and 26, pp. 409ff.

First, (1) there are the eunuchs, mutilated (says Christ), "who have been so from birth, and there are eunuchs who have been made eunuchs by men, and there are eunuchs who have made themselves eunuchs for the sake of the kingdom of heaven. He who is able to receive this, understand it," Matt. 19:12.

Here Christ surely shows that those who for God's sake keep their virginity do well, for virginity is much better and more beneficial to the kingdom of God than marriage and widowhood, as we can also thoroughly prove from Paul when he says:

"It is well for a man not to touch a woman.... To the unmarried and widows I say it is well for them to remain as I am. Concerning the virgins, I have no command of the Lord, but I give my opinion as one who by the Lord's mercy is truthworthy. I think that in view of the prevailing[28] distress it is well for a person to remain as he is. Are you married to a wife? Do not seek a divorce. Are you separated from a wife? Do not seek one. But if you marry, you have not sinned. If a girl marries she does not sin. Yet such will have sadness of the flesh. The unmarried man is anxious about the affairs of the Lord, how to please the Lord; but the married man is anxious about worldly affairs, how to please his wife, and he is divided. An unmarried woman or virgin is attentive to the affairs of the Lord, in order to become holy in body and spirit; but the married woman is attentive to worldly affairs, how to please her husband. I say this for your own benefit, not to lay any restraint upon you, but to foster what is honorable and enables you to pray without ceasing /480/ to the Lord. In short, whoever is firmly established in his heart, standing fast, being under no necessity but having his desire under control, and has determined this in his heart to keep his virgin (that is, her virginity)[29] he does well. So that he who marries his virgin does well; and he who does not marry her does better, 1 Cor. 7.

From these words it is easy to understand first of all that virginity is superior to marriage and also without doubt to

---

[28] What most translations of 1 Cor. 7:26 render as "impending" can also be translated "present"; Hubmaier makes it literally "daily."

[29] The parenthetical words are Hubmaier's own, whereas all the rest of the paragraph digests the words of Paul.

widowhood, as John also writes: (2) "These are they who have never been defiled with women, for they are virgin. They follow the Lamb wherever he goes," Rev. 14:4. There are many other Scriptures in the Old and New Testaments which refer to virginity with high praise, as (3) Jephtha's daughter, Judges 11, (4) Mary, Luke 1, (5) the four daughters of Philip, Acts 21, and the like.

Second, Paul teaches us that he who marries is also doing no wrong, and especially he who cannot sustain his chastity without lust, for such it is better to marry than to burn, 1 Cor. 7:9.

Third, concerning widowhood, Paul speaks of two kinds of widows, young and old; to both he grants freedom to remarry or to remain widows. Nevertheless, it is more honorable to the aged henceforth to pray and to serve God, but to the young widows he says they should not be admitted to the temple below the age of sixty, but should marry and bear children so that no occasion to revile may be given the enemy. But the aged, honorable, and virtuous widows who are forsaken and have nobody shall be enrolled in the temple. That is Paul's teaching, 1 Tim. 3ff. But in this very connection I must raise the complaint, as I have frequently done in my booklets and sermons with weeping eyes about and against all those who, on the authority of these Scriptures on taking husbands and wives, claim to be oh, so evangelical and boast greatly of their Christian freedom, but may the lament be faithfully made to God, it is nothing but carnal liberty, for the other dogmas of our Christian faith with the exception of carnal pleasure are bitterer to them than vinegar and gall. Such persons create great offense and scandal in the church; woe to the person through whom offenses come.

The Nineteenth Article, On Fasting

Although to the Christian all days are fast days, in the sense that he should use food and drink with seemliness and thanksgiving, /481/ nevertheless, for the chastisement of the body, also in order to be better fitted to pray on some days, one may himself choose and set aside a particular day. Likewise, a king may also do so with his people and the particular church.

In confirmation of this article I shall refer to some of the many Scripture passages. First, when Jonah cried out over the city of Nineveh, (1) " 'Yet forty days, and Nineveh shall be overthrown!' the Ninevites believed him and proclaimed a fast. They dressed in sackcloth and ashes from the greatest to the least of them. When the cry reached the king of Nineveh he arose from his throne, cast off his robe, covered himself with sackcloth, and sat in ashes. He proclaimed and said throughout Nineveh: By the decree of the king and his nobles: Let neither humans nor beasts, oxen nor cattle, taste anything; let them not pasture, nor drink water, but let people dress in sackcloth, and let the cattle also cry mightily to the God of strength. Let everyone turn from his evil way and from the wickedness which is in his hands. Who knows, God may yet be moved and forgive us and turn from his fierce anger, so that we may not thus perish. And God saw their works how they turned from their evil ways, and repented of the evil which he had said he would do to them; and he did not do it," Jonah 3:4-10.

Likewise, (2) Anna, the prophetess, is praised in the Scriptures because she fasted, Luke 1; 3:37. (3) Christ also fasted, Matt. 4; Luke 4, and (4) spoke of a certain kind of devils that cannot be cast out but by prayer and fasting, Matt. 9; Luke 17. Anyone who wishes to examine more Scripture on fasting may look at Isaiah 58, Jeremiah 14:36; Matthew 6; Acts 10; 13; 14.

In brief, I think highly of fasting and of self-denial if one does it voluntarily with regard to food and drink so that his evil and worthless flesh does not grow too wicked and thus, like the uncontrolled oxen, run without discipline and throw the ark of God's commandments into the mud, 2 Sam. 6. And if I were to give advice in these dangerous times, I would advise, and also do it myself, that one should fast often and hold general assemblies in prayer, that God may graciously turn his anger and wrath away from us and aid us to come again to peace in soul and body (as we read that the children of Israel also did this, Ezra 10 and Dan. 9, and at many other places), in good hope and confidence in God that it would soon get better. But with the way we are now living, we shall call down upon ourselves fire from heaven, burning, war, prison, pestilence, /482/ famine, terrible storms and punishments, sudden death, strange fevers, unusual sicknesses, and Egyptian boils. A foreign Gogish and Magogish people also will overcome us,[30] whose language we do not understand who will terrify us so mercilessly that we will cry out: " 'Blessed are the barren, and the wombs that never bore, and the breast that never gave suck!' Yea, we shall say to the mountains, 'fall upon us,' and to the hills, 'cover us!'" Wisdom 3; Isa. 54:2; Hos. 10; Ezek. 38; 39; Rev. 6; 20. Yes indeed, we will have to pray and fast or it will finally come to the point where, even though we raise our hands to God, he will turn his eyes from us; and even though we engage in much praying, he will not hear us. If one reads Isaiah 1; 2; and 3 and the book of Wisdom, he will find something that we need as a warning.

The Twentieth Article, On the Sabbath

Although to a Christian every day is a Sabbath Day, in that he should rest from sinning, Sunday is especially mentioned in Scripture as being the Lord's Day.

Since the almighty God created heaven and earth in six days and rested on the seventh day, Gen. 1; 2, it is now indicated to us by the light that burns in our heart, Psalm 4, that it is reasonable and right for the people in return to devote to him a time for praise, honor, and thanksgiving and to rest, as God afterward very seriously commanded us to celebrate that same day and said, "Remember to keep the seventh day holy. Six days you shall labor and do all your works; but on the seventh day, the day of the Lord your God; you shall not do any work, you, or your son, or your daughter, your manservant, or your maidservant, or your cattle, or the sojourner who is within your gates; for in six days God made heaven and earth, the sea, and all that is in them, and rested the seventh day; therefore the Lord blessed the seventh day and hallowed it," Exod. 20:8-11; Deut. 5:14.

But that now among Christians the Sabbath has changed to Sunday, I consider to have been a good change; for when Joshua was in battle the sun and moon, in the providence of

---

[30] Cf. Ezekiel 38:1ff and Rev. 20:7. Even when concerned to seem orthodox to Catholic readers, Hubmaier retains an apocalyptic reading of his times.

God, stood still for twenty-four hours /483/ until the people
had their revenge on their foes according to the divine command.[31] These twenty-four hours make one natural day.
Accordingly, when Christ Jesus, our Joshua, had overcome his
enemy and had victoriously ascended into heaven, this type
was taken up into its actual fulfillment. Thus the Sabbath was
moved forward twenty-four hours, that is, it was transformed
into Sunday, which Sunday John calls the Lord's Day, Rev.
1:10. I do not, however, herewith want to reject other reasons
the theologians may give.

The works of the Sabbath are: to rest in God, to preach
his Word, to read, hear, pray, consider the hour to be reconciled to God and to perform deeds of mercy toward one's
neighbor, as one finds that Christ and Paul also did, Luke 4;
John 5; 9; Acts 13; 15; 17; 18. This is what I have hitherto
been teaching concerning the Sabbath.

As to some other holidays, such as Christmas, Easter,
Pentecost, etc., I am satisfied, but there should not be so
many, as I publicly argued, twenty years ago at Freyburg im
Breußgew,[32] the thesis *de non multiplicandis festis* (that feast
days are not to be multiplied).

The Twenty-first Article, On Food

I have preached, and have also practiced, that all food is
clean for human use with moderation and thankfulness. What
goes into the mouth (says Christ) does not defile a person,
Matt. 15:17. Nevertheless, it has been, and still is, my intention to eat nothing which might result in causing my neighbor
to stumble, as Paul also teaches, saying, "Everything is indeed
clean, but they are unclean for the person whose eating
causes stumbling," Rom. 14:20.

Yes, in particular I have always and everywhere felt a
very great disapproval toward those people who seek their
gospel alone in eating meat and taking wives. Oh, they are
truly evangelical, so they say, but with the exception of these
two points one feels in them not a spark that resembles the
gospel. This means turning Christian liberty back again into

---

[31] Josh. 10:12ff.
[32] I.e., during his theological studies.

carnal license, as I have frequently lamented from the public pulpit and in my booklets (if I recall correctly) on the ban, that we now take hold of the gospel with the deeds that are pleasing to the body, but otherwise, unfortunately, to God be it lamented, we remain in all the vices of this world and in all sensuality. /484/

The Twenty-second Article, On the Ten Commandments

Christian necessity demands that the commandments of God be held before the people very frequently, especially in these dark days, so that the people do not deviate to the right or to the left but stay on the right way of the Lord our God and be saved.

How earnestly and zealously Moses presented God's commands to the people, as described in Exodus 20 and Deuteronomy 5. All Scripture is full of this; namely how he called heaven and earth to witness that he was setting before man blessing and curse, good and evil, life and death, and has given him the free choice to choose what he wished, Deut. 30. Nor could anyone excuse himself from keeping God's commandments on the ground of impossibility, for the Word, by which God gives strength to keep his commandments, is not in heaven or beyond the sea, but near us in our mouths and hearts. In the strength of this Word of God the power and might is given us to do everything that God commands (not by compulsion but voluntarily); but if we will not, we can leave it undone out of our own wickedness, for without our faith and will God will not work in us, Heb. 4, as also Christ did not perform many miracles in his homeland because of their unbelief, Matt. 13:58.

This is exactly the difference between a man's Word and God's word, for a man's word does not give the strength to perform what it commands, as for example, Pharaoh's magicians were unable to imitate Moses' signs and wonders. They were defeated because their words were human words, Exod. 8. But whatever God commands, he gives power and strength to those who believe and who will it, that we may do it without compulsion, for therein is the finger of God, Exod. 8, that all things are possible to the believer, Mark 9:23. For

God simply refuses to be responsible for our damnation. Therefore he lets us be the judge, Isa. 5. In explanation of this point I have in my booklets and teaching always and everywhere used the parable, when Christ said to the thirty-nine-year-old bedridden man: "Rise, take up your bed and walk," John 5:8. On the authority of this word the sick man now received strength and power to stand up, but the power to lie still was not taken away from him. But as he believed and desired, so it happened. Likewise, when Peter cried out to Christ on the sea: "Lord, command me to come to you," Christ said, "Come!" Matt. 14. Now on the authority of this word of Christ, Peter could have walked dry-shod across the water to Christ and into his boat. But as much as Peter doubted, just so far did Christ let him sink. I have therefore often taught this, so that no one could make excuses and say it is impossible for him /485/ to keep God's commandments, an error firmly implanted in the hearts of men in these times by false doctrines, that is an eternal curse; even if we had no word but this one word of Christ when he said to man, "If you would enter life, keep the commandments," Matt. 19:17. In the strength of this one word, i.e., "keep the commandments," enough strength is given us to keep them, that is, if we, we, we want to. O God, grant grace that this misleading doctrine be rooted out again. Now let us hear the Scriptures.

(1) "Cursed be whoever does not abide in the words of this law and does not fulfill them, and the whole people shall say Amen," Deut. 27:26.

(2) "My son, keep my words and receive my commandments; keep my commandments and you shall live. Keep my law as the apple of your eye; bind it on your fingers, write it on the tablet of your heart," Prov. 7:1-3.

(3) "He who says he knows God" but does not keep his commandments is deceitful, and the truth is not in him," 1 John 2:4.

(4) "For it is not the hearers of the law who are righteous before God, but the doers of the law who will be justified," Rom. 2:13.

(5) "Go," says King Josiah, "inquire of the counsel of the Lord for me, and for the people, and for all Judah, concerning the words of this law book that has been found; for a great wrath of God is kindled against us, because our fathers have

not obeyed the law of this book, to do according to all that is written concerning us," 2 Kings 22:13. In brief, hearing and doing the commandments of God belong together. Although the flesh does not want to undertake it, it still must undertake it, for on the authority of the divine Word the soul is master; with it, according to its will, the flesh must go into the fire against its own will. Thus I have taught hitherto about the Ten Commandments, presented them faithfully to the people, as I confirm with my catechism, in which I have set the Ten Commandments as the first beginning of a Christian life.[33]

The Twenty-third Article, On the Ban

The ban instituted by Christ is in Christendom so necessary a medicine that where it does not exist there is nothing but sin, shame, and vice. To attest to this article I shall let Christ speak through the Scriptures.

(1) "If your brother sins against you, go and rebuke him, between you and him alone. If he listens to you, you have won your brother. But if he does not listen, take one or two others along with you, that every word may be confirmed by the evidence of two or three witnesses. If he refuses to listen to you, tell it to the church; and if he refuses to listen even to the church, let him be to you as a Gentile /486/ and a tax collector. Truly, I say to you, whatever you bind on earth shall be bound also in heaven, and whatever you loose on earth shall be loosed also in heaven," Matt. 18:15-18.

(2) Likewise Paul pronounced the ban on the Corinthian who sinned with his stepmother, 1 Cor. 5.

(3) But when he repented and desisted from his sin he was received again with joy, 2 Cor. 2.

(4) Likewise, he delivered Hymenaeus and Alexander to Satan when they made shipwreck of their faith, 1 Tim. 1:20.

(5) Likewise, he pronounced the ban on the slothful and lazy who conducted themselves disorderly among the Thessalonians, 2 Thess. 3:6.

(6) Thus heretics and antichrists should also be dealt with, Titus 3:10; 2 John 1:10f.

---

[33] Cf. above, text 21, p. 345.

It is not necessary to write further on the ban, for I have published a special booklet about it[34] in which one clearly sees that I am very firm on the ban for without the key of the ban the church cannot remain upright.

The Twenty-Fourth Article,
On the Intercession of the Saints

Because our Head, Christ Jesus, intercedes for us with the Father, I hold that also the dear saints who are in heaven and are of one will with their Head, Christ, and with members of his body, intercede along with him, for their will is subject to the will of Christ. But I know of no Scripture at all that says we are to call upon them for help and salvation in our needs, for all the Scriptures point us to Christ as our advocate and mediator, Matt. 11; 1 Tim. 2:5; 1 John 2:1; Rom. 8:34; as I have also noted in my catechism.

The Twenty-fifth and Twenty-sixth Articles,
On Baptism and the Sacrament

Most august, great and mighty King, most gracious Sovereign, with regard to baptism and the sacrament, I am very dissatisfied with the way Johann Hut and his followers taught and practiced these two articles and intend to stand against it in my teaching and writing all my life as God gives me strength. For on the basis of the divine Word and with a good conscience I can say that he has misused both doctrines, contrary to the institution of Christ. Also I have no doubt that with God's help I could soon set aside his baptism and Supper. Nevertheless, I will say here, as I must give an account to Christ on the judgment day, that I am convinced and powerfully compelled in my conscience that I will stand by what I have written in my books /487/ on these two points.[35] For I have taught nothing else regarding baptism except that it is a public and oral confession of the Christian faith, and a renunciation that one must address to the devil and his works, so

---

[34] Cf. above, text 26, p. 409ff.
[35] Cf. above, texts 7, 11, 18, 24, and 25, pp. 73ff., 95ff., 275ff., 386ff., 393ff.

that a person, in the power of God the Father and the Son and the Holy Spirit, may yield himself in such surrender that he is willing with Christ to suffer, die, and be buried, in the faith that he will arise with him to everlasting life, Rom. 6:4; this he testifies by receiving water baptism. But concerning the Lord's Supper I have taught that it is a testimonial of brotherly love, that as Christ loved us unto death so we should also love one another and each perform toward one another the works of mercy, concerning which Christ will demand an account on the judgment day, Matt. 25:40. By this people will know that we are true disciples of Christ, John 13:35. This witness of love occurs through the breaking of the bread, which is eaten in memory of Christ's suffering which he endured for us out of love, for the remission of our sins, which I have written still more clearly in my booklets on baptism, on the Lord's Supper, and in the theses against Hutt.[36] Therefore the baptism that I taught and the baptism that Hutt promoted are as far apart as heaven and hell, east and west, Christ and Belial. Likewise, with the Lord's Supper, I hope to God I will not bear his charge.

But in order that your Royal Majesty may see yet further that I do not want to be obstinate or stubborn, I offer to postpone these two articles as I have taught them, and other matters concerning the faith, until the next Christian council which (if God will) shall soon be assembled and held by the providence of God working through the Imperial and your Royal Majesty.[37] Until then I will submit to the holy Christian church and gladly accept instruction on these points from divine Scriptures, also meanwhile I will leave these articles in suspense and with the others, namely, on faith, good works, against carnal liberty, on the fear of God, a good conscience, against the error that all things happen of necessity, against

---

[36] See preceding note. Regarding the "Theses against Hut," cf. above note 21, and below note 39. There may have been another (not extant) text on baptism and the Supper written by Hubmaier for Fabri. Cf. Bergsten 1961, p. 479.

[37] The expectation of a reform council was widespread in the 1520s. Since the pope would not call a council to reform the papacy, it was expected that the emperor would convene it. Ferdinand's brother Emperor Charles V (elected 1519), had been in Spain since 1522. Hubmaier is both realistic and complimentary in suggesting that if there were to be such a council, Ferdinand might have a hand in convening it.

the captive will, on remorse and repentance, on the virginity of Mary and that Christ is true God, on inherited sin, fasting, confessing, prayer, the authority of the church, Ten Commandments, Sunday, the ban, on the obedience of subjects and the avoidance of all rebellion, I will with divine help teach and practice in such a way that Your Royal Majesty will be especially pleased with it and will also visibly find and feel that I have worked well and fruitfully./488/

However, if Your Royal Majesty does not want to wait for a council, I offer to appear before Your Royal Majesty yourself, before your praiseworthy council and universities, to give an answer with the holy Scriptures on all the articles that are ascribed to me. Your Royal Majesty may then after hearing my answers be the judge according to the Word of God, for I would like to conduct myself always in such a way that I maintain a good conscience toward God, and may be able to stand with my soul before the judgment seat of Christ at the last judgment—that God knows. I will also earnestly ask God day and night that he might by virtue of his divine mercy cause me to know means and ways by which Your Royal Majesty and all Christendom may arrive at Christian welfare and peace. The God who is with me in my wretchedness will hear me. And if it should be Your Royal Majesty's pleasure, I would gladly delineate and describe an order for a Christian government, whereby everyone, with the grace of God and the help of the Imperial and Your Royal Majesties, could soon come everywhere to peace and unity. God's will be done. Amen.

The Twenty-seventh Article, On Government

The Word of God teaches love, peace, unity, and not rebellion, yea especially that one should be obedient unto death to all authority in everything that is not contrary to God, pray for them earnestly, and render tribute, taxes, fear, and honor, and also to offer one's life and goods for the protection of the peace of the land.

As the article states, so Christ teaches us that we should love not only those who do good to us, but also our enemies who do evil to us. He also adds the reward and says, "Blessed are the peacemakers, for they shall be called children of

God," Matt. 5:9. Paul also teaches that we should keep peace with all men as far as it lies in us, Rom. 12:15. Thus Christ orders Peter to sheathe his sword, for he who takes the sword will perish by the sword, Matt. 26:52. Those persons "take" the sword who have no command to use it according to God's order. But those who are in power "wield" the sword as special ministers of God, ordained for the protection of the righteous and the punishment of evildoers, Rom. 13:4. To them we owe obedience at the cost of honor, property, body, and life, unto death, for body and the goods belong to the emperor, that is, the government, but the soul belongs to God, as I have expressly taught in my booklet on the sword.[38] Now I shall also present sufficient Scripture on the question.

(1) First, St. Paul writes thus to the Romans: "Let every person be subject to the government and authority. For there is no authority /489/ except from God. The authority, however, which is everywhere, is ordained by God. Therefore he who resists the authorities resists God's order, and those who resist will incur judgment. For rulers are not a terror to those who do good, but to the evil. Would you not fear them? Then do what is good, and you will receive their approval, for he is God's servant for your good. But if you do wrong, be afraid, for government does not bear the sword in vain; he is the servant of God, an avenger of wrath on the wrongdoer. You must therefore now be subject, necessarily, not only for the sake of God's wrath but also for the sake of conscience. For the same reason you also must pay taxes, for they are God's servants, who should provide such protection. Pay each of them their. dues, tribute to whom tributes are due, toll to whom toll, honor to whom honor, fear to whom fear," Rom. 13:1-7.

(2) St. Peter also has something to say about it. Thus: "Be subject for the Lord's sake to every human creature, to the king as supreme, to princes as sent by him to punish those who do wrong and to praise those who do right." Then Peter adds a brief word which comprehends the entire matter: "Fear God. Honor the emperor," 1 Pet. 2:13-17.

(3) Paul teaches further: "Remind the people to be submissive, to rulers and authorities, to obey their commands, to be ready for any good work," Tit. 3:1. He writes further,

---

[38] See above, no. 29, p. 492ff.

(4) "First of all, then, I urge that prayers, supplications, intercessions, and thanksgiving be made for all men, for kings and all who are in high positions, that we may lead a quiet and peaceable life, in all piety and respectability," 1 Tim. 2:1f.

Here anyone who has ears can hear that on the authority of these Scriptures we are to be completely docile, submissive, and obedient to the authorities and ready to prevent and repudiate all disturbances, rebellion, and disunity. For this reason I am greatly displeased with Hanns Hutt and his followers for stirring up and misleading the populace secretly in corners, provoking conspiracy and sedition under the pretense of baptism and the Supper of Christ as if one had to take up the sword and the like. No, No! That is not the way. A Christian does not fight, strike, or kill unless he is in a seat of authority and is ordered to do it or is called to do it by the properly instituted government. Otherwise, before a Christian draws a sword he will give up his cloak and coat. He also offers the other cheek, yea even his body and life. Christian conduct is so peaceable because this is the Christian's victory, our faith, which overcomes the world, 1 John 5:4. Accordingly, a Christian's life is set toward suffering /490/ in order that he may in some measure become like Christ in suffering, fulfill Christ's suffering in his body and with his cross, follow in the path that he has prepared for us and on which he himself has gone before us with his cross and suffering. Then we shall also inherit eternal life with him, Rom. 8:17; Col. 1:24; Luke 24; Acts 14:22. This is what I told Hut and others to their face, and reproved them severally for their seductive and seditious doctrines, as one finds in my theses that I publicly presented against him and his followers.

Thus I had very great difficulties especially in the upper country[39] with those who held that no Christian should hold

---

[39] Probably an allusion to Hubmaier's debates around Nikolsburg, with Hut and the so-called *Stäbler*. Hubmaier's difference on this matter was not only with Hut at Nikolsburg but also with the "Swiss Brethren" with whom he had had to do earlier. Yet from the earlier period we have no records of his arguing the matter. The paradoxical tragedy of Hubmaier's fate is that though he tried hard to relate positively to governments and to distance himself from other Anabaptists in that respect, it seems still to be the accusation of "rebellion" that caused him to be brought to Vienna for trial and execution. As far as the Vienna government is concerned, the reproach goes back to Waldshut's uprising in 1525.

governmental office or bear the sword. Against them and their false teaching I have written and have preached so firmly that they criticized me in a public church service for holding so strongly and firmly on the sword, that a Christian may according to God's institution also bear the sword, indeed far better than an unbeliever who takes neither Christ nor his Word to heart. That is why I wrote my booklet and preached on the sword. In it one finds plain and clear the basis for this article of faith. To this very day I am still ready and willing, with grace granted by God, to advise and help toward peace and unity[40] and also to prevent secret conspiracy and opposition wherever I may learn of them, as far as my body and life can reach, as could be seen and recognized in deed.

Now, O great, mighty, and most gracious King, for the sake of God's and your own mercy, I beg Your Royal Majesty, as the gentle ruler of Austria, to whose house this praise and title of gentleness has always and ever been ascribed above others, and particularly because Lord Dr. Johann Fabri, Your Royal Majesty's Councillor, also Lord Marx Beckh, your Vice-regent in Austria, and Lord Saltzer, Rector of the University of Vienna, praised to me Your Royal Majesty's great mercy and virtue,[41] may Your Royal Highness pardon me, a prisoner and distressed man lying here in great sickness, cold, and wretchedness, and be gracious and merciful even to me. For with God's help I will henceforth conduct myself in such a way that your Royal Highness will be pleased, and will direct the people with great earnestness and high zeal to worship, to the fear of God and obedience, in whatever place I am appointed to.[42] Your Royal Majesty shall have no doubt of my consent, for Your Royal Majesty and Milord your brother, His Imperial Majesty possess nearly all of Christendom, hence I would not care to take residence anywhere else; to this my yea shall be yea and be found as yea on the judgment day, to which may God help me. Amen. I herewith want to have com-

---

[40] A vague allusion to a possible role for Hubmaier in encouraging other dissenters to conform. Cf. above p., 157, note 19, and below, note 42.

[41] The men sent to debate with Hubmaier seem seriously to have hoped for a complete recantation. Their official correspondence demonstrates that this text was not acceptable.

[42] Hubmaier hopes not merely to be spared but to be appointed to a pastoral role.

mended and subjected myself in all submissiveness to Your Royal Majesty. Given in my bonds in Kreuzenstein Castle on January 3, 1528.

To God Be Praise!

31

Vienna Testimony

Dr. John Heigerlin (1478-1541) was usually called Faber. Besides Hubmaier's own teacher, John Eck, Faber was the most weighty anti-Protestant polemist of Austrian Catholicism. He had been the representative of the See of Constance at the disputation of January 29, 1523, which marked Zurich's move into the Reformation.

When Hubmaier was brought to Kreuzenstein, Faber was chaplain to Ferdinand I of Austria. In 1530 Faber was to become bishop of Vienna. With Ferdinand's permission, he debated three days with Hubmaier, covering the entire scope of Christian doctrine. The result was Faber's massive Defense of the Orthodox Catholic Faith Against Dr. Balthasar Pacimontanus,[1] *published in the summer of 1528 and again in 1537.*

The day after Hubmaier's execution Faber published a pamphlet, Reason Why Dr. Balthasar Hubmayr, Head and Founder of the Anabaptists, Was at Vienna March 10, 1528.[2] *Faber recounts Hubmaier's progressive falling-away from the Roman faith, accusing him of the authorship of the* Ten Articles *of the rebellious peasants. To his account of his own meeting with Hubmaier, Faber then appends the following testimony (*urgicht*), which he says was "read publicly in the presence of many thousands."[3]*

Testimony, as read publicly:

First, Dr. Balthasar Hubmayer confessed how at Waltzhut he preached rebellious things against the government which

---

[1] Full title in ME II, p. 285f. Partially translated in Crismon 1949 and reproduced by Estep 1976, pp. 140ff.

[2] Reprinted in Loserth 1893, pp. 210ff. Quoted in Vedder 1905, p. 240.

[3] Our source is Böhmer 1933, pp. 13f. Translated by Estep 1967, p. 139. What "read publicly" means is not evident, since the text is in the third person. Was the hearing public from which this record was taken? Did the court recorder read this record in public? Does Faber mean that Hubmaier read the court document in public, speaking of himself in the third person? It is most likely that there were two events with the same content, one public and one in court.

did not contribute to peace but were counter to God, justice, and his conscience, whence much contentiousness and rebellion against government and much bloodshed have sprung.[4]

Further he confessed having helped those of Waltzhut[5] to deliberate and write letters to His Royal Highness (then his princely Majesty) which contributed more to rejection than to obedience.

Further he confessed that he went into the homes of those of Waltzhut and spoke with them saying they had every claim and right, they should stand by it in death or life. He also advised and aided them twice to swear an oath together that they would resist all those who would not want to let them stay by the doctrine he had preached. This too he confesses was against God and his conscience, as well as against the government.

Further he confessed concerning the articles of the peasants, which were brought to him from their army, that he expanded and exposited them, and convinced the same [army] to accept them as Christian and reasonable. He confesses[6] also that in so doing he erred and did wrong.

Further he confessed how it happened that numerous of the councilmen of Waltzhut went to Laufenburg. Meanwhile the architect Hans Müller, in the Mayor's stead, convened the assembly in the Council Hall and announced, in the name of the Tribunal and the Town, the report that the Imperial alliance was ready, on behalf of His Royal Highness (then His Princely Majesty), to attack the city and punish the citizenry. To accept which,[7] whoever did not wish to do so could leave the city until things would get better. Whereupon he, Dr.

---

[4] From this accent on the "testimony," as well as from Faber's account, it seems clear that the accusation of civil rebellion was a more weighty accusation than that of religious heresy. This is evident in the relative space given here to the details of the Waldshut unrest.

[5] Hubmaier seems to have had a part in the deliberations of Waldshut's town council: cf. Bergsten 1961, pp. 58, 144ff., 192ff., 277ff.

[6] The variation in tenses is in the original. Each paragraph begins with the legal formula, past tense "er hat bekannt," yet as the narrative goes on the recorder slips into the present. Stayer 1988, pp. 106-111, updates the analysis of Hubmaier's contribution to the documents of the peasants' revolt.

[7] Hans Müller in his function as deputy mayor recommends surrender, accepting the alliance's terms to avoid the attack. The recommendation is stated in an incomplete clause.

Balthasar, publicly took his leave of everyone and returned home saying he would not be part of such a settlement. The next morning after breakfast he left the city, after which he came to Zürich, and there was taken captive because of the second baptism, for the same is against Zwingli, to whom those of Zürich adhere. Because of rebaptism he was also racked[8] there; he had to say who had moved him to such baptism, and whom he had baptized in their territories. Wherefore he publicly recanted concerning infant baptism.

Further he confessed that he thus preached and gave advice and aid in order to have a good life and be a Lord! He confesses to have done all that wrongly. Also that their reason and objective had been to have no government but rather to call forth and elect one from their midst.

Further said Dr. Balthasar confesses that he thinks nothing of the sacrament of the altar or of infant baptism.[9]

---

[8] I.e., tortured. The euphemistic official term was "painfully interrogated" (*peinlich verhört*).

[9] Here the recorder condenses so much that we cannot tell what Hubmaier meant. The text of the testimony from the court record ends here. Faber concludes his report with two paragraphs of his own, reporting that Hubmaier died unrepentant, as his own handwritten text (our text, number 30, above) demonstrates.

32

"Rejoice, Rejoice"

The following text has been attributed to Hubmaier by The
Hutterite Chronicle[1] *and by Hošek,[2] Beck,[3] Loserth, and Vedder. The great hymnologist Wackernagel[4] recorded but doubted
its attribution by some to Erasmus Albert. Nothing of its content proves or disproves Hubmaier's authorship. Nothing of its
content is specifically Anabaptist. Stronger reason for doubting
the attribution to Hubmaier is its appearance in a Lutheran
hymnal published in Leipzig in 1545.[5] A very similar text, dif-
fering only in the first few words, was published in Wittenberg
in 1530,[6] attributed to "a young earl."*

*H. C. Vedder prepared this metrical rendering, "in which
the attempt has been made to follow the original as closely as
the exigencies of English versification would admit."[7] Estep
reproduced it.[8]*

*The Chronicle indicates two possible melodies: "So weiss
ich eins das mich erfreut" and "Sohn Davids." The former,
previously a secular tune, is reproduced below in two versions.[9]
The latter has not been identified by Zahn.*

*A more literal rendering than Vedder's is suggested only at
some points where his versification sacrificed significant
nuances. Our German version and the preface are from the
Hutterite collection.[10]*

---

[1] The source of the German version and the preface are the *Chronicle*
1987, p. 49; *Die Lieder der Hutterischen Brüder*, Scottdale, Herald Press,
1914, pp. 23-25.
[2] Cf. Hošek, p. 511.
[3] ME I, p. 258.
[4] Wackernagel 1870, Vol. III, no. 165, p. 126.
[5] Zahn 1963, Vol. III, items 5693a and 5693b, pp. 500 and 501.
[6] Zahn 1963, item 5692, Vol III, p. 500.
[7] Vedder 1905, p. 311. Vedder's internal rhyme in each seventh line
renders something similar in each eighth line of the German. His uniform
eighth line renders the uniform seventh line of the German.
[8] Estep 1976, p. 169.
[9] Source: Zahn 1963, III, loc. cit. Zahn preserves a wording of the first
verse which differs from Wackernagel in small ways, and may be earlier.
[10] *Die Lieder der Hutterischen Brüder*, Scottdale, Herald Press, 1914, pp.
23-25.

Balthasar Hubmaier was burned at the stake in Vienna March 10, 1528. There would be much to write about him, known to many as leader and founder in Moravia.[11] In prison

---

[11] *Principal und Anfanger.*

he became aware that he had improperly resisted Hans Hut on several points. He acknowledged that he had yielded too far to the carnal liberty to retain the sword. He was moved to write to Nikolsburg, especially to his assistant, Martin Göschel, Provost in Kannitz,[12] saying that he and they[13] should renounce everything. He also said: if Hans Hut were here now, we could soon agree.[14] There are two songs known in the church, which he composed, of which only one is known.[15]

---

[12] Göschl was Hubmaier's predecessor, not his assistant.

[13] The "they" alludes to unnamed persons, part of the collectivity "Nikolsburg."

[14] There is no historical truth in the importance given here to the estrangement between Hut and Hubmaier, and the reference to the sword as the theme of the breach. See above, p. 557, note 36. Apart from the Hutterite sources, there is no evidence for this notion that Hubmaier recanted at those points where he disagreed with Hut.

[15] Since the hymnal itself gathered (when edited) all the extant sources, the notion that there had been a second hymn must have been an oral reminiscence.

1. Rejoice, rejoice, ye Christians all,
   And break forth into singing!
   Since far and wide on every side
   The Word of God is ringing.[16]
   And well we know, no human foe
   Our souls from Christ can sever;
   For to the base, and men of grace,
   God's Word stands sure forever.

Freut euch, freut euch in dieser Zeit
Ihr wahren Christen alle.
Wann jetzt in allen Länder weit
Gotts Wort herdringt mit Schalle.
Es ist kein Mann ders wehren kann,
Das habt ihr wohl vernommen.
Denn Gottes Wort bleibt ewig bstan
Den Bösen als den Frommen.

2. O Adam, Adam, first of men,[17]
   What future did fate send you?
   After your Fall in Paradise
   How did your God befriend you?
   His holy Word from him you heard,
   That Word which faileth never,
   To tend'rest age, to hoary sage,
   God's Word stands sure forever.

Adam, Adam, du alter Greis,
Wie hat es dir ergangen.
Nach deinem Fahl im Paradeis
Hast du von Gott empfangen.
Sein göttlich Wort genommen an
Und bist dadurch erhalten.
Denn Gottes Wort bleibt ewig bstan
Den Jungen als den Alten.

3. O Noah, Noah, man of God,
   Thy God hath thee selected
   And sworn to thee an oath, since thou
   His Word hast not rejected:
   "With flood again to drown all men
   My wrath shall hasten never";
   To swollen pelf, to want itself,[18]
   God's Word stands sure forever.

Noah, Noah, du Gottesmann,
Gott hat dich auserkoren.
Dass du sein Wort hast genommen an
Hat er zu dir geschworen.
Mit Wasser nicht ertrinken lan
Wollt von sein Zorn abweichen.
Dann Gottes Wort bleibt ewig bstan
Den Armen als den Reichen.

4. And Abraham believed his God,
   And so, for his devotion,
   His faith became his righteousness,
   His seed like sands of ocean.
   Thus has God done for every one,[19]
   Who trust him perish never;
   To every one who builds thereon
   God's Word stands sure forever.

Abram, Abram, gab gut Bescheid,
Er glaubet Gott sein Herren.
Das ward ihm gzählt zur Gerechtigkeit,
Sein Samen wollt er mehren.
Also hat Gott den Alten tan
Die seinen Wort vertrauen.
Dann Gottes Wort bleibt ewig bstan
Den die darauf tun bauen.

5. And Lot, devout, God-fearing man,
   Two angels came to find him,
   And lead him out from Sodom safe,
   Nor should he look behind him.
   God's fiery flood therein withstood
   No living thing whatever:
   All men, like Lot, must pay their scot,
   God's Word stands sure forever.

Lot, Lot, ein fromm gottsfürchtig Mann,
Gott tät zwei Engel senden
Hiess ihm aus Sodom ziehen tun
Und sollt sich nicht umwenden.
Alsbald hub Gott zu regnen an
Mit Schwefel und mit Feuer.
Dann Gottes Wort bleibt ewig bstan
Kommt uns allen zu Steuer.

6. O David, David, king and lord,
   A man of God's own choosing,
   God's truth he hid within his heart
   Beyond all fear of losing.
   From David's seed Christ should proceed,
   He swore who changeth never;
   In heaven and on earth the same
   God's Word stands sure forever.

David, David, ein Knecht und Herr,
Ein Mann nach Gottes Willen.
Hat angenommen Gottes Lehr,
Damit sein Wort erfüllet.
Aus seinem Stamm Gott g'lobet an.
Wollt er geboren werden.
Dann Gottes Wort bleibt ewig bstan
Im Himmel und auf Erden.

---

[16] The original accentuates the *present* tense: literally, "Rejoice *in this time* ... as *now* in all lands...."

[17] Literally: "you old man."

[18] Literally: "to the poor as to the rich."

[19] Literally: "for the ancients," i.e., the saints of the old covenant.

7. Jesus the Christ, of Mary born
     And of the Holy Spirit
  What all the prophets promised
     We shall in him inherit.
  "Hear him," the call of God to all,
     to save us his endeavor;
  To him all praise and honor raise—
     God's Word stands sure forever.

Jesus Christ, Maria Sohn,
Vom heiligen Geist empfangen.
Was all Propheten Gesaget han
Ist alls an ihm ergangen.
Das hat Gott alls durch ihn gethan
Und spricht, den sollt ihr hören.
Dann Gottes Wort bleibt ewig bstan
Den sollen wir loben und ehren.

8. Now hear, now hear, and mark with care
     What else for us is written,
  And learn from his new covenant
     What more to do we're bidden.
  And what of old has been foretold
     Of Christ our Lord and Savior;
  To latest hour, in vaster power,
     God's Word stands sure forever.

Nun hört, nun hört und merkt mit Fleiss,
Was uns fürder beschrieben
Im Testament auf neue weiss,
Darin sie tun verbleiben.
Was vormals jegesaget war
Von Christo unsern Herren.
Dann Gottes Wort bleibt ewig bstan
Und wird sich allzeit mehren.

9. Matthew, the first evangelist,
     From Roman service taken,
  Has now become chief counselor
     And has his sins forsaken:
  Hears Jesus call, who says to all,
     "Follow with best endeavor."[20]
  In ample frame, always the same,
     God's Word stands sure forever.

Matthäus, Levi, Evangelist,
Ein Mann vom Zoll berufen.
Der erste Canzler worden ist,
Lehret allein zu suchen
Diesen Heiland, der selber spricht:
Kommt her, ihr Betrübten alle.
Dann Gottes Wort bleibt ewig bstan
Mit Pracht und grossem Schalle.

10. And Mark, yes Mark, the second is,
     And richly he has taught us
  The knowledge of that mighty power
     Wherewith our Lord has brought us
  To faith in God, to which is owed
     All goodness whatsoever;
  For all men's tears, for all men's jeers.
     God's Word stands sure forever.

Markus, Markus, der andre ist,
Der auch reichlich ausbreitet
Mirakel gross von diesem Christ,
Damit er hat geleitet.
Zum Glauben brecht, dass er allein
Gerecht und fromm tut machen.
Dann Gottes Wort bleibt ewig bstan
Sie weinen uder lachen.

11. Luke also follows in the train
     And tells the gospel story:
  The wondrous works of Christ, and how
     From heaven the God of glory
  To men undone has sent his Son
     That men might perish never;[21]
  Believe we must, or bite the dust,
     God's Word stands sure forever.

Lukas auch in die Ordnung tritt,
Gross Wundertat uns zeiget.
Zu schreiben aus ist er der dritt,
Wie hoch uns Gott geneiget.
Dass er uns schickt von Himmel herab
Sein Sohn freundlich lässt locken
Dann Gottes Wort bleibt ewig bstan
Wer dass nicht glaubt, muss pocken.

12. And John, the fourth evangelist,
     A youth of wondrous beauty,
  Reveals to us the Word divine
     And teaches us our duty.
  With faith and love your calling prove
     And seek no other lever;
  It gives no aid to hoe or spade,
     But God's Word stands forever.

Johannes, Johannes, der Jüngling schon,
Jst auch der vierte worden.
Das Wort er führt in gleichen Ton
Lehrt uns den Christen Orden.
Mit Glaub und Lieb beweisen recht,
Und sonst anderst nicht suchen.
Dann Gottes Wort bleibt ewig bstan
Es hilft kein Scharren noch Bochen.

---

[20] Literally: "teaches to seek only the Savior, who speaks, 'come to me, you who are oppressed.'"

[21] The original has no reference to "perishing"; literally: "he has his son amiably entice us."

13. And Saul,[22] God's chosen vessel he,
His early sin repented:
He stormed and strove against the saints
As if he were demented.
In vain the age 'gainst us shall rage,
Our souls from Christ to sever;
In time of ill our stronghold still,
God's Word stands sure forever.

Saulus, Paulus, erwähltes Fass,
Ist erst der rechte Kören.
Der uns erregt den reid und Hass,
Davon so zornig werden.
Die Welt und ihr gross Hofgesindt,
Die also toben und wüten.
Dann Gottes Wort bleibt ewig bstan
Vor dem wird ers behüten.

14. O Paul, O Paul, what fruit of all
Thy writings in their season!
The truth thou hast declared shall stand
Against all human reason.
Sin is o'erthrown by faith alone,
And, though the great and clever
Were all employed to make it void,
God's Word stands sure forever.

O Paul, O Paul, was richtst du an
Mit deinen teuren Schreiben.
Menschlich Vernunft hoch fichtest an,
Willst ihre Werk vertreiben.
Allein den Glauben richten aus,
Der soll alles ausrichten.
Dann Gottes Wort bleibt ewig bstan
Wie wohl sie es vernichten.

15. And Peter, Jude, and James, all three
follow in this teaching;
Repentance and confession they
Through Christ our Lord are preaching.
In him men must put all their trust,
Or they shall see God never;
The wolf may tear, the lion, bear—
God's Word stands sure forever.

Petrus, Judas, und Jacobus
Folgen auch diefer Lehre.
Dass sie uns lehren Reu und Buss.
Durch Christum unsern Herrn,
Auf dass sie all uns weisen tun.
Ohn ihm wird nicht geholfen.
Dann Gottes Wort bliebt ewig bstan
Vor Löwen, Bären und Wölfen.

16. Ah, man, blind man, now hear the Word,
Make sure your state and calling;
Believe the Scripture is the power
By which we're kept from falling.
Your valued lore at once give o'er,
Renounce your vain endeavor;
This shows the way, no longer stray,
God's Word stands sure forever.

Ach Mensch, ach Mensch, schick dich nur drein
Lass deinen Dünkel fahren.
Und glaub der Schrift und Worten sein,
Damit du mögst bewahren
Dein Gwissen und auch all dein Tun,
Treulich darauf verlassen.
Dann Gottes Word bleibt ewig bstan
Zeigt uns den Weg und Strassen.

17. O Jesus Christ, thou Son of God,
Let us not lack thy favor,
For what shall be our just reward
If the salt shall lose its savor?
With angry flame to efface thy name
In vain shall men endeavor;
Not for a day, the same for aye,
God's Word stands sure forever.

O Jesu Christ, du Gottes Sohn,
Lass uns von dir nicht weichen.
Dass uns nicht werd ein Böser Lohn,
So Menschenlehr herstreichen.
Mit schöner Gstalt und Wütrichs Gwalt.
Zu tilgen deinen Namen.
Dann Gottes Wort bleibt ewig bstan
Von nun und ewig Amen.

18. Praise God, praise God in unity,
Ye Christian people sweetly,
That he his Word has spread abroad—
His Word, his work completely.
No human hand can him withstand,
No name how high soever;
And sing we then our glad Amen!
God's Word stands sure forever.

Lobt Gott, Lobt Gott in Ewigkeit,
Ihr Christen allgemeine.
Dass er sein Wort hat ausgebreit,
Das ist sein Werk alleine.
Kein Menschen Wahn nicht helfen kan,
Wie hoch er sei mit Namen.
Dann Gottes Wort bleibt ewig bstan
Nun singen wir fröhlich Amen. Amen.

---

[22] The original uses both names: "Saul" and "Paul."

Bibliography

Sources cited only by initials:

CIC   Aemilius Friedberg, *Corpus iuris canonici*. Graz: Akademische Druck und Verlagsanstalt, 1959.

DLA   Desiderius Erasmus, *De Libero Arbitrio*, ed. by Winfried Lesowsky. Vol. 4: Ausgewälte Schriften. Darmstadt: Wissenschaftliche Buchgellschaft, 1969.

HS   Westin/Bergsten, *Balthasar Hubmaier Schriften*. Gütersloh, 1962.

LW   *Luther's Works*. Concordia Publishing House and Fortress Press, 1955—.

Mansi   J. D. Mansi, *Sacrorum Conciliorum nova et amplissima collectio*, 31 vols. Florence/Venice, 1757-98.

ME   *The Mennonite Encyclopedia*. Scottdale: Mennonite Publishing House, 1955.

MPG   J. -P. Migne, ed., *Patrologiae cursus completus*. Series Graeca, 163 vols. Paris: J. -P. Migne, 1857-1866.

MPL   J. -P. Migne, ed., *Patrologiae cursus completus*. Series Latina, 218 vols. Paris: J. -P. Migne, 1866ff.

MQR   *Mennonite Quarterly Review.*

vMS   Leonhard von Muralt and Walter Schmidt, *Quellen zur Geschichte der Täufer in der Schweiz. Band I, Zürich*. Zurich 1952.

WA   *D. Martin Luthers Werke*. Weimar: Böhlau, 1883—.

ZL   *The Latin Works of Huldreich Zwingli*. Vol. 1: Samuel Jackson, ed., New York: G. P. Putnam's Sons, 1912. Vol. 2: William J. Hinke, ed., Philadelphia: The Heidelberg Press, 1922. Vol. 3: Clarence N. Heller, ed., Philadelphia: The Heidelberg Press, 1929.

Z   *Huldreich Zwingli Sämtliche Werke*, Band II. Leipzig Hensius, 1908.

Sources cited by author and date:

Armour 1966   Rollin Stely Armour, *Anabaptist Baptism: A Representative Study*. Vol. 11: Studies in Anabaptist and Mennonite History. Scottdale: Herald Press.

Basil 1950   M. Monica Wagner, C.S.C., translator, *Saint Basil: Ascetical Works*. Washington: Catholic University of America Press, Vol. 9 in *The Fathers of the Church: A New Translation*.

Basil 1963   Agnes Clare Way, C.D.P., translator, *Saint Basil, Exegetical Homilies*. Washington: Catholic University of America Press, Vol. 46 in *The Fathers of the Church: A New Translation*.

Bender 1950   Harold Stauffer Bender, *Conrad Grebel*. Goshen: Mennonite Historical Society.

Bergsten 1978   Torsten Bergsten and W. R. Estep, Jr., ed., *Balthasar Hubmaier, Anabaptist Theologian and Martyr*. Valley Forge: Judson Press.

Bergsten 1961   Torsten Bergsten, *Balthasar Hubmaier: Seine Stellung zu Reformation und Täufertum*. Kassel: Oncken Verlag.

Blanke 1961   Fritz Blanke, *Brothers in Christ*. Scottdale: Herald Press.

Blickle 1981   Peter Blickle, *The Revolution of 1525*, Baltimore, Johns Hopkins University Press.

Bromiley 1953   G. W. Bromiley, *Zwingli and Bullinger*. Vol. 24: The Library of Christian Classics. Philadelphia: Westminster.

Bullinger 1878   J. J. Hottinger and H. H. Vögeli, eds., *Heinrich Bullinger's Reformationsgeschichte*. Beyel: Frauenfeld.

Chronicle 1987   *The Chronicle of the Hutterian Brethren Volume I*, translated and edited by the Hutterian Brethren. Rifton: Plough Publishing House.

Cochrane 1966   Arthur Cochrane, *Reformed Confessions of the 16th Century*. Philadelphia: The Westminster Press.

Courvoisier 1947 Jacques Courvoisier, *Zwingli*. Geneva.

Courvoisier 1963 Jacques Courvoisier, *Zwingli: A Reformed Theologian*. Atlanta: John Knox Press.

Crismon 1949   Leo T. Crismon, "The Interview Between John Faber and Balthasar Hubmaier, Vienna, December 1527-January 1528" in *The Review and Expositor*, Vol. XLVI, No. 1 (January 1949), pp. 38ff.

Davidson 1939   George Diuguid Davidson, translator, *The Writings of Balthasar Hubmaier*. Vol. 1-3, collected and photocopied by W. O. Lewis. Cited from a partial microfilm copy in the Mennonite Historical Library, Goshen, Indiana. A more complete version, edited by Walter Klaassen, is at Conrad Grebel College, Waterloo. It is cited where the page citation is above 400.

Deppermann 1979	Klaus Deppermann, *Melchior Hoffman*. Göttingen: Vandenhoek & Ruprecht.
Englebert 1951	Omar Englebert, *The Lives of the Saints*. New York: David McKay, Co.
Erasmus 1961	Desiderius Erasmus, *Opera Omnia*. Hildesheim: Georg Olms, 1961 (1706)
Estep 1976	William R. Estep, Jr., ed., *Anabaptist Beginnings: A Source Book*. Nieuwkoop: de Graaf.
Farner 1954	Oscar Farner, *Huldrych Zwingli, Seine Verkündigung und Seine ersten Früchte*. Zurich: Zwingli Verlag, 1954.
Fast 1973	Heinold Fast, *Quellen zur Geschichte der Täufer in der Schweiz, Zweiter Band, Ostschweiz*. Zurich: Theologischer Verlag.
Fellmann 1956	*Hans Denck*: Schriften; *2. Teil: Religiöse Schriften, Gütersloh, Bertelsmann*, part of Vol. XXIV in *Quellen und Forschungen zur Reformationsgeschichte*. Bd. VI in *Quellen zur Geschichte der Täufer*.
Frend 1952	W. H. C. Frend, *The Donatist Church*. Oxford: Clarendon Press.
Furcha 1975	Edward J. Furcha with Ford Lewis Battles, *Selected Writings of Hans Denck*. Pittsburgh: Pickwick Press.
Furcha/Pipkin 1984	E. J. Furcha and H. W. Pipkin, *Prophet, Pastor, Protestant: The Work of Huldrych Zwingli*. Pickwick.
Furcha 1984	E. J. Furcha, *Huldrych Zwingli, Writings*, Vol. I: *The Defense of the Reformed Faith*. Allison Park: Pickwick Publications.
Gagliardi 1952	Ernst Gagliardi, Hans Müller, Fritz Büsser, et al., *Johannes Stumpfs Schweizer und Reformationschronik*. Vol. 5: Quellen zur Schweizer Geschichte. Basel: Verlag Birkhäuser.
Goertz 1975	Hans-Jürgen Goertz, ed., *Umstrittenes Täufertum, 1525-1975*. Göttingen: Vandenhoeck & Ruprecht: pp. 111-137.
Goertz 1980	Hans-Jürgen Goertz, *Die Täufer, Geschichte und Deutung*. München: Verlag Beck.
Goertz 1982	H. J. Goertz, ed., *Profiles of Radical Reformers*. Herald Press.
Hall 1961	Thor Hall, "Possibilities of Erasmian Influence on Denck and Hubmaier in Their Views on the Freedom of the Will," MQR 30, pp. 149-170.

Harder 1985   Leland Harder, *The Sources of Swiss Anabaptism*. Scott-
                 dale: Herald Press.

Hertzsch 1957   Erich Hertzsch, *Karlstadt's Schriften*. Part II, Halle: Max
                 Niemeyer Verlag.

Hošek 1891f.   "Life of Balthasar Hubmeyer, the founder of 'New
                 Christianity' in Moravia," tr. W. W. Everts, *Texas Baptist
                 Hist. and Biographical Magazine*, 1891: pp. 118-148, 226-
                 256, 321-329, 502-559; 1892: pp. 19-32, 127-155, 189-
                 209, 251-268, 313-328, 375-386, 435-445, 497-511.

Hillerbrand 1962 Hans Joachim Hillerbrand, *A Bibliography of Anabaptism
                 1520-1630*. Elkhart: Institute of Mennonite Studies.

Jackson 1900   Samuel Macauley Jackson, *Huldreich Zwingli: The
                 Reformer of German Switzerland*. New York: G. P. Put-
                 nam's Sons.

Jackson 1901   Samuel Macauley Jackson, *Selected Works of Huldrych
                 Zwingli*. Philadelphia: University of Pennsylvania Press.

Janz 1982   Denis Janz, *Three Reformation Catechisms*. Toronto:
                 Edwin Mellen.

Jerome 1954   W. H. Fremantle, et al, translators, *St. Jerome: Letters
                 and Select Works*. Grand Rapids: Eerdmans, Vol. 6 in
                 Schaff NPNF.

Klaassen 1981   Walter Klaassen, *Anabaptism in Outline*. Scottdale:
                 Herald Press.

Köhler 1925   Walther Köhler, "Urkunder des Zürcher Rates,"
                 Zwingliana IV.

Loserth 1891   Johan Loserth, *Die Stadt Waldshut und die vorder öster-
                 reichische Regierung*, Vol. 77, in *Archiv für österreich-
                 ische Geschichte*. Vienna.

Loserth 1893   *Dr. Balthazar Hubmaier und die Anfänge der Wiedertaufe
                 in Mähren*. Brünn 1893 MHL/B/H861.

McNeill/Battles John T. McNeill, ed., and Ford Lewis Battles, trans., *Cal-
1960   vin: Institutes of the Christian Religion*, Vols. 20-21: Li-
                 brary of Christian Classics, Philadelphia: Westminster
                 Press.

McGlothlin 1906 W. J. McGlothlin, "An Anabaptist Liturgy of the Lord's
                 Supper," *The Baptist Review and Expositor*, III (1906),
                 pp. 82ff.

Moore 1981   Walter L. Moore, Jr., "Catholic Teacher and Anabaptist
                 Pupil: The Relationship between John Eck and Balthasar
                 Hubmaier," *Archive for Reformation History*, Vol. 72, pp.
                 68-97.

Oecolampadius 1525	Johannes Oecolampadius, *In epistolam B. Pauli apost. ad Rhomanos*. Basel.
Odlozilik 1925	"Der Widerhall der Lehre Zwinglis in Mähren," *Zwingliana*, Vol. 4, No. 9, 1524, pp. 257ff.
Packull 1973	Werner Packull, "Denck's Alleged Baptism by Hubmaier," MQR 47 (1973): pp. 327-338.
Pegis 1945	Anton C. Pegis, *Basic Writings of Saint Thomas Aquinas*. 2 vols. New York: Random House.
Pipkin 1984	H. Wayne Pipkin, *Huldrych Zwingli: Writings*, Vol. II: *In Search of True Religion: Reformation, Pastoral and Eucharistic Writings*. Allison Park: Pickwick Publications.
Potter 1977	G. R. Potter, *Huldrych Zwingli*. New York: St. Martin's Press.
Roberts 1981	Alexander Roberts, James Donaldson, *The Ante-Nicene Fathers*. Grand Rapids: Eerdmans. (1885-96)
Rupp 1959	E. Gordon Rupp, Philip S. Watson, *Luther and Erasmus: Free Will and Salvation*. Vol. 17, Library of Christian Classics, Philadelphia: Westminster Press.
Sachsse 1914	Carl Sachsse, *D. Balthasar Hubmaier als Theologe*. Berlin: Trowitsch, 1914, reprinted Scientia Verlag, Aalen.
Schaff 1931	Philip Schaff, *The Creeds of Christendom*. Vol. 2, Sixth Edition, Grand Rapids: Baker Book House. (1877)
Schaff 1956	Philip Schaff, *A Select Library of the Nicene and Post-Nicene Fathers*. First Series, Grand Rapids: Eerdmans. (1887-94)
Schaff 1979	Philip Schaff, Henry Wace, *A Select Library of the Nicene and Post-Nicene Fathers*. Second Series, Grand Rapids: Eerdmans. (1890-1900)
Schlabach 1977	Ervin Schlabach, *The Rule of Christ Among the Early Swiss Anabaptists*. Th.D. Dissertation, Chicago Theological Seminary.
Schopp 1962	Ludwig Schopp, et al, *The Fathers of the Church*. Washington: Catholic University of America, 1962—.
Scribner/Benecke 1979	Bob Scribner, Gerhard Benecke, eds., *The German Peasant War of 1525. New Viewpoints*. London: Allen Unwin.
Seebass 1972	Gottfried Seebass: *Müntzer's Erbe: Werk, Leben und Theologie des Hans Hut*. Theology Dissertation, Erlangen.
Séguenny 1980	André Séguenny, *Bibliotheca Dissidentium*. Tome I, Baden-Baden: Valentin Koerner.

Staehelin 1927   Ernst Staehelin, *Briefe und Akten zum Leben Oekolampads.* [Vol. I] Leipzig, 1927: M. Heinsius Nachfolger.

Staehelin 1934   Ernst Staehelin, *Briefe und Akten zum Leben Oekolampads.* Vol. II: 1527-1553, Leipzig: M. Heinsius Nachfolger.

Stayer 1972   James M. Stayer, *Anabaptists and the Sword.* Lawrence, Kans.: second edition, 1976.

Stayer 1975   James M. Stayer, "Die Anfänge des schweizerischen Täufertums im reformierten Kongregationalismus" in Goertz 1975, pp. 19-49.

Stayer 1977a   James M. Stayer, "Reflections and Retractions on *Anabaptists and the Sword.*" MQR 1977, pp. 196-212.

Stayer 1977b   James M. Stayer, "Reublin and Brötli: The Revolutionary Beginnings of Swiss Anabaptism" in Marc Lienhard, ed., *The Origins and Characteristics of Anabaptism.* The Hague: Nijhoff, 1977, pp. 83-102.

Stayer 1981   James M. Stayer, "Zwingli Before Zurich: Humanist Reformer and Papal Partisan," *Archive for Reformation History*, Vol. 72, pp. 55-68.

Stayer 1985a   James M. Stayer, "Zwingli and Radical Early Zwinglianism," in E. J. Furcha, ed., *Huldrych Zwingli, 1484-1531: A Legacy of Radical Reform.* Montreal: ARC Supplement Nr. 2., pp. 62-82.

Stayer 1985b   James M. Stayer, "Radikaler Frühzwinglianismus: Balthasar Hubmaier, Fabers 'Ursach' und die Programme der Bauern," MGB 42/37 1985, pp. 43-59.

Stayer 1988   James M. Stayer, "Anabaptists and Future Anabaptists in the Peasants' War," MQR LXII/2, April 1988, pp. 99-139.

Steinmetz 1979   David C. Steinmetz, "The Baptism of John and the Baptism of Jesus in Huldrych Zwingli, Balthasar Hubmaier and late Medieval Theology," Forrester Church and Timothy George, eds., *Continuity and Discontinuity in Church History.* Leiden: E. J. Brill: pp. 169-181.

Stupperich 1960   Robert Stupperich, *Martin Bucers Deutsche Schriften.* Vol. I. Gütersloh: Gerd Mohn.

Thomas 1914   *The "Summa Theologica" of St. Thomas Aquinas,* trans. by Fathers of the English Dominican Province. London: Burns, Oates, and Washbourne, Ltd.

Vedder 1905   Henry C. Vedder, *Balthasar Hubmaier The Leader of the Anabaptists.* New York: Putnam.

Wackernagel 1870   Philipp Wackernagel, *Das Deutsche Kirchenlied*. Leipzig.

Williams 1957   George Huntston Williams and Angel M. Mergal, eds., *Spiritual and Anabaptist Writers, Library of Christian Classics*. Philadelphia: Westminster.

Windhorst 1975   Christoph Windhorst, "Das Gedächtnis des Leidens Christi und Pflichtzeichen brüderlicher Liebe, Zum Verständnis des Abendmahls bei Balthasar Hubmaier," in Goertz 1975, pp. 111-137.

Windhorst 1976   Christoph Windhorst, *Täuferisches Taufverstandnis: Balthasar Hubmaiers Lehre Zwischen Traditioneller und Reformatorischer Theologie*. Vol. 16: Studies in Medieval and Reformation Thought, Leiden: E. J. Brill.

Windhorst 1982   Christof Windhorst, "Professor, Preacher, Politician," in Goertz 1982: pp. 144-157.

Yoder 1959   John H. Yoder, "Balthasar Hubmaier and the Beginnings of Swiss Anabaptism." MQR, 1959, pp. 5-17.

Yoder 1962   John H. Yoder, *Täufertum und Reformation in der Schweiz, I: Die Gespräch zwischen Täufern und Reformatoren, 1523-1538*. Karlsruhe: H. Schneider.

Yoder 1968   John H. Yoder, *Täufertum und Reformation im Gespräch*. Vol. 13: Basler Studien zur Historischen und Systematischen Theologie, Zurich: EVZ.

Yoder 1973   John H. Yoder, *The Legacy of Michael Sattler*, Vol 1: Classics of the Radical Reformation. Scottdale: Herald Press.

Yoder 1983   John H. Yoder, *Christian Attitudes to War, Peace and Revolution*. Elkhart: Co-op Bookstore.

Zahn 1963   *Die Melodien der deutschen evangelischen Kirchenlieder*. OLMS Verlag, Hildesheim (reprint of 1890 Gütersloh edition).

Zeman 1967   Jarold Knox Zeman, "Historical Topography of Moravian Anabaptism" in MQR, Vols. XL (1966) and XLI (1967).

Zeman 1969   Jarold Knox Zeman, *The Anabaptists and the Czech Brethren in Moravia, 1526-1628*. The Hague, Paris: Mouton.

Scripture Index

Index of Proper Names

Index of Place Names

Index of Scholars

Subject Index

The Editors

H. Wayne Pipkin has been Professor of Anabaptist and Sixteenth-Century Studies at the Associated Mennonite Biblical Seminaries and Associate Director of the Institute of Mennonite Studies, Elkhart, Indiana, since 1989. He is a native of Houston, Texas. Educated in Texas, he left Texas in order to study in New England. He received the M.A. in history from the University of Connecticut in 1963 and the Ph.D. in church history from the Hartford Seminary Foundation in 1968. He was a Fulbright Scholar at the University of Vienna in 1968-69, where he studied with Professor Grete Mecenseffey, the Austrian Anabaptist scholar.

He served as associate director of the Consortium for Higher Education Religion Studies (CHERS), the Ohio consortium of theological seminaries and directed their interseminary D.Min. program. He also worked as coordinator of the Columbus branch of the University Without Walls/Ohio, where he was also director of the Institute for Community Science and Appropriate Technology. While in Ohio he was active in hunger concerns and was for some time the Ohio state coordinator of Bread for the World and served on the board of the Franklin County Hunger Task Force. He was also involved as an associate in the New Wineskins Center for Research and Development.

Pipkin was professor of church history at the Baptist Theological Seminary, Rüschlikon, Switzerland, from 1979 to 1989. In 1984 he founded the Institute for Baptist and Anabaptist Studies at Rüschlikon and was the director of that institute to 1989. He has written for numerous scholarly journals. He has published *A Zwingli Bibliography* (1972), Volume II of *Huldrych Zwingli: Selected Writings* (1984), and edited *Seek Peace and Pursue It: Proceedings from the 1988 International Baptist Peace Conference* (1989). He wrote *Christian Meditation: Its Art and Practice* (1976). He also translated two modern volumes into English.

In addition to his teaching and scholarly work, he has served as Baptist theological consultant to the first international conversations of the Baptist World Alliance and the Lutheran World Federation which began in 1986 and concluded in

1989. He was particularly involved in the discussion on the condemnation of the Anabaptist which are contained in the Lutheran confessions of the sixteenth century.

Wayne is married to Arlene Schenk Pipkin, who directs the Habitat for Humanity Program of Elkhart County. They have two daughters: Nancy Gail Pipkin (born 1969) and Heather Michelle Pipkin (born 1972). Wayne and Arlene are members of the First Baptist Church of South Bend, an American Baptist congregation.

John H. Yoder is professor of theology at the University of Notre Dame. He has served the Mennonite denomination in overseas relief and mission administration, in ecumenical relations, and in theological education as professor of theology (1965-84) and president (1970-73) of Goshen Biblical Seminary.

Born in 1927, he studied at the College of Wooster, Goshen College, and at the University of Basel. His doctoral research investigated the conversations between Anabaptists and Reformers in the early Swiss Reformation. He translated and edited *The Legacy of Michael Sattler* (Herald Press, 1973), volume one in the Classics of the Radical Reformation series.

His best-known writings are in the field of Christian social ethics, especially *The Politics of Jesus* (1972, 1994) and *The Priestly Kingdom* (1984). With Herald Press he has published *The Original Revolution* (1971), *Nevertheless* (1972), *The Legacy of Michael Sattler* (1973), *What Would You Do?* (1983, 1992), *He Came Preaching Peace* (1985), *A Declaration on Peace* (with others, 1990), *The Royal Priesthood* (1994, 1998), and other books.

John is married to Anne Marie Guth. They are the parents of six living children and are members of the Prairie Street Mennonite Church, Elkhart, Indiana.

Added for the 2001 reprint:

John H. Yoder died on December 30, 1997. A comprehensive bibliography of his writings, prepared by Mark Thiessen Nation, is available from *The Mennonite Quarterly Review* (Goshen, Ind.).

the region in which

Balthasar Hubmaier

lived and ministered

Contemporary borders added for easier orientation

Leipz

Erfurt

Jena

Zwickau

Frankfurt

Main

GERMANY

Bayreuth

Mainz

Darmstadt

hessen

Worms

Neckar

Nürnberg

Speyer

Heidelberg

the Rhine

Regensburg

BAVARIA

Karlsruhe

Stuttgart

WÜRTTEMBERG

Ingolstadt

Danube

ALSACE

BADEN

Strasbourg

Rottenburg

Horb

Ulm

Augsburg

Friedberg

München

Colmar

Villingen

Ensisheim

Freiburg
im Breisgau

Schleitheim

KLETTGAU

Mulhouse

Waldshut

Schaffhausen

Radolfzell

Constance

Sankt Gallen

Innsbruck

Basel

Baden

Zurich

Zollikon

Küssnacht

Grüningen

Appenzell

S.TIRO

Kappel

Einsiedeln

Luzern

SWISS

Bern

Schwyz

Chur

CONFEDERATION

the Rhine

Inn

It

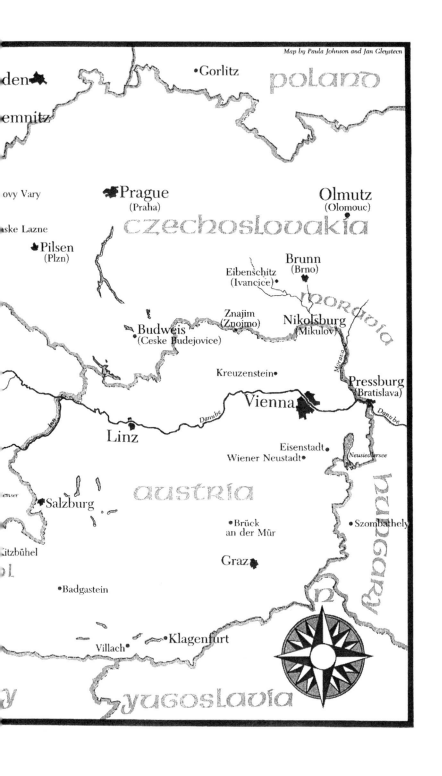

•Gorlitz

poland

den🕊

emnitz

ovy Vary

🕊Prague
(Praha)

Olmutz
(Olomouc)

czechoslovakia

aske Lazne

🍁Pilsen
(Plzn)

Brunn
(Brno)

Eibenschitz
(Ivancice)•

moravia

Znajim
(Znojmo)

Nikolsburg
(Mikulov)

Budweis
(Ceske Budejovice)

Morava

Kreuzenstein•

Pressburg
(Bratislava)

Vienna

Danube

Danube

Linz

Eisenstadt•
Wiener Neustadt•

Neusiedlersee

Inn

enser

🕊Salzburg

austria

hungary

•Brück
an der Mür

•Szombathely

itzbühel

ol

Graz🕊

•Badgastein

•Klagenfurt

Villach•

y

yugoslavia

Lightning Source UK Ltd.
Milton Keynes UK
27 October 2010

161999UK00001B/28/P

9 780836 131031